MKTG

PRINCIPLES OF MARKETING

FIFTH CANADIAN EDITION

CHARLES W. LAMB
TEXAS CHRISTIAN UNIVERSITY

JOE F. HAIR
UNIVERSITY OF SOUTH ALABAMA

CARL McDANIEL
UNIVERSITY OF TEXAS, ARLINGTON

MARC BOIVIN
UNIVERSITY OF CALGARY

DAVID GAUDET
SOUTHERN ALBERTA INSTITUTE OF
TECHNOLOGY

KIM SNOW
YORK UNIVERSITY

 CENGAGE

Australia • Brazil • Canada • Mexico • Singapore • United Kingdom • United States

MKTG, Fifth Canadian Edition
Charles W. Lamb, Joe F. Hair, Carl
McDaniel, Marc Boivin, David Gaudet,
Kim Snow

Senior Director, Product: Jackie Wood

Senior Portfolio Managers: Leanna MacLean,
Alexis Hood

Marketing Manager: Lindsay Shipman

Director, Content and Production: Toula DiLeo

Content Development Manager: Courtney Thorne

Senior Content Production Manager: Imoinda
Romain

IP Analyst: Christine Myaskovsky

IP Project Manager: Julie Pratt

Production Service: MPS Limited

Copy Editor: Karen Rolfe

Compositor: MPS Limited

Text Designer: Diane Robertson

Cover Designer: Courtney Hellam

Printed in Canada
Print Number: 01   Print Year: 2020

For product information and technology assistance, contact us at
Canada Support, canadasupport@cengage.com.

For permission to use material from this text or product, submit all requests online at **www.cengage.com/permissions.**

Library and Archives Canada Cataloguing in Publication:

Title: MKTG : principles of marketing / Charles W. Lamb (Texas Christian University), Mark Boivin (University of Calgary), Joe F. Hair (University of South Alabama), David Gaudet (Southern Alberta Institute of Technology), Carl McDaniel (University of Texas, Arlington), Kim Snow (York University).

Other titles: Marketing | Principles of marketing

Names: Lamb, Charles W., author. | Boivin, Marc, author. | Hair, Joseph F., Jr., author. | Gaudet, David, author. | McDaniel, Carl, Jr., author. | Snow, Kim, author.

Description: Fifth Canadian edition. | Includes bibliographical references and index.

Identifiers: Canadiana (print) 20200343513 | Canadiana (ebook) 20200343610 | ISBN 9780176910075 (softcover) | ISBN 9780176930219 (PDF)

Subjects: LCSH: Marketing—Textbooks. | LCSH: Marketing—Management—Textbooks. | LCGFT: Textbooks.

Classification: LCC HF5415 .L34 2020 | DDC 658.8—dc23

Print text ISBN-13: 978-0-17-691007-5
Print text ISBN-10: 0-17-691007-7
Ebook ISBN-13: 978-0-17-691013-1
Ebook ISBN-10: 0-17-691013-1

Cengage Canada
333 Bay Street, #2400
Toronto, ON M5H 2T6
Canada

Cengage is a leading provider of customized learning solutions with employees residing in nearly 40 different countries and sales in more than 125 countries around the world. Find your local representative at **www.cengage.com.**

To learn more about Cengage platforms and services, register or access your online learning solution, or purchase materials for your course, visit **www.cengage.ca.**

MKTG

BRIEF CONTENTS

PART 1 MARKETING—LET'S GET STARTED

1 An Introduction to Marketing 2

2 The Marketing Environment, Social Responsibility, and Ethics 14

3 Strategic Planning for Competitive Advantage 36

PART 2 ANALYZING MARKETING OPPORTUNITIES

4 Marketing Research and Analytics 52

5 Consumer Decision Making 74

6 Business Marketing 96

7 Segmenting, Targeting, and Positioning 114

8 Customer Relationship Management (CRM) 132

PART 3 PRODUCT DECISIONS

9 Product Concepts 156

10 Developing and Managing Products 176

11 Services and Non-profit Organization Marketing 196

PART 4 PRICING DECISIONS

12 Setting the Right Price 218

PART 5 DISTRIBUTING DECISIONS

13 Marketing Channels and Supply Chain Management 240

14 Retailing 262

PART 6 PROMOTION DECISIONS

15 Marketing Communications 284

16 Advertising, Public Relations, and Direct Response 306

17 Sales Promotion and Personal Selling 330

18 Social Media and Digital Strategies 346

19 (Online Chapter) Developing a Global Vision 19-1

Glossary 367

Endnotes 380

Index 390

Tear-Out Cards

CONTENTS

Preface xiii

Features xiv

Supplements for Success xvi

About the Canadian Authors xvii

Acknowledgments xviii

Part 1
MARKETING—LET'S GET STARTED

1 An Introduction to Marketing 2

1-1 What Is Marketing? 2

    1-1a What Is Marketing? 2

1-2 The Evolution of Marketing 4

    1-2a The Production Era 4

    1-2b The Sales Era 4

    1-2c The Marketing Company Era 5

    1-2d Societal Marketing Era 6

    1-2e Relationship Marketing Era 6

1-3 Key Marketing Terms 7

    1-3a Exchange 8

1-4 Why Marketing Matters 10

    1-4a Marketing Is Part of Every Company 10

    1-4b Marketing Is a Rewarding Career 10

1-4c Marketing Provides an Important Skill Set 10

1-4d Marketing Is Part of Everyday Life 11

Awake Chocolate Continuing Case: A Delicious Way to Get Energy 12

2 The Marketing Environment, Social Responsibility, and Ethics 14

2-1 The External Marketing Environment 14

    2-1a Understanding the External Environment 15

2-2 Competitive Factors 16

2-3 Regulatory Factors 16

    2-3a Federal Legislation 17

    2-3b Provincial and Territorial Laws 17

    2-3c Self-Regulation 18

2-4 Economic Factors 18

    2-4a Consumers' Incomes 18

    2-4b Purchasing Power 19

    2-4c Inflation 19

    2-4d Recession 20

2-5 Social Factors 21

    2-5a Marketing-Oriented Values 22

    2-5b The Growth of Component Lifestyles 22

    2-5c Families Today 22

2-6 Demographic Factors 23

    2-6a Generation Z 23

    2-6b Generation Y 24

    2-6c Generation X 25

    2-6d Baby Boomers—A Mass Market 26

    2-6e Population Shifts in Canada 26

    2-6f Ethnic and Cultural Diversity 26

2-7 Technological Factors 27

    2-7a Research 28

    2-7b Technology and the Future of Businesses 28

2-8 Corporate Social Responsibility and Ethical Behaviour in Business 29

2-8a Growth of Social Responsibility 30

2-8b Green Marketing 31

2-8c Ethical Behaviour in Business 31

2-8d Morality and Business Ethics 32

2-8e Ethical Decision Making 32

2-8f Ethical Guidelines 32

Awake Chocolate Continuing Case: Doing Right by Resources 34

3 Strategic Planning for Competitive Advantage 36

3-1 The Importance of Strategic Planning 36

3-1a Strategic Business Units 37

3-1b Corporate Planning—Defining the Business Mission 38

3-2 Strategic Directions—Designing the Business Portfolio 39

3-2a Conducting a SWOT Analysis 39

3-2b Strategic Alternatives—Linking SWOT to Growth Strategies 39

3-2c Selecting a Strategic Alternative 41

3-3 Business Planning for Competitive Advantage 41

3-3a Competitive Advantage 41

3-3b Cost Competitive Advantage 41

3-3c Product Differentiation Competitive Advantage 42

3-3d Niche Competitive Advantage 43

3-3e Building Sustainable Competitive Advantage 43

3-4 Marketing Planning 44

3-4a Setting Marketing Plan Objectives 44

3-4b Target Market Strategy 44

3-4c The Marketing Mix 45

3-4d Product Strategies 45

3-4e Pricing Strategies 46

3-4f Place (Distribution) Strategies 46

3-4g Promotion Strategies 46

3-5 Marketing Plan Implementation, Evaluation, and Control 46

3-5a Implementation 46

3-5b Evaluation and Control 46

3-6 Effective Strategic Planning 47

Awake Chocolate Continuing Case: Marketing Strategy with Energy 48

Part 1 Case: Uber-izing Food Delivery Shows Limitations 50

Part 2 ANALYZING MARKETING OPPORTUNITIES

4 Marketing Research and Analytics 52

4-1 Marketing Research and Marketing Analytics 52

4-2 The Marketing Research Process 53

4-2a Step 1: Identify and Formulate the Problem/Opportunity 53

4-2b Step 2: Plan the Research Design and Gather Secondary Data 54

4-2c Step 3: Specify the Sampling Procedures 55

4-2d Step 4: Collect Primary Data 56

4-2e Step 5: Analyze the Data 61

4-2f Step 6: Prepare and Present the Report 62

4-2g Step 7: Provide Follow-Up 62

4-3 The Impact of Technology on Marketing Research and Marketing Analytics 62

4-3a Uses of the Internet 63

4-3b Online Research Panels 63

4-3c Online Focus Groups 63

4-3d Online Research Communities 64

4-3e Mobile Marketing Research 64

4-3f Social Media Marketing Research 64

4-3g The Rise of Big Data 65

4-4 Marketing Analytics and Marketing Strategy 65

4-4a Data Used in Marketing Analytics 67

4-4b Organizing the Data 67

4-4c Analyzing the Data 67

4-4d Categories of Data for Marketing Analytics 68

4-4e Marketing Analytics Techniques 69

4-5 Data Collection Concerns 70

4-5a Intrusive Methods of Data Collection 70

4-5b Lack of Transparency about Data Sharing 70

4-6 When to Use Market Research or Marketing Analytics 71

Awake Chocolate Continuing Case: Scrappy Little Research 72

5 Consumer Decision Making 74

5-1 The Importance of Understanding Consumer Behaviour 74

5-2 Consumer Decision-Making Process 75

5-2a Step 1: Need Recognition 75

5-2b Step 2: Information Search 76

5-2c Steps 3 and 4: Evaluation of Alternatives and Purchase 78

5-2d Step 5: Postpurchase Behaviour 78

5-3 Types of Consumer Buying Decisions and the Significance of Consumer Involvement 79

5-3a Factors Determining the Level of Consumer Involvement 80

5-3b Marketing Implications of Involvement 80

5-3c Factors Influencing Consumer Buying Decisions 81

5-4 Cultural and Social Factors Affect Consumer Buying Decisions 83

5-4a Cultural Influences on Consumer Buying Decisions 83

5-4b Social Influences on Consumer Buying Decisions 85

5-5 Individual Influences on Consumer Buying Decisions 87

5-5a Gender 87

5-5b Age and Family Life-Cycle Stage 87

5-5c Personality, Self-Concept, and Lifestyle 89

5-6 Psychological Influences on Consumer Buying Decisions 90

5-6a Perception 90

5-6b Motivation 91

5-6c Learning 92

5-6d Beliefs and Attitudes 93

5-6e Consumer Behaviour Elements—Working Together 93

Awake Chocolate Continuing Case: Taste Drives Decisions 94

6 Business Marketing 96

6-1 What Is Business Marketing? 96

6-2 Business versus Consumer Marketing 97

6-3 The Network and Relationships Approach to Business Marketing 98

6-3a Relationships in Business Marketing 98

6-3b Interaction in Business Marketing 99

6-3c Networks in Business Marketing 99

6-4 Fundamental Aspects of Business Marketing 102

6-4a Types of Demand 102

6-4b Number of Customers 102

6-4c Location of Buyers 103

6-4d Type of Negotiations 103

6-4e Use of Reciprocity 103

6-4f Use of Leasing 103

6-4g Types of Business Products 104

6-5 Classifying Business Customers 105

6-5a Major Categories of Business Customers 105

6-5b Classification by Industry 106

6-6 Business Buying Behaviour 107

6-6a Buying Centres 107

6-6b Buying Situations 108

6-6c Evaluative Criteria for Business Buyers 109

6-7 Business Marketing Online 110

6-7a Trends in B2B Online Marketing 111

Awake Chocolate Continuing Case: 2B2B or Not 2B2B 112

7 Segmenting, Targeting, and Positioning 114

7-1 Market Segmentation 114

7-1a The Importance of Market Segmentation 115

7-2 Bases for Segmenting Consumer Markets 115

7-2a Geographic Segmentation 116

7-2b Demographic Segmentation 116

7-2c Psychographic Segmentation 119

7-2d Benefit Segmentation 121

7-2e Usage-Rate Segmentation 122

7-2f Bases for Segmenting Business Markets 122

7-3 Criteria for Successful Segmentation 123

7-4 Steps in Segmenting a Market 123

7-5 Strategies for Selecting Target Markets 124

7-5a Undifferentiated Targeting 124

7-5b Concentrated Targeting 125

7-5c Multisegment Targeting 125

7-5d One-to-One Marketing 126

7-6 Positioning 127

7-6a Perceptual Mapping 128

7-6b Positioning Bases 128

7-6c Repositioning 129

7-6d Developing a Positioning Statement 129

Awake Chocolate Continuing Case: Target Market Time Traveller 130

8 Customer Relationship Management (CRM) 132

8-1 What Is Customer Relationship Management? 132

8-1a The Other CRM 133

8-2 The CRM Cycle 134

8-3 Steps in the CRM Cycle 134

8-3a The CRM Cycle—Stage 1 (Marketing Research) 134

8-3b The CRM Cycle—Stage 2 (Business Development) 136

8-3c The CRM Cycle—Stage 3 (Customer Feedback) 145

8-4 Privacy Concerns and CRM 148

8-5 The Future of CRM 149

Awake Chocolate Continuing Case: Mindset More than Machine 151

Part 2 Case: Indigo Where? 153

Part 3 PRODUCT DECISIONS

9 Product Concepts 156

9-1 What Is a Product? 156

9-2 Types of Consumer Products 157

9-2a Convenience Products 158

9-2b Shopping Products 158

9-2c Specialty Products 159

9-2d Unsought Products 159

9-3 Product Items, Lines, and Mixes 160

 9-3a Adjustments to Product Items, Lines, and Mixes 161

9-4 Branding 163

 9-4a Benefits of Branding 164

 9-4b Branding Strategies 164

 9-4c Trademarks 167

9-5 Packaging 168

 9-5a Packaging Functions 168

 9-5b Labelling 169

 9-5c Universal Product Codes (UPCs) 170

9-6 Global Issues in Branding and Packaging 170

9-7 Product Warranties 172

Awake Chocolate Continuing Case: Approachable Packaging 173

10 Developing and Managing Products 176

10-1 The Importance of New Products 176

 10-1a Categories of New Products 177

10-2 The New-Product Development Process 178

 10-2a New-Product Strategy 178

 10-2b Idea Generation 179

 10-2c Idea Screening 181

 10-2d Business Analysis 181

 10-2e Development 182

 10-2f Test Marketing 182

 10-2g Commercialization 184

10-3 Global Issues in New-Product Development 186

10-4 The Spread of New Products 186

 10-4a Diffusion of Innovation 186

 10-4b Product Characteristics and the Rate of Adoption 187

 10-4c Marketing Implications of the Adoption Process 188

10-5 Product Life Cycles 188

 10-5a Introductory Stage 189

 10-5b Growth Stage 191

 10-5c Maturity Stage 191

 10-5d Decline Stage 191

 10-5e Implications for Marketing Management 192

Awake Chocolate Continuing Case: Disrupting Energy 193

11 Services and Non-profit Organization Marketing 196

11-1 How Services Differ from Goods 196

 11-1a Intangibility 196

 11-1b Inseparability 198

 11-1c Heterogeneity 198

 11-1d Perishability 198

11-2 Service Quality 199

 11-2a Evaluating Service Quality 199

 11-2b The Gap Model of Service Quality 199

11-3 Marketing Mixes for Services 203

 11-3a Product (Service) Strategy 203

 11-3b Process Strategy 204

 11-3c People Strategy 205

 11-3d Place (Distribution) Strategy 205

 11-3e Physical Evidence Strategy 206

 11-3f Promotion Strategy 206

 11-3g Price Strategy 206

 11-3h Productivity Strategy 207

11-4 Relationship Marketing in Services 207

11-5 Internal Marketing in Service Companies 208

11-6 Non-profit Organization Marketing 209

 11-6a What Is Non-profit Organization Marketing? 210

 11-6b Unique Aspects of Non-profit Organization Marketing Strategies 210

Awake Chocolate Continuing Case: Essential Service of Caffeine 213

Part 3 Case: Hershey's Focus on Innovation 216

Part 4
PRICING DECISIONS

12 Setting the Right Price 218

12-1 The Importance of Price and the Pricing Process 218

    12-1a What Is Price? 218

    12-1b The Importance of Price to Marketing Managers 219

12-2 The Pricing Process 220

    12-2a Step 1—Establishing Pricing Objectives 220

    12-2b Step 2—Estimating Demand, Costs, and Profits 222

    12-2c Step 3—Choosing a Price Strategy 225

    12-2d Step 4—Using a Price Tactic 228

12-3 The Legality and Ethics of Setting a Price 233

    12-3a Bait Pricing 233

    12-3b Deceptive Pricing 234

    12-3c Price Fixing 234

    12-3d Predatory Pricing 234

    12-3e Resale Price Maintenance 235

    12-3f Price Discrimination 235

Awake Chocolate Continuing Case: Sell Value over Price 236

Part 4 Case: Pricing Tactics at Costco 238

Part 5
DISTRIBUTING DECISIONS

13 Marketing Channels and Supply Chain Management 240

13-1 The Nature of Marketing Channels 240

    13-1a Change the Channel 240

    13-1b The Marketing Channel and Intermediaries Defined 242

    13-1c How Intermediaries Help the Supply Chain 242

13-2 Channel Intermediaries and Their Functions 245

    13-2a Channel Functions Performed by Intermediaries 245

13-3 Types of Marketing Channels 246

    13-3a Channels for Consumer Products 246

    13-3b Channels for Business and Industrial Products 247

    13-3c Alternative Channel Arrangements 248

13-4 Making Channel Strategy Decisions 249

    13-4a Factors Affecting Channel Choice 249

    13-4b Levels of Distribution Intensity 251

13-5 Handling Channel Relationships 252

    13-5a Channel Power, Control, and Leadership 252

    13-5b Channel Conflict 252

    13-5c Channel Partnering 253

13-6 Managing the Supply Chain 254

    13-6a Benefits of Supply Chain Management 254

    13-6b Managing Logistics in the Supply Chain 255

    13-6c Sourcing and Procurement 255

    13-6d Production Scheduling 255

    13-6e Order Processing 256

    13-6f Inventory Control 257

13-7 Distribution Challenges in World Markets 258

    13-7a Developing Global Marketing Channels 258

    13-7b Electronic Distribution 258

Awake Chocolate Continuing Case: A Taste for Channel Success 260

14 Retailing 262

14-1 The Role of Retailing 262

14-2 Classification and Types of Retail Operations 263

    14-2a Classification of Retail Operations 263

    14-2b Major Types of Retail Operations 264

14-3 The Rise of Nonstore Retailing 267

    14-3a Automatic Vending 268

    14-3b Self-Service Technologies (SST) 268

    14-3c Direct Retailing 268

    14-3d Direct Marketing (DM) 268

    14-3e Online Retailing or E-tailing 269

    14-3f Sharing Economy 269

14-4 Franchising 270

14-5 Retail Marketing Strategy 271

    14-5a Defining a Target Market 271

    14-5b Choosing the Retailing Mix 271

    14-5c Retailing Decisions for Services 276

14-6 Addressing Retail Product/Service Failures 277

14-7 Retailer and Retail Consumer Trends and Advancements 277

    14-7a Big Data 277

    14-7b Shopper Marketing and Analytics 278

    14-7c Future Developments in Retail Management 278

Awake Chocolate Continuing Case: Micro Mart, Macro Potential 280

Part 5 Case: Apocalypse… Soon? 282

Part 6 PROMOTION DECISIONS

JeremyRichards/Shutterstock.com

15 Marketing Communications 284

15-1 The Role of Promotion in the Marketing Mix 284

15-2 Marketing Communication 286

    15-2a The Communication Process 287

15-3 The Goals of Promotion 290

    15-3a Informing 290

    15-3b Persuading 291

    15-3c Reminding 291

    15-3d Connecting 291

15-4 The Promotional Mix (AKA Integrated Marketing Communications—IMC) 291

    15-4a Advertising 292

    15-4b Public Relations (PR) and Publicity 292

    15-4c Sales Promotion 293

    15-4d Personal Selling 293

    15-4e Direct-Response Communication 294

    15-4f Online Marketing, Content Marketing, and Social Media 294

    15-4g The Communication Process and the Promotional Mix 295

15-5 Promotional Goals and the AIDA Concept 297

    15-5a AIDA and the Promotional Mix 298

15-6 Integrated Marketing Communications and the Promotional Mix 299

    15-6a Factors Affecting the Promotional Mix 299

Awake Chocolate Continuing Case: Nevil, the Communicator 304

16 Advertising, Public Relations, and Direct Response 306

16-1 What Is Advertising? 306
16-1a Advertising and Market Share 307
16-1b The Effects of Advertising on Consumers 308
16-2 Major Types of Advertising 308
16-2a Institutional Advertising 309
16-2b Product Advertising 309
16-3 Creative Decisions in Advertising 310
16-3a Identifying Product Benefits 310
16-3b Developing and Evaluating Advertising Appeals 311
16-3c Executing the Message 312
16-3d Postcampaign Evaluation 312
16-4 Media Decisions in Advertising 313
16-4a Media Types 314
16-4b Media Selection Considerations 318
16-4c Media Scheduling 320
16-4d Media Buying 320
16-5 Public Relations 321
16-5a Major Public Relations Tools 321
16-5b Managing Unfavourable Publicity 324
16-6 Direct-Response Communication 324
16-6a The Tools of Direct-Response Communication 325
Awake Chocolate Continuing Case: Terms of Engagement 327

17 Sales Promotion and Personal Selling 330

17-1 What Is Sales Promotion? 330
17-1a The Sales Promotion Target 331
17-1b The Objectives of Sales Promotion 332
17-2 Tools for Consumer Sales Promotion 333
17-2a Discounts and Coupons 333
17-2b Rebates 334
17-2c Premiums 334
17-2d Loyalty Marketing Programs 335
17-2e Contests and Sweepstakes 335
17-2f Sampling 336
17-2g Shopper Marketing 336

17-3 Tools for Trade Sales Promotion 336
17-4 Personal Selling 337
17-5 Relationship Selling 338
17-6 The Selling Process 339
17-6a Some Key Issues in Each Step of the Selling Process 340
17-6b Personal Selling in a Global Marketplace 343
17-6c The Impact of Technology on Personal Selling 343
Awake Chocolate Continuing Case: Strategic Sampling 344

18 Social Media and Digital Strategies 346

18-1 What Is Social Media's Role in Integrated Marketing Communications? 346
18-1a How Canadians Use Social Media 348
18-2 The Tools of Social Engagement 350
18-2a Social Networks 350
18-2b Social News Sites 352
18-2c Blogs 353
18-2d Microblogs 353
18-2e Location-Based Social Networking Sites 354
18-2f Review Sites 354
18-2g Audio: Podcasts and Beyond 355
18-2h Virtual Worlds and Online Gaming 355
18-2i Evaluation and Measurement of Social Media 355
18-2j The Changing World of Social Media 356
18-3 Mobile's Role in Digital Marketing 356
18-3a Mobile and Smartphone Technology 356
18-3b The Second Coming of Text 357
18-3c Apps and Widgets 357
18-4 Search: SEO and SEM 358
18-5 Designing a Digital Marketing Strategy 360
18-5a The Listening System 360
Awake Chocolate Continuing Case: Influencers at the Ready 362

Part 6 Case: Connection in a Contagion 364

19 (Online Chapter) Developing a Global Vision 19-1

19-1 Rewards of Global Marketing 19-1

    19-1a Importance of Global Marketing to Canada 19-3

19-2 Multinational Companies 19-4

    19-2a Global Marketing Standardization 19-5

19-3 External Environment—Facing Global Marketers 19-5

    19-3a Culture 19-5

    19-3b Economic and Technological Development 19-6

    19-3c The Global Economy 19-6

    19-3d Political Structure and Actions 19-7

    19-3e Demographic Makeup 19-12

    19-3f Natural Resources 19-13

19-4 Global Marketing by the Individual Company 19-13

    19-4a Exporting 19-13

    19-4b Licensing and Franchising 19-14

    19-4c Contract Manufacturing 19-15

    19-4d Joint Venture 19-15

    19-4e Direct Investment 19-16

19-5 The Global Marketing Mix 19-16

    19-5a Product Decisions 19-17

    19-5b Promotion Adaptation 19-18

    19-5c Place (Distribution) 19-18

    19-5d Pricing 19-18

19-6 The Impact of the Internet 19-20

Glossary 367

Endnotes 380

Index 390

Tear-Out Cards

The fifth Canadian edition of *MKTG* and the accompanying MindTap is the number one, most used textbook in Canada for the Introduction to Marketing course. This resource was developed in consultation with instructors and more than 400 students over the course of more than 10 years, with the goal of creating a comprehensive yet efficient resource that engages, develops critical thinking skills, and helps learners to move up Bloom's Taxonomy, from memorization to mastery of course concepts.

In *MKTG,* Fifth Canadian Edition, we begin in Part 1 with an introduction to marketing, including a look at social responsibility and ethics. In Part 2, we take a deep look at the kinds of market research businesses should do, segmenting, targeting and positioning, and customer relationship management. In Part 3, we focus on developing and managing products from concept to execution. In Part 4, the importance of setting the right price is explored in great detail. In Part 5, the details of marketing channels and supply chain management are explored. In Part 6, we look at decisions related to promotions including the ways in which marketers communicate to the target audience through advertising, public relations, and direct response. Further, there is a focus on sales promotion and personal selling and strategies related to social media.

FEATURES

MINDTAP

MKTG, Fifth Canadian Edition, is a digital learning solution that presents concepts in a way that resonates with the needs of today's learners. This resource not only helps introduce students to all the important concepts that they need to learn in the Introduction to Marketing course, but also does so through interactive, media-rich activities that help them better retain those concepts and get the hands-on decision-making practice they need for continued success in school and in business.

MindTap can be fully integrated with most Learning Management Systems (LMS), providing students with one place to log in, and allowing you to sync to your LMS gradebook if you wish. MindTap can be personalized for your course needs. You can hide lessons, move content around, and assign the things you find most useful!

Learn, Apply, Succeed

To meet the needs of today's students and to ultimately provide a more interactive course experience, the MindTap for *MKTG*, Fifth Canadian Edition, encourages students to learn, apply, and succeed in mastering the concepts featured throughout the book. MindTap for *MKTG* presents the core concepts taught in the Introduction to Marketing course in a variety of ways, including short paragraphs of text and the following assets that appear right in-line in the ebook:

- **Interactive Figures** allow students to apply the key concepts of each lesson by manipulating content and therefore deepening their understanding of concepts.

- **Concept Checks** appear throughout the ebook. This formative assessment ensures that students understand each concept before moving on to the next.

Through extensive research with Canadian students, we have seen that students respond to this type of format and come to class more prepared and engaged.

Additionally, the MindTap Reader has the following functionality to engage students and support self-study:

- **ReadSpeaker** will read the text aloud.

- **Highlighting** and **Note Taking** allow students to highlight text and make notes in the MindTap Reader. These notes will flow into Evernote, the electronic notebook app that you can access anywhere when it's time to study for the exam.

Within MindTap, students also have access to study tools, including the following:

- **Adaptive Test Prep**, which reduces exam anxiety and allows students to create practice quizzes covering multiple chapters in a low-stakes environment. Students receive immediate feedback so they know where they need additional help, and the test bank–like questions prepare students for what to expect on the exam.

- **Flashcards**, which are prepopulated to provide a jump-start for review; there is an option to create new ones.

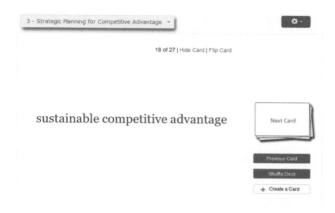

sustainable competitive advantage

Next Card

Previous Card

Shuffle Deck

+ Create a Card

Connecting Concepts through Multimedia and Active Learning

MindTap for *MKTG*, Fifth Canadian Edition, also contains a variety of activities intended to help students deepen their understanding of concepts and move from memorization to mastery. These activities include

- **Three Different Types of Cases**

  - The **Continuing Case** at the end of each chapter features the Awake Chocolate Company, a Canadian caffeinated-chocolate company.

  - **Chapter Case Studies** ask students to provide solutions and recommendations to a variety of real challenges facing Canadian and global businesses.

  - **Part Cases** ask students to respond to business situations that relate to multiple chapters at a time.

- **Mini Simulations** help students focus on thinking critically. These activities place students in interactive scenarios and ask them to make decisions on behalf of the company. The scenario changes at each decision point so that students receive a unique experience based on the choices they make. The effectiveness of the business decisions they make along the way will result in success, failure, or something in between.

Part 5: You Make the Decision - Product Decisions

Introduction · Quality or Affordability · Quality · Hire vet techs or Extend the brand

Click for Transcript

How should CanineCare enhance its perceived quality?

○ Hire vet techs.

○ Extend the brand to a luxury product line.

- **Mind Doodle videos** are whiteboard animation–style videos that engage and prepare students for the content in the ebook.

- **Interviews with industry professionals:** Canadian professionals from a cross-section of industries reinforce the readings, activities, and highlighted skills of chapter concepts. Students watch and receive multiple choice questions to assess their understanding.

- **Multitude of activities**, including **Application Exercises**, **Review/Discussion Questions,** and **Ethics Exercises**

SUPPLEMENTS FOR SUCCESS

INSTRUCTOR RESOURCES

The following instructor resources have been created for *MKTG*, Fifth Canadian Edition. Access these ultimate tools for customizing lectures and presentations at http://login.cengage.com.

Annually Updated Integrative Cases

A unique feature to the *MKTG*, Fifth Canadian Edition, resource package is the annually updated Integrative Casebank. Each case features accompanying questions with answers and teaching notes.

Test Bank

The Test Bank for *MKTG*, Fifth Canadian Edition, is

available in Cognero®, a secure online testing system that allows instructors to author, edit, and manage test bank content from anywhere Internet access is available. No special installations or downloads are needed, and the desktop-inspired interface, with its drop-down menus and familiar, intuitive tools, allows instructors to create and manage tests with ease. Multiple test versions can be created in an instant, and content can be imported or exported into other systems. Tests can be delivered from a learning management system, the classroom, or wherever an instructor chooses. Cognero for *MKTG*, Fifth Canadian Edition, can be accessed through http://login.cengage.com.

PowerPoint Presentations

Microsoft® PowerPoint® lecture slides for every lesson feature key figures, tables, and photographs from *MKTG*, Fifth Canadian Edition. Principles of clear design and engaging content have been incorporated throughout, making it simple for instructors to customize for their courses.

Image Library

This resource consists of digital copies of figures, short tables, and photographs used in the book. Instructors may use these jpegs to customize the PowerPoints or create their own PowerPoint presentations.

Instructor Guide

This resource is organized according to the lessons and addresses and key educational concerns. Other features include classroom activity and discussion suggestions and additional exercises.

Microlearning Presentations

These narrative-based PowerPoint Presentations provide different stories to illustrate marketing concepts. Scripts, discussion questions, and activities are included.

Marketing Math Lessons Plans and Workbook

These tutorials introduce students to key marketing math concepts and tools used by marketers to analyze, develop, support, and evaluate their marketing plans.

Marketing Plan and Planning Worksheets

This comprises a series of exercises to guide students through the development of a marketing plan for a chosen company.

ABOUT THE CANADIAN AUTHORS

MARC BOIVIN

Marc Boivin is a Senior Instructor at the Haskayne School of Business at the University of Calgary. He has been a faculty member of the marketing department at Haskayne since 2005. He coordinates and teaches the Marketing Principles course, in addition to teaching senior marketing electives in marketing strategy and business-to-business marketing. Marc received his Bachelor of Commerce degree in Marketing from the University of Calgary and has an MBA in Strategy from McGill University. His work experience includes international trade, new product development, marketing research, non-profit consulting, strategy consulting, and academic research and writing. His main area of research focuses on competencies and competency-based education. When not working or writing textbooks, Marc enjoys spending time with his wonderful wife and two amazing daughters.

DAVID GAUDET

David Gaudet is an instructor/course designer at The Southern Alberta Institute of Technology. He has also taught and developed business courses for the University of Calgary and Mount Royal University. He is a contributing author to marketing textbooks in the United States and Canada and provides consulting services to a variety of companies through his marketing firm, Triceratops Brand Logic Inc.

David is also a graduate of SAIT, jumping into a broadcast/media career in the mid-1980s that spanned 15 years, during which he helped launch and manage some of Canada's most successful radio stations. This evolved into his first entrepreneurial pursuit—a market research company that studied media audience trends. This expanded into channeling his passion for communications across a broad variety of industries, advising and producing content for companies in energy, hospitality, transportation, entertainment, and education sectors.

David completed his MBA from the University of Southern Queensland in Australia, with High Distinction.

These days, when not teaching, consulting or helping raise his two daughters, he can be found podcasting and producing digital content either for clients or his own companies.

KIM SNOW

Kim Snow is an associate professor of marketing at York University in Toronto. Dr. Snow received her MBA and PhD from the University of Bradford, UK and her Diploma in Business Administration from Wilfrid Laurier University, Waterloo, Ontario. She has taught undergraduate and graduate programs both in Canada and Europe. She has published articles in the area of service marketing, customer satisfaction, and marketing research. She has coauthored Canadian editions of textbooks in management and marketing. She has worked with the American Marketing Association to develop student chapters and has been a judge on several international competitions for the American Marketing Association. Kim also spent 17 years working in the financial services industry.

ACKNOWLEDGMENTS

The authors would like to gratefully acknowledge the original authors of the American edition for the thoughtful structure and text with which to work and the entire Cengage Canada team who have supported us in this endeavour. Our thanks in particular to Leanna MacLean, Senior Portfolio Manager; Jackie Wood, Senior Product Director; and Imoinda Romain, Senior Content Production Manager, for championing this dynamic product, as well as to Courtney Thorne, Content Development Manager; Alexis Hood, previously Portfolio Manager; and our detailed and thorough copyeditor Karen Rolfe. Their guidance throughout the development and production of this fifth Canadian edition have been invaluable.

The authors would also like to thank the following reviewers for their time and feedback: Sara Mercier, Durham College; Jack Michienzi, Fanshawe College; Margaret O'Brien, Algonquin College; Keith Penhall, Red River College; and Victor Sousa, Centennial College.

1 | An Introduction to Marketing

LEARNING OUTCOMES

1-1 Define marketing

1-2 Describe the evolution of marketing

1-3 Define key marketing terms

1-4 Explain why marketing matters

"Good marketing makes the company look smart. Great marketing makes the customer feel smart."

—Joe Chernov[1]

1-1 | WHAT IS MARKETING?

Anyone who has picked up this book and is reading this first chapter has a preconceived notion of what marketing is. The term *marketing* is misused and overused in discussions about companies, celebrities, and all aspects of business. Because the term is so broadly interpreted, we end up in a situation where the word itself begins to lose its meaning.

And this meaning is most often associated with a few words that are attached to the promotional activities of marketing: sales, advertising, and social media. This is likely because these types of activities are what we as consumers see all the time, on our phones, online, or even out in public. Any message delivered by a company is simplified down to becoming part of a company's *marketing*.

But marketing is not only seen as a noun. Marketing is also used as a verb: "this company sure is marketing their services." Here the function of marketing is distilled down to, once again, promotional efforts related to advertising or other forms of promotion.

And so the term *marketing* is used in a variety of ways and misrepresented in many others. But without marketing, there is no customer. Most departments in a business—whether accounting or finance or operations—are internally focused on achieving goals related to their functional area. Marketing's sole focus is on the customer and understanding what makes them tick. Without marketing to identify a customer to create revenues and profit, there is no need for an accounting department or manufacturing facility.

It has become a marketer's job to understand the customer, and in doing so, transition marketing from something that is misused and misunderstood to a key component in an organization. Being able to bring an external customer-based approach, marketing can inform other parts of the organization to focus on the needs of customers when undertaking any action or decision. Because, as the quote at the start of this chapter suggests, the customer is the focus of marketing, not the company.

1-1a | What Is Marketing?

Marketing is about understanding the **needs** of the customer. No other aspect of business has this focus. Marketing helps to shape the products and services of a company, based on an understanding of what the customer is looking for. Marketing is about engaging in a conversation with that customer and

guiding the delivery of what is required to satisfy those needs.

The goal of marketing is summarized nicely by the marketing concept. At its core, the marketing concept is about offering the customer what they are looking for. It includes the following:

- Focusing on customer wants and needs so that the organization can distinguish its offerings from those of its competitors
- Integrating all the organization's activities, including production, to satisfy customers' wants
- Achieving long-term goals for the organization by satisfying customers' wants and needs legally and responsibly

Marketing is becoming a conversation with the customer rather than a distraction. Companies are finding innovative ways in which to lead this conversation, and with access to more tools (Instagram, TikTok), consumers are now, more than ever, able to talk back.

As we can see from the Dilbert cartoon, there is an issue with how marketing is perceived. Understanding

marketing
the activities that develop an offering in order to satisfy a customer need

need
a state of being where we desire something that we do not possess but yearn to acquire

where marketing came from and how it has evolved should help to provide the necessary context to understand the importance and relevance of marketing to any company in the marketplace today.

1-2 | THE EVOLUTION OF MARKETING

The misconceptions surrounding marketing come from the evolution of how marketing has been used in businesses for more than a century. The conceptualization of marketing into distinct eras began back in 1960, with a seminal article written in the *Journal of Marketing*. Titled "The Marketing Revolution," the article was written by Robert J. Keith, who was not an academic at the time, but rather the executive vice president of the Pillsbury Company.[2] Keith split up the history of marketing, going back to the 19th century, in three eras: production oriented, sales oriented, and marketing oriented. Since his article, more eras have been added to the history of marketing, reflecting the shift away from selling and products toward consumer and societal focuses.

Numerous terms and ideologies are used to describe these shifts in thinking, and below are the eras in marketing that have been part of these periodic shifts. It is important to investigate some prior perspectives on marketing to provide a better understanding of how marketing is perceived today and why there is so much confusion around what truly constitutes marketing.

1-2a | The Production Era

The **production era** focuses on marketing as a messenger. Marketing is seen as a way to let customers know about products and assumes that those customers will beat a path to the producer's door.

This perspective can best be described as the "Field of Dreams" era, thanks to the movie of the same name in which a character states, "If you build it, they will come." The production era focuses on products because of a lack of product options in the marketplace. Companies are free to create whatever products they deem appropriate, and customers have to accept what is offered.

production era
a focus on manufacturing and production quantity in which customers are meant to choose based on what is most abundantly available

sales era
hard selling to the customer, who has greater choice thanks to more competition in the marketplace

1-2b | The Sales Era

The **sales era** is highlighted by the increased power of customer choice. Companies no longer simply produce a product and expect customers to be waiting to buy whatever they are selling. Sales techniques were established and evolved to convince consumers to buy, giving consumers choice and ensuring companies focused on creating market share and building sales volume in a highly competitive environment.

Sales pitches are encouraged during this era, in which savvy salespeople use their understanding of human nature to convince customers to purchase their products. Answer the door at home to a company using the sales-era approach, and you may see a well-dressed person attempting to sell vacuum cleaners or encyclopedias.

The need to coax the customer is paramount in the sales era. Behind this belief, companies place resources, specifically sales materials (brochures, print ads, etc.) that are used in great quantities to encourage sales of their products. Companies respond to a marketplace with more competition by overwhelming customers with promotional activities that focus on the hard sell.

Today, some companies still believe in the importance of hard selling to customers. Companies are still using aggressive sales tactics to entice customers, which is why consumers associate marketing with selling and why marketing is often considered intrusive.

The majority of companies and marketers do not subscribe to a marketing approach heavy only on selling. While

Henry Ford of the Ford Motor Company once stated, "Any customer can have a car painted any colour that he wants, so long as it is black." Ford was describing the line of Model T cars that were available to the customer. His perspective is a great example of the production era way of thinking.

Chronicle/Alamy Stock Photo

sales makes up an important part of the marketing offering, it is only one part of the promotional activities available to today's marketer. Management thinker and innovator Peter Drucker put it best: "There will always, one can assume, be a need for some selling. But the aim of marketing is to make selling superfluous. The aim of marketing is to know and understand the customer so well that the product or service fits him and sells itself. Ideally, marketing should result in a customer who is ready to buy."[3]

1-2c | The Marketing Company Era

The **marketing company era** is highlighted by the coordination of marketing activities—advertising, sales, and public relations—into one department in an organization. Much of how a marketing department is organized is based on the need to include those elements. The job of this department is to better understand the customer rather than just trying to sell to them.

As society evolves and consumers become more sophisticated, products and services previously seen as exclusive and out of reach are now seen as possible purchases. In this era, customers are grouped into market segments, with marketing professionals tasked with understanding their customer before making their move.

A term that is important in many eras, and very much so in a marketing company era, is the *marketing concept*. The marketing concept focuses on linking the needs of customers with the competencies of an organization seeking to meet those needs.

In bringing the elements of the marketing company era together, it becomes clear that marketing and persuasion are intermixed. Marketing professionals focus on how to be shrewder about convincing customers to buy. Emotions are tied to basic-need products, higher-order benefits are attached to everyday products, and the customer is as much of a target of focus as the product.

However, this stage in the marketing era process is not devoid of any counteraction from the customer. Consumers are becoming shrewd themselves, as they begin to ask for more from the companies providing them products and services. While consumers are focused on aspects of value and service, they begin to seek out new ways to satisfy their needs. As seen by the prominence of the sharing phenomenon, through companies like Uber and Airbnb, consumers flock toward new offerings that satisfy their needs in ways not previously considered. Companies can no longer simply focus on persuasion to a passive customer; the customer begins to demand more from the companies that serve them, both for the individual and for society at large.

marketing company era
a strong emphasis on the marketing concept and development of a more comprehensive approach to understanding the customer

BODY OF WORK

In the era of socially responsible marketing, the Body Shop stands out. The company was founded by Anita Roddick in 1976 on principles of sustainability long before the term became the norm in business and society. Over the years, the company spearheaded campaigns to raise awareness on social and environmental issues while creating value for customers with product lines that were innovative and often environmentally sustainable at the same time. Roddick was an activist and human rights campaigner, and took pride in the company's stance on no animal testing just as much as the products produced by the multinational company.

All of which made the sale of the Body Shop to L'Oreal, the large French cosmetics company that was linked to animal testing so difficult for customers to accept. The result was a downward spiral for the Body Shop, as many customers went elsewhere.

However, in 2017, the Body Shop was sold by L'Oreal to Brazil's largest cosmetics company, Natura. This purchase made much more sense, and customers began to re-engage with the Body Shop as a company aligned with their social and ethical beliefs. In 2016, the Body Shop had announced a new company focus of "Enrich not Exploit." The company listed 14 efforts that would help the business move as a leader in the societal marketing space.[4] Getting back to its green roots was the overall purpose of the new direction, but the company had a lot to do in order to meet its lofty goals.

In late 2019, the Body Shop announced it would not be able to meet all of its 2016 goals. It had done well with biodiversity goals but fell behind in promised innovations in sustainable product packaging. Some "closed-loop" packaging goals the company had targeted for 2020 had to be moved to 2025.[5]

The case of the Body Shop shows us the inherent challenge of the societal marketing era: it is very difficult to do right by the environment and the bottom line. Most companies that try to achieve sustainability goals are faced with challenges that range from financing large-scale projects to keeping shareholders satisfied.

JHVEPhoto/Shutterstock.com

1-2d | Societal Marketing Era

It is apparent when we distill the marketing concept down to a basic idea (give customers what they want) that its pursuit can have potentially unsavoury consequences (what if what they want isn't good for them?). Dealing with this challenge created the **societal marketing era**, where a dual emphasis results: looking at not only what the customer wants but also what society wants.

Societal marketing examines the longer-term impacts on the customer and the environment when customers seek to satisfy needs. New movements, such as recycling and waste reduction, sought out companies' solutions to deal with greater consumerism. Health issues relating to product use are at the forefront of this era, with greater awareness of the safety and dietary issues attached to products. This era brings a greater government involvement in consumer needs and wants. Thanks to better customer education and extremely strict promotional restrictions, sales of products such as cigarettes have dropped drastically. Industries and companies are placing an emphasis on self-regulation before more strict government involvement created bottom-line and public relations issues.

1-2e | Relationship Marketing Era

Today, the relationship marketing era is about developing a real and sustainable relationship with the customer. The key movement in this era has to do with moving from interruption to interaction in a company's marketing efforts.[6] Marketing can no longer look for a

societal marketing era looking not only at the customer but expanding marketing efforts to include aspects from the external environment that go beyond a company's customers, suppliers, and competitors

one-off sale; marketing has to focus on taking steps to truly engage with the customer. Interruptions involve asking the customer to stop doing what they are interested in doing to listen to a company's message. This interruption frustrates customers and often results in their negative views on whichever company is the source of the interruption. As companies look to move away from interruption, they see the benefit of looking for a series of transactions that turn into a true interaction. Engagement is the focus of this era, aided by the use of two essential customer-based strategies: customer satisfaction and relationship marketing.

CUSTOMER SATISFACTION Customer satisfaction is the customer's evaluation of a good or service in terms of whether that good or service has met the customer's needs and expectations. Failure to meet a customer's needs and expectations results in the customer's dissatisfaction with the good or service.[7] Keeping current customers satisfied is just as important as attracting new customers—and a lot less expensive. Customer attrition, also known as churn rate, involves customers removing themselves from relationships with businesses due to concerns or issues they feel go unaddressed. A recent study by Qualtrics, a leading marketing research survey provider, found customers who left a company did so because of "poor service," and more than half said that the company could have changed their mind but did not even try.[8]

Another study showed that a 2 percent increase in customer retention has the same effect on profits as cutting costs by 10 percent.[9] Businesses that have a reputation for delivering high levels of customer satisfaction tend to do things differently from their competitors. When top management is obsessed with customer satisfaction, employees throughout the organization are more likely to understand the link between how they perform their job and the satisfaction of customers. The culture of such an organization focuses on delighting customers rather than on selling products.

RELATIONSHIP MARKETING Relationship marketing is a strategy that focuses on keeping and improving relationships with current customers. This strategy assumes that many consumers and business customers prefer to keep an ongoing relationship with one organization rather than to switch continually among providers in their search for value.

Disney is a good example of an organization focused on building long-term relationships with its customers. Most easily observed at its parks around the world, Disney managers understand that their company creates products and experiences that become an important part of people's lives and memories. This understanding has made Disney a leader in doing "right by the customer"—starting with the front-line cast members who interact directly with the public and encompassing all employees in all departments, who assess each decision based on how it will affect the customers and their relationship with the Disney brand.

CUSTOMER RELATIONSHIP MANAGEMENT
An important result of the relationship marketing era has been the concept of customer relationship management (CRM). Although created as a data-mining system to help marketers understand each customer on an individual level, CRM best serves the ultimate goal of meeting the needs of customers and building relationships.

A key aspect of relationships—and any CRM system—is trust. To build trust, companies have to be willing to share their stories with customers and listen to and act on what customers desire. Doing this has not always been possible when companies use data mining from various sources, but it is possible with social and mobile marketing.

Creating a 24/7/365 relationship with customers is now possible, if companies are willing to use the online world, an arena not only for exchange but also for true communication.

In the days of Henry Ford, door-to-door salesmen, and real-life Mad Men, there was never the opportunity to understand and target individual customers. However, this goal is now possible. Just head to any popular social media site, and you will find an interactive world with endless potential.

Chapter 8 focuses on CRM and will show the possibility of truly evolving from "interruption to interaction."

1-3 | KEY MARKETING TERMS

Now that we have seen the past and given an indication of the future of marketing, it is important to cover some of the fundamental aspects of marketing that every student of marketing should know. These ideas will form the basis of all remaining chapters and will provide you with the necessary tools to discuss and learn about marketing.

customer satisfaction customers' evaluation of a good or service in terms of whether it has met their needs and expectations

relationship marketing a strategy that focuses on keeping and improving relationships with current customers

CONDITIONS OF EXCHANGE

An exchange can take place only if the following five conditions exist:

1. At least two parties are involved.
2. Each party has something that may be of value to the other party.
3. Each party is capable of communication and delivery.
4. Each party is free to accept or reject the exchange offer.
5. Each party believes it is appropriate or desirable to deal with the other party.

Source: Philip Kotler, *Marketing Management*, 11th ed. (Upper Saddle River, NJ: Prentice-Hall, 2003), 12.

1-3a | Exchange

One desired outcome of marketing is an **exchange**—people giving up one thing to receive another thing they would rather have. Normally, we think of money as the medium of exchange. We "give up" money to "receive" the goods and services we want. Exchange does not, however, require money. Two people may barter or trade items such as baseball cards or oil paintings.

CUSTOMER VALUE Customer value is the relationship between benefits and the sacrifice necessary to obtain those benefits. Customer value is not simply a matter of high quality. A high-quality product that is available only at a high price will not be perceived as good value, nor will bare-bones service or low-quality goods selling for a low price. Instead, customers value goods and services that are of the quality they expect and are sold at prices they are willing to pay. Value can be used to sell both a Tesla and a $5 frozen pizza.

MARKET SEGMENTS Market segments are groups of individuals, families, or companies that are placed together because it is believed that they share similar needs. As we saw in the discussion of the evolution of marketing earlier in this chapter, segmentation has gone from not being done at all to being done at an almost individual level. Market segments form the core of marketing efforts because they represent the source of customer needs.

To target specific market segments, much has to be done to research the lives, trends, and needs of a particular group.

Later in the book, we will look at how marketing research (Chapter 4), consumer decision making (Chapter 5), and business marketing (Chapter 6) help provide the necessary tools to develop strong market segments (Chapter 7).

BUILDING RELATIONSHIPS Attracting new customers to a business is only the beginning. The best companies view new-customer attraction as the launching point for developing and enhancing a long-term relationship. Companies can expand their market share in three ways: attracting new customers, increasing business with existing customers, and retaining current customers. Building relationships with existing customers directly addresses two of the three possibilities and indirectly addresses the other.

THE MARKETING MIX The marketing mix—also known as the 4Ps of marketing—refers to product, price, place, and promotion. Each of the 4Ps must be studied and developed to create a proper strategy to go after a market segment:

- **Product** relates to the tangible and intangible aspects of a company's offering. A product could be a can of soup or a virtuoso ballet performance; both companies will need to look at what needs are being satisfied and how to best package all the aspects of the offering so that the consumer will be satisfied.

- **Price** relates to the quantifying of a value in exchange for a company's offering. Competition is a significant issue here, as are customer perception and economic factors. Setting the right price is all about taking those factors into consideration and making the best decision that satisfies the bottom line and the customer.

- **Place** relates to much of the behind-the-scenes activities of making an offering available to the customer. This is the world of channels and logistics, where

exchange
people giving up one thing to receive another thing they would rather have

customer value
the relationship between benefits and the sacrifice necessary to obtain those benefits

DISNEY CUSTOMER MAGIC

Anyone who has visited a Disney theme park can relate to the feeling of being overwhelmed, be it by the crowds, lines, or just the overall environment. For some, this overstimulation can be too much. In 2019 at Walt Disney World in Florida, Brody Bergner, a young autistic boy had had enough while waiting in line to see Disney characters. Brody had what his mother described as a "meltdown." Noticing this, a Disney employee dressed as Snow White took Brody's hand and took him away from the noise and bustle. She sat down with him, engaged at a one-to-one level that was likely a nice change from the chaos of a theme park. When Brody's mom posted a series of images on Facebook, it didn't take long for media attention and those pictures to make their rounds online and in the media. The pictures of Brody and Snow White are not only heart-warming but also represent what companies can do to train employees to go beyond basic expectations and offer experiences for their customers that are long lasting and impactful.

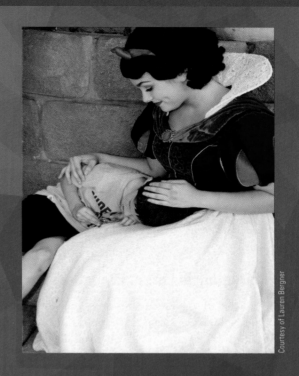

Courtesy of Lauren Bergner

Sources: "This Snow White actress at Disney World is being praised for helping an autistic child" August 28, 2019, Daily Dot, www.dailydot.com/irl/disney-world-snow-white-helps-autistic-child; Caitlin O'Kane, "Snow White comforts boy with autism who had a 'meltdown' in Disney World," September 4, 2019, www.cbsnews.com/news/snow-white-comforts-boy-with-autism-who-had-a-meltdown-in-disney-world.

CUSTOMER VALUE

Marketers interested in customer value

- offer products that perform,
- earn trust through loyalty programs,
- avoid unrealistic pricing by communicating clearly,
- give consumers the facts and the opportunity to learn more,
- offer an organization-wide commitment to service and after-sales support, and
- partner with consumers to cocreate experiences that consumers want.

decisions made on how to get a company's product to market could be more important than the product itself.

- **Promotion** relates to what most people believe marketing to be about. These are the most visible activities of marketing, the ones that get into the news and the faces of customers. Trying to find the right balance of what techniques to use (including advertising) is a constant challenge, as is keeping a consistent feel and look.

1-4 | WHY MARKETING MATTERS

Given that this chapter started out by proclaiming the death of marketing, the question that needs to be asked is *Why does marketing matter?* Here are a few compelling reasons.

1-4a | Marketing Is Part of Every Company

No matter what discipline in business you choose to pursue, you will have customers. If you do not concern yourself with the customer, you will cease to have any (just ask BlackBerry).

All companies, from multinationals to independent consultants, need to be customer focused. We know now that marketing provides this customer focus; therefore, understanding marketing means understanding your customer.

Successful companies have a strong understanding of the importance of marketing. Apple, the incredibly successful technology company, created a three-point marketing philosophy when it was founded in 1977. The first point of that philosophy is the most telling: "Empathy—we will truly understand [the customer's] needs better than any company." This fundamental belief lies at the core of many successful organizations, including Apple.[10]

1-4b | Marketing Is a Rewarding Career

Marketing can provide both financial and personal rewards. Marketing graduates have the flexibility of seeking employment in any industry, profit or non-profit, public or private. This is because there is an inherent need for marketing in any organization that has a customer—whether final consumers or businesses' customers.

Careers in marketing are varied and offer many opportunities to those looking for a constantly evolving and changing marketplace. There are entry-level positions such as marketing coordinators and marketing analysts; these positions offer an opportunity for aspiring marketers to learn the skill set necessary to be successful in marketing. These are often challenging roles that are rewarded with greater opportunity and responsibility. As you become versed in the world of marketing, more senior-level positions become available. Job titles like marketing manager, project manager, and vice president of marketing all display the importance of leadership and management while still applying the basic concepts of marketing along with advance techniques of analysis and strategy.

A great advantage to a career in marketing lies in the variety of industries in which marketing jobs are present. Although there are many jobs in the areas of advertising, product management, and marketing research, there are also many opportunities to apply the concepts of marketing to various situations. Numerous marketing opportunities can be found in government (at the municipal level especially), but also in sports, the arts, and nonprofit worlds. There is no shortage of opportunity in the field of marketing—finding the right opening often comes down to how well students can learn the material (such as reading a textbook like this) and combine that with skills that are invaluable in creating a career in marketing.

To excel and advance in the field of marketing, strong communication and analytical skills are essential. Now that we know that marketing forms a fundamental part of any organization, a good marketer will understand the importance of working with other departments to ensure customer needs are met. As well, managers in marketing will deal constantly with uncertainty, so being able to analyze diverse and often divergent information will be key in becoming a successful marketing professional.

1-4c | Marketing Provides an Important Skill Set

Even if your career aspirations are not in the field of marketing, you will still need to sell yourself to a future employer. Skills developed when learning marketing—how to understand needs, research trends, create an offering, and communicate benefits—all relate back to a person's job search.

Anyone with aspirations of a career in marketing should think of the hard and soft skills needed to be successful. On the hard skill side, a new marketer should seek to possess the ability to analyze data and communicate their findings via the digital space. In the past,

Marketing—A Tough Task

The irony should be clear—marketing as a discipline has a marketing problem. More specifically, an image problem. As mentioned earlier in the chapter, marketing is often known by what it is compared to—advertising, selling, and social media. And this gets perpetuated in the business press, where all you have to do is go into a news site and type in the word *marketing* and you will get an endless list of articles such as the "Top 10 Social Media Marketing Tips" or "Digital Marketing Tools." And while there is nothing wrong with these lists or tools, associating marketing primarily or only with these limits what marketing is truly about. A recent study asked nonmarketing workers about the value that marketers can bring. Only 13 percent of respondents thought the marketing team would have any influence on business strategy, and only 10 percent believed they had anything to do with product development in an organization.[12]

"Business has only two functions — marketing and innovation." — Milan Kundera

marketing was much more focused on brand- and product-related skills, but recent studies have shown a significant gap being created between what skills aspiring marketing professionals bring to the workplace and the necessary skill set that industry is increasingly seeking.

A 2019 report by recruiting company Hays found that the most in-demand job titles relating to marketing included digital project managers, data insight analysts, and content managers. The report also noted that marketers entering the marketplace should focus on building a wide variety of skills, and not focus on just one media channel or social media platform.[11]

1-4d | Marketing Is Part of Everyday Life

The tasks in marketing, as we have seen in this chapter, go well beyond a simple advertisement or sales call. Marketing includes important tasks that may not always be associated with marketing—such as distribution—that ensure that the products are on store shelves or delivered from a website.

Being informed about marketing means being an informed consumer. Most Canadians' lives are full of activities and tasks that will have them confronting marketing messages from numerous organizations. By learning about marketing, you will be better able to discern a good message from a bad one and hold those companies that are targeting you to a higher standard.

You now have the necessary background and understanding of marketing. But most importantly, you have learned not to limit marketing to just a few basic tactics. Now you can turn the page to start learning about what marketing has to offer.

AWAKE CHOCOLATE
CONTINUING CASE

AWAKE Chocolate

A Delicious Way to Get Energy

In February 2013, the founders of Awake Chocolate faced the scrutiny of the *Dragon's Den*. One pointed question from former Dragon Kevin O'Leary concerned cash flow in the anticipated first year of business for their new product. One of the founders, Adam Deremo, stated that the company would likely be in the red in the first year because, as he stated, "... we need to make an investment in marketing."[1]

It is clear that Awake Chocolate appreciates and understands the importance of marketing for the company's success. This running case will look at how a group of former big-company executives made the shift from drinking coffees in boardrooms to making chocolate energy products destined to replace those boardroom coffees.

When asked how Awake Chocolate came to be, Deremo stated that he along with cofounders Matt Schnarr and Dan Tzotzis were focused on one thing: understanding the customer. He noted that the idea for Awake Chocolate "... came complexly from a place of consumer insight." Adam was referring to the focus on understanding customer need before actually designing or making a product.

This initial focus on what customers want before making what *you* want is an important lesson for anyone starting their own business. Too often would-be entrepreneurs are focused on a solution to a problem that either does not exist or has not been proven by asking the most important part of any successful business—the customer.

The belief that created the foundation of Awake Chocolate was that consumers were searching to solve a problem: they could not find a pleasing way to consume products that provided them with energy. Adam noted that the unmet need was: "The ability to get energy in a way that tasted good."

All of Awake's founders had experience with consumer products before starting the company. Most notably, experience working at Kraft and Pepsi allowed the founders of Awake to see what was happening in marketplace. Adam Deremo noted during his time at Pepsico that consumer tastes were impacting product choices by consumer product companies: "Competitors of Pepsi in granola bar space had added functional ingredients to bars." Companies began to realize that products that provided a notable energy boost were not that appealing, and there was opportunity for companies to add energy-based ingredients to other products.

And a fundamental need in the food and drink space is, of course, taste. It would seem that customers seeking energy products were having to make sacrifices in order to get that burst. Adam observed: "The number one consumer objection to energy drinks was taste. Same problem that coffee had."

So the idea for Awake Chocolate arose from a consumer dislike. The founders of Awake chose the vehicle of chocolate to deliver something that was normally presented to consumer in forms other than food. The result was Awake Chocolate, a North American success story in the food and energy product markets. By focusing on customer needs before anything else, the founders were able to create a novel product to meet those needs and create, as Adam Deremo said, "energy benefit in a food product."

QUESTIONS

1. Explain in which era of marketing that Awake Chocolate currently resides. Describe some ways in which the company can move beyond the current stage into the next era of marketing.

2. Review the Awake Chocolate website (awakechocolate.ca) and determine where the focus on customer needs is apparent in the various pages of the website. Look over social media sites owned by Awake to assess needs as well.

3. The concept of value is a key concept in Chapter 1, and is evidenced in the above case without using the term *value*. Look back through the chapter and your notes to determine how value is represented in the above case.

NOTE

1. CBC.ca at www.cbc.ca/dragonsden/m_pitches/awake-chocolate

AWAKE Chocolate

AWAKE Chocolate

AWAKE CAFFEINATED CHOCOLATE™

2 | The Marketing Environment, Social Responsibility, and Ethics

LEARNING OUTCOMES

2-1 Discuss the external environment of marketing, and explain how it affects a company

2-2 Describe the competitive factors that affect marketing

2-3 Describe the regulatory factors that affect marketing

2-4 Describe the economic factors that affect marketing

2-5 Describe the social factors that affect marketing

2-6 Explain the importance to marketing managers of current demographic trends

2-7 Describe the technological factors that affect marketing

2-8 Discuss the role of corporate social responsibility and ethics in business

"Nothing is more important than preparation."

—Simon Sinek[1]

2-1 | THE EXTERNAL MARKETING ENVIRONMENT

target market
a group of people or organizations for which an organization designs, implements, and maintains a marketing mix intended to meet the needs of that group

Marketing managers oversee the marketing mix of a company. Chapter 1 described the marketing mix as a unique combination of product, price, place (distribution), and promotion strategies. (The marketing mix is also addressed in Chapter 3.) The marketing mix is ultimately designed, developed, and maintained by the company to appeal to a specific group of potential buyers—the target market. A **target market** is the group of potential customers for whom a company's product offers the greatest value.

While the marketing mix, management, HR, and finance are the major business elements a company controls, it operates within a galaxy of external forces over which it has little or no control. Key among these forces is the evolution of the target market itself. Businesses must adjust the marketing mix to reflect the changing needs and composition of the target market, brought on by the changes in the environment in which consumers live, work, and make purchases. While new consumers may become part of the target market, others will inevitably drop out. But even those who

remain will have different tastes, needs, incomes, lifestyles, and buying habits than the original target consumers. They, along with their behaviours, will also be affected by fluctuations in the economy and changes in sociopolitical and technological events, as well as offerings from other businesses hoping to steal them away.

Controllable and uncontrollable or internal and external variables affect the target market, whether that market consists of individual or business purchasers. Although companies can control the marketing mix, as well as other internal activities of the business, they cannot control elements in the external environment that continually evolve, thus moulding and reshaping the target market. Marketers must shape and reshape the marketing mix to react to the external environment in an attempt to influence the target market. However, they have the ability, more than ever before, to anticipate changes in the environment and therefore proactively revise their marketing mix.

2-1a | Understanding the External Environment

By understanding the external environment, marketing managers and the businesses they work for can plan strategically. However, the environment, likened previously to a "galaxy," is forever in motion and endlessly mysterious.

This "unknown" renders some marketers completely at the mercy of the environment, forever reacting too late to changes or missing them all together. If these changes negatively impact the company, they are threats, which can put a company out of business. Positive changes are opportunities that can lift a business to unexpected heights if it is paying attention. But "paying attention" must be formalized into a structured process, where the marketing team influences a corporate culture of environmental intel informants. While it is the team's job to catch all glimmers of change in the environment, it needs buy-in from the front line all the way up the ladder to senior executives. What's more, in the digital uber-connected world in which we live, businesses can compel and involve their customers in this information gathering as well. This process called *environmental scanning*.

The most important part of the process is developing a framework within which these external environmental forces can be categorized. Various systems exist but they are all variations of the CREST model, which organizes external forces into competitive, regulatory, economic, social, and technological categories. As shown in Exhibit 2.1, the forces of CREST impact not only the business but also one another. Moreover, they almost always originate from the social force. Consider the movement toward plant-based proteins in the 2010s as

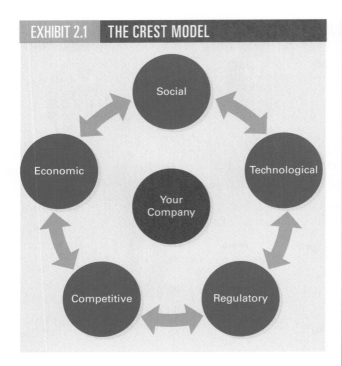

EXHIBIT 2.1 THE CREST MODEL

Social

Economic

Technological

Your Company

Competitive

Regulatory

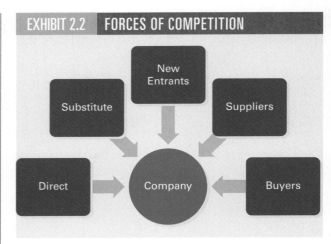

EXHIBIT 2.2 FORCES OF COMPETITION

New Entrants

Substitute

Suppliers

Direct

Company

Buyers

an example. Social concerns with inhumane treatment of animals, health hazards associated with meat-based fat consumption, environmental impact of livestock production, and so on, all conspired to trigger a domino effect of new entrants (competitors), regulations (Health Canada), economics (new industries), and technology (GMO).

2-2 | COMPETITIVE FACTORS

The competitive environment includes competitors to a business, both directly and indirectly, as well as the size and number of competitors. Companies have little control over the competitive environment, but they can influence it greatly through their own actions and strategic planning. Even since his 1979 *Harvard Business Review* article "How Competitive Forces Shape Strategy," business guru Michael Porter's five forces of competition[2] still serves as a relevant model to organize, anticipate, and strategically plan for competitors (see Exhibit 2.2):

- *Direct competitors:* competitors most closely matching a business's product offering

- *Substitutes:* competitors whose products satisfy the same need, but in varying ways

- *New entrants:* competitors who might emerge when barriers to entry in the industry are lowered

- *Suppliers:* business partners, such as materials producers, motivated to charge the highest price to the company to maximize profit

- *Buyers:* business partners, such as retailers, motivated to pay the least for products purchased from the company, once again, to maximize profit

The five forces of competition demonstrate how competition is not always for market share, as it is between two competing companies targeting the same market. It is also about competition over dollars, as seen in Exhibit 2.2, between a company and its suppliers and buyers. Competition is its own environment—a microcosm of the larger external environment covered in this chapter—fraught with unpredictability, turbulence, and opportunities and threats. Marketers must constantly plan and adjust across all marketing mix elements to keep up with, or conquer competition.

This creates a double-edged sword for companies in gathering information on any form of competition. Competitors are leveraging the power of big data, analytics, and social media to gather information about the company's customers and then relate to them across a host of different platforms, most of which are open for public viewing. The problem is that when the company gathers intelligence on its competitors, it is also being viewed by its competitors, creating an obvious dilemma. Businesses *must* use social media to tell their story and build community, but in doing so they leave themselves open to being viewed by competitors.

2-3 | REGULATORY FACTORS

Like every aspect of running a business, the marketing mix is also subject to laws and restrictions created by regulators. It is the duty of marketing managers and their legal counsel not only to understand these laws and conform to them today but also to track and predict the shaping and reshaping of laws. Failure to

EXHIBIT 2.3 SPECIALIZED FEDERAL LEGISLATION AFFECTING BUSINESS

Legislation	Major Provisions
Competition Act	Promotes the efficiency and adaptability of the Canadian economy. Expands opportunities for Canadian participation in world markets while at the same time recognizing the role of foreign competition in Canada. Ensures that small- and medium-sized enterprises have an equitable opportunity to participate in the Canadian economy. Provides consumers with competitive prices and product choices.
Consumer Packaging and Labelling Act	Requires prepackaged consumer products to bear accurate and meaningful labelling information to help consumers make informed purchasing decisions. It prohibits false or misleading representations and sets out specifications for mandatory label information.
Trade-marks Act	Regulates and protects trade names and trademarks.
Textile Labelling Act	Requires that textile articles bear accurate and meaningful labelling information to help consumers make informed purchasing decisions. It prohibits false or misleading representations and sets out specifications for mandatory label information.
Health Canada's Food and Drugs Act & Regulations	Establishes standards for the safety and nutritional quality of all foods sold in Canada.
Motor Vehicle Safety Act	Regulates the safely standards for the manufacture and importation of motor vehicles.
Personal Information Protection and Electronic Documents Act	Supports and promotes electronic commerce by protecting personal information that is collected, used, or disclosed in certain circumstances, by providing for the use of electronic means to communicate or record information or transactions.
Privacy Act	Governs the personal information handling practices of federal government institutions. Applies to all the personal information the federal government collects, uses, and discloses—whether about individuals or federal employees.

Sources: Zikmund/D'Amico/Browne/Anthony/Monk/Donville. *Effective Marketing*, 1E. © 2008 Nelson Education Ltd.; Competition Bureau (https://www.competitionbureau.gc.ca; accessed January 17, 2017); Health Canada (https://www.canada.ca/en/health-canada.html; accessed January 17, 2017); Justice Laws Website (https://www.laws-lois.justice.gc.ca; accessed January 17, 2017); Office of the Privacy Commissioner of Canada (https://www.priv.gc.ca (accessed January 17, 2017).

comply with regulations can have major consequences for a business. Sometimes just sensing trends and taking corrective action before a government agency acts can help avoid the negative effects of regulation.

Regulations don't just appear suddenly and unexpectedly. As indicated earlier, they are, in fact, a product of social forces, shaped by people who respond to events that affect them personally and eventually grow in public awareness. The frequent breaches of personal data collected by businesses throughout the last decade, only to be compromised by hackers, has triggered never-ending adjustments to the Consumer Privacy Act in Canada.

2-3a | Federal Legislation

The federal legislation affecting how business is conducted in Canada is administered by the **Competition Bureau**, an independent agency of Industry Canada. This bureau encompasses several branches and is responsible for enforcing laws covering areas such as bankruptcy, trade practices, competition, credit, labelling and packaging, copyrights, hazardous products, patents, and trademarks.[3] Some of the specialized federal legislation that affects businesses and business dealings is listed in Exhibit 2.3.

2-3b | Provincial and Territorial Laws

In Canada, our constitution divides legal jurisdictions between the provincial or territorial legislatures and the federal government, thus allowing each level of government to legislate in the areas for which it has been given responsibility. For example, Québec's Bill 101 restricts the use of the English language in certain advertising and promotion material. A national company, such as Tim Hortons, may have to alter its advertising and store signage in Québec to be in compliance. Alberta allows the sale of recreational cannabis by private retailers, whereas Ontario has provincially run stores operating as Liquor Control Board of Ontario (LCBO) outlets. Airlines, on the other hand, are under federal jurisdiction, and the provinces do not have direct powers to regulate airline companies.

Marketing managers, especially those working for national companies, must be aware of the differences in each province's and territory's legal environment, and

Competition Bureau
the federal department charged with administering most marketplace laws

they also need a sound understanding of federal legislation that affects their industry.

2-3c | Self-Regulation

Instead of facing explicit legislation from either the provincial, territorial, or federal governments, many business groups in Canada have formed associations that police themselves. This arrangement is called **self-regulation**. One such association is Advertising Standards Canada (ASC), established by Canada's advertising industry to monitor honesty and fairness in advertising. Advertising is a very visible form of communication strategy, and some businesses come under fire from consumer groups regarding deception in their advertising. The ASC provides clear ethical guidelines to both advertisers and advertising agencies in its document "The Canadian Code of Advertising Standards."[4] Another group, the Canadian Association of Petroleum Producers (CAPP), has established a code of ethics for its member oil and gas companies. The Canadian Marketing Association (CMA) continues to develop guidelines and ethical practices for its member marketing companies.

CONSUMER PRIVACY A marketing manager must also be aware of the increasingly important area of consumer privacy, especially because of the vast amounts of data that almost any company can collect and store by using the latest cloud technology. Everything from customer information to survey data is valuable to companies, but privacy issues need to be addressed. Businesses should be able to justify the type of information they have and how it is to be used. Other issues of note are the security of information storage and the sale or transfer of information to others. Increasingly, and largely as a result of pressure from consumers' groups, governments are looking at developing, or have already developed, privacy legislation.

The January 1, 2019, update to Canada's Personal Information Protection and Electronic Documents act (PIPEDA) pointed out the domino effect of external forces upon a business. First is the social force of more and more people using digital devices. Next, this increased use of technology sets in motion a range of aggressive moves by companies to get a competitive advantage in data collection. The competitiveness then spurs technological changes in the environment as tech companies accommodate the desires of companies. Then citizens learn their privacy is at risk, resulting in distrust. All of which, in turn, leads to the regulatory tightening.

Canada's federal government, like the governments of many other countries, already has legislation relating to privacy. The Privacy Act (PA) and the Personal Information Protection and Electronic Documents Act (PIPEDA) were put in place to protect the privacy of our personal information and to ensure that its collection, use, and disclosure are both legal and ethical. The latest protection, established in July 2014 by the federal government to improve and protect consumer privacy, is referred to as the Canadian Anti-Spam Legislation (CASL). Its intent is to deter the most damaging and deceptive forms of spam. The CASL, which is enforced by the Canadian Radio-television and Telecommunications Commission (CRTC), the Competition Bureau, and the Privacy Commissioner, undergoes review and updates as deemed necessary. Canadian consumers are concerned about their privacy, but most are unaware of the details of this legislation. Therefore, marketers must be proactive in ensuring consumer privacy.

2-4 | ECONOMIC FACTORS

In addition to competitive and regulatory factors, marketing managers must understand, forecast, and react to the economic environment. The four economic areas of greatest concern to most marketers are consumers' incomes, purchasing power, inflation, and recession.

2-4a | Consumers' Incomes

As disposable (or after-tax) incomes rise, more families and individuals can afford the "good life." The median total family income in Canada was $92 700.[5] That means half of all Canadian households earned less than and the other half earned more than that amount.

Education is the primary determinant of a person's earning potential. According to Human Resources and Skills Development Canada, the benefits of higher education include higher earnings, greater savings and assets, higher growth in earnings, and higher income during retirement. In addition, higher education reduces the risk of experiencing low income and unemployment. The benefits of higher education are consistent across all provinces.[6]

Along with ability to make purchases, income is a key demographic determinant of markets businesses choose to target. Marketers of high-priced products will naturally target high income earners, while the opposite is true for

self-regulation
programs voluntarily adopted by business groups to regulate the activities of their members

those marketing low-priced items. This targeting can easily be geographically based as well, as wealthy people tend to live in larger, more expensive homes in higher-end neighborhoods. Our digital footprint, however, can often be confusing even for the sophisticated algorithms of Google and FaceBook, which will automatically place ads on the screens of those who visit a company's website, whether they can afford products from that company or not. That said, the average household spends more than it earns. In 2019, our household debt in Canada had reached a total of $2.16 trillion, the highest rate of debt relative to GDP of any of the G7 countries.[7]

Our disposable income goes toward living expenses after income tax. Specifically, 19 percent goes toward mortgage or rent; 7 percent on food.[8] But even before we're able to make those expenditures, 18 percent of our earnings, on average, goes to Canada Revenue Agency. Discretionary income is what's left over after essentials and taxes, and this is typically where Canadians get themselves into debt. Thirteen percent of household income goes to private transportation; 5.5 percent toward household operations; 4 percent on clothing and accessories; 3 percent on eating out; and more than 3 percent is spent on recreational services and/or equipment.[9]

When we carry debt, we must eventually use our income to make interest payments instead of buying more goods and services. The compounding nature of interest payments, combined with the consumer behavioural trait of credit-based spending, can have serious negative results on individuals, which leads to reduced spending. With less spending, of course, companies sell fewer items at the retail level, and manufacturing in turn slows down. The result, as you can see, become a negative cycle for all involved.

2-4b | Purchasing Power

Purchasing power is measured by comparing income to the relative cost of a set standard of goods

SpeedKingz/Shutterstock.com

and services in different geographic areas, usually referred to as the cost of living. Another way to think of purchasing power is income minus the cost of living (i.e., expenses). In general, a cost-of-living index takes into account the costs of housing, food and groceries, transportation, utilities, healthcare, and miscellaneous expenses, such as clothing, services, and entertainment. In Canada, we have seen the cost of living soar in Toronto and Vancouver, particularly in housing. While these world-class urban centres have become the subject of great envy to many (due to the amenities offered by cities of such stature), Calgary, still mired in a slow economy in 2019, outranked both Toronto and Vancouver in the *Economist*'s most desirable cities to live in the world. It placed fifth, ahead of Vancouver, 6 and Toronto, 7.[10]

When income is high relative to the cost of living, people have more **discretionary income**. That means they have more money to spend on nonessential items, as defined previously. This information is important to marketers for obvious reasons. Consumers with high purchasing power can afford to spend more money without jeopardizing their budget for necessities such as food, housing, and utilities. They also have the ability to purchase higher-priced items, such as a more expensive car, a home in a more expensive neighbourhood, or a designer handbag versus one from a discount store.

2-4c | Inflation

Inflation is generally considered to be a measure of price increases in the cost of living, but it is more accurately defined as the decrease in the value of money. Thus, in simple terms, an inflation rate of 5 percent means 5 percent more money is needed today to buy the same basket of products that was purchased last year. If inflation is 5 percent, you can expect that, on average, prices have risen about 5 percent over prices in the previous year. Of course,

purchasing power
a comparison of income versus the relative cost of a set standard of goods and services in different geographic areas

discretionary income
the amount of money people have to spend on nonessential items

disposable income
the amount of money people have to spend after taxes

gross income
The amount of money people earn before taxes and expenses

inflation
a measure of the decrease in the value of money, expressed as the percentage reduction in value since the previous year

EXHIBIT 2.4 THE PERSONAL SPENDING OF CANADIANS

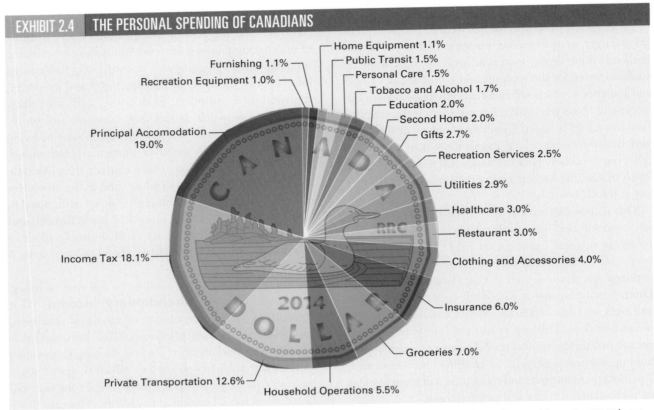

Home Equipment 1.1%
Public Transit 1.5%
Furnishing 1.1%
Personal Care 1.5%
Recreation Equipment 1.0%
Tobacco and Alcohol 1.7%
Education 2.0%
Second Home 2.0%
Principal Accomodation 19.0%
Gifts 2.7%
Recreation Services 2.5%
Utilities 2.9%
Healthcare 3.0%
Income Tax 18.1%
Restaurant 3.0%
Clothing and Accessories 4.0%
Insurance 6.0%
Groceries 7.0%
Private Transportation 12.6%
Household Operations 5.5%

Source: Doug Murray, "Where do Canadians spend the most money each year?" Slice.ca, June 25, 2019. https://www.slice.ca/where-do-canadians-spend-the-most-money-each-year.

if pay raises are matching the rate of inflation, then employees will be no worse (or better) off with regard to the immediate purchasing power of their salaries. However, in Canada, where the general state of the economy varies greatly from province to province, this is rarely the case. Inflation rises, while salaries remain flat, or worse, decreased. See Exhibit 2.4.

Inflation pressures consumers to make more economically practical purchases and still maintain their standard of living. This is where consumer behaviour becomes both fascinating and problematic. Either way, marketers must develop strategies that acknowledge the impact of inflation but still compel consumers to make purchases—often ones they cannot afford. In this regard, marketers, or more broadly, brands, are often perceived as taking advantage of a vulnerable buying public. Financial services, in particular, are called out for this, seen as taking advantage of the discretionary spending addiction of Canadians, extending to them a lifeline of credit, only to collect interest rate payments many cannot sustain.

recession
a period of economic activity characterized by negative growth, which reduces demand for goods and services

2-4d | Recession

A **recession** is a period of economic activity characterized by negative growth. More precisely, a recession occurs when the gross domestic product falls for two consecutive quarters. The recession that began in December 2007, spurred by a surge in underpriced mortgages, eventually coming due and triggering a domino effect around the world, affected Canada less than our neighbours to the south. Canada experienced a recession that was less severe and shorter than in the other G7 nations, and our financial institutions ended up in a much better position than those in the United States, where many required government aid to stay afloat.

However, the collapse of the world price of oil in 2013 resulted in a much different story. With so much of its economy based on the production of natural resources, such as fossil fuels, the global drop in demand for oil, resulting in a price per barrel decrease from over $110 to less than $30 in the span of a few short months, was catastrophic.[11] The Alberta economy in particular, the main producer of the resource, was the hardest hit, with job losses in the tens of thousands, but the ripple effect was felt across the country. Unfortunately, the crash endured longer in Canada, where our reliance on the oilsands resource in northern Alberta, portrayed internationally

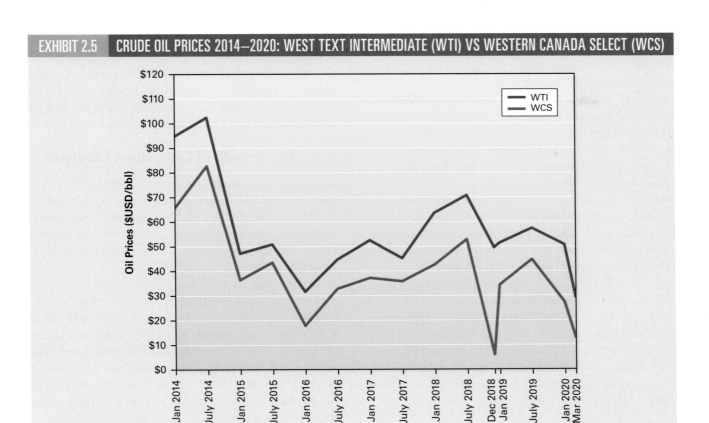

Source: Trevor Tombe, "Why producing less oil is likely to help Alberta—and Canada—earn more," CBC News, Dec. 4, 2018. https://www.cbc.ca/news/canada/calgary /alberta-production-cuts-trevor-tombe-impact-analysis-1.4930691.

as a key contributor to global warming, offset any chance that demand would pick back up any time soon. Transport of Alberta's "heavy" oil became a divisive federal and provincial election platform, that had still not sorted itself out by late 2019. And thus, a "pseudorecession" continues in Alberta. See Exhibit 2.5.

From 2014 to 2016, Alberta's GDP fell by 6.5 percent.[12] To add insult to injury, wildfires in 2016 led to the evacuation of over 80 000 residents of Fort McMurray, Alberta, and temporarily shut down production of oil sands operations. The cost of the shutdown alone shaved another 0.33 percent off Alberta's GDP and was significant enough to make a minor dent in the Canadian GDP.[13] The wildfires are a good example of an **environmental factor**. Environmental factors are often treated separately, as part of the natural environment. Like any of the environmental forces described here, the natural environment cannot be controlled by businesses. That said, natural disasters, aside from the obvious human toll, usually end up affecting the economic environment, which is why we are discussing them here. Either way, in cases of geographically isolated peaks and valleys in the economy, national brands in particular have to manage their marketing strategy accordingly, providing one plan for the isolated area, and another for the rest of the country.

2-5 | SOCIAL FACTORS

Social change may be the most difficult of the environmental forces to forecast, but as mentioned previously, all other forces originate at the social level, and thus, it is incumbent upon marketers to do their due diligence in seeing social patterns develop, then seizing them early.

Social factors include demographics, values, and lifestyles but, most importantly, the needs people are demanding to be met. Social factors influence the products people buy, the prices paid for products, the effectiveness of specific promotions, and how, where, and when people expect to purchase products.

environmental factors
noncontrollable factors caused by natural disasters, which negatively or positively affect organizations

2-5a | Marketing-Oriented Values

A *value* is a strongly held and enduring belief. Our values are key determinants of what is important and not important, what actions we take or do not take, and how we behave in social situations. Our values are typically formed through our interactions with family, friends, and other influencers, such as teachers, religious leaders, and politicians. The influence of celebrities, both the traditional celebrity (entertainer or athlete) and the emerging new sway held by social media celebrities cannot be ignored, despite the biases marketers might feel about them personally. This is particularly true of Gen Zs, those born from 1995 to 2009. Almost all of those older than 13 have a smart phone, and the majority are online up to 3 to 10 hours a day—many finding out about news and new products on social media.[14]

Despite the conclusions one might draw from those statistics, it is important to note that Canadians still hold on passionately to core values, which have nothing to do with digital communications. A 2016 survey by Nanos is summarized below, showing the most common responses to the question "What do Canadians value most?"[15]

- 16 percent: Rights and freedoms

- 12 percent: Respect for others

- 11 percent: Kindness and compassion

Another 32 percent of the responses clustered around similar themes such as diversity, inclusion, tolerance, acceptance, social justice, and equality. Clearly, we're not quite as narrowly focused upon the trappings within our devices as we might perceive.

These core values hold for a majority of Canadians today and have led to the perception that Canadians are fair and socially conscious. Additionally, we are known to be tolerant and respectful of other cultures.

What does this tell marketers about our buying habits? We place a high value on fairness at the cash register, but also in what transpired getting the product to the cash register. Today's consumers are demanding, inquisitive, and discriminating when it comes to supply chains. We expect ethical treatment of people, animals, and our planet. Companies caught taking short cuts or bending ethical standards in this regard experience significant loss of credibility and/or financial damage as well. The 2019 scandal involving Québec-based engineering and procurement company SNC Lavalin and the federal government played out for months, tarnishing the reputation of the global corporation and the trustworthiness of Prime Minister Justin Trudeau. Nevertheles, by year's end he and his Liberal Party had once again been elected.

2-5b | The Growth of Component Lifestyles

Canadian consumers today are piecing together **component lifestyles**. A lifestyle is a mode of living; it is the way we decide to live our lives. In other words, we choose products and services that meet our diverse needs and interests rather than conforming to traditional stereotypes.

In the past, a person's profession—for instance, banker—defined their lifestyle. Today, a person can be a banker and also a gourmet cook, a fitness enthusiast, a dedicated single parent, and an Internet guru. Each of these lifestyles is associated with different goods and services and represents a target audience. Component lifestyles increase the complexity of consumers' buying habits. The unique lifestyles of every consumer can require a different marketing mix.

2-5c | Families Today

The Vanier Institute of the Family defines the family today as "any combination of two or more persons who are bound together over time by ties of mutual consent, birth and/or adoption or placement and who, together, assume responsibilities for variant combinations of some of the following:

- Physical maintenance and care of group members
- Addition of new members through procreation or adoption
- Socialization of children
- Social control of members
- Production, consumption, distribution of goods and services
- Affective nurturance—love"[16]

Despite a great deal of media coverage on the changing role of the family, it isn't so much the *role* of the family that has changed but the *makeup* of the family. Canadian families have an unprecedented level of diversity. Some men and women are raising children on their own without a partner; others are living together unmarried, with or without children; and gay and lesbian couples are caring for each other and raising children together. In addition, some adult children are following a trend of returning to the nest and living with their

component lifestyles
mode of living that involves choosing goods and services that meet one's diverse needs and interests rather than conforming to a single, traditional lifestyle

parents, and an increasing number of people are living alone.[17] Families today still demonstrate how, as individuals, we accept responsibility for each other.[18]

We face significant challenges in how we carry out our family responsibilities. For families today, two key resources are required—time and money—and they are both in short supply. To meet financial obligations, most couples work and even, in some cases, hold multiple jobs. This situation results in further time poverty and affects the consumption choices that a family makes. The recent developments in technology combined with the time poverty of Canadian families has led to an increase in the use of social media not only as a communication tool but also as an information-gathering and shopping tool. Decision makers in families are increasingly using the Internet to do chores, plan trips, research products, find health information, read the news, seek out specials, and get coupons or participate in group savings. Consumers freely share the information they find with everyone in their personal networks.

2-6 | DEMOGRAPHIC FACTORS

Another variable in the external environment and one extremely important to marketing managers is **demography**—the study of people's vital statistics, such as their age, race and ethnicity, and location. Demographics are significant because they are strongly related to consumer behaviour in the marketplace.

We turn our attention now to a closer look at age groups, their impact, and the opportunities they present for marketers. Why does tailoring the merchandise to particular age groups matter? One reason is that each generation enters a life stage with its own tastes and biases, and tailoring products to what customers value is key to sales. The cohorts have been named Generation Z, Generation Y/millennials, Generation X, and baby boomers. You will find that each cohort group has its own needs, values, and consumption patterns.

2-6a | Generation Z

Members of **Generation Z**, increasingly referred to as snowflakes (because they have been called "special and unique" by their parents), are preadolescents and early adolescents born between 1995 and 2009. With attitudes, access to information, brand consciousness, technical sophistication well beyond their years, and purchasing power to match, these young consumers increasingly represent an attractive segment for marketers of all kinds of products.

The number of young Gen Zs (also called tweens) who own cellphones has increased significantly over the years. They have now overtaken Gen Ys/millennials in world population, becoming the second largest demographic cohort—second only to the baby boomers. Given that they were practically born with a smart phone in their hand, it is not surprising their ownership and usage rates of devices. With cellphone ownership among Grade 4 students at 25 percent and 50 percent for those in Grade 7,[19] this age group represents the fastest-growing segment in the cellphone market.[20] Add to this the dollar amounts that parents will spend on their tweens, teens, and young adults, and one grasps the importance and potential of this market. Gen Zs overwhelmingly (92 percent) recognize television commercials for what they are—just advertising—and indicate that they tune out ads simply because they are boring. Despite tweens' tech-savvy attitude, major social network sites are off limits to tweens under age 13 because of privacy and safety concerns.

In 2017, TikTok, a social platform for kids, was launched and it acquired Music.ly in 2018. By 2019, TikTok had over half a billion users, and changed the way social media was being used.[21] This sudden influence of the platform caught even its own Chinese-based ownership offguard. The surge of usership by kids under 13, and subsequent collection of their data, led to a $5.7 million fine in 2019 by the FTC (Federal Trade Commission).[22]

The older Gen-Zs, those born between 1995 and 2000, represent just over 2.1 million people in Canada.[23] As a group, they are extremely important to marketers because they wield significant purchasing power and are key influencers in family purchases. Young adults are avid shoppers, spending on fashion, makeup, food, and entertainment.

demography
the study of people's vital statistics, such as their age, race and ethnicity, and location

Generation Z
people born between 1995 and 2009

They are computer savvy, heavy users of social media, and active digital music and movie downloaders.

2-6b | Generation Y

Those designated as **Generation Y** were born between 1979 and 2000. They began hitting their purchasing power around the turn of the millennium—hence the increasingly familiar cohort term of *millennials*. Though Gen-Ys represent a smaller group than the baby boomers, whose birthdates span nearly 20 years, they are plentiful enough to put their own footprints on society. You will also note that inconsistencies within the study of demography often result in age overlap, as we note here, where the last five years of Gen Y overlap with the first five years of Gen Z.

Environics, a national research firm, estimates there are over 9 million Gen-Ys in Canada, accounting for over 27 percent of the country's population. But while Gen-Ys are smaller in population than the baby boomer segment, Environics predicts the Gen-Ys will soon overtake baby boomers because boomers will be decreasing due to mortality.[24] Gen-Ys range from new career entrants to those in their early 40s. Those starting their careers are already making major purchases, such as cars and homes, and have a heightened sense of social responsibility. A survey conducted by Leger Marketing found a growing attitude among young Canadians of expecting their employer to be aware of their impact on the environment, and one-third reported they would quit their job over the environmental policies of their company.[25] Gen-Ys have been referred to as "trophy kids" as a result of their high expectations in the workforce and their increased sense of entitlement, which leads to a desire for a better work–life balance. Most Gen-Ys are the children of baby boomers and so are sometimes referred to as echo boomers. Because of economic necessity, many baby boomers in Canada are working well into their retirement age, thus shrinking the employment opportunities for Gen-Ys. As a result, Gen-Ys are facing unstable employment opportunities and struggling to establish themselves professionally. Those who have launched their careers often find themselves working side by side with baby boomers. The workplace dynamics of this demographic integration have not created widespread issues, according to an IBM Institute for Business Value study, which concluded both cohorts had similar values and goals, thus minimizing negative effects.[26]

Generation Y
people born between 1979 and 2000

Demographic patterns and economic realities make it still commonplace to find baby boomers and Gen-Ys doing essentially the same job in the same company.

SeventyFour/Shutterstock.com

When the traditional "job hunt" fails to fulfill Gen-Ys with a dream career, they are more likely to be entrepreneurial. They have grown up in the face of a global financial crisis and significant meltdown in the financial markets. They are thus able to work with an uncertainty that other generations can't. They have the ability to network and can use social media to their advantage. They have seen people all around them forced out of work and are able to reinvent themselves as freelancers or consultants.

The ultimate test for Gen Ys' ability to pivot, of course, was the COVID-19 pandemic of 2020. This unprecedented event tested the entrepreneurial mindset of even the most entrepreneurial. The durability of this, or any other generation, through this period in history is still playing out.

Researchers have found Gen-Ys to be

- *Impatient:* Because they have grown up in a world that has always been automated, they expect instant gratification.

- *Family oriented:* Gen-Ys had relatively stable childhoods and grew up in a very family-focused era, so they tend to have a stronger family orientation than the generation that preceded them.

- *Inquisitive:* Gen-Ys tend to want to know why things happen, how things work, and what they can do next.

- *Opinionated:* Gen-Ys have been encouraged to share their opinions by everyone around them. As a result, they feel that their opinions are always needed and welcomed.

- *Diverse:* Gen Y is the most ethnically diverse generation the nation has ever seen, so they're much more accepting overall of people who are different from themselves.

Gen-Ys pursue balance in life, often integrating their children into activities that cultivate this value.

- *Good managers of time:* Their entire lives have been scheduled—from playdates to hockey to dance—so they've picked up a knack for planning along the way.
- *Savvy:* Having been exposed to the Internet and 24-hour cable TV news at a young age, Gen-Ys are not easily shocked. They're much more aware of the world around them than earlier generations were.[27]
- *Connected:* Gen-Ys use social networks, such as Facebook and Twitter, for both communication and commerce.
- *Life-balance seekers:* Having watched their baby boomer parents burn out from work, many Gen-Ys are more inclined to take care of themselves holistically, especially when raising their own families.

Finally, older millennials are now parenting and are breaking the cycle of "helicopter parenting" initiated by the youngest of today's baby boomers and almost the entire Gen-X cohort.[28] This will likely pave the way for more independent future generations of Canadians.

2-6c | Generation X

Generation X—people born between 1966 and 1978—consists of more than 7 million consumers across Canada, including Justin Trudeau, who was sworn in as Canada's prime minister in 2015 at age 43, then elected to a second term in 2019. It is the first generation of latchkey children—products of dual-career households or, in roughly half the cases, of divorced or separated parents. Gen-Xs have been bombarded by multiple media since their cradle days; thus, they are savvy and cynical consumers.

Their careers launched and their families started, Gen-Xs are at the stage in life when a host of demands are competing for their time—and their budgets. As a result, Gen X spending is quite diffuse: food, housing, and transportation. Time is at a premium for harried Gen-Xs, so they're outsourcing the tasks of daily life, which include responsibilities such as housecleaning, dog walking, and lawn care. Because of demands on their time, Gen-Xs spend much more on personal services than any other age group.[29] Many Gen-Xs work from home.

Gen-Xs face the reality, however, that the generation ahead of them, having experienced a financial recession that started in late 2007, may opt not to retire, thereby affecting the Gen-Xs' ability to maximize their income. In addition, as an impending pension crisis looms, the Gen-Xs may find themselves funding the retirement years of the baby boomers. Finally, as with Gen Y, this generation too, many of whom had finally felt a level of comfort financially, had their world rocked by the COVID-19 pandemic of 2020. Many will be forced to spend additional years in the workforce to make up for job/income loss.[30] Because Gen-Xs are a large group who make and spend significant amounts of money, companies

Generation X
people born between 1966 and 1978

Due to the volatility of Canada's economy since 2008, and lost retirement savings related to the recession, which began that year, many baby boomers have been forced to stay in their careers for prolonged periods. The youngest of the baby boomers, still part of the workforce in 2020, would have also been impacted by the COVID-19 pandemic, throwing off, as it did, for all other demographics, their best laid plans.

cannot overlook them, despite how big the baby boomers and Gen Y are by comparison.

2-6d | Baby Boomers—A Mass Market

Baby boomers make up the largest demographic segment of today's Canadian population. There are 9 million **baby boomers** (people born between 1947 and 1965). The oldest are now 75. There are now more people 65 and over in Canada than there are aged 15 and younger.[31] With average life expectancy increasing, more and more Canadians over the age of 50 consider middle age to be a new start on life. People now in their 50s, given better health and uncertain economic cycles, may well work longer than any previous generation.

Many commentators have been predicting a "baby-boom bust" around the world, due to this cohort's sheer size and its eventual exit first from the workforce, and then as it develops more reliance on the health system and ultimately dies. But while the burden on the health system is bothersome to

baby boomers
people born between 1947 and 1965

multiculturalism
the peaceful and equitable coexistence of different cultures, rather than one national culture, in a country

some analysts, a CBC report suggests that, with proper planning, there will be benefits to this older generation as it lives out the last one to two decades of its life.[32] First, the report says, the majority of boomers are living their lives until their mid-80s, with many working well past the age of 65. This, the report suggests, could create a ratio of the working population supporting the nonworking population, similar to that of the 1950s—one of the most robust economic periods in modern history.[33] Boomers are a powerful demographic (as they have always been) with a spending power of more than $1 trillion.

2-6e | Population Shifts in Canada

Canada is a large country with a relatively small population that was, historically, spread out between rural and urban areas. Since the mid-1970s, however, the population has shifted out of rural areas so that now over 82 percent of Canadians are considered to be urban dwellers. The majority of urban dwellers live in census metropolitan areas (CMAs), regions defined by Statistics Canada as comprising one or more municipalities situated around a major urban core, with a total population of at least 100 000.[34]

According to Statistics Canada, the Canadian population topped 36 million in October 2015.[35] More than 50 percent of the Canadian population lives in four major urban regions in Canada: the Golden Horseshoe in Ontario; Montreal and surrounding area; British Columbia's Lower Mainland; and the Calgary–Edmonton corridor. A Statistics Canada study observed that new parents and those between the ages of 25 and 44 were more likely than any others to move from an urban central municipality to a surrounding municipality or suburb.[36] Most of Canada's population growth comes from immigration, and 2015 to 2016 was a banner year for this growth with over 320 000 immigrants, close to 10 percent of whom were Syrian refugees.[37] The majority of immigrants are settling within Canada's largest urban centres, namely Toronto, Montréal, and Vancouver.[38] As a result, these urban core areas are the focus of many marketing programs by companies that are interested in reaching a large national yet very multicultural market.

2-6f | Ethnic and Cultural Diversity

Multiculturalism refers to the peaceful and equitable coexistence of different cultures, rather than one national culture, in a country. More than 200 different languages are spoken in Canada and the trend in Canada is toward greater multiculturalism.

More and more people are arriving in Canada every year from around the world and starting new lives as Canadian residents.

the four

THE HIDDEN DNA OF AMAZON, APPLE, FACEBOOK, AND GOOGLE

Scott Galloway

One of Canada's highest values is its multiculturalism. It turns out that this is not only something that we appreciate about ourselves at an emotional level but also good for our economy. Without immigration, our population would have flatlined decades ago. The population of Canada simply wasn't large enough to be producing a significant growth[39] rate naturally, through childbirth; growth had to happen through immigration.

A decades-long program to attract migrants from around the world reached a pinnacle between 2017 and 2018, when more than half a million people arrived here.[40] This was the largest single intake of immigrants in the country's history, and represented its highest annual population growth rate, 1.4 percent, since the late 80s. The same report declared Canada as having the highest growth rate of any of the G7 nations—double that of the closest rival, the United States, which had a growth rate of 0.7 percent.[41] The cultural diversity of our country and the trend to multiculturalism will require multicultural marketing right at home. More than 20 percent of the visible minority population is under 15 years of age. This group will have a great impact in the decades ahead. Many of these young people can understand and converse in multiple languages and have adapted elements of numerous cultures into their lifestyle. These cultures influence their response to marketing messages and ultimately determine their buying behaviour. What does being a Canadian really mean to a marketer?

Depending upon their country of origin, age, and personal circumstances, it is likely that recent immigrants to Canada are tech savvy. Young people from most cultures have been using the Internet for accessing information and making purchases, which has spawned new strategies for using the Internet to reach diverse youth markets. Like Canadian-born youth, most of them have never used or even seen a payphone or home phone connected to a cord. Every cultural group has access to websites that cater to their specific culture—such as social networks, products, events, and links to their native country. These culture-specific websites present opportunities for businesses to target specific ethnic groups.

2-7 | TECHNOLOGICAL FACTORS

Technology is an external force because, like the others discussed here, it evolves, morphs, advances, and disrupts irrespective of what a company is doing. That said, there are tech companies creating the technology to such an extent that they must now be considered a "force within the force" of tech. Google, Apple, Facebook, and Amazon (popularized as "The Four" in Scott Galloway's 2017 book of the same name, and often referred to as "GAFA") as separate companies have the size, resources, and some might argue, willingness, to be external forces on their own. The products (or companies) they have created are so ubiquitous in our lives that marketers must treat them as external forces. We search and research for information on Google; connect and interconnect with people through Facebook (or its sister company Instagram); shop through Amazon and do all of these through a small device that fits in our pocket, made by Apple. While other businesses are present in each of these scenarios, their market share is minimal compared to GAFA, or they have been reduced to simply following what GAFA does, copying it, and extracting a small sliver of market share.

These powerhouse tech companies (and you could throw in a few others like Microsoft and Netflix) can certainly be considered a technological force. When you consider the definition of *technology* as "the practical application of knowledge especially in a particular area,"[42] you begin to get the sense that there is still a lot of externality to this force that goes way beyond even GAFA.°

But even here, some students stumble into the trap of believing technology isn't an external force, but rather a strength of companies that "apply knowledge." Without question, entrepreneurial thinking over the generations has produced companies which create wildly successful companies on the back of the products that they create, often using their own technology. But to assume that tech is therefore "internal" rather than external, is to miss the foundational understanding of what constitutes an external force of the marketing environment—it happens irrespective of a business. Furthermore, it happens because society wants it to happen. And if companies themselves cannot apply knowledge to solution, then it will be done at an institutional level—that's right, at universities and colleges around the world, where research and technology are applied to solve real-world problems.

Technology is a critical factor in every company's external environment. Our ability, as a nation, to maintain and build wealth depends in large part on the speed and effectiveness with which we invent and adopt machines and technologies that lift productivity. External technology is important to managers for two reasons. First, by acquiring a technology, a company may be able to operate more efficiently or create a better product.

°Technology definitions contained herein are used with permission from https://www.merriam-webster.com/dictionary/technology, © 2020 by Merriam-Webster, Incorporated.

basic research
pure research that aims to confirm an existing theory or to learn more about a concept or phenomenon

applied research
an attempt by marketers to use research to develop new or improved products

Second, a new technology may render existing products obsolete, as in the case of the traditional film-based camera being replaced by digital camera technology. Staying technologically relevant requires a great deal of research and a willingness to adopt new technologies.

2-7a | Research

Basic research (or pure *research*) attempts to expand the frontiers of knowledge but is not aimed at a specific, pragmatic problem. Basic research aims to confirm an existing theory or to learn more about a concept or phenomenon. For example, basic research might focus on high-energy physics. **Applied research**, in contrast, attempts to develop new or improved products.

2-7b | Technology and the Future of Businesses

Of all the external environmental forces, technology is the fastest changing with, perhaps, the most significant impact on businesses. New technologies will create not only new industries but also new ways to develop products, compete, and meet customer needs. Such is the accelerated rate of technology that the very topics written here in this textbook may be "old news" by the time it ends up in your hands. With that disclaimer out of the way, here is Tech Republic's Five Tech Trends, it said, in 2019, businesses cannot afford to ignore.[43]

1. *Internet of Things (IoT):* Sensors everywhere in everything have already connected us in very obvious ways such as our phone to our watch to our ears. But we now expect sensors to tether us to all household appliances and mechanical operations. The business equivalent of IoT comes in the form of RFID (radio frequency identification) and mobile card readers.

2. *Artificial intelligence (AI):* Quickly becoming the most commonly used, and misused, abbreviation in business, AI is not synonymous with robotics, nor is its trajectory into a cyborg apocalypse. And, importantly, AI is not exclusive domain of highly capitalized companies. Like the technological force itself, AI is simply applying knowledge to practical solutions. When businesses today automate things as mundane and routine as data entry and analysis, they are using AI. The sky is the limit, but for now, using things already available here at ground level is a start.

3. *Telecommuting:* Research shows half of all people in the workforce do at least some work from home,

or places other than their office at the site of their employer. This number is of course closer to 100 percent for entrepreneurs who work entirely out of their home. The reason this is an important tech trend for businesses, is that it affords them time flexibility and cost savings on things like extravagant video conference rooms that now seem rather redundant. Certainly the COVID-19 pandemic of 2020 amplified this new reality, as businesses of all sizes were forced to streamline operations through increased use of virtual communication.

4. *Customer relationship management (CRM):* This is perhaps the most mature technology in Tech Republic's ranking. But like those mentioned previously, it is on the list due to its potential impact on businesses. Salesforce, a CRM superpower, could be to businesses what GAFA companies have become to consumers. The sophistication, ease of use, and sheer speed of today's CRMs make it perilous for companies not to be using some form of it inside their operations.

5. *Voice search:* While for its first couple of years considered a novelty, the smart speaker has become the fastest adopted technology since the smart phone. And, while more and more consumers are using Amazon, Google, and Apple speakers to perform tasks ranging from weather reports to exercise regimes, companies too are adopting voice search into their employees' arsenal of tools for productivity.

As an aside to the list above, it might also be added that, through the sheer will of companies like Amazon to make its Echo speakers and Alexa voice ecosystem the market leader, it is becoming increasingly important for companies to have a "sonic brand," a space in the growing ecosystem of podcasts, and content available through smart speakers.

2-8 | CORPORATE SOCIAL RESPONSIBILITY AND ETHICAL BEHAVIOUR IN BUSINESS

Social responsibility and ethics go hand in hand. **Corporate social responsibility (CSR)** is a business's concern for social and environmental welfare. But really, CSR is the culmination of decades of accrued forces of the collective external environment (CREST), as explained so far in this chapter (see Exhibit 2.6). Since

The Salesforce Tower, completed in 2018 and dominating the San Francisco skyline, serves as a visual statement of not only the company's position in the CRM space but also the necessity of CRM to businesses.

the end of World War II, these forces have accelerated along parallel tracks, helping businesses grow rapidly, but ultimately converging to a point where the advancement of society, caused largely through the growth of companies, has left the planet in a state of depleted resources, alarming environmental concerns, and wealth inequality. With due awareness and concern of these and other related issues, society has forced companies to pursue the **triple bottom line**—profitability, care for the planet, and care for people. Thus, at a high level, CSR has evolved into a core value of any successful company, while at a nuts and bolts level, it is indeed a cost of doing business.

The integrated forces of the CREST environment have ultimately resulted in a very high standard of living in the developed world, while at the same time drying up the earth's resources, creating a wealth divide, and risking environmental sustainability. This process of **social acceleration**, fuelled by the business cycle, has resulted in the need

corporate social responsibility
a business's concern for society's welfare

triple bottom line
a business philosophy seen as the pursuit of profit while also benefiting society and the environment

social acceleration
the concept of exponentially rapid growth starting with human desire for improved products, spurring competitive pursuit of market share, driving innovation and technology, and resulting in a higher standard of living but with new socio environmental problems

EXHIBIT 2.6 | CORPORATE SOCIAL RESPONSIBILITY

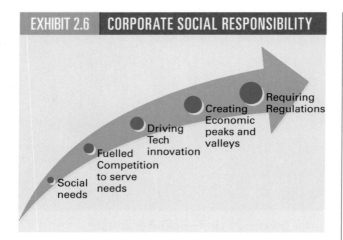

EXHIBIT 2.7 | PYRAMID OF CORPORATE SOCIAL RESPONSIBILITY

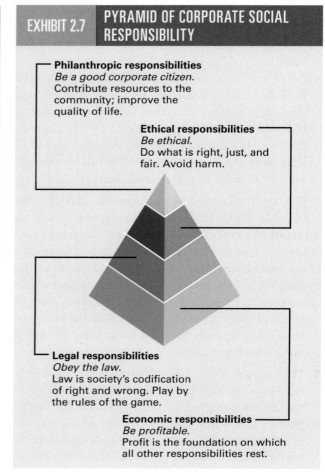

to implement heightened regulations of business practices regionally, federally, and internationally to protect people and the planet from the blind pursuit of profit by business. It has also introduced a permanent ethical dimension to business, summed up by the concept of corporate social responsibility.

Total corporate social responsibility has four components: economic, legal, ethical, and philanthropic.[44] The **pyramid of corporate social responsibility** portrays economic responsibility as the foundation for the other three responsibilities (see Exhibit 2.7). At the same time that a business pursues profits (economic responsibility), however, it is also expected to obey the law (legal responsibility); to do what is right, just, and fair (ethical responsibilities); and to be a good corporate citizen (philanthropic responsibility). These four components are distinct but together constitute the whole. This reminds us that, at its roots, in its DNA, a business must be profitable in order to accommodate not only the needs of its customers and owners but also the needs of society and the environment. Viewed this way, the pyramid of corporate social responsibility has, in effect, morphed into a cycle of corporate social responsibility.

2-8a | Growth of Social Responsibility

The social responsibility of businesses is growing globally; a 2015 study of CSR practices conducted by the *Harvard Business Review* of 142 executives attending Harvard Business School over a four-year period found

pyramid of corporate social responsibility
a model that suggests corporate social responsibility is composed of economic, legal, ethical, and philanthropic responsibilities and that the company's economic performance supports the entire structure

a wide array of differing definitions and degrees of CSR implementation. In their summarizing article, "The Truth About CSR," researchers concluded that "most companies practice a multifaceted version of CSR that runs the gamut from pure philanthropy to environmental sustainability to the active pursuit of shared value. Moreover, well-managed companies seem less interested in totally integrating CSR with their business strategies and goals than in devising a cogent CSR program aligned with the company's purpose and values."[45] This is the inevitable CSR conundrum: companies must do good, but if they say they are doing good, it renders their goodwill as nothing more than brand promotion. It has thus become a very tricky aspect of a business to integrate social responsibility into its operations and not be seen as having non-altruistic intents.

In Canada social responsibility has become increasingly professionalized and integrated across all levels within most organizations. According to Imagine Canada, a national program supporting public and corporate charitable giving, businesses have moved beyond simply writing a cheque to a more engaged and integrated approach to social responsibility that includes in-kind gifts, employee volunteerism, and sponsorships.[46]

Businesses are realizing that corporate social responsibility isn't easy or quick. It works only when a company engages a long-term strategy and effort and the strategy is coordinated throughout the organization. It doesn't always come cheap, and the payoff, both to society and to the company itself, isn't always immediate. But consumers will patronize businesses that are socially responsible, providing that they are convinced the business's intent starts from a place of authenticity.

2-8b | Green Marketing

An outgrowth of the social responsibility movement is **green marketing**—the development and marketing of products designed to minimize negative effects on the physical environment. Not only can a company aid the environment through green marketing, but also green marketing can help the bottom line. (This is not to be confused with "green-washing," the practice of using marketing communications to position a company as environmentally conscious, but really offering little in terms of actual operational commitment toward protecting the environment.) Environmentally aware consumers tend to earn more and are more willing to pay a premium for green products.

To protect consumers from companies capitalizing on the green movement without substance, the Canadian Competition Bureau launched a guide that provides the business community with green marketing guidelines. While the guide is not law, the Competition Bureau will pursue deceptive environmental claims, fine violators, or remove products from store shelves. The guide suggests that environmental claims should be clear, specific, accurate, and not misleading, and that all environmental claims should be verified and substantiated.

A company known for its green marketing practices is S. C. Johnson & Son. This company developed the Greenlist process, which requires that its scientists evaluate all the company's product ingredients to determine their impact on the environment and to reformulate products to reduce that impact.[48] The use of this patented process led to the reformulation of Windex, resulting in a greener and more effective product.

2-8c | Ethical Behaviour in Business

Ethics refers to the moral principles or values that generally govern the conduct of an individual or a group. Ethics can also be viewed as the standard of behaviour by which conduct is judged. Standards that are legal may not always be ethical and vice versa. Laws

calimedia/Shutterstock.com

Clorox's Canadian office is leading the way in sustainability by diverting from landfill more than 90 percent of the company's waste and improving the manufacturing process for greater sustainability.[47]

are the values and standards enforceable by the courts. Ethics consists of personal moral principles and values rather than societal prescriptions.

Defining the boundaries of ethicality and legality can be difficult. Often, judgment is needed to determine whether an action that may be legal is an ethical or unethical act. Also, judgment is required to determine whether an unethical act is legal or illegal.

Morals are the rules people develop as a result of cultural values and norms. Culture is a socializing force that dictates what is right and wrong. Moral standards may also reflect the laws and regulations that affect social and economic behaviour. Thus, morals can be considered a foundation of ethical behaviour.

Morals are usually characterized as good or bad. *Good* and *bad* have different connotations, including effective and ineffective. A good salesperson makes or exceeds the assigned quota. If the salesperson sells a new stereo or television set to a disadvantaged consumer—knowing full well that the person can't keep up the monthly payments—is the salesperson still considered to be good? What if the sale enables the salesperson to exceed their quota?

Good and bad can also refer to conforming and

green marketing
the development and marketing of products designed to minimize negative effects on the physical environment

ethics
the moral principles or values that generally govern the conduct of an individual or a group

morals
the rules people develop as a result of cultural values and norms

deviant behaviours. Any doctor in Canada who charges extra fees for fast-tracking patients on waiting lists for provincially funded procedures would be considered unprofessional. Such a doctor would not be conforming to the norms and laws of the medical profession or to the laws regarding universal healthcare set by our provincial or territorial legislatures and federal government. *Bad* and *good* are also used to express the distinction between criminal and law-abiding behaviour. And finally, different religions define good and bad in markedly different ways. A Muslim who eats pork would be considered bad, as would a fundamentalist Christian who drinks whisky.

2-8d | Morality and Business Ethics

Today's business ethics consist of a subset of major life values learned since birth. The values businesspeople use to make decisions have been acquired through family and educational and religious institutions.

Ethical values are situation specific and time oriented. Nevertheless, everyone must have an ethical base that applies to conduct in the business world and in personal life. One approach to developing a personal set of ethics is to examine the consequences of a particular act. Who is helped or hurt? How long lasting are the consequences? What actions produce the greatest good for the greatest number of people? A second approach stresses the importance of rules. Rules come in the form of customs, laws, professional standards, and common sense. "Always treat others as you would like to be treated" is an example of a rule.

The last approach emphasizes the development of moral character within individuals. Ethical development can be thought of as having three levels:[49]

- *Preconventional morality,* the most basic level, is child-like. It is calculating, self-centred, even selfish, and is based on what will be immediately punished or rewarded.
- *Conventional morality* moves from an egocentric viewpoint toward the expectations of society. Loyalty and obedience to the organization (or society) become paramount. A marketing decision maker at this level would be concerned only with whether the proposed action is legal and how it will be viewed by others.
- *Postconventional morality* represents the morality of the mature adult. At this level, people are less concerned about how others might see

code of ethics
a guideline to help marketing managers and other employees make better decisions

them and more concerned about how they see and judge themselves over the long run. A marketing decision maker who has attained a postconventional level of morality might ask, "Even though it is legal and will increase company profits, is it right in the long run?"

2-8e | Ethical Decision Making

Ethical questions rarely have cut-and-dried answers. Studies show that the following factors tend to influence ethical decision making and judgments[50]:

- *Extent of ethical problems within the organization:* Marketing professionals who perceive fewer ethical problems in their organizations tend to disapprove more strongly of unethical or questionable practices than those who perceive more ethical problems. Apparently, the healthier the ethical environment, the more likely marketers will take a strong stand against questionable practices.
- *Top-management actions on ethics:* Top managers can influence the behaviour of marketing professionals by encouraging ethical behaviour and discouraging unethical behaviour.
- *Potential magnitude of the consequences:* The greater the harm done to victims, the more likely marketing professionals will recognize the behaviour as unethical.
- *Social consensus:* The greater the degree of agreement among managerial peers that an action is harmful, the more likely marketers will recognize the action as unethical.
- *Probability of a harmful outcome:* The greater the likelihood that an action will result in a harmful outcome, the more likely marketers will recognize the action as unethical.
- *Length of time between the decision and the onset of consequences:* The shorter the length of time between the action and the onset of negative consequences, the more likely it is that marketers will perceive the action as unethical.
- *Number of people to be affected:* The greater the number of persons affected by a negative outcome, the more likely it is that marketers will recognize the behaviour as unethical.

2-8f | Ethical Guidelines

Many organizations have become more interested in ethical issues. Companies of all sizes have developed a **code of ethics** as a guideline to help marketing managers and other employees make better decisions.

Creating ethics guidelines has several advantages:

- The guidelines help employees identify the business practices their company recognizes as being acceptable.
- A code of ethics can be an effective internal control on behaviour, which is more desirable than external controls, such as government regulation.
- A written code helps employees avoid confusion when determining whether their decisions are ethical.
- The process of formulating the code of ethics facilitates discussion among employees about what is right and wrong, which ultimately leads to better decisions.

Businesses must be careful, however, not to make their code of ethics too vague or too detailed. Codes that are too vague give little or no guidance to employees in their day-to-day activities. Codes that are too detailed encourage employees to substitute rules for judgment. For instance, if employees are involved in questionable behaviour, they may use the absence of a written rule as a reason to continue their behaviour, even though their conscience may be telling them otherwise. Following a set of ethical guidelines will not guarantee the "rightness" of a decision, but it will improve the chances that the decision will be ethical.

Although many companies have issued policies on ethical behaviour, marketing managers must still put the policies into effect. They must address the classic "matter of degree" issue. For example, marketing researchers often resort to deception to obtain unbiased answers to their research questions. Asking for a few minutes of a respondent's time is dishonest if the researcher knows the interview will last 45 minutes. Management must not only post a code of ethics but also give examples of what is ethical and unethical for each item in the code. Moreover, top management must stress to all employees the importance of adhering to the company's code of ethics. Without a detailed code of ethics and top management's support, creating ethical guidelines becomes an empty exercise. The Canadian Marketing Association's code of ethics outlines its purpose (see Bullseye box).

WHAT'S EXPECTED OF CANADIAN MARKETERS

The Canadian Marketing Association has recently undergone a rework of its Marketing Code of Ethics and Standards, a comprehensive self-regulatory framework governing members' conduct that is mandatory for members. Members are expected to be stewards of CMA's code of ethics, which, in its simplest terms, is established to "contribute to an environment where consumers are protected and businesses can thrive." Members of the Canadian Marketing Association recognize their obligation—to the consumers and businesses they serve—to maintain the highest standards of honesty, truth, accuracy, fairness, and professionalism.

Source: Canadian Marketing Association, https://www.the-cma.org/about.

AWAKE CHOCOLATE CONTINUING CASE

AWAKE Chocolate

Doing Right by Resources

With the business experience of Awake's three founders tied significantly to Pepsico, one of the world's largest consumer packaged goods (CPG) companies, it could be reasonably expected that an operational objective would focus on cost efficiency. To be sure, lessons learned in this regard from the soft drink and snack giant were not entirely lost on Adam, Matt, and Dan, but from the very beginning, when it came to product and packaging they were not willing to cut corners where values came into play.

"There was an agreement amongst the three of us that, first, we were only going to include ingredients in our bars which the consumer actually needed. So no extraneous ingredients," asserted CEO Adam Deremo. "But also," he continued, "we were going to do right by the resources we were consuming as a company. So making sure that when we buy cocoa, making sure that everyone involved in the harvest has been paid properly."

But it isn't just the ingredients of what Awake fans were eating that Adam and his team were steadfast about. The philosophy of doing right by resources extended into their entire supply management and operations: "Making sure that all of our caddies (packaging) and cases were made from paper that had been recycled. In other words, not cutting corners for the sake of saving a penny here or there."

Of course, these days, one would expect a food company to executive to say all of these things. Furthermore, it would be reasonable to assume that the company would not only do the right thing but also use every means and channel possible to say they are doing the right thing. And yet, at the time of this writing, there is no mention of Awake's environmental, fair trade, or any other policy pertaining to corporate social responsibility.

This omission, it turned out, was deliberate for both practical and philosophical reasons, and may be one of the most honest things you'll hear coming from the mouth of an executive in an age where purchase decisions are often calibrated by the perception the purchaser has of the producer's corporate social responsibility. "When you are a brand trying to build awareness," began Deremo, "you have to remember that you can only command so much of your customer's attention. And so you have to prioritize what you say."

Deremo believes that if a company is going to hang its entire brand's position on some sort of social or environmental cause, then whatever that cause is most certainly must be a part of its customer-facing story. However, for Awake, in 2020, the message had to be about the product's benefit, again, given its relatively low market awareness. "In our case that [message] was, 'Awake delivers a valuable consumer benefit that you're not going to find somewhere else.'"

On the other hand, even if Awake were a more recognized brand, you get the feeling that the CSR story would remain under-emphasized if mentioned at all. "I think sometimes its enough to just do the right thing. You don't need everyone to know about it, and you certainly don't need a pat on the head for it," stated Deremo. He went further to suggest that consumer demand for exemplary corporate behaviour, and the in-turn reaction companies have to manufacture their own halo effect, is by now seen with cynicism rather than respect.

"I kind of take a sideways glance at brands who base their entire marketing persona on doing the right thing. There's a fine line between CSR and green-washing." The latter is a less than flattering term used to describe companies that attempt to hitch their wagon to some sort of socio-environmental movement in order to capitalize on the halo effect by association, but at the end of the day demonstrate little if any authentic or measurable CSR.

Thus, Awake will continue to operate under an ethos of doing good by benefit provided, as well as resourcing, but will do so as a matter of understated but deeply held values: making sure its customers needs are met without robbing from the needs of people or planet.

QUESTIONS

1. Identify and describe any corporate social responsibility Awake is engaged in at present. Go online to www.awakechocolate.com, and its social media feeds as part of your research.

2. In this chapter, the concept of corporate social responsibility is presented as a part of the value proposition. Based on what you read in this case, and what you were able to identify in your research, do you believe that Awake is doing enough to communicate its CSR activities?

3. Awake's CEO Adam Deremo appears to be protecting his brand, by refusing to make a lot of noise around CSR activities. In what way(s) could Awake draw more attention to its CSR activities, without appearing to be "green-washing"?

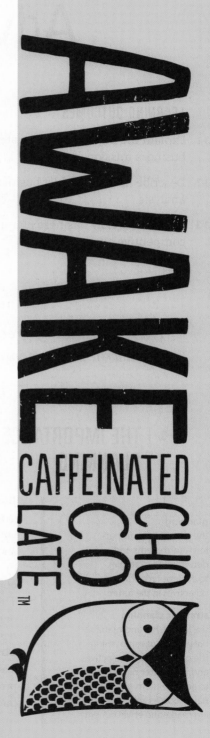

3 Strategic Planning for Competitive Advantage

LEARNING OUTCOMES

3-1 Explain the importance of strategic planning and a business mission statement

3-2 Describe how to conduct business portfolio analysis

3-3 Summarize how business planning is used for competitive advantage

3-4 Discuss marketing planning, identification of target markets and the elements of the marketing mix

3-5 Explain why implementation, evaluation, and control of the marketing plan are necessary

3-6 Identify several techniques that help make strategic planning effective

"There are a lot of great ideas that have come and gone in [the digital advertising] industry. Implementation many times is more important than the actual idea."

—David Moore, CEO of 24/7 Real Media[1]

3-1 | THE IMPORTANCE OF STRATEGIC PLANNING

planning
the process of anticipating future events and determining strategies to achieve organizational objectives in the future

strategic planning
the leadership and managerial process of establishing the organization's objectives and then determining how to achieve them given internal resources and the evolving marketing environment

Business **planning** in general is the process of anticipating future events and determining strategies to achieve organizational objectives in the future. This should happen in an organization at the strategic and tactical levels. **Strategic planning** is the leadership and managerial process of establishing the organization's objectives and then determining how to achieve them given internal resources and the evolving **marketing environment**. The marketing environment is the entire set of situational conditions, both internal (strengths and weaknesses) and external (opportunities and threats), within which a business operates. The goal of strategic planning is long-run profitability and growth. Thus strategic decisions require long-term commitments of resources. A strategic error can threaten a company's survival. On the other hand, a good strategic plan can help protect and grow the business's resources.

Organizations are increasingly becoming complex, and modern businesses, especially large corporations, constitute a set of diverse business interests spread over several business areas and markets. These diverse businesses within a corporation are linked by common corporate goals and interdependent business strategies that must be coordinated to obtain maximum advantage for the business and its customers. In a large business setting, strategic planning is a complex set of activities that

takes place at three levels: (1) corporate, (2) business, and (3) marketing. The corporate strategic planning takes place at the highest level of an organization and sets the direction and scope of the overall corporation through its mission statement, the identification of key business opportunities and constraints, and the allocation of resources.

3-1a | Strategic Business Units

Corporate planning leads to objectives for business- and marketing-level planning that address issues related to when, where, how, and against whom to compete. Business planning is undertaken at the **strategic business unit (SBU)** level, which is a subgroup of a single business or a collection of related businesses within the larger organization. A properly defined SBU should have a distinct mission and specific target market, as well as control over its resources, its own competitors, and plans independent of the other SBUs in the organization. The goal of business-level planning is to formulate strategies that deal with issues related to the competitive advantage a business intends to achieve through various means—including, for example, the supply chain, strategic partnerships, and the development and capitalization of distinctive competencies. The marketing

planning activities are aimed at a target market and marketing mix considerations that cover, for example, product lines, branding, pricing, and communication strategies. The corporate planning guides business and marketing planning; however, at the same time the corporate planning is also based on input from the other two lower levels.

Strategic decisions are made at all three levels, whereas tactical decisions are limited to the implementation of marketing plans at the lowest operational level. A strategic decision is a decision that is wider in scope and long term in its orientation, whereas a tactical decision is narrower in scope and is short term. Strategic decisions, like that of Bon-Look (the Montreal-based online eyewear retailer) to open retail stores, affect an organization's long-run course, its allocation of resources, and ultimately its financial success.[2] In

marketing environment
The entire set of situational conditions, both internal (strengths and weaknesses) and external (opportunities and threats), within which a business operates

strategic business unit (SBU)
a subgroup of a single business or a collection of related businesses within the larger organization

Online eyewear businesses such as BonLook deciding to open retail stores would be a strategic decision.

nd3000/Shutterstock.com

EXHIBIT 3.1   ELEMENTS OF A MARKETING PLAN

Corporate-Level Planning

Corporate strategy
- Define the mission statement.
- Set organizational goals and objectives.

Set strategic directions
- Situation (SWOT) analysis
- Portfolio analysis
- Identify growth strategies.

Business Unit–Level Planning

Business strategy
- Develop competitive advantage.
- Identify core competencies.

Marketing-Level Planning

Marketing strategy
- Identify target markets.
- Develop the marketing mix.
  - Product
  - Price
  - Place
  - Promotion

Implement, evaluate, and control
- Marketing audits
- Annual marketing plan review

contrast, a tactical decision, such as changing the package design for Iögo, probably won't have a big impact on the long-run profitability of the company.

How do companies go about developing strategic marketing? The answer is a strategic plan that addresses all three levels of planning (see Exhibit 3.1). Strategic planning spawns a marketing plan, which is a written document that acts as a guidebook of marketing analysis and activities for the marketing manager. In this chapter, you will learn the importance of marketing analysis and strategic planning. And it all begins by setting a company's mission statement.

3-1b | Corporate Planning—Defining the Business Mission

The foundation of any strategic direction, much less the marketing plan it spawns, is the business's **mission statement**, which answers the question "What value do we provide for customers?" The way a business defines—and lives—its mission profoundly affects the business's long-run resource allocation, profitability, and survival. The mission statement is based on a careful analysis of benefits sought by present and potential customers and an analysis of existing and anticipated environmental conditions. The business's mission statement establishes boundaries for all subsequent decisions, objectives, and strategies. Thus a mission statement should focus on the market or markets the organization is attempting to serve rather than on the goods or services offered. Otherwise, a new technology may quickly make the goods or services obsolete and the mission statement irrelevant to company functions.

Mission statements that are stated too narrowly define a business by its goods and services rather than by the benefits that customers seek. On the other hand, missions stated too broadly will provide neither focus for strategic planning nor the differentiation that customers are often attracted to. Care must be taken to state the

mission statement
a statement of the business's value based on a careful analysis of benefits sought by present and potential customers and an analysis of existing and anticipated environmental conditions

business a company is in and to emphasize the distinct benefits that customers seek before the foundation for the marketing plan is set.

The organization may also need to develop a mission statement and objectives for a strategic business unit (SBU). Thus a large business such as Procter & Gamble may have marketing plans for each of its SBUs, which include beauty, hygiene, homecare, and health and grooming.

3-2 | STRATEGIC DIRECTIONS— DESIGNING THE BUSINESS PORTFOLIO

To set an organization's strategic direction, businesses must thoroughly understand their current environment and any potential environment in which they will be operating. This goal is accomplished by conducting a **SWOT analysis** of an organization's internal environment of strengths (S) and weaknesses (W) in the context of its external environment of opportunities (O) and threats (T). Exhibit 3.2 provides an outline of a SWOT analysis.

3-2a | Conducting a SWOT Analysis

When examining internal strengths and weaknesses, marketers should focus on three key organizational categories—financial, management, and marketing. The financial category, for instance, would include things such as cash on hand and access to funding. Management would cover production costs, HR processes, and supply chain management. Marketing would be made up of value of offerings, number of customers, brand reputation, pricing strategy, distribution, and communication—in other words, anything within the four Ps. In fact, the very practice of strategic planning and SWOT

EXHIBIT 3.2	SWOT ANALYSIS		
		Strengths	**Weaknesses**
Internal	Financial		
	Management		
	Marketing		
		Opportunities	**Threats**
External	Competitive		
	Regulatory		
	Economic		
	Social		
	Technological		

analysis could be viewed as either a strength or weakness depending upon how or even if a company chooses to use the SWOT tool in the first place. All participants in the SWOT analysis must be able to step back from their biased view of the company and provide a rigorous and honest depiction of what works and what doesn't.

When examining external forces of opportunities and threats, marketers must analyze aspects of the marketing environment. This process is called **environmental scanning**—the collection and interpretation of information about forces, events, and relationships in the external environment that may affect the future of the organization or the implementation of the marketing plan. These are inherently uncontrollable by the company. That is, the company neither initiates them nor stops them; rather, companies can only prepare to act upon them. Environmental scanning is at its best when it foresees business opportunities and threats at an early stage so that trends identified may be acted upon to either make or save money. See the box about Loblaw as an example of how companies use environmental scanning.

SWOT analysis helps identify the strategic direction the company should follow. That is, if done properly, SWOT analysis findings will often be so compelling that companies can proceed with confidence with a growth strategy.

3-2b | Strategic Alternatives—Linking SWOT to Growth Strategies

Once an organization fully identifies strengths, weaknesses, opportunities, and threats, certain ideas will emerge in the form of alternative growth strategies. These can be easily categorized using Ansoff's strategic opportunity matrix (see Exhibit 3.3), which matches products with markets. The grid produces the following four options:

- **Market penetration:** A company using the market penetration alternative tries to increase market share among existing customers by selling more of its current products.

SWOT analysis
identifying internal environment of strengths (S) and weaknesses (W) as well as external opportunities (O) and threats (T)

environmental scanning
the collection and interpretation of information about forces, events, and relationships in the external environment that may affect the future of the organization or the implementation of the marketing plan

market penetration
a marketing strategy that tries to increase market share among existing customers by using existing products

LOBLAW REACTS TO THE CHANGING ENVIRONMENT

On a regular basis Statistics Canada releases information regarding retail sales. For companies such as Loblaw, the giant grocery and drug retailer, these statistics show trends in the shopping habits of consumers. One recent report showed that specialty food stores sales grew by almost 6 percent but grocery store sales grew by only a little more than 2 percent over a three-month period. Another trend that could affect companies like Loblaw was the fact online sales were increasing at a rate of almost 30 percent for the year. Loblaw used information in reports like these to alter its distribution and promotional strategies.

Paul McKinnon/Shutterstock.com

Loblaw introduced a "click and collect" service. Customers could order their groceries online and pick them up at a store that was convenient. This service was expanded to include grocery pick up at some GO train stations in the Toronto region. An agreement between Metrolinx, the GO train operation, and Loblaw offered commuters the opportunity to pick up their grocery order at five Go Train stations from Whitby to Oakville. Customers could place their grocery order online by midnight the night before and pick them up on their way home from work the following day. Loblaw hoped these changes would appeal to the growing number of online shoppers.

Loblaw attempted to appeal to the consumer who was increasingly shopping at specialty food stores and those consumers who wanted to feel more comfortable shopping for specialty foods. The company did this by using special promotions. The advertisements showed that it was not a problem to make mistakes with food with the message that "anyone who cares that much how and what they eat" makes the customers a food lover.

Loblaw and other companies monitor changing consumer behaviour by paying attention to reports produced by organizations such as Statistics Canada.

Sources: Josh Kolm, "Loblaws Unites Around Thanksgiving," Strategy Online, http://strategyonline.ca/2019/10/01/loblaw-unites-around-thanksgiving, October 1, 2019; Justin Dallaire, "Loblaw Emphasizes Customers' Passion for Food," Strategy online, https://strategyonline.ca/2018/12/13/loblaw-emphasizes-customers-passion-for-food, December 13, 2019; Francine Kopun, "Commuters Can Soon Order Groceries Online and Pick Them Up at Go Stations," Toronto Star, https://www.thestar.com/business/2018/02/26/commuters-can-soon-order-groceries-online-and-pick-them-up-at-go-stations.html, February 26, 2018; Josh Kolm, "Canadian Retail Growth Continues to Stumble," Strategy Online, http://strategyonline.ca/2019/09/27/canadian-retail-growth-continues-to-stumble, September 27, 2019.The five most often studied macroenvironmental forces are competitive, regulatory, economic, social, and technological. These forces were examined in detail in Chapter 2.

Tim Hortons' introducing their all-day breakfast menu across the country is an example of a market penetration strategy.[3]

- **Market development:** Market development involves attracting new customers to existing products. For example, Tim Hortons opened its first restaurant in Shanghai, China in 2019. The restaurant will serve the chain's classic coffee and Timbits with some

market development
a marketing strategy that involves attracting new customers to existing products

product development
a marketing strategy that entails the creation of new products for current customers

EXHIBIT 3.3	ANSOFF'S STRATEGIC OPPORTUNITY MATRIX	
	Current Product	**New Product**
Current Market	*Market Penetration* Starbucks sells more coffee to customers who register their reloadable Starbucks cards.	*Product Development* Starbucks develops powdered instant coffee called Via.
New Market	*Market Development* Starbucks opens stores in Brazil and Chile.	*Diversification* Starbucks launches Hear Music and buys Ethos Water.

minor additions specifically for the Chinese market.[4]

- **Product development:** A product development strategy entails the creation of new products for current markets. Pushed not only by evolutionary social taste preferences but also by competition, Tim Hortons must constantly be aware of up-and-coming food trends in quick-service restaurants and be able to spring into action with the trends that are suitable for its operations. It regularly introduces new soups, sandwiches, and sides, as well as new doughnut flavours and baked goods. A recent new product for Tim Hortons is the "Double Double" coffee bar, similar to a chocolate bar but made with coffee beans.[5]

- **Diversification:** Diversification is a strategy of increasing sales by introducing new products into new markets. By far the riskiest of the four strategies, diversification, is often necessary to combat competitive forces or to exploit new social trends. Indigo Books and Music has transitioned from a bookstore to home, fashion and baby products. Indigo's most recent diversification is into wellness products.[6]

3-2c | Selecting a Strategic Alternative

Selecting which alternative to pursue depends on the overall company philosophy and culture. Clearly, the goal of for-profit companies is just that—profit. However, a company may face a situation, as identified through SWOT, in which it's necessary to place profit at a lower priority and choose a strategy that may not reap profits in the near term. Companies generally have one of two philosophies about when they expect profits. Even though market share—the percentage of sales in a market owned by a company—and profitability are compatible long-term goals, companies might pursue profits right away or first seek to build market share and/or awareness before going after profit.

The four strategic alternatives supported by Ansoff's matrix generally befit any given situation. Companies often need to prioritize between where there is the greatest gain and where there is the least harm. For instance, in assessing whether to grow by penetration, product development, market development, or diversification, a company needs to look at what jumps out of the SWOT analysis most urgently. Is there an underused strength that needs to be fully leveraged? A craft brewery, for example, may be constantly running out of a particular beer. Ramping up production of this product and selling more of it to the brewery's current customers may be the most effective and profitable strategy—that is, market penetration. On the other hand, that same brewery, noting the growth in demand for ciders in the female market, may decide that it should leverage its strengths of operations and distribution and develop a cider (new product) for women (new market), thereby arriving at a diversification strategy.

Either way, companies cannot run away with an idea that seems obvious upon completion of SWOT any more than they should jump at a growth strategy from Ansoff's matrix, without pushing the two tools together and critically thinking through all options.

3-3 | BUSINESS PLANNING FOR COMPETITIVE ADVANTAGE

Once an organization has thoroughly scanned its internal and external environment via SWOT analysis and considered the most appropriate growth strategy by combining SWOT with Ansoff's matrix, it needs to begin outlining *how* to go about implementing and executing the strategy. At this stage, more detailed planning is required at the strategic business unit (SBU) level as to how a business will achieve a sustainable competitive advantage. Leaders of SBUs must identify the **core competencies**, key unique strengths that are hard to imitate and underlie the functioning of an organization, that will help them attain a competitive advantage. In other words, SWOT must be conducted at an SBU level as well to identify SBU-related factors not evident in the corporate analysis.

3-3a | Competitive Advantage

A **competitive advantage** is a set of unique features of a company and its products that are perceived by the target market as significant and superior to the competition and thus results in customers choosing one company over its competitors. There are a variety of competitive advantage strategies to pursue, most of which fall into the category of cost, product differentiation, or niche strategies.

3-3b | Cost Competitive Advantage

Cost leadership can result from obtaining inexpensive raw materials, creating an efficient scale of plant operations, designing products for ease of manufacture, controlling overhead costs, and avoiding marginal customers. WestJet Airlines has been successful at keeping its airfares lower than its competitors while

diversification
a strategy of increasing sales by introducing new products into new markets

core competencies
key unique strengths that are hard to imitate and underlie the functioning of an organization

competitive advantage
the set of unique features of a company and its products that are perceived by the target market as significant and superior to the competition

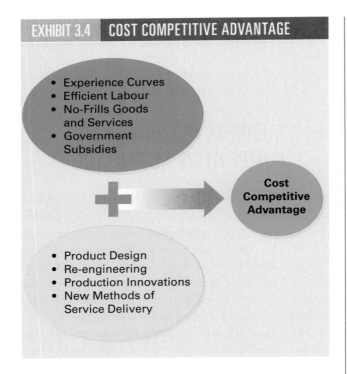

EXHIBIT 3.4 COST COMPETITIVE ADVANTAGE

- Experience Curves
- Efficient Labour
- No-Frills Goods and Services
- Government Subsidies

+ → Cost Competitive Advantage

- Product Design
- Re-engineering
- Production Innovations
- New Methods of Service Delivery

still providing customers with the inflight services they want.[7] Having a **cost competitive advantage** means being the low-cost competitor in an industry while maintaining satisfactory profit margins.

Costs can be reduced in a variety of ways as shown in Exhibit 3.4.

- *Experience curves:* **Experience curves** demonstrate that costs decline at a predictable rate as experience with a product increases. The experience curve effect encompasses a broad range of manufacturing, marketing, and administrative costs. Experience curves reflect learning by doing, technological advances, and economies of scale. Businesses use historical experience curves as a basis for predicting and setting prices. Experience curves allow management to forecast costs and set prices based on anticipated costs as opposed to current costs.

- *Efficient labour:* Labour costs can be an important component of total costs in low-skill, labour-intensive industries, such as product assembly and apparel manufacturing. Many Canadian manufacturers have gone offshore to achieve cheaper manufacturing costs. Many Canadian companies are

also outsourcing activities such as data entry and other labour-intensive jobs.[8]

- *No-frills goods and services:* Marketers can lower costs by removing frills and options from a product or service. Jetlines, for example, aims to be to the Canadian airline that WestJet was when it launched in the mid-1990s. Jetlines offers low fares with no frills. The assumption is that low prices give Jetlines a higher load factor and greater economies of scale, which, in turn, mean even lower prices.[9]

- *Government subsidies:* Governments may provide grants and interest-free loans to target industries. There are government grants and loans available for everything from technology innovation projects to developing export markets.[10]

- *Product design:* Cutting-edge design technology can help offset high labour costs. Reverse engineering—the process of disassembling a product piece by piece to learn its components and obtain clues as to the manufacturing process—can also mean savings. Reverse-engineering a low-cost competitor's product can save research and design costs.

- *Re-engineering:* Re-engineering entails fundamental rethinking and redesign of business processes to achieve dramatic improvements in critical measures of performance. It often involves reorganizing from functional departments, such as sales, engineering, and production, to cross-disciplinary teams. Uber, partnering with Toyota, is working on re-engineering cars to be driverless. Research has shown that driverless cars could increase Uber's revenues by up to 70 percent.[11]

- *Production innovations:* Production innovations, such as new technology and simplified production techniques, help lower the average cost of production. Technologies such as computer-aided design and computer-aided manufacturing (CAD/CAM) and increasingly sophisticated robots help companies reduce their manufacturing costs.

- *New methods of service delivery:* While all banks, not to mention household utility service providers, have gone paperless with statements and billing, Tangerine, a subsidiary of Scotiabank, has gone to the extreme of cost reduction by replacing expensive bricks-and-mortar buildings with cafés and pop-up kiosks, driving its younger target market toward a total mobile banking experience.[12]

3-3c | Product Differentiation Competitive Advantage

Because cost competitive advantages are subject to continual erosion (costs can be pushed only so low), product/service

cost competitive advantage
being the low-cost competitor in an industry while maintaining satisfactory profit margins

experience curves
curves that show costs declining at a predictable rate as experience with a product increases

Roberto Machado Noa/LightRocket/Getty Images

Nathan Legiehn for Greenhouse

differentiation tends to provide a longer-lasting competitive advantage. The durability of this strategy tends to make it more attractive to many top managers. A **product/service differentiation competitive advantage** exists when a company provides a unique benefit that is valuable to buyers beyond simply offering a low price. Examples are brand names, a strong dealer network, product reliability, image, or service. An example of product differentiation is Nicecream, a frozen fruit dessert. Company founder Brooke Hammer developed a process to produce fruit-only frozen desserts while attending Trent University. The all-natural product is only 50 to 60 calories per serving and fat free, appealing to the health-conscious consumer. Nicecream also appeals to consumers who want to move away from large food and beverage companies to brands that better align with their own their values. Loblaw started carrying the product in a few stores and plans to carry it in all stores across the country eventually.[13]

3-3d | Niche Competitive Advantage

A **niche competitive advantage** seeks to target and effectively serve a single segment of the market (see Chapter 7). For small companies with limited resources that potentially face giant competitors, carving out a niche strategy may be the only viable option. A market segment that has good growth potential but is not crucial to the success of major competitors is a good candidate for developing a niche strategy. Many companies using a niche strategy serve only a limited geographic market. Other companies focus their product lines on specific types of products, as is the case with the Canadian Greenhouse Juice Company, whose mission is to "to offer widespread, sustainable access to plant-based nutrition and wellness of the highest quality." Since opening its doors in January 2014 the company has focused only on plant-based beverages like cold-pressed juices produced in small batches from organic produce. The company has expanded the production facilities and now has more than 10 stores and national distribution but still produces only organic, plant-based beverages.[14]

3-3e | Building Sustainable Competitive Advantage

The key to having a competitive advantage is the ability to sustain that advantage. A **sustainable competitive advantage** is an advantage that cannot be copied by the competition. Examples of companies with a sustainable competitive advantage are Rolex (high-quality watches), Harry Rosen stores (customized service), and Cirque du Soleil (top-notch entertainment). When a company or organization doesn't have a competitive advantage, target customers don't perceive any reason to patronize one organization over its competitors.

The notion of competitive advantage means that a successful business will stake out a position unique in some manner from its rivals.

product/service differentiation competitive advantage
the provision of a unique benefit that is valuable to buyers beyond simply offering a low price

niche competitive advantage
the advantage achieved when a company seeks to target and effectively serve a single segment of the market

sustainable competitive advantage
an advantage that cannot be copied by the competition

Imitation by competitors indicates a lack of competitive advantage and almost ensures their mediocre performance. Moreover, competitors rarely stand still, so it is not surprising that imitation causes marketers to feel trapped in a seemingly endless game of catch-up. They are regularly surprised by the new accomplishments of their rivals.

Companies need to build their own competitive advantages rather than copy a competitor. The sources of tomorrow's competitive advantages are the skills and assets of the organization. Skills are functions, such as customer service and promotion, that the business performs better than its competitors. Assets include patents, copyrights, locations, and equipment and technology that are superior to those of the competition. Marketing leaders should continually focus the business's skills and assets on sustaining and creating competitive advantages.

3-4 | MARKETING PLANNING

After the corporate level and SBU level, the third level of planning is aimed at developing **marketing strategy**, which involves the activities of selecting and describing one or more target markets and developing and maintaining a marketing mix that will produce mutually satisfying exchanges with target markets.

marketing strategy
the activities of selecting and describing one or more target markets and developing and maintaining a marketing mix that will produce mutually satisfying exchanges with target markets

marketing objective
a statement of what is to be accomplished through marketing activities

market opportunity analysis (MOA)
the description and estimation of the size and sales potential of market segments that are of interest to the business and the assessment of key competitors in these market segments

3-4a | Setting Marketing Plan Objectives

Before the details of a marketing plan can be developed, objectives for the plan must be stated. Without objectives, a business has no basis for measuring the success of its marketing plan activities.

A **marketing objective** is a statement of what is to be accomplished through marketing activities. To be useful, stated objectives should meet five criteria, easily developed through the SMART method. First, objectives should be *specific*, meaning that they must be worded in a way that leaves little guessing or generality. Second, they need to be *measurable*, using a unit of measure, such as dollar amount, so that a level of achievement can be literally witnessed. Third, objectives must be *attainable*, or realistically within the reach of the business. Fourth, they should be *relevant* to the organization, in that they are on-brand or parallel to the business's mission. Finally, they should be *time bound*, by assigning some sort of time window for the objective to be achieved. It is tempting to state that the objective is "to be Canada's leading publisher of postsecondary marketing textbooks." However, what is "leading" for one company might mean selling 10 000 units, whereas another company might view "leading" as having cutting-edge digital textbook supplements. "Leading" in this statement is neither specific nor measurable. We therefore have no idea whether it is attainable, nor do we know when the objective should be met. A SMART objective might read, "Achieve sales of 10 000 units of the *Introduction to Marketing* textbook to postsecondary business students, by June 1, 2021." Objectives are the main intersection of a company's marketing strategies. Specifically, objectives flow from the situational analysis and mission statement and drive the decisions made for the future in the marketing plan.

Carefully specified objectives serve several functions. First, they communicate marketing management philosophies and provide direction for lower-level marketing managers so that marketing efforts are integrated and pointed in a consistent direction. Objectives also serve as motivators by creating goals for employees to strive toward. When objectives are attainable and challenging, they motivate those charged with achieving the objectives. Additionally, the process of writing specific objectives forces executives to clarify their thinking. Finally, objectives form a basis for control; the effectiveness of a plan can be gauged in light of the stated objectives.

3-4b | Target Market Strategy

A market segment is a group of individuals or organizations that share one or more characteristics. As we'll see in Chapter 7, a segment isn't necessarily the same as a target market, until it can be established that one of these characteristics is an actual need for the product being offered. For example, parents of young babies may need formula, diapers, and special foods.

The target market strategy identifies the market segment or segments on which to focus. This process begins with a **market opportunity analysis (MOA)**—the description and estimation of the size and sales potential of market segments that are of interest to the business and the assessment of key competitors in these market segments.

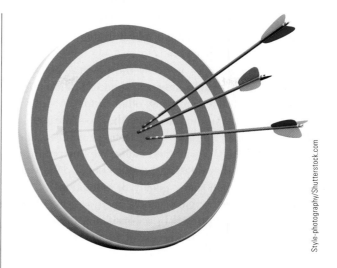

Style-photography/Shutterstock.com

After the business describes the market segments, it may choose to target one or more of these segments. Marketers use three general strategies for selecting target markets.

Target markets can be selected by appealing to the entire market with one marketing mix, concentrating on one segment, or appealing to multiple market segments using multiple marketing mixes. The characteristics, advantages, and disadvantages of each strategic option are examined in Chapter 7. Target markets could be individuals who are concerned about sensitive teeth (the target of Sensodyne toothpaste) or young urban professionals who need inexpensive transportation on demand (Car2Go).

Any market segment that is targeted must be fully described. Geographics, demographics, psychographics, and buyer behaviour should be assessed. Buyer behaviour is covered in Chapters 5 and 6. If segments are differentiated by ethnicity, multicultural aspects of the marketing mix should be examined. If the target market is international, it is especially important to describe differences in culture, economic and technological development, and political structure that may affect the marketing plan.

3-4c | The Marketing Mix

The term **marketing mix** refers to a unique blend of product, price, place (distribution), and promotion strategies (often referred to as the **four Ps**) designed to produce mutually satisfying exchanges with a target market. The marketing manager can control each component of the marketing mix, but the strategies for all four components must be blended to achieve optimal results. Any marketing mix is only as good as its weakest component. The best promotion and the lowest price cannot save a poor product. Similarly, excellent products with poor placing, pricing, or promotion will likely fail.

Variations in marketing mixes do not occur by chance. Astute marketers devise marketing strategies to gain advantages over competitors and best serve the needs and wants of a particular target market segment. By manipulating elements of the marketing mix, marketing managers can fine-tune the customer offering and achieve competitive success.

3-4d | Product Strategies

Typically, the marketing mix starts with the product, as this is essentially where marketing starts. The product is the literal satisfaction of the discovered need. The heart of the marketing mix, the starting point, is the product offering and product

marketing mix
a unique blend of product, price, place, and promotion, strategies designed to produce mutually satisfying exchanges with a target market

four Ps
product, price, place, and promotion, which together make up the marketing mix

strategy. Without knowing the product to be marketed, it is difficult to design a pricing or place strategy, or decide on a promotion campaign.

The product includes not only the physical unit but also its package, warranty, after-sale service, brand name, company image, value, and many other factors. A Godiva chocolate has many product elements: the chocolate itself, a fancy gold wrapper, a customer satisfaction guarantee, and the prestige of the Godiva brand name. We buy products not only for what they do (their benefits) but also for what they mean to us (their status, quality, or reputation).

Products can be tangible goods, such as computers; ideas, such as those offered by a consultant; or services, such as medical care. To be successful, products must offer customer value. Product decisions are covered in Chapters 9 and 10, and services marketing is detailed in Chapter 11.

3-4e | Pricing Strategies

Price is what a buyer must give up to obtain a product. Thus, it is often viewed in a subconscious (or conscious) calculation of value by a consumer. It is often the most flexible of the four marketing mix elements because it is the quickest element to change. Marketers can raise or lower prices more frequently and easily than they can change other marketing mix variables. Price is an important competitive weapon and is very important to the organization because price multiplied by the number of units sold equals total revenue for the business. Pricing decisions are covered in Chapter 12.

3-4f | Place (Distribution) Strategies

Place, or distribution, strategies are concerned with making products available when and where customers want them. Would you rather buy a kiwi fruit at the 24-hour grocery store within walking distance or fly to New Zealand to pick your own? A part of the place is physical distribution, which involves all the business activities concerned with storing and transporting raw materials or finished products. The goal is to ensure products arrive in usable condition at designated places when needed. Place strategies are covered in Chapters 13 and 14.

3-4g | Promotion Strategies

Elements of the promotional mix, or integrated marketing communications (IMC), include advertising, direct marketing, public relations, sales promotion, personal selling, and digital marketing. Promotion's role in the marketing mix is to introduce, facilitate, or sustain conversation and community between companies and their customers. It does this by informing, educating, persuading, and reminding consumers of the benefits of an organization or a product. A good promotion strategy can dramatically increase sales. Good promotional strategies, however, are not the same as costly promotional strategies. Each element of the promotion is coordinated and managed with the others to create a promotional blend or mix. These integrated marketing communications activities are described in Chapters 15, 16, 17, and 18.

3-5 | MARKETING PLAN IMPLEMENTATION, EVALUATION, AND CONTROL

One of the keys to success overlooked by many businesses is to actively follow up on the marketing plan. The time spent researching, developing, and writing a useful and accurate marketing plan goes to waste if the plan is not used by the organization. One of the best ways to get the most of a marketing plan is to correctly implement it. Once the first steps to implementation are taken, evaluation and control will help guide the organization to success as laid out by the marketing plan.

3-5a | Implementation

Implementation is the process that turns a marketing plan into action assignments and, in theory, ensures that these assignments are executed in a way that accomplishes the plan's objectives. Implementation activities may involve detailed job assignments, activity descriptions, timelines, budgets, and lots of communication. Although implementation is essentially "doing what you said you were going to do," many organizations repeatedly experience failures in strategy implementation. Brilliant marketing plans are doomed to fail if they are not properly implemented. Strategies that envision lofty and ambitious growth for a company cannot be supported by the strength of their potential alone; tangible tactics will provide the building blocks to strategies.

3-5b | Evaluation and Control

After a marketing plan is implemented, it should be evaluated. **Evaluation** involves gauging the extent to which marketing objectives have been achieved during

---

implementation
the process that turns a marketing plan into action assignments and ensures that these assignments are executed in a way that accomplishes the plan's objectives

evaluation
gauging the extent to which the marketing objectives have been achieved during the specified period

FOUR CHARACTERISTICS OF A MARKETING AUDIT

- *Comprehensive:* covers all major marketing issues facing an organization and not just trouble spots.
- *Systematic:* takes place in an orderly sequence and covers the organization's marketing environment, internal marketing system, and specific marketing activities. The diagnosis is followed by an action plan with both short-term and long- term proposals for improving overall marketing effectiveness.
- *Independent:* normally conducted by an inside or outside party that is independent enough to have top management's confidence and to be objective.
- *Periodic:* for maximum benefit, should be carried out on a regular schedule instead of only in a crisis.

the specified time. Four common reasons for failing to achieve a marketing objective are unrealistic marketing objectives, inappropriate marketing strategies in the plan, poor implementation, and changes in the environment after the objective was specified and the strategy was implemented. It is important to note here that both implementation and evaluation are written into a marketing plan before the plan is approved, as a means of demonstrating to executives, who sign off on these plans, that there is follow-through on the plan's objectives.

Once a plan is chosen and implemented, its effectiveness must be monitored. **Control** provides the mechanisms both for evaluating marketing results in light of the plan's objectives and for correcting actions that do not help the organization reach those objectives within budget guidelines. Businesses need to establish formal and informal control programs to make the entire operation more efficient.

Perhaps the broadest control device available to marketing managers is the **marketing audit**—a thorough, systematic, periodic evaluation of the objectives, strategies, structure, and performance of the marketing organization. A marketing audit helps management allocate marketing resources efficiently.

Although the main purpose of the marketing audit is to develop a full profile of the organization's marketing effort and to provide a basis for developing and revising the marketing plan, it is also an excellent way to improve communication and raise the level of marketing consciousness within the organization. A marketing audit is a useful vehicle for selling the philosophy and techniques of strategic marketing to other members of the organization.

3-6 | EFFECTIVE STRATEGIC PLANNING

Effective strategic planning requires continual attention, creativity, and management commitment. Strategic planning should not be an annual exercise, in which managers go through the motions and forget about strategic planning until the next year. It should be an ongoing process because the environment is continually changing and the business's resources and capabilities are continually evolving.

Sound strategic planning is based on creative thinking. Marketers should challenge assumptions about the business and the environment and establish new strategies. And above all, the most critical element in successful strategic planning is top management's support and participation.

control
provides the mechanisms both for evaluating marketing results in light of the plan's objectives and for correcting actions that do not help the organization reach those objectives within budget guidelines

marketing audit
a thorough, systematic, periodic evaluation of the objectives, strategies, structure, and performance of the marketing organization

AWAKE CHOCOLATE CONTINUING CASE

AWAKE Chocolate

Marketing Strategy with Energy

With the founders of Awake having emerged from careers in consumer goods such as Pepsico, there is a keen awareness of the need to continually innovate. While the business adage "innovate or die" might seem a little extreme, it is not far from the truth for companies that decide to rest on past success instead of looking around and seeing what is going on around them (see: Blockbuster Video).

Much of what Awake tries to achieve around its marketing strategy is the creation of two things: new products and new customers. While the company is not actively moving away from a loyal customer, the leaders believe in the importance of creating an infrastructure of innovation that will continually push the company to create a new product and then seek out the consumer segment that they believe will gain the most value from consuming this particular product.

Awake cofounder Adam Deremo noted that by "bringing more new products to market, we have more reason to go out and talk with our customers on a more frequent basis than we ever had before." This "excuse" for customer engagement is a great way to not only assess new product ideas but also get the name of the brand in front of consumers on a more consistent basis.

And once again, the backbone of marketing (needs) is front and centre in Awake's approach to its marketing strategy. One of the most misunderstood aspects of marketing surrounds the concept of strategy. Often companies, journalists, and even business students will assume that marketing strategy is all about tactical concepts such as creating great content or developing an advertisement.

For Awake, the ability to come up with "new" is central to its strategic aspirations. Deremo asserted: "Having a more robust innovation pipeline, and bringing new products to market more frequently, I think is a good marketing strategy. It meets consumer needs."

And as new Awake products arrive on store shelves, the focus is squarely on creating something incremental that builds upon what is already available to consumers. Awake listens to customer feedback and shifts gears whenever necessary. In recalling a recent new product introduction, Adam Deremo described how a shift in consumer preferences shifted what the company offered: "The ways we can make it better is: one, the format. So we launched in a full-size bar that had 200 calories with between 20 and 30 grams of sugar. We subsequently brought out a format that was a third its size and less than 100 calories per serving and fewer than 9 grams of sugar. Consumers seem to value that."

If you go looking for Awake Chocolate on store shelves, you will not only find the original chocolate bar that started it all on *Dragon's Den*. You will find a number of new innovations, including different sizes and flavours, but also different formats like bite-sized snacks and granola.

And there are no signs of Awake stopping anytime soon. The company continues to come up with new ideas, test markets, and concept assessments. The cupboards of Awake's product ideas are far from bare, as Deremo stated: "At this point in the lifetime of the brand, we have the deepest innovation pipeline that we have ever had." For competitors in the market, including the larger more established brands like Quaker and KitKat, this pipeline should be a concern. The company is still small enough to be nimble and make adjustments on the fly that would be challenging for large multinationals.

And the company's plan is to make sure its marketing strategy never has the company standing still. "It's about maximizing consumer reach. In simple terms, the more dissimilar you can make your next project, the more likely you are to reach a new consumer." Deremo's makes it clear that the beaten path is of no interest for Awake. There are simply too many ideas based on continually evolving consumer needs. And for that reason, Awake has a marketing strategy with real energy.

QUESTIONS

1. **Conduct a SWOT analysis for Awake Chocolate. Use the information from the case at the end of Chapters 1 and 2, along with your own research on the internal and external environments facing the company.**

2. **Adam Deremo was quoted as saying: "We are trying to expand the footprint of Awake as much as we can—to make sure that when we bring new products, we're reaching new consumers." Using the Ansoff matrix, describe which type of marketing strategy this approach is supporting.**

3. **It is clear that Awake Chocolate has a very aggressive marketing strategy. Create a short pitch for a more conservative approach to marketing strategy than the one Awake currently undertakes.**

AWAKE Chocolate

Marketing—Let's Get Started, Part 1 Case

Uber-izing Food Delivery Shows Limitations

As the new millennium entered its second decade, the platform economy was the new world order, Uber one of its largest kingdoms, and Travis Kalanick, the crown prince. There were the TED Talks, keynotes, the life of a rock star, and the wealth of royalty. Especially after Uber, a company he co-founded with Canadian Garrett Camp in 2009, rocketed to almost $50 billion valuation 8 years later.

However, by the time of the ride sharing company's 2019 IPO, Kallanick had been ousted as CEO. His apparent cut-throat/take-no-prisoners mentality and obsession with winning had figured prominently in a corporate culture exposed in 2017 by the *New York Times* as being overrun by an "aggressive, unrestrained workplace culture." The IPO opened at $45 a share in May 2019, closed at $41 at the end of trading, and has spent more time below the initial valuation ever since.

But this is not a story about Kalanick, Uber, or even the platform economy both were so instrumental in creating. No, this is a story about human behaviour and how understanding it is the most valuable knowledge a company can have.

DoorDash, arguably the first company to launch an app connecting hungry customers with profit-hungry restaurants, together with UberEats and GrubHub command over 75 percent of the food delivery service space in the United States. Canada's first entrant, Skip The Dishes, began as a service for working professionals to provide quick and easy access to a wider variety of restaurants. This differed from the opportunity-need the American companies were tackling—food convenience for customers (beyond pizza and Chinese food, which had been staples of food delivery since the telephone era). As well, food delivery services would connect restaurants without delivery services with customers looking for delivery, resulting in a new market category for restaurant owners. This would help everyone from quick-service restaurants, such as McDonalds, to five-star restaurants, which would have previously shunned delivery and thus not even provided a delivery option for customers. As with Uber, the macro-opportunity was convenience, satisfying a time-starved market.

In the beginning, it seemed to be working as convenience trumped all. Even at 20 to 30 percent commission rates, restaurants were quickly jumping on to the growing number of platforms. If they didn't see the value in the service itself, they looked at it as a competitive necessity because everyone else was doing it. And everyone was doing it because customers wanted the convenience.

Customers enjoyed this new platform that brought any food from any restaurant to their home, office, or school. In Canada's cold climate, the convenience went further. We could jump on to our favorite food delivery platform and choose a meal from our favorite restaurant then eat it in the comfort of our kitchen table. No warming up the car, driving through winter storms, or brushing snow off the windshield. You could also have more than one glass of wine with your meal without fear of impaired driving.

By early 2019, the sky was the limit for the food delivery industry, with some analysts pegging the market value globally at as high as $3 trillion. Canadians ordered $1 billion worth of meals through delivery apps in 2018, and another $3 billion on meal kits such as Blue Apron.

TOO MANY COOKS?

Despite the sharp growth in market use and revenue, the food delivery space began taking on water almost as soon as it got off the ground. The central issue, as always, had to do with costs. Commissions were eating away at restaurant profits, while the major app platforms were also squeaking by on "very, very thin margins," according to Foodora Canada's General Manager David Albert.

Some restaurants accepted the toll but opted out of the program due to reliability issues. These include infractions ranging from the predictable, such as late or neglected order pickups to the downright creepy, such as drivers nibbling on orders prior to delivery; a survey conducted by US Foods found that 28 percent of food delivery drivers admitted to this behaviour, casting a whole new meaning to the term *distracted driving*.

On the other hand, perhaps drivers are merely trying to balance the books in terms of their remuneration. A class action lawsuit was filed in Winnipeg in 2018 by a former Skip the Dishes driver who claimed he and his counterparts were not being fairly compensated by the company. The lawsuit claimed everything about Skip's hiring, training, and fee processes smack of employment, and yet drivers do not receive minimum wage, vacation, or overtime. The lawsuit in question was put on hold in November 2019 pending the outcome of a similar case brought up against Uber Eats by one of its drivers in Toronto.

All of which brings us back to one rather unexpected consequence of food delivery services: teenagers. With dual-income households scrambling to get lunches into backpacks as kids scurry out the door, someone came up with the novel idea of having said child's meal delivered to them via app instead. The problem became so great by spring semester of 2019 that school districts across Canada were forced to create food-delivery policies. Said James Johnston, principal at Semiahmoo Secondary School in Surrey, BC, after noting delivery drivers showing up throughout the day and traipsing through his school, "We started thinking about that as a bit of a safety issue."

Finally, we end discussion in the same place much of the food delivery packaging winds up—in landfills. While not yet raising environmental alarm bells in North America, scientists estimate that food delivery in China resulted in 2 million tons of packaging waste in 2018. While it should be pointed out that China far exceeds any other country on earth in its use of food delivery apps, the US market is actually greater per capita. Either way, China, the United States, Canada or any other country where food delivery apps have entered into ubiquity will have to eventually come to terms with increased pressure brought to their already over-burdened sustainability programs.

QUESTIONS

1. Suppose you are a new intern for Skip the Dishes. On your first day on the job, your boss decides to see what you are made of, and asks you to prepare a SWOT analysis of your new employer. Using this case, and any other resources available to you,

JPstock/Shutterstock.com

prepare a simplified SWOT, showing what you consider to be, at minimum, three most important strengths, weaknesses, opportunities, and threats currently facing the company.

2. The case you have just read was written in early 2020. What opportunities and threats have entered into the food-delivery market that were not noted in the case? Use the CREST model for your responses.

3. A growing trend in the food delivery industry is "ghost kitchens." This concept is made possible specifically because of the demand for food delivery and consumers' penchant for variety. Find an example of ghost kitchen operation within your community and elaborate.

4. Food delivery apps introduced a new way of accessing and consuming meals. Around the same time that these were showing up, meal-kit delivery companies such as Blue Apron and Good Food were penetrating the meal market as well. List the main differences between these two entrants into the food industry.

SOURCES

Trefis Team, "Breaking Down Uber's Valuation: An Interactive Analysis," Forbes, 2018; Avery Hartmans and Paige Leskin, "The History of How Uber Went from the Most Feared Startup in the World to Its Massive IPO" Business Insider, 2019; Money, MSN, "Uber Technologies Inc. NYSE History,". 2019; James Wang, "Food-as-a-Service: The $3 Trillion Meal Delivery Market," Ark Invest, 2019; Dianne Buckner, "Consumers Love Food Delivery Apps, but High Commissions Eat at Restaurant Owners" CBC News, Toronto, 2019; Jackie Salo, "More Than 1 in 4 Delivery Drivers Eat Your Food Order: Study," *New York Post*, 2019; Andrew Chang and Ian Hanomansing, "Skip the Dishes Driver Wants Class-Action against Company." CBC, The National, Toronto, 2018; Katie May, "Proposed Skip the Dishes Lawsuit Awaits Ruling on Uber," Winnipeg Free Press, 2019; Chris Purdy, "There's An App for That: Students Opt for Delivery Over Bag Lunches, Cafeterias" Canadian Press, 2019; Raymond Zhong, "Food Delivery Apps Are Drowning China in Plastic," *New York Times*, 2019.

4 | Marketing Research and Analytics

LEARNING OUTCOMES

4-1 Explain marketing research and marketing analytics

4-2 List the steps in the marketing research process

4-3 Discuss the impact of technology on marketing research and marketing analytics

4-4 Explain how marketing analytics is used to develop a marketing strategy

4-5 Summarize the concerns related to the collection and use of marketing data

4-6 Describe when to conduct marketing research or when to use marketing analytics

"It's a digital world out there! Everything from TV, to phone, to in-store shopping and transportation modes, are somehow connected. The marketing research world is no exception, and in fact must be at the heart of it. That's where the consumer lives."

—Tamer El Araby, Managing Director, Nielsen Insights[1]

4-1 | MARKETING RESEARCH AND MARKETING ANALYTICS

The challenges for marketing managers can be great, as the marketplace is constantly changing, and customers are not always clear (whether intentionally or not) about what their needs are or how they would like them satisfied. Marketing managers turn to marketing research and marketing analytics to help them make decisions to meet the challenges of today's marketplace. **Marketing research** is the process of planning, collecting, and analyzing data relevant to a marketing decision. The results of this analysis are then communicated to management.

Closely related to marketing research, **marketing analytics** is the use of data to optimize marketing decisions.

In the past, access to marketing data was relatively limited; the data came from company records such as sales reports or from the marketing research process. As technology has developed, marketers have access to more data from more sources. This increase in data availability has impacted how and when marketing managers undertake marketing research projects to collect data and when and how to use technology to collect data for marketing analytics. The use of technology to collect data has led to rapid advances in marketing analytic techniques to help marketing managers make decisions.

marketing research
the process of planning, collecting, and analyzing data relevant to a marketing decision

marketing analytics
the use of data to optimize marketing decisions

An important note about marketing research and marketing analytics is that these processes alone do not solve any problem; they are invaluable in helping companies better understand their customers, the marketplace, and the inherent challenges of meeting customer needs.

THREE FUNCTIONAL ROLES OF MARKETING RESEARCH AND ANALYTICS

There are three functional roles marketing research and marketing analytics can play in an organization:

1. *Descriptive role*—presenting factual statements. For example, What are the historic sales trends in the industry? What are consumers' attitudes toward a product and its advertising?

2. *Diagnostic role*—explaining relationships within data. For example, What is the impact on a product's sales if the colour of the packaging is changed?

3. *Predictive role*—predicting results of a marketing decision. For example, What is the impact of a new product introduction on market share?

4-2 | THE MARKETING RESEARCH PROCESS

Virtually all companies engage in some market research because it offers decision makers many benefits. The market research process is a scientific approach to decision making that maximizes the chance of receiving accurate and meaning results. Exhibit 4.1 traces the seven steps in the research process and provides the basis from which marketing research is undertaken.

4-2a | Step 1: Identify and Formulate the Problem/Opportunity

Identifying the problem is the most important stage of the entire marketing research process. Without a defined problem statement, marketing research will be nothing more than a series of tasks without direction or purpose. This first stage is best explained by a phrase used in information technology: "garbage in, garbage out"; the integrity of the output (results) is dependent on the integrity of the input (the problem).

This means that a researcher should first determine whether there is enough information to clearly define a problem before embarking on the full marketing research process. Decision makers must be able to diagnose the right situation for conducting marketing research. We'll discuss this further in the section titled When to Conduct Market Research or Marketing Analytics later in the chapter.

4-2b | Step 2: Plan the Research Design and Gather Secondary Data

The **research design** specifies which research questions must be answered, how and when data will be gathered, and how the data will be analyzed. The research design is about creating a roadmap for the research process.

To gather the necessary information to answer the research question, a researcher must decide on the type of research design to use. There are two types of research design: exploratory and conclusive.

Exploratory research is an informal discovery process that attempts to gain insights and a better understanding of the management and research problems. It is done to help explore the problem further, and because the parameters of exploratory research are not always clearly defined, researchers have more flexibility in how the research is conducted. There are a number of different methods of exploratory research: focus groups, expert interviews, literature search, and case studies.

Conclusive research is a more specific type of research that attempts to provide clarity to a decision maker by identifying specific courses of action. It is focused on developing conclusions and courses of actions.

There are two kinds of conclusive research: descriptive and causal. **Descriptive research**,

research design
specifies which research questions must be answered, how and when data will be gathered, and how the data will be analyzed

exploratory research
an informal discovery process that attempts to gain insights and a better understanding of the management and research problems

conclusive research
a more specific type of research that attempts to provide clarity to a decision maker by identifying specific courses of action

descriptive research
a type of conclusive research that attempts to describe marketing phenomena and characteristics

causal research
a type of conclusive research that focuses on the cause and effect of two variables and attempts to find some relationship between them

secondary data
data previously collected for any purpose other than the one at hand

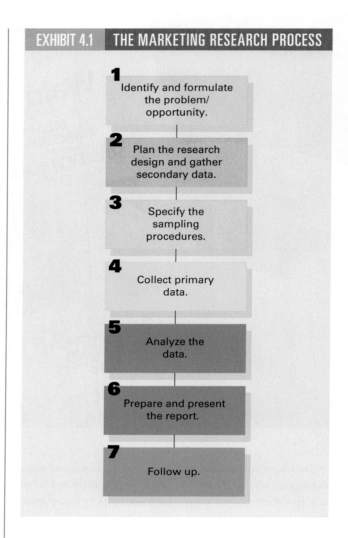

EXHIBIT 4.1   THE MARKETING RESEARCH PROCESS

1. Identify and formulate the problem/opportunity.
2. Plan the research design and gather secondary data.
3. Specify the sampling procedures.
4. Collect primary data.
5. Analyze the data.
6. Prepare and present the report.
7. Follow up.

by far the more common type of conclusive research used in business, attempts to describe marketing phenomena and characteristics. **Causal research** focuses on the cause and effect of two variables and attempts to find some relationship between them. This type of conclusive research is used often in academic and research environments.

In deciding on a research design, it should be noted that this is not an "either–or" situation where only one type of research design can be chosen. The best way to consider research design is as a process, described in Exhibit 4.2.

SECONDARY DATA The temptation for researchers is to begin collecting their own data to answer their research question. But it is vital to examine the data that already exist.

Secondary data are data previously collected for a purpose other than the one at hand. Secondary data may not be able to completely answer your research question.

EXHIBIT 4.2   THE RESEARCH DESIGN PROCESS

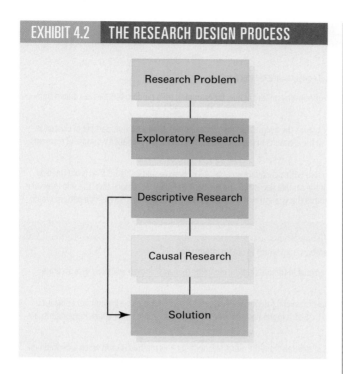

EXHIBIT 4.3   ADVANTAGES AND DISADVANTAGES OF SECONDARY DATA

Advantages of Secondary Data	Disadvantages of Secondary Data
Inexpensive	Collected for another purpose
Clarifies problem	Questionable sources
Fast to collect	Quickly outdated

There are two main sources of secondary data: sources inside the organization conducting the research and external sources that are publicly available, sometimes at a price. Secondary information originating from within the company includes documents such as annual reports and reports to shareholders.

There are many outside sources of secondary information, including government departments and agencies such as Statistics Canada. Still more data are available from online journals and research studies. Marketing associations, such as the Marketing Research and Intelligence Association (MRIA) and the Canadian Institute of Marketing (CIM), also provide information. Trade and industry associations publish secondary data that can be found in business periodicals and other news media which regularly publish studies and articles on the economy, specific industries, and individual companies. In addition, information on many topics, such as industry trends and brands, can be derived from polls, focus groups, surveys, panels, and interviews and is available from companies such as Environics Research Group and other sources online.

The advantages and disadvantages of secondary data are shown in Exhibit 4.3.

4-2c | Step 3: Specify the Sampling Procedures

Once the researchers have designed the research and collected secondary data, their next step is to select the sampling procedures to use. A company can seldom interview or take a census of all possible people they want to include in the research. Therefore, the company must select a sample of the group to be interviewed. A **sample** is a subset from a larger population.

Several questions must be answered before a sampling plan is chosen. First, the population of interest must be defined. It should include all the people whose opinions, behaviours, preferences, attitudes, and so on are of interest to the marketer. For example, in a study whose purpose is to determine the market for a new canned dog food, the population might be defined to include all current buyers of canned dog food.

After the population has been defined, the next question is whether the sample must be representative of that population. If the answer is yes, a probability sample is needed. Otherwise, a nonprobability sample might be considered.

A **probability sample** is a sample in which every element in the population has a known statistical likelihood of being selected. Its most desirable feature is that scientific rules can be used to ensure that the sample represents the population. Any sample in which little or no attempt is made to have a representative cross-section of the population can be considered a **nonprobability sample**. Therefore, the probability of each sampling unit being selected is not known. Nonprobability samples are acceptable as long as the researcher understands their nonrepresentative nature. Because of their lower cost, nonprobability samples are the basis of much marketing research.

Common forms of probability and nonprobability samples are shown in Exhibit 4.4.

TYPES OF ERRORS

When ever a sample is used in marketing research, two major types of error may occur: measurement error

sample
a subset from a larger population

probability sample
a sample in which every element in the population has a known statistical likelihood of being selected

nonprobability sample
any sample in which little or no attempt is made to have a representative cross-section of the population

EXHIBIT 4.4 TYPES OF SAMPLES

	Probability Samples
Simple Random Sample	Every member of the population has a known and equal chance of selection.
Stratified Sample	The population is divided into mutually exclusive groups (by gender or age, for example), then random samples are drawn from each group.
Cluster Sample	The population is divided into mutually exclusive groups (by geographic area, for example); then a random sample of clusters is selected. The researcher then collects data from all the elements in the selected clusters or from a probability sample of elements within each selected cluster.
Systematic Sample	A list of the population is obtained—e.g., all persons with a chequing account at XYZ Bank—and a skip interval is obtained by dividing the sample size by the population size. If the sample size is 100 and the bank has 1000 customers, then the skip interval is 10. The beginning number is randomly chosen within the skip interval. If the beginning number is 8, then the skip pattern would be 8, 18, 28, etc.
	Nonprobability Samples
Convenience Sample	The researcher selects the easiest population members from which to obtain information.
Judgment Sample	The researcher's selection criteria are based on personal judgment that the elements (persons) chosen will likely give accurate information.
Quota Sample	The researcher finds a prescribed number of people in several categories—e.g., researcher selects a specific number of business students, arts students, science students, etc., so that each group has a specific number represented in the study. Respondents are not selected on probability sampling criteria.
Snowball Sample	Additional respondents are selected on the basis of referrals from the initial respondents. This method is used when a desired type of respondent is difficult to find—e.g., persons who have taken round-the-world cruises in the last three years are asked to refer others they know who have taken long cruises and could be involved in the research study.

and sampling error. **Measurement error** occurs when the information desired by the researcher differs from the information provided by the measurement process. For example, people may tell an interviewer that they purchase Crest toothpaste when they do not. Measurement error generally tends to be larger than sampling error.

Sampling error occurs when a sample does not represent the target population. A sampling error can be one of several types. A nonresponse error occurs when the sample interviewed differs from the sample drawn. This error happens because the original people selected to be interviewed either refused to cooperate or were inaccessible.

4-2d | Step 4: Collect Primary Data

Now that the research design has been chosen, it is time to collect the primary data. An important early decision at this stage of the process is what mix of secondary and primary research will be used.

measurement error
an error that occurs when the information desired by the researcher differs from the information provided by the measurement process

sampling error
an error that occurs when a sample does not represent the target population

primary data
information that is collected for the first time and is used for solving the particular issue under investigation

Primary data, or information collected for the first time, are used for solving the particular issue under investigation. The main advantage of primary data is that they will answer a specific research question that secondary data cannot answer. For example, suppose Pillsbury has two new recipes for refrigerated dough for sugar cookies. Which one will consumers like better? Secondary data will not help answer this question. Instead, targeted consumers must try each recipe and evaluate the taste, texture, and appearance of each cookie. The advantages and disadvantages of primary data are shown in Exhibit 4.5 and the types of primary data are shown in Exhibit 4.6.

QUALITATIVE AND QUANTITATIVE RESEARCH

Primary data is collected through either qualitative or quantitative research methods. Qualitative research is best used when a researcher still needs to clear up aspects of the research problem or requires a better

EXHIBIT 4.5 ADVANTAGES AND DISADVANTAGES OF PRIMARY DATA

Advantages of Primary Data	Disadvantages of Primary Data
Focuses on solving a specific problem	Expensive
Sources are known	Time consuming
Results more accurate	Requires specific skills sets

Campbell Soup Company regularly performs primary research such as studying consumers' reactions to different pictures of soup. The research has resulted in the company using bigger and clearer pictures of steaming soup with fewer pictures of spoons on the packaging.[2]

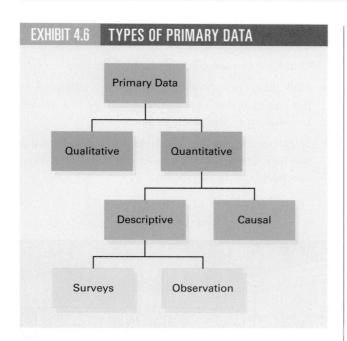

EXHIBIT 4.6   TYPES OF PRIMARY DATA

Primary Data
- Qualitative
- Quantitative
  - Descriptive
    - Surveys
    - Observation
  - Causal

understanding of a research situation. Quantitative research methods are best used when a researcher wants specific numbers and the ability to analyze the data to provide statistical conclusions.

The difference between qualitative and quantitative research methods brings us back to research design (step 2)

and the three types of design: exploratory, descriptive, and causal. Exploratory research includes the collection of secondary data and qualitative data collection. Both descriptive and causal research are included under quantitative data collection. Descriptive research seeks to describe phenomena that are observed and collected. Causal research looks for relationships and interactions between variables that are identified before research begins.

QUALITATIVE DATA COLLECTION METHODS

DEPTH INTERVIEWS A **depth interview** involves a discussion between a well-trained researcher and a respondent who is asked about attitudes and perspectives on a topic. The interview is one on one, a process that is very costly. First, individuals must be identified and located, which can be expensive and time consuming. Once a qualified person is located, the next step is to convince that person to agree to be interviewed and to set a time for the interview. An interviewer must also arrange to have the discussion recorded and transcribed.

> **depth interview**
> an interview that involves a discussion between a well-trained researcher and a respondent who is asked about attitudes and perspectives on a topic

FOCUS GROUPS A **focus group** is a small group of recruited participants engaged in a nonstructured discussion in a casual environment. Often recruited by random telephone screening, these qualified consumers are usually offered a monetary incentive to participate in a group discussion.

The meeting place is usually a typical business meeting room with a large conference table in the centre. The room is equipped with audio and video taping capabilities (which the participants are aware of). One wall of the focus group room has a one-way mirror that allows the client to view the proceedings. A moderator sits at the head of the table and leads the discussion with the participants.

The discussion is guided and directed by the moderator, who uses a moderator's guide (a series of questions developed by the researchers) to discuss a variety of topics in an open discussion. Focus groups can be used to gauge consumer response to a product or promotion and are occasionally used to brainstorm new product ideas or to screen concepts for new products.

Focus groups are a popular technique with companies, as the format and discussion are often engaging and entertaining for the clients watching the proceedings from behind the one-way mirror. But focus groups should never be confused with quantitative data collection methods such as surveys. The unstructured nature of focus group discussions allows for very few conclusive statements. The opinions, no matter how passionately presented in a focus group session, are still those of only a handful of people.

iStock.com/Eltoddo

ONLINE SURVEYS According to Statistics Canada, the percentage of adult Canadians with Internet access in their homes in 2018 reached more the 90 percent.[3] Online surveys have become a popular survey method because of the number of people with Internet access and better online survey tools such as SurveyMonkey, as well as the following advantages:

- *Rapid development, real-time reporting:* Internet surveys can be broadcast to thousands of potential respondents simultaneously.

- *Dramatically reduced costs:* The Internet can cut costs significantly and provide results in half the time required for traditional telephone surveys.

- *Improved respondent participation:* Internet surveys enjoy much higher response rates.

- *Contact with the difficult-to-reach:* Certain groups—doctors, high-income professionals, top management—are among the most surveyed individuals on the planet and the most difficult to reach.

Other survey methods include the following:

- *Mall intercept interviews,* which are conducted in the common area of a shopping mall or in a market research office within the mall.

- *Telephone interviews,* which are conducted from a specially designed phone room called a central-location telephone (CLT) facility.

QUANTITATIVE DATA COLLECTION METHODS

focus group
a small group of recruited participants engaged in a nonstructured discussion in a casual environment

survey research
the most popular method for gathering primary data, in which a researcher interacts with people to obtain facts, opinions, and attitudes

SURVEY RESEARCH The most popular quantitative data collection method for gathering primary data is **survey research**, in which a researcher interacts with people to obtain facts, opinions, and attitudes. Exhibit 4.7 summarizes the characteristics of different types of survey research and the box *Is It True* describes the results of some survey research.

Marmaduke St. John/Alamy Stock Photo

Is It True?

Marketers have different reasons for doing research. When there are significant changes in environmental factors, such as when COVID-19 struck Canada, marketers may do some research to monitor the changes in consumer behaviour.

In the early stages of the pandemic in Canada, research company Angus Reid surveyed over 900 Canadians to understand behaviours and attitudes toward the virus. The results showed that concern over the virus related to age group; people aged 18 to 24 continued to interact with friends, thinking that social distancing was less important than close contact with friends. These results confirmed what researchers thought was happening. What did surprise researchers was that people aged 35 to 44 were also interacting with friends. The age group that most complied with the social distancing recommendations were those aged 65 and older.

During this same period, the generation Z cohort (those born between 1995 and 2009) stayed home with family. This group did not change their behaviour significantly with many spending their time shopping online, with more than 25 percent of them shopping as often as did before the virus struck. Research completed by Mintel found that seniors did change their shopping behaviour, with many also turning to online shopping particularly for their groceries, in order to reduce their interactions with others.

Research studies that start out to confirm what marketers think is happening often also provide new trends that have not been predicted.

Sources: Christopher Lombardo, "Seniors are Embracing Tech and Online Shopping," Strategy online website, https://strategyonline.ca/2020/04/03/seniors-are-embracing-technology-and-online-shopping, April 3, 2020; Christopher Lombardo, "Young People Least Concerned About COVID-19," Strategy Online website, https://strategyonline.ca/2020/03/30/younger-canadians-least-concerned-about-social-distancing, March 30, 2020.

- *Mail surveys* are not as popular as they once were. Mail surveys can be one-time events or panels where participants are asked to complete surveys on an ongoing basis. The benefits of mail surveys include their relatively low cost, elimination of interviewers and field supervisors, centralized control, and actual or promised anonymity for respondents (which may draw more candid responses).

QUESTIONNAIRE DESIGN All forms of survey research require a questionnaire. Questionnaires ensure

EXHIBIT 4.7 CHARACTERISTICS OF SURVEY RESEARCH

Characteristic	Online Surveys	Mall Intercept Interviews	Central-Location Telephone Interviews	Self-Administered and One-Time Mail Surveys	Mail Panel Surveys
Cost	Low	Moderate	Moderate	Low	Moderate
Time span	Fast	Moderate	Fast	Slow	Relatively slow
Use of interviewer probes	No	Yes	Yes	No	No
Ability to show concepts to respondent	No	Yes (also taste tests)	No	Yes	Yes
Management control over interviewer	n/a	Moderate	High	n/a	n/a
General data quality	Moderate	Moderate	High to moderate	Moderate to low	Moderate
Ability to collect large amounts of data	High	Moderate	Moderate to low	Low to moderate	Moderate
Ability to handle complex questionnaires	Low	Moderate	High, if computer-aided	Low	Low

Surveys where respondents select an answer from a list or rate the intensity of their response on a scale are relatively easy to evaluate.

Kaspars Grinvalds/Shutterstock.com

that all respondents will be asked the same series of questions. Questionnaires include three basic types of questions: open-ended, closed-ended, and scaled-response. An **open-ended question** encourages an answer phrased in the respondent's own words. Researchers receive a rich array of information that is based on the respondent's frame of reference (e.g., "What do you think about the new flavour?"). In contrast, a **closed-ended question** asks the respondent to make a selection from a limited list of responses. Closed-ended questions can either be what marketing researchers call dichotomous (e.g., "Do you like the new flavour? Yes or No") or *multiple choice*. A **scaled-response question** is a closed-ended question designed to measure the intensity of a respondent's answer.

Good questions address each of the previously set research objectives. Questions must also be clear and concise, and

open-ended question an interview question that encourages an answer phrased in the respondent's own words

closed-ended question an interview questions that asks the respondent to make a selection from a limited list of responses

scaled-response question a closed-ended question designed to measure the intensity of a respondent's answer

observation research a systematic process of recording the behavioural patterns of people, objects, and occurrences with or without questioning them

mystery shoppers researchers posing as customers who gather observational data about a store and collect data about customer–employee interactions

ambiguous language must be avoided. The answer to the question "Do you live within 10 minutes of here?" depends on the mode of transportation (maybe the person walks), driving speed, perceived time, and other factors. Language should also be clear. Thus, jargon should be avoided, and wording should be geared to the target audience. A question such as "What is the level of efficacy of your preponderant dishwasher soap?" would probably be greeted by blank stares. It would be much simpler to say "Are you (1) very satisfied, (2) somewhat satisfied, or (3) not satisfied with your current brand of dishwasher soap?"

Finally, to ensure clarity, the interviewer should avoid asking two questions in one; for example, "How did you like the taste and texture of the Betty Crocker coffee cake?" This should be divided into two questions, one concerning taste and the other texture.

OBSERVATION RESEARCH Observation is categorized as another method of descriptive quantitative research, but instead of asking questions to respondents, **observation research** depends on watching what people do. In order to qualify as descriptive, observation must be completed in a structured manner, with data being collected and tracked by participant. Specifically, observation is the systematic process of recording the behavioural patterns of people, objects, and occurrences with or without questioning them. A marketing researcher uses the observation technique and witnesses and records information as events occur or compiles evidence from records of past events. While there are observation methods that are more qualitative in nature, the focus often is on using observation as a means to supplement and complement a quantitative research program.

A common form of people-watching-people research are mystery shoppers. **Mystery shoppers** are researchers posing as customers who gather observational data about a store (i.e., are the shelves neatly stocked?) and collect data about customer–employee interactions. The interaction is not an interview, and communication occurs only so that the mystery shopper can observe the actions and comments of the employee. Mystery shopping is, therefore, classified as an observational marketing research method even though communication is often involved.

ETHNOGRAPHIC RESEARCH Ethnographic research comes to marketing from the field of anthropology. The technique is becoming increasingly popular in commer-

Mystery shoppers are tasked with (and paid for!) assessing a company's operations without its staff realizing their true intentions. Mystery shopping can be a helpful aspect of a retailer's overall marketing research efforts.

cial marketing research. **Ethnographic research**, or the study of human behaviour in its natural context, involves observation of behaviour and physical setting. Ethnographers, such as Canadian-based marketing research firm Environics, directly observe the population they are studying. As "participant observers," ethnographers can use their intimacy with the people they are studying to gain richer, deeper insights into culture and behaviour—in short, learning what makes people do what they do. While ethnographic research in anthropology often uses qualitative methods of data collection (e.g., semistructured interviews), there is a greater prevalence of the use of more quantitative methods such as surveys and questionnaires.[4]

The key focus for ethnographic research is to watch people in their "natural setting," much like anthropologist Jane Goodall's seminal work with chimpanzees. In the marketing world, Procter & Gamble (P&G) sends researchers to people's homes for extended periods of time to see how customers do household chores such as laundry and vacuuming. In a famous case, P&G discovered the design and use for the now-famous Swiffer Mop from conducting ethnographic research by observing people mopping their floors. The key finding from watching this mundane chore: people spent more time cleaning their mop than cleaning their floor. Promotions for Swiffer often focus on the time-saving benefit of using the product instead of conventional methods of cleaning.[5]

EXPERIMENTS An **experiment** is a causal method a researcher can use to gather primary data to determine cause and effect. The researcher alters one or more variables—price, package design, shelf space, advertising theme, and advertising expenditures—while observing the effects of those alterations on another variable (usually sales). The best experiments are those in which all factors are held constant except the ones being manipulated. The researcher can then observe, for example, how sales change as a result of changes in the amount of money spent on advertising.

There are two types of settings for experimental design: laboratory and field. A laboratory environment can be any situation where the researcher can create and control a set of variables to measure. An example of laboratory testing is a test store or simulated supermarket, where shoppers interact in a real or virtual environment that simulates a shopping experience. A field environment is much less controllable than a laboratory; however, field experiments provide a more realistic environment in which a respondent will display relevant behaviours and attitudes.

4-2e | Step 5: Analyze the Data

After collecting the data, the marketing researcher proceeds to the next step in the research process: data analysis. The purpose of this analysis is to interpret and draw conclusions from the mass of collected data. The marketing researcher tries to organize and analyze those data by using one or more techniques.

Researchers can use many powerful and sophisticated statistical techniques, such as proportion testing, measures of association, and regression analysis. A description of these techniques goes beyond the scope of this book but can be found in any good marketing research textbook. The use of sophisticated

ethnographic research
the study of human behaviour in its natural context; involves observation of behaviour and physical setting

experiment
a method a researcher uses to gather primary data to determine cause and effect

statistical techniques depends on the researchers' objectives and the nature of the data gathered.

4-2f | Step 6: Prepare and Present the Report

After data analysis has been completed, the researcher must prepare the report and communicate the conclusions and recommendations to management. This is a key step in the process. If the marketing researcher wants managers to carry out the recommendations, they must convince managers that the results are credible and justified by the data collected.

Researchers are usually required to present both written and oral reports on the project. They should begin with a clear, concise statement of the research issue studied, the research objectives, and a complete but brief and simple explanation of the research design or methodology employed, including the nature of the sample and how it was selected. A summary of major findings should come next. The way in which this section is written is very important, as this is the part of the report that will build a case as to how the marketing research will help solve the research problem. Staying away from technical jargon is vital; the report has to be written in an accessible manner for the manager who will be making a decision based on the information provided. The findings can be presented in a number of formats, including tables, line charts, and flow charts. Having a mix of writing and visuals will keep the attention of the reader and provide for a more compelling presentation than writing alone.

The conclusion of the report should also present recommendations to management. Any research report should present limitations that might have affected the research. These limitations will warn or advise the readers of any issues that could affect the reliability and validity of the research. Awareness of these limitations may also help future researchers and may serve as cautions to managers when making their decision.

Most people who enter marketing will become research users rather than research suppliers. Thus, they must know what items to take note of in a report. As with many items we purchase, quality is not always readily apparent, and a high price does not guarantee superior quality. The basis for measuring the quality of a marketing research report is the research proposal. Were the correct type of data collection methods used given the nature of the problem? Did the research meet the objectives established in the proposal? Was the methodology outlined in the proposal followed? Are the conclusions based on logical deductions from the data analysis?

Do the recommendations seem prudent, given the conclusions?

4-2g | Step 7: Provide Follow-Up

The final step in the marketing research process is to follow up. The way in which follow-up is conducted will depend on whether the marketing researcher is an internal or external provider.

Internal providers of marketing research will have the opportunity for greater interaction and feedback into the report and research efforts. They should be prepared to answer any questions and be available to discuss the project and its ramifications. The internal researcher should keep track of the project that relates to the research. Questions to ask include the following:

- Was sufficient decision-making information included?
- What could have been done to make the report more useful to management?

External marketing research providers will not have the same level of access to the decision makers as someone who works within an organization. For the external provider, managing the client is a very important part of the research process and can ensure that there is the possibility of future work with that client. The external researcher may be asked to be part of implementing aspects of the research report. If they are not part of this process, it is important to agree with the client on a follow-up schedule. Often post-report meetings are included in research contracts, with some meetings occurring years after the final report has been handed in. A fundamental question to ask a client is whether they found that the research had been conducted properly and accurately. In other words, did the researcher solve the research problem and help in making a management problem clearer?

4-3 | THE IMPACT OF TECHNOLOGY ON MARKETING RESEARCH AND MARKETING ANALYTICS

As in all areas of business and our personal lives, marketing research and marketing analytics use technology to improve results. The Internet can be used to administer a survey, provide feedback to organizations on products and services, or discuss the effectiveness of promotional activities. Research conducted on mobile devices such as smartphones, research involving social media, and the growth of big data are also tremendously helpful.

4-3a | Uses of the Internet

Marketing managers use the Internet to administer surveys, conduct focus groups, and perform a variety of other types of marketing research.

The Internet is often used to conduct online surveys discussed earlier in the chapter. There are several basic methods for conducting online surveys: web survey systems, survey design, and online research panels.

Web survey and survey design systems are software systems specifically designed for web questionnaire construction and delivery. They consist of an integrated questionnaire designer, web server, database, and data delivery program designed for use by nonprogrammers. A **database** collects, organizes, and stores electronic data for easy retrieval. The web server distributes the questionnaire and files responses in a database. The user can query the server at any time using the web for completion statistics, descriptive statistics on responses, and graphic displays of data. One popular survey research software is SurveyMonkey but there are others.

Feng Yu/Shutterstock.com. Bank note image used with the permission of the Bank of Canada.

Companies can now purchase online focus group software, which can be very cost efficient, and, depending on the provider, even free. This compares favourably to conventional focus groups, which can cost thousands of dollars.

4-3b | Online Research Panels

An **online research panel** is a sample of individuals who have agreed to complete surveys via the Internet.[6] Often, researchers use online panel providers for a ready-made sample population. Online panel providers such as e-Rewards pre-recruit people who agree to participate in online market research surveys. Some online panels are created for specific industries and may have a few thousand panel members, while the large commercial online panels have millions of people waiting to be surveyed. When people join online panels, they answer an extensive profiling questionnaire that enables the panel provider to target research efforts to panel members who meet specific criteria.

Some critics of online panels suggest that they are not representative of the target population. Others claim that offering incentives to join a panel leads to bias and misleading results. Online panel researchers contend that they use a number of interventions to detect poor-quality online surveys.

4-3c | Online Focus Groups

The exploratory research method of focus groups has also found a home online. A number of organizations are currently offering this new means of conducting focus groups. The process is fairly simple. The research firm builds a database of respondents via a screening questionnaire on its website. When a client comes to a company with a need for a particular focus group, the firm goes to its database and identifies individuals who appear to qualify. The firm sends an email to these individuals, asking them to log on to a particular site at a particular time scheduled for the group. Many times, these groups are joined by respondents on mobile devices. Like in-person focus groups, the respondents are paid an incentive for their participation. However, the two types of focus groups are not alike when it comes to costs. Beyond providing the moderator and the online capabilities for supporting the focus group session, research companies save on a number of costs for online focus groups compared to in-person focus groups. Items like room rentals, food costs, and travel reimbursement are all nonissues for online focus groups, providing a real cost savings along with convenience as key benefits of going online for focus groups.

The firm develops a moderator's guide similar to the one used for a conventional focus group, and a moderator runs the group by typing in questions online for all to see. The group operates in an environment similar to that of a chat room so that all participants see all questions and all responses. The complete text of the focus group is captured and made available for review after the group has finished.

Online focus groups also allow respondents to view things such as a concept statement, a mock-up of a print ad, or a short product demonstration video. The moderator simply provides a URL for the respondents to open in another browser window.

web survey and design systems
software systems specifically designed for web questionnaire construction and delivery

database
where electronic data is collected, organized, and stored for easy retrieval

online research panel
a sample of persons who have agreed to complete surveys via the Internet

Benefits of Online Research Communities

The popularity and marketing power of online research communities stems from several key benefits:

- provide cost-effective, flexible research
- help companies create customer-focused organizations by putting employees into directly contact with consumers
- achieve customer-derived innovation

- establish brand advocates who are emotionally invested in a company's success
- engage customers in a space where they are comfortable, allowing clients to interact with them on a deeper level
- offer real-time results, enabling clients to explore ideas that normal time constraints prohibit

4-3d | Online Research Communities

An online research community is a carefully selected group of consumers who agree to participate in an ongoing dialogue with a particular corporation. All community interaction takes place on a custom-designed website. During the life of the community—which may last anywhere from six months to a year or more—community members respond to questions posed by the corporation on a regular basis. In addition to responding to the corporation's questions, community members talk to one another about topics that are of interest to them.

4-3e | Mobile Marketing Research

It is estimated that by 2023 more than 30 million Canadians will have a smartphone.[7] Because so many people are connected through their phones, mobile is a natural vehicle for conducting marketing research surveys.

Mobile surveys are designed to fit into the brief cracks of time that open up when a person waits for a plane, is early for an appointment, or stands in line. Marketers strive to engage respondents "in the moment" because mobile research provides immediate feedback when a consumer makes a decision to purchase or consume a product, or experiences some form of promotion. With mobile research, participants can not only send and respond to direct and immediate questions but also share the videos, photos, stories, and moments that are important to them. As new and better apps make the survey experience easier and more intuitive, the use of mobile surveys will continue

to rise. New responsive design technology automatically adjusts the content and navigation of a website to fit the dimensions and resolution of any screen it is viewed on.

4-3f | Social Media Marketing Research

Facebook owns and controls data collected from roughly 2.5 billion monthly users.[8] The user databases of social media sites like Twitter, Pinterest, and Facebook tell these companies' marketers a lot about who you are and what you are like, through often on an anonymous basis.

In an effort to expand their information databases even further, social media sites like Facebook are now combining their databases with third-party information like data collected from loyalty programs.

Social media analytical tools are available to help keep track of all the conversations on social media about companies, brands, perceptions, and attitudes—a veritable gold mine for companies and researchers.

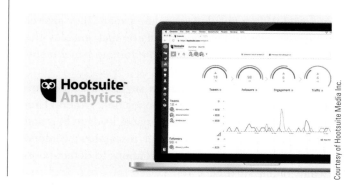

The challenge with social media marketing research is trying to find a way to extract meaningful data from the millions of conversations happening on social media. Hootsuite provides a means of helping organizations manage social media activity and track what is being said about a brand or marketing campaign. From its Vancouver head office, Hootsuite provides organizations with a dashboard from which data from multiple social media networks can be tracked and analyzed.

The Hootsuite dashboard provides a centralized hub for managing social media insights and analytics. Organizations can evaluate and report on the effectiveness of their social media efforts against key performance indicators relevant to their business. Having a centralized dashboard provides great value to companies that need to manage a myriad of activities, actions, and interactions across social media networks that can be volatile and overwhelming at times.[9]

4-3g | The Rise of Big Data

Big data is the exponential growth in the volume, variety, and velocity of information and the development of complex new tools to analyze and create meaning from such data. Today data are constantly streaming in from social media as well as other sources. Advanced big data databases allow the analysis of unstructured data such as emails, audio files, and YouTube videos.

Big data are gathered both online and offline. Even if data are collected and entered into databases manually, big data tool sets allow companies to catalogue customer attributes and analyze which characteristics they have in common.

The ability to crunch numbers means nothing, however, if humans cannot use or even access that information. Modern databases sometimes contain billions of pieces of data, so the question quickly arose as to how big data could be presented in a meaningful way. The answer to this question is data visualization. Visualization acts as an engine for bringing patterns to light—even the subtlest of patterns woven into the largest of data sets. It also enables managers to share, describe, and explain what big data has uncovered. Big data analytics focuses not only on gathering data but also on learning and adapting based on that data.

While it is clear that big data could be quite disruptive to marketing research, it is also clear that there is room for both big data and marketing research in trying to help companies make better decisions. For example, a company could glean from big data that customers purchased a certain amount of their products, and there could be demographic information tied into those purchases based on credit card and customer database information. But what is still missing from this picture is *why* they bought the product. The "why" aspect could definitively be answered only by conducting some form of marketing research that would ask the customer directly, via surveys, focus groups, or other traditional methods of marketing research.

Therefore, in order to bring meaning to big data and its role in marketing research, it will be vital to search for an interpretive structure. The question is, does this structure already exist? Some uses of big data are highlighted in the box *Companies Use Big Data for Different Reasons*.

4-4 | MARKETING ANALYTICS AND MARKETING STRATEGY

The goal of marketing analytics is to use data to gain insights and make better decisions. While this field overlaps considerably with traditional marketing research, it differs in two ways.

1. Marketing research often uses simpler data analysis methods, while marketing analytics usually involves larger data sets and more complex data analysis methods.

2. Marketing research typically uses data to answer predefined research questions, while marketing analytics seeks to find new insights that might be missed otherwise. For example, a market researcher at a clothing and outdoor recreational retailer might ask, "Which of our customer segments are most likely to buy ski coats this winter?," while marketing analytics might discover that "winter spending among our customers in the western provinces who have families of five or more is 30% higher than any other current customer group."

The field of marketing analytics is growing rapidly, and its role in marketing is increasingly valuable. While using data to make informed decisions has always been important, the sheer scope and volume of data available to marketers today make it essential to utilize that information to gain insights about customers, products, and market opportunities. Keep in mind that competitors are using their data for the same purpose.

big data
the exponential growth in the volume, variety, and velocity of information and the development of complex new tools to analyze and create meaning from such data

Companies Use Big Data for Different Reasons

Companies like the TD Bank Group, Coca-Cola, Pepsi, Netflix, and Amazon are all using the information generated from analyzing the vast amounts of data each has been collecting.

The most obvious use of the information is to improve the customer's relationship with a company. The TD Bank Group started with this goal in mind when it revamped its customer databases. The bank already had a functioning data infrastructure in place but believed it could do better. The bank built a new system giving employees and customers access to more relevant information by expanding its existing data structures through cloud-based technology.

Coca-Cola had the same goal of customer service in mind when designing its customer loyalty program. Coke has monitored the opinions of customers through various feedback methods including social media. The company has used the information to develop advertising content specifically for different audiences.

Netflix also uses information gained from data analysis to target its messages to certain audiences. Based on the viewing history of its more than 187 million subscribers, Netflix sends messages to customers recommending movies they might enjoy based on their individual viewing history. These recommendations account for the viewing patterns of 80 percent of the content streamed.

Pepsi and Amazon have used their data analysis programs for different reasons. Amazon used the results to understand how customers purchase groceries and how to set up the supply chain for the Amazon Fresh and Whole Food operations. Pepsi used the information from its data system to manage its supply chain. Using point-of-sale and inventory information provided by customers, the company is able to ensure that store shelves are stocked with the best-selling products.

Companies have invested significant funds in order to implement these information systems. However, the success of these data programs relies on more than the funds needed to develop them. Because the field of big data analysis is relatively new, there are a limited number of people with the skill sets to develop the programs and analyze the data. These companies also need a corporate culture that enables them to act quickly when the information provided by these programs suggests changes to their current ways of conducting business.

Sources: Ryan Ayers, "How to Innovate with Big Data: 4 Essentials," Innovation Management website, https://innovationmanagement.se/2019/04/11/how-to-innovate-with-big-data-4-essentials/, March 11, 2019; John Kopanakis, "5 Real-World Examples of How Brands are Using Big Data Analytics," Mentionlytics website, innovationmanagement.se/2019/04/11/how-to-innovate-with-big-data-4-essentials/, March 11, 2019; Bernard Marr, "The Amazing Ways TD Bank, Canada's Second-Largest Bank, Uses Big Data, AI & Machine Learning," Forbes website, www.forbes.com/sites/bernardmarr/2018/12/18/the-amazing-ways-td-bank-canadas-second-largest-bank-uses-big-data-ai-machine-learning/#7bf8adb165be, December 18, 2018.

Even before advances in technology, it was possible for marketers to collect useful data. However, it was a manual process. If a retailer was choosing between three possible new locations, they could have employees stand at each site for a few days and count the foot and car traffic that goes by. Also, marketers have long collected feedback from prospective customers using surveys and focus groups. Technically, data like this could be collected and analyzed with nothing more than pen and paper.

However, technology has enhanced our ability to collect information that is useful in marketing analytics.

- Data is collected on a much larger scale because of technology. For example, companies can collect their own data through the various types of technology discussed earlier in the chapter or they can purchase data from outside companies.

- The data being collected today is more detailed, making it easier for data analysts to find patterns of consumer behaviour in the data.

- Data comes from more sources. A lot of consumer activity that takes place online is recorded automatically. Website visits and purchases, social media activity, and mobile "check-ins" at various locations all provide marketers new insights that weren't available before consumers lived more of their lives on computers and mobile devices.

4-4a | Data Used in Marketing Analytics

With so much data potentially available, how do marketing managers exploit it using marketing analytic techniques? The first step is to make sure the data is actually being collected. For example, an e-commerce website that does not have analytics software connected will not be able to measure how many people visited and which pages were visited most. And a large set of data available for purchase from a marketing research firm is valuable only if a marketing analyst can actually access and use that data.

Useful data can come from a variety of sources *inside* the company, including the following:

- sales data from checkout-scanning software (sales history and trends)

- website data from an e-commerce store (visits, sales, and times spent on site)

- interaction on social media sites (user profile, engagement with content, and customer service interactions)

- communications by phone, email, or in person (reservations, check-ins, and customer service)

This information goes into a database, which contains a number of files called tables. Tables are similar to spreadsheets, except each table contains a very specific chunk of information. For example, a database would contain separate tables for customer names and addresses, company products, company store locations, and all sales transactions. A database makes it easy to link these tables so that specific questions, or queries, can be answered. For instance, hardware stores can ask their database, "How many customers purchased lawn mowers from our Vancouver stores in June?" The database will scan the various tables and compile an accurate answer to this question—in the blink of an eye.

A common type of database is a company's customer relationship management (CRM) software, which records all interactions between a company and its customers, including sales transactions and customer service interactions. This information can be used to serve customers better.

In addition to data collected inside the company, data can also come from a variety of sources *outside* the company, including the following:

- Government sources, such as census data that provides detailed demographic information about people and households.

- Supply chain partners that can provide data about activity within the supply chain. For example, Walmart can give data on lightbulb sales to General Electric (GE) so that GE can better understand current demand and update its production schedules accordingly.

- Commercial data sources, such as market research companies, that collect and sell data that companies can integrate with their internal data to gain additional insights.

4-4b | Organizing the Data

Gaining insights from data collection is not possible by merely dumping massive amounts of data into a database, especially as data from various sources inside and outside the company might be assembled differently. When dealing with big data, the data sets are often so large and complex that traditional database-processing tools are inadequate.

To be truly useful, data must be organized in a way that is both structured but flexible for discovering insights. A **data warehouse** is a type of database specifically designed to collect and organize large sets of data used for analytics. These data warehouses form the basis for more comprehensive information systems, such as **marketing information systems (MIS)** that help companies collect, analyze, and communicate information throughout the organization.

4-4c | Analyzing the Data

To provide insight into marketing situations and allow marketers to make better decisions many analysts use a technique called **data mining**, which is the process of sorting through large sets of data to find patterns and relationships. Data mining uses complex statistical analysis, machine learning, and even artificial intelligence to find insights that would be nearly impossible for a person to uncover using traditional analysis techniques.

An essential aspect of data analysis is to communicate insights in a way that decision makers can understand and act upon them. That's why marketers often rely on **data visualization**, which involves presenting data in a pictorial or graphical format.[10] A basic example of data visualization is a pie chart showing the market

data warehouse
a type of database specifically designed to collect and organize large sets of data used for analytics

marketing information systems (MIS)
help companies collect, analyze, and communicate information throughout the organization

data mining
the process of sorting through large sets of data to find patterns and relationships

data visualization
presenting data in a pictorial or graphical format

EXHIBIT 4.8   EXAMPLE OF DATA VISUALIZATION

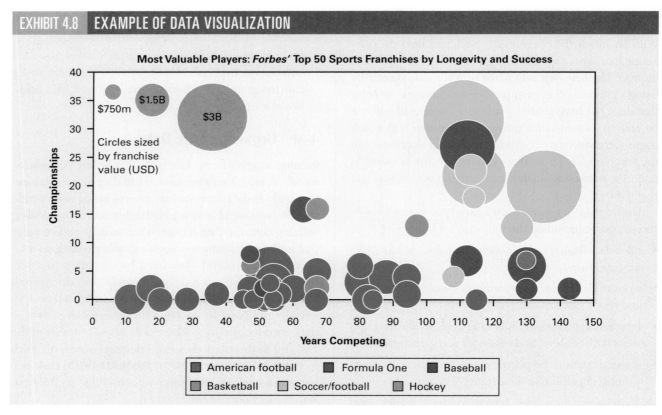

Most Valuable Players: *Forbes'* Top 50 Sports Franchises by Longevity and Success

Source: Adapted with permission from Column Five, "Most Valuable Sports Franchises Interactive." https://www.columnfivemedia.com/work-items/interactive -most-valuable-sports-franchises

share for companies within a product category. Data visualization can quickly communicate more complex relationships between data points. See Exhibit 4.8 as an example.

A common use of data visualization is in a **marketing dashboard**, where marketing metrics and insights from marketing analytics are compiled in one place. Marketing dashboards give marketers real-time awareness of their marketing programs' performance.

4-4d | Categories of Data for Marketing Analytics

The reason data can lead to marketing insights is that it measures something. If sales results for a drugstore chain are going up in every region except one (descriptive analytics), the team would gather more data that might explain why (diagnostic analytics) such as sales by category, store traffic counts, and promotional spending by region.

The challenge is that data comes in many different forms, which sometimes makes it harder to measure. Imagine that marketers at Samsung wanted feedback on a new design for their Galaxy phone. One option is to email an online survey to existing customers asking them to rate the phone design on a scale of 1–10 (with 10 being best). The survey results can easily be calculated into an average numerical score. But what if the team instead emailed an online survey asking customers to write their comments about the design. This method would likely yield more profound customer insights about the phone design that could inform the product development process; however interpreting the comments would take extra work. If there is a relatively small number of responses, they could be read manually and discussed by the marketing team. But what if there were thousands or even millions of responses? These would be nearly impossible to analyze manually due to the time and effort required. As a traditional database isn't designed to process this type of data, what should the marketers do? This example illustrates the difference between structured and unstructured data.

Structured data is data that is easily defined and organized. It's similar to information you might find in an Excel spreadsheet, in that each field belongs to a clear category and has a precise value. If you have a

marketing dashboard
marketing metrics and insights from marketing analytics are compiled in one place

structured data
data that is easily defined and organized

list of customer names and addresses, it's easy to find out how many customers live in each province. If you have a raw list of sales transactions for each item in your store, it's easy to add up the total sales revenue for each item.

Unstructured data is data that is not easily defined and organized, including audio, video, photos, written messages, presentation slides, and anything else where the contents of the data don't belong to a clear category or have precisely defined values. Examples would be social media posts, blog articles, emails, photos uploaded to Instagram, and videos uploaded to Twitter. See Exhibit 4.9 for examples of structured and unstructured data.

Vast amounts of insight are available from unstructured data. But the sheer volume of this data can be daunting. Fortunately, technology is making it possible to scan all of this unstructured data and group it in ways that resemble structured data so it can be analyzed. For example, **sentiment analysis** is the use of text analysis to mine and categorize unstructured data from social media posts. For example, market research companies can monitor social media mentions for brands to track whether posts and tweets are positive, negative, or neutral. This is done by looking for the sentiment expressed in various keywords. If Samsung's new phone design results in a lot of posts and tweets containing words and phrases like "beautiful," "sleek," or "where do I buy," the company will know it is on the right track. But if that sentiment analysis uncovered words and phrases like "ugly," "clunky," and "switch to iPhone," Samsung would have early warning of potential problems.

4-4e | Marketing Analytics Techniques

Marketing analytic techniques are used throughout the marketing strategy development process. Examples are shown in Exhibit 4.10.

unstructured data
data that is not easily defined and organized

sentiment analysis
the use of text analysis to mine and categorize unstructured data from social media posts

EXHIBIT 4.9	EXAMPLES OF DIFFERENT CATEGORIES OF DATA	
Structured Data	**Unstructured Data**
Customer lists	Social media posts (text, photo, or video)
Sales transaction lists	Emails
Store traffic counts	Instant messages
Census and other demographic data	YouTube videos
Website traffic statistics	Customer service call transcripts

EXHIBIT 4.10	USES OF MARKETING ANALYTICS FOR STRATEGY DEVELOPMENT		
Marketing Strategy	**Analytic Technique**		**Example**
Product Development and Management	Advanced customer segmentation	Taking data from online activities together with traditional market research data to provide companies with more accurate segmentation information	Netflix
	Pattern recognition	Scanning blog posts and social media sites and combining this with previous purchase behaviour to uncover patterns	Fashion industry
	Predictive modelling	Taking into account several variables that could influence the success or failure of new products	Retail locations
Promotion	Improved merchandising	Using analytic techniques to decide what products to carry and where to place them within a store	Retail
	Personalized recommendations	Based on Internet search patterns, purchase history of a customer and other customers data analytics can make suggestions about what products a customer might be interested in	Retail
	Audience targeting	Social media sites can send ads to a specific target market based on information on file, keyword searches, etc.	Online retail
	Return on marketing investment	Using analytic techniques, marketers can more accurately assign costs to the revenues that were generated, providing more accurate return on investment	Marketing planning
Customer Service and Retention	Maximizing engagement	Using analytic techniques to recommend other products or services based on previous usage patterns	Online retail
	Customizing rewards	Using reward programs to collect data on customer usage patterns and designing promotions based on products or services the customer purchases	Loyalty programs
	Improving efficiency	Using data about when customers are in the store or delivery routes operations can help determine how many people to schedule during peak times or the most efficient delivery routes	Retail or delivery services

4-5 | DATA COLLECTION CONCERNS

Big data has many benefits. From the marketer's perspective, instead of using limited information and making educated guesses, big data and marketing analytics can drastically increase the quality of marketing decisions and maximize the return on investment. From a consumer's perspective, instead of being offered one-size-fits-all products and having to wade through irrelevant ads every day, the shift toward personalization and customization gives us access to products and offers that are more likely to fit our individual needs.

With that said, there are some downsides. These include intrusive methods of data collection and lack of transparency about data sharing.

4-5a | Intrusive Methods of Data Collection

Whether they realize it or not, consumers routinely trade away their privacy in exchange for convenience or discounts. But usually, these are small and reasonably contained trade-offs such as signing up for a free email service; information on a social media profile to connect with friends; registering a recent purchase online to receive the warranty protection; activating location services on your phone to enable the mapping app; and uploading your private files and photos to a free, online backup service.

A distinction about these examples is that they are voluntary and the user can easily understand the impact of the decision. However, an issue arises when the company involved expands the reach of its data collection without a clear understanding or consent from the user. For example,

- While Gmail offers convenient and free email, many consumers were concerned to find out that Google scans the contents of those emails. While the use of these scans to personalize ads was discontinued in 2017, emails are still scanned and the data integrated into other features and apps, such as Smart Reply.[11]

- While Google and Apple utilize location services on your phone to upgrade the user experience, such as by providing accurate mapping, both companies were accused of collecting far more data than they openly disclose. For example, Google used data collected from cell towers to approximate the location of users, even users who had turned off location services or removed their SIM card.[12]

- Facebook (which owns Instagram and WhatsApp) can track your browser activity online and use location services to track where you shop *offline*. This data is used to customize the ads you see in its apps. Facebook has also disclosed that, through the various services it provides to other applications and websites, it can track activity for users who aren't logged into Facebook or those who don't even have an account.[13]

These issues are likely to become even more important as companies like Apple, Amazon, and Google expand the use of voice-integrated devices into the home, where personal conversations can be heard and recorded, even when not activated by the user.[14] Privacy concerns related to voice-integrated devices can come from unlikely places, which Mattel found out after a backlash over its talking Barbie doll. While the intent was to allow users to talk with the toy, the idea of kids being recorded in their homes raised concerns from parents and privacy advocates.[15]

In many cases, companies will state that their data collection methods fall within the terms of service that consumers agree to when signing up for a service or logging into an app for the first time. The issue for marketers is whether terms of service, with their small type and legal language, actually represent informed consent on the part of the consumers.

4-5b | Lack of Transparency about Data Sharing

Even if a consumer generally understands the trade-off in providing their data to a single company in exchange for a service, another concern is whether consumers are aware of how and when that data is shared. This sharing can show up in two primary ways:

- *Sharing among apps and program:* The "Login with Facebook" option in many third party (i.e., non-Facebook) apps is meant to provide a convenient way for you to activate new apps without having to re-enter your personal information. However, when you use "Login with Facebook," not only does Facebook share certain aspects of your Facebook profile with that third-party app, but Facebook itself can track some of your activity within that third-party app.[16] Facebook also has disclosed that it shared deep user data with 61 hardware and software manufacturers, even after stating it had discontinued this practice in 2015.[17]

- *Data sold to other companies:* While a core benefit of marketing analytics is better ad targeting and measurement, sometimes these efforts can go too far. In 2018, Google and MasterCard brokered a deal where Google received data on billions of customer credit card transactions. This data helped Google track whether ads that ran online resulted in offline purchases. This tracking is valuable data for online advertisers, which is why Facebook has also looked into acquiring user data from financial services companies.[18]

While these practices raise privacy concerns, it's important to distinguish between different types of user data. **Personally identifiable information** is data that can be used to identify a particular person. If a marketer has the name, address, and phone number of a specific person, they can locate that person easily. **Anonymized data** is data where personally identifiable information has been removed. If a marketer has a list of 1 million credit card transactions that represent spending from 10 000 users over the last year, it's not possible to identify the users of those credit cards with that data alone.

Typically, anonymizing data is a high priority for companies that share data. The location data from phones, the information Facebook receives from third-party apps, and the list of transactions Google received from MasterCard are examples of anonymized data sharing. Technically, this means the data is relatively safe to share. However, a researcher at MIT found that he could analyze a list of "anonymized" credit card transactions and group transactions by individual users 90 percent of the time; and by cross-referencing the transactions with other data, he would likely be able to identify the individuals who made each those purchases.[19]

The concerns related to data privacy and security are complex. Technology gives consumers new ways to interact with friends, shop, manage our finances, and stay entertained. And the data collected from these activities allows marketers to serve customers even better. Today's marketers must carefully consider how to use this data responsibly to retain trust among their consumers and protect the integrity of their brand.

4-6 | WHEN TO USE MARKET RESEARCH OR MARKETING ANALYTICS

When managers have several possible solutions to a problem, they should not instinctively call for market research or analytics. In fact, the first decision to make is whether to look to marketing research or analytics to solve the problem at all.

The first step is to clearly understand the problem. As information is gathered, it may become clear that marketing research or analytics may not be necessary. Some companies with big brands and large budgets, like Procter & Gamble, can afford to cut down on the research done to introduce new products in markets where they control a large part of the market share. Marketing research may also not be required if sufficient information can be determined from ongoing analysis from other sources such as websites. However, most companies benefit from as much information as possible when making decisions.

Gathering the right information can require a great deal of time and expense. However, the potential expense to a company when introducing a new product or entering a new market without the right information can be catastrophic. Even if a company can afford to do only some secondary research, the value of the information to the decision process is immense. With technology making this information more accessible and the data more detailed, it is incumbent upon any business decision maker to include some aspect of additional information.

Marketers can combine information from an external environmental analysis with marketing research or marketing analytic data to help make important strategic decisions. Since competitive advantage is a significant goal in any business, being able to understand other companies can be of great value, especially in highly competitive industries. **Competitive intelligence (CI)** helps managers assess their competitors and their vendors and create a more efficient and effective company. *Intelligence* is analyzed information. It becomes *decision-making intelligence* when it has implications for the organization. For example, a primary competitor may have plans to introduce a product with performance standards equal to a company's current product but with a 15 percent cost advantage. The new product will reach the market in eight months. This intelligence has important decision-making and policy consequences for management. Competitive intelligence and environmental scanning combine to create *marketing intelligence*.

Regardless of where the information to assist marketing managers with decision making comes from, there are two important considerations. How much will it cost to get the information and how much time will it take?

personally identifiable information
data that can be used to identify a particular person

anonymized data
data from which personally identifiable information has been removed

competitive intelligence (CI)
an intelligence system that helps managers assess their competition and vendors in order to become more efficient and effective competitors

AWAKE
CHOCOLATE
CONTINUING CASE

AWAKE Chocolate

Scrappy Little Research

The approach taken by Awake with regard to conducting marketing research is described by co-founder Adam Deremo as being "scrappy." And while this characterization could have one thinking of an underdog, the marketing research done at Awake is like most aspects of the business: carefully thought through and executed without much waste or indecision.

Awake does not designate a certain amount of money for research purposes; rather, the company focuses on learning more about its customers' needs. "People always have questions that we want to answer. Our approach to that has always been just to try to go out and do it in the most cost-effective and fastest way possible."

One way in which Awake strives to gain more knowledge from customers is by aligning research with existing promotional opportunities. Adam Deremo described this as "… sometimes [when] we are doing campus speaking or a sampling event on a campus, we'll just ask people what they think of our new product ideas, or what flavour they would launch next if they ran our brand." One challenge of taking this approach is that generally one is speaking to people who are already invested or positive about the company and are already likely to make future purchases of existing or new product offerings.

Awake realizes the inherent bias in this approach and endeavours to look at doing more organized and representative research. But once again, the path of least resistance (and cost) is seen as best; "Other times the questions are more complicated and when that happens, we will generally do online research. The nice thing about that is you can generally get a good data set of respondents quickly and affordably. Things that used to cost tens of thousands of dollars and take months to do can now be answered with maybe a couple thousand dollars and a few days."

When things are more complicated, Awake will look at more established and tested approaches such as panels. Recently, Awake was interested in getting a clear sense of why consumers were buying their products. Instead of asking in an ad hoc way through a campus visit or focus group of Awake customers; the company dug a bit further. Adam Deremo described it: "We addressed that question by recruiting a panel of respondents online and asking them a lot of questions, from which we could iteratively boil down the number of potential answers. We were able to get to a fairly concrete response, which in that case was the unique combination of flavour and efficacy. And it was important for us to know because we're trying to build a communications message around what the most important attribute around our product is. The financial consequences of guessing on that were significant to us. It was worth running a few thousand dollars' worth of surveys on that."

So, while there is a reluctance on the part of Awake to spend large sums of money on marketing research, there is still a healthy respect for what solid marketing research can provide. There are some very important questions companies must ask of stakeholders in marketplace, and not just loyal customers. Adam Deremo admitted that while the company does not use much paid research, as compared to ad hoc and interview style, Awake had used a large sample of respondents to conduct research on a new product idea.

So, as Awake continues to grow, it will be important to find a place of marketing research in the overall marketing direction of the company. When large competitors are gathering data and insights into the customers in the marketplace, Awake will need more than just scrappiness to make better decisions.

QUESTIONS

1. **Prepare a five-slide presentation for Awake on the marketing research process. Keep in mind Awake's current approach versus what you have read in your textbook and class notes.**

2. **How could analytics help Awake with its marketing research goals? Provide at least two examples (only one related to social media) in order to show the increased importance of analytics in marketing research.**

3. **Awake conducted in-depth research on an open-ended question: "What are the most important attributes of Awake's products that compel you to buy our product?" Develop a series of closed-ended questions that could also help answer this question.**

AWAKE Chocolate

5 Consumer Decision Making

LEARNING OUTCOMES

5-1 Explain why marketing managers should understand consumer behaviour

5-2 Analyze the components of the consumer decision-making process

5-3 Identify the types of consumer buying decisions and discuss the significance of consumer involvement

5-4 Identify and understand the cultural and social factors that affect consumer buying decisions

5-5 Identify and understand the individual factors that affect consumer buying decisions

5-6 Identify and understand the psychological factors that affect consumer buying decisions

"Human behaviour flows from three main sources: desire, emotion and knowledge."
—Attributed to Plato

5-1 | THE IMPORTANCE OF UNDERSTANDING CONSUMER BEHAVIOUR

Consumers' product and service preferences are constantly changing. Marketing managers must have a thorough knowledge of consumer behaviour in order to create a proper marketing mix for a well-defined market. **Consumer behaviour** describes how consumers make purchase decisions and how they use and dispose of the purchased goods or services. The study of consumer behaviour also includes an analysis of factors that influence purchase decisions and product use.

Understanding how consumers make purchase decisions can help marketers in several ways.

consumer behaviour
how consumers make purchase decisions and how they use and dispose of purchased goods or services; also includes the factors that influence purchase decisions and product use

For example, if they know through research that having low carbon emissions is the most important attribute in an automobile for a certain target market, they can redesign the product to meet that criterion. If the company cannot change the product design in the short run, they can use other marketing elements in an effort to change consumers' decision-making criteria. When Tesla realized that many drivers loved the concept of Tesla's electric car, but simply couldn't afford it, Tesla developed a new model, bearing all the expected Tesla traits, but making it more affordable. The Tesla 3 joined the Model X and Model S. It was roughly half the price of the Model X, yet it maintained the environmentally friendly promise that came with the Tesla brand.[1] But was it just price driving these purchase decisions? Maybe it was an altruistic sense of personal environmental responsibility. On the other hand, it might have been that silent but provocative voice of the customers' ideal self coaxing them to make a commitment not to a car they cared little about, but to a sense of the type of person they wanted to be. Elon Musk, founder of Tesla, knew that all of these

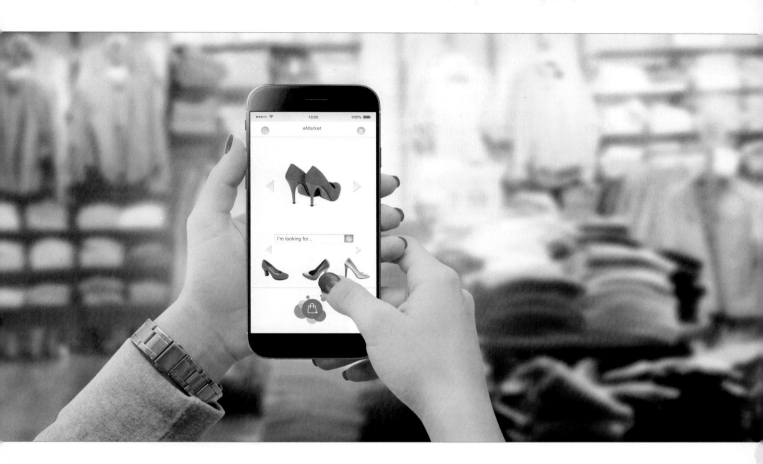

factors—price, environmental impact, and how customers viewed themselves—and others, would affect the Tesla value proposition.

5-2 | CONSUMER DECISION-MAKING PROCESS

When buying products, consumers generally follow a series of steps known as the **consumer decision-making process**, shown in Exhibit 5.1. The steps in the process are (1) need recognition, (2) information search, (3) evaluation of alternatives, (4) purchase, and (5) postpurchase behaviour. These five steps represent a general process that can be used as a guide for studying how consumers make decisions. This guideline does not assume that consumers' decisions will proceed in order through all the steps of the process. In fact, the consumer may end the process at any time or may not even make a purchase. Note too that technology is changing how people make decisions. The section on the types of consumer buying decisions later in the chapter discusses why a consumer's progression through these steps may vary. Before addressing this issue, however, we will describe each step in the process in detail.

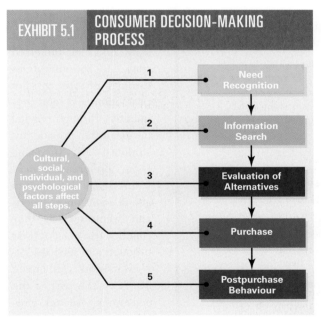

EXHIBIT 5.1 **CONSUMER DECISION-MAKING PROCESS**

1. Need Recognition
2. Information Search
3. Evaluation of Alternatives
4. Purchase
5. Postpurchase Behaviour

Cultural, social, individual, and psychological factors affect all steps.

5-2a | Step 1: Need Recognition

The first stage in the consumer decision-making process is need recognition.

consumer decision-making process
a five-step process used by consumers when buying goods or services

Need recognition occurs when consumers are faced with an imbalance between actual and desired states. This imbalance is triggered when a consumer is exposed to an internal or external **stimulus,** which is any unit of input affecting one or more of the five senses: sight, smell, taste, touch, or hearing. *Internal stimuli* are occurrences you experience, such as hunger or thirst. *External stimuli* are influences from an outside source, such as someone's recommendation of a new restaurant, the design of a package, or an advertisement on television or radio. In today's digital age, stimuli can come from a multitude of sources.

Marketers know, however, that wants and needs are not the same thing. The **need** is a state of being where we desire something that we do not possess but yearn to acquire and a **want** is for a particular product or service that the consumer perceives as being unfulfilled or satisfying the need. It can be for a specific product, or it can be for a certain attribute or feature of a product. For example, if you lose your cellphone, you'll need to buy a replacement, but you'll also need to decide whether you need the new version, as it comes with the latest technology.

Therefore, a key objective for marketers is to get consumers to recognize an imbalance between their current status and their preferred state. Communications through advertising, sales promotion, and more frequently through digital devices, often provide this stimulus. By surveying buyer preferences, marketers gain information about consumer needs and wants, which they can then use to tailor their products and services.

Marketers can create wants on the part of the consumer. An ad promoting a healthy, active lifestyle and the fun of fitness tracking may inspire you to purchase a wearable fitness tracker like a Fitbit. A want can be for a specific product, or it can be for a certain attribute

Antony McAulay/Shutterstock.com

or feature of the product. A runner may purchase the Fitbit model with the Real-Time Pace and Distance feature because it will map out the route for their run.[2]

Consumers recognize unfulfilled needs in various ways. The two most common occur when a current product isn't performing properly and when the consumer is about to run out of something that is generally kept on hand. Consumers may also recognize unfulfilled wants if they become aware of a product that seems superior to the one they currently use.

5-2b | Step 2: Information Search

After recognizing a need, consumers search for information about the various alternatives available to satisfy it. An information search can occur internally, externally, or both. An **internal information search** is the process of recalling information stored in one's memory. This stored information stems largely from previous experience with a product—for example, recalling whether a hotel where you stayed earlier in the year had clean rooms and friendly service.

In contrast, an **external information search** is the process of seeking information in the outside environment. Historically, there have been two basic types of external information sources: nonmarketing-controlled

need recognition
the result of an imbalance between actual and desired states

stimulus
any unit of input affecting one or more of the five senses: sight, smell, taste, touch, hearing

need
a state of being where we desire something that we do not possess but yearn to acquire

want
a particular product or service that will satisfy a need

internal information search
the process of recalling information stored in one's memory

external information search
the process of seeking information in the outside environment

and marketing-controlled. A **nonmarketing-controlled information source** is one that doesn't originate from the company(ies) making the product. These information sources include personal experiences (trying or observing a new product); personal sources (family, friends, acquaintances, and coworkers who may recommend a product or service); and public sources, such as *Consumer Reports* and other rating organizations that comment on products and services. For example, if you feel like streaming a movie, you may search your memory for past experiences with different service providers such as Shaw, Rogers, or Netflix (personal experience). To choose which movie to see, you may rely on the recommendation of a friend or family member (personal sources), or you may read the critical reviews as contributed by others who've watched the movie and have rated it through a third-party website (public sources).

Social media are playing an ever-increasing role in consumers' information searches. More than 40 percent of Canadians who responded to a recent survey said that they used social media to research products.[3] Although the use of a mobile device to make purchases is rising, consumers primarily use their smartphones and tablets to research products before buying.

On the other hand, a **marketing-controlled information source** originates with marketers promoting the product. Marketing-controlled information sources include mass-media advertising (out-of-home, radio, newspaper, television, digital, and magazine advertising), sales promotions (contests, displays, and premiums), salespeople, public relations, product labels, packaging, and social media. Many consumers, however, are wary of the information they receive from marketing-controlled sources, believing that most marketing campaigns stress the product's attributes and ignore its faults. These sentiments tend to be stronger among better-educated and higher-income consumers. Social media are being used extensively by consumers to seek product information from both marketer and nonmarketer sources.

The increase of platform-based businesses, such as Uber, Airbnb, or Amazon, has introduced an additional, and perhaps most valuable, information source where past consumers of a product purchased through one of these platforms post reviews about their experience. This form of external information source is called consumer-to-consumer (C2C) reviews. The aggregated reviews are then made available to would-be purchasers. Unlike consumer reports in nonpartisan publications, C2C reviews are willingly and transparently posted directly through the vendors' sites. You have instant exposure to reviews of Uber drivers or Airbnb hosts (and guests) within the Web or the mobile apps of these companies. This trend is reshaping the business landscape because it is reshaping how customers make purchase decisions. In the meantime, marketers in turn are exposed to enormous new information sources to use to figure out and attract customers.

The extent to which an individual conducts an external search depends on their perceived risk, knowledge, prior experience, confidence in their decision-making ability and level of interest in the good or service. Generally, as the perceived risk of the purchase increases, the consumer expands the search and considers alternative brands. For example, you would spend more time researching the purchase of a car than the purchase of an energy drink. A consumer's knowledge about the product or service will also affect the extent of an external information search. A consumer who is knowledgeable and well informed about a potential purchase is less likely to search for additional information and will conduct the search more efficiently, thereby requiring less time to search.

The extent of a consumer's external search is also affected by confidence in one's decision-making ability. A confident consumer not only has sufficient stored information about the product but also feels self-assured about making the right decision. People lacking this confidence will continue an information search even when they know a great deal about the product. Finally, the extent of the search is positively related to the amount of interest a consumer has in a product. A consumer who is more interested in a product will spend more time searching for information and alternatives. A dedicated runner searching for a new pair of running shoes may enjoy reading about the new brands available and, as a result, may spend more time and effort than other buyers in deciding on the next shoe purchase.

The consumer's information search should yield a group of the most preferred alternatives called the **evoked set** (or **consideration set**), which a buyer can further

nonmarketing-controlled information source
a product information source that doesn't originate from the company(ies) making the product

marketing-controlled information source
a product information source that originates with marketers promoting the product

evoked set (consideration set)
a group of the most preferred alternatives resulting from an information search, which a buyer can further evaluate to make a final choice

evaluate to make a final choice. Consumers do not consider all brands available in a product category, but they do seriously consider a much smaller set. The hardcore runner mentioned in the previous paragraph may be loyal to Nike, for instance, but may have been told by peers about the benefits of other brands and thus includes these additional brands as her evoked set. Having too many choices can, in fact, confuse consumers and cause them to delay the decision to buy or, in some instances, can cause them to not buy at all.

5-2c | Steps 3 and 4: Evaluation of Alternatives and Purchase

After acquiring information and constructing a set of alternative products, the consumer is ready to make a decision. A consumer will use the information stored in memory and obtained from outside sources to develop a set of criteria. These standards help them to evaluate and compare alternatives. One way to begin narrowing the number of choices in the consideration set is to pick a product attribute and then exclude all products in the set without that attribute. For example, if you are buying a car and live in the mountains, you will probably exclude all cars without four-wheel drive.

Another way to narrow the number of choices is to use cutoffs. Cutoffs are either minimum or maximum levels of an attribute that an alternative must pass to be considered. If your budget for that new car is $25 000, you will not consider any four-wheel-drive vehicle above that price. A final way to narrow the choices is to rank the attributes under consideration in order of importance and evaluate the products on how well each performs on the most important attributes.

If new brands are added to an evoked set, the consumer's evaluation of the existing brands in that set changes. As a result, certain brands in the original set may become more desirable. If you discover that you can get the exact car you want, used, for $18 000 instead of spending $25 000 for a new model, you may revise your criteria and select the used car.

The goal of the marketing manager is to determine which attributes have the most influence on a consumer's choice. Several attributes may collectively affect a consumer's evaluation

Menno Schaefer/Shutterstock.com

of products. A single attribute, such as price, may not adequately explain how consumers form their evoked set. Moreover, attributes the marketer thinks are important may not be very important to the consumer. A brand name can also have a significant impact on a consumer's ultimate choice. By providing consumers with a certain set of promises, brands in essence simplify the consumer decision-making process so consumers do not have to rethink their options every time they need something.[4] Following the evaluation of alternatives, the consumer decides which product to buy or decides not to buy a product at all. If they decide to make a purchase, the next step in the process is an evaluation of the product after the purchase.

5-2d | Step 5: Postpurchase Behaviour

When buying products, consumers expect certain outcomes from the purchase. How well these expectations are met determines whether the consumer is satisfied or dissatisfied with the purchase. For the marketer, an important element of any postpurchase marketing activity is reducing any lingering doubts that the decision was sound. Eliminating such doubts is particularly important to increase consumer satisfaction with their purchases. Marketers thus must provide **decision confirmation** support beginning at the evaluation of alternatives stage, through the purchase itself, and into postpurchase. The decision confirmation is the reaffirmation of the wisdom of the decision a consumer has made, and such a need is stronger among consumers after making an important purchase.

A failure to confirm one's decision may result in **cognitive dissonance**—also popularly known as buyer's remorse—induced by constant doubt about one's choice. Cognitive dissonance is defined as an inner tension that a consumer experiences after recognizing an inconsistency between behaviour and values or opinions.

decision confirmation
the reaffirmation of the wisdom of the decision a consumer has made

cognitive dissonance
the inner tension that a consumer experiences after recognizing an inconsistency between behaviour and values or opinions

For example, suppose a consumer is looking to purchase a mountain bike that is light, yet durable, with disc brakes and priced under $1000. In such a situation, not one of the alternatives he has in his evoked set is clearly offering all the key attributes he is seeking. Thus proceeding with the purchase is likely to result in cognitive dissonance.

Marketing managers can help reduce dissonance through effective communication with purchasers. Postpurchase communication by sellers and dissonance-reducing statements in instruction booklets may help customers to feel more at ease with their purchase. Advertising that displays the product's superiority over competing brands or guarantees can also help relieve the possible dissonance of someone who has already bought the product. Ultimately, the marketer's goal is to ensure that the outcome meets or exceeds the customer's expectations rather than being a disappointment.

5-3 | TYPES OF CONSUMER BUYING DECISIONS AND THE SIGNIFICANCE OF CONSUMER INVOLVEMENT

All consumer buying decisions generally fall along a continuum of three broad categories: routine response behaviour, limited decision making, and extensive decision making (see Exhibit 5.2). Goods and services in these three categories can best be described in terms of five factors:

- level of consumer involvement
- length of time to make a decision
- cost of the good or service
- degree of information search
- the number of alternatives considered

The level of consumer involvement is perhaps the most significant determinant in classifying buying decisions. **Involvement** is the amount of time and effort a buyer invests in the search, evaluation, and decision processes of consumer behaviour.

Frequently purchased, low-cost goods and services are generally associated with **routine response behaviour**. These goods and services can also be called low-involvement products because consumers spend little time on the search and decision before making the purchase. Usually, buyers are familiar with several different brands in the product category but stick with one brand. Consumers engaged in routine response behaviour normally don't experience need recognition until they are exposed to advertising or see the product displayed on a store shelf. These consumers buy first and evaluate later, whereas the reverse is true for consumers who engage in extensive decision making.

Limited decision making requires a moderate amount of time for gathering information and deliberating about an unfamiliar brand in a familiar product category. It typically occurs when a consumer has previous product experience but is unfamiliar with the current brands available. Limited decision making is also associated with lower levels of involvement (although higher than routine decisions) because consumers expend only moderate effort in searching for information or in considering various alternatives. If a consumer's usual

involvement
the amount of time and effort a buyer invests in the search, evaluation, and decision processes of consumer behaviour

routine response behaviour
the type of decision making exhibited by consumers buying frequently purchased, low-cost goods and services; requires little search and decision time

limited decision making
the type of decision making that requires a moderate amount of time for gathering information and deliberating about an unfamiliar brand in a familiar product category

EXHIBIT 5.2	CONTINUUM OF CONSUMER BUYING DECISIONS		
	Routine	**Limited**	**Extensive**
Involvement	Low	Low to moderate	High
Time	Short	Short to moderate	Long
Cost	Low	Low to moderate	High
Information Search	Internal only	Mostly internal	Internal and external
Number of Alternatives	One	Few	Many
Examples	Shampoo, toothpaste	Clothes, technology	Car, college or university program

brand is sold out, they will likely evaluate several other brands before making a final decision.

Consumers practise **extensive decision making** when considering the purchase of an unfamiliar, expensive product or an infrequently purchased item. This process is the most complex type of consumer buying decision and is associated with high involvement on the part of the consumer. The process resembles the model outlined in Exhibit 5.1. Because these consumers want to make the right decision, they want to know as much as they can about the product category and the available brands. Buyers use several criteria for evaluating their options and spend more time seeking information. Buying a home or a car, for example, requires extensive decision making.

The type of decision making that consumers use to purchase a product does not necessarily remain constant. If a routinely purchased product no longer satisfies, consumers may practise limited or extensive decision making to switch to another brand. Consumers who first use extensive decision making may then use limited or routine decision making for future purchases. For example, a family may spend a lot of time figuring out that their new puppy prefers hard food to soft, but once they know, the purchase will become routine.

5-3a | Factors Determining the Level of Consumer Involvement

The level of involvement in the purchase depends on the following five factors:

- *Previous experience:* When consumers have had previous experience with a good or service, the level of involvement typically decreases. After repeated product trials, consumers learn to make quick choices. Because consumers are familiar with the product and know whether it will satisfy their needs, they become less involved in the purchase.

- *Interest:* Involvement is directly related to consumer interests, as in cars, music, movies, bicycling, or electronics. Naturally, these areas of interest vary from one individual to another. A person highly involved

in bike racing will be more interested in the type of bike she owns than someone who rides a bike only for recreation.

- *Perceived risk of negative consequences:* As the perceived risk in purchasing a product increases, so does a consumer's level of involvement. The types of risks that concern consumers include financial risk, social risk, and psychological risk.

  – Financial risk is exposure to loss of wealth or purchasing power. Because high risk is associated with high-priced purchases, consumers tend to become extremely involved. Therefore, price and involvement are usually directly related: as price increases, so does the level of involvement.

  – Social risks occur when consumers buy products that can affect people's social opinions of them (e.g., driving an old, beat-up car or wearing unstylish clothes).

  – Psychological risk occurs if consumers feel that making the wrong decision might cause some concern or anxiety (e.g., some consumers feel guilty about eating foods that are not healthy, such as regular ice cream rather than fat-free frozen yogurt).

- *Situation:* The circumstances of a purchase may temporarily transform a low-involvement decision into a high-involvement one. High involvement comes into play when the consumer perceives risk in a specific situation. For example, an individual might routinely buy frozen fruit and vegetables, but for dinner parties shop for high-quality fresh produce.

- *Social visibility:* Involvement also increases as the social visibility of a product increases. Products that are often on social display include clothing (especially designer labels), jewellery, cars, and furniture. All these items make a statement about the purchaser and, therefore, carry a social risk.

5-3b | Marketing Implications of Involvement

Marketing strategy varies according to the level of involvement associated with the product. For high-involvement product purchases, marketing managers have several responsibilities. First, promotion to the target market should be extensive and informative. A good ad gives consumers the information they need to make the purchase decision and specifies the benefits and unique advantages of owning the product.

extensive decision making
the most complex type of consumer decision making, used when considering the purchase of an unfamiliar, expensive product or an infrequently purchased item; requires the use of several criteria for evaluating options and more time for seeking information

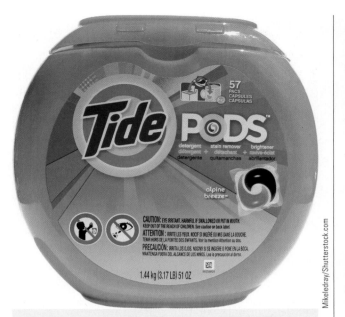

Tide uses bright, eye-catching packaging to draw customers to what is otherwise a low-involvement product.

For low-involvement product purchases, consumers may not recognize their wants until they are in the store. Therefore, marketers focus on package design so the product will be eye catching and easily recognized on the shelf. In-store promotions and displays also stimulate sales of low-involvement products. A good display can explain the product's purpose and prompt recognition of a want. Coupons, cents-off deals, and two-for-one offers also effectively promote low-involvement items.

At the opposite end of the spectrum, marketers can draw from their knowledge of the marketing environment to assist customers in their decision about extensive-involvement purchases. For instance, when buying a home, purchasers are forever weighing not only the immediate costs of a down payment but also the future costs of monthly mortgage payments. During economic periods when the interest rates on loans are low, marketers can reinforce the importance of timing their purchase to would-be home buyers. This tactic not only compels buyers to act in a timely manner but also pre-empts or reduces cognitive dissonance.

5-3c | Factors Influencing Consumer Buying Decisions

The consumer decision-making process does not occur in a vacuum. On the contrary, the decision process is strongly influenced by underlying cultural, social, individual, and psychological factors. These factors are central to the deeper concept of consumer behaviour and have an effect from the time a consumer perceives a stimulus through to the time of postpurchase behaviour. Cultural factors, which include culture and values, subculture, and social class, exert the broadest influence over consumer decision making. Social factors sum up the social interactions between a consumer and influential groups of people, such as reference groups, opinion leaders, and family members. Individual factors, which include gender, age, family life-cycle stage, personality, self-concept, and lifestyle, are unique to each individual and play a major role in the type of products and services consumers want. Psychological factors determine how consumers perceive and interact with their environments and influence the ultimate decisions consumers make. They include perception, motivation, learning, beliefs, and attitudes. Exhibit 5.3 summarizes these influences.

Rethinking the Consumer Decision-Making Process

Rapid changes in digital technology have given consumers unprecedented power to express likes and dislikes, compare prices, find the best deals, sift through huge numbers of recommendations and have items delivered. In short, the balance of power has shifted largely from the marketer to the consumer. Because of these changes, many marketers today are rethinking the consumer decision-making process.

Researchers have determined that how consumers make decisions can best be described as a journey as shown below.

The consumer decision journey begins when some stimulus like an advertisement causes the consumer to consider a number of products or services to meet their needs. Even at this early stage, the consumer may drop a number of items from the potential purchase set. The second stage of the journey begins when the consumer evaluates the alternatives, using input from peers, reviewers, the brand itself, and competitors. At this stage, new brands may be added, and options from the initial set may be dropped as the selection criteria shift. The consumer then buys (or doesn't buy) the product and, if they enjoy the purchase, may advocate and bond with the brand. This feedback loop of ratings, rankings, and referrals pressures brands to deliver a superior experience on an ongoing basis.

Progressive companies armed with new technologies are actively working to exert greater influence over the decision-making journey. In order to minimize (or in some cases eliminate) the "consider and evaluate" phases of the consumer journey, a company must have four distinct but interconnected capabilities:

- *automation* that streamlines the steps;
- *proactive personalization* uses of information to instantaneously customize the customer experience;
- *contextual interaction* that uses knowledge about where a customer is in the journey to deliver the next set of interactions; and
- *journey innovation* that extends customer interactions to new sources of value, like related products.

Researchers have found two levels of loyalty among customers of the companies using this new technology to assist consumers through the decision journey: the satisfied and the committed. The satisfied are those who buy regularly, often out of habit, because they are satisfied with the brand's performance over a long period. The committed have a more intense and involved relationship with the brand.

Classic Journey

In the classic journey, consumers engage in an extended consideration and evaluation phase before either entering into the loyalty loop or proceeding into a new round of consideration and evaluation that may lead to the subsequent purchase of a different brand.

New Journey

The new journey compresses the consider step and shortens or entirely eliminates the evaluate step, delivering customers directly into the loyalty loop and locking them within it.

Sources: David Edelmand and Mark Singer, "Competing on Customer Journeys," *Harvard Business Review*, November 2015; David Aaker and Andrew Marcum, "The Satisfied vs Committed Brand Loyalist and What Drives Them," *Marketing News*, January 2017, pp. 24–25.

EXHIBIT 5.3   FACTORS THAT AFFECT THE CONSUMER DECISION-MAKING PROCESS

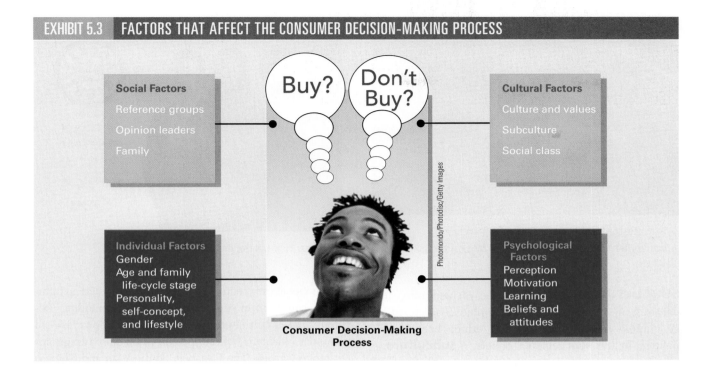

Consumer Decision-Making Process

5-4 | CULTURAL AND SOCIAL FACTORS AFFECT CONSUMER BUYING DECISIONS

5-4a | Cultural Influences on Consumer Buying Decisions

CULTURE AND VALUES Cultural factors exert a deep influence on consumer decision making. Marketers must understand the way people's **culture** and its accompanying values, as well as their subculture and social class, influence their buying behaviour. Culture comprises the set of values, norms, attitudes, and other meaningful symbols that shape human behaviour and the artifacts, or products, of that behaviour as they are transmitted from one generation to the next. Culture is the essential character of a society that distinguishes it from other cultural groups.

Culture is

- *Pervasive:* Culture encompasses all the things consumers do without conscious choice because their culture's values, customs, and rituals are ingrained in their daily habits.

- *Functional:* Human interaction creates values and prescribes acceptable behaviour for each culture. By establishing common expectations, culture gives order to society.

- *Learned:* Consumers are not born knowing the values and norms of their society. Instead, they must learn what is acceptable from family and friends.

- *Dynamic:* It adapts to changing needs and an evolving environment. The rapid growth of technology in today's world has accelerated the rate of cultural change

The most defining element of a culture is its **values**—the enduring beliefs shared by a society that a specific mode of conduct is personally or socially preferable to another mode of conduct. People's value systems have a great effect on their consumer behaviour. Consumers with similar value systems tend to react similarly to various marketing-related inducements. Values also correspond to consumption patterns. For example, Canadians place a high value on convenience, as we are in a time-starved society. This value has created lucrative markets for products such as breakfast bars, energy bars, and nutrition bars that allow consumers to eat on the go.

culture
the set of values, norms, attitudes, and other meaningful symbols that shape human behaviour and the artifacts, or products, of that behaviour as they are transmitted from one generation to the next

value
the enduring belief shared by a society that a specific mode of conduct is personally or socially preferable to another mode of conduct

Tim Horton's breakfast sandwiches are very convenient for Canadians to eat while on the go.

Hockey Night in Canada Punjabi

SUBCULTURE A culture can be divided into subcultures on the basis of demographic characteristics, geographic regions, national and ethnic background, political beliefs, and religious beliefs. A **subculture** is a homogeneous group of people who share elements of the overall culture and also have their own unique cultural elements. Within subcultures, people's attitudes, values, and purchase decisions are even more similar than they are within the broader culture. Subcultural differences may result in considerable variation within a culture with regard to how, when, and where people buy goods and services, and what they buy.

In Canada's multicultural society, French Canadians represent a dominant subculture. While this subculture is mainly based in Quebec, Canada is officially a bilingual nation, and marketers in all regions of the country must be knowledgeable about the language and lifestyle values of the French Canadian subculture. It is important to note that the nature of bilingualism in Canada is changing: an increasing proportion of the population is bilingual not in English and French but in English and one of the immigrant languages.

Once marketers identify subcultures, they can design special marketing programs to serve their needs. There are large South Asian and Chinese markets in British Columbia that the BC Dairy Association wanted to target as part of an ongoing promotional campaign. The Association launched an influencer campaign in support of their larger branding program. Research showed that dairy consumption was high in India and China but dropped off when these two groups came to Canada. The Canadian South Asian and Chinese markets were chosen because they represent approximately 30 percent of the population in British Columbia.[5]

SOCIAL CLASS A **social class** is a group of people who are considered nearly equal in status or community esteem, who regularly socialize among themselves both formally and informally, and who share behavioural norms.

The majority of Canadians today define themselves as middle class, regardless of their actual income or educational attainment. This phenomenon most likely occurs because working-class Canadians tend to aspire to the middle-class lifestyle while some of those who achieve affluence may downwardly aspire to respectable middle-class status as a matter of principle.

Social class is typically measured as a combination of occupation, income, education, wealth, and other variables. For instance, affluent upper-class consumers are more likely to be salaried executives or self-employed professionals with at least an undergraduate degree. Working-class or middle-class consumers are more likely to be hourly service workers or blue-collar employees with only a high-school education. Educational attainment, however, seems to be the most reliable indicator of a person's social and economic status. Those with university or college degrees or graduate degrees are more likely to fall into the upper classes, while those people with some postsecondary experience fall closer to traditional concepts of the middle class.

Marketers are interested in social class as an integral part of segmentation and targeting, covered in Chapter 7. Segmentation is a process where marketers

subculture

a homogeneous group of people who share elements of the overall culture and also have their own unique cultural elements

social class

a group of people who are considered nearly equal in status or community esteem, who regularly socialize among themselves both formally and informally, and who share behavioural norms

Education is usually a reliable indicator of a person's social and economic status. Those with postsecondary degrees are more likely to fall into the upper classes, while those with some postsecondary experience tend to fall into the middle class.

divide larger populations into groups based upon a number of variables, including demographics. Among many other descriptors, demographics can be represented by individual and household income, a telltale sign as to how much money people have to spend on goods and services. Targeting is the directed pursuit of a given segment based on its attractiveness to a company. Thus Lululemon, with its high-end yoga-lifestyle apparel, will target not only image- and fit-conscious consumers (mostly women), but also those with some discretionary income to spend on a relatively expensive item.

5-4b | Social Influences on Consumer Buying Decisions

Most consumers are likely to seek out the opinions of others to reduce their search and evaluation effort or uncertainty, especially as the perceived risk of the decision increases. Consumers may also seek out others' opinions for guidance on new products or services, products with image-related attributes, expensive products, or products where attribute information is lacking or uninformative. Specifically, consumers interact socially with reference groups, opinion leaders, and family members to obtain product information and decision approval.

REFERENCE GROUPS All the formal and informal groups that influence the purchasing behaviour of an individual are that person's **reference groups**. Consumers may use products or brands to identify with or to become a member of a group. Consumers observe how members of their reference groups consume, and they use the same criteria to make their own consumer decisions.

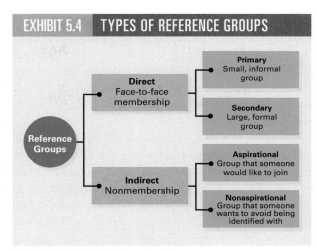

EXHIBIT 5.4 | TYPES OF REFERENCE GROUPS

Reference Groups

- Direct — Face-to-face membership
  - Primary — Small, informal group
  - Secondary — Large, formal group
- Indirect — Nonmembership
  - Aspirational — Group that someone would like to join
  - Nonaspirational — Group that someone wants to avoid being identified with

Reference groups can be broadly categorized as being either direct or indirect (see Exhibit 5.4). Direct reference groups are face-to-face membership groups that touch people's lives directly. They can be either primary or secondary. **Primary membership groups** include all groups with which people interact regularly in an informal, face-to-face manner, such as family, friends, and coworkers. In contrast, people associate with **secondary membership groups** less consistently and more formally. These groups might include clubs, professional associations, and people who share a religious affiliation.

Consumers are also influenced by many indirect, nonmembership reference groups they do not belong to. **Aspirational reference groups** are those groups that a person would like to join. To join an aspirational group, a person must conform to that group's **norms**—that is, the values and attitudes deemed acceptable by the group. Thus a person who wants to be elected to public office may begin to dress more conservatively, to match the attire of other politicians. Athletes are an aspirational group for several market segments.

reference group
a group in society that influences an individual's purchasing behaviour

primary membership groups
groups with which individuals interact regularly in an informal, face-to-face manner

secondary membership groups
groups with which individuals interact less consistently and more formally than with primary membership groups

aspirational reference groups
groups that an individual would like to join

norms
the values and attitudes deemed acceptable by a group

Nonaspirational reference groups, or **dissociative groups**, influence our behaviour because we try to maintain distance from them. A consumer may avoid buying some types of clothing or cars, going to certain restaurants or stores, or even buying a home in a certain neighbourhood to avoid being associated with a particular group.

The activities, values, and goals of reference groups directly influence consumer behaviour. For marketers, reference groups have three important implications: (1) they serve as information sources and influence perceptions; (2) they affect an individual's aspiration levels; and (3) their norms either constrain or stimulate consumer behaviour. Understanding the effect of reference groups on a product is important for marketers as they track the life cycle of their products. Marketers continually face the challenge of identifying the trendsetters in a particular target market. For example, a snowboard manufacturer can determine what is considered cool in the snowboard market by seeking out the trendsetters on their favourite slopes. The unique ways in which these snowboarders personalize their equipment and clothing can be looked on as being desirable and thus may be modified by the influencers who are seeking to express their own individual character. Once the fad look is embraced by the influencers, it has the potential to be adopted by the others in that sociogeographic group. However, as the adoption of the latest trend becomes more common, that trend loses its appeal to the trendsetters, and they seek new ways to express their individualism. The effects of reference groups are especially important both for products that satisfy such visible, unique, socially desirable, high-involvement needs as wine, fashion, and the latest foods, and for personal services, such as spa treatments and vacation destinations and activities. Thus, marketers must understand and track the effects of reference groups on the sales of a product as it moves through its life cycle.

OPINION LEADERS Reference groups frequently include individuals known as group leaders, or **opinion leaders**—those who influence others. Obviously, it is important for marketing managers to persuade such people to purchase their goods or services.

Opinion leaders are often the first to try new products and services, usually as the result of pure curiosity. They are typically self-indul-

gent, making them more likely to explore unproven but intriguing products and services. Technology companies have found that teenagers, because of their willingness to experiment, are key opinion leaders for the success of new technologies: texting became popular with teenagers before it gained widespread appeal.

Social media have made identification of opinion leaders easier than ever before. There are several social media monitoring software products available that collect data from social networks and search date from the Internet to measure a person's influence. Some software also monitors offline data as well to see how often an individual is mentioned in traditional media like magazines and newspapers.[6]

After identifying potential opinion leaders, marketers will often endeavour to engage these people to support their products. On a wider scale, large companies, groups, associations, and causes will seek out recognized organizations or individuals in sports, business, entertainment, religion, or politics to endorse or support the promotion of their product. The organization's or individual's familiarity, attractiveness, credibility, and relative association can greatly influence a target group. A recent study shows that influencers on social media play a role in fashion purchases, particularly for purchases made online. The study showed that more than 20 percent of online fashion purchases were influenced by social media and more than 40 percent of online shoppers made a purchase that an influencer promoted.[7]

FAMILY The family is the most important social institution for many consumers, strongly influencing their values, attitudes, self-concepts, and buying behaviour. For example, a family that strongly values good health will have a grocery list distinctly different from that of a

John Tavares endorsed the Casper mattress in the "Sleep Better, Hockey Harder" campaign to reach out to those who also "live at the rink."

Alamy Stock Photo

family that views every dinner as a gourmet event. Moreover, the family is responsible for the **socialization process**—the passing down of cultural values and norms to children. Because children learn by observing their parents' consumption patterns, they will tend to shop in a similar pattern.

Decision-making roles among family members tend to vary significantly, depending on the types of items purchased. Family members assume a variety of roles in the purchase process. *Initiators* suggest, initiate, or plant the seed for the purchase process. The initiator can be any member of the family. For example, a sister might initiate the product search by asking for a new bicycle as a birthday present. *Influencers* are those members of the family whose opinions are valued. In our example, Mom might function as a price-range watchdog, an influencer whose main role is to veto or approve price ranges. A brother may give his opinion on certain makes of bicycles. The *decision maker* is the family member who actually makes the decision to buy or not to buy. For example, a parent is likely to choose the final brand and model of bicycle to buy after seeking further information from the sister regarding cosmetic features, such as colour, and after imposing additional parental criteria, such as durability and safety. The *purchaser* (probably a parent) is the one who actually exchanges money for the product. Finally, the *consumer* is the actual user—the sister, in the case of the bicycle.

Marketers should consider family purchase situations along with the distribution of consumer and decision-maker roles among family members. Ordinary marketing views the individual as both decision maker and consumer. Family marketing adds several other possibilities: sometimes more than one family member or all family members are involved in the decision; sometimes only children are involved in the decision; sometimes more than one consumer is involved; and sometimes the decision maker and the consumer are different people.

5-5 | INDIVIDUAL INFLUENCES ON CONSUMER BUYING DECISIONS

A person's buying decisions are also influenced by personal characteristics that are unique to each individual, such as gender; age and life-cycle stage; and personality, self-concept, and lifestyle. Individual characteristics are generally stable over the course of one's life. For instance, most people do not change their gender, and the act of changing personality or lifestyle requires a complete reorientation of one's life. In the case of age and life-cycle stage, these changes occur gradually over time.

5-5a | Gender

Physiological differences between men and women result in different needs. Just as important are the distinct cultural, social, and economic roles played by men and women and the effects that these roles have on their decision-making processes. Most car manufacturers have realized that men and women tend to look at different features when purchasing a vehicle. Generally, men gravitate toward performance-related items, while women prefer to focus on durability and safety features.[8]

Indeed, men and women do shop differently. Studies show that both men and women go through the same decision-making process when purchasing products. Women, however, are looking to make the perfect decision and therefore may go through each stage of the decision-making process more than once. Men take a more direct route to a good purchase decision.[9]

Trends in gender marketing are influenced by the changing roles of men and women in society. Companies must develop new strategies that reflect the changing roles of men and women both at home and at work. As *Canadian Grocer* points out, in 60 percent of Canadian households, a male is either the primary or shared grocery shopper, due largely to the sharp increase of stay-at-home dads, which had risen to 12 percent of households by 2015.[10]

5-5b | Age and Family Life-Cycle Stage

The age and family life-cycle stage of a consumer can have a significant impact on consumer behaviour. How old a consumer is generally indicates the products they may be interested in purchasing and how they purchase the products. Consumer tastes in food, clothing, technology, cars, furniture, and recreation are often age related. A survey of how consumers planned to shop during a holiday season revealed that more millennials planned to shop online while more of the younger Gen Z planned to shop in retail stores.[11]

Related to a person's age is their place in the family life cycle. As Chapter 7 explains in more detail, the *family life cycle* is an orderly series of stages through which consumers' attitudes and behavioural tendencies evolve through maturity, experience, and changing income and status. Marketers often define their target markets in terms of family life cycle, such as "young singles," "young married with children," and "middle-aged

socialization process
the passing down of cultural values and norms to children

Changes to Customer Purchasing Behaviour

Consumer purchasing patterns are constantly changing. There are many factors causing this change. The rapid increase in the use of technology is only one of these factors. Recent research into Global Consumer Trends also suggests that the overall aging of the world population, the global increase in the number of middle class, and the speed of urbanization internationally are also influencing consumer purchasing patterns. The Global Trends research also identified seven drivers of change: well-being, surroundings, technology, rights, identity, value, and experiences.

The well-being driver includes trends like the reduced rate of alcohol consumption, particularly within younger age groups. It also includes dietary changes such as less red meat being consumed but not a total switch by much of the population to a vegetarian diet. The surroundings driver includes environmental issues such as the move toward modular and movable homes and brands offering returnable products such as furniture. The technology driver includes factors like the impact of 5G and the acceptance of consumers of retail stores without sales personnel. The rights driver includes privacy, particularly privacy over information being collected about us and what the data can be used for. The identity driver includes the trend that young adults will continue to challenge the traditional ideas of gender and sexuality. The identity driver also includes the increasing power of the small group of consumers who fit into the Gen Z group. Until recently companies paid little attention to this group because it was so small, but they are becoming more vocal about what they want and won't accept less. The value driver includes the trend toward consuming less and purchasing products that will last longer even if these products are more expensive. The final driver is experiences. This driver moves consumers to experience traditions and celebrations where people can interact.

Identifying the trends affecting consumer behaviour is only part of what companies need to understand about how consumers are making decisions today. KPMG, the international professional services firm, has developed a new framework to explain the decision making of Canadian consumers. The framework consists of the "Five Mys" including My motivation, My attention, My connection, My watch, and My wallet. The "My motivation" element involves customer expectations and where consumers look for information. "My attention" focuses on the abundance of information available for today's consumers and how the attention span of today's customers is falling. "My connection" looks at the impact of the consumer's digital interactions and "My watch" looks at the influence our time- pressured lifestyles have on our purchase decisions. The "My wallet" element looks at the relationship between life events and spending patterns.

Sources: Justin Dallaire, "Consumers in 2020 and Beyond," Strategy online, https://strategyonline.ca/2020/01/10/consumers-in-2020-and-beyond/, January 10, 2020; KPMG website, Me, my Canadian life, my wallet: An in-depth look at the Canadian customer; kpmg.ca/customer-insights, accessed January 15, 2020; "Consumer Trends 2030," Mintel website, https://downloads.mintel.com/private/80Eae/files/792831/ accessed Jan 15, 2020; "Consumer Trends 2030," Mintel website, https://downloads.mintel.com/private/80Eae/files/792831.

married without children." As you can imagine, the spending habits of young singles, young parents, and empty nesters are very different. For instance, the presence of children in the home is the most significant determinant of the type of vehicle that's driven off the new-car lot. Parents are the ultimate need-driven car consumers, requiring larger cars and trucks to haul their children and all their belongings, which explains why sport utility vehicles (SUVs) and minivans were selling at a brisk pace before rising fuel costs became a major consideration when purchasing a vehicle.

Marketers should also be aware of the many nontraditional life-cycle paths that are common today and provide insights into the needs and wants of such consumers as divorced parents, lifelong singles, and childless couples.

For many consumers, the family is the single most important social institution. Family strongly influences a person's values, attitudes, self-concept, and buying behaviour.

5-5c | Personality, Self-Concept, and Lifestyle

Each consumer has a unique personality. **Personality** is a broad concept that can be thought of as a way of organizing and grouping the consistency of an individual's reactions to situations. Thus personality combines psychological makeup and environmental forces. It also includes people's underlying dispositions, especially their most dominant characteristics. Some marketers believe that personality influences the types and brands of products purchased. For instance, the type of car, clothes, or jewellery a consumer buys may reflect one or more personality traits.

Self-concept, or self-perception, is how consumers perceive themselves in terms of attitudes, perceptions, beliefs, and self-evaluations. Although a self-concept may change, the change is often gradual. Through self-concept, people define their identity, which in turn provides for consistent and coherent behaviour.

Self-concept combines the **ideal self-image** (the way an individual would like to be) and the **real self-image** (the way an individual actually perceives themself to be). Generally, we try to raise our real self-image toward our ideal (or at least narrow the gap). Consumers seldom buy products that jeopardize their self-image. For example, a woman who sees herself as a trendsetter wouldn't buy clothing that doesn't project a contemporary image.

Human behaviour depends largely on self-concept. Because consumers want to protect their identity as individuals, the products they buy, the stores they patronize, and the credit cards they carry support their self-image. By influencing the degree to which consumers perceive a good or service to be self-relevant, marketers can affect consumers' motivation to learn about, shop for, and buy a certain brand. Marketers also consider self-concept important because it helps explain the relationship between individuals' perceptions of themselves and their consumer behaviour.

An important component of self-concept is *body image,* the perception of the attractiveness of one's own physical features. For example, a person's perception of body image can be a stronger reason for weight loss than either good health or other social factors.[12] With the median age of Canadians rising, many companies are introducing products and services aimed at aging baby boomers who are concerned about their age and physical appearance. Marketers are also seeing boomers respond to products aimed at younger audiences. For instance, Home Hardware introduced an app that allows customers to see what the rooms in their homes would look like painted a different colour. The app was aimed at younger consumers but many older consumers are using it as well.[13]

Personality and self-concept are reflected in lifestyle. A **lifestyle** is a mode of living, as identified by a person's activities, interests, and opinions. *Psychographics* is the analytical technique used to examine consumer lifestyles and to categorize consumers. Unlike personality characteristics, which can be difficult to describe and measure, lifestyle characteristics are useful in segmenting and targeting consumers. We, as consumers, are ever-changing in our affluence (income and spending focus), where we live (urban, suburban, or rural), and our relationships (family stage or life-stage groups). Lifestyle and psychographic analyses explicitly address the way consumers outwardly express their inner selves in their social and cultural environment. For example, to better understand their market segments, many Canadian companies now use psychographics such as PRIZM, which segments consumers into 68 different groups.[14] Psychographics and lifestyle segmentation are discussed in more detail in Chapter 7.

personality
a way of organizing and grouping the consistency of an individual's reactions to situations

self-concept
how consumers perceive themselves in terms of attitudes, perceptions, beliefs, and self-evaluations

ideal self-image
the way an individual would like to be

real self-image
the way an individual actually perceives themself to be

lifestyle
a mode of living as identified by a person's activities, interests, and opinions

5-6 | PSYCHOLOGICAL INFLUENCES ON CONSUMER BUYING DECISIONS

An individual's buying decisions are further influenced by **psychological factors**: perception, motivation, learning, beliefs, and attitudes. These factors are what consumers use to interact with their world, recognize their feelings, gather and analyze information, formulate thoughts and opinions, and take action. Unlike the other three influences on consumer behaviour, psychological influences can be affected by a person's environment because they are applied on specific occasions. For example, you will perceive different stimuli and process these stimuli in different ways depending on whether you are sitting in class concentrating on the instructor, sitting outside class talking to friends, or sitting in your dorm room watching television.

5-6a | Perception

psychological factors
tools that consumers use to interact with their world, recognize their feelings, gather and analyze information, formulate thoughts and opinions, and take action

perception
the process by which people select, organize, and interpret stimuli into a meaningful and coherent picture

selective exposure
the process whereby a consumer decides which stimuli to notice and which to ignore

selective distortion
a process whereby consumers change or distort information that conflicts with their feelings or beliefs

selective retention
a process whereby consumers remember only information that supports their personal feelings or beliefs

The world is full of stimuli. A stimulus is any unit of input affecting one or more of the five senses: sight, smell, taste, touch, or hearing. The process by which we select, organize, and interpret these stimuli into a meaningful and coherent picture is called **perception**. In essence, perception is how we see the world around us and how we recognize that we need some help in making a purchasing decision.

People cannot perceive every stimulus in their environment. Therefore, they use **selective exposure**, a process whereby a consumer decides which stimuli to notice and which to ignore. The familiarity of an object, as well as its contrast, movement, intensity (such as increased volume), and smell, are cues that influ-ence perception. Consumers use these cues to identify and define products and brands. The shape of a product's packaging, such as Coca-Cola's signature contour bottle, can influence perception. Colour is another cue, and it plays a key role in consumers' perceptions. Packaged food manufacturers use colour to trigger unconscious associations for grocery shoppers who typically make their shopping decisions in the blink of an eye. Food marketers use green to signal environmental well-being and healthy, low-fat foods, whereas black, brown, and gold are used to convey premium ingredients.[15] The shape and look of a product's packaging can also influence perception.

What is perceived by consumers may also depend on the vividness or shock value of the stimulus. Graphic warnings of the hazards associated with a product's use are perceived more readily and remembered more accurately than less vivid warnings or warnings that are written in text. Sexier ads excel at attracting the attention of younger consumers. Some companies use sensuous ads to "cut through the clutter" of competing ads and other stimuli to capture the attention of the target audience.

Two other concepts closely related to selective exposure are selective distortion and selective retention. **Selective distortion** occurs when consumers change or distort information that conflicts with their feelings or beliefs. For example, suppose you buy a new iPhone. After the purchase, if you receive new information about an alternative brand, such as the Google Pixel, you may distort the information to make it more consistent with the prior view that the iPhone is just as good as the Pixel, if not better.

Selective retention is a process whereby consumers remember only information that supports their personal feelings or beliefs. The consumer forgets all information that may be inconsistent. Consumers may see a news report on suspected illegal practices by their favourite retail store but soon forget the reason the store was featured on the news.

Which stimuli will be perceived often depends on the individual. People can be exposed to the same stimuli under identical conditions but perceive them very differently. For example, two people viewing a TV commercial may have different interpretations of the advertising message. One person may be thoroughly engrossed by the message and become highly motivated to buy the product. Thirty seconds after the ad ends, the second person may not be able to recall the content of the message or even the product advertised.

MARKETING IMPLICATIONS OF PERCEPTION

Marketers must recognize the importance of cues, or signals, in consumers' perception of products. Marketing managers first identify the important attributes that the targeted consumers want in a product, such as price, social acceptance, or quantity, and then design signals to communicate these attributes. Gibson Guitar Corporation briefly cut prices on many of its guitars to compete with Japanese rivals Yamaha and Ibanez but found instead that it sold more guitars when it charged more. Consumers perceived the higher price as indicating a better-quality instrument.[16]

Marketing managers are also interested in the *threshold level of perception:* the minimum difference in a stimulus that the consumer will notice. This concept is sometimes referred to as the "just-noticeable difference." For example, how much would Apple have to drop the price of its watch before consumers recognized it as a bargain—$25? $50? or more? One study found that the just-noticeable difference in a stimulus is about a 20 percent change. That is, consumers will likely notice a 20 percent price decrease more quickly than a 15 percent decrease. This marketing principle can also be applied to other marketing variables, such as package size or loudness of a broadcast advertisement.[17]

Another study showed that the bargain-price threshold for a name brand is lower than that for a store brand. In other words, consumers perceive a bargain more readily when stores offer a small discount on a name-brand item than when they offer the same discount on a store brand; a larger discount is needed to achieve a similar effect for a store brand.[18] Researchers also found that for low-cost grocery items, consumers typically do not see past the second digit in the price. For instance, consumers do not perceive any real difference between two comparable cans of tuna, one priced at $1.52 and the other at $1.59, because they ignore the last digit.[19]

Marketing managers who intend to do business in global markets should be aware of how foreign consumers perceive their products. For instance, in Japan, product labels are often written in English or French, even though they may not translate into anything meaningful. Many Japanese associate the foreign words with products that are exotic, expensive, and of high quality.

5-6b | Motivation

By studying motivation, marketers can analyze the major forces influencing consumers to buy or not buy products. When you buy a product, you usually do so to fulfill some kind of need. These needs become motives when aroused sufficiently. For instance, you can be motivated by hunger to stop at McDonald's for, say, an Egg McMuffin before an early-morning class. **Motives** are the driving forces that cause a person to take action to satisfy specific needs.

Why are people driven by particular needs at particular times? One popular theory is **Maslow's**

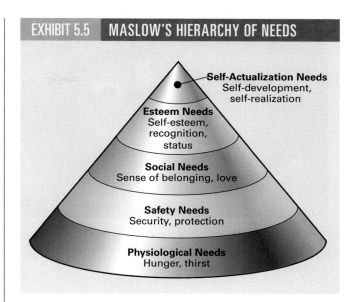

EXHIBIT 5.5 MASLOW'S HIERARCHY OF NEEDS

Self-Actualization Needs
Self-development, self-realization

Esteem Needs
Self-esteem, recognition, status

Social Needs
Sense of belonging, love

Safety Needs
Security, protection

Physiological Needs
Hunger, thirst

hierarchy of needs, shown in Exhibit 5.5, which arranges needs in ascending order of importance: physiological, safety, social, esteem, and self-actualization. As a person learns how to satisfy a need at one level, a higher-level need becomes the next challenge.

The most basic human needs are *physiological*—that is, the needs for food, water, and shelter. Because these needs are essential to survival, they must be satisfied first. *Safety* needs include security and freedom from pain, discomfort, and anxiety. Marketers sometimes appeal to consumers' fears about safety and their well-being in order to sell their products.

After physiological and safety needs have been fulfilled, *social needs*—especially love and a sense of belonging—become the focus. Love includes acceptance by one's peers, as well as sexual and romantic love. Over the latter part of the 20th century and into the 21st century, marketers have recognized our vulnerability at this level of need and have thus zeroed in on the abundant resulting marketing opportunities. The need to belong is also a favourite of marketers, especially those marketing products to teens.

Self-esteem needs are the needs to feel good about ourselves, including self-respect and a sense of accomplishment. Esteem needs also include prestige, fame, and recognition of one's accomplishments. Indeed, marketers of luxury

motives
driving forces that cause a person to take action to satisfy specific needs

Maslow's hierarchy of needs
a method of classifying human needs into five categories in ascending order of importance: physiological, safety, social, esteem, and self-actualization

More than one motive may drive a consumer's purchase. Consumers often look to products that satisfy multiple needs such as status and the value of family.

products, such as Dom Pérignon, Louboutin, Prada, and Mercedes-Benz, find that demand for their products is so strong among image-conscious consumers that their sales are generally unaffected by economic downturns. Beyond impressing others, self-esteem needs also motivate us to indulge in purchases that truly reflect who we are.

The highest human need of Maslow's hierarchy—which we become aware of last—is *self-actualization*. It refers to realizing our true potential, or discovering our true purpose. Maslow felt that very few people ever attain this level. Even so, marketers churn out products and accompany them with messages focusing on this type of need by appealing to consumers' ambition, such as encouraging adults to go back to school, look for better career opportunities, or volunteer for charities that are consistent with their values and goals.

Maslow's hierarchy at a first glance seems to suggest rigid boundaries and a linear sequential escalation between different levels but this would be an oversimplification of the theory. Do we need to *fully* meet all our needs at one level before we move to the next higher level? Do we stop satisfying a need after moving on to the next? Can an individual try to meet needs at two different levels at the same time? In fact, we do not need to meet all our needs at one level before moving to the next. New university graduates, for example, tend to rent their first apartment (a physiological need) before buying a larger house at a later stage in life. At the same time, the new graduates spend money on clothing to meet their self-esteem needs and make friends and join dating sites to

learning
a process that creates changes in behaviour, immediate or expected, through experience and practice

look for potential mates. This pattern suggests that consumers must realize some level of achievement at one level before moving to the next higher level and effortlessly move between different levels at the same time.

5-6c | Learning

Almost all consumer behaviour results from **learning**, which is the process that creates changes in behaviour, immediate or expected, through experience and practice. It is not possible to observe learning directly, but we can infer when it has occurred by a person's actions. For example, suppose you see an advertisement for a new and improved cold medicine. If you go to the store that day and buy that remedy, you have most likely learned something about the cold medicine.

There are two types of learning: experiential and conceptual. *Experiential learning* occurs when an experience changes your behaviour. For example, if the new cold medicine does not relieve your symptoms, you may not buy that brand again. *Conceptual learning*, which is not acquired through direct experience, is the second type of learning. Assume, for example, that you are a habitual bottled-water drinker and you see someone from an aspirational reference group drinking from a trendy S'well reusable bottle. You note that it looks good, and then your ideal self-image kicks in, imploring you to stop using disposable bottles. This new learning motivates you to buy the S'well bottle and change your behaviour. You have learned a new behaviour without even trying out the S'well bottle first.

Reinforcement and repetition boost learning. Reinforcement can be positive or negative. For example, if you see a vendor selling frozen yogurt (a stimulus), and you buy it (your response), you may find the yogurt to be quite refreshing (your reward). In this example, your behaviour

has been positively reinforced. On the other hand, if you buy a new flavour of yogurt and it does not taste good (negative reinforcement), you will not buy that flavour of yogurt again (your response). Without positive or negative reinforcement, a person will not be motivated to repeat the behaviour pattern or to avoid it. Thus, if a new brand evokes neutral feelings, some marketing activity, such as a price change or an increase in promotion, may be required to induce further consumption. Learning theory is helpful for reminding marketers that concrete and timely actions are what reinforce desired consumer behaviour.

Repetition is a key strategy in promotional campaigns because it can lead to increased learning. Most marketers use repetitious advertising so that consumers will learn their unique advantage over the competition. Generally, to heighten learning, advertising messages should be spread over time rather than clustered together.

5-6d | Beliefs and Attitudes

Beliefs and attitudes are closely linked to values. A **belief** is an organized pattern of knowledge that an individual holds as true about their world. A consumer may believe that GoPro makes the videos of their active lifestyle look exciting, that the camera is tough and durable, and that it's reasonably priced. These beliefs may be based on knowledge, faith, or hearsay. Consumers tend to develop a set of beliefs about a product's attributes and then, through these beliefs, form a *brand image*—a set of beliefs about a particular brand. In turn, the brand image shapes consumers' attitudes toward the product.

An **attitude** is a learned tendency to respond consistently toward a given object, such as a brand. Attitudes rest on an individual's value system, which represents personal standards of good and bad, right and wrong, and so forth; therefore, attitudes tend to be more enduring and complex than beliefs. For an example of the nature of attitudes, consider the differing attitudes of millennial and baby boomer consumers toward the practice of purchasing on credit. Millennials don't think twice about charging goods and services and are willing to pay high interest rates for the privilege of postponing payment. To older baby boomer consumers, however, doing what amounts to taking out a loan, even a small one, to pay for anything seems absurd.

CHANGING BELIEFS If a good or service is meeting its profit goals, positive attitudes toward the product merely need to be reinforced. If the brand is not succeeding, however, the marketing manager must strive to change target consumers' attitudes toward it. This change can be accomplished in three ways: (1) changing beliefs about the brand's attributes, (2) changing the relative importance of these beliefs, or (3) adding new beliefs. The first technique is to turn neutral or negative beliefs about product attributes into positive beliefs. For example, many younger consumers believe that Harley-Davidson is a motorcycle brand targeted at their fathers or even grandfathers. In 2016, however, Harley-Davidson introduced a completely different looking motorcycle, the Street series, featuring a sleeker, more youthful look, with a weight and price much more befitting a younger market that had been quickly disappearing.[20]

Changing consumers' beliefs about a service can be more difficult because service attributes are intangible. Convincing consumers to switch hairstylists or lawyers or to go to a mall dental clinic can be much more difficult than getting them to change their brand of razor blades. Image, which is also largely intangible, significantly determines service patronage. Service marketing is explored in detail in Chapter 11.

The second approach to modifying attitudes is to change the relative importance of beliefs about an attribute. For example, milk has always been considered a healthy beverage for children and adults. Now, however, dairies are aware of milk's added benefits, primarily the importance of calcium for bone strength, which they now actively promote on their packaging. The third approach to transforming attitudes is to add new beliefs, such as that LinkedIn is not only for job seekers and recruiters, but also a social medium for professionals to connect and exchange ideas.

5-6e | Consumer Behaviour Elements— Working Together

As a result of their environment, individuals change, which, in turn, changes the nature of the goods and services they consume. By using the stages of the buying process to make the best choices, consumers become more experienced. This experience changes the parts of the buying process they use, the degree of effort and time they spend on each stage of buying, and the importance of each of the psychological influences in their final buying decision. Effective marketers will carefully study their target markets, noting these changes and the degrees of difference. Then, after understanding the consumers' needs, these marketers can adjust their approach to the various elements in the marketing mix to meet the consumers' needs and help them move through the buying process.

belief
an organized pattern of knowledge that an individual holds as true about their world

attitude
a learned tendency to respond consistently toward a given object

AWAKE CHOCOLATE
CONTINUING CASE

AWAKE Chocolate

Taste Drives Decisions

As mentioned after in the Awake case in Chapter 1, the clear focus for the company was to understand consumer needs. This focus on needs describes very well the first stage of the Consumer Decision Process described in this chapter.

When Awake Chocolate was formed, determining how to meet a consumer need was paramount. Awake CEO Adam Deremo noted that the rallying cry when starting up Awake was focused on "… delivering the energy benefit in food format. And we are not aware of anything better tasting than chocolate, [so] that's what we focused on."

And thus taste is what drove Awake Chocolate, and was the stimulus that would compel consumers to try to solve the problem of a lack of energy with food products instead of beverages like coffee and energy drinks. And the form that has been the most popular for Awake Chocolate has been with chocolate bar type products.

When taste is not a clear advantage, often Awake will shy away from pushing new products to the market with an offering that does not engage their customers. Awake is continually looking at innovative ways to solve consumer problems, and this is often in the form of different forms of delivery—in this case a bite-sized candy instead of the more traditional Awake chocolate bar.

"Imagine if Awake was like an M&M type product, but better." And Awake realized through various trials and tribulations (like granola) that the main deciding factor for consumers will be taste. When looking for food and drink, consumers aim to achieve benefits that go beyond simply satisfying thirst and hunger. Consumers today have so many different alternatives that they can look for multiple benefits. For Awake, the inclusion of energy into a chocolate bar was the "aha" moment that caught the attention of Canadians from Dragons to regular consumers.

When looking at consumers' needs, it is important to look at the ways and environment environments in which they are will solve problems to meet their needs. For example, when consumers go to the movie theatre, they are tempted by a number of food and beverage choices. While the prices of these products seem exorbitant, there is the temptation that comes along with movie-watching experience. Awake Chocolate tried a pilot program in movie theatres to see how consumers enjoyed their products. The pilot was not very successful, largely because the format of pilot product did not suit the environment in which consumers were making decisions. Adam said, "I think we were trying to sell them the wrong product. We were selling them our full-sized caramel chocolate bar. And I think that something that is a little more bite sized and snackable, I think that's the right application there. … "Because if you just look at what people are buying in movie theatres, it's generally not chocolate bars. It's usually bags of bite sized chocolate pieces, or candies or popcorn."

So when Awake introduced "Bites," bite-sized individually wrapped chocolates with a caffeine equivalent of a half cup of coffee, its use in the workplace and on campus made a lot of sense given the portability and ease of consumption. These two factors are significant in another setting—the movie theatre. And Awake Chocolate hopes to one day have the chance to sell the candy-coated treat in theatres.

QUESTIONS

1. Prepare a defence of the following statement: "Awake Chocolate is unique in the food marketplace because, unlike other new products in this area, it is truly an engineered need."

2. Describe how psychological factors identified in this chapter may prevent some consumers loyal to existing products like M&Ms from trying the new Awake bite-sized candy products once they enter the market.

3. Using the concepts from this chapter, provide clear justification that Awake products are a more involved purchase than traditional chocolate bars and candies.

AWAKE Chocolate

6 | Business Marketing

Mirexon/Shutterstock.com

LEARNING OUTCOMES

6-1 Describe business marketing

6-2 Explain the differences between business and consumer marketing

6-3 Summarize the network and relationships approach to business marketing

6-4 State the fundamental aspects of business marketing

6-5 Classify business customers

6-6 Identify aspects of business buying behaviour

6-7 Describe the ways in which business marketing has gone online

"Pulling a good network together takes effort, sincerity and time."

—Alan Collins[1]

6-1 | WHAT IS BUSINESS MARKETING?

Describing business marketing is not as simple as inserting the word *business* in front of marketing terms and concluding that this is how it is different from consumer marketing. Business marketing is not only differentiated because of the volume of transactions between businesses or because there are unique jobs and career paths in business marketing.

business-to-business (B2B) marketing
the process of matching capabilities between two nonconsumer entities to create value for both organizations and the "customer's customer"; also referred to as *business marketing*

Business marketing is marketing. But it is marketing done differently. Business marketing is often referred to as **business-to-business (B2B) marketing**; it is a connection between two entities, and it is that which is vital to understanding the concept of business marketing. Too often when discussing marketing in textbooks like this one, B2B is treated as an afterthought or as a footnote to traditional marketing. But as you will find out, much of what traditional marketing does today is based on trends and efforts seen in B2B marketing for decades. Since we do not see B2B marketing happen in front of us like we do with consumer-focused marketing, we assume the B2B version of marketing lacks the importance of business-to-consumer (B2C) marketing; however, nothing could be further from the truth.

In Chapter 1, you encountered the concept of relationships and learned how successful marketers seek to build relationships with customers over time. The challenge in forming such relationships is to figure out how to create a system to keep track of all those customers (see Chapter 8 on customer relationship management). In business marketing, the number of customers is also the challenge in building relationships—not because there are so many but the exact opposite: because there are so few.

With limited options to choose from, it becomes important to treat any relationship with care and attention.

Marketing to consumers is often described as creating a marketing mix (recall the four Ps) and delivering it to a consumer. There is a sense that marketing when focused on promotion is an activity done separate from the consumer. In business marketing, there needs to be an active interaction between businesses to ensure needs are met. There needs to be trust, mutual respect, and an understanding that both parties working together can achieving both companies' goals.

6-2 | BUSINESS VERSUS CONSUMER MARKETING

In trying to describe marketing of any kind, we'll use examples that you can relate to: a consumer (the buyer) goes into a store and purchases a widely distributed product from a store (the seller). Often the discussion surrounds what the seller can do to better understand the needs of this customer, to determine why the consumer is buying the product, and to figure out how to influence this and future purchases. But what this explanation implies is that the customer is passive, simply waiting to be researched, analyzed, and retained.

In business marketing, neither the seller nor the buyer can afford to be passive. Neither business interest can rely on the other party doing all the work—there needs to be effort and cooperation on both sides of the exchange. This level of cooperation is not yet seen in consumer marketing, but that may change.

Consumer marketing is now seeing a more engaged buyer. Aided by the information and options afforded by technology, specifically the Internet and social media, consumers are taking a more active role in the exchange process of marketing. For example, term life insurance policy premiums were reduced quite significantly with the emergence of online insurance quote websites. Once consumers were given access to choice and information, they became less passive and more willing to actively involve themselves in the role of buyer.[2] For example, KANETIX. ca, a Canadian online insurance comparison website, offers consumers multiple quotes from a variety of insurance providers in Canada. In addition to comparing insurance rates, consumers can also check rates for home insurance, life insurance, and even pet insurance. Kanetix published results of a survey of Canadians that showed that almost half of respondents would be willing to share more information through their devices (e.g., Onstar for car insurance) if it meant reduced insurance premiums. In

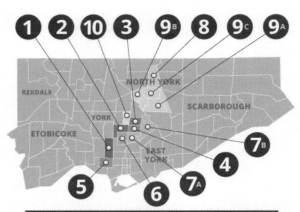

THE CHEAPEST
CAR INSURANCE RATES IN TORONTO

RANK	POSTAL CODE	AVG. RATE	MAIN INTERSECTION
1	**M6G**	**$1,479**	**Downtown Toronto (Christie)**
2	M5P	$1,486	Central Toronto (Forest Hill North)
3	M4P	$1,503	Central Toronto (Davisville North)
4	M4S	$1,505	Central Toronto (Davisville)
5	M6J	$1,511	West Toronto (Trinity)
6	M4V	$1,513	Central Toronto (Summerhill/Forest Hill)
7-A	M4T	$1,515	Central Toronto (Moore Park/Summerhill East)
7-B	M4G	$1,515	East York (Leaside)
8	M2K	$1,529	North York (Bayview Village)
9-A	M3B	$1,530	North York (Don Mills North)
9-B	M2P	$1,530	North York (York Mills)
9-C	M2L	$1,530	North York (York Mills)
10	M4R	$1,532	Central Toronto (North Toronto West)

*Average rates as determined by Kanetix.ca

KANETIX.CA
INSURANCE · MORTGAGES · CREDIT CARDS

Courtesy of Kanetix.ca

the same survey, though, over one third were concerned that this information could be hacked.[3] Developing trust with customers is essential to any business relationship (read more about this in Chapter 8).

Therefore, what has to be created in business marketing is a sense of involved self-interest mixed with mutual benefit. The Canadian Marketing Association, a leading advocate for the marketing community in Canada, has taken on this approach of mutual benefit when describing business marketing:

> What makes B2B different than consumer marketing is the complex nature of *relationships* and *interactions* that form a buying process and customer lifecycle that lasts months or years. It involves a *network* of individuals from buyer, seller, and even third-party partners who have different needs and interests.[4]

The terms provided in this quotation—*relationships*, *interactions*, and *networks*—are not always ones associated with marketing and need to be explained further. Let's now consider what these terms mean in the context of business marketing.

6-3 | THE NETWORK AND RELATIONSHIPS APPROACH TO BUSINESS MARKETING

In looking at business marketing from a network and relationships perspective, one must understand how each of these terms is meant and applied.

6-3a | Relationships in Business Marketing

Clearly, relationships are important in marketing, but they are usually the result of greater effort on one side (the seller). In business marketing, business relationships are more complex, as they involve greater commitment from both sides, and thus more company resources and effort. There are two particularly important aspects of such relationships: commitment and trust.

Relationship commitment is a business's belief that an ongoing relationship with some other business is so important that it warrants maximum efforts at maintaining it indefinitely.[5] A perceived breakdown in commitment by one of the parties often leads to a reduction in the relationship from the other party.

Trust exists when one party has confidence in an exchange partner's reliability and integrity.[6] It has been noted extensively that power plays a large role in trust between two business entities in a relationship. However, there was never agreement on whether having a large or small difference in power between partners is a good thing until a 2015 study in 2015 showed that power in fact plays a much smaller role in building trust between B2B partners. So what is the most important factor to ensure trust if it's not power? Goal congruence. The study published in *Industrial Marketing Management* magazine found that it was most important that the strategies of the two businesses were compatible. If this was true, there was a better chance that a shared vision could be reached, thus allowing for trust to be built.[7]

relationship commitment
a business's belief that an ongoing relationship with another business is so important that the relationship warrants maximum efforts at maintaining it indefinitely

trust
confidence in an exchange partner's reliability and integrity

The concepts of trust and commitment show the importance of collaboration between entities in a B2B relationship. To build and develop a relationship requires a level of cooperation that is not always comfortable for businesses used to competing for market share and industry profits. North American businesses often believe that laws and regulations are the most important components in maintaining business relationships. However, in many parts of the world, cooperation is a vital part of conducting business. In Japan, for example, exchange between businesses is based on personal relationships that are developed through what is called *amae*, or indulgent dependency. *Amae* is the feeling of nurturing concern for, and dependence on, another. Reciprocity and personal relationships contribute to *amae*. Relationships between companies can develop into a *keiretsu*—a network of interlocking corporate affiliates.

6-3b | Interaction in Business Marketing

There is a movement in marketing away from interruption toward interaction. Interruption marketing is often viewed as invasive ways in which companies have tried to insert their messages to consumers. It could be a direct mail piece in a company's shipment or a pop-up advertisement in an email to a customer.

What this interruption approach achieves are a series of one-off transactions, which generate short-term revenue and profits, but little in long-term gain. The movement toward interaction has to do with engaging with customer and creating content and experiences that the customer is interested in sharing.[8] A long-term perspective is precisely what interaction is about. An interaction can be seen as the culmination of numerous transactions (sales) between two business entities that build over time. Interaction includes not only transactions but also negotiations, discussions, and customizations—anything that is part of the relationship between the two organizations.

An example of transaction versus interaction can be seen with buying versus leasing an automobile. Car companies often prefer to lease vehicles, as evidenced by the many incentive programs offered for leasing vehicles. Through leasing programs, a car company can develop a relationship with the customer over time. If a customer buys a vehicle, on the other hand, the relationship may be limited to warranty issues and may end as soon as the customer drives off the lot.

The Industrial Marketing and Purchasing Group (IMP Group), a leading group of researchers in business marketing, developed an interaction model that provides a good explanation of interaction: "Business exchange cannot be understood as a series of disembedded and independent transactions of given resources—but rather as complex relationships between buying and selling organisations, where what is exchanged is created in interaction."[9]

6-3c | Networks in Business Marketing

The Canadian Marketing Association's definition of B2B marketing describes a "network" of buyers, sellers, and other third parties. This network approach to business marketing takes the interactions and relationships and places them into a bigger context.

To understand the network approach, we must note how it differs from other approaches to business marketing:

- *The sales approach:* If you look for "B2B marketing" on any search engine, most of the results will focus on sales and selling to companies. The sales approach is focused on generating leads and new business through various persuasion techniques. This approach focuses on what a company has to offer to other businesses, but very little time is spent on understanding the problems facing potential customers.

- *The market management approach:* This approach looks at B2B marketing much like B2C marketing. Develop a product, price it, place it, and promote it—all to a waiting set of customers. This approach focuses on that passive customer and assumes that all customers will have the same needs and will respond in a similar way.

- *The network approach:* This approach looks at the factors and forces around a company and the other companies that will have an impact on their business—suppliers, customers, and even competitors. Companies are encouraged to research the external marketplace and by doing so should develop an idea of the forces and challenges facing them and the rest of the companies in their network.

Companies in a network can then develop their relationships through interaction over time. Cooperation gets built into these networks as it becomes evident that working together can achieve goals that might not have been possible if one business had tried to work on its own or just on a transaction basis. See Exhibit 6.1 for an example of a representation of a business network.

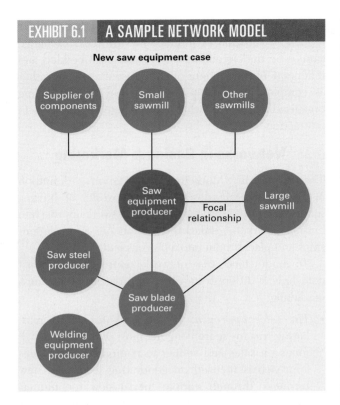
interaction and denotes mutual dependence and respect, and a network called a *keiretsu* is developed based on *amae*. Within a *keiretsu*, executives may sit on the boards of their customers or their suppliers. Members of a *keiretsu* trade with each other whenever possible and often engage in joint product development, finance, and marketing activity. Toyota's *keiretsu* functions best when its suppliers see themselves as not only connected to Toyota but also to each other. (See Exhibit 6.2.) And while there may be a risk that these companies must be adversaries in other car maker networks, it's vital that the advantages of the network approach outweigh more primal competitive concerns. Recently, an executive at Toyota's largest supplier, Denso, made an observation that is key to the network approach: "(Other suppliers) are all rivals. But they also might be future partners. In this era, it is very difficult to work alone. So, we also need to be well prepared to collaborate."[10]

In China, *guanxi* is a term that loosely means "relationships" or "networking," and in business, *guanxi* refers to a network of businesses tied together based on not only economic relationships but also personal relationships. *Guanxi* networks help to distinguish collaborators from competitors and serve to build trust in business relationships.[11] There can be negative aspects to the *guanxi* network model, as it can lead to a group of insiders unwilling to interact with external businesses and creating internal rules and regulations that fall outside the law. Many Canadian businesses have found that the best way to compete in Asian countries is to form relationships with Asian companies in order to properly and efficiently enter the market.

The concept of business networks is not new. Cooperation and making a profit are not seen as two competing forces in places like Japan and China. As mentioned earlier, in Japan, the concept of *amae* is used in business

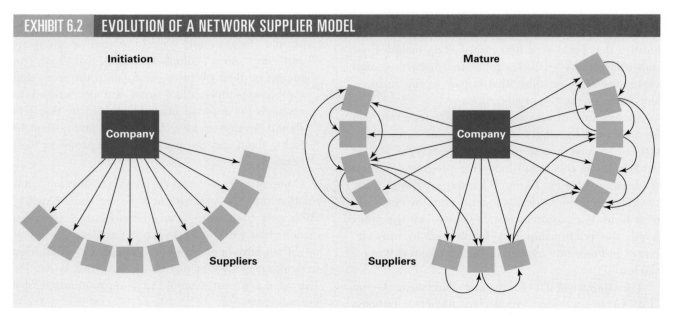

EXHIBIT 6.2 EVOLUTION OF A NETWORK SUPPLIER MODEL

Initiation

Company

Suppliers

Mature

Company

Suppliers

Trickle-Down Effect

As stories about layoffs and strikes at large automobile manufacturers appear in our news feed, we often think of the employees of those businesses and the impact on the local economy. And while these are clearly significant concerns, it is not often we think about the companies that supply those car companies and the impact of layoffs and closures on interrelated companies. For every car manufacturer, there are hundreds of supply companies that can be negatively affected by labour strife. In the case of General Motors 2019 employee strike, a number of *just-in-time* suppliers of GM parts like door panels had to shut down operations while waiting out the strike. Some suppliers had more than one-third of their overall business tied to General Motors.[12] In situations like this, it is important to see the importance of creating broad networks instead of relying on a concentrated group of companies for business survival.

Cole Burston/Bloomberg/Getty Images

BUMPER CROP—A FRUITFUL NETWORK

GARDN, the Green Aviation Research and Development Network, is an entity dedicated to fostering the development of technologies for quiet, clean, and sustainable air travel to increase the competitiveness of the Canadian aerospace industry. GARDN is a product of the funded and successful initiative from the Government of Canada called the Business-Led Networks of Centres of Excellence program (BL-NCE). The BL-NCE "funds large-scale collaborative research networks that bring a wide range of research expertise to bear on specific challenges identified by an industrial sector." Since its inception in 2009, GARDN has spearheaded 35 research and development projects, from improving engine core technologies on airplanes to recycling aerospace manufacturing materials into other commercial uses. Programs developed by GARDN include Canadian businesses like Bombardier, Bell Flight, Air Canada, Pratt & Whitney, and 15 universities across Canada in a network of 60+ members. One major achievement for GARDN was the development of the world's first civilian jet powered entirely by biofuel.

Sustainable
Aviation Fuels:
A Canadian
Perspective

2019

Courtesy of GARDN

Sources: Government of Canada, Networks of Centres of Excellence of Canada, "Green Aviation and Research and Development Network—GARDN," www.nce-rce.gc.ca/NetworksCentres-CentresReseaux/BLNCE-RCEE/GARDN_eng.asp (accessed July 8, 2020); GARDN, "GARDN Projects I 2009–2014," https://gardn.org/projects/gardn-i-projects-2009-2014/?lang=en (accessed July 8, 2020); GARDN, "GARDN Projects II 2014–2019," https://gardn.org/projects/gardn-ii-projects-2014-2019/?lang=en (accessed July 8, 2020); NCE Secretariat News Release: Strengthening an Electronics Manufacturing Ecosystem for Canada, April 16, 2019. https://www.nce-rce.gc.ca/Media-Medias/news-communiques/News-Communique_eng.asp?ID=200.

6-4 | FUNDAMENTAL ASPECTS OF BUSINESS MARKETING

Now that we can appreciate the importance of relationships and networks, let's look at the fundamental aspects of business marketing. These aspects highlight the importance of the purchasing relationship between buyer and seller in a business interaction. Without knowledge of the types of buyers, buying situations, products, and services in business marketing, it would be virtually impossible to create a network of strong relationships.

iStock.com/onurdongel

6-4a | Types of Demand

Because demand in business markets is driven by comparatively fewer buyers, there are aspects of demand that are important to consider. These include derived, inelastic, and joint demand.

DERIVED DEMAND The demand for business products is called **derived demand** because organizations buy products to be used in producing their customers' products. For example, the market for lithium, glass screens, and microchips are derived from the demand for cellular phones. These items are valuable only as components of cellular phones. Demand for these items rises and falls with the demand for cellular phones.

Because demand is derived, business marketers must carefully monitor demand patterns and changing preferences in final consumer markets, even though their customers are not in those markets. Moreover, business marketers must carefully monitor their customers' forecasts because derived demand is based on expectations of future demand for those customers' products.

Some business also try to influence final consumer demand. For example, aluminum producers use television and magazine advertisements to point out the convenience and recycling opportunities that aluminum offers to consumers who can choose to purchase juice and soft drinks in either aluminum or plastic containers.

INELASTIC DEMAND The demand for many business products is inelastic with regard to price. *Inelastic demand* means that an increase or a decrease in the price of the product will not significantly affect demand for the product.

The price of a product used either in the production of another product or as part of another product is often a minor portion of the final product's total price. Therefore, demand for the final consumer product is not affected. If the price of pill casings for pharmaceutical drugs went up 200 percent in one year, would the price increase affect the introduction of new drugs in a given year? That's highly doubtful. That's inelastic demand.

JOINT DEMAND Joint demand refers to the demand for two or more items used together in a final product. For example, a decline in the availability of memory chips will slow the production of tablets like an iPad, which will in turn reduce the demand for disk drives. Likewise, the demand for the Apple operating system (iOS) exists as long as there is demand for Apple devices. Sales of the two products are directly linked.

FLUCTUATING DEMAND The demand for business products, particularly for new plants and equipment, tends to be less stable than the demand for consumer products. A small increase or decrease in consumer demand can produce a much larger change in demand for the facilities and equipment needed to make the consumer product. Economists refer to this phenomenon as the **multiplier effect** (or **accelerator principle**).

6-4b | Number of Customers

Business marketers usually have far fewer customers than consumer marketers. The advantage is that it is much easier to identify prospective buyers, monitor

---

derived demand
demand in the business market that comes from demand in the consumer market

joint demand
the demand for two or more items used together in a final product

multiplier effect (accelerator principle)
the phenomenon in which a small increase or decrease in consumer demand can produce a much larger change in demand for the facilities and equipment needed to make the consumer product

current customers' needs and levels of satisfaction, and personally attend to existing customers. The main disadvantage is that each customer becomes crucial—especially for those manufacturers that have only one customer. In many cases, this customer is the Canadian government. The success or failure of one bid can make the difference between prosperity and bankruptcy.

6-4c | Location of Buyers

Business customers tend to be much more geographically concentrated than consumers. For instance, many of Canada's largest B2B buyers are located in or around the large urban centres of Canada: Toronto, Montréal, Calgary, and Vancouver. The oil and gas industry is centred in Alberta and Saskatchewan, the automotive industry in southwestern Ontario, and the wine industry primarily in British Columbia and southern Ontario.

6-4d | Type of Negotiations

Consumers are used to negotiating prices on automobiles and real estate. In most cases, however, Canadian consumers expect sellers to set the price and other conditions of sale, such as time of delivery and credit terms. In contrast, negotiating is common in business marketing. Buyers and sellers negotiate product specifications, delivery dates, payment terms, and other pricing matters. Sometimes these negotiations occur during many meetings over several months. Final contracts are often very long and detailed.

6-4e | Use of Reciprocity

Business purchasers often choose to buy from their own customers, a practice known as **reciprocity**. Once trust is developed in a business network, reciprocity is a natural progression where companies will become each other's best customers. For example, General Motors (GM) buys engines for use in its automobiles and trucks from BorgWarner, which in turn buys many of the automobiles and trucks it needs from GM. This practice is neither unethical nor illegal unless one party coerces the other and the result is unfair competition. The Japanese *keiretsu* and Chinese *guanxi* are good examples of systems that encourage reciprocity.

6-4f | Use of Leasing

Consumers normally buy products rather than lease them. But businesses commonly lease expensive equipment, such as computers, construction equipment and vehicles, and automobiles. Leasing allows businesses to reduce their capital outflow, acquire a seller's latest products, receive better services, and gain tax advantages.

The lessor, the business providing the product, may be either the manufacturer or an independent business. The benefits to the lessor include greater total revenue from leasing compared with selling and an opportunity to do business with customers who cannot afford to buy.

> **reciprocity**
> a practice where business purchasers choose to buy from their own customers

Education Derivation

Here is a quick activity to help you understand derived demand better: take the textbook you have in your hands (or on your laptop or mobile phone). First, think about all the companies that had to work together for this textbook to have been published. Done? Your list should have included pulp and paper companies, ink producers, binding companies (for the hard copy of the book), the publisher, the companies with pictures in the textbook, and of course the postsecondary institutions (instructors, bookstore). The question that remains is, What is the consumer demand that the demand for a marketing textbook is derived from? (Answer: see the picture beside.)

EXHIBIT 6.3 | TYPES OF BUSINESS PRODUCTS

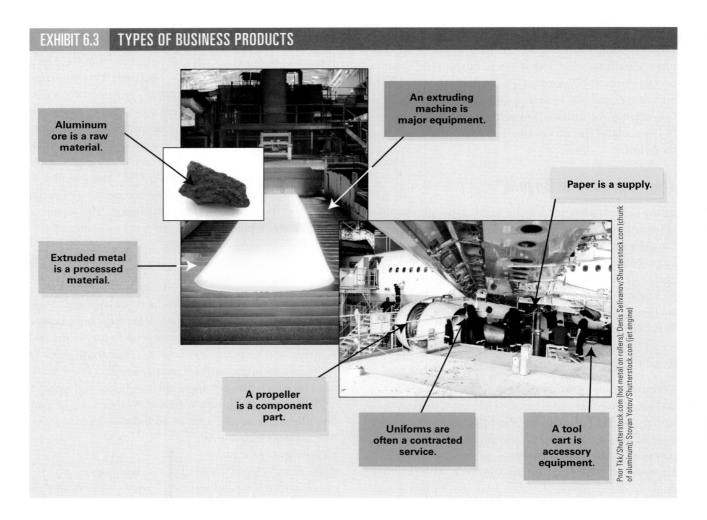

Aluminum ore is a raw material.

An extruding machine is major equipment.

Paper is a supply.

Extruded metal is a processed material.

A propeller is a component part.

Uniforms are often a contracted service.

A tool cart is accessory equipment.

Pnor Tkk/Shutterstock.com (hot metal on rollers); Denis Selivanov/Shutterstock.com (chunk of aluminum); Stoyan Yotov/Shutterstock.com (jet engine)

The concept of leasing fits well into the relationships and network model. A lease provides the basis for a long-term interaction, where two companies are reliant on each other for either payment for or use of a leased product.

6-4g | Types of Business Products

There are numerous types of business products, and there are different classification systems used for them. (See Exhibit 6.3.) Here are the main categories:

- *Major equipment:* large and expensive purchases that depreciate over time (e.g., buildings, machinery);

- *Accessory equipment:* smaller in size and expense than major equipment, this equipment is more standardized and often sold to consumers as well (e.g., power tools, printers);

- *Raw materials:* unprocessed or untapped materials that are extracted or harvested for consumption of further processing (e.g., oil, canola, potash);

- *Component parts and materials:* finished products ready for assembly or requiring very little in the way of further processing to become part of other products (e.g., engines, pulp paper, chemicals); and

- *Supplies:* consumable items that are not part of the final product but provide some solution to a business's needs (e.g., pencils, paper, coffee).

BUSINESS SERVICES Business services include a number of actions that are not necessarily part of the final product but may have a direct impact on the customer's willingness to buy and maintain a relationship over time. While services can be as basic as hiring janitorial staff to clean an office on a weekend, there are important services that can be provided to customers.

Providing a support or help line for customers to help with or troubleshoot any challenges with a product is one example of an important business service. With the rising importance of leasing options for a number of

business services
complementary and ancillary actions that companies undertake to meet business customers' needs

industries, the product becomes only part of the interaction, as much of the focus is placed on the services that are needed during the leasing period.

6-5 | CLASSIFYING BUSINESS CUSTOMERS

Now that the major components of business marketing have been identified, it is time to turn our attention to the business customer. While traditional means of segmentation are not as useful in business marketing because of the unique nature of the business customer, there are still means with which to organize and structure business customers.

6-5a | Major Categories of Business Customers

The business market consists of four major categories of customers: producers, resellers, governments, and institutions.

PRODUCERS The producer segment of the business market includes profit-oriented individuals and organizations that use purchased goods and services to produce other products, to incorporate into other products, or to facilitate the daily operations of the organization. Examples of producers are construction, manufacturing, transportation, finance, real estate, and food service businesses. In the early 2000s, Canada was a major exporter of cars, pulp and paper, and electronics. Today, all those areas of production have lower export numbers. These areas of production have been replaced by oil and gas, minerals, chemicals, and food products.[13] It is believed that some of the jobs lost from the car industry earlier in the century might return. However, it is likely these "jobs" will be taken by artificial intelligence of some kind—be it computer or robot.

Producers are often called **original equipment manufacturers (OEMs)**. This term includes all individuals and organizations that buy business goods and incorporate them into the products that they produce for eventual sale to other producers or to

original equipment manufacturers (OEMs) individuals and organizations that buy business goods and incorporate them into the products that they produce for eventual sale to other producers or to consumers

IMPORTANCE OF BEING MALLEY-ABLE

Malley Industries is a New Brunswick–based manufacturer of specialized vehicles and automotive-related aftermarket components. The unique nature of its ambulance interior is what differentiates Malley in the highly competitive US market. Malley ambulances are manufactured using the company's lightweight thermo-formed composite interior that increases workable space, reduces operating costs, and improves safety due to providing rounded surfaces and angled access to equipment. The company uses the same design principles to manufacture partitions and wall liner kits for commercial automotive fleets and provides similar innovations in the vehicles it adapts for wheelchair securement for special care facilities and individuals. This company has been successful by meeting clients' varying needs and ensuring that its products exceed customer expectations. Its growth has been a result of its ability to diversify and develop creative methods and products to solve problems for their expanding customer base. The company's innovative approach to meeting customer needs has made it a leading provider of ambulances and custom components across North America. Malley ambulances are in service in Haiti, Chile, Israel, Puerto Rico, and more.

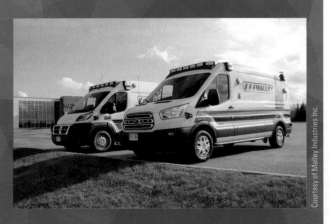

Courtesy of Malley Industries Inc.

Sources: Inda Intiar, "Dieppe's Malley Industries Enters New Market With Ambulance Delivery to Israel" Huddle website, October 1, 2019. https://huddle.today/dieppes-malley-industries-enters-new-market-with-ambulance-delivery-to-israel/ (accessed Feb 6, 2020); "Malley: About Us," www.malleyindustries.com/about/ (accessed Feb 6, 2020).

consumers. Companies such as General Motors that buy steel, paint, tires, and batteries are said to be OEMs.

RESELLERS The reseller market includes retail and wholesale businesses that buy finished goods and resell them for a profit. A retailer sells mainly to final consumers; wholesalers sell mostly to retailers and other organizational customers. Wholesalers are predominately smaller business (98 percent have fewer than 100 employees) with 76 percent of companies making a profit.[14]

Consumer product businesses, such as Procter & Gamble, McCain Foods, and Canada Dry Motts, sell directly to large retailers and retail chains and through wholesalers to smaller retail units. Retailing is explored in detail in Chapter 14.

Business product distributors are wholesalers that buy business products and resell them to business customers. They often carry thousands of items in stock and employ sales forces to call on business customers. Businesses that want to buy a gross of pencils or a hundred kilograms of fertilizer typically purchase these items from local distributors rather than directly from manufacturers.

GOVERNMENTS A third major segment of the business market is government. Government organizations include thousands of federal, provincial or territorial, and municipal buying units. They make up what may be the largest single market for goods and services in Canada.

Contracts for government purchases are often put out for bid. Interested vendors submit bids (usually sealed) to provide specified products during a particular time. Sometimes the lowest bidder is awarded the contract. When the lowest bidder is not awarded the contract, strong evidence must be presented to justify the decision. Grounds for rejecting the lowest bid include lack of experience, inadequate financing, or poor past performance. Bidding allows all potential suppliers a fair chance at winning government contracts and helps ensure that public funds are spent wisely.

FEDERAL GOVERNMENT Name just about any good or service and chances are that someone in the federal government uses it. The federal government buys goods and services valued at approximately $16.05 billion per year, making it the country's largest customer.[15]

Although much of the federal government's buying is centralized, no single federal agency contracts for all the government's requirements, and no single buyer in any agency purchases all that the agency needs. We can view the federal government as a combination of several large companies with overlapping responsibilities and thousands of small independent units.

MUNICIPAL, ACADEMIC, SOCIAL, AND HOSPITALS (MASH) Many of the entities in this category are run by either provincial, territorial, or local governments. These are significant customers in their size and scope in the Canadian market: health and social services institutions employ 2.52 million people, while educational services employ over 1.4 million.[16]

In Canada, each province and territory sets its own regulations and buying procedures within this municipal, academic, social, and hospitals (MASH) sector. The potential for both large and small vendors is great, however, as more than 6000 municipal clients are spread across all the provinces and territories.

INSTITUTIONS The fourth major segment of the business market consists of institutions that seek to achieve goals other than the standard business goals of profit, market share, and return on investment. Excluding the MASH sector, this segment includes places of worship, labour unions, fraternal organizations, civic clubs, foundations, and other so-called nonbusiness organizations. Many businesses have a separate sales force that calls on these customers.

6-5b | Classification by Industry

If you are looking for more detail than a general classification of business customers provides, you can look to the NAICS system. The **North American Industry Classification System (NAICS)** is an industry classification system for North American business establishments. The system, developed jointly by the United States, Canada, and Mexico, provides a common industry classification system. It had been established as part of the basis of the North American Free Trade Act established in 1994. With the ratification in late 2019 of the new United States–Mexico–Canada Agreement (USMCA) agreement between the three countries, it remains to be seen if there will be any changes to how the NAICS system is arranged.

In the current NAICS system, goods- or service- producing businesses that use identical or similar production processes are grouped together. (See Exhibit 6.4.) This makes searching for, and finding, companies that provide products and services in hundreds of different industries across North America more efficient.

North American Industry Classification System (NAICS)
an industry classification system developed by the United States, Canada, and Mexico to classify North American business establishments by their main production processes

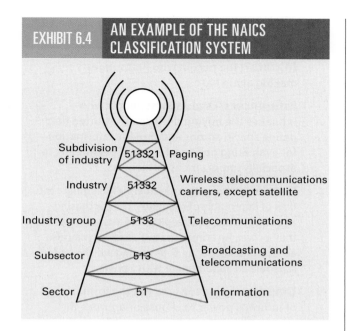

EXHIBIT 6.4 | AN EXAMPLE OF THE NAICS CLASSIFICATION SYSTEM

Subdivision of industry	513321	Paging
Industry	51332	Wireless telecommunications carriers, except satellite
Industry group	5133	Telecommunications
Subsector	513	Broadcasting and telecommunications
Sector	51	Information

NAICS is an extremely valuable tool for business marketers engaged in analyzing, segmenting, and targeting markets. Each classification group is relatively homogeneous with regard to raw materials required, components used, manufacturing processes employed, and problems faced. The more digits in a code, the more homogeneous the group is. Therefore, if a supplier understands the needs and requirements of a few companies within a classification, requirements can be projected for all companies in that category. The number, size, and geographic dispersion of companies can also be identified. This information can be converted to market potential estimates, market share estimates, and sales forecasts. It can also be used for identifying potential new customers. NAICS codes can help identify companies that may be prospective users of a supplier's goods and services. For a complete listing of all NAICS codes, visit www.naics.com.

6-6 | BUSINESS BUYING BEHAVIOUR

Once you are able to identify your customers, you still have to understand how they make purchase decisions. Learning about the makeup and motivation behind business buying provides excellent insights for marketers on how to create products and services that meet the needs of business customers.

6-6a | Buying Centres

A **buying centre** includes all those people in an organization who become involved in the purchase decision.

Membership and influence vary from company to company. For instance, in engineering-dominated companies, such as Bell Helicopter, the buying centre may consist almost entirely of engineers. In marketing-oriented companies, such as Toyota and IBM, marketing and engineering have almost equal authority. In consumer goods companies, such as Procter & Gamble, product managers and other marketing decision makers may dominate the buying centre. In a small manufacturing company, almost everyone may be a member.

The number of people involved in a buying centre varies with the complexity and importance of the purchase decision. The composition of the buying group will usually change from one purchase to another and sometimes even during various stages of the buying process. To make matters more complicated, buying centres do not appear on formal organization charts.

For example, although a formal committee may have been set up to choose a new plant site, such a committee is only part of the buying centre. Other people, such as the company president, often play informal yet powerful roles. In a lengthy decision-making process, such as finding a new plant location, some members may drop out of the buying centre when they can no longer play a useful role. Others whose talents are needed then become part of the centre. No formal announcement is ever made concerning "who is in" and "who is out."

NATURE OF BUYING Unlike consumers, business buyers usually approach purchasing rather formally. Businesses use professionally trained purchasing agents or buyers who spend their entire career purchasing a limited number of items. They get to know the items and the sellers well. Some professional purchasers earn the designation of Certified Purchasing Manager (CPM) after participating in a rigorous certification program.

NATURE OF BUYING INFLUENCE Typically, more people are involved in a single business purchase decision than in a consumer purchase.

ROLES IN THE BUYING CENTRE Compared to consumer buying decisions, several people may play a role in the business purchase process.

IMPLICATIONS OF BUYING CENTRES FOR THE MARKETING MANAGER Successful vendors realize the importance of identifying who is in the decision-making unit, each member's relative influence in the buying decision, and each

> **buying centre**
> all those people in an organization who become involved in the purchase decision

member's evaluative criteria. Successful selling strategies often focus on determining the most important buying influences and tailoring sales presentations to the evaluative criteria most important to these buying-centre members. For example, Loctite Corporation, the manufacturer of Super Glue and industrial adhesives and sealants, found that engineers were the most important influencers and deciders in adhesive and sealant purchase decisions. As a result, Loctite focused its marketing efforts on production and maintenance engineers.

6-6b | Buying Situations

Business companies, especially manufacturers, must often decide whether to make something or buy it from an outside supplier. The decision is essentially one of economics. Can an item of similar quality be bought at a lower price elsewhere? If not, is manufacturing it in-house the best use of limited company resources? For example, Briggs & Stratton Corporation, a major manufacturer of four-cycle engines, might be able to save $150 000 annually on outside purchases by spending $500 000 on the equipment needed to produce gas throttles internally. Yet Briggs & Stratton could also use that $500 000 to upgrade its carburetor assembly line, which would save $225 000 annually. If a company does decide to buy a product instead of making it, the purchase will either be a new task buy, a modified rebuy, or a straight rebuy.

NEW TASK BUY A **new task buy** is a situation requiring the purchase of a product for the first time. For example, suppose a manufacturing company needs a better way to page managers while they are working on the shop floor. Currently, each of the several managers has a distinct ring—for example, two short and one long, which sounds over the plant intercom when a manager is being paged in the factory. The company decides to replace its buzzer system of paging with hand-held wireless radio technology that will allow managers to communicate immediately with the department initiating the page. This situation represents the greatest opportunity for new vendors. No long-term relationship has been established for this product, specifications may be somewhat fluid, and the buyers are generally more open to new vendors.

new task buy
a situation requiring the purchase of a product for the first time

modified rebuy
a situation where the purchaser wants some change in the original good or service

---

BUSINESS PURCHASING ROLES

- **Initiator:** the person who first suggests making a purchase.

- **Influencers/Evaluators:** people who influence the buying decision. They often help define specifications and provide information for evaluating options. Technical personnel are especially important as influencers.

- **Gatekeepers:** group members who regulate the flow of information. Frequently, the purchasing agent views the gatekeeping role as a source of their power. An administrative assistant may also act as a gatekeeper by determining which vendors schedule an appointment with a buyer.

- **Decider:** the person who has the formal or informal power to choose or approve the selection of the supplier or brand. In complex situations, it is often difficult to determine who makes the final decision.

- **Purchaser:** the person who actually negotiates the purchase. It could be anyone from the president of the company to the purchasing agent, depending on the importance of the decision.

- **Users:** members of the organization who will actually use the product. Users often initiate the buying process and help define product specifications.

If the new item is a raw material or a critical component part, the buyer cannot afford to run out of supply. The seller must be able to convince the buyer that the seller's company consistently delivers a high-quality product on time.

MODIFIED REBUY A **modified rebuy** is normally less critical and less time consuming than a new buy. In

MONOPOLY919/Shutterstock.com

a modified-rebuy situation, the purchaser wants some change in the original good or service. It may be a new colour, greater tensile strength in a component part, more respondents in a marketing research study, or additional services in a janitorial contract.

Because the two parties are familiar with each other and credibility has been established, buyer and seller can concentrate on the specifics of the modification. In some cases, though, modified rebuys are open to outside bidders. The purchaser uses this strategy to ensure that the new terms are competitive. An example is a manufacturing company buying radios with a vibrating feature for managers who have trouble hearing the ring over the factory noise. The company may open the bidding to examine the price/quality offerings of several suppliers.

STRAIGHT REBUY A **straight rebuy** is the situation vendors prefer. The purchaser is not looking for new information or new suppliers. An order is placed and the product is provided as in previous orders. Usually, a straight rebuy is routine because the terms of the purchase have been agreed to in earlier negotiations. An example would be the previously cited manufacturing company purchasing, on a regular basis, additional radios from the same supplier.

One common instrument used in straight-rebuy situations is the purchasing contract. Purchasing contracts are used with high-volume products that are bought frequently. In essence, because of the purchasing contract, the buyer's decision making becomes routine and the salesperson is promised a sure sale. The advantage to the buyer is a quick, confident decision, and the advantage to the salesperson is reduced or eliminated competition.

Suppliers must remember not to take straight-rebuy relationships for granted. Retaining existing customers is much easier than attracting new ones.

6-6c | Evaluative Criteria for Business Buyers

Business buyers evaluate products and suppliers against three important criteria: quality, service, and price—often in that order.

QUALITY In evaluative criteria, quality refers to technical suitability. A superior tool can do a better job in the production process, and superior packaging can increase dealer and consumer acceptance of a brand. Evaluation of quality also applies to the salesperson and the salesperson's company. Business buyers want to deal with reputable salespeople and companies that are financially responsible. Quality improvement should be part of every organization's marketing strategy.

SERVICE Almost as much as business buyers want satisfactory products, they also want satisfactory service. A purchase offers several opportunities for service. Suppose a vendor is selling heavy equipment. Prepurchase service could include a survey of the buyer's needs. After thorough analysis of the survey findings, the vendor could prepare a report and recommendations in the form of a purchasing proposal. If a purchase results, postpurchase service might consist of installing the equipment and training those who will be using it. Postpurchase services may also include maintenance and repairs. Another service that business buyers seek is dependability of supply. They must be able to count on delivery of their order when it is scheduled to be delivered. Buyers also welcome services that help them to sell their finished products. Services of this sort are especially appropriate when the seller's product is an identifiable part of the buyer's end product.

PRICE Business buyers want to buy at low prices—at the lowest prices, in most circumstances. However, when a buyer pressures a supplier to cut prices to a point where the supplier loses money, the supplier is almost forced to take shortcuts on quality. The buyer also may, in effect, force the supplier to quit selling to the buyer, which will then need to find a new source of supply.

SUPPLIER–BUYER RELATIONSHIP The three buying situations described above provide a context to the changing nature of supplier–buyer relationships. While there can be some stability with a straight rebuy, often buyers are looking for the supplier to make adjustments and improvement to maintain the relationship over time. The supplier–buyer relationship has been called "the backbone of economic activities in the modern world." A recent study looked at the supplier–buyer relationship by examining 130 suppliers and the multinational company with which they were conducting business. It was determined that the average number of years of a supplier–buyer relationship was slightly over six. The suppliers came from different industries and provided different products ranging from machinery and equipment to component parts and materials. The researchers in this study also noted that the more of an identity that suppliers create in their networks, the stronger and more sustainable the relationships become.[17]

straight rebuy
a situation in which the purchaser reorders the same goods or services without looking for new information or new suppliers

6-7 | BUSINESS MARKETING ONLINE

The online world presents a great opportunity for business marketing. Given the challenge of trying to find customers and suppliers to create a network of solid relationships, companies are looking online for help. While the possibilities for business marketing online are immense, the B2B world is still trying to find the best way to conduct business online.

The creation and growth of business marketing online followed a pattern similar to that of the Internet. As websites became more advanced and online security was improved, businesses began to conduct business online. The term *e-commerce* was first attached to the B2B world and described the transactions that were taking place between businesses online. Given the sheer volume of products and services exchanged between businesses around the world, the ability to complete transactions online created a buzz.

Huge sales numbers were published, touting an online e-commerce world with billions of dollars changing hands in transactions. Canadian consumers are becoming more comfortable purchasing online, with 87 percent making a recent online purchase and 47 percent of respondents making a recent purchase on their mobile phone.[18] It is becoming more important that businesses offer a clear and consistent online presence, as two-thirds of respondents stated they would be more likely to purchase from a company that has a website, and 49 percent would be more likely to give to a charity with an online site.[19]

With new technologies creating excellent online interfaces, it is perplexing why Canadian B2B companies do not invest more time and effort to create a stronger online presence. Companies that reported selling to consumers had a much higher likelihood of having a website than businesses focused on selling to other businesses.

A recent BDC study of Canadian businesses with an online presence showed that only 4 out of 10 companies sell, receive, or take orders online. Reasons why 60 percent of respondents are not taking advantage of an online presence were: data concerns (32), lack of understanding of online purchasing requirements (25%), and the challenges in hiring appropriate talent to complete the necessary tasks for online engagement (24%).[20] See Exhibit 6.5 for usage rates of specific B2B marketing tactics.

Another study found that the most likely reason that Canadian companies do not invest in a more interactive online presence is concerns over data breaches. More than one quarter (28) of companies surveyed stated that they had been a victim of an online data breach. Even more concerning was that 25 percent of companies queried stated they had no plans for recovery if an attack took place and, most concerning,

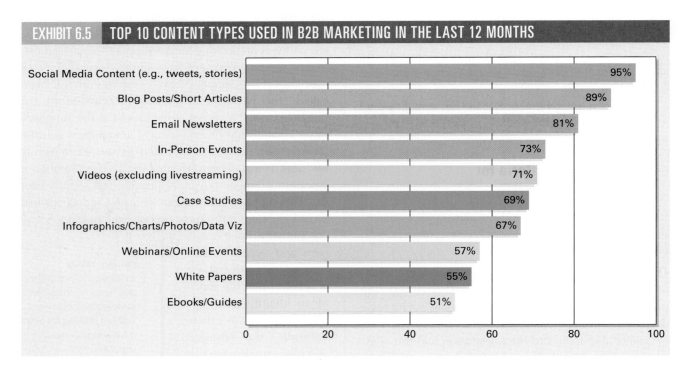

EXHIBIT 6.5 TOP 10 CONTENT TYPES USED IN B2B MARKETING IN THE LAST 12 MONTHS

Content Type	Percentage
Social Media Content (e.g., tweets, stories)	95%
Blog Posts/Short Articles	89%
Email Newsletters	81%
In-Person Events	73%
Videos (excluding livestreaming)	71%
Case Studies	69%
Infographics/Charts/Photos/Data Viz	67%
Webinars/Online Events	57%
White Papers	55%
Ebooks/Guides	51%

Source: Content Marketing Institute, B2B Content Marketing 2020: Benchmarks, Budgets, and Trends – North America. https://contentmarketinginstitute.com/wp-content/uploads/2019/10/2020_B2B_Research_Final.pdf

almost half said they would not inform customers of a cyberattack.[21]

There are many roadblocks for online B2B marketing in Canada, but there are some trends in the marketplace that might make this move forward a little easier.

6-7a | Trends in B2B Online Marketing

A number of new technologies and approaches can help businesses improve online presence and sales.

THE GROWTH OF MOBILE The numbers relating to mobile phone usage and commerce in Canada continue to grow in comparison to all types of media. In 2019, for the first time, mobile phone usage (90%) was greater than Internet access (89%). More households owned mobile phones (89.5%) than home computers (84.1).[22]

As more consumers become comfortable with mobile technologies at home, there is a greater likelihood for them to find comfort in using mobile technologies for business and work purposes.

IMPORTANCE OF CONTENT MARKETING Borrowing from the B2C market is another solid trend for business marketers. An area of greater importance for B2B marketers online is getting the word out about their company—which is what content marketing is all about. Recently, the B2B Content Marketing Benchmarks Report was published, and it reported that 65 percent of companies surveyed had a documented content marketing strategy, up 3 percent from the year before.[23] Much of that content marketing is happening online with B2B online content marketing tools, such as blogs, articles on websites, e-newsletters, videos, and the most popular—social media.

SOCIAL MEDIA GROWTH While many view social media as a consumer-driven phenomenon, it is important to remember that some of the earliest adopters of social media were companies with a strong B2B component: IBM, Sun Microsystems, and Hewlett Packard. Given the importance of each relationship in business marketing, companies need to put a great deal of time and effort into making sure their social media presence is handled properly.

However, it is becoming clearer that simply a presence in social media will not be good enough to create true engagement. Customers are beginning to use social media as a method of inquiry, be it for more information about a company or to voice concern over an issue with a company. Companies using social media send 20 times more promotional messages over social media than actual responses to

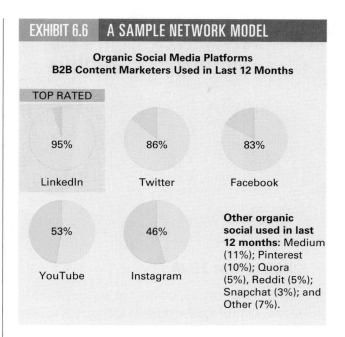

EXHIBIT 6.6   A SAMPLE NETWORK MODEL

Organic Social Media Platforms B2B Content Marketers Used in Last 12 Months

TOP RATED

LinkedIn 95%
Twitter 86%
Facebook 83%
YouTube 53%
Instagram 46%

Other organic social used in last 12 months: Medium (11%); Pinterest (10%); Quora (5%), Reddit (5%); Snapchat (3%); and Other (7%).

Source: Content Marketing Institute, B2B Content Marketing 2020: Benchmarks, Budgets, and Trends – North America. https://contentmarketinginstitute.com/wp-content/uploads/2019/10/2020_B2B_Research_Final.pdf

customer queries. This can be quite problematic in a B2B environment where both the speed and nature of a response can have a significant impact on the relationship between two companies. Therefore, it is vital that companies embarking in the social space for B2B have a clear policy for ensuring that any account representing a company will do so in a responsible and responsive manner.

Research shows that social media has great value for B2B decision makers: 75 percent of B2B buyers and 84 percent of executives use social media to help make purchase decisions. Top salespeople have noted that using social media platforms is a key element in being able to secure and finalize business deals.[24] The most effective social media platform continues to be LinkedIn, as seen in Exhibit 6.6.

With regard to social media effectiveness for B2B interactions, it is clear that LinkedIn still leads the way. As a social media platform, LinkedIn is seen as a great resource for human resources looking for new talent, but lead generation for sales and networking for executives are becoming even more popular than any human resource function. The LinkedIn environment can be a potential source for finding new vendors, partners, and other business interactions. According to Hubspot, LinkedIn is 277 percent more effective at lead generation than Facebook and Twitter.[25]

AWAKE CHOCOLATE
CONTINUING CASE

AWAKE Chocolate

2B2B or Not 2B2B

Awake Chocolate is a Canadian success story, but one that is playing out mostly south of the 49th parallel. The founders of Awake have chosen to focus their efforts more on the US market than Canada. This can be seen even when searching for Awake online: you will be taken to one of two websites. Both sites look identical, with the exception of the Canadian and American flags adorning the top right corner of each page.

The only real difference between the two sites is that the US site has a few more product options, including granola products (which were mentioned in Chapter 5). Ironically, both sites offer the ability to search for retailers; however, both sites ask for the US-based zip code.

These two different sites bely the two different B2B approaches taken by Awake Chocolate. Awake cofounder Matt Schnarr notes that the focus on US markets makes sense from a financial perspective: "There are a few elements that are deliberate about (the US focus), population is not the only reason. We make our product in Canada and sell it in the US, right off the bat (revenues) are 30 percent bigger for the same amount of effort."

But currency rates are not the only reason for Awake's US-based focus. Due to a lack of competition, the Canadian retail market presents a bit of a challenge for consumer product companies like Awake. Major food retailers such as Loblaw's, Sobeys, and Metro all charge listing fees, which is money paid to a retailer by a manufacturer or other intermediary in order to get their product on store shelves. Matt Schnarr observes that in the United States "nobody charges listing fees. It's a totally different way to do business."

In the United States, there seems to be more opportunity to build relationships with different businesses. As mentioned previously, Awake often conducts market research at postsecondary campuses. Schnarr states there are approximately 40 to 60 schools that Awake could sell to in Canada versus thousands in the United States. As well, "Amazon is a major, major driver for our business there (US), and we still consider ourselves to be in the infancy of the Amazon funnel. ...They are a major part of our business."

Through Amazon Awake can not only sell its products and achieve exposure but also sell excess product. At most retailers in Canada, the 40 percent or so excess product would simply be returned and not sold—something that is challenging for a relatively small producer like Awake.

Awake has created two unique approaches to B2B interactions. One approach involves a more traditional B2B model, where a sales team is hired to try to push products onto store shelves. But Schnarr noted, "I would say that … 70 percent of our business is specialty/e-commerce versus … traditional."

No matter which side of the border they are on, the focus is on finding unique ways to answer the question that Matt Schnarr feels is fundamental: "Where am I going to be when I'm tired?" And the way in which Awake structures its business relationships, the hope is that that an Awake product will be there.

QUESTIONS

1. **Create the business network for Awake Chocolate. Be sure to include the traditional and specialty relationships that exist for the company using its two approaches.**

2. **Describe the importance of Awake creating interactions in its business network, and how this type of relationship is important in a competitive market like Canada.**

3. **Explain the following statement: the MASH group of business organizations is the most important for Awake Chocolate.**

AWAKE Chocolate

7 | Segmenting, Targeting, and Positioning

LEARNING OUTCOMES

7-1 Discuss markets, market segments, and the importance of market segmentation

7-2 Describe the bases commonly used to segment consumer and business markets

7-3 Discuss criteria for successful market segmentation

7-4 List the steps involved in segmenting markets

7-5 Discuss alternative strategies for selecting target markets

7-6 Explain how and why companies implement positioning strategies and how product differentiation plays a role

"In the business world, the rearview mirror is always clearer than the windshield."

—Warren Buffet[1]

7-1 | MARKET SEGMENTATION

The term **market** means different things to different people. We are all familiar with the supermarket, stock market, labour market, fish market, and flea market. All these types of markets share several characteristics. First, they are composed of people (consumer markets) or organizations (business markets). Second, these people or organizations have wants and needs that can be satisfied by particular product categories. Third, they have the ability to buy the products they seek. Fourth, they are willing to exchange their resources, usually money or credit, for desired products. In sum, a market is (1) people or organizations with (2) needs or wants and with (3) the ability and (4) the willingness to buy. A group of people or an organization that lacks any one of these characteristics is not a market.

Within a market, a **market segment** is a subgroup of people or organizations sharing one or more characteristics that cause them to have similar product needs. At one extreme, we can define every person and every organization in the world as a market segment because each is unique. At the other extreme, we can define the entire consumer market as one large market segment and the business market as another large segment. All people have some similar characteristics and needs, as do all organizations.

From a marketing perspective, market segments can be described as being somewhere between the two extremes. The process of dividing a market into meaningful, relatively similar, and identifiable segments or groups is called **market segmentation**. The purpose of market segmentation is to enable the marketer to

market
people or organizations with needs or wants and the ability and willingness to buy

market segment
a subgroup of people or organizations sharing one or more characteristics that cause them to have similar product needs

market segmentation
the process of dividing a market into meaningful, relatively similar, and identifiable segments or groups

tailor marketing mixes to meet the needs of one or more specific segments.

7-1a | The Importance of Market Segmentation

Until the 1960s, few companies practised market segmentation. When they did, it was more likely a haphazard effort rather than a formal marketing strategy. Before 1960, for example, the Coca-Cola Company produced only one beverage and aimed it at the entire soft drink market. Today, Coca-Cola offers more than a dozen different products to market segments on the basis of diverse consumer preferences for flavours and for calorie and caffeine content. Coca-Cola offers traditional soft drink flavours, energy drinks (Powerade), organic bottled tea (Honest Tea), fruit drinks (Minute Maid, Simply Orange), and water (Dasani).[2]

Market segmentation plays a key role in the marketing strategy of most successful organizations and is a powerful marketing tool. Market segmentation enables marketers to identify groups of customers with similar needs and to analyze the characteristics and buying behaviour of these groups. That information forms the basis of marketing mixes designed specifically with the characteristics and desires of one or more segments. Because market segments differ in size and potential, segmentation helps decision makers to more accurately define marketing objectives and better allocate resources. In turn, performance can be better evaluated when objectives are more precise. The 60-year-old company Canada Goose has stayed true to its roots and brand promise, creating luxury "Made in Canada" outdoor apparel for extreme weather conditions for consumers who are willing to pay a premium for the Canada Goose guarantee of warmth in extreme conditions.[3]

7-2 | BASES FOR SEGMENTING CONSUMER MARKETS

Marketers use **segmentation bases**, or **variables**, which are characteristics of individuals, groups, or organizations, to divide a total market into segments. The choice of

segmentation bases (variables)
characteristics of individuals, groups, or organizations

segmentation bases is crucial because an inappropriate segmentation strategy may lead to lost sales and missed profit opportunities. The key is to identify bases that will produce substantial, measurable, and accessible segments that exhibit different response patterns to marketing mixes.

Markets can be segmented by using a single variable, such as age group, or by using several variables, such as age group, gender, and education. Although a single-variable segmentation is less precise, it has the advantage of being simpler and easier to use than multiple-variable segmentation. The disadvantages of multiple-variable segmentation are that it is often more difficult to use than single-variable segmentation; usable secondary data are less likely to be available; and, as the number of segmentation bases increases, the size of the resulting segments decreases. Nevertheless, the current trend is toward using more rather than fewer variables to segment most markets. Multiple-variable segmentation is clearly more precise than single-variable segmentation.

To maximize the potential of multiple-variable segmentation, marketers often turn to data-driven consulting firms such as Environics Analytics, which utilizes data-driven research and an extensive suite of data-based products and services to help organizations better understand their customer segments to create marketing campaigns that maximize return on investment. As an example, Arc'teryx, an outdoor equipment and sports clothing manufacturer headquartered in Vancouver was seeking to expand its branded stores beyond its single location in Montreal, but wasn't sure which geographic areas would be most profitable. Environics analysts identified geographic concentrations of customers, collected sales data from bricks-and-mortar and e-commerce transactions of their distributors over a five-year period, and then used a proprietary database to create target groups of core customers based on demographics, lifestyles, and social values. In calculating where to open a branded store, Environics researchers completed an analysis that identified demographics and lifestyles that predicted sales. They then mapped the results to ensure that a new location would not compete with the current distributor network. The result was 12 prospective branded store locations in Canada and the United States described by sales potential, new and current customers, and competition.[4]

geographic segmentation
segmenting markets by region of a country or the world, market size, market density, or climate

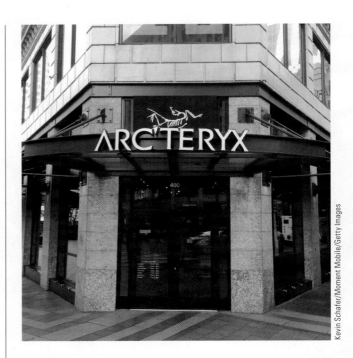

Kevin Schafer/Moment Mobile/Getty Images

Consumer goods marketers commonly use one or more of the following characteristics to segment markets: geography, demographics, psychographics, benefits sought, and usage rate.

7-2a | Geographic Segmentation

Geographic segmentation refers to segmenting markets by a region of a country or a region of the world, market size, market density, or climate. Market density means the number of people within a unit of land. Climate is commonly used for geographic segmentation because of its dramatic impact on residents' needs and purchasing behaviour. Snow blowers, water and snow skis, clothing, and air-conditioning and heating systems are products with varying appeal, depending on climate.

Consumer goods companies often take a geographic approach to marketing. Walmart uses this approach when testing new technology. When testing what it called the "Urban Supercentre" concept, the retail giant chose a store in Toronto's west end. The tech-savvy customers in this neighbourhood can scan their purchases using their phones as they shop and have their credit card charged on their way out of the store.[5]

7-2b | Demographic Segmentation

Marketers often segment markets on the basis of demographic information because such information is widely available and often relates to consumers' buying and consuming behaviour. Some common bases of

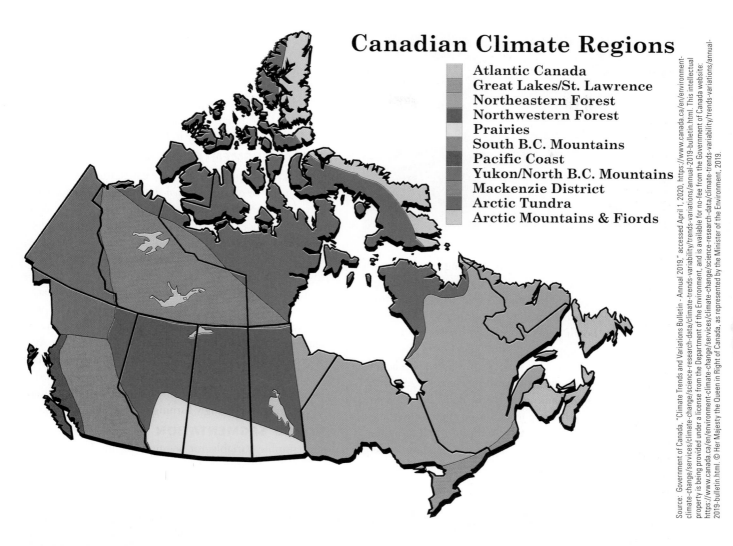

Canadian Climate Regions

Atlantic Canada
Great Lakes/St. Lawrence
Northeastern Forest
Northwestern Forest
Prairies
South B.C. Mountains
Pacific Coast
Yukon/North B.C. Mountains
Mackenzie District
Arctic Tundra
Arctic Mountains & Fiords

demographic segmentation are age, gender, income, ethnic background, occupation, and family life cycle (FLC).

AGE SEGMENTATION Marketers use a variety of terms to refer to different age groups: newborns, infants, preschoolers, young children, tweens, teens, young adults, baby boomers, millennials, Generation X, Generation Y, and seniors. Age segmentation can be an important tool identifying potential profitable market segments with unique needs and wants.

Many companies have long targeted parents of babies and young children with products such as disposable diapers, baby food, and toys. Recently, other companies that have not traditionally marketed to young children are developing products and services to attract this group. For example, the high-intensity fitness company CrossFit developed a program for kids.[6]

Children, through the spending of their allowances, earnings, and gifts, account for and influence a great deal of consumption. Tweens (ages 10 to 14) comprise approximately 2 million of Canada's total population. The teenage market (ages 15 to 19) includes more than 2 million individuals, and, like tweens, this market accounts for substantial purchasing power.[7] This age group is concerned about social and environmental issues and will force brands to be more responsible in these areas. Social media is good way to connect with these consumers, who are technology savvy but have a short attention span and focused on brand names.[8]

Generation Y—or as they are often called, *Gen-Ys* or *millennials*—are those born between 1979 and 2000. With about 10 million Canadians in this demographic group, millennials are a significant segment to consider. Millennials represent over 27 percent of the population and 35 percent of them are still living at home with their parents. The spending

> **demographic segmentation**
> segmenting markets by age, gender, income, ethnic background, occupation, and family life cycle

patterns of this groups varies depending on if they are still living at home with their parents or if they have a family of their own. They make fewer trips to the store than other age group but they spend more in each trip.[9]

The baby boom generation, born between 1947 and 1965, represents approximately 27 percent of the entire Canadian population. This generation is quickly reaching retirement age, bringing a host of new challenges to the Canadian economy and marketers. Baby boomers are often nostalgic and eager to continue their active lives, and many can now afford to buy top-of-the-line models of products from their youth. Baby boomers are leading the luxury real estate market and are driving demand for luxury holidays. About 19 percent of baby boomers are

now considered seniors (those aged 65 and older) and this group is especially attracted to companies that build relationships by taking the time to get to know them and their preferences.[10] Canadian seniors are increasingly using technology to communicate with others. In the 65- to 74-year-old age range, 81 percent are using the Internet. Senior men are more likely to be online than women.[11]

GENDER SEGMENTATION Segmenting the market by gender is simple and, in many cases, the obvious variable to use. For example, facial shaving products for men. In recent years, however, segmenting the market along traditional gender roles has been challenged. As younger consumers, who grew up challenging gender stereotypes, become more important to marketers' gender boundaries are becoming blurred.[12] Many products that were once identified as male or female, such as earrings or facial creams, are now marketed to both genders. The way companies are portraying gender in their advertising is changing as described in the Unilever Is Changing Attitudes again box. The shopping habits of male and female consumers are also changing in part due to social media. For example, men are more informed and proactive shoppers who are increasingly turning to e-commerce.[13]

INCOME SEGMENTATION Income is a popular demographic variable for segmenting markets because income level influences consumers' wants and determines their buying power. Many markets are segmented

UNILEVER IS CHANGING ATTITUDES AGAIN

When Unilever launched the award-winning marketing campaign "Real Beauty" in an attempt to change attitudes about what was beautiful, it started a major change in how the company promoted personal care products. The company is now taking the same approach to their products aimed at men.

About 10 years ago, Unilever launched its Dove Men+Care line of personal care . The company wanted to build on the success of the Real Beauty campaign and launched its "Real Heroes" that strove to break gender stereotypes. The ads attempted to change the perspective on masculinity—that the caring side of men is a sign of strength. The ads presented everyday dads as heroes.

Sources: Christopher Lombardo, "Dove Men+Care Funds Documentary About Dads at TIFF," Strategy online, http://strategyonline.ca/2019/09/06/dove-mencare-funds-documentary-about-dads-at-tiff/, September 6, 2019; Melissa Dunne, "MOY 2019: Sharon MacLeod Builds Bridges to the Next Generation of Men," Strategy online, http://strategy online. ca/2019/01/07/moy-2019-sharon-macleod-builds-bridges-to-the-next-generation-of-men, January 7, 2019; Unilever website, www.unilever.com, accessed January 20, 2020.

by income, including the markets for housing, clothing, automobiles, and food. For example, in the auto industry, many car manufacturers have two different brands aimed at different income groups, such as Honda and Acura; Nissan and Infiniti; Toyota and Lexus.

ETHNIC SEGMENTATION Canada is a very culturally diverse country, and Canadian marketers are strongly aware of the multicultural makeup of the market. When considering Canada's ethnic communities, marketers might first focus on French Canadian and English Canadian markets, which are the largest, but they will then consider the other ethnic populations. Many companies are segmenting their markets according to ethnicity, and some marketers are developing unique approaches to sizable ethnic segments.

Tracking ethnic communities is one of a multicultural marketer's most challenging and most important tasks. Some companies have found that segmenting according to the main ethnicities is not precise enough.

OCCUPATION SEGMENTATION As a college or university student, you purchase products related to your school program—computers, special equipment, and so on. The same goes for any occupation. Nurses need to purchase uniforms, and workers in the construction trades need to purchase tools. Segmenting the market based on occupation makes sense for those products that are used in particular occupations. Segmenting the market by occupation is more common in business-to-business markets but can be used in the consumer market for some products.

FAMILY LIFE-CYCLE SEGMENTATION Consumer buying behaviour varies, and the variations are often not sufficiently explained by the demographic factors of gender, age, and income. The consumption patterns among people of the same age and gender frequently differ because they are in different stages of the **family life cycle (FLC)**. The FLC is a series of stages determined by a combination of age, marital status, and the presence or absence of children.

Hurst Photo/Shutterstock.com

As of July 2019, Statistics Canada estimates that there more than 10 million families in Canada. Out of this number, more than 80 percent are classified as couple family and the remainder as single-parent families.[14]

Exhibit 7.1 illustrates numerous FLC patterns and shows how families' needs, incomes, resources, and expenditures differ at each stage. The horizontal flow shows the traditional FLC. The lower part of the exhibit lists some of the characteristics and purchasing patterns of families in each stage of the traditional life cycle. The exhibit also acknowledges that about half of all first marriages end in divorce. When young married couples move into the young-divorced stage, their consumption patterns often revert to those of the young-single stage of the cycle. About four out of five divorced persons remarry by middle age and re-enter the traditional life cycle, as indicated in the exhibit by the recycled flow.

At certain points in the life cycle, consumers are especially receptive to marketing efforts. Soon-to-be-married couples are typically considered to be the most receptive because they are making brand decisions about products that could last longer than their marriages. Similarly, young parents are targeted by companies promoting baby products, as these parents expect to have higher expenses. A thorough understanding of the FLC can help marketers to design, develop, and successfully sell their products in the most competitive manner.

7-2c | Psychographic Segmentation

Age, gender, income, ethnicity, FLC stage, and other demographic variables are usually helpful in developing segmentation strategies, but often they don't paint the entire picture. Demographics provide the skeleton, but psychographics add meat to the bones. **Psychographic segmentation** is market segmentation on the basis of the following variables:

- *Personality:* Personality is a person's traits, attitudes, and habits. Clothing is the ultimate personality descriptor. Fashionistas wear high-end trendy clothes while hipsters enjoy jeans and T-shirts with tennis shoes. People buy clothes that they feel represent their personalities and give others an idea of who they are.

family life cycle (FLC)
a series of stages determined by a combination of age, marital status, and the presence or absence of children

psychographic segmentation
market segmentation on the basis of personality, motives, lifestyles, and geodemographic categories

EXHIBIT 7.1   FAMILY LIFE CYCLE

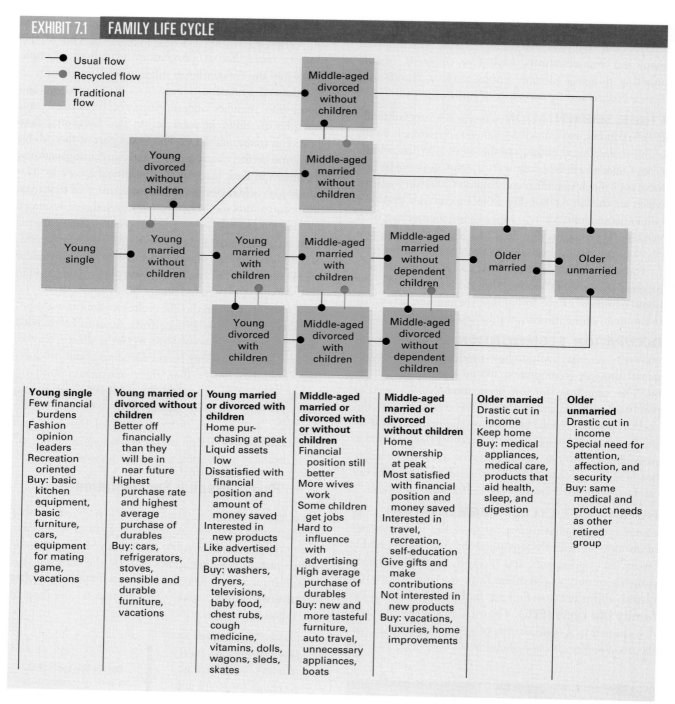

- Usual flow
- Recycled flow
- Traditional flow

Young single	Young married or divorced without children	Young married or divorced with children	Middle-aged married or divorced with or without children	Middle-aged married or divorced without children	Older married	Older unmarried
Few financial burdens	Better off financially than they will be in near future	Home purchasing at peak	Financial position still better	Home ownership at peak	Drastic cut in income	Drastic cut in income
Fashion opinion leaders	Highest purchase rate and highest average purchase of durables	Liquid assets low	More wives work	Most satisfied with financial position and money saved	Keep home	Special need for attention, affection, and security
Recreation oriented	Buy: cars, refrigerators, stoves, sensible and durable furniture, vacations	Dissatisfied with financial position and amount of money saved	Some children get jobs	Interested in travel, recreation, self-education	Buy: medical appliances, medical care, products that aid health, sleep, and digestion	Buy: same medical and product needs as other retired group
Buy: basic kitchen equipment, basic furniture, cars, equipment for mating game, vacations		Interested in new products	Hard to influence with advertising	Give gifts and make contributions		
		Like advertised products	High average purchase of durables	Not interested in new products		
		Buy: washers, dryers, televisions, baby food, chest rubs, cough medicine, vitamins, dolls, wagons, sleds, skates	Buy: new and more tasteful furniture, auto travel, unnecessary appliances, boats	Buy: vacations, luxuries, home improvements		

- *Motives:* Marketers of baby products and life insurance appeal to consumers' emotional motives—namely, to care for their loved ones. Using appeals to economy, reliability, and dependability, carmakers such as Subaru target customers by appealing to their rational motives. Car makers like Mercedes-Benz, Jaguar, and Cadillac appeal to customers with status-related motives.

- *Lifestyles:* Lifestyle segmentation divides people into groups according to the way they spend their time, the importance of the things around them, their beliefs, and socioeconomic characteristics such as income and education. For example, record stores specializing in vinyl are targeting young people who enjoy listening to independent labels and pride themselves on being independent of big business. LEED-certified appliances appeal to environmentally conscious "green" consumers. PepsiCo is promoting its no-calorie, sugar-free, flavoured water, Aquafina FlavorSplash, to consumers who are health conscious.[15]

- *Geodemographics:* **Geodemographic segmentation** clusters potential customers into neighbourhood lifestyle categories. It combines geographic, demographic, and lifestyle segmentations. Geodemographic segmentation helps marketers develop marketing programs tailored to prospective buyers who live in small geographic regions, such as neighbourhoods, or who have very specific lifestyle and demographic characteristics. Canadian Blood Services was able to utilize geodemographics and social values to identify communities that had a high potential of blood donors and then open clinics in those areas. The data not only supported the opening of new clinics, but also assisted in evaluating performance of the clinic against realistic benchmarks, ensuring subsequent marketing strategies were appropriately created.[16]

Psychographic variables can be used individually to segment markets or can be combined with other variables to provide more detailed descriptions of market segments. Environics Analytics has created a statistical tool that divides the Canadian population into 68 different lifestyle types. The clusters combine basic demographic data, such as age, ethnicity, and income, with lifestyle information, such as media and sports preferences, taken from consumer surveys. For example, the "Satellite Burbs" group comprises older, upscale, exurban couples and families with an average household income of $143 173 who enjoy spending time with tight-knit groups but have a global consciousness. Satellite Burbs are family-centric, active in their religious community, and enthusiastic about purchasing products and services; they see themselves as opinion leaders and influencers to their peers. They are more likely to drive a domestic sports vehicle, enjoy The Movie Network, purchase books online, and frequent Pinterest. They prefer Canadian whisky and enjoy shopping at factory outlet stores.[17] This information, combined with other information, can be extremely helpful to marketers.

7-2d | Benefit Segmentation

Benefit segmentation is the process of grouping customers into market segments according to the benefits they seek from the product. Most types of market segmentation are based on the assumption that related subgroups of people or organizations share one or more characteristics that cause them to have similar product needs. Benefit segmentation is different because it groups potential customers on the basis of their needs or wants rather than some other characteristic, such as age or gender. Mobile phone customers, for example, can be divided into three benefit segments: work-oriented customers, highly social customers, and customers who consider mobile phones as a status symbol.[18]

Customer profiles can be developed by examining demographic information associated with people seeking certain benefits. This information can be used to match marketing strategies to selected target markets. A Tesco grocery store in Scotland is testing what it calls a "relaxed checkout line." It is slower paced than normal lines and is staffed by employees trained by an Alzheimer's group. This checkout line has benefits for anyone who feels they need extra time, such as those with dementia, or perhaps parents with small children.[19] Sobeys grocery stores in Canada have implemented a similar program aimed at customers with autism or those who are sensitive to sound and light. During certain hours of the week the stores have "sensory friendly" shopping. The store lighting is turned down and noise is reduced as much as possible by turning off the music.[20]

geodemographic segmentation
clusters potential customers into neighbourhood lifestyle categories

benefit segmentation
the process of grouping customers into market segments according to the benefits they seek from the product

7-2e | Usage-Rate Segmentation

Usage-rate segmentation divides a market by the amount of product bought or consumed. Categories vary depending on the product, but they are likely to include some combination of the following: former users, potential users, first-time users, light or irregular users, medium users, and heavy users. Segmenting by usage rate enables marketers to focus their efforts on heavy users or to develop multiple marketing mixes aimed at different segments. Because heavy users often account for a sizable portion of all product sales, some marketers focus on the heavy-user segment. Developing customers into heavy users is the goal behind many frequency and loyalty programs.

The **Pareto Principle (80/20 rule)** holds that approximately 20 percent of all customers generate around 80 percent of the demand. Although the percentages usually are not exact, the general idea often holds true.

7-2f | Bases for Segmenting Business Markets

The business market consists of four broad groups: producers, resellers, government, and institutions (for a detailed discussion of the characteristics of these segments, see Chapter 6). Whether marketers focus on only one or on all four of these groups, they are likely to find diversity among potential customers. Thus further market segmentation offers just as many benefits to business marketers as it does to consumer-product marketers.

COMPANY CHARACTERISTICS Company characteristics, such as geographic location, type of company, company size, and product use, can be important segmentation variables. Some markets tend to be regional because buyers prefer to purchase from local suppliers, and distant suppliers may have difficulty competing in price and service. Therefore, companies that sell to geographically concentrated industries benefit by locating close to their markets.

Segmenting by customer type allows business marketers to tailor their marketing mixes to the unique needs of particular types of organizations or industries. Many companies are finding this form of segmentation to be quite effective. For example, Lowes, one of the largest do-it-yourself retailers in Canada, has targeted professional repair and remodelling contractors in addition to consumers.

A commonly used basis for business segmentation is volume of purchase (heavy, moderate, light). Another is the buying organization's size, which may affect its purchasing procedures, the types and quantities of products it needs, and its responses to different marketing mixes. Many products, especially raw materials, such as steel, wood, and petroleum, have diverse applications. How customers use a product may influence the amount they buy, their buying criteria, and their selection of vendors.

BUYING PROCESSES Many business marketers find it helpful to segment current and prospective customers on the basis of how they buy. For example, companies can segment some business markets by ranking key purchasing criteria, such as price, quality, technical support, and service. Atlas Corporation developed a commanding position in the industrial door market by providing customized products in just four weeks, which was much faster than the industry average of 12 to 15 weeks. Atlas's primary market is companies with an immediate need for customized doors.

The purchasing strategies of buyers may provide useful segments. Two purchasing profiles that have been identified are satisficers and optimizers. **Satisficers** are business customers who place their order with the first familiar supplier to satisfy their product and delivery requirements. **Optimizers**, on the other hand, are business customers who consider numerous suppliers (both familiar and unfamiliar), solicit bids, and study all proposals carefully before selecting one.

dragon_fang/Shutterstock.com

Piotr Marcinski/Shutterstock.com

---

usage-rate segmentation
dividing a market by the amount of product bought or consumed

Pareto Principle (80/20 rule)
a principle holding that approximately 20 percent of all customers generate around 80 percent of the demand

satisficers
business customers who place their order with the first familiar supplier to satisfy their product and delivery requirements

optimizers
business customers who consider numerous suppliers, both familiar and unfamiliar, solicit bids, and study all proposals carefully before selecting one

The personal characteristics of the buyers themselves (their demographic characteristics, decision styles, tolerance for risk, confidence levels, job responsibilities, etc.) influence their buying behaviour and thus offer a viable basis for segmenting some business markets.

7-3 | CRITERIA FOR SUCCESSFUL SEGMENTATION

To be useful, a segmentation scheme must produce segments that meet four basic criteria:

1. *Substantiality:* A segment must be large enough to warrant developing and maintaining a special marketing mix. This criterion does not necessarily mean that a segment must have many potential customers. Marketers of custom-designed homes and business buildings, commercial airplanes, and large computer systems typically develop marketing programs tailored to each potential customer's needs. In most cases, however, a market segment needs many potential customers to make commercial sense.

2. *Identifiability and measurability:* Segments must be identifiable and their size measurable. Data on the population within geographic boundaries, the number of people in various age categories, and other social and demographic characteristics are often easy to get, and they provide fairly concrete measures of segment size.

3. *Accessibility:* The company must be able to reach members of targeted segments with customized marketing mixes. Some market segments are more difficult to reach—for example, senior citizens (especially those with reading or hearing disabilities), individuals who don't speak English, and people who are illiterate.

4. *Responsiveness:* Markets can be segmented by using any criteria that seem logical. Unless one market segment responds to a marketing mix differently from other segments, however, that segment need not be treated separately. For instance, if all customers are equally price conscious about a product, marketers have no need to offer high-, medium-, and low-priced versions to different segments.

7-4 | STEPS IN SEGMENTING A MARKET

The purpose of market segmentation, in both consumer and business markets, is to identify marketing opportunities. Markets are dynamic, so it is important that companies proactively monitor their segmentation strategies over time. Often, once customers or prospects have been assigned to a segment, marketers think their task is done. After customers are assigned to an age segment, for example, they stay there until they reach the next age bracket or category, which could be 10 years in the future. Thus the segmentation classifications are static, but the customers and prospects are changing. Marketing managers typically follow these six steps to segment a market based on the criteria described in the previous sections:

1. *Select a market or product category for study.* Define the overall market or product category to be studied. It may be a market in which the company already competes, a new but related market or product category, or a totally new market or category.

2. *Choose a basis or bases for segmenting the market.* This step requires managerial insight, creativity, and market knowledge. No scientific procedures guide the selection of segmentation variables. However, a successful segmentation scheme must produce segments that meet the four basic criteria discussed earlier in this chapter.

3. *Select segmentation descriptors.* After choosing one or more bases, the marketer must select the segmentation descriptors. Descriptors identify the specific segmentation variables to use. For example, a company that selects usage segmentation needs to decide whether to pursue heavy users, nonusers, or light users.

4. *Profile and analyze segments.* The profile should include the segments' sizes, expected growth, purchase frequency, current brand usage, brand loyalty, and long-term sales and profit potential. This information can then be used to rank potential market segments by profit opportunity, risk, consistency with organizational mission and objectives, and other factors important to the company. Included in the profile is the creation of a target persona, which is a holistic description of the target group that creates a three-dimensional picture. It is a composite sketch that aids in the creation of strong and targeted communications strategies.

5. *Select target markets.* Selecting target markets is not a part of the segmentation process but is a natural outcome of the segmentation process. It is a major decision that influences and often directly determines the company's marketing mix. This topic is examined in detail later in this chapter.

EXHIBIT 7.2 ADVANTAGES AND DISADVANTAGES OF TARGET MARKETING STRATEGIES

Targeting Strategy	Advantages	Disadvantages
Undifferentiated targeting	Potential savings on production/marketing costs	Unimaginative product offerings
		Company more susceptible to competition
Concentrated targeting	Concentrates resources	Segments too small or changing
	Can better meet the needs of a narrowly defined segment	Large competitors may more effectively market to niche segment
	Allows some small companies to better compete with larger companies	
	Provides strong positioning	
Multisegment targeting	Greater financial success	High costs
	Economies of scale in producing/marketing	Cannibalization
One-to-One targeting	Delivers highly customized service	High costs
	High customer engagement/retention	
	Increasing revenue through loyalty	

6. *Design, implement, and maintain appropriate marketing mixes.* The marketing mix has been described as product, place (distribution), promotion, and pricing strategies intended to bring about mutually satisfying exchange relationships with target markets. Chapters 9 through 18 explore these topics in detail.

Not all segments are stable over time and dynamic segmentation reflects real-time changes made to market segments based on a customer's ongoing search and shopping behaviours. For example, the website of Chapters Indigo, the bookselling chain, suggests book titles based on a site visitor's browsing and purchase pattern. Similar segmentation techniques are also used by Netflix and many companies utilizing online marketing today. Dynamic segmentation uses advanced mathematical and computer programming techniques to offer highly customized solutions to customers.

7-5 | STRATEGIES FOR SELECTING TARGET MARKETS

So far, this chapter has focused on the market segmentation process, which is only the first step in deciding whom to approach about buying a product. The next task is to choose one or more target markets. A target market is a group of people or organizations for which an organization designs, implements, and maintains a marketing mix intended to meet the needs of that group, resulting in mutually satisfying exchanges.

undifferentiated targeting strategy
a marketing approach that views the market as one big market with no individual segments and thus uses a single marketing mix

Because most markets will include customers with different characteristics, lifestyles, backgrounds, and income levels, a single marketing mix is unlikely to attract all segments of the market. Thus, if a marketer wants to appeal to more than one segment of the market, it must develop different marketing mixes. Four general strategies are used for selecting target markets—undifferentiated, concentrated, multisegment, and one-to-one targeting. Exhibit 7.2 illustrates the advantages and disadvantages of each targeting strategy.

7-5a | Undifferentiated Targeting

A company using an **undifferentiated targeting strategy** essentially adopts a mass-market philosophy, viewing the market as one big one with no individual segments. The company uses one marketing mix for the entire market. A company that adopts an undifferentiated targeting strategy assumes that individual customers have similar needs that can be met through a common marketing mix. Thus marketers of commodity products, such as flour and sugar, are likely to use an undifferentiated targeting strategy.

The first company in an industry sometimes uses an undifferentiated targeting strategy. With no competition, the company may not need to tailor marketing mixes to the preferences of market segments. At one time, Coca-Cola used this strategy with its single product offered in a single size in a familiar shaped bottle. Undifferentiated marketing allows companies to save on production and marketing and achieve economies of mass production. Also, marketing costs may be lower when a company has only one product to promote and a single channel of distribution.

Too often, however, an undifferentiated strategy emerges by default rather than by design, reflecting a failure to consider the advantages of a segmented approach. The result is often sterile, unimaginative product offerings that have little appeal to anyone. Another problem associated with undifferentiated targeting is the company's greater susceptibility to competitive inroads. Coca-Cola forfeited its position as the leading cola seller in supermarkets to Pepsi-Cola in the late 1950s, when Pepsi began offering its cola in several sizes.

Undifferentiated marketing can succeed. A grocery store in a small, isolated town may define all the people who live in the town as its target market. It may offer one marketing mix that generally satisfies everyone. This strategy is not likely to be as effective, however, when a community has three or four grocery stores.

7-5b | Concentrated Targeting

Companies using a **concentrated targeting strategy** select a market **niche** (one segment of a market) to target their marketing efforts. Because the company is appealing to a single segment, it can concentrate on understanding the needs, motives, and satisfactions of that segment's members and on developing and maintaining a highly specialized marketing mix. Some companies find that concentrating resources and meeting the needs of a narrowly defined market segment is more profitable than spreading resources over several different segments.

Small companies often adopt a concentrated targeting strategy to compete effectively with much larger companies. This strategy is often used by smaller family-owned restaurants in order to compete with the larger fast-food restaurant chains.

Concentrated targeting violates the old adage "Don't put all your eggs in one basket." If the chosen segment is too small or if it shrinks because of environmental changes, the company may suffer negative consequences. For instance, OshKosh B'gosh was highly successful selling children's clothing in the 1980s. It was so successful, however, that children's clothing came to define the company image to the extent that the company could not sell clothes to anyone else. Attempts to market clothing to other market segments were unsuccessful. Recognizing that it was in the children's wear business, the company expanded into products such as children's eyeglasses, shoes, and other accessories. A concentrated strategy can also be disastrous for a company that is not successful in its narrowly defined target market. For example, before Procter & Gamble introduced Head & Shoulders shampoo, several small companies were already selling antidandruff shampoos. Head & Shoulders was intro-

KK Stock/Shutterstock.com

duced with a large promotional campaign, and the new brand immediately captured over half the market. Within a year, several of the companies that had been concentrating on this market segment went out of business.

7-5c | Multisegment Targeting

A company that chooses to serve two or more well-defined market segments and develops a distinct marketing mix for each has a **multisegment targeting strategy**. Maple Leaf Foods offers many different kinds of bacon, such as regular and salt-reduced bacon. For convenience-seeking consumers, the company has developed Ready Crisp microwaveable bacon. For health-conscious segments, it offers turkey and chicken bacons.

Multisegment targeting is used for stores and shopping formats, not just for brands. Gap Inc. uses multisegment targeting to reach more than one customer segment with different brands within the store portfolio. The Gap brand itself targets individuals interested in a casual style, Athleta targets the fitness-minded women, Banana Republic reaches a slightly more sophisticated and less price-conscious shopper, while Old Navy is targeting a shopper interested in style but concerned with price.[21]

Multisegment targeting offers many potential benefits to companies, including

concentrated targeting strategy
a strategy used to select one segment of a market to target marketing efforts

niche
one segment of a market

multisegment targeting strategy
a strategy that chooses two or more well-defined market segments and develops a distinct marketing mix for each

greater sales volume, higher profits, larger market share, and economies of scale in manufacturing and marketing. Yet it may also involve greater product design, production, promotion, inventory, marketing research, and management costs. Before deciding to use this strategy, companies should compare the benefits and costs of multisegment targeting to those of undifferentiated and concentrated targeting.

Another potential cost of multisegment targeting is **cannibalization**, which occurs when sales of a new product cut into sales of a company's existing products. In many cases, however, companies prefer to steal sales from their own brands rather than lose sales to a competitor. Marketers may also be willing to cannibalize existing business to build new business.

7-5d | One-to-One Marketing

Most businesses today use a mass-marketing approach designed to increase *market share* by selling their products to the greatest number of people. For many businesses, however, a more efficient and profitable strategy is to use **one-to-one marketing** to increase their *share of customers*—in other words, to sell more products to each customer. The goal is to reduce costs through customer retention while increasing revenue through customer loyalty. Infinit Nutrition Canada is an energy beverage company that recognizes that athletes compete at different levels in different sports. This variability requires an energy beverage designed for each athlete's calorie, electrolyte, and carbohydrate requirements, as well as flavour preferences and strength. Using an online tool or through one-on-one consultations, the right beverage is created. With a 100 percent guarantee, athletes can vary the formulation until one that suits their unique needs is created.[22]

As many companies have discovered, a detailed and segmented understanding of the customer can be advantageous. There are at least four trends that will lead to the continuing growth of one-to-one marketing:

- *Personalization:* The one-size-fits-all marketing of the past is no longer relevant. Consumers want to be treated as the individuals they are, with their own unique sets of needs and wants. By its personalized nature, one-to-one marketing can fulfill this desire.

- *Time savings:* Consumers will have little or no time to spend shopping and making purchase decisions. Because of the personal and targeted nature of one-to-one marketing, consumers can spend less time making purchase decisions and more time doing the things that are important.

- *Loyalty:* Consumers will be loyal only to those companies and brands that have earned their loyalty and reinforced it at every purchase occasion. One-to-one marketing techniques focus on finding a company's best customers, rewarding them for their loyalty, and thanking them for their business.

- *Technology:* Advances in marketing research and database technology will allow marketers to collect detailed information on their customers, not only the approximation offered by demographics but also specific names and addresses. Mass-media approaches will decline in importance as new technology and new media offer one-to-one marketers a more cost-effective way to reach customers and enable businesses to personalize their messages to customers. With the help of database technology, one-to-one marketers can track their customers as individuals, even if they number in the millions.

cannibalization
a situation that occurs when sales of a new product cut into sales of a company's existing products

one-to-one marketing
an individualized marketing method that uses data generated through interactions between carefully defined groups of customers and the company to build long-term, personalized, and profitable relationships with each customer

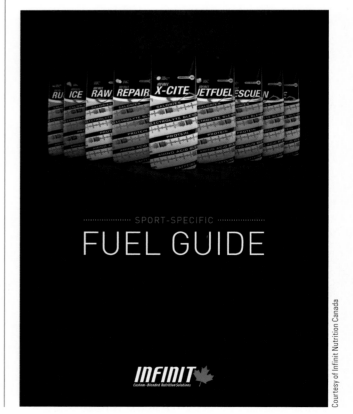

SPORT-SPECIFIC

FUEL GUIDE

INFINIT
Custom-Blended Nutrition Solutions

Courtesy of Infinit Nutrition Canada

Although mass marketing will probably continue to be used, especially to create brand awareness or to remind consumers of a product, the advantages of one-to-one marketing cannot be ignored.

7-6 | POSITIONING

The development of any marketing mix depends on **positioning**, a process that influences potential customers' overall perception of a brand, a product line, or an organization in general. **Position** is the place a product, brand, or group of products occupies in consumers' minds relative to competing offerings. Consumer goods marketers are particularly concerned with positioning. Coca-Cola has multiple cola brands, each positioned to target a different segment of the market. Diet Coke is positioned as the same great taste without the calories, while Coca-Cola Zero is positioned as having a bolder taste and zero calories.

Positioning assumes that consumers compare products on the basis of important features. Marketing efforts that emphasize irrelevant features are therefore likely to misfire. Effective positioning requires assessing the positions occupied by competing products, determining the important dimensions underlying these positions, and choosing a position in the market where the organization's marketing efforts will have the greatest impact. For example, research indicates that roughly a third of luxury car purchases in Canada are made around the same time as a new luxury home purchase. The BMW Canada dealership in Toronto partnered with Royal LePage Real Estate to position itself with the high-end real estate market. The photos taken of the houses for promotional material include a high-end BMW parked in the driveway. When there is an open house scheduled there, arrangements are made to have a BMW parked in the driveway.[23]

One positioning strategy that many companies use to distinguish their products from competitors is based on **product differentiation.** The distinctions can be either real or perceived. Companies can develop products that offer very real advantages for the target market. However, many everyday products, such as bleach, acetaminophen, unleaded regular gasoline, and some soaps, are differentiated by means such as brand names, packaging, colour, smell, or secret additives. The marketer attempts to convince consumers that a particular brand is distinctive and that they should demand it over competing brands.

Instead of using product differentiation, some companies position their products as being similar to competing products or brands. For example, artificial sweeteners are advertised as tasting like sugar, and margarine is touted as tasting like butter.

positioning
a process that influences potential customers' overall perception of a brand, a product line, or an organization in general

position
the place a product, brand, or group of products occupies in consumers' minds relative to competing offerings

product differentiation
a positioning strategy that some companies use to distinguish their products from those of competitors

7-6a | Perceptual Mapping

Perceptual mapping is a means of displaying or graphing, in two or more dimensions, the location of products, brands, or groups of products in customers' minds. For example, Lululemon has strengthened its position as a yoga-inspired technical athletic apparel company by expanding its product mix beyond yoga into running, cycling, and training for both men and women. The resulting product mix, its retail stores, its website image, and its culture have resulted in a unique place in the minds of consumers for Lululemon.

Exhibit 7.3 presents a perceptual map that shows positioning for soft drinks.

7-6b | Positioning Bases

Companies use a variety of bases for positioning, including the following:

- *Attribute:* A product is associated with an attribute, a product feature, or a customer benefit. Clorox Green Works line of household cleaning products has positioned the line as all-natural products. The products are plant or mineral based and biodegradable.[24]

- *Price and quality:* This positioning base may stress high price as a signal of quality or emphasize low price as an indication of value. Walmart has successfully followed the low-price and value strategy. By purchasing Saks Fifth Avenue, HBC has ventured into the high-price, high-quality retail market, for that is how Saks is positioned in consumers' minds.[25]

- *Use or application:* A company can stress a product's uses or applications as an effective means of positioning it with buyers. Hello Fresh, the meal in a box service, is an example of use or application positioning.[26]

- *Product user:* This positioning base focuses on a personality or type of user. In the highly competitive soft drink market, young millennials are the prime market for single product purchases particularly during the summer months. In order to reach this group of socially active consumers, Pepsi created the "Snap It With Pepsi" campaign. This Snapchat-based campaign worked for this user group because research showed that more than 65 percent of them checked Snapchat more than six times a day. Pepsi created unique Snapchat lenses that consumers could unlock by scanning Snapcode on selected Pepsi products.[27]

- *Product class:* The objective here is to position the product as being associated with a particular category of products—for example, positioning a margarine brand with butter. Alternatively, products can be disassociated from a category.

- *Competitor:* Positioning against competitors is part of any positioning strategy. Apple positions the iPhone as cooler and more up-to-date, and Samsung positions the Galaxy series as cooler and more up-to-date than the iPhone.

EXHIBIT 7.3 | PERCEPTUAL MAP AND POSITIONING STRATEGY FOR SOFT DRINKS

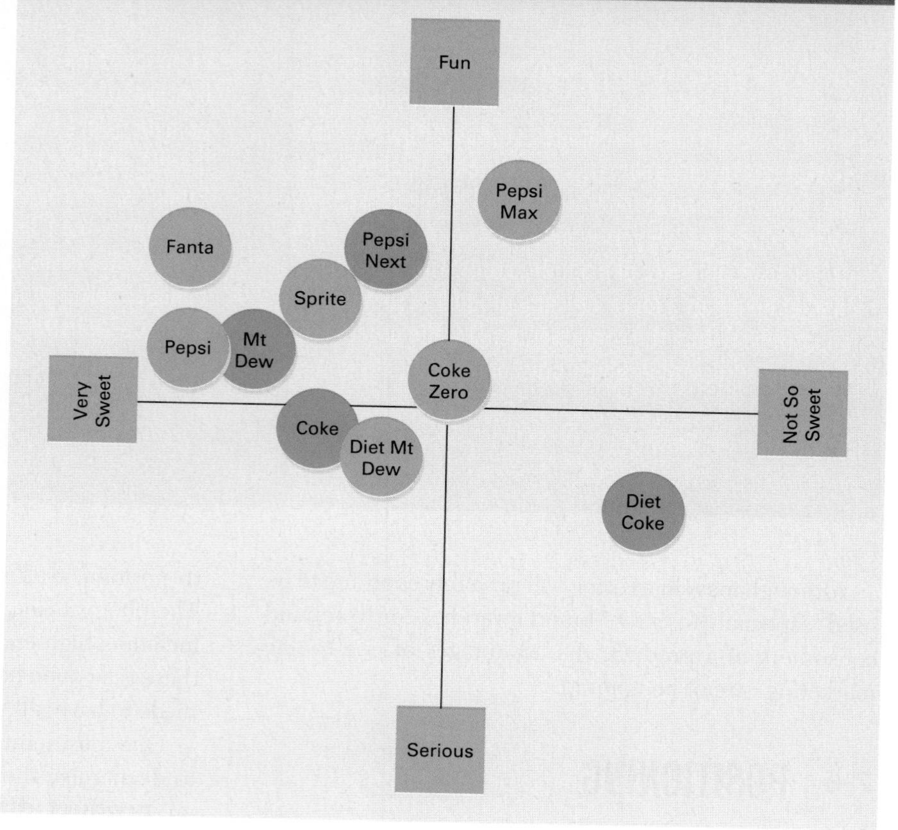

Source: Perceptual Maps for Marketing, http://www.perceptualmaps.com/example-maps/

perceptual mapping
a means of displaying or graphing, in two or more dimensions, the location of products, brands, or groups of products in customers' minds

- *Emotion:* Positioning that uses emotion focuses on how the product makes customers feel. A number of companies use this approach. For example, Nike's "Just Do It" campaign did not tell consumers what "it" is, but most got the emotional message of achievement and courage. Nike continues to build on the "Just Do It" theme. One project included the "Just Do It HQ at the Church." Nike turned a church located in Chicago's inner city into a basketball facility for neighbour youth running training sessions and workshops for young athletes.[28]

It is not unusual for a marketer to use more than one of these bases. In a campaign launched by McDonald's for the Big Mac with Bacon, the company promotes a debate on whether a Big Mac with bacon is really a Big Mac. McDonald's is using the following bases:

- *Product attribute/benefit:* The addition of bacon to a Big Mac is a benefit for those who love bacon.

- *Product user:* The promotion is based on an argument suggesting that those involved in the argument are loyal Big Mac consumers.

- *Emotion:* Again because the promotion is based on an argument, there is clearly a strong emotional connection with the brand.[29]

7-6c | Repositioning

Sometimes products or companies are repositioned to sustain growth in slow markets or to correct positioning mistakes. **Repositioning** refers to changing consumers' perceptions of a brand in relation to competing brands.

For example, in its early years, the Hyundai brand was synonymous with cheap, low-quality cars. To reposition its brand, Hyundai redesigned its cars to be more contemporary looking and started a supportive warranty program. Consumer perceptions changed because customers appreciated the new designs and were reassured of the cars' performance by the

VanderWolf Images/Shutterstock.com

generous warranties. Today, Hyundai's brand reputation has vastly improved.[30]

7-6d | Developing a Positioning Statement

Segmenting, targeting, and positioning are key managerial activities that go beyond simply understanding the process of how to complete each task. Marketing managers often fail to develop and communicate effective positioning statements for their products/brands even though they might have developed effective market segments; thus they fail to state how the business will compete in a given market segment. A positioning statement is also critical for consumers to understand the specific benefits they will obtain from a product.

Following is an excellent positioning statement from Black & Decker for its DeWalt power tools: "To the tradesman who uses his power tools to make a living and cannot afford downtime on the job [target], DeWalt professional power tools [frame of reference] are more dependable than other brands of professional power tools [point of difference] because they are engineered to the brand's historic high-quality standards and are backed by Black & Decker's extensive service network and guarantee to repair or replace any tool within 48 hours [reasons to believe]."[32]

repositioning changing consumers' perceptions of a brand in relation to competing brands

GUIDELINES FOR DEVELOPING A POSITIONING STATEMENT

Research by Tybout and Sternthal of the Kellogg School of Management provide guidelines for crafting a positioning statement:

1. **Targeted consumers:** Develop a brief statement of the target market in terms of their segment description.

2. **Frame of reference:** Develop a statement of the goal for the target market about the product benefit, thus identifying the consumption situations in which the product/brand is to be used.

3. **Point of difference:** Develop a statement asserting why the product/brand being offered is superior.

4. **Reason to believe:** Provide evidence to support the claim provided in the frame of reference.[31]

AWAKE CHOCOLATE
CONTINUING CASE

Konontsev Artem/Shutterstock.com

Target Market Time Traveller

When the founders of Awake first contemplated their target market, they had college students squarely in their cross-hairs. This is aimed at a segment of people who are notorious for both all-night socializing and all-night studying. Either way, they are often very tired.

So when Awake hit campus convenience stores in 2012, the quirky combination of colourful packaging with a caffeinated kick attracted the first loyal consumers. But rather than stay bound solely to students as its target market, Awake moved with it. As CEO Adam Deremo contemplates, "One of the interesting things that happens if you operate a brand for long enough [is that] you see a transition point, where now our most important consumer from a buying standpoint is a millennial female who works in an office." But as Deremo points out, this has nothing to do with Awake shifting its focus, but more to do with Awake's initial consumers falling in love with the brand and staying loyal to it while transitioning from one life stage to another. "Just to prove the connectedness of consumer groups, when we ask that female millennial office worker where she first discovered the brand, there's a good subset of them who tell us they were first introduced to us when they were in college."

Many companies will discover an unmet need for a particular segment, zone in upon that cohort, analyze it to confirm that the need exists and that the segment represents a large enough market to warrant the development of a produce, and then keep serving that target market as consumers grow into and out of it. But many companies aren't built around a product that can be easily ported from one life stage to the next.

While Deremo maintains that this "brand partnership" as he calls it, was all part of the original plan—creating lifelong customer loyalty—not even he and his cofounders expected something this interdependent. "That's actually one of the only long-term predictions we got right," he jokes. "But the reality is it's kind of the law of numbers. You have 4 to 5 years in college, then 20 to 30 years in the work in your career. So eventually there had to be more consumers in the workforce than in university, and I'm just glad their brand affection has persisted."

Brand affection, as Deremo refers to it, speaks to an indelible subcomponent of behavioural segmentation, an often misunderstood and underappreciated component in target marketing. Companies often get hung up on geopsychodemographics. They make a product—skater shoes, for instance—and market it primarily toward teenaged boys in urban centres, particularly on the West Coast. But then they're stuck when that segment grows up, and the incoming segment is disinterested in the fashion of its predecessor. Thus, companies are constantly redesigning products to cater to the values and attitudes of the successor.

In Awake's case, the flavour and functionality, portability, and appealing branding elements zoned in on the behavioural aspect of its consumers. The need being satisfied—finding a healthy, effective, and flavourful way to overcome mid-afternoon fatigue—created the brand partnership of which Deremo speaks. Customer loyalty is a core human behaviour to track in marketing. How committed customers are to a specific brand in a sea of alternatives largely comes back to familiarity and trust. Awake provided college students with a reliable solution to solve a common problem. But then it met them on the other side of graduation. It was there as a familiar and functional product to satisfy the same need but at a different stage of the life cycle.

The longstanding affection for Awake is primarily the result of a value-oriented product, but also one of having a flexible approach to target marketing. "It testifies to the quality of the product, but also to the fact that we were meeting the needs of the market that we set out to meet both then and now."

QUESTIONS

1. Create a table on your computer, with four columns, labelled Geographic, Demographic, Psychographic, and Behavioural. Using the material in this chapter, provide a minimum of two specific descriptors of Awake's target market.

2. Of the four different segmentation variables, rank them in order of importance from the perspective of Awake.

3. Behavioural segmentation, as mentioned in the case, is often either misunderstood or underappreciated in target marketing. In your own words, explain the difference between psychographic and behavioural segmentation characteristics.

8 | Customer Relationship Management (CRM)

LEARNING OUTCOMES

8-1 Summarize customer relationship management

8-2 Explain the CRM cycle

8-3 Describe the three stages in the CRM cycle: marketing research, business development, and customer feedback

8-4 Identify privacy issues in CRM

8-5 Determine the future challenges for CRM

> *"Focusing on the customer makes a company more resilient."*
>
> —Jeff Bezos[1]

8-1 | WHAT IS CUSTOMER RELATIONSHIP MANAGEMENT?

Customer relationship management (CRM) is the evolution of the importance of relationships to marketing success. Much of the early work done by business-to-business marketing research in the early 1980s provided the framework for looking at the importance of relationships and harnessing their immense potential. Companies working on the frontlines with customers realized that customers hold a lot of information and thus a lot of value to companies.

CRM is tasked with identifying those profitable customers and finding ways to interact with them, with the goal of maximizing the value of that customer relationship. As the concept of CRM has evolved over the past few decades, it has become a vital part of most companies' marketing activities. Any organization with customers should strive to know them better, and CRM provides the tools to do that. CRM is now often seen as a process to help improve relationships, to work with people in the company (employees) and the external customer, and to incorporate technological systems to manage those people and processes.

If we go back to Chapter 1, you will recall that marketing is about meeting the needs of customers. To do this, you must learn more about your customer by doing research, learning about customers' behaviours, segmenting them, and delivering something of value (the four Ps) to them. In Chapter 4, we discussed how to conduct research to learn more about the customer. What is next is to bring those tools together into one focused objective. And that objective is CRM. CRM is about building customer loyalty and retaining those valued customers. It is about delivering on the promises made and establishing a system that will continue to deliver over time. To return to another concept we've looked at in this book, CRM is about interaction with your customer

customer relationship management (CRM)
a system that gathers information about customers that can help to build customer loyalty and retain those loyal customers

Marketing Research

Business Development

Customer Feedback

Campaigns

CRM
Customer Relationship
Management

Privacy

Information Technologies

Customer Relationships

over the long term, not just tracking transactions over the short term.

This leads us to an important statement: CRM is not just about tracking customer information. If you were to do an Internet search for "customer relationship management," you might get the impression that CRM is about building a computer system that captures information about your customers. In fact, in the 1990s and early 2000s, companies created information systems that were referred to as "CRM systems." These systems were costly, and most companies could not find the value in using IT systems to create better customer relationships. Faith in IT-based CRM solutions wavered as sales of CRM systems were drastically reduced in the early 2000s. Some saw CRM as just "another overhyped IT investment."[2]

While IT is part of the development of a strong CRM program, information about customers is useless without knowing how to attract and keep those customers over the long term. In the end, the value is not how much you can squeeze out of each customer through a computer program; the value is in developing a customer who will be investing in maintaining a mutually beneficial interaction.

8-1a | The Other CRM

Hardware and software are needed to gather consumer information for CRM. In fact, this focus on database creation is another CRM abbreviation—customer relationship marketing.

The two CRMs have seemingly been melded together by most companies; however, it is important to understand the difference between the two. *Customer relationship marketing* is more focused on *acquiring* the necessary hardware and software to create a database or system to gather and track customer information. It references *relationship marketing*, the term used since the 1920s to describe the importance of close customer relationships. *Customer relationship management* is an *overall* company strategy that a company employs to understand the needs of customers, keep updated on their needs, and satisfy them over the long term. The heavy emphasis on technology in CRM is understandable given the goals of trying to track customers down to an individual level, but it is still important to remember that this process has to be managed and assessed. See Exhibit 8.1.

EXHIBIT 8.1 — WHAT'S IN A NAME? CUSTOMER RELATIONSHIP MANAGEMENT VS. CUSTOMER RELATIONSHIP MARKETING

Factor	Customer Relationship *Marketing*	Customer Relationship *Management*
Action	Does things **to** people	Does things **with** people
Response	Concerned with achieving a response to stimulus	Concerned about the "how" and "why" of a response
Measurement	"Do you like what we are sending?"	"Tell me why what we sent was useful."
Collection	Data—addresses, purchases	Data plus intention
Focus	Buyer–seller	Supplier–customer

8-2 | THE CRM CYCLE

In a report titled "State of Customer Relationship Management," the Government of Canada presented a three step CRM cycle: (1) marketing and market research, (2) business development, and (3) customer feedback (Exhibit 8.2). This comprehensive assessment of a CRM system was based on a seminal article in the *Harvard Business Review* on CRM, shortly after the downfall of IT-based CRM systems in the early 2000s.

CRM has often been described as a closed-loop system that builds relationships with customers. However, too often CRM has been reduced to a tool for selling software that promises to identify customers and provide information at a microscopic level. Little thought was given to using CRM as a tool to build long-term relationships with customers.

At its core, CRM is a relationship-building tool, and the sections that follow explain each stage of the CRM cycle. Stage 1 requires that companies understand what they have to offer to their customers and the marketing and market research tools that can help them use the four Ps. Stage 2 focuses on the use of technology to systematically identify customers, gather information on them, and store that information. Finally, in Stage 3 companies

look at ways to use the information about customers to retain them in the long term by satisfying their needs.

Stage 2 of the CRM cycle includes many of the CRM tools and concepts a company offering these types of solutions to companies would use. However, without an understanding of the context in Stage 1 and the ramifications of those CRM tools in Stage 3, CRM is a one-sided effort that lacks cooperation and inclusion of a most vital component—the customer.

8-3 | STEPS IN THE CRM CYCLE

8-3a | The CRM Cycle—Stage 1 (Marketing Research)

During the first stage of creating a CRM system, companies must create an offering. This can be a product or service (or some combination of the two) that satisfies a customer need. Here is where marketing research can be helpful. As you recall from Chapter 5, conducting marketing research can help to identify customer needs, helping the marketer better understand the external marketplace where the company's offering will be sold.

Tools such as surveys, customer panels, and competitive intelligence are all helpful devices during this first stage for understanding the consumer and the marketplace. Product development and design (see Chapters 9 and 10) are also part of this initial stage, as companies develop ideas and concepts to prepare them for commercialization.

Companies should collect as much information as possible about the market and customer during this process. This will ensure that the offering supplied by the company reflects the current needs of customers. Companies can then make the right decisions about price (Chapter 12), place (Chapters 13 and 14), and promotion (Chapters 15 to 18) to provide an offering with the greatest opportunity for success in the marketplace.

Essentially, the first stage of developing a proper CRM system involves using the tools and techniques you have been learning about in the previous chapters. By

EXHIBIT 8.2 THE CRM CYCLE

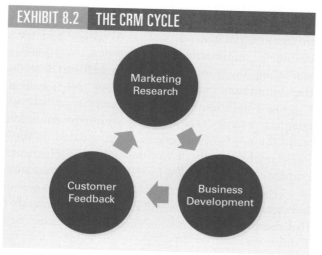

Marketing Research in a CRM— The Case of NPS

An NPS (Net Promoter Score) is a marketing research tool, usually in the form of a questionnaire, that tries to measure how loyal your customers are. It inquires about how likely your customer would recommend you to others, and how the actions of your company have impacted their future willingness to purchase.

The "score" part of NPS is a number from –100 to +100. The final NPS score is based on a scale in a question such as "How likely are you to recommend Company A to your friends and family?" Based on a 10-point scale, consumer answers are collected and interpreted. Each company decides what each number represents. Most often, top scores of 9–10 are coded as "Promoters," while scores below 5 are often seen as "Detractors." The numbers are then totalled to get a final number. In the case of NPS, a zero is a good score, above 50 is great, and anything in the negatives is obviously bad.

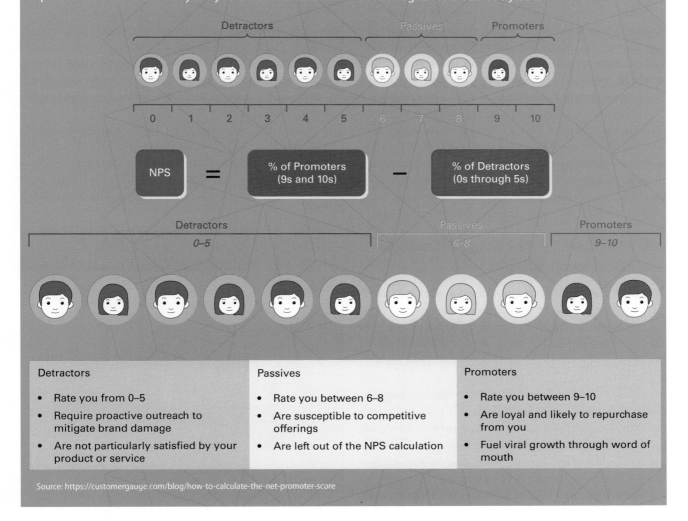

Detractors	Passives	Promoters
Rate you from 0–5	Rate you between 6–8	Rate you between 9–10
Require proactive outreach to mitigate brand damage	Are susceptible to competitive offerings	Are loyal and likely to repurchase from you
Are not particularly satisfied by your product or service	Are left out of the NPS calculation	Fuel viral growth through word of mouth

Source: https://customergauge.com/blog/how-to-calculate-the-net-promoter-score

creating an offering that reflects and satisfies customer needs, a company will develop a holistic CRM system. The data acquired through various IT methods (discussed in the section on Stage 2) will be only as useful as the marketing strategies created by a company that truly understands what marketing is about.

A *Journal of Marketing* article identified the qualities necessary for an effective CRM program: "CRM provides

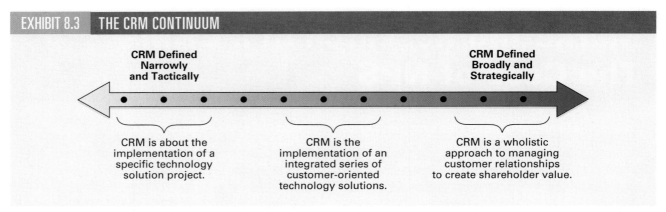

EXHIBIT 8.3   THE CRM CONTINUUM

CRM Defined Narrowly and Tactically

CRM Defined Broadly and Strategically

CRM is about the implementation of a specific technology solution project.

CRM is the implementation of an integrated series of customer-oriented technology solutions.

CRM is a wholistic approach to managing customer relationships to create shareholder value.

Source: Republished with permission of Sage Publications Inc. Journals, from Adrian Payne, Pennie Frow (2005) A Strategic Framework for Customer Relationship Management. *Journal of Marketing*: October 2005, Vol. 69, No. 4, pp. 167-176; permission conveyed through Copyright Clearance Center, Inc.

enhanced opportunities to use data and information to both understand customers and co-create value with them. This requires a cross-functional integration of processes, people, operations, and marketing capabilities that is enabled through information, technology, and applications."[3] The article also provided a continuum of CRM programs similar to the one shown in Exhibit 8.3.

The continuum highlights the importance of developing a CRM system that not only is technology based but also considers strategy and marketing. By using what is known about marketing, from marketing research through to the four Ps, companies can establish the foundation for an effective CRM program. Once these foundations are created, the technology can be introduced.

8-3b | The CRM Cycle—Stage 2 (Business Development)

Now that an offering has been developed that satisfies an identified customer need, the technology tools can be unleashed to seek out more detailed information on these customers. Exhibit 8.4 provides a flow model of the process of the technology stage of the CRM cycle.

To initiate Stage 2 of CRM cycle, a company must first identify customer relationships with the organization. This step may simply involve learning who the company's customers are or where they are located, or it may require more detailed information about the products and services these customers are using. Bridgestone Canada Inc., a tire service company that produces Firestone tires, uses a CRM system called OnDemand5, which initially gathers data from a point-of-sale interaction.[4] The information includes basic demographic information, the frequency of consumers' purchases, how much they purchase, and how far they drive.

Next, the company must understand its interactions with current customers. Companies accomplish this

task by collecting data on all types of communications a customer has with the company. Using its OnDemand5 system, Bridgestone Canada Inc. can add information that is based on additional interactions with the consumer, such as multiple visits to a physical store location and purchasing history. In this phase, companies build on the initial information collected and develop a more useful database.

Using this knowledge of its customers and their interactions, the company then captures relevant customer data on interactions. As an example, Bridgestone/Firestone can collect relevant information such as the date of the last communication with a customer,

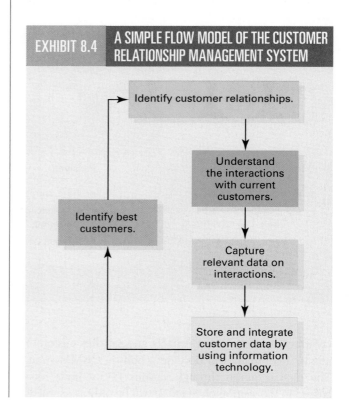

EXHIBIT 8.4   A SIMPLE FLOW MODEL OF THE CUSTOMER RELATIONSHIP MANAGEMENT SYSTEM

Identify customer relationships.

Understand the interactions with current customers.

Identify best customers.

Capture relevant data on interactions.

Store and integrate customer data by using information technology.

how often the customer makes purchases, and whether the customer has redeemed coupons sent through direct mail.

How can marketers realistically analyze and communicate with individual customers? The answer lies in how information technology is used to implement the CRM system. Fundamentally, a CRM approach is no more than the relationship cultivated by a salesperson with the customer. A successful salesperson builds a relationship over time, constantly thinks about what the customer needs and wants, and is mindful of the trends and patterns in the customer's purchase history. The salesperson may also inform, educate, and instruct the customer about new products, technology, or applications in anticipation of the customer's future needs or requirements.

This kind of thoughtful attention is the basis of successful IT CRM flow systems. Information technology is used not only to enhance the collection of customer data but also to store and integrate customer data throughout the company and, ultimately, to get to know customers on a personal level. A recent survey from LinkedIn found that 64.2 percent of companies using a CRM rated the technology as "impactful" or "very impactful" to their ability to produce great results and grow their businesses.[5]

Customer data are the firsthand responses obtained from customers through investigation or by asking direct questions. These initial data, which might include individual answers to questionnaires, responses on warranty cards, or lists of purchases recorded by electronic cash registers, have not yet been analyzed or interpreted.

The value of customer data depends on the system that stores the data and the consistency and accuracy of the data captured. Obtaining high-quality, actionable data from various sources is a key element in any CRM system. Bridgestone Canada Inc. accomplishes this task by managing all information in a central database accessible by marketers. Different kinds of database management software are available, from extremely high-tech, expensive, custom-designed databases to standardized programs.

Every customer wants to be a company's main priority, but not all customers are equally important in the eyes of a business. Consequently, the company must identify its profitable and unprofitable customers. The Pareto principle (mentioned in Chapter 7) indicates that 80 percent of a business's profit comes from 20 percent of its customers.

Data mining is an analytical process that compiles actionable data on the purchase habits of a company's current and potential customers. Essentially, data mining transforms customer data into customer information that a company can use to make managerial decisions. Bridgestone Canada Inc. uses OnDemand5 to analyze its data to determine which customers qualify for the MasterCare Select program.

Once customer data are analyzed and transformed into usable information, the information must be leveraged. The CRM system sends the customer information to all areas of a business because the ultimate customer interacts with all aspects of the business. Essentially, the company is trying to enhance customer relationships by getting the right information to the right person in the right place at the right time.

Bridgestone Canada Inc. uses the information in its database to develop different marketing campaigns for each type of customer. Customers are also targeted with promotions aimed at increasing their store visits, upgrading their tires to higher-end models, and encouraging their purchases of additional services. Since the company customized its mailings to each type of customer, visits to stores have increased by more than 50 percent.[6]

IDENTIFY CUSTOMER RELATIONSHIPS Companies that have a CRM system follow a customer-centric

data mining
an analytical process that compiles actionable data on the purchase habits of a company's current and potential customers

focus or model. Being **customer-centric** refers to an internal management philosophy similar to the marketing concept discussed in Chapter 1. Under this philosophy, the company customizes its product and service offerings based on data generated through interactions between the customer and the company. This philosophy transcends all functional areas of the business, producing an internal system where all of the company's decisions and actions are a direct result of customer information.

A customer-centric company builds long-lasting relationships by focusing on what satisfies and retains valuable customers. For example, Sony PlayStation's website (https://www.playstation.com/en-ca) focuses on learning, customer knowledge management, and empowerment to market its PlayStation gaming entertainment systems. The website offers online shopping, opportunities to try new games, customer support, and information on news, events, and promotions. The interactive features include online gaming and message boards.

The PlayStation site is designed to support Sony's CRM system. When PlayStation users want to access amenities on the site, they must log in and supply information, such as their name, email address, and birthdate. Users can opt to complete a survey that asks questions about the types of computer entertainment systems they own, how many games are owned for each console, expected future game purchases, time spent playing games, types of games played, and level of Internet connectivity. Armed with this information, Sony mar-

charnsitr/Shutterstock.com

keters are then able to tailor the site, new games, and PlayStation hardware to the players' replies to the survey and their use of the website.[7]

Customer-centric companies continually learn ways to enhance their product and service offerings. **Learning** in a CRM environment involves the informal process of collecting customer information through comments and feedback on product and service performance.

Each unit of a business typically has its own way of recording what it learns and may even have its own customer information system. The departments' different interests make it difficult to pull all the customer information together in one place using a common format. To overcome this problem, companies using CRM rely on **knowledge management**, a process by which learned information from customers is centralized and shared to enhance the relationship between customers and the organization. Information collected includes experiential observations, comments, customer actions, and qualitative facts about the customer.

Empowerment involves delegating authority to solve customers' problems quickly, usually by the first person who learns of the problem. In other words, **empowerment** is the latitude organizations give their representatives to negotiate mutually satisfying commitments with customers. Usually, organizational representatives are able to make changes during interactions with customers through email or by phone, or face to face.

An **interaction** occurs when a customer and a company representative exchange information and develop learning relationships. With CRM, the customer, not the organization, defines the terms of the interaction, often by stating their preferences. The organization responds by designing products and services around customers' desired experiences. For example, students in Canada can purchase the Student Price Card, a loyalty card, for $10 per year and use it to obtain discounts from affiliated retailers, such as Booster Juice, Aldo, and Banana

customer-centric
a philosophy under which the company customizes its product and service offerings based on data generated through interactions between the customer and the company

learning (CRM)
in a CRM environment, the informal process of collecting customer data through customer comments and feedback on product or service performance

knowledge management
the process by which learned information from customers is centralized and shared for the purpose of enhancing the relationship between customers and the organization

empowerment
delegation of authority to solve customers' problems quickly—usually by the first person who learns of the customer's problem

interaction
the point at which a customer and a company representative exchange information and develop learning relationships

Republic.[8] Student Advantage tracks the cardholders' spending patterns and behaviours to gain a better understanding of what student customers want. Student Advantage then communicates this information to the affiliated retailers, which can tailor their discounts to meet students' needs.[9]

The success of CRM—building lasting and profitable relationships—can be directly measured by the effectiveness of the interaction between the customer and the organization. In fact, CRM is further differentiated from other strategic initiatives by the organization's ability to establish and manage interactions with its current customer base. The more latitude (empowerment) a company gives its representatives, the more likely the interaction will conclude in a way that satisfies the customer.

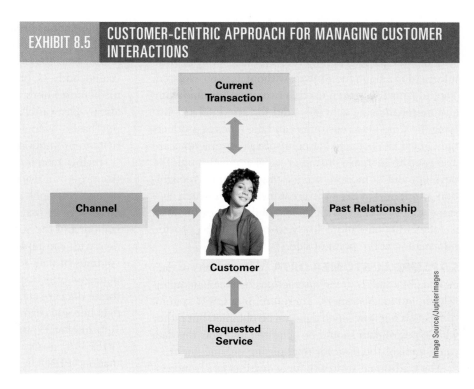

EXHIBIT 8.5 CUSTOMER-CENTRIC APPROACH FOR MANAGING CUSTOMER INTERACTIONS

Current Transaction

Channel

Past Relationship

Customer

Requested Service

Image Source/Jupiterimages

UNDERSTAND INTERACTIONS OF THE CURRENT CUSTOMER BASE
The interaction between the customer and the organization is the foundation on which a CRM system is built. Only through effective interactions can organizations learn about the expectations of their customers, generate and manage knowledge about customers, negotiate mutually satisfying commitments, and build long-term relationships.

Exhibit 8.5 illustrates the customer-centric approach for managing customer interactions. Following a customer-centric approach, an interaction can occur through a formal or direct communication channel, such as a phone, the Internet, or a salesperson. Any activity or touch point a customer has with an organization, either directly or indirectly, constitutes an interaction.

Companies that effectively manage customer interactions recognize that customers provide data to the organization that affect a wide variety of touch points. In a CRM system, **touch points** are all possible areas of a business where customers have contact with that business and data might be gathered. Touch points might include a customer registering for a particular service; a customer communicating with customer service for product information; a customer making direct contact electronically via email or website visit; a customer completing and returning the warranty information card for a product; or a customer talking with salespeople, delivery personnel, and product installers. Data gathered at these touch points, once interpreted, provide information that affects touch points inside the company. Interpreted information may be redirected to marketing research to develop profiles of extended warranty purchasers; to production to analyze recurring problems and repair components; and to accounting to establish cost-control models for repair service calls.

Web-based interactions are an increasingly popular touch point for customers to communicate with companies on their own terms. Web users can evaluate and purchase products, make reservations, input preferential data, and provide customer feedback on services and products. Data from these Web-based interactions are then captured, compiled, and used to segment customers, refine marketing efforts, develop new products, and deliver a degree of individual customization to improve customer relationships.

Another touch point is **point-of-sale interactions**, communications between customers

touch points
all possible areas of a business where customers have contact with that business

point-of-sale interactions
communications between customers and organizations that occur at the point of sale, usually in a store

and organizations that occur at the point of sale, usually in a store but also at information kiosks. Many point-of-sale software packages enable customers to easily provide information about themselves without feeling violated. The information is then used in two ways: for marketing and merchandising activities, and for accurately identifying the store's best customers and the types of products they buy. Data collected at point-of-sale interactions are also used to increase customer satisfaction through the development of in-store services and customer recognition promotions. Given the greater ease with which consumers can now pay, with their mobile phones or smart watches, they are more likely to be willing to provide information at the point of sale.

CAPTURE CUSTOMER DATA Vast amounts of data can be obtained from the interactions between an organization and its customers. Therefore, in a CRM system, the issue is not how much data can be obtained but rather what types of data should be acquired and how the data can effectively be used for relationship enhancement.

The traditional approach for acquiring data from customers is through channel interactions, which include store visits, conversations with salespeople, interactions via the Web, traditional phone conversations, and wireless communications. In a CRM system, channel interactions are viewed as prime information sources that are based on the channel selected to initiate the interaction rather than on the data acquired. For example, if a consumer logs on to the Sony website to find out why a Sony device is not functioning properly and the answer is not available online, the consumer is then referred to a page where they can describe the problem. The website then emails the problem description to a company representative, who will research the problem and reply via email.

Point-of-sale interactions enable customers to provide information about themselves.

Interactions between the company and the customer facilitate the collection of large amounts of data. Companies can obtain not only simple contact information (name, address, phone number) but also data pertaining to the customer's current relationship with the organization—past purchase history, quantity and frequency of purchases, average amount spent on purchases, sensitivity to promotional activities, and so forth.

In this manner, much information can be captured from one individual customer across several touch points. Multiply this information by the thousands of customers across all the touch points within an organization, and the volume of data that company personnel deal with can rapidly become unmanageable. The large volumes of data resulting from a CRM initiative can be managed effectively only through technology. Once customer data are collected, the question of who owns those data becomes extremely salient. In Canada, the Personal Information Protection and Electronic Documents Act (PIPEDA) deals with the protection of personal information. PIPEDA does not address the selling of the information as a business asset. In June 2019, Canadian credit union Desjardins announced that 4.2 million of its members had their personal information compromised. The breach was not caused by an external third party, but instead from a Desjardins employee who had access to this information and forwarded it on to a third party. Later in 2019, it was found out that this employee also had access to a further 1.8 million credit card holders. The number of consumers who were affected by this data breach is quite concerning, especially since only recently did the Government of Canada require companies like Desjardins to report breaches publicly rather than voluntarily as in the past (read more about this and PIPEDA in the following box).[10]

STORE AND INTEGRATE CUSTOMER DATA Customer data are only as valuable as both their consistency and accuracy and the system in which they are stored. Gathering data is complicated because data needed by one unit of the organization, such as sales and marketing, are often generated by another area of the business or even a third-party supplier, such as an independent marketing research company. Thus, companies must use information technology to capture, store, and integrate strategically important customer information. This process of centralizing data in a CRM system is referred to as data warehousing.

A data warehouse is a central repository (database) of data collected by an organization. Essentially, it is a large computerized file of all information collected in the previous stage of the CRM process—for example,

PIPEDA—Into the Breach

PIPEDA (the Personal Information Protection and Electronic Documents Act) is an important piece of legislation that affects all Canadians. Signed into law in 2001 with much fanfare, PIPEDA sets out the rules on how companies can use information customers supply when they buy something or enter a contest or other promotion. Through PIPEDA, you can request to see your personal information possessed by an organization with which you have had dealings. In November 2018, PIPEDA took on greater regulations for industry with regard to data breaches. Companies were mandated to report any data breaches, instead of self-reporting, and the numbers were telling. For a one-year period, ending on October 31, 2019, Canadian companies submitted 680 breach reports. More than half the reports involved unauthorized access, while 147 of the reports involved companies accidentally disclosing information about customers. With a stronger mandate and greater disclosure, these 680 reports represented a huge uptick in reporting of cases to the Office of the Privacy Commissioner (OPC). And now with greater tools of enforcement, PIPEDA can now truly begin to protect consumers as was promised to Canadian consumers almost 20 years ago.

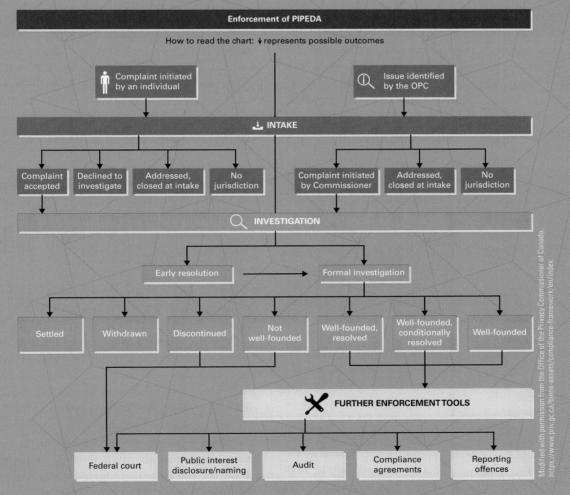

Modified with permission from the Office of the Privacy Commissioner of Canada. https://www.priv.gc.ca/biens.assets/compliance-framework/en/index.

Sources: "A Guide for Individuals: Protecting Your Privacy: An Overview of the Office of the Privacy Commissioner of Canada and Federal Privacy Legislation," Office of the Privacy Commissioner of Canada, March 2014, www.priv.gc.ca/information/02_05_d_08_e.asp (accessed August 24, 2014); "The Case for Reforming the Personal Information Protection and Electronic Documents Act," http://www.mondaq.com/canada/x/870082/Data+Protection+Privacy/Once+More+Unto+The+Data+BreachLooking+Back+At+Twelve+Months+Of+Mandatory+Breach+Notifications

information collected in channel, transaction, and product or service touch points. The core of the data warehouse is the **database**, "a collection of data, especially one that can be accessed and manipulated by computer software."[11] The CRM database focuses on collecting vital statistics on consumers, their purchasing habits, transactions methods, and product usage in a centralized repository that is accessible by all functional areas of a company. By using a data warehouse, marketing managers can quickly access vast amounts of information to make decisions.

When a company builds its database, usually the first step is to develop a list. A **response list** is a customer list that includes the names and addresses of individuals who have responded to an offer of some kind, such as by website, email, mail, telephone, direct-response television, product rebates, contests or sweepstakes, or billing inserts. It can also be a compiled list, created by an outside company that has collected names and contact information for potential consumers. Response lists tend to be especially valuable because past behaviour is a strong predictor of future behaviour and because consumers who have indicated interest in the product or service are more likely to purchase in the future. **Compiled lists** usually are prepared by an outside company and are available for purchase. A compiled list is a customer list that was developed by gathering names and addresses gleaned from telephone directories or membership rosters, sometimes enhanced with information from public records, such as census data, auto registrations, birth announcements, business start-ups, or bankruptcies. Lists range from those owned by large list companies, such as Dun & Bradstreet, for business-to-business data, and InfoCanada, for consumer lists, to small groups or associations that are willing to sell their membership lists. Data compiled by large data-gathering companies are usually very accurate.

response list
a customer list that includes the names and addresses of individuals who have responded to an offer of some kind, such as by website, email, mail, telephone, direct-response television, product rebates, contests or sweepstakes, or billing inserts

compiled lists
customer lists that are developed by gathering names and addresses gleaned from telephone directories and membership rosters, sometimes enhanced with information from public records, such as census data, auto registrations, birth announcements, business start-ups, or bankruptcies

In this phase, companies usually collect channel, transaction, product, and service information, such as stores, salespersons, communication channels, contacts information, relationships, and brands.

A customer database becomes even more useful to marketing managers when it is enhanced to include more than simply a customer's or prospect's name, address, telephone number, and transaction history. Database enhancement involves purchasing information on customers or prospects to better describe their needs or to determine how responsive they might be to marketing programs. Enhancement data typically include demographic, lifestyle, or behavioural information.

Database enhancement can increase the effectiveness of marketing programs. By learning more about their best and most profitable customers, marketers can maximize the effectiveness of their marketing communications and cross-selling. Database enhancement also helps a company find new prospects.

Multinational companies building worldwide databases often face difficult problems when pulling together internal data about their customers. Differences in language, computer systems, and data-collection methods can be huge obstacles to overcome. In spite of the challenges, many global companies are committed to building databases. And despite challenges raised from regulations like PIPEDA, companies are still looking to create a reliable database in order to help them make better decisions. Coca Cola invested in a company that creates databases called FileMaker. The beverage multinational is aware of the need to track data, and realizes that programs that can help provide this information in real time around the world is an incredibly valuable asset.[12]

IDENTIFYING THE BEST CUSTOMERS CRM manages interactions between a company and its customers. To be successful, companies need to identify those customers who yield high profits or high potential profits. To do this, significant amounts of data must be gathered from customers, stored and integrated in the data warehouse, and then analyzed and interpreted for common patterns that can identify homogeneous customers who differ from other customer segments. Because not all customers are the same, organizations often develop interactions that target the top 20 percent high-value customers' wants and needs. In a CRM system, data mining is used to identify these customers.

DATA MINING Data mining is used to find hidden patterns and relationships in the customer data stored in the data warehouse. A data analysis approach identi-

Chris Wylie, owner of AggregateIO

When using data mining, it is important to remember that the real value is in the company's ability to transform its data from operational bits and bytes into information marketers' need for successful marketing strategies. Companies must analyze the data to identify and profile the best customers, calculate their lifetime value (LTV), and ultimately predict purchasing behaviour through statistical modelling. London Drugs uses data mining to identify commonly purchased items that should be displayed together on shelves and to learn which soft drinks sell best in different parts of the country.

Before the information is leveraged, several types of analysis are often run on the data. These analyses include customer segmentation, recency-frequency-monetary (RFM) analysis, LTV analysis, and predictive modelling.

CUSTOMER SEGMENTATION Recall that customer segmentation is the process of breaking large groups of customers into smaller, more homogeneous groups. This type of analysis generates a profile, or picture, of the customers' similar demographic, geographic, and psychographic traits, in addition to their previous purchase behaviour; it focuses particularly on the best customers. Profiles of the best customers can be compared and contrasted with other customer segments. For example, a bank can segment consumers on their frequency of usage, credit, age, and turnover.

Once a profile of the best customer is developed by using these criteria, this profile can be used to screen other potential consumers. Similarly, customer profiles can be used to introduce customers selectively to specific marketing actions. For example, young customers with an open mind can be introduced to online banking. See Chapter 7 for a detailed discussion of segmentation.

RECENCY-FREQUENCY-MONETARY (RFM) ANALYSIS Recency-frequency-monetary (RFM) analysis allows companies to identify customers who have purchased recently and often and who have spent considerable money, because they are most likely to purchase again (see Exhibit 8.6). Companies develop equations to identify their best customers (often the top 20 percent of the customer base) by assigning a score to their customer records in the database based on how often, how recently, and how much customers have spent. Customers are

fies patterns of characteristics that relate to particular customers or customer groups. Although businesses have been conducting such analyses for many years, the procedures typically were performed on small data sets containing as few as 300 to 400 customers. Today, with the development of sophisticated data warehouses, millions of customers' shopping patterns can be analyzed.

Data mining can have a dark side, as seen in the Cambridge Analytica scandal around the Brexit campaign in the United Kingdom and the 2016 US presidential election. Cambridge Analytica was a British data mining company that reportedly took information from 87 million Facebook users in an effort to sway votes and elections. Canadian data mining company AggregateIQ was accused of being connected to Cambridge Analytica and the Brexit "Vote Leave" campaign, and subsequently lost all Facebook access in the scandal.

Using data mining, marketers can search the data warehouse, capture relevant data, categorize significant characteristics, and develop customer profiles.

recency-frequency-monetary (RFM) analysis the analysis of customer activity by recency, frequency, and monetary value

then ranked to determine which will move to the top of the list and which will fall to the bottom. The ranking provides the basis for maximizing profits by enabling the company to use the information to select those persons who have proved to be good sources of revenue. Based on an analysis of recency and frequency, customers are given scores from 1 to 5, with 5 being the most desirable score for a customer. See Exhibit 8.7 for an example of an RFM table score.

LIFETIME VALUE (LTV) ANALYSIS Recency, frequency, and monetary data can also be used to create a LTV model on customers in the database. Whereas RFM looks at how valuable a customer currently is to a company, **lifetime value (LTV) analysis** projects the future value of the customer over a period of years. An example of LTV for a female 20 to 30 years old who has her hair done four times a year at an average cost of $120 per visit, given data-mined information of an average typical patronage life of five years, is $2400 ($120/visit × 4 visits/year × 5 years). One of the basic assumptions in any LTV calculation is that marketing to repeat customers is more profitable than marketing to first-time buyers. That is, it costs more to find a new customer, in terms of promotion and gaining trust, than to sell more to a customer who is already loyal.

Customer LTV has numerous benefits. It shows marketers how much they can spend to acquire new customers, it tells them the level of spending to retain customers, and it facilitates targeting new customers who are identified as likely to be profitable. While these are strong benefits, LTV can be problematic if companies treat customers like the numbers that appear on the screen. While keeping customers is a noble goal, the reasons should go beyond the numbers, and companies should remember that they need specific systems in place (e.g., customer satisfaction measurement) to maintain a relationship over time.

PREDICTIVE MODELLING The ability to reasonably predict future customer behaviour gives marketers a significant competitive advantage. Through **predictive modelling**, a data manipulation technique, marketers try to determine, using a past set of occurrences, the odds that some other occurrence, such as an inquiry or a purchase, will take place in the future. IBM SPSS

lifetime value (LTV) analysis
a data manipulation technique that projects the future value of the customer over a period of years by using the assumption that marketing to repeat customers is more profitable than marketing to first-time buyers

predictive modelling
a data manipulation technique in which marketers try to determine, based on some past set of occurrences, the odds that some other occurrence, such as an inquiry or a purchase, will take place in the future

EXHIBIT 8.7	SAMPLE RFM SCORES						
Customer ID	**Name**	**Recency**	**RScore**	**Frequency**	**FScore**	**Monetary**	**MScore**
8217	Anya Merrick	8	5	53	5	98 700 000	5
667	Asha Khan	66	5	79	5	1 900 000	2
5911	Jin Lu	3	5	13	2	34 000 000	5
1099	Charlotte Walker	4	5	4	1	8 400 000	4
832	Nolan Randall	197	1	1	1	1 336 000	2

Predictive Marketing is one tool marketers can use to answer questions about their consumers. The software requires minimal knowledge of statistical analysis. Users operate from a prebuilt model, which generates profiles in three to four days. SPSS also has an online product that predicts website users' behaviour.

8-3c | The CRM Cycle—Stage 3 (Customer Feedback)

As is clear from Stage 2 of the CRM cycle, technology is an important driver of a successful CRM system. However, an overreliance on technology and data down to the individual customer level can lead to companies losing sight of the real goal of CRM—maintaining long-term relationships with those who buy the products and services.

As long as companies can see CRM as a means to build a relationship with customers, and not as a sales tool or technology solution, they will see the need to complete the cycle. This is done by implementing measures of customer satisfaction to establish whether what the company is doing is meeting the needs of those customers.

In the *MIT Sloan Management Review*, an article entitled "Putting the 'Relationship' Back into CRM" highlighted some of the concerns over how companies use CRM. The authors came up with three ways the current practice of CRM is failing companies:[13]

1. CRM programs focus too much on transactions and not on other aspects of the customer's life.

2. Relationships cannot be solely about achieving loyalty, and companies need to find multiple ways to retain their customers.

3. A relationship is dynamic and two sided. It is not enough to get a list of customers and their spending habits; the relationship will evolve with each transaction, and CRM systems must as well.

The third concern is the most serious. If marketing is about understanding and meeting customer needs, it is important to appreciate that those needs and how to meet them will change over time. Any relationship (whether it's between a business and a consumer, a business and another business, or even between family members) involves a series of interactions. The relationship builds over time with more of these interactions. The needs of both parties change, and the other party has to be willing to adjust to those changes to be successful. Companies that ignore this do so at their own peril.

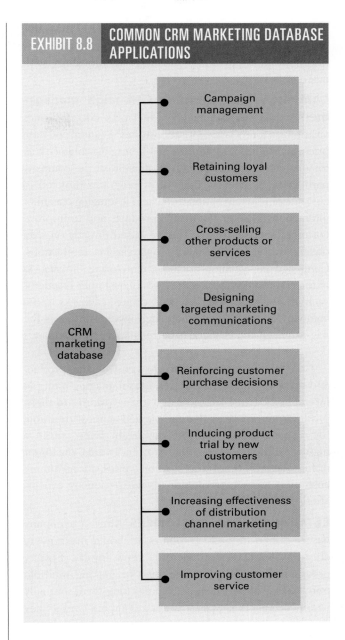

EXHIBIT 8.8 COMMON CRM MARKETING DATABASE APPLICATIONS

To create a two-sided relationship that focuses on more than just loyalty, companies must leverage the customer information they have gathered. While there is an adage that states keeping an existing customer is cheaper than finding a new customer, a CRM system has to have the ability to move beyond just finding those loyal customers. A company can undertake to best leverage the information gathered through the database and IT solutions from Stage 2. Some of the benefits that can be gained by gathering this information can be seen in Exhibit 8.8.

LEVERAGE CUSTOMER FEEDBACK Data mining identifies the most profitable customers and prospects. Managers can then design tailored marketing strategies to best appeal to the identified segments. In CRM, this activity is commonly referred to as leveraging customer information to facilitate enhanced relationships with customers.

CAMPAIGN MANAGEMENT Campaign management refers to developing product or service offerings customized for the appropriate customer segment and then pricing and communicating these offerings to enhance customer relationships. Through it, all areas of the company participate in the development of programs targeted to customers. It involves monitoring and leveraging customer interactions to sell a company's products and to improve customer service. Campaigns are based directly on data obtained from customers through various interactions. Campaign management includes monitoring the success of the communications on the basis of customer reactions, such as customer inquiries, sales, orders, callbacks to the company, and the like. If a campaign appears unsuccessful, it is evaluated and changed to better achieve the company's desired objective.

Campaign management involves customizing product and service offerings, which requires managing multiple interactions with customers and giving priority to those products and services that are viewed as most desirable for a specifically designated customer. Even within a highly defined market segment, individual customer differences will emerge. Therefore, interactions among customers must focus on individual experiences, expectations, and desires.

RETAINING LOYAL CUSTOMERS After a company has identified its best customers, it should make every effort to maintain and increase their loyalty. Loyalty programs reward loyal customers for making multiple purchases. The objective is to build long-term mutually beneficial relationships between a company and its key customers. Marriott, Hilton, and Starwood Hotels, for instance, reward their best customers with special perks not available to customers who stay less frequently. Travellers who spend a specified number of nights per year receive reservation guarantees, welcome gifts such as fruit baskets and wine in their rooms, and access to concierge lounges. Loyal members who sign up to collect points can use their accumulated points to receive discounts at hotels in exotic locations, free nights, free flights, and reduced rates on car rentals.

campaign management
developing product or service offerings customized for the appropriate customer segment and then pricing and communicating these offerings to enhance customer relationships

In addition to rewarding good customers, loyalty programs provide businesses with a wealth of information about their customers and shopping trends that can be used to make future business decisions. A yearly report released by Canadian-based Bond Brand Loyalty examines the most critical factors to success for loyalty programs. It asks for information from more than 55 000 North American consumers and assesses programs in more than 20 markets worldwide in order to develop data on the success factors in the loyalty reward program business.[14] The top drivers of loyalty program satisfaction are that it meets consumer needs, the customer enjoys participating in the program, the program makes the brand experience better, there is consistency with other interactions, and the overall reward is seen as a benefit.[15] The report also highlights some concerning trends for loyalty programs among Canadians: only 33 percent of those surveyed were very satisfied with their loyalty card program, down from 36 percent in 2018.[16] And what made a trustworthy and strong loyalty program? It came down to personal interaction. Customers who felt there was an attempt to personalize their loyalty reward program were much more likely to be satisfied or very satisfied with the program.

The report also ranked the top (and bottom) loyalty programs in Canada. Before you look at the list in Exhibit 8.9, what would your experiences with loyalty programs tell you about good and bad loyalty programs? The categories are retail, grocery and drug store, quick service restaurants (QSR), coalition (multiple businesses), consumer packaged goods (CPG), and cobranded debit (two companies joining together).

CROSS-SELLING OTHER PRODUCTS AND SERVICES CRM provides many opportunities to cross-sell related products. Marketers can use the database to match product profiles with consumer profiles, enabling the cross-selling of products that match consumers' demographic, lifestyle, or behavioural characteristics. Ingersoll Rand, a global manufacturer of everything from air compressors to refrigeration units, saw the benefits of cross-selling. One of Ingersoll Rand's business units, Club Car, sells golf carts. The company soon found out that Club Car's customers were also potential customers in other areas, such as for excavators and loaders. Ingersoll Rand began to share information about customers across all of the more than 30 business units of the organization. In the first year of doing this, Ingersoll Rand brought in $6.2 million in incremental cross-selling revenue.[17]

Online companies use product and customer profiling to reveal cross-selling opportunities while a visitor

EXHIBIT 8.9	THE TOP 3 LOYALTY PROGRAMS SCORES IN CANADA BASED ON MEMBER ENGAGEMENT		
	First Place	**Second Place**	**Third Place**
Coffee	McDonald's	Starbucks	Second Cup
Airline	WestJet	Porter	Air Canada
Grocery	Co-op	Metro	PC Optimum
Retail	Amazon Prime	MEC	Cineplex Scene
Gas & Convenience	Petro Points	7-11 Rewards	Fas Gas Plus
Hospitality	Wyndham	Marriot	IHG Club
Department	Simons	Nordstroms	Hudson's Bay
Coalition	Student Plus Card	More Rewards	Air Miles

Source: Bond, The Loyalty Report '19. https://cdn2.hubspot.net/hubfs/352767/TLR%202019/Bond_CAN_TLR19_Exec%20Summary_Launch%20Edition.pdf

is on their site. Past purchases on a particular website and the website a visitor comes from provide online marketers with clues about the visitor's interests and what items to cross-sell. Similarly, profiles on customers enable sales representatives or customer service people to personalize their communications while the customer is shopping. Knowing a customer's past purchases and preferences can enable the employee to provide more advice or suggestions that fit with the customer's tastes.

DESIGNING TARGETED MARKETING COMMUNICATIONS By using transaction and purchase data, a database allows marketers to track customers' relationships to the company's products and services and to then modify their marketing message accordingly. By creating this database, companies can answer a question that would seem at first to be an obvious one: "How many customers do we have?" But it is surprising how many companies focus on units sold or other metrics. Once the number of customers is determined, there can be a focus on "how much"—as in, how much are your customers worth to your brand? Transaction and purchase data provide insights into average purchase volume, purchase by location, and other factors. Once these records are organized in a clear database, a company can get on to the important focus of "Who is our customer?" Customers can also be segmented into infrequent users, moderate users, and heavy users. A segmented communications strategy can then be developed to target the customer segment. Communications to infrequent users might encourage repeat purchases through a direct incentive, such as a limited-time coupon or price discount. Communications to moderate users may use fewer incentives and more reinforcement of their past purchase decisions. Communications to heavy users would be designed around loyalty and reinforcement of the purchase rather than price promotions.

REINFORCING CUSTOMER PURCHASE DECISIONS As you learned in Chapter 5, cognitive dissonance is the feeling consumers get when they recognize an inconsistency between their values and opinions and their purchase behaviour. In other words, they doubt the soundness of their purchase decision and feel anxious. CRM offers marketers an excellent opportunity to reach out to customers to reinforce the purchase decision. By thanking customers for their purchases and telling customers they are important, marketers can help cement a long-term, profitable relationship.

Updating customers periodically regarding the status of their order reinforces purchase decisions. Post sale emails also afford the chance to provide more customer service or cross-sell other products. There is a movement for companies who sell high involvement and high-priced offerings to consider sending a "thank-you letter" to customers to not only express thanks but also to look to the future by discussing their current order and potential future orders.

INDUCING PRODUCT TRIAL BY NEW CUSTOMERS Although significant time and money are expended on encouraging repeat purchases by the best customers, a marketing database is also used to identify new customers. Because a company using a marketing database already has a profile of its best customers, it can easily use the results of modelling to profile potential customers. Bell Canada uses modelling to identify prospective residential and commercial telephone customers and successfully attract their business.

Marketing managers generally use demographic and behavioural data overlaid on existing customer data to develop a detailed customer profile that is a powerful tool for evaluating lists of prospects. For instance, if a company's best customers are 35 to 50 years of age, live in suburban areas, and enjoy mountain climbing, the company can match this profile to prospects already in its database or to customers currently identified as using a competitor's product.

INCREASING EFFECTIVENESS OF DISTRIBUTION CHANNEL MARKETING A marketing channel is a business structure of interdependent organizations, such as wholesalers and retailers, which move a product from the producer to the ultimate consumer (you will read more about this in Chapter 13). Most marketers rely on indirect channels to move their products to the end user. Thus marketers often lose touch with customers as individuals because the relationship is really between the retailer and the consumers. Marketers in this predicament often view their customers as aggregate statistics because specific customer information is difficult to gather.

Using CRM databases, manufacturers now have a tool to gain insight into who is buying their products.

Sephora offers a Beauty Insider Rewards program free for customers to join. The program awards points to members for every dollar spent, a free gift in the member's birthday month, and special discounts. Members also benefit from beauty services in Sephora stores.

Instead of simply unloading products into the distribution channel and leaving marketing and relationship building to dealers, auto manufacturers today are using websites to keep in touch with customers and prospects, to learn about their lifestyles and hobbies, to understand their vehicle needs, and to develop relationships in hopes these consumers will reward them with brand loyalty in the future. BMW and other vehicle manufacturers have databases filled with contact information on the millions of consumers who have expressed an interest in their products.

With many bricks-and-mortar stores setting up shop online, companies are now challenged to monitor the purchases of customers who shop both in-store and online. This concept is referred to as multichannel marketing. Canadian footwear brand Manitoba Mukluks has used pop-up stores in Canadian shopping malls in 2018 and 2019 in order to build on its multichannel approach that includes the company's websites and sales in retail footwear stores across Canada.[18]

IMPROVING CUSTOMER SERVICE CRM marketing techniques are increasingly being used to improve customer service. Many companies are using information and training webinars for their product or service to make personal contact with interested customers. Those interested in a topic are asked to register and provide a bit of information about themselves and their company's needs. Before or immediately after the webinar, a representative will contact them to answer questions and provide further information. Other companies, such as Starbucks, follow up customers' visits to the store with a short survey to determine each customer's level of service satisfaction. Consumers contacted are given Starbucks Rewards points as an incentive to provide feedback.

8-4 | PRIVACY CONCERNS AND CRM

Before rushing out to invest in a CRM system and build a database, marketers should consider consumers' reactions to the growing use of databases. Many customers are concerned about databases because of the potential for invasion of privacy. The sheer volume of information that is aggregated in databases makes this information vulnerable to unauthorized access and use. A fundamental aspect of marketing using CRM databases is providing valuable services to customers based on knowledge of what customers really value. It is critical, however, that marketers remember that these relationships should be built on trust. Although database technology enables marketers to compile ever-richer information about their customers that can be used to build and manage relationships, if these customers feel their privacy is being violated, then the relationship becomes a liability.

The popularity of the Internet for customer data collection and as a repository for sensitive customer data has alarmed privacy-minded customers. Online users complain loudly about being spammed, and online users, including children, are routinely asked to divulge personal information to access certain screens or to purchase goods or services. Internet users are disturbed by the amount of information businesses collect on them as they visit various sites in cyberspace. Indeed, many users are unaware of how personal information is collected, used, and distributed. The government actively sells huge amounts of personal information to list companies. Consumer credit databases are often used by credit-card marketers to prescreen targets for solicitations. Online and off-line privacy concerns are growing and ultimately will have to be dealt with by businesses and regulators.

As we have discussed, privacy policies for Canadian companies are regulated by PIPEDA and the Privacy Act. But collecting data on consumers outside Canada is a different matter. For database marketers venturing beyond our borders, success requires careful navigation of foreign privacy laws. For example, under the European Union's European Data Protection Directive, any business that trades with a European organization must comply with the EU's rules for handling information about individuals or risk prosecution. More than 50 nations have developed, or are developing, privacy legislation. The EU nations have the strictest legislation regarding the collection and use of customer data, and other countries look to that legislation when formulating their policies.

8-5 | THE FUTURE OF CRM

Some think CRM as it exists now will soon be obsolete. An article in the *Harvard Business Review* stated, "CRM isn't dead [yet], but [users] will cease to use it unless it can

Salesforce of Nature

It would be impossible to discuss CRM, or to get through a page of Google results on CRM, without mention of Salesforce. The company is one of the most recognizable enterprise software companies in the world, and Salesforce is now used interchangeably with CRM. Founded in 1999 by Marc Benioff, the company changed the way in which companies dealt with acquiring CRM systems. In the past, companies had to make large upfront payments for systems that could take months or years to properly implement. However, moving with the Software as a Service (SaaS) model of monthly subscriptions, Salesforce was able to make CRM accessible to companies of any size. Today, Salesforce is the world's leading CRM Software (based on sales and on the company's website) and brings elements of sales, marketing research, and customer service together in a cloud-based environment that does not require the large upfront fees and setup time. Large companies seeking to use Salesforce will likely have to create and pay for adjustments and upgrades, but it

is much more cost-effective compared to older CRM systems. Salesforce's challenge for future growth lies squarely on trying to get the general public, the fledgling entrepreneur, to understand exactly what Salesforce does. In a 2019 global brand campaign, Salesforce explained by creating the tag line "We Bring Companies and Customers Together." Simple in concept yet incredibly challenging in execution; such is the world of CRM.

get smart and save them time, rather than burden them with time-intensive data entry and lookup."[19] So while technology has been an important part of the growth and success of CRM, continued use of the newest and best technologies will be vital to CRM maintaining its relevance. Other than the introduction of cloud storage systems to keep track of data (like customer loyalty information), technological innovations have not been as impactful as the use of cloud storage

While the CRM systems that have been described in this chapter do help to create efficiencies for organizations, there is greater concern as to the amount of time needed to input data into these systems and manage the information that comes out. Research shows that sales representatives are spending less time actually selling, and more time on what are deemed "administrative" tasks that often include the upkeep and management of the CRM systems.

However, there is a movement in CRM toward customer relationship automation, given the pressures of continuous improvement in organizations and the prevalence of predictive technologies and relational databases. This is best exemplified by Amazon's highly sophisticated technologies related to CRM. Anyone who has an Amazon account is often mystified by how well Amazon can track your preferences by your search history and previous purchases.

The emergence of **on-demand marketing** is taking CRM to a new level. As technology evolves and becomes more sophisticated, consumers' expectations of their decision- and buying-related experiences have risen. Consumers (1) want to interact anywhere, anytime; (2) want to do new things with varied kinds of information in ways that create value; (3) expect data stored about them to be targeted specifically to their needs or to personalize their experiences; and (4) expect all interactions with a company to be easy. In response to these expectations, companies are developing new ways to integrate and personalize each stage of a customer's decision journey, which in turn should increase relationship-related behaviours from customers. On-demand marketing delivers relevant experiences throughout the consumer's decision and buying process that are integrated across both physical and virtual environments. Trends such as the growth of mobile connectivity, better-designed websites, inexpensive communication through technology, and advances in handling big data have allowed companies to start designing on-demand marketing programs that appeal to consumers. For on-demand marketing to be successful, companies must deliver high-quality experiences across all touch points with the customer, including sales, service, product use, and marketing.

Many more companies are offering on-demand services. For example, Instacart will deliver groceries to a customer's door, typically within an hour of ordering. Many restaurant chains are now a part of online service GrubHub, which allows customers to type in their postal codes, pick a restaurant, and order items for delivery—all without leaving the GrubHub website. Uber and Lyft provide on-demand transportation by connecting customers to drivers using their own cars—a service that Uber has leveraged into a GrubHub competitor called UberEats.[20]

on-demand marketing delivering relevant experiences, integrated across both physical and virtual environments, throughout the consumer's decision and buying process

AWAKE CHOCOLATE
CONTINUING CASE

Mindset More than Machine

The belief that CRM goes beyond technology solutions is evidenced by Awake's approach to managing its customer relationships. Early in its existence, Awake founders did concern themselves with the minutiae of customer tracking, as described by Matt Schnarr: "We have used some [CRM technologies], we have used HubSpot. That was at a point in our business where we tried to call on every university in the US. It got to a point where we couldn't do it in Excel anymore." But creating a CRM was not all about finding the right computer program for Awake; it had to involve something more grounded in the tenets of the company and the way it has grown and succeeded over the last decade.

But as Awake realized a traditional approach to building a customer base would not work for the company, it had to adjust the way in which it established and tracked customer relationships. Matt Schnarr went on to say, "As we started to focus on selling to the distributor instead of to the university[,] that's required us to have less touchpoints and be more scalable." This has meant that larger software programs like Salesforce were not as relevant for Awake as a company, so it had to shift focus and start building key relationships rather than simply gathering data.

Therefore, it comes as no surprise that Awake no longer relies on high-tech solutions to manage its CRM systems because the company does not have such large buying cycles, nor long lists of customers. Instead, it takes a more pragmatic approach, focusing on "relationships, when they are ongoing and day to day." This still requires organization and structure like that described in the chapter, but with a focus on building relationships instead of databases. "No one here calls more than 50 to 100 customers. So, there is no need for an elaborate machine." Hence the "machinery" being used by Awake must rely on human resources to develop and manage customer relationships.

The first characteristic Awake looks for in a customer manager is character, something Matt Schnarr noted as "somewhere between accountable and trustworthy." With fewer customers than before because of its approach to B2B interactions, Awake looks for managing customer relationships in a more personal and engaging manner.

The other characteristic of an Awake staff member charged with managing customers is someone who is adding value, doing something more than just following the basic instructions about CRM; it's more about, as Matt puts it, "putting your strategic hat on." It's easy to forget that imply reaching out to customers and getting updates on their situations can be just as impactful as inquiring about future sales.

For Awake, the path to customer relationship management clearly veers more toward customer support than business development. This does not mean that Awake is unconcerned about building its network of customers but believes that the ideal approach is through relationship building that is more personal in nature. Therefore, the CRM at Awake is less about bytes and storage, and more about critical thinking and problem-solving skill sets.

QUESTIONS

1. Since Stage 3 of the CRM cycle is where Awake places a lot of emphasis, use Exhibit 8.6 to highlight the top three applications that the company could use to best develop its CRM.

2. Awake has turned away from software applications as the focus of its CRM approach. Scan this chapter and look for reasons that a more structured database would be helpful for the company to continue to evolve.

3. Take on the role of a CRM manager at Awake. You have just been notified that there is a heightened occurrence of hacking of company's customer databases. Write an email to Matt Schnarr to show how you would handle this situation.

Analyzing Marketing Opportunities, Part 2 Case

Indigo Where?

The story of Indigo Books & Music is one of constant renewal. The company Indigo started in 1997, but the makeup of the company started during World War II.

In 1940, the Coles brothers started a bookstore in Toronto. The Coles name was synonymous with booksellers in Canada for most of the 20th century, including the creation of the world's largest bookstore in Toronto. Around the same time, the United Kingdom–based bookseller W.H. Smith opened stores in Canada and grew.

As the Internet began its ascent in the mid-1990s, Coles and W.H. Smith merged to become Chapters Inc. and around the same time Indigo Books & Music opened its first location in Burlington, Ontario. In 2001, Chapters and Indigo merged, using the Indigo name but still keeping the Chapters name in some stores up until a few years ago.[1]

Since then, Indigo has made multiple attempts to stave off the barbarians at the gate for the bookseller industry in Canada. And those barbarians take many different forms, from online giants to societal trends.

Overall book sales in Canada have been flat for a number of years. The most recent data from the Canadian Book Market 2019 report shows 806 000 unique books (ISBNs), which accounted for 54 million units sold and $1.1 billion in industry revenue.[2]

Another report from IBIS World predicted a decline in industry revenues for booksellers in Canada, due to what it called "… high levels of external competition from online retailers and e-books, which offer alternative and more affordable channels through which consumers are able to purchase industry goods."[3]

So, it's not only behemoths such as Amazon that Canadian booksellers like Indigo need to be wary of, but even the local library that increasingly offers print and digital alternatives for consumers to digest books at a fraction (if any) of the cost of a book in a bookstore.

In response, Indigo has introduced a number of new product lines; many would consider them to be brand extensions (see Chapters 9 and 10). These products include home accessories like blankets, pillows, and throws; and infant products like stuffed animals and bottles. There now seems to be more space in Indigo stores for water bottles, stocking stuffers, and kids' toys than for books. This is partly due to the changing nature of the book customer. With

Vince Talotta/Toronto Star/Getty Images

Vince Talotta/Toronto Star/Getty Images

more options, consumers now use technology and choice to sometimes delay purchase decisions. Consumers can go into a bricks-and-mortar bookstore like Indigo, browse through a book, and order the same book through Amazon at a cheaper price, to arrive at their home within hours.

Indigo started shipping products from its website around the time of the merger with Chapters, but it has always struggled with shipping times. Offering delivery in weeks when competitors offer it in days has been a real hindrance.

As sales numbers and share price continued to tumble since the merger, Indigo has had to focus on other aspects of its business. The company started hosting events at stores, including what one would normally expect from a bookstore: book signings. But the company needed to attract a younger audience, so it started hosting children's events where kids and their parents would come to the store to play games, read books, and interact with Indigo products. During March break, Indigo often hosts daily events to provide parents and kids a break from their spring break.[4]

Realizing the advantage of a physical presence in the market, Indigo began opening larger stores, concept stores, and other formats in order to better engage with customers. Creating experiences included creating special shops: from Indigotech stores selling phones and technology to American Girl Doll boutiques that offer everything from dollhouses to hair and makeup services (for the dolls).

Indigo has also focused on being a good Canadian citizen, another way to differentiate it from large online adversaries. While it is challenging for Indigo to offer same-day delivery, it can focus on Canadian authors and children learning to read in Canada. For Canada's 150th birthday in 2017, Indigo honoured Canadian authors by selling books and collections focused on authors from the Great White North.

The Indigo Love of Reading Foundation, Indigo Literacy Fund Grant, and Indigo Adopt-A-School all display a commitment to give back to a community that, it is hoped, become future book consumers.[5] The Foundation has raised more than $29 million for schools in Canada since its founding in 2004.

In 2011, Indigo entered the world of loyalty programs by introducing the Plum Rewards program. The bookseller seemed a little late to the game of customer tracking and rewards, and the Plum program was seen as a good but not great program. In 2019, the company announced plum PLUS, a higher-end loyalty program that charges a $39 fee but provides discounts on most purchases.[6]

But as the ideas increase, the numbers continue to fall. The company's stock price flirted with $21 per share in early 2018, but early 2020 it had fallen close to the $3 mark.[7] And with every quarterly reporting noting a decline from the previous period the year before, one wonders how much longer the biggest Canadian bookseller can survive.

But according to Indigo CEO Heather Reisman, there is actually hope in these declining numbers. The company embarked in 2020 on a cost-cutting mission, looking in all places for ways to reduce expenses, whether in administrative, operating, or general areas of the company. The goal, it would seem, is to be sleeker and more efficient and to make the best out of the infrastructure it currently possesses.

In February 2020, Reisman said, "We are in the early stages of a fundamental repositioning of Indigo—one that will fully build on our customer affection for our brand but that will allow us to thrive in an environment which is totally different from the one we were 'born into.'"[8]

However, what that new position will be is still up for interpretation. As you know, there is a lot to be done in marketing before worrying about advertising or selling. Your experience so far in the areas of marketing research, consumer behaviour, business-to-business interactions, segmentation, and customer relationship management should guide you in helping Indigo Books & Music Inc. to escape the world in which it was "born into."

With the questions that follow, you are given a blank page on which to make the changes necessary to achieve success in the bookselling market in Canada.

Spencer Weiner/Los Angeles Times/Getty Images

QUESTIONS

1. Conduct a proper SWOT analysis for Indigo Books & Music.

2. Assess Heather Reisman's statement in terms of what you know about positioning from Chapter 7.

3. Create a market segment for a consumer and a business segment for Indigo's new position, using your assessment from Question 2. Provide the necessary characteristics in order to ensure that you have properly segmented the market.

NOTES

1. Indigo, "Our Company, Timeline," www.chapters.indigo.ca/en-ca/our-company/timeline (accessed July 3, 2020).

2. BookNet, "The Canadian Book Market 2019," April 1, 2020, www.booknetcanada.ca/blog/2020/4/1/the-canadian-book-market-2019 (accessed July 3, 2020).

3. www.ibisworld.com/canada/market-research-reports/book-stores-industry

4. Indigo, "Kids Break," www.chapters.indigo.ca/en-ca/march-break (accessed July 3, 2020).

5. Indigo, "Our Company, Timeline," www.chapters.indigo.ca/en-ca/our-company/timeline (accessed July 3, 2020).

6. Cision, "Membership Program That Offers Canadians More Rewards Than Ever," September 25, 2019, www.newswire.ca/news-releases/indigo-launches-plum-plus-a-new-membership-program-that-offers-canadians-more-rewards-than-ever-890454073.html (accessed July 3, 2020).

7. Indigo, "Investor Relations," www.chapters.indigo.ca/en-ca/investor-relations (accessed July 3, 2020).

8. Cision, "Indigo Reports Third Quarter Fiscal 2020 Financial Results—Focus on Profitability Drives Net Earnings Growth of 20%" February 6, 2020, www.newswire.ca/news-releases/indigo-reports-third-quarter-fiscal-2020-financial-results-focus-on-profitability-drives-net-earnings-growth-of-20--875420979.html (accessed July 3, 2020).

9 | Product Concepts

LEARNING OUTCOMES

9-1 Define the term *product*

9-2 Classify consumer products

9-3 Define the terms *product item*, *product line*, and *product mix*

9-4 Describe marketing uses of branding

9-5 Describe marketing uses of packaging and labelling

9-6 Discuss global issues in branding and packaging

9-7 Describe how and why product warranties are important marketing tools

"My philosophy is that everything starts with a great product"

—Steve Jobs, Apple[1]

9-1 | WHAT IS A PRODUCT?

The product offering, at the heart of an organization's marketing efforts, is usually the starting point in creating a marketing mix. Many marketing mix decisions are made simultaneously; however, a marketing manager cannot determine a price, design a promotion strategy, or create a distribution channel until the company has a product or service to sell. Moreover, an excellent distribution channel, a persuasive promotional campaign, and a fair price have no value when a company's offering is poor or inadequate.

product
anything, both favourable and unfavourable, received by a person in an exchange for possession, consumption, attention, or short-term use

A **product** may be defined as anything, both favourable and unfavourable, received by a person in an exchange for possession, consumption, attention, or short-term use. It is important to note that not all products received by someone can be owned by them because a product may be a tangible good (a pair of shoes), a service (a haircut), an idea ("don't litter"), a person (a political candidate or a celebrity), a place (a tourism destination "For Glowing Hearts"), or any combination of these. Customers can own a tangible product, like a pair of shoes, but they only use a service, such as staying at a hotel (for more on services, please see Chapter 11). For a tangible good, packaging, style, colour, options, and size are some typical product features. Just as important are intangibles such as service, the seller's image, the manufacturer's reputation, and the way consumers believe others will view the product.

To most people, the term *product* means a tangible good, but product can also include services, ideas, persons, and places as these are all part of what companies offer to customers. (Chapter 11 focuses specifically on the unique aspects of marketing services.)

The concept of a product will continue to evolve with the inclusion of technology into the mix. One technology that is already seeping into the way

Special Price

Special Price

Special Price

Special Price

products will be defined, identified, and sold is augmented reality (AR). Not to be confused with virtual reality, AR is defined by business management consultants Accenture as "the overlaying of physical environments with digital content and images to provide users an enhanced (or augmented) experience of reality."[2] The popularity of AR has been helped immensely by the popularity of Snapchat, which allows users to enhance photos by using elements of AR. Snapchat's AR elements, seen in the smartphone screen on the Snapchat app, will be key to how the company grows in the future. One of the most popular AR filters recently is the Time Machine AR, which shows the user as a child, at their current age, and in old age.

As of 2019, Snapchat had 210 million users, and those users interacted with the company's AR features 30 times a day on average.

The future of AR lies in the ability of companies to use it to promote their brand—or even other company's brands. Snapchat uses some AR filters that showcase an advertiser's brand immersed in the world of the user. Some retailers are creating apps that allow consumers to interact with retail environments, such as allowing customers to visualize what a piece of clothing might look like on them.

9-2 | TYPES OF CONSUMER PRODUCTS

Products can be broadly classified as either business or consumer products, depending on the buyer's intentions. The key distinction, as discussed earlier in the book, between the two types of products is their intended use. If the intended use is a business purpose, the product is classified as a business or industrial product. As explained in Chapter 6, a **business product** is used to manufacture other goods or provide services, to facilitate an organization's operations, or to resell to other customers. A **consumer product** is bought to satisfy an individual's personal wants. Sometimes the same item can be classified as either a business or a consumer product, depending on its intended use. Examples are light bulbs, pencils and paper, and computers.

We need to know about product classifications because different products are marketed differently: They are marketed

business product
a product used to manufacture other goods or services, to facilitate an organization's operations, or to resell to other customers

consumer product
a product bought to satisfy an individual's personal wants

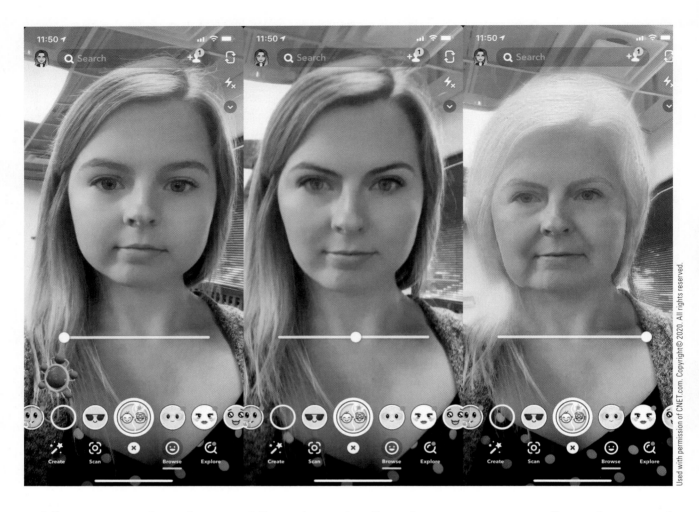

to different target markets, often using different distribution, promotion, and pricing strategies.

Chapter 6 examined seven categories of business products and services: major equipment, accessory equipment, component parts, processed materials, raw materials, supplies, and services. This chapter examines an effective way of categorizing consumer products. Although they can be classified in several ways, the most popular approach includes these four types: convenience products, shopping products, specialty products, and unsought products.

This approach classifies products according to how much effort is normally used to shop for them.

9-2a | Convenience Products

A **convenience product** is a relatively inexpensive item that merits little shopping effort—that is, a consumer is unwilling or does not need to shop extensively for such an item. Grocery items fall into the convenience product category.

Consumers buy convenience products regularly, usually without much planning. Nevertheless, consumers do know the brand names of popular convenience products, such as Monster Energy Drinks, Mr. Clean, Axe deodorants, and Rice Krispie treats. Convenience products normally require wide distribution to be easily accessible to consumers. For example, Skittles is available everywhere, including at Shoppers Drug Mart, 7-Eleven, vending machines, and Amazon.ca.

Impulse products are a type of convenience products that consumers purchase without any planning; they are placed near the front of retail stores for consumers to see and purchase at the last minute. For example, batteries, soft drinks, magazines, and gift cards fall into this category.

9-2b | Shopping Products

A **shopping product** requires comparison shopping because it is usually more expensive than a convenience product and is found in fewer stores. Consumers usually

convenience product
a relatively inexpensive item that merits little shopping effort

shopping product
a product that requires comparison shopping because it is usually more expensive than a convenience product and is found in fewer stores

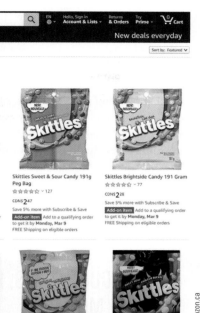

buy a shopping product only after comparing different brands' style, practicality, price, and lifestyle compatibility. Shoppers are typically willing to invest some effort in this process to get their desired benefits.

Shopping products can be divided into two types: homogeneous and heterogeneous. Consumers perceive *homogeneous* shopping products as being basically similar in their functions and features—for example, toasters, kettles, and other kitchen appliances tend to be similar. When shopping for homogeneous shopping products, consumers typically look for the lowest-priced brand that has the desired features. For example, consumers might compare Black & Decker, Betty Crocker, and Sunbeam toasters, perceive them to be similar, and select the one with the lowest price.

In contrast, consumers perceive *heterogeneous* shopping products as essentially different in their features, quality, and performance—for example, furniture, clothing, housing, and postsecondary institutions. Consumers often have trouble comparing heterogeneous shopping products because the prices, quality, and features vary so much. The benefit of comparing heterogeneous shopping products is that consumers can find the best product or brand for their needs, a decision that is often highly individual. For example, it can be difficult to compare a small technical college with a large, public university.

9-2c | Specialty Products

When consumers search extensively for a particular item with unique characteristics and are very reluctant to accept substitutes, that item is known as a **specialty product**. Specialty products don't have to be expensive; however, most expensive products, such as Bang & Olufson speakers, Tesla automobiles, and Ruth's Chris Steak House, are generally considered specialty products. A relatively inexpensive product can also be considered a specialty item if it possesses a unique product or brand attribute; for example, people visiting Canada will often seek out real maple syrup and will pay a premium in comparison to inexpensive grocery store options. This is due to the unique taste, limited availability, and overall connection of the product to Canadian culture.

Marketers of specialty products often use selective advertising to maintain their product's exclusive image. Distribution is often limited to one or a very few outlets in a geographic area. Brand names and quality of service are often very important.

9-2d | Unsought Products

A product unknown to the potential buyer or a known product that the buyer does not actively seek is referred to as an **unsought product**. New products fall into

specialty product
a particular item with unique characteristics for which consumers search extensively and for which they are very reluctant to accept substitutes

unsought product
a product unknown to the potential buyer or a known product that the buyer does not actively seek

this category until consumer awareness of them is increased through advertising and distribution.

Some goods are always marketed as unsought items, especially needed products that we do not like to think about or do not care to spend money on. Insurance, burial plots, and similar items require aggressive personal selling and highly persuasive advertising. Salespeople actively seek leads to potential buyers. Because consumers usually do not seek out this type of product, the company must focus on discussing the importance of dealing with this issue without reminding consumers of any negative connotations. Often the focus of message with unsought goods relates to the classic advertising tactic of "peace of mind."

9-3 | PRODUCT ITEMS, LINES, AND MIXES

Rarely does a company sell a single product. More often, it sells a variety of products. Marketing managers make important decisions regarding the number and type of products a company should sell under a brand name in a given market. A **product item** is a specific version of a product that can be designated as a distinct offering among an organization's products. Campbell's Cream of Chicken Soup is an example of a product item (see Exhibit 9.1).

A group of closely related product items is a **product line**. For example, the column in Exhibit 9.1 titled "Soups" represents one of Campbell's product lines. Different container sizes and shapes also distinguish items in a product line. Diet Coke, for example, is available in cans and various plastic containers. Each size and each container is a separate product item. When Diet Coke announced new flavours in 2018, which included Ginger Lime, Twisted Mango, and Feisty Cherry, the

product item
a specific version of a product that can be designated as a distinct offering among an organization's products

product line
a group of closely related product items

product mix
all products that an organization sells

product mix width
the number of product lines an organization offers

product line length
the number of product items in a product line

product line depth
the different versions of a product item in a product line

company also introduced a new sleeker packaging and overall look to the products.

An organization's **product mix** includes all the products it sells. All Campbell's products—soups, sauces, beverages, and biscuits—constitute its product mix. Each product item in the product mix may require a separate marketing strategy. In some cases, however, product lines and even entire product mixes share some marketing strategy components. Chapstick has numerous but related product lines, all with the familiar brand name emblazoned on the products. From higher-end "Total Hydration" to the classic candy-cane flavoured product, the look and feel for Chapstick is the same. Companies derive several benefits from organizing related items into product lines.

The product mix of a business organization can be described in terms of product mix width, product line length, and depth.

Product mix width (or breadth) refers to the number of product lines an organization offers. In Exhibit 9.1, for example, the width of Campbell's product mix continues to grow from a few lines (mostly soups) to including gravies, salsas, cookies, and crackers. **Product line length** is the number of product items in a product line. As shown in Exhibit 9.1, the sauces product line consists of four product items; while the line of soups has so many items it would take up at least two pages of this textbook. **Product line depth** refers to the number of types and sizes offered for each product in the line. For example, Campbell's soup offers different sizes of the tomato soups that also come in different flavours.

Companies increase the *width* of their product mix to diversify risk. To generate sales and boost profits, companies spread risk across many product lines rather than depending on only one or two. Companies also widen

EXHIBIT 9.1 | CAMPBELL'S PRODUCT LINES AND PRODUCT MIX

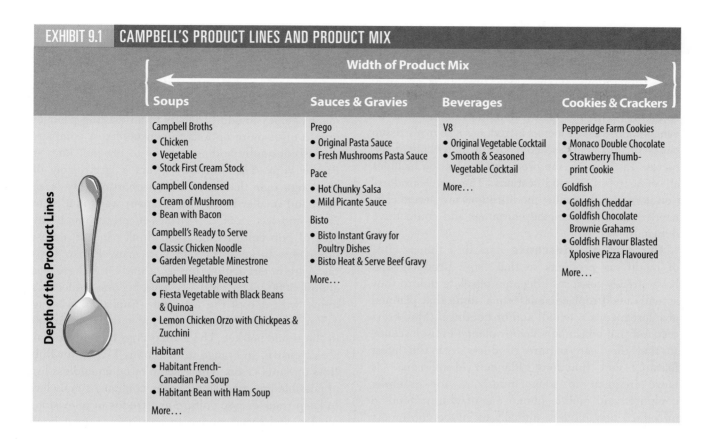

Width of Product Mix

Depth of the Product Lines

Soups	Sauces & Gravies	Beverages	Cookies & Crackers
Campbell Broths • Chicken • Vegetable • Stock First Cream Stock **Campbell Condensed** • Cream of Mushroom • Bean with Bacon **Campbell's Ready to Serve** • Classic Chicken Noodle • Garden Vegetable Minestrone **Campbell Healthy Request** • Fiesta Vegetable with Black Beans & Quinoa • Lemon Chicken Orzo with Chickpeas & Zucchini **Habitant** • Habitant French-Canadian Pea Soup • Habitant Bean with Ham Soup More…	**Prego** • Original Pasta Sauce • Fresh Mushrooms Pasta Sauce **Pace** • Hot Chunky Salsa • Mild Picante Sauce **Bisto** • Bisto Instant Gravy for Poultry Dishes • Bisto Heat & Serve Beef Gravy More…	**V8** • Original Vegetable Cocktail • Smooth & Seasoned Vegetable Cocktail More…	**Pepperidge Farm Cookies** • Monaco Double Chocolate • Strawberry Thumb-print Cookie **Goldfish** • Goldfish Cheddar • Goldfish Chocolate Brownie Grahams • Goldfish Flavour Blasted Xplosive Pizza Flavoured More…

their product mix to capitalize on established reputations. Reese's started out with a successful pair of chocolate bars; the Reese's Pieces and Reese's Peanut Butter Cups. But now you can find Reese's breakfast cereal, Reese's Peanut Butter, and Reese's ice cream topping.

Companies increase the *length* and *depth* of their product lines to attract buyers with different preferences, to increase sales and profits by further segmenting the market, to capitalize on economies of scale in production and marketing, and to even out seasonal sales patterns. P&G is adding some lower-priced versions of its namesake brands, including Bounty Basic and Charmin Basic. These brands are targeted to more price-sensitive customers, a segment that Procter & Gamble had not been serving with its more premium brands.[3]

9-3a | Adjustments to Product Items, Lines, and Mixes

Over time, companies change product items, lines, and mixes to take advantage of new technical or product developments or to respond to changes in the environment. They may adjust by modifying products, repositioning products, or extending or contracting product lines.

PRODUCT MODIFICATION Marketing managers must decide whether and when to modify existing products. **Product modification** changes one or more of a product's characteristics:

- Quality modification: a change in a product's dependability or durability. Reducing a product's quality may allow the manufacturer to lower the price, thereby appealing to target markets unable to afford the original product. Conversely, increasing quality can help the company compete with rival companies. Increasing quality can also result in increased brand loyalty, greater ability to raise prices, or new opportunities for market segmentation. Inexpensive ink-jet printers have improved in quality to the point that they can now produce photo-quality images.

- Functional modification: a change in a product's versatility, effectiveness, convenience, or safety. Tide with Downy combines into one product the functions of both cleaning power and fabric softening.[4]

- Style modification: an aesthetic product change, rather than a quality or functional change. Clothing and auto manufacturers also commonly use style modifications to motivate customers to replace products before they are worn out.

product modification
changing one or more of a product's characteristics

Companies often introduce changes that may focus on one of three types of modifications one at a time, or sometimes modifications may include two or more dimensions at the same time. For example, Kleenex might introduce four-ply tissue paper that could be termed a quality modification only. However, suppose that Kleenex introduces a four-ply tissue paper in pink that also comes with or without moisturizer. In this case, the product introduction includes all three types of modifications. The key consideration here is that product modifications are periodically needed to meet changing consumer and competitive demands.

Planned obsolescence describes the practice of modifying products so that those products that have already been sold become obsolete before they actually need replacement. Some argue that planned obsolescence is wasteful and/or unethical. Marketers respond that consumers favour planned obsolescence so that they can acquire products with the latest features and functions. Planned obsolescence is more frequent in some industries; for example, computer and mobile phone manufacturers tend to introduce new models annually to entice consumers into replacing their older version of the products. Apple has created numerous public relations events where newer versions of its products (iPhone, iPad, Mac) are introduced and older versions are phased out, making them less compatible or completely incompatible with the newer operating systems and product accessories.

REPOSITIONING Repositioning, as Chapter 7 explained, involves changing consumers' perceptions of a brand. Recently, Listerine, known for its antibacterial mouthwash qualities, introduced, among others, Listerine Whitening Plus Restoring, Listerine Total Care, and Listerine Zero to emphasize its new product positioning in the market. Similarly, Head & Shoulders has repositioned itself away from being a dandruff-only shampoo and introduced multiple different variations to suit different hair care needs, including ones targeted specifically for men. Changing demo-graphics, declining sales, or changes in the social environment often motivate companies to reposition established brands.

PRODUCT LINE EXTENSIONS A **product line extension** occurs when a company's management decides to add products to an existing product line to offer more options to consumers. A company that is constantly adding options to product lines is Funko Pops. The company offers a large array of vinyl figurines that have a disproportionately large head and smaller body. The company was founded in 2011, and has created figurines in pretty much any area of pop culture you could think of. It is almost impossible to keep track of how many Funko Pops there are in circulation, but as of mid 2018 there was almost 9000.[5] The products have become collector's items, with one of the most rare Funko Pops being a Star Wars Darth Maul valued at more than $2000 in the resale market. The Funko Pops line extensions are extensive, and range from famous TV painter Bob Ross to Santa Claus. There seem to be an endless list of possible line extensions, as the company simply has to keep track of pop culture and trends in television, movies, and social media. In late 2019, Funko Pops launched more than 20 new products for the launch of the movie *Frozen 2*.

PRODUCT LINE CONTRACTION Sometimes marketers can get carried away with product extensions (does the world really need 41 varieties of Crest toothpaste?), and some extensions are not embraced by the market, such as Doritos Wow Chips, which were promoted as fat free but contained the now discredited additive olestra. Other times, contracting product lines is a strategic move. Heinz deleted a number of product lines, such as vegetables, poultry, frozen foods, and seafood, to concentrate instead on

planned obsolescence
the practice of modifying products so those that have already been sold become obsolete before they actually need replacement

product line extension
adding products to an existing product line to offer more options to consumers

Dave J Hogan/Getty Images

the products it sells best: ketchup, sauces, frozen snacks, and baby food.[6]

Three major benefits are likely when a company contracts its overextended product lines. First, resources become concentrated on the most important products. Second, managers no longer waste resources trying to improve the sales and profits of poorly performing products. Third, new product items have a greater chance of being successful because more financial and human resources are available to manage them.

9-4 | BRANDING

The success of any business or consumer product depends in part on the target market's ability to distinguish one product from another. Branding is the main tool marketers use to distinguish their products from the competition's.

And it seems that there are as many lists of top brands as there are actual brands. While the lists try to measure different metrics, top brands in any country can provide insights into industries and consumer behaviour. Canadian marketing magazine *Strategy* ranks brands based in Canada on company value and opinions of the Canadians. See Exhibit 9.2.

According to the American Marketing Association (AMA), a **brand** is a name, term, symbol, design, or combination thereof that identifies a seller's products and differentiates them from competitors' products.[7] However, in a broader sense a brand is much more than the name and symbols that a company can create: what a brand stands for also involves consumers and is the sum total of their expectations, feelings, thoughts, and actions that are associated with a brand. This deeper meaning of a brand is created by consumers over time when they hear, experience, and interact with a brand in various situations. Astute marketers strive to shape consumers' creation and interpretation of brand meaning through effective marketing programs and customer service.

A **brand name** is that part of a brand that can be spoken, including letters (RBC, CIBC), words (Lululemon), and numbers (G2, 7-Eleven). The elements of a brand

brand
a name, term, symbol, design, or combination thereof that identifies a seller's products and differentiates them from competitors' products

brand name
that part of a brand that can be spoken, including letters, words, and numbers

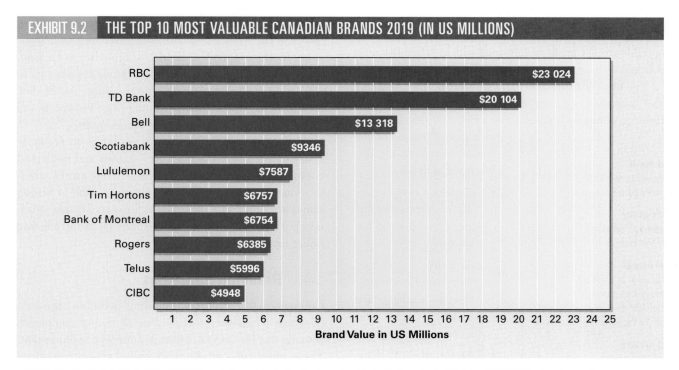

EXHIBIT 9.2 THE TOP 10 MOST VALUABLE CANADIAN BRANDS 2019 (IN US MILLIONS)

Brand	Brand Value in US Millions
RBC	$23 024
TD Bank	$20 104
Bell	$13 318
Scotiabank	$9346
Lululemon	$7587
Tim Hortons	$6757
Bank of Montreal	$6754
Rogers	$6385
Telus	$5996
CIBC	$4948

Source: Adapted from Justin Dallaire, "RBC, TD top ranking of most valuable Canadian brands," Strategy (online) October 30, 2019. http://strategyonline. ca/2019/10/30/rbc-td-top-ranking-of-most-valuable-canadian-brands/

ValeStock/Shutterstock.com

360b/Shutterstock.com

that cannot be spoken are called the **brand mark**—for example, the well-known Canadian Tire and Air Canada symbols.

9-4a | Benefits of Branding

Branding has three main purposes: product identification, repeat sales, and new-product sales. The most important purpose is *product identification*. Branding allows marketers to distinguish their products from all others. Many brand names are familiar to consumers and indicate quality.

The term **brand equity** refers to the value of company and brand names. A brand that invokes strong and favourable thoughts, feelings, and actions and has high awareness, high perceived quality, and high brand loyalty among customers is said to have high brand equity. RBC, TD Bank, and Bell are all Canadian companies with high brand equity. A brand with strong brand equity is a valuable asset.

The term **global brand**, in general, refers to a brand that is available in many different countries at the same time. A company that is considering the development of a global brand should consider undertaking the following activities:

- Conduct research in the countries that are being considered for entry.

- Identify factors that would identify which markets are most attractive to enter.

- Determine if decisions will be made at the local level or centrally.

- Assess any aspects of a brand that might need to be altered or adjusted to foreign markets (e.g., colours, symbols, images, tag lines, etc.).[8]

Yum! Brands, which owns Pizza Hut, KFC, and Taco Bell, is a good example of a company that has developed strong global brands. Yum! believes in adapting its restaurants to local tastes and different cultural and political climates. For example, in Japan, KFC sells tempura crispy strips; in northern England, it offers gravy and potatoes; and in Thailand, it sells rice with soy or sweet chili sauce.

The best generator of *repeat sales* is satisfied customers. Branding helps consumers identify those products they want to buy again and avoid those they do not. **Brand loyalty**, a consistent preference for one brand over all others, is quite high in some product categories. More than half the users in product categories such as mayonnaise, toothpaste, coffee, headache remedies, bath soap, and ketchup are loyal to one brand. Many students go to college or university and purchase the same brands they used at home rather than becoming price buyers. Brand identity is essential to developing brand loyalty.

The third main purpose of branding is to *facilitate new-product sales*. Having a well-known and respected company and brand name is extremely useful when introducing new products. Companies with a strong brand not only can look at line extensions for new products but also can take the riskier approach by introducing brand extensions.

9-4b | Branding Strategies

Companies face complex branding decisions, the first of which is whether to brand at all. Some companies actually use the lack of a brand name as a selling point. These unbranded products are called generic products. Companies that decide to brand their products may choose to follow a policy of using manufacturers' brands, private (distributor) brands, or both. In either case, they

---

brand mark
the elements of a brand that cannot be spoken

brand equity
the value of company and brand names

global brand
a brand with at least 20 percent of the product sold outside its home country or region

brand loyalty
a consistent preference for one brand over all others

Key Advantages of Carrying Manufacturers' Brands	Key Advantages of Carrying Private Brands
Heavy advertising to the consumer by well-known manufacturers, such as Procter & Gamble, helps develop strong consumer loyalties.	A wholesaler or retailer can usually earn higher profits on its own brands. In addition, because the private brand is exclusive, the retailer is under less pressure to mark the price down to meet competition.
Well-known manufacturers' brands, such as LG and Method	A manufacturer can decide to drop a brand or a reseller at any time or even to become a direct competitor to its dealers.
Many manufacturers offer rapid delivery, enabling the dealer to carry less inventory.	A private brand ties the customer to the wholesaler or retailer. A person who wants MotoMaster batteries must go to Canadian Tire.
If a dealer happens to sell a manufacturer's brand of poor quality, the customer may simply switch brands and remain loyal to the dealer.	Wholesalers and retailers have no control over the intensity of distribution of manufacturers' brands. Canadian Tire store managers don't have to worry about competing with other sellers of MotoMaster automotive products. They know that these brands are sold only at Canadian Tire.

must then decide among a policy of individual branding (different brands for different products), family branding (common names for different products), or a combination of individual branding and family branding.

GENERIC PRODUCTS VERSUS BRANDED PRODUCTS

A **generic product** is typically a no-frills, no-brand-name, low-cost product that is simply identified by its product category.

The main appeal of generics is their low price. Generic grocery products are usually 30 to 40 percent less expensive than manufacturers' brands in the same product category and 20 to 25 percent less expensive than retailer-owned brands. Pharmaceuticals are one example of a product category where generics have made large inroads. When patents on successful pharmaceutical products expire, low-cost generics rapidly appear on the market.

MANUFACTURERS' BRANDS VERSUS PRIVATE BRANDS

The brand name of a manufacturer—such as Samsung, La-Z-Boy, and Cheemo Perogies—is called a **manufacturer's brand**. Sometimes *national brand* is used as a synonym for *manufacturer's brand*; however, *national brand* is not always an accurate term because many manufacturers serve only regional markets. Using the term *manufacturer's brand* more precisely defines the brand's owner.

A **private brand**, also known as a private label or store brand, is a brand name owned by a wholesaler or a retailer. Private label brands are different from generic products in that generic products do not have any branding associated with them at all. Private-label products made exclusively by retailers account for one of every five items sold in Canada, representing a large part of sales in some retail sectors.[9] The image of private label brands as a low-cost alternative to manufacturers' brands has changed over the years. In a recent Neilsen survey, 70 percent of Canadians surveyed stated that private brands were a good alternative to national brands. For almost two-thirds of those surveyed, price was the main reason Canadians buy a private brand.[10] Some of the major private label brands in Canada are President's Choice from Loblaws, Life from Shoppers Drug Mart, Selection from Metro, and MasterCraft from Canadian Tire.

Exhibit 9.3 illustrates key issues that wholesalers and retailers should consider in deciding whether to sell manufacturers' brands or private brands. Many companies offer a combination of both. Retailers love consumers' greater acceptance of private brands. Because their overhead is low and these products have no marketing costs, private-label products bring 10 percent higher margins, on average, than manufacturers' brands. More than that, a trusted store brand can differentiate a chain from its competitors.

The Canadian Press/Francis Vachon

generic product
a no-frills, no-brand-name, low-cost product that is simply identified by its product category

manufacturer's brand
the brand name of a manufacturer

private brand
a brand name owned by a wholesaler or a retailer

Better Letters?

According to Lexicon Branding, an established branding business, there are a few options available to companies when selecting a brand. There are five types of names that can be used when choosing a brand name:

Type	Examples
Real words	Apple, Sharp
Real words stemming from Greek, Latin, or Sanskrit	Sonos, Dasani
Shrunken words	Impreza, Optima
Constructed words	OnStar, DreamWorks
Coined solutions	Xerox, Kodak

The use of linguistics is also seen as important when devising a brand name, with the letter *B* being one of the top letters to use because of the universal agreement in how to pronounce words with it as a primary letter. David Placek, founder and CEO of Lexicon Branding has been using linguistics and the five types of words to help create brands for companies from BlackBerry to Tangerine. The fruits of branding labour are easy to see when you use some creativity and knowledge.

Sources: https://www.cnn.com/2019/09/06/success/david-placek-lexicon-branding/index.html (accessed January 2020) and https://www.theglobeandmail.com/report-on-business/industry-news/marketing/the-art-and-science-of-creating-a-brand-name/article18915415/ (Accessed January 2020).

INDIVIDUAL BRANDS VERSUS FAMILY Many companies use different brand names for different products, a practice referred to as **individual branding**. Companies use individual brands when their products vary greatly in use or performance. For instance, it would not make sense to use the same brand name for a pair of dress socks and a baseball bat. Procter & Gamble targets different segments of the laundry detergent market with Bold, Cheer, Dash, Dreft, Era, Gain, Ivory Snow, Oxydol, Solo, and Tide.

In contrast, a company that markets several different products under the same brand name is using a **family brand**. Apple's family brand includes phones, desktop computers, laptops, watches, tablets, and streaming services. Some companies have a family brand where the brand name, as in Apple, is not attached to every product. The Swatch Group, which sells timepieces of different varieties, has a total of 18 different brands. These include Omega, Tissot, and Longines.

individual branding
the use of different brand names for different products

family brand
the marketing of several different products under the same brand name

TOP FIVE GLOBAL AND CANADIAN BRANDS—GLOBAL FINANCE

Top Five Global—2020	Top Canadian Firms in Global 500
1. Amazon	TD Bank—113th
2. Google	RBC—117th
3. Apple	Scotiabank—180th
4. Microsoft	BMO—190th
5. Samsung	CIBC—246th

Source: https://brandirectorypublic.s3.eu-west-2.amazonaws.com/reports_free/brand-finance-global-500-2020-preview.pdf

COBRANDING Cobranding involves placing two or more brand names on a product or its package. Three common types of cobranding are ingredient branding, cooperative branding, and complementary branding. *Ingredient branding* identifies the brand of a part that makes up the product—for example, an Intel microprocessor in a digital device, such an Apple computer. *Cooperative branding* occurs when two brands receiving equal treatment (in the context of an advertisement) borrow on each other's brand equity. This type of cobranding happens quite often with tourism-related products and services. Hotels work with credit card companies to create branded cards with specific benefits for customers staying at their properties. If you visit most travel sites, there are incentives for customers to combine flights, rental cars, and hotels, often based on cooperative branding agreements. Finally, with *complementary branding*, products are advertised or marketed together to suggest usage, such as the agreement between coffee giant Starbucks and tea brand Teavana to sell Starbucks Teavana Iced Tea drinks. In the summer of 2019, three very successful flavours were introduced: Peach Green Tea Lemonade, Guava White Tea Lemonade, and Blueberry Black Tea Lemonade.

Cobranding is a useful strategy when a combination of brand names enhances the prestige or perceived value of a product or when it benefits brand owners and users. Cobranding may be used to increase a company's presence in markets where it has little or no market share. For example, online content curator Flipboard was looking to attract more readers who had interest in travel and visiting the world. Flipboard partnered with Airbnb to create a very successful cobranding relationship, where Airbnb created a magazine within the Flipboard app, and Airbnb offered trips to locations around the world for loyal Flipboard customers. This partnership has been a win-win![11]

Prachana Thong-on/Shutterstock.com

9-4c | Trademarks

A **trademark** is the exclusive right to use a brand or part of a brand. Others are prohibited from using the brand without permission. A **service mark** performs the same function for services, such as H&R Block and Weight Watchers. Parts of a brand or other product identification may qualify for trademark protection. Some examples are

- shapes, such as the Coca-Cola bottle or Toblerone's triangular shape
- ornamental colour or design, such as the decoration on Nike shoes, the black-and-copper colour combination of a Duracell battery, or the noticeable green colour of the Garnier Fructis bottles of hair and body care products.
- catchy phrases, such as Subway's "Eat Fresh," Nike's "Just do it," and KFC's "Finger Lickin' Good"
- abbreviations, such as LG, H&M, or FedEx
- sounds, like the THX "Deep Note" that plays at the start of movies using this technology

It is important to understand that trademark rights come from use rather than registration. In Canada, trademarks are registered under the Trade-marks Act and Regulations. When a company registers a trademark, it must have a genuine intention to use it and must actually use it within three years of the application being granted. Trademark protection typically lasts for 15 years. To renew the trademark, the company must prove it is using the mark. Rights to a trademark last as long as the mark is used. Normally, if the company does not use a trademark for an extended period, it is considered abandoned, allowing a new user to claim exclusive ownership.

The Canadian Intellectual Property Office is responsible for registering trademarks and patents. Canada's Trademarks Act and Regulations were updated in 2012 to include the trademarking of sounds like the MGM lion's roar.[12]

Companies that fail to protect their trademarks face the possibility that their product names will become generic. A **generic product name**

cobranding
placing two or more brand names on a product or its package

trademark
the exclusive right to use a brand or part of a brand

service mark
a trademark for a service

generic product name
a term that identifies a product by class or type and cannot be trademarked

Brand Mark

Registered Trademark (™)

CIRQUE DU SOLEIL.

identifies a product by class or type and cannot be trademarked. Former brand names that were not sufficiently protected by their owners and were subsequently declared to be generic product names by courts include cellophane, linoleum, thermos, kerosene, rollerblades, and shredded wheat.

Companies such as Rolls-Royce, Cross, Xerox, Levi Strauss, Frigidaire, and McDonald's aggressively enforce their trademarks. Rolls-Royce, Coca-Cola, and Xerox even run newspaper and magazine ads stating that their names are trademarks and should not be used as descriptive or generic terms. Some ads threaten lawsuits against competitors that violate trademarks.

Despite severe penalties for trademark violations, trademark infringement lawsuits are not uncommon. Some of the major battles involve brand names that closely resemble an established brand name. Donna Karan filed a lawsuit against Donnkenny, Inc., whose NASDAQ trading symbol—DNKY—was too close to Karan's DKNY trademark.

Companies must also contend with fake or unauthorized brands. Knockoffs of Burberry's trademarked tan, black, white, and red plaid are easy to find in cheap shops all over the world, and loose imitations are also found in some reputable department stores. Counterfeiting and knockoff brands are rampant online, where anyone with basic computer skills can create a website with a stolen or heavily borrowed logo and a "Buy" button. In 2019, online giant Amazon introduced Project Zero, a system put in place where companies themselves are in charge of finding and deleting Amazon listings of counterfeit products. Instead of companies reacting to competing Amazon listings from counterfeiters by lowering their prices, reputable brands are tasked with finding and then removing fake listings featuring their brands.

9-5 | PACKAGING

Packages have always served a practical function—that is, they hold contents together and protect goods as

they move through the distribution channel. Today, however, packaging is also a container for promoting the product and making it easier and safer to use.

9-5a | Packaging Functions

The three most important functions of packaging are to contain and protect products, to promote products, and to facilitate the storage, use, and convenience of products. A fourth function of packaging that is becoming increasingly important is to facilitate recycling and reduce environmental damage.

CONTAINING AND PROTECTING PRODUCTS The most obvious function of packaging is to contain products that are liquid, granular, or otherwise divisible. Packaging also enables manufacturers, wholesalers, and retailers to market products in specific quantities, such as kilograms.

Physical protection is another obvious function of packaging. Most products are handled several times between the time they are manufactured, harvested, or otherwise produced and the time they are consumed or used. Many products are shipped, stored, and inspected several times between production and consumption. Some products, such as milk, need to be refrigerated. Others, such as beer, are sensitive to light. Still others, such as medicines and bandages, need to be kept sterile. Packages protect products from breakage, evaporation, spillage, spoilage, light, heat, cold, infestation, and many other conditions.

PROMOTING PRODUCTS Packaging does more than identify the brand, list the ingredients, specify features, and give directions. A package differentiates a product from competing products and may associate a new product with a family of other products from the same manufacturer. Welch's repackaged its line of grape juice–based jams, jellies, and juices to unify the line and get more impact on the shelf.

Packages use designs, colours, shapes, and materials to try to influence consumers' perceptions and buying behaviour. For example, marketing research shows that health-conscious consumers are likely to think that any food is probably good for them as long as it comes in green packaging. Packaging can also influence consumer perceptions of quality and prestige.

However, sometimes packaging is used for the exact opposite purpose. Enter the Canadian government's attempt to create the most unappealing packaging in the entire country for cigarettes. In order to deter young

The Canadian Press/Justin Tang

people from smoking, the government introduced new packaging in late 2019 with "the ugliest colour in the world"—a drab unappealing shade of brown. In addition, there are the requisite disturbing pictures showing the ill effects of smoking meant to shock those who intend to smoke despite the warnings. And, of course, the packaging of cigarettes includes something unthinkable for any other package: a warning NOT to use the product.

FACILITATING STORAGE, USE, AND CONVENIENCE
Wholesalers and retailers prefer packages that are easy to ship, store, and stock on shelves. They also like packages that protect products, prevent spoilage or breakage, and extend the product's shelf life.

Consumers' requirements for storage, use, and convenience cover many dimensions. Consumers are constantly seeking items that are easy to handle, open, and reclose, and some consumers want packages that are tamperproof or childproof. Research indicates that hard-to-open packages are among consumers' top complaints.[14] Surveys conducted by *Sales & Marketing Management* magazine revealed that consumers dislike—and avoid buying—leaky ice cream boxes, overly heavy or fat vinegar bottles, immovable pry-up lids on glass bottles, key-opener sardine cans, and hard-to-pour cereal boxes. Packaging innovations such as zipper tear strips, hinged lids, tab slots, screw-on tops, and pour spouts were introduced to solve these and other problems. Easy openings are especially important for kids and older consumers.

Some companies use packaging to segment markets. Dasani creates small packages for use with meals on airplanes and in hotels and sells larger packages of its products to retail outlets that sell to consumers. Differently sized packages appeal to heavy, moderate, and light users. Campbell's soup is packaged in single-serving cans aimed at the seniors and singles market segments. Packaging convenience can increase a product's utility and, therefore, its market share and profits.

FACILITATING RECYCLING AND REDUCING ENVIRONMENTAL DAMAGE
One of the most important packaging issues today is compatibility with the environment. Some companies use their packaging to target environmentally concerned market segments. Brocato International markets shampoo and hair conditioner in bottles that are biodegradable in landfills. Products as different as deodorant and furniture polish are packaged in eco-friendly, pump-spray packages that do not rely on aerosol propellants.

The concept of reducing and recycling has led to the "circular economy" movement. The concept has to do with companies focusing on the full life of their product packaging, which looks at the materials used to make the products and the proper disposal of the products to recycling or landfill facilities. Unilever has made a commitment to ensure that all of its plastic packaging would be fully recyclable, reusable, or compostable by 2025. Hellman's Canada announced that it will use 100 percent recyclable plastic by March 2020, saving up to 1 million kilograms of virgin plastic. [15]

The recent decriminalizing of marijuana has led to a negative health impact that has nothing to do with cannabis. Early in the sales of cannabis in Canada, it was estimated that for every gram of the product that was sold, there were 70 grams of packaging waste.[16] The first year of legalized sales of marijuana resulted in 10 000 tons of packaging waste.[17] Government and industry have been quick to identify the problems, and are searching for solutions, which include greener packaging and organized recycling programs for cannabis product waste.

9-5b | Labelling

An integral part of any package is its label. Labelling generally takes one of two forms: persuasive or informational.

Persuasive labelling focuses on a promotional theme or logo, and consumer information is secondary. Note that the standard promotional claims—such as *new*, *improved*, and *super*—are no longer very persuasive. Consumers have been saturated with "newness" and thus discount these claims.

Informational labelling, in contrast,

persuasive labelling
package labelling that focuses on a promotional theme or logo; consumer information is secondary

informational labelling
package labelling designed to help consumers make proper product selections and to lower their cognitive dissonance after the purchase

Unilever has promised that 100% recycled plastic will be used for all of Hellmann's Mayonnaise packaging by 2020.

The **universal product codes (UPCs)** that now appear on most items in supermarkets and other high-volume outlets were first introduced in 1974. Because the numerical codes appear as a series of thick and thin vertical lines, they are often called *bar codes*. The lines are read by computerized optical scanners that match the codes to brand names, package sizes, and prices. They also print information on cash register tapes and help retailers rapidly and accurately prepare records of customer purchases, control inventories, and track sales.

9-6 | GLOBAL ISSUES IN BRANDING AND PACKAGING

When planning to enter a foreign market with an existing product, a company has three options for handling the brand name:

- One brand name everywhere: This strategy is useful when the company markets mainly one product and the brand name does not have negative connotations in any local market. The Coca-Cola Company uses a one-brand-name strategy in more than 200 countries around the world. The advantages of a one-brand-name strategy are greater identification of the product from market to market and ease of coordinating the promotion from market to market.

- Adaptations and modifications: A one-brand-name strategy is not possible when the name cannot be pronounced in the local language, when the brand name is owned by someone else, or when the brand name has a negative or vulgar connotation in the local language. In 2019, Heinz introduced a new product called "Mayochup" which was a combination of mayonnaise and ketchup. The problem with this name was that in the Indigenous Cree language, the two sounds that make up the name represent the words "feces" and "face."[19]

- Different brand names in different markets: local brand names are often used when translation or pronunciation problems occur, when the marketer wants the brand to appear to be a local brand, or when regulations require localization. Henkel's Silkience hair conditioner is called Soyance in France and Sientel in Italy. The adaptations were deemed to be more appealing in the local markets. Unilever's Axe line of male grooming products is called Lynx in England, Ireland, Australia, and

is designed to help consumers make proper product selections and to lower their cognitive dissonance after the purchase. In Canada, the responsibility for labelling of packaged foods is shared by Health Canada and the Canadian Food Inspection Agency (CFIA). When it comes to products that consumers will be putting their bodies, it is vital that this labelling provides the necessary information between consumer and products. The Consumer Packaging and Labelling Act mandates detailed nutritional information on most food packages and standards for health claims on food packaging. An important outcome of this legislation has been guidelines from Health Canada for the use of terms such as *low fat, light, reduced cholesterol, low sodium, low calorie, low carb,* and *fresh*. See Exhibit 9.4.

Another important section of the act mandates the requirement that all information on a product label in Canada be in both French and English except for the dealer's name and address, which can be in either language. There are a few exceptions to this rule, including test market products that are exempt for up to one year, and products that require knowledge of either French or English for its proper use (e.g., books, greeting cards).[18] However, the requirement for both languages on products in Canada creates an extra step for companies first entering the Canadian market.

universal product codes (UPCs)
a series of thick and thin vertical lines (bar codes), readable by computerized optical scanners that match the codes to brand names, package sizes, and prices

EXHIBIT 9.4   LABELLING REQUIREMENTS FOR CANADIAN PACKAGING

Nutrition Facts Table

The Nutrition Facts table is a standardized table that lists the nutrient content information of the product, including energy (calories) and 13 core nutrients. This table must be shown on the package in English and in French.

List of Ingredients

The ingredients must be listed in descending order of proportion by weight. This is the weight of each ingredient determined prior to being combined to make the food. This information is required on most prepackaged foods and must be listed in English and in French. It may appear anywhere on the package, except the bottom.

Date Marking

The date marking ("best before") is the predicted amount of time that an unopened food product will retain quality characteristics when stored under the proper conditions. The "best before" date can be listed anywhere on the package, though exceptions exist if it appears on the bottom. It is mandatory that the "best before" date is shown on prepackaged foods if the shelf life is 90 days or less. It is suggested that the best before date is shown on foods if the shelf life longer is than 90 days. The date marking must be shown in English and in French.

Origin Claim

Companies are encouraged to note either Product of Canada or the qualified Made in Canada to help customers quickly and easily identify Canadian made foods. There are specific guidelines about what constitutes a Canadian product.

The Canadian government assists companies entering the Canadian market by providing clear guidelines and pictures (like the one above) to provide specific details on packaging such as the requirement for bilingual labelling.

New Zealand. Coca-Cola's Sprite brand had to be renamed Kin in Korea to satisfy a government prohibition on the unnecessary use of foreign words.

In addition to making global branding decisions, companies must consider global packaging needs. Three aspects of packaging especially important in international marketing are labelling, aesthetics, and climate considerations. The major concern is properly translating ingredient, promotional, and instructional information on labels. Care must also be employed in meeting all local labelling requirements. Several years ago, an Italian judge ordered that all bottles of Coca-Cola be removed from retail shelves because the ingredients were not properly labelled.

Package *aesthetics* may also require some attention. Even though simple visual elements of the brand, such as a symbol or logo, can be a standardizing element across products and countries, marketers must stay attuned to cultural traits in host countries. For example, colours may have different connotations. In some countries, red is associated with witchcraft, green may be a sign of danger, and white may be symbolic of death. Aesthetics also influence package sizes. Soft drinks are not sold in six-packs in countries that lack refrigeration. In some countries, products such as detergent may be bought only in small quantities because of a lack of storage space. Other products, such as cigarettes, may be bought in small quantities, and even single units, because of the low purchasing power of buyers.

Extreme *climates* and long-distance shipping necessitate sturdier and more durable packages for goods sold overseas. Spillage, spoilage, and breakage are all more important concerns when products are shipped long distances or are frequently handled during shipping and storage. Packages may also have to ensure a longer product life if the time between production and consumption lengthens significantly.

9-7 | PRODUCT WARRANTIES

Just as a package is designed to protect the product, a **warranty** protects the buyer and provides essential information about the product. A warranty confirms the quality or performance of a good or service. An **express warranty** is a written guarantee. Express warranties range from simple statements—such as "100 percent cotton" (a guarantee of quality) and "complete satisfaction guaranteed" (a statement of performance)—to extensive documents written in technical language. In contrast, an **implied warranty** is an unwritten guarantee that the good or service is fit for the purpose for which it was sold.

Although court rulings might suggest that all products sold in Canada carry an implied warranty, actual warranties do vary depending on the province or territory. At the federal level, protection against misleading warranties is provided under the Competition Act. In general, products sold must be free from encumbrances (the seller must have clear title to ownership), the descriptions of the product on the package must be accurate, the product must be fit for its intended purpose, and the product must be of reasonable durability.

warranty
a confirmation of the quality or performance of a good or service

express warranty
a written guarantee

implied warranty
an unwritten guarantee that the good or service is fit for the purpose for which it was sold

AWAKE CHOCOLATE
CONTINUING CASE

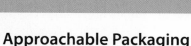

AWAKE Chocolate

Approachable Packaging

There are some schools of thought that say there should be more than the "4P's" of marketing. One of the candidates nominated for this would be "packaging," a close relative of "product" and an invaluable yet somewhat immeasurable component of branding. For three consumer packaged goods veterans, having spent most of their time with Pepsico, Awake founders Adam Deremo, Matt Schnarr and Dan Tzotzis knew a thing or two about all of these concepts. They had been part of developing and managing several products within the packaged food category.

When they identified the missing element in the market—the energy boost of caffeine, wrapped cleverly in chocolate, targeting overworked, underrested people—the name Awake came quickly and naturally. The packaging for their innovative product, however, was a rather iterative and costly endeavour.

Cofounder and Chief Operating Officer Dan Tzotzis remembers clearly the costly mistake, which might have proved costlier had they not eaten the costs of their mistake. "We actually developed a prototype that was completely different to the current branding we have," he begins. "It played far more on the energy side of things than on the flavour side of things. It had 'Awake Energy Chocolate' all over it. We spent money on the film, developed finished goods around it, made moulds to carry the branding on the chocolate. It was north of fifty thousand dollars that we spent on all of this stuff."

In the early stages of product development entrepreneurs do not typically have $50 000 to spend, never mind throw away, but that's exactly what the Awake partners did upon realizing the packaging did not speak to the brand's messaging. This realization, Tzotzis recalls, came from two different directions, one more subtle than the other.

"The product was not moving off shelves the way we had expected it to," he recalls. "Subsequent research suggested that the emphasis on energy may have been drawing mild interest from males, but little to no interest from females." Down but not out on their initial endeavour, around the time the product was about to launch the founders met with a potential strategic investor, to whom they presented samples wrapped inside the newly minted packaging. "I love the taste. I love the product that you've created," the investor assessed but, he noted, the packaging was awful. Ouch.

Humbled by a very disappointing market test, and further demoralized by the tough-loving words of a would-be investor, Tzotzis and company took the investor's advice and turned to a new branding agency to bring the packaging and all other associated branding elements to life. The product inside the wrapping remained identical, and the name was changed slightly, from Awake Energy Chocolate to Awake Caffeinated Chocolate. But the change in wardrobe essentially turned around the fate of Awake. "The formula remained the same. The only thing that changed was the way the brand looked. And that made all the difference in the world."

Once the Awake crew moved past flushing a large sum of money away, and had become laser focussed on branding elements deemed "more approachable," as Tzotzis put it, the product turned the corner almost instantly. "From the moment that we hit our first college campus, it was like they immediately understood what we were trying to do, with little explanation and a lot of excitement around the brand." The guerrilla marketing tactics, arriving on campuses in decal-covered school buses to give away samples, was followed by placement in campus stores for sale—the truest test of brand awareness. "The moment we put the product into those stores, the movement was beyond our wildest dreams."

The power of packaging is an important takeaway for this chapter. While many companies are content to treat it as an afterthought, particularly in this era of minimal viable product (MVP) thinking, there is enough science surrounding cognitive connections with symbols, words, and colours to support spending considerable time and effort on packaging.[1] In Awake's case, the costly lesson learned in getting the packaging right paid off.

QUESTIONS

1. In consumer packaged goods (CPGs) that second word is vitally important to not only to distinguish a product from its competitors on the shelf, but also communicate brand values and attitudes. Suppose you wish to purchase something from your campus store. Visit one on your campus and take a picture of Awake (if your campus stocks it) along with other confectionary brands on the shelves. Pay particular attention to energy or health-oriented packaged goods. Describe the differences in packaging that might guide your purchase decision.

2. Make a list of other consumer package goods companies that you feel have done a good job of distinguishing themselves while also representing their brands in a consistent and effective way. Explain the packaging elements you feel are particularly appealing.

3. Awake's brand mascot, an owl named Nevil, is omnipresent in virtually every visible branding element created by Awake. Describe the different ways in which this symbol effectively communicates the brand's message.

NOTE

1. www.iosrjournals.org/iosr-jbm/papers/Vol16-issue7/Version-2/I016726164.pdf

10 | Developing and Managing Products

LEARNING OUTCOMES

10-1 Explain the importance of developing new products and describe the six categories of new products

10-2 Explain the steps in the new-product development process

10-3 Discuss global issues in new-product development

10-4 Explain the diffusion process through which new products are adopted

10-5 Explain the concept of product life cycles

"Anyone developing new products and new technology needs one characteristic above all else: hope."[1]

—James Dyson

10-1 | THE IMPORTANCE OF NEW PRODUCTS

New products are important to sustain growth, increase revenues and profits, and replace obsolete items. New-product development and introduction are also important to meet ever-changing consumer wants and are compounded by the developing of new technologies and shrinking product life cycles (PLCs).

A 2019 study asked more than 18 000 Canadians about new products. Two-thirds of those who responded felt that for new products to resonate with them, the products would have to make their life easier. An even greater percentage, 79 percent, desired new products introduced into Canada to be environmentally friendly, with 37 percent stating that they would pay more for a product that was sustainable.[2]

At the same time, the new-product development process is replete with failures and high introduction costs. Businesses must introduce new products to stay competitive or risk being pushed out of the market; however, despite spending huge sums on (R&D) and development, most companies have many more failures than successes.

Nevertheless, the companies that succeed in introducing new products reap substantial financial and market rewards. While there is no magic trick involved in launching a successful product, there are certain actions companies should take to be successful. Market research firm Neilsen produces a list of breakthrough innovative products each year and identifies five key areas that companies should focus on in order to be successful with a new product launch: brand incrementality, mass potential, category distinction, longevity, and appeal to a specific target market.[3]

Almost every business publication has a list for "most innovative company" and the results are almost always different depending on the source. The Boston Consulting Group had Alphabet (Google) as the most innovative company in 2019, with Amazon and Apple filling out the top three.[4] Meanwhile, *Forbes* magazine has a top three that is surprising, with ServiceNow (cloud computing), Workday (software vendor), and Salesforce (CRM software) at the top of its list.[5] Companies we would normally expect to see, like Tesla, Microsoft, and Amazon, were in the top 10, but this seeming changing of the guard shows how innovation and new-product development are changing.

Innovative companies from Canada do sometimes make the above lists; however, most Canadian-based rankings of companies end up being a "who exactly is who here" feel to them with mostly unfamiliar companies. This lack of top lists should not give the impression that Canada is devoid of innovation; Canada has been the home of a number of important inventions over the years, many of which have had an impact on how people live their lives. Some truly Canadian inventions include the following:

- insulin
- IMAX
- basketball
- electric wheelchair
- JAVA programming language
- peanut butter[6]

10-1a | Categories of New Products

The term **new product** can be confusing because its meaning varies widely and has several correct definitions. A new product doesn't carry the same level of newness in different markets or companies: a product can be new to the market, new to the producer or seller, new to the world, or new to some combination of these (see Exhibit 10.1). The degree of newness even for the same product varies from one market to the other and from one company to the next. Based on the degree of newness, new products can be classified into six categories:

EXHIBIT 10.1 NEW PRODUCT CATEGORIES

New to the Company (vertical axis) — New to the Market (horizontal axis)

- New Product Lines
- New to the World
- Improvements or Revisions of Existing Products
- Additions to Existing Product Lines
- Lower-priced Products
- Repositioned Products

new product
a product new to the world, new to the market, new to the producer or seller, or new to some combination of these

- *New-to-the-world products (also called discontinuous innovations):* These products create an entirely new market. New-to-the-world products represent the smallest category of new products, since few products are seen as completely new by everyone.

- *New product lines:* These products, which the company has not previously offered, allow the company to enter an established market. Tim Hortons has created new product lines in its retail locations, with the introduction of soups, chilis, and hot sandwiches over the last 20 years. The Canadian coffee giant has also made an impression in the grocery aisles, with the introduction of new products in the area of instant coffee, candy bars, and most recently cereal (Timbits!).[7]

- *Additions to existing product lines:* This category includes new products that supplement a company's established line. Examples of product line additions are Huggies Pull-Ups, Pampers Kandoo baby wipes, and other personal care products for kids.

- *Improvements or revisions of existing products:* The new and improved product may be significantly or slightly changed. Gillette's Fusion 5 Proshield and Skinguard Sensitive razors are examples of product improvements. Another type of revision is package improvement. Many of the products listed in *Canadian Living's* Best New Product Awards are improvements on existing products—health care (Neutrogena Acne Spot Treatment), household care (Downy Unstopables laundry beads), and food (Black River Cheese Cubes). The products on this list are move revisions of existing products than entirely new products.[8] Most new products fit into the revision or improvement category.

- *Repositioned products:* These are existing products targeted at new markets or new market segments. In 2020, Sylvania, a company that focused most of its time and efforts on selling lighting solutions to other businesses, launched a new consumer-focused campaign. The title of the campaign is "Find Your Tru Light," which uses the company's TruWave technology that mimics natural light. This turn toward the consumer market required the company to focus on benefits for natural living using natural light—something that was not a concern when selling to OEMs (original equipment manufacturers) and car companies.[9]

new-product strategy
a plan that links the new-product development process with the objectives of the marketing department, the business unit, and the corporation

- *Lower-priced products:* This category refers to products that provide performance similar to that of competing brands at a lower price. For decades, homeowners turned to home security systems to help provide them with piece of mind when away from home. But these systems were expensive to install, and then often quite expensive for the monthly monitoring costs. With the advent of smart and connected devices, the world of home security is much cheaper. A Ring video doorbell allows consumers to be constantly connected to their home via the front entrance, and can be had at a price that is less than one month's monitoring fee for some security firms.[10]

10-2 | THE NEW-PRODUCT DEVELOPMENT PROCESS

Management consulting firm Booz Allen Hamilton has studied the new-product development process for more than 35 years. After analyzing five major studies undertaken during this period, the company concluded that the companies most likely to succeed in developing and introducing new products are those that take the following actions:

- Make the long-term commitment needed to support innovation and new-product development.

- Use a company-specific approach, driven by corporate objectives and strategies, with a well-defined new-product strategy at its core.

- Capitalize on experience to achieve and maintain competitive advantage.

- Establish an environment—a management style, an organizational structure, and a degree of top-management support—conducive to achieving company-specific new-product and corporate objectives.

Most companies follow a formal new-product development process, usually starting with a new-product strategy. Exhibit 10.2 traces the seven-step process, which is discussed in this section. The exhibit is funnel-shaped to highlight the fact that each stage acts as a screen. The purpose is to filter out unworkable ideas.

10-2a | New-Product Strategy

A **new-product strategy** links the new-product development process with the objectives of the marketing department, the business unit, and the corporation. A new-product strategy must be compatible with

EXHIBIT 10.2

NEW-PRODUCT DEVELOPMENT PROCESS

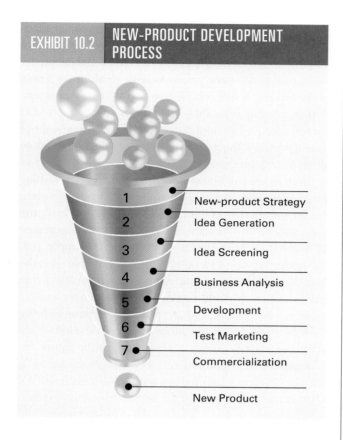

1 New-product Strategy
2 Idea Generation
3 Idea Screening
4 Business Analysis
5 Development
6 Test Marketing
7 Commercialization

New Product

these objectives, and, in turn, all three objectives must be consistent with one another.

A new-product strategy is part of the organization's overall marketing strategy. It sharpens the focus and provides general guidelines for generating, screening, and evaluating new-product ideas. The new-product strategy specifies the roles that new products must play in the organization's overall plan and describes the characteristics of products the organization wants to offer and the markets it wants to serve. Some companies, like Apple, apply the new product strategy to each of their existing lines, punctuating with public events to unveil new features and benefits of a new product.[11] While other businesses that may not be able to compete at the scale of Apple may slow things down, LG announced in 2018 it would introduce new products only "when the technological landscape necessitates it."[12]

As discussed at the beginning of this chapter, companies with successful new-product introduction programs derive a substantial percentage of their total sales from new-product introductions. These companies tend to have numerous new-product ideas at various stages of development at the same time and realize that very few of their ideas will be successful in the market.

10-2b | Idea Generation

New-product ideas come from many sources, including customers, employees, distributors, competitors, vendors, research and development (R&D), and consultants.

CUSTOMERS The marketing concept suggests that customers' wants and needs should be the springboard for developing new products. Many of today's most innovative and successful marketers have taken the approach of introducing fewer new products but taking steps to ensure these chosen few are truly unique, better, and, above all, really do address unmet consumer needs. How do they do that? They begin and end development with the customer.[13] The most common techniques for gathering new-product ideas from consumers are surveys, focus groups, observation, and the analysis of social media posts.

Innovative companies are also gathering a variety of R&D input from customers online. For example, leading manufacturer of power tools DeWALT recently created an online community called the DeWALT Insights Forum. Customers can use this forum both to provide feedback about current products and to submit ideas for new products. Twelve thousand members participate in DeWALT's Insights Forum community.[14]

EMPLOYEES Marketing personnel—advertising and marketing research employees, as well as salespeople—often create new-product ideas because they analyze and are involved in the marketplace. Encouraging employees from different divisions to exchange ideas is also a useful strategy.

Fashion companies have turned to the software world for inspiration when it comes to engaging employees for new ideas. Using the "hackathon" model where people come together to solve software problems in a finite amount of time, companies like Kering, Prada, and Zalando are "hacking" for employee ingenuity. A key area of concern for employees and industry is sustainability—trying to find ways for their fashion brands to cover the world but in a way that is environmentally aware. The results of the hackathons have included eco-designs and supply chain waste reduction.[15]

Bloomicon/Shutterstock.com

Customers use DeWalt's Insights Forum to provide feedback about current products and to submit ideas for new products.

digitalreflections/Shutterstock.com

DISTRIBUTORS A well-trained sales force routinely asks distributors about needs that are not being met. Because distributors are closer to end users, they are often more aware of customer needs than are manufacturers. The inspiration for Rubbermaid's Sidekick, a litter-free lunch box, came from a distributor's suggestion that the company place some of its plastic containers inside a lunch box and sell the set as an alternative to wrapping lunches in plastic wrap and paper bags.

COMPETITORS No companies rely solely on internally generated ideas for new products. A big part of any organization's marketing intelligence system should be monitoring the performance of competitors' products. One purpose of competitive monitoring is to determine which, if any, of the competitors' products should be copied. Many companies form alliances with competitors to market new and existing products. Procter & Gamble and Clorox combined the patented adhesive-film technology that P&G uses in its packaging to develop Glad Press'n Seal food storage wrap.[16]

VENDORS 7-Eleven regularly forges partnerships with vendors to create proprietary products, such as Jones Soda Big Gulps and Blue Vanilla Laffy Taffy Rope candy, developed by Nestlé's Wonka division exclusively for 7-Eleven.

RESEARCH AND DEVELOPMENT R&D is carried out in four distinct ways. You learned about basic research and applied research in Chapter 4. The other two ways are product development and product modification. Product development goes beyond applied research by converting applications into marketable

products. Product modification makes cosmetic or functional changes to existing products. Many new-product breakthroughs come from R&D activities. Balancing the need to develop new products with pressure to lower costs creates a difficult dilemma for many managers. Although companies spend billions of dollars every year on research and development, as many as 40 percent of managers think their companies are not doing enough to develop new products.[17]

Both companies and governments are establishing innovation laboratories to complement or even replace traditional R&D programs. In the 2017 Budget, the Government of Canada clearly laid out the importance of innovation and R&D: "Innovation is, simply put, the understanding that better is always possible. It is the key that unlocks possibilities and opportunities. From urban centres to rural farms, from researchers looking to secure new patents to entrepreneurs working to bring their products to market, innovation is what allows Canadians to adapt to change and prepare for the future."[18]

Canada has a number of factors in its favour as it tries to become a hub for innovation. Canada leads the OECD and G-7 countries for higher education graduation rates and higher education R&D performance. And Canada generates 4 percent of the world's knowledge while representing only 0.5 percent of the population of the world.[19]

Despite the important role that idea labs play in the systematic development of new products, it is critical to realize that not all new products are developed in this manner. For example, the glass touchscreen used on iPhones was initially developed by Corning, but it was never commercially produced. In a conversation with the then-CEO of Corning, Steve Jobs, realized that Corning had the capability to produce the kind of glass he wanted for iPhone screens. Called Gorilla Glass, Corning's glass screens have adorned every single iPhone since the product revolutionized mobile phones in 2007. Apple believes so strongly in the technology that it continues to fund Corning to advance it even more, to the tune of $250 million in late 2019.[20]

CONSULTANTS Outside consultants are always available to examine a business and recommend product ideas. Examples include Booz Allen Hamilton and Management Decisions. Traditionally, consultants determine whether a company has a balanced portfolio of products and, if not, which new-product ideas are needed to offset the imbalance. Both of these Canadian-based innovation consultants have developed a list of the most innovative companies in Canada. Booz Allen Hamilton can leverage the presentation of this list to discuss innovation and R&D issues in Canada, and raise the profile of companies on the list that are far from household names. Often it is lists of innovative companies that garner publicity and create a level of awareness that is often challenging for startups and new companies to achieve.

Creativity is the wellspring of new-product ideas, regardless of who comes up with them. Although a variety of approaches and techniques have been developed to stimulate creative thinking, the two considered most useful for generating new-product ideas are brainstorming and focus-group exercises. The goal of **brainstorming** is to get a group to think of unlimited ways to vary a product or solve a problem. Group members avoid criticism of an idea, no matter how ridiculous it may seem, and objective evaluation is postponed; the sheer quantity of ideas is what matters. As noted in Chapter 4, an objective of focus-group interviews is to stimulate insightful comments through group interaction. **Focus groups** usually consist of anywhere from 6 to 12 people. Sometimes consumer focus groups generate excellent new-product ideas. In the industrial market, focus groups have led to the evolution of machine tools, keyboard designs, and aircraft interiors.

10-2c | Idea Screening

After new ideas have been generated, they pass through the first filter in the product-development process. This stage, called **screening**, eliminates ideas that are inconsistent with the organization's new-product strategy or are inappropriate for some other reason. Managers screening new-product ideas must have a clear understanding of what their business is about. Some companies have a very broad definition of what is consistent with their business objectives. Alphabet (Google) acquired fitness tracking pioneer Fitbit in late 2019. At the time of purchase, Google noted that it had made the purchase to "help spur innovation in wearables." But the tech giant

already had made similar purchases of R&D departments of other fitness tracking devices (Fossil Group). Some were wondering if Google is more interested in the data of millions of Fitbit users around the world.[21] In screening new-product ideas, companies need to have a certain degree of tolerance for risk and uncertainty.

Concept tests are often used at the screening stage to rate concept (or product) alternatives. A **concept test** is an evaluation of a new-product idea, usually before any prototype has been created. Typically, researchers survey consumer reactions to descriptions and visual representations of a proposed product.

Concept tests are considered fairly good predictors of success for line extensions. They have also been relatively precise predictors of success for new products that are not copycat items, are not easily classified into existing product categories, and do not require major changes in consumer behaviour—such as Planters Creamy peanut butter. Concept tests are often laid out in terms of benefits, attributes, and claims; and these descriptions are placed on a piece of paper; and delivered to a potential customer to answer questions. The most important metric in concept tests are the DWB scores: "Definitely Would Buy." A score of 30 percent of respondents stating they "DWB" is a good score, showing that success at this stage is not easily attained.[22]

10-2d | Business Analysis

New-product ideas that survive the initial screening process move to the **business analysis** stage, the second stage of the screening process, where preliminary figures for demand, cost, sales, and profitability are calculated. For the first time, costs and revenues are estimated and compared. Depending on the nature of the product and the company, this process may be simple or complex.

The newness of the product, the size of the market, and the nature of the competition all affect the accuracy of revenue

REUTERS/Steve Marcus

brainstorming
the process of getting a group to think of unlimited ways to vary a product or solve a problem

screening
the first filter in the product-development process, which eliminates ideas that are inconsistent with the organization's new product strategy or are obviously inappropriate for some other reason

concept test
evaluation of a new-product idea, usually before any prototype has been created

business analysis
the second stage of the screening process, where preliminary figures for demand, cost, sales, and profitability are calculated

projections. In an established market, such as the soft drink business, industry estimates of total market size are available. Forecasting market share for a new entry is a bigger challenge.

Analyzing overall economic trends and their impact on estimated sales is especially important in product categories that are sensitive to fluctuations in the business cycle. If consumers view the economy as uncertain and risky, they will put off buying durable goods, such as major home appliances, automobiles, and homes. Likewise, business buyers postpone major equipment purchases if they expect a recession.

Answering questions during the business analysis stage may require studying the new product's markets, competition, costs, and technical capabilities. But at the end of this stage, management should have a good understanding of the product's market potential. This understanding is important because costs increase dramatically once a product idea enters the development stage.

10-2e | Development

In the early stage of **development**, the R&D or engineering department may develop a prototype of the product. During this stage, the company should start sketching a marketing strategy. The marketing department should decide on the product's packaging, branding, labelling, and so forth. In addition, it should map out strategies for the product's preliminary promotion, price, and distribution. The feasibility of manufacturing the product at an acceptable cost should be thoroughly examined. The development stage can last a long time and thus be very expensive. It took 11 years to develop Crest toothpaste, 15 years to develop the Xerox copy machine, 18 years to develop Minute Rice, and 51 years to develop television. In Canada, the average amount of time it takes for a pharmaceutical drug to go from research to clinic studies to approval is 12 years. This is slightly less than in the United States.[23]

Laboratory tests are often conducted on prototype models during the development stage. User safety is an important aspect of laboratory testing, which subjects products to much more severe treatment than is expected by end users. The Canada

development
the stage in the product-development process in which a prototype is developed and a marketing strategy is outlined

test marketing
the limited introduction of a product and a marketing program to determine the reactions of potential customers in a market situation

Apple introduced its Apple Watch in late 2014, with sales beginning in April 2015. Eighteen months later the Apple Watch Series 2 came out alongside the iPhone 7, and the Apple Watch Series 3 went on sale in September 2017. Right on cue, Apple Watch Series 4 was released in September 2018, and Series 5 one year later in 2019.

Consumer Product Safety Act requires manufacturers to conduct a reasonable testing program to ensure that their products conform to established safety standards.

Many product prototypes that test well in the laboratory are also tried out in homes or businesses. Examples of product categories well suited for such tests include human and pet food products, household cleaning products, and industrial chemicals and supplies. These products are all relatively inexpensive, and their performance characteristics are apparent to users.

10-2f | Test Marketing

After products and marketing programs have been developed, they are usually tested in the marketplace. **Test marketing** is the limited introduction of a product and associated marketing program to determine the reactions of potential customers in a market situation. It allows management to evaluate alternative strategies and to assess how well the various aspects of the marketing mix fit together. Even established products are test marketed to assess new marketing strategies.

It is important that the value of the test market be tempered by critically assessing the specific aspects of a company's offering. The locations chosen as test sites should reflect market conditions in the new product's projected market area as much as possible. Yet no test city exists that can universally represent actual market conditions, and a product's success or failure in one city doesn't guarantee its success or failure in the national

Crowdfunding and Product Development

The popularity of social media has affected many aspects of marketing, including product development. Crowdfunding is a way that companies can solicit investment from a large number of donors. With the advent of social networks like Instagram, it was inevitable that crowdfunding would have its own online networks. The top for-profit crowdfunding sites are Kickstarter as well as indiegogo, which funds causes focusing on non-profit social and cultural issues.[24]

However, the success rate of product development from crowdfunding campaigns is under some scrutiny. An article in the journal *Design Science* describes how of 144 successfully funded projects on Kickstarter, only 32 percent managed to produce a product on time. There were more Kickstarter projects that had *not* delivered in more than a year than there were successful products. Those who supported the campaigns, called backers, had the following issues with unsuccessful crowdfunding campaigns:

- **lack of features that were promised**
- **low quality in material used**
- **fundamental design flaws**
- **usability not meeting expectations[25]**

Campaign	FAQ	Updates	Comments	Community

Product Set-Up: Prototype Issues

We have received the ocean clean-water prototype from the factory and were excited to test it out. Our initial tests show that a number of modifications must be made to the design for optimal performance. These include

- Adjustments to the size of the switch

- The angle of rotation off by 2 degrees

Work Is Underway

It is important that we get this right. Our goal is a product that is lightweight but durable to withstand ocean currents and significant weather events. Once these adjustments are complete, production will begin in earnest.

market. When selecting test market cities, researchers should therefore find locations where the demographics and purchasing habits mirror the overall market. Some businesses can test market their products in their retail locations. For example, McDonald's is known to test-market new products in its own restaurants in select cities. Likewise, Starbucks conducts extensive test marketing before introducing various products in its stores, as the risk of its failing and thus damaging the parent brand is always a serious concern.

THE HIGH COSTS OF TEST MARKETING Test marketing frequently takes one year or longer, and costs can often inflate into the millions. Some products remain in test markets even longer. Despite the cost, many companies believe it is much better to fail in a test market than in a national introduction. Because test marketing is so expensive, some companies do not test line extensions of well-known brands. For example, because its Sara Lee brand is well known, Consolidated Foods Kitchen faced little risk in distributing its frozen croissants nationally. Other products introduced without being test marketed include General Foods' International Coffees and Quaker Oats' Chewy Granola Bars.

The high cost of test marketing is not just financial. One unavoidable problem is that test marketing exposes the new product and its marketing mix to competitors before its introduction. Thus the element of surprise is lost. Competitors can also sabotage, or jam, a testing program by introducing their own sales promotion, pricing, or advertising campaign. The purpose is to hide or distort the normal conditions that the testing company might expect in the market.

South by Southwest—A Testing Market

Nestled between Toronto and Detroit, London, Ontario, is the perfect test market: it's not too big and not too small. While large markets are attractive due to the sheer number of potential customers, a good test market needs to have a nice variety of characteristics. There needs to be a good mix of demographics, industries, and educational facilities. London has a rounded representation of ethnicity; manufacturing, health care, and technology industries; and the University of Western Ontario. These factors are very attractive for companies to test their products. It would seem that Southwestern Ontario is a popular place in general for test marketing, as McDonald's used the area for testing its plant-based burger (the PLT.) and Tim Hortons tested out the not-so-popular plant-based offerings at their restaurants.[26]

REUTERS/Moe Doiron

ALTERNATIVES TO TEST MARKETING Many companies are looking for cheaper, faster, and safer alternatives to traditional test marketing. In the early 1980s, Information Resources pioneered one alternative: single-source research using supermarket scanner data. Another alternative to traditional test marketing is **simulated (laboratory) market testing**, which involves the presentation of advertising and other promotional materials for several products, including the test product, to members of the product's target market. These people are then taken to shop at a mock or real store, where their purchases are recorded. Shopper behaviour, including repeat purchasing, is monitored to assess the product's likely performance under true market conditions. Computer simulation is also used extensively to test-market certain types of new products. For example, Google and Amazon extensively conduct test-market experiments to examine the effectiveness of various marketing programs.

Despite these alternatives, most companies still consider test marketing essential for most new products. The high price of failure simply prohibits the widespread introduction of most new products without testing. Many companies are finding that the Internet offers a fast, cost-effective way to conduct test marketing. Procter & Gamble is an avid proponent of using the Internet as a means of gauging customer demand for potential new products. The company tested out a refillable skincare product through olay.com, where customers could try out the new packaging and provide feedback on the refilling process. The product, Olay Whips, is the first of many Procter and Gamble offerings that will focus on reusable packaging.[27]

10-2g | Commercialization

The final stage in the new-product development process is **commercialization**, the decision to market a product. This decision sets several tasks in motion: ordering production materials and equipment, starting production, building inventories, shipping the product to field distribution points, training the sales force, announcing the new product to the trade, and advertising to potential customers.

The time from the initial commercialization decision to the product's actual introduction varies. It can range from a few weeks for simple products that use existing equipment to several years for technical products that require custom manufacturing equipment. And the total

simulated (laboratory) market testing
the presentation of advertising and other promotion materials for several products, including the test product, to members of the product's target market

commercialization
the decision to market a product

CO-LAB-ORATION

Two Canadian companies have come together to create a real-life laboratory for a technology that could change everything for technology companies: 5G. 5G is the fifth generation of digital networks that support wireless and digital technologies. Higher efficiency, ultra-low latency (near instantaneous responsiveness), massive device connectivity (Internet of things), and lower energy consumption (5G networks are said to use 90 percent less energy than 4G) are some of the key aspects of 5G that make it such a compelling technology. The challenge is that no one really knows what can be done with 5G until it is online. Which is why TELUS, one of Canada's largest telecommunications companies, and Zú, a non-profit organization tasked to promote creative endeavours in the entertainment sector, provide such a compelling match. The resulting laboratory is called 5G TELUS Lab in collaboration with Lenovo, and is a creative space for companies and entrepreneurs to create new concepts around mobile gaming, virtual and augmented reality, 3D holograms, and 4K live streaming. The laboratory in Montreal houses multiple facilities to encourage creativity and exploration.

Courtesy of Lenovo, TELUS, and Zú

Sources: www.bctechnology.com/news/2019/9/20/Zu-Partners-With-TELUS-to-Establish-Experimental-5G-Laboratory-in-Canada.cfm; https://zumtl.com/en/page/creative-lab

cost of development and initial introduction can be staggering. Gillette spent US$750 million developing the Mach3 razor, and the first-year marketing budget for the new three-bladed razor was US$300 million.

The most important factor in successful new-product introduction is a good match between the product and market needs—as the marketing concept would predict. Successful new products deliver a meaningful and perceivable benefit to a sizable number of people or organizations and are different in some significant way from their intended substitutes.

chanonnat srisura/Shutterstock.com

Olay sells eco-friendly refills for its Whip line to save on packaging.

CHARACTERISTICS OF COMPANIES WITH SUCCESSFUL NEW-PRODUCT INTRODUCTIONS

Companies that routinely experience success in new-product introductions tend to share the following characteristics:

- a history of carefully listening to customers
- a vision of what the market will be like in the future
- strong leadership
- a commitment to new-product development
- a project-based team approach to new-product development
- an insistence on getting every aspect of the product-development process right

Often products fail due to the inaction or misguided actions of a company:

- Incongruity between the product and the chosen target market;
- Development process too long, leading to delayed market entry;
- Company resources, from financial to human resources, ill-equipped to handle growth;
- Poor initial product reviews, combined with few changes made based on customer feedback; and
- Poor execution of the marketing-mix activities necessary to execute strategy.

10-3 | GLOBAL ISSUES IN NEW-PRODUCT DEVELOPMENT

Increasing globalization of markets and of competition encourages multinational companies to consider new-product development from a worldwide perspective. A company that starts with a global strategy is better able to develop products that are marketable worldwide. In many multinational corporations, every product is developed for potential worldwide distribution, and unique market requirements are built in whenever possible.

Some global marketers design their products to meet regulations in their major markets and then, if necessary, meet smaller markets' requirements country by country. For years, Domino's Pizza was in the second tier of fast food chains, until it began to understand the importance of having a strong international marketing approach. The basic product was still pizza: bread, sauce, and cheese. But the company now offers specific menu items based on where the pizza is being sold, from seafood and fish in Asia, to curry in India.[28] Some products, however, have little potential for global market penetration without modification. In other cases, companies cannot sell their product at affordable prices and still make a profit in many countries. We often hear about the popularity of American products in foreign countries. Recently, Canadian companies have been finding that products popular in foreign markets can become hits in Canada. For example, Häagen-Dazs introduced dulce de leche ice cream in Canada after successfully introducing it in Argentina.

adopter
a consumer who was satisfied enough with their trial experience with a product to use it again

innovation
a product perceived as new by a potential adopter

diffusion
the process by which the adoption of an innovation spreads

10-4 | THE SPREAD OF NEW PRODUCTS

Managers have a better chance of successfully marketing new products if they understand how consumers learn about and adopt products. A person who buys a new product they have never before tried may ultimately become an **adopter**, a consumer who was happy enough with the trial experience with a product to use it again.

10-4a | Diffusion of Innovation

An **innovation** is a product perceived as new by a potential adopter. It really doesn't matter whether the product is new to the world or belongs to some other category of new product. If the product is new to a potential adopter, in this context, it is considered an innovation. **Diffusion** is the process by which the adoption of an innovation spreads.

Five categories of adopters participate in the diffusion process:

- *Innovators:* The first 2.5 percent of all those who adopt the product. Innovators are eager to try new ideas and products—almost to the point of obsession. In addition to having higher incomes, innovators are typically more worldly and more active outside their communities than noninnovators. Innovators also rely less on group norms and are more self-confident. Because they tend to be well educated, they are more likely to get their information from scientific sources and experts. Innovators are characterized as being venturesome.

- *Early adopters:* The next 13.5 percent to adopt the product. Although early adopters are not the very first, they do adopt early in the product's life cycle. Compared with innovators, early adopters rely much more on group norms and values. They are also more oriented to the local community, in contrast to the innovators' worldly outlook. Early adopters are more likely than innovators to be opinion leaders because of their closer affiliation with groups. The respect of others is a dominant characteristic of early adopters.

- *Early majority:* The next 34 percent to adopt. The early majority weighs the pros and cons before adopting a new product. They are likely to collect more information and evaluate more brands than early adopters, thereby extending the adoption process. They rely on the group for information but are unlikely to be opinion leaders themselves. Instead, they tend to be opinion leaders' friends and neighbours. The early majority is an important link in the process of diffusing new ideas because they are positioned between earlier and later adopters. A dominant characteristic of the early majority is deliberateness. Most of the first residential broadband users were classic early adopters—white males, well educated, and wealthy, with a great deal of Internet experience.

- *Late majority:* The next 34 percent to adopt. The late majority adopts a new product because most of their friends have already adopted it. Because they also rely on group norms, their adoption stems from pressure to conform. This group tends to be older and below average in income and education. They depend mainly on word-of-mouth communication rather than on the mass media. The dominant characteristic of the late majority is skepticism.

- *Laggards:* The final 16 percent to adopt. Like innovators, laggards do not rely on group norms. Their independence is rooted in their ties to tradition. Thus, the past heavily influences their decisions. By the time laggards adopt an innovation, it has probably been outmoded and replaced by something else. For example, they may have bought their first digital camera once film cameras were no longer being produced. Laggards have the longest adoption time and the lowest socioeconomic status. They tend to be suspicious of new products and alienated from a rapidly advancing society. The dominant value of laggards is tradition. Marketers can benefit from laggards by introducing no-frills, low-cost products to this segment.

Note that some product categories may never be adopted by 100 percent of the population. The percentages noted in the adopter categories above refer to the percentage of all of those who will eventually adopt a product, not to percentages of the entire population.

10-4b | Product Characteristics and the Rate of Adoption

Five product characteristics can be used to predict and explain the rate of acceptance and diffusion of a new product:

- *Complexity:* The degree of difficulty involved in understanding and using a new product. The more complex the product, the slower its diffusion.

Beautyimage/Shutterstock.com

According to *Canadian Grocer*, the early adopters for shopping for groceries online are between 18 and 29, tech savvy, stay-at-home types that are driven by value for money. And with Canada set to become the sixth most attractive market in the world for online purchasing by 2022, it makes sense that Canadian grocery stores take some time get to know these early adopters.[29]

- *Compatibility:* The degree to which the new product is consistent with existing values and product knowledge, past experiences, and current needs. Incompatible products diffuse more slowly than compatible products.

- *Relative advantage:* The degree to which a product is perceived as superior to existing substitutes. Due to the improved camera technology in cell phones, the convenience of using phones over digital cameras has created a significant relative advantage.

- *Observability:* The degree to which the benefits or other results of using the product can be observed by others and communicated to target customers. For instance, fashion items and automobiles are highly visible and more observable than personal-care items.

- *Trialability:* The degree to which a product can be tried on a limited basis. Products that can be tried on a limited basis have a better chance of being adopted. It is much easier to try a new toothpaste or breakfast cereal than a new automobile or microcomputer. However, many products that are trying to enter into a crowded marketplace will often offer a free trial period to encourage trial. Netflix uses a 30-day free trial to entice customers, while Disney+ hopes its customers will make a decision within a week. The various adoption rates found in Exhibit 10.3 shows how important it is to take into consideration as many of these product characteristics as possible.

EXHIBIT 10.3 TECHNOLOGY ADOPTIONS IN US HOUSEHOLDS

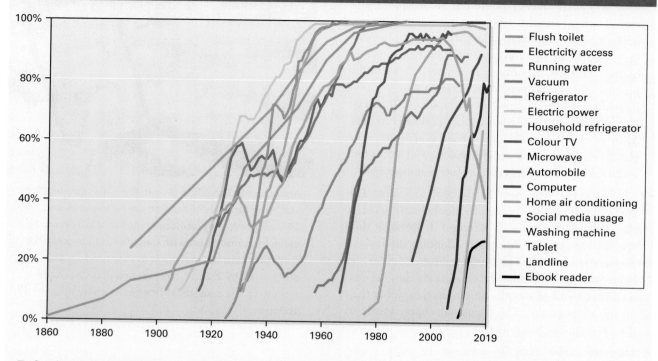

Technology adaptation rates, measured as the percentage of households in the United States using a particular technology

Source: Hannah Ritchie and Max Roser (2019), "Technology Adoption". Published online at OurWorldInData.org. Retrieved from: 'https://ourworldindata.org/technology-adoption' [Online Resource]

10-4c | Marketing Implications of the Adoption Process

Two types of communication aid the diffusion process. One is *word-of-mouth communication,* both traditional and digital among consumers and communication from marketers to consumers. Word-of-mouth communication within and across groups speeds diffusion. Opinion leaders discuss new products with their followers and with other opinion leaders. Marketers must therefore ensure that opinion leaders receive the types of information that are desired in the media they use. Suppliers of some products, such as professional and healthcare services, rely almost solely on word-of-mouth communication for new business.

The second type of communication aiding the diffusion process is *communication directly from the marketer to potential adopters.* Messages directed toward early adopters should normally use different appeals than messages directed toward the early majority, the late majority, or the laggards. Early adopters are more important than innovators because they make up a larger group, are more socially active, and are usually opinion leaders.

As the focus of a promotional campaign shifts from early adopters to the early majority and the late majority, marketers should study these target markets' dominant characteristics, buying behaviour, and media characteristics. They should then revise their messages and media strategy to fit these target markets. The diffusion model helps guide marketers in developing and implementing promotion strategy.

10-5 | PRODUCT LIFE CYCLES

The **product life cycle (PLC)**, one of the most familiar concepts in marketing, traces the stages of a product's

product life cycle (PLC)
a concept that traces the stages of a product's acceptance, from its introduction (birth) to its decline (death)

acceptance, from its introduction (birth) to its decline (death). Few other general concepts have been so widely discussed. Although some researchers and consultants have challenged the theoretical basis and managerial value of the PLC, many believe it is a useful marketing management diagnostic tool and a general guide for marketing planning in various life-cycle stages.[30]

As Exhibit 10.4 shows, a product progresses through four major stages: introduction, growth, maturity, and decline.

The PLC concept can be used to analyze a product category (e.g., motor vehicle), product form (i.e., four-wheel drive), and brand (Jeep). The PLC for a product form is usually longer than the PLC for any one brand. The exception would be a brand that was the first and last competitor in a product form market, meaning it occupied a space that had little competition in the product form space. In that situation, the brand and product form life cycles would be equal in length. Product categories have the longest life cycles. A **product category** includes all brands that satisfy a particular type of need, such as shaving products, passenger automobiles, or colas.

The time a product spends in any one stage of the life cycle may vary dramatically. Some products, such as trendy items, move through the entire cycle in weeks. Others, such as electric clothes washers and dryers, stay in the maturity stage for decades. Exhibit 10.4 illustrates the typical life cycle for a consumer durable good, such as a washer or dryer. In contrast, Exhibit 10.5 illustrates typical life cycles for styles (such as formal, business, or casual clothing), fashions (such as high-waisted jeans and bucket hats), and fads (such as man-buns). Changes in a product's uses, its image, or its positioning can extend that product's life cycle.

The PLC concept does not tell managers the length of a product's life cycle or its duration in any stage. It does not dictate marketing strategy. It is simply a tool to help marketers forecast future events and suggest appropriate strategies.

10-5a | Introductory Stage

The **introductory stage** of the PLC represents the full-scale launch of a new product into the marketplace. Product categories that have recently entered the PLC include computer databases for personal use, room-deodorizing air-conditioning filters, and wind-powered home electric generators. A high failure rate, little competition, frequent product modification,

EXHIBIT 10.4 FOUR STAGES OF THE PRODUCT LIFE CYCLE

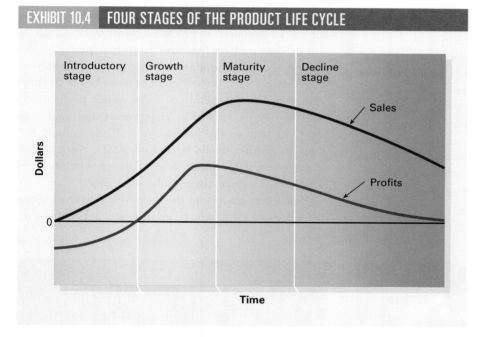

EXHIBIT 10.5 PRODUCT LIFE CYCLES FOR STYLES, FASHIONS, AND FADS

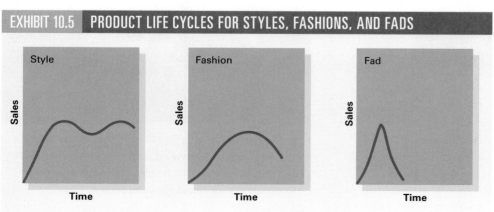

product category
all brands that satisfy a particular type of need

introductory stage
the full-scale launch of a new product into the marketplace

Is it a toy? A tool to relieve nervous energy? Both? The fidget spinner, that small device that fits in the palm of your hand, was hugely popular in 2017 but soon became the bane of teachers' existence everywhere.

Once adorning wrists of many in support of the fight against cancer, these ubiquitous yellow wristbands became trash when Lance Armstrong was accused of and admitted to doping during cycling races.

and limited distribution typify the introductory stage of the PLC.

Marketing costs in the introductory stage are normally high for several reasons. High dealer margins are often needed to obtain adequate distribution, and incentives are needed to convince consumers to try the new product. Advertising expenses are high because of the need to educate consumers about the new product's benefits. Production costs are also often high in this stage, as a result of product and manufacturing flaws being identified and then corrected and because of efforts undertaken to develop mass-production economies.

Sales normally increase slowly during the introductory stage. Moreover, profits are usually negative because of R&D costs, factory tooling, and high introduction costs. The length of the introductory phase is largely determined by product characteristics, such as the product's advantages over substitute products, the educational effort required to make the product known, and management's commitment of resources to the new item. A short introductory period is usually preferred to help reduce the impact of negative earnings and cash flows. As soon as the product gets off the ground, the financial burden should begin to diminish. Also, a short introduction helps dispel some of the uncertainty as to whether the new product will be successful.

Promotion strategy in the introductory stage focuses on developing product awareness and informing

Pokemon Go is an augmented reality game that was all the rage in 2016. And while the game is still around, there are not as many people wandering around looking for a virtual Pikachu.

In the mid 1990s, kids had to have this virtual pet, one that required care, grew up, and even left home. While the product is still sold, it lacks the computing power to compete with cellphones and tablets.

consumers about the product category's potential benefits. At this stage, the communication challenge is to stimulate primary demand—demand for the product in general rather than for a specific brand. Intensive personal selling is often required to gain acceptance for the product among wholesalers and retailers. Promotion of convenience products often requires heavy consumer sampling and couponing. Shopping and specialty products demand educational advertising and personal selling to the final consumer.

10-5b | Growth Stage

If a product category survives the introductory stage, it advances to the **growth stage** of the life cycle. The growth stage is the second stage of the PLC, when sales typically grow at an increasing rate, many competitors enter the market, large companies may start to acquire small pioneering companies, and profits are healthy. Profits rise rapidly in the growth stage, reach their peak, and begin declining as competition intensifies. Emphasis switches from primary demand promotion (for example, promoting tablets) to aggressive brand advertising and communication of the differences between brands (for example, promoting the Apple iPhone versus Samsung Galaxy).

Distribution becomes a major key to success during the growth stage and later stages. Manufacturers scramble to sign up dealers and distributors and to build long-term relationships. Without adequate distribution, it is impossible to establish a strong market position.

10-5c | Maturity Stage

A period during which sales increase at a decreasing rate signals the beginning of the **maturity stage** of the life cycle. New users cannot be added indefinitely, and, sooner or later, the market approaches saturation. Normally, the maturity stage is the longest stage of the PLC. Many major household appliances are in the maturity stage of their life cycles.

For shopping products, such as durable goods and electronics, and for many specialty products, annual models begin to appear during the maturity stage. Product lines are lengthened to appeal to additional market segments. Service and repair assume more important roles as manufacturers strive to distinguish their products from others. Product design changes tend to become stylistic (How can the product be made different?) rather than functional (How can the product be made better?).

As prices and profits continue to fall, marginal competitors start dropping out of the market. Dealer margins also shrink, resulting in less shelf space for mature items, lower dealer inventories, and a general reluctance to promote the product. Thus, promotion to dealers often intensifies during this stage to retain loyalty.

Heavy consumer promotion by the manufacturer is also required to maintain market share. Cutthroat competition during this stage can lead to price wars. Another characteristic of the maturity stage is the emergence of niche marketers that target narrow, well-defined, underserved segments of a market. Starbucks Coffee targets its gourmet line at the only segment of the coffee market that is growing: new, younger, more affluent coffee drinkers.

10-5d | Decline Stage

A long-run drop in sales signals the beginning of the **decline stage**. The rate of decline is governed by how rapidly consumer tastes change or substitute products are adopted. Many convenience products and trendy items lose their market overnight, leaving large inventories of unsold items, such as designer jeans. Others die more slowly. Video rental stores like Blockbuster went out of business and were replaced by Netflix and other forms of digital entertainment.

Some companies have developed successful

growth stage
the second stage of the product life cycle when sales typically grow at an increasing rate, many competitors enter the market, large companies may start to acquire small pioneering companies, and profits are healthy

maturity stage
a period during which sales increase at a decreasing rate

decline stage
a long-run drop in sales

And then there was one. The world's last Blockbuster is in Oregon, USA. Blockbuster used to have over 9000 locations worldwide.

strategies for marketing products in the decline stage of the PLC. They eliminate all nonessential marketing expenses and let sales decline as more and more customers discontinue purchasing the products. Eventually, the product is withdrawn from the market.

Management sage Peter Drucker said that all companies should practise organized abandonment, which involves reviewing every product, service, and policy every two or three years and asking the critical question "If we didn't do this already, would we launch it now?" If the answer is no, it's time to begin the abandonment process.[31]

10-5e | Implications for Marketing Management

The PLC concept encourages marketing managers to plan so that they can take the initiative instead of reacting to past events. The PLC is especially useful as a predicting, or forecasting, tool. Because products pass through distinctive stages, it is often possible to estimate a product's location on the curve by using historical data. Profits, like sales, tend to follow a predictable path over a product's life cycle.

The first digital camera went on sale in 1975. With the rise of smartphone camera technology, this discontinuous innovation is surely headed toward the end of its product life cycle.

Exhibit 10.6 shows the relationship between the adopter categories and the stages of the PLC. Note that the various categories of adopters first buy products in different stages of the life cycle. Almost all sales in the maturity and decline stages represent repeat purchasing.

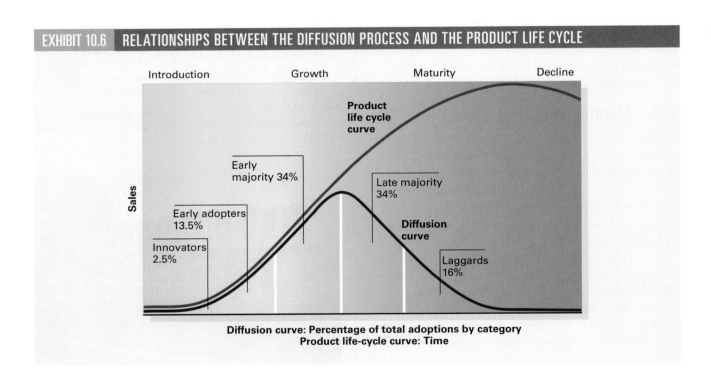

EXHIBIT 10.6   RELATIONSHIPS BETWEEN THE DIFFUSION PROCESS AND THE PRODUCT LIFE CYCLE

AWAKE Chocolate

AWAKE CHOCOLATE CONTINUING CASE

Disrupting Energy

Every company that devises a new product hopes it will be unique in some significant way. The hope is that a new product will get people's attention, from consumers willing to try it to competitors concerned about its presence in the marketplace.

But often a new product will simply be an addition to the market, maybe a new approach or flavour, but not something disruptive. Often these revisions are welcome in the market, and they may garner attention at the start, but the challenge is for companies to keep up any momentum gained.

In the case of Awake Chocolate, the momentum started early—even earlier than the *Dragon's Den* appearance in 2013 mentioned in Chapter 1. In 2012, Awake had managed to, as COO and CFO Dan Tzotzis, recalled, "raise enough capital to visit 40 different schools across Canada. We bought two school buses, decorated [them] in Awake logos and design … it was in those moments when students started engaging that we realized there was something special there."

This feeling of something special was also shared by fellow Awake founder Adam Deremo. He looked at the development of a new product like Awake as something truly seismic in the energy food market. He observed, "We're into incremental part of our innovation; our disruptive part of our innovation was delivering the energy benefit in a food form. Our incremental part of innovation is about making the disruptive innovation a little better each day."

This hybrid model of new product development, combining disruptive and incremental innovation, seems to be appropriate for Awake given its meteoric rise since launching in 2012. And it was not only infusion of capital from their business contacts, a few Dragons, and others that laid the foundation for Awake; the company's continual focus on innovation is the real key to the success of Awake Chocolate. Whether it's marketing research or B2B relationships, the company continues to see the importance of devising new ways of approaching all aspects of its business. Deremo noted that exact point: "Innovation is something that keeps your brand relevant; it creates authentic news to talk about."

So, with every new innovation, from granola to bite-sized candy to whatever the company comes up with next, Awake is well positioned to handle the challenging consumer goods market in North America.

As discussed in the marketing research chapter (Chapter 4), Awake does not eagerly spend money conducting primary research such as surveys or focus groups. Often the company will develop a new product and then find ways to use its target market as respondents. Adam Deremo stated that "[marketing research] can be a simple and cost-effective way to do concept screening, because it's not always easy to see the difference between an idea and a business opportunity when it's your own idea."

And these ideas continue to flow from the Awake Chocolate new product development process; the pipeline of new products seems to be endless. At the writing of this case, Awake was in talks to develop an entirely new product line, possibly even a brand extension. Take a moment to go to the Awake website (https://awakechocolate.ca) and see if you can find the newest innovation brought to the market.

QUESTIONS

1. Read the original article about disruptive innovation from your school's library or online.[1] Based on your understanding of the concept, test Adam Deremo's claim that Awake Chocolate is a disruptive innovation in the marketplace.

2. Use the new-product development process in this chapter to provide a "how-to" guide using Awake Chocolate as your focus. Use each stage of the process and explain it based on your understanding of Awake's process.

3. Draw the diffusion of innovation model and place Awake's chocolate bars at a point in the curve. Use the textbook and your notes to justify your answer.

NOTE

1. Bower, J. L., and C. M. Christensen. "Disruptive Technologies: Catching the Wave." *Harvard Business Review* 73, no. 1 (January–February 1995): 43–53.

11 | Services and Non-profit Organization Marketing

LEARNING OUTCOMES

11-1 Discuss the differences between services and goods

11-2 Describe the components of service quality and the gap model of service quality

11-3 Develop marketing mixes for services

11-4 Discuss relationship marketing in services

11-5 Explain internal marketing in services

11-6 Describe non-profit organization marketing

"Great things in business are never done by one person, they're done by a team of people."[1]

—Steve Jobs

A **service** is the result of applying human or mechanical efforts to people or objects. Services involve a deed, a performance, or an effort that cannot be physically possessed. Today, the service sector substantially influences the Canadian economy. According to Statistics Canada, in 2019 the service sector accounted for more than 80 percent of all employment in Canada.[2] The service sector is important to the overall health of the Canadian economy, with more than 70 percent of Canadian GDP coming from services.[3] The service-oriented industries contributing to much of this output includes technology, financial services, and retail.

The marketing process discussed in Chapter 1 is the same for all types of products, whether they are goods or services. In addition, although a comparison of goods and services marketing can be beneficial, in reality it is hard to distinguish clearly between manufacturing and service companies because many manufacturing companies can point to service as a major factor in their success. For example, maintenance and repair services offered by the manufacturer are important to buyers of office equipment. Services do have some unique characteristics that distinguish them from goods, and marketing strategies need to be adjusted for these characteristics.

11-1 | HOW SERVICES DIFFER FROM GOODS

Services have four unique characteristics that distinguish them from goods. Services are intangible, inseparable, heterogeneous, and perishable.

11-1a | Intangibility

The basic difference between services and goods is that services are intangible performances. Because of their **intangibility**, they cannot be touched, seen, tasted,

service
the result of applying human or mechanical efforts to people or objects

intangibility
the inability of services to be touched, seen, tasted, heard, or felt in the same manner that goods can be sensed

heard, or felt in the same manner that goods can be sensed.

Evaluating the quality of services before or even after making a purchase is harder than evaluating the quality of goods because, compared with goods, services tend to exhibit fewer search qualities. A **search quality** is a characteristic that can be easily assessed before purchase—for instance, the colour of a car or the size of a smartphone. At the same time, services tend to exhibit more experience and credence qualities. An **experience quality** is a characteristic that can be assessed only after use, such as the quality of a meal in a restaurant. A **credence quality** is a characteristic that consumers may have difficulty assessing even after purchase because they do not have the necessary knowledge or experience. Medical and consulting services are examples of services that exhibit credence qualities.

These characteristics also make it more difficult for marketers to communicate the benefits of an intangible service than to communicate the benefits of tangible goods. Thus marketers often rely on tangible cues to communicate a service's nature and quality. For example, the amazon.ca logo has an arrow from the "a" to the "z," communicating that Amazon has everything from a to z.

The facilities that customers visit, or from which services are delivered, are a critical tangible part of the total service offering. Messages about the organization are communicated to customers through elements such as the decor, the clutter or neatness of service areas, and the staff's manners and dress. Hotels know that guests form opinions quickly and are more willing than ever before to tweet them within 15 minutes of their stay. Therefore, some hotels go to great lengths to make their guests feel at home. For example, Four Seasons makes sure that the locks on the hotel room doors make the right click when the door closes to ensure the guests feel secure. The company also gives all of its employees—from parking attendants to managers—the authority to act instantly when a guest makes a request. This allows Four Seasons to offer excellent personalized service from check-in to check-out.[4]

search quality
a characteristic that can be easily assessed before purchase

experience quality
a characteristic that can be assessed only after use

credence quality
a characteristic that consumers may have difficulty assessing even after purchase because they do not have the necessary knowledge or experience

Everything from "a" to "z" with a smile.

11-1b | Inseparability

Goods are produced without requiring any involvement of the consumer, sold, and then consumed. In contrast, services are often sold, and then produced and consumed at the same time. In other words, their production and consumption are inseparable activities with the consumer involved at the beginning of the process instead of partway through. This **inseparability** means that because consumers must be present during the production of services, such as haircuts or surgery, they are actually involved in the production of the services they buy. That type of consumer involvement is rare in goods manufacturing.

Simultaneous production and consumption also means that services normally cannot be produced in a centralized location and consumed in decentralized locations, as goods typically are. Services are also inseparable from the perspective of the service provider. Thus the quality of service that companies are able to deliver depends on the quality of their employees.

inseparability
the inability of the production and consumption of a service to be separated; consumers must be present during the production

heterogeneity
the variability of the inputs and outputs of services, which causes services to tend to be less standardized and uniform than goods

perishability
the inability of services to be stored, warehoused, or inventoried

11-1c | Heterogeneity

One great strength of McDonald's is consistency. Whether customers order a Big Mac in Tokyo or Moscow, they know exactly what they will get. This is not the case with many service companies. Because services have **heterogeneity**, or variability of inputs and outputs, they tend to be less standardized and uniform than goods. For example, physicians in a group practice or hairstylists in a salon differ in their technical and interpersonal skills. Because services tend to be labour intensive and production and consumption are inseparable, consistency and quality control can be difficult to achieve.

Standardization, training, uniforms, procedures, and manuals help increase consistency and reliability. In the competitive retail landscape, consistency of service quality is often key to building a competitive advantage. Saje Natural Wellness is a 27-year-old family-run Canadian business with 50 locations across North America and a 1017 percent growth over the past five years. The owners—a husband and wife team—are a perfect complement to one another to ensure continued growth and long-term success. Jean-Pierre LeBlanc has a background in corporate chemistry, which led to the launch of their initial products, still available at Saje today. Kate Ross, on the other hand, grew up in the retail industry and as she would tell you, "It is in my DNA to create outrageous customer experiences." Saje's corporate philosophy is that all employees report to the customer. Sales staff educate the customer to ensure the products purchased meet the customer's needs. At the same time Saje invests in the tangible product, ensuring that the product mix is composed of high-quality natural products.[5]

11-1d | Perishability

Perishability is the fourth characteristic of services. Perishability refers to the inability of services to be stored, warehoused, or inventoried. An empty hotel room or airplane seat produces no revenue that day. Yet service organizations are often forced to turn away full-price customers during peak periods.

One of the most important challenges in many service industries is finding ways to synchronize supply and demand. The philosophy that some revenue is better than none has prompted many hotels to offer deep discounts on weekends and during the off-season.

11-2 | SERVICE QUALITY

Because of the four unique characteristics of services, service quality is more difficult to define and measure than the quality of tangible goods. Business executives rank the improvement of service quality as one of the most critical challenges facing them today.

11-2a | Evaluating Service Quality

Research has shown that customers evaluate service quality by the following five components[6]:

- **Reliability**: The ability to perform the service dependably, accurately, and consistently. Reliability refers to performing the service right the first time and every time. This component has been found to be the one most important to consumers. Reliability of delivery will create brand loyalty, which in the highly competitive service industry is coveted. Take, for example, the Calgary Philharmonic Orchestra (CPO). With a renowned conductor as music director and talented musicians offering a variety of consistently high-quality musical performances, it has come to be known as an orchestra of exceptional artistic excellence. This level of ongoing excellence has led to sold-out performances.

- **Responsiveness**: The ability to provide prompt service. Examples of responsiveness are returning customers' calls quickly, serving lunch fast to someone in a hurry, or ensuring that the consumer does not have to wait past the appointment time. The ultimate in responsiveness is offering service 24 hours a day, 7 days a week. The importance of responsiveness to customers is shown in the growth of the online travel sites like Expedia.ca. Worldwide, the growth of digital travel sales is more than 15 percent.[7]

- **Assurance**: The knowledge and courtesy of employees and their ability to convey trust. Skilled employees exemplify assurance when they treat customers with respect and when they make customers feel that they can trust the company.

- **Empathy**: Caring, individualized attention paid to customers. Companies whose employees recognize customers and learn their specific requirements are providing empathy. Again, empowering employees to be partners provides the opportunity for Starbucks' baristas to be empathetic. The emphasis on creating connections is the stimulus for the barista–customer relationship that many Starbucks' baristas and customers have come to enjoy.

- **Tangibles**: The physical evidence of the service. The tangible parts of a service include the physical facilities, tools, and equipment used to provide the service, and the appearance of personnel. Starbucks' physical facility reinforces its desire to create and foster connections. Starbucks promotes socializing in the restaurants—they are neighbourhood gathering places offering comfortable seating, WiFi, and newspapers. The stores are a haven from the stresses of the day.[8]

Overall service quality is measured by combining customers' evaluations for all five components. Some companies use different methods to measure service quality as described in Measuring Service Quality and Customer Satisfaction.

11-2b | The Gap Model of Service Quality

A model of service quality called the **gap model** identifies five gaps that can cause problems in service delivery and influence customer evaluations of service quality (see Exhibit 11.1)[9]:

- *Gap 1:* Knowledge gap—the gap between what customers want and what management thinks customers want. This gap results from a lack of understanding or a misinterpretation of

reliability
the ability to perform a service dependably, accurately, and consistently

responsiveness
the ability to provide prompt service

assurance
the knowledge and courtesy of employees and their ability to convey trust

empathy
caring, individualized attention paid to customers

tangibles
the physical evidence of a service, including the physical facilities, tools, and equipment used to provide the service

gap model
a model identifying five gaps that can cause problems in service delivery and influence customer evaluations of service quality

EXHIBIT 11.1   GAP MODEL OF SERVICE QUALITY

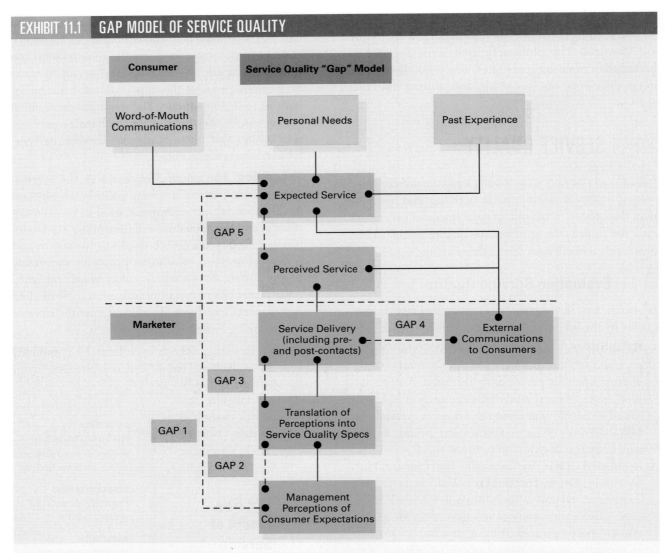

Service Quality "Gap" Model

Consumer

Word-of-Mouth Communications

Personal Needs

Past Experience

Expected Service

GAP 5

Perceived Service

Marketer

GAP 4

Service Delivery (including pre- and post-contacts)

External Communications to Consumers

GAP 3

Translation of Perceptions into Service Quality Specs

GAP 1

GAP 2

Management Perceptions of Consumer Expectations

The gap analysis model measures consumer perceptions of service quality. Managers use the model to analyze sources of quality problems and to understand how service quality can be improved.

the customers' needs, wants, or desires. A consumer's expectations may vary for a variety of reasons, including past experiences and the type of situation. A company that does little or no customer satisfaction research is likely to experience this gap. To close gap 1, companies must stay attuned to customer wants by researching customer needs and satisfaction.

- *Gap 2:* Standards gap—the gap between what management think customers want and the quality specifications that management develops to provide the service. Essentially, this gap is the result of management's inability to translate customers' needs into delivery systems within the company. In other words, the gap is a result of manage-

ment not having provided the appropriate service designs and standards. The reduction in this gap is achieved through the creation of policies and procedures related to the delivery of the service, the establishment of metrics to measure performance on an ongoing basis, and the training and development of employees.

- *Gap 3:* Delivery gap—the gap between the service quality specifications and the service that is actually provided. If both gaps 1 and 2 have been closed, then gap 3 results from the inability of management and employees to do what should be done. Management needs to ensure that employees have the skills and the proper tools to perform their jobs, including effective training programs and ongoing feedback.

The importance of the service quality component responsiveness is shown by online travel sites such as Expedia

Piotr Swat/Shutterstock.com

- *Gap 4:* Communication gap—the gap between what the company provides and what the customer is told it provides. This gap may be caused by misleading or deceptive advertising campaigns promising more than the company can deliver or doing "whatever it takes" to get the business. To close this gap, companies need to create realistic customer expectations through honest, accurate communication regarding what they can provide.

- *Gap 5:* Expectation gap—the gap between the service that customers expect they should receive and the perceived service that customers actually receive. This gap can be positive or negative. Ongoing research is necessary to understand consumers' perceptions and to manage their expectations. In this age of social media, where conversations are happening online in real time on a number of online forums, companies can monitor these conversations to ensure timely responses.

Measuring Service Quality and Customer Satisfaction

One way that the banks in Canada measure service quality is through customer satisfaction ratings. J.D. Power, a global research company, reaches out annually to more than 15 000 bank customers to ask their opinion on how satisfied they are with their banking services.

In the J.D. Power research, the banks are rated on a scale of 0 to 1000 on six factors including communication, convenience, and problem resolution. The finding are released in two categories: the Big Five banks and medium-sized banks. The group in the medium-sized banks rated higher than the Big Five. The study indicates whether the overall satisfaction with banks increases or declines year over year and whether there are specific areas of customer satisfaction that increased or declined more than others. For example, in one recent year the study showed that customers in the under-40-years-of-age category showed a decline in their satisfaction levels while customers in other age groups actually showed an increase in their satisfaction levels.

J.D. Power also looks at customer satisfaction ratings with individual products or services within the bank. For example, it did a study that measured customer satisfaction with digital banking and credit cards. This study found that while overall customer rates were improving, banks and credit card companies needed to do a better job educating their customers on all the digital features of the products.

Some companies measure customer satisfaction and service quality based on the SERVQUAL model developed by Valerie Zeithaml, A. Parasuraman, and Leonard Berry. These are the same researchers who developed the gap model (previous page). The SERVQUAL model is based on the difference between what customers expect from a service experience before entering into the service and what the customer perceived about the service after the service encounter.

Whether a service company uses a research company such as J.D. Power or develops their measure of customer service and service quality based on the SERVQUAL model, most service companies understand the importance of customer service and service quality.

(Continued)

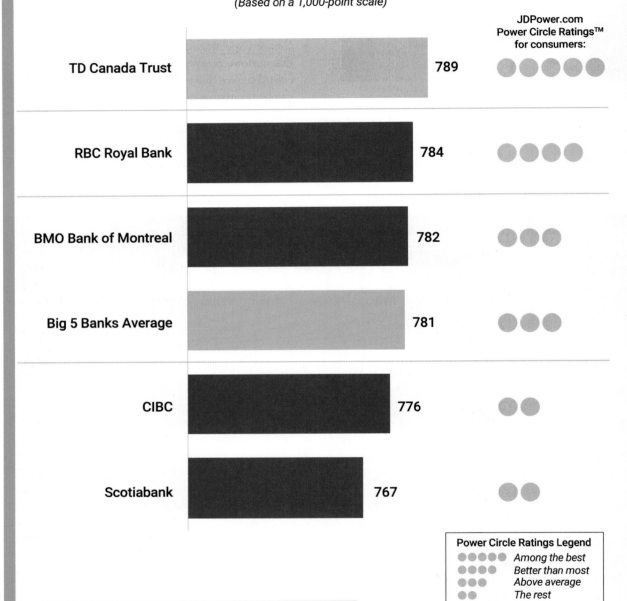

A season's pass to the games of a Canadian Football League (CFL) team is a mental stimulus–processing service where the quality of the product (the service) is very much dependent on the quality of the players and the coaching staff.

When one or more of these gaps is large, service quality is perceived as being low. As the gaps shrink, service quality perception improves.

11-3 | MARKETING MIXES FOR SERVICES

Services' unique characteristics—intangibility, inseparability of production and consumption, heterogeneity, and perishability—make the marketing of services more challenging. Elements of the marketing mix (product, place, promotion, and pricing) need to be adjusted to meet the special needs created by these characteristics. In addition, effective marketing of services requires the management of four additional Ps: people, process, productivity, and physical environment.

11-3a | Product (Service) Strategy

A product, as defined in Chapter 9, is everything a person receives in an exchange. In the case of a service organization, the product offering is intangible and is part of a process or a series of processes. Product strategies for service offerings include decisions on the type of process involved, core and supplementary services, standardization or customization of the service product, and the service mix.

SERVICE AS A PROCESS Two broad categories of things are processed in service organizations: people and objects. In some cases, the process is physical, or tangible; in other cases, the process is intangible. Using these characteristics, service processes can be placed into one of four categories[10]:

- *People processing* takes place when the service is directed at a customer. Examples are transportation services and healthcare.

- *Possession processing* occurs when the service is directed at customers' physical possessions. Examples are lawn care and veterinary services.

- *Mental stimulus processing* refers to services directed at people's minds. Examples are theatre performances and education.

- *Information processing* describes services that use technology or brainpower directed at a customer's assets. Examples are insurance and consulting.

Because customers' experiences and involvement differ for each of these types of services processes, marketing strategies may also differ. Take, for example, a season's pass to the games of a Canadian Football League (CFL) team. It is a mental-stimulus–processing service where the quality of the product (the service) is very much dependent on the quality of the players and the coaching staff. The game outcome can never be controlled, but the individual clubs can control other aspects of the game to ensure the game attendee has a positive experience. The half-time shows, the game-day giveaways, the stadium itself, and the food and drink are elements of the product that can be controlled to enhance the service experience.

CORE AND SUPPLEMENTARY SERVICE PRODUCTS The service offering can be viewed as a bundle of activities that includes the **core service**, which is the most basic benefit the customer is buying, and a group of **supplementary services** that support or enhance the core service. Exhibit 11.2 illustrates these concepts for a hotel like the Hyatt. The core service is providing bedrooms for rent, which involves people processing. The supplemental services might include food services, reservations, parking, WiFi, and television services. In many service industries, the core product becomes a commodity as competition increases. Thus companies usually emphasize supplemental services to create a competitive advantage. On the other hand, some companies are positioning themselves in the marketplace

core service
the most basic benefit the consumer is buying

supplementary services
a group of services that support or enhance the core service

EXHIBIT 11.2 CORE AND SUPPLEMENTARY SERVICES FOR A LUXURY HOTEL

Reservation

Room Phone

Parking

Core Delivery Process

Room Service

Overnight rental of a bedroom

Check-in/ Check-out

Pay TV

Supplementary Services

Porter

Meal

Delivery Processes for Supplementary Services

Source: Lovelock, Christopher H.; Wirtz, Jochen, *Services Marketing*, 7th, © 2011. Electronically reproduced by permission of Pearson Education, Inc., Upper Saddle River, New Jersey.

Trucking companies are an example of a possession-processing service. This type of service focuses less on the attractiveness of its physical environment than would a people-processing service, such as a massage therapist, but emphasis is still placed on the logo and the look of the physical cues that represent the company.

Bayne Stanley/Alamy Stock Photo

mass customization
a strategy that uses technology to deliver customized services on a mass basis

by greatly reducing supplemental services.

CUSTOMIZATION/ STANDARDIZATION An important issue in developing the

service offering is whether to customize or standardize it. Customized services are more flexible and respond to individual customers' needs. They also usually command a higher price. Standardized services are more efficient and cost less.

Instead of choosing to either standardize or customize a service, a company may incorporate elements of both by adopting an emerging strategy called **mass customization**. Mass customization uses technology to deliver customized services on a mass basis, which results in giving each customer whatever they ask for. To mass-customize coffee drinks, Starbucks uses different kinds of coffee, dairy, flavour shots, and temperature levels, resulting in more than 150 000 different combinations.[11]

THE SERVICE MIX Many service organizations market more than one service. For example, Vancouver City Savings Credit Union, more commonly known as Vancity, is a financial cooperative offering a wide range of banking and investment services to both individuals and organizations. Each service within the organization's service mix represents a set of opportunities, risks, and challenges. Each part of the service mix makes a different contribution to achieving the company's overall goals. To succeed, each service may also need a different level of financial support. Designing a service strategy therefore means deciding what new services to introduce to which target market, what existing services to maintain, and what services to eliminate.

Vancity

Courtesy of Vancity

11-3b | Process Strategy

Because services are delivered before or while being consumed, the marketing mix for services includes the strategic decisions surrounding the process. Here, *process* refers to the establishing of standards to ensure the service delivery is consistent and compatible with the service positioning. To establish these processes, the knowledge gap must be reduced through market research that seeks to understand consumer expectations; a process protocol must then be established to ensure the service delivery meets customers' expectations. Process is fluid, which means that customer satisfaction should be evaluated on an ongoing basis and processes should be updated to ensure service delivery continues to meet expectations.

The more standardized the delivery, the less likely the need for ongoing evaluation of process.

11-3c | People Strategy

The standards gap and the delivery gap must be managed to improve the service. The service is provided by a service provider, but distinguishing between the two is often very difficult. Thus managing the employee who is the service provider is highly strategic. Strategies include providing incentives, training, and recognition programs that management consistently supports. Employees who are well trained, empowered, and rewarded will deliver on the service promise.

11-3d | Place (Distribution) Strategy

Distribution strategies for service organizations must focus on issues such as convenience, number of outlets, direct versus indirect distribution, location, and scheduling. One of the key factors influencing the selection of a service provider is *convenience*. Tim Hortons is using its new downtown Toronto location for more than one objective as described in the feature box.

An interesting example of this are the meal delivery kit services such as Goodfood. Each week all the fresh ingredients you need to make delicious meals at home are delivered in a refrigerated box to your door.

An important distribution objective for many service companies is the *number of outlets* to use or the number of outlets to open during a certain time. Generally, the intensity of distribution should meet, but not exceed, the target market's needs and preferences. Having too few outlets may inconvenience customers; having too many outlets may boost costs unnecessarily. Intensity of distribution may also depend on the image desired. Having only a few outlets may make the service seem more exclusive or selective.

The next service distribution decision is whether to distribute services to end-users *directly* or *indirectly* through other companies. Because of the nature of services, many service companies choose to use direct distribution or

TIM HORTONS OPENS INNOVATION CAFÉ

Tim Hortons has opened a location in the heart of Toronto's financial district to test new products and a new design to attract a new portion of guests housed in the coffee and baked good market.

The traditional Tim Hortons brand is about coffee, donuts and hockey. While the new Innovation Café still maintains these values, the goal of its modern design and offerings is to expand the core values in order to attract the professional urban millennials and generation Z guests. Tim Hortons is not the only restaurant in the quick service market to go upscale, McDonald's and Boston Pizza have already a made the move in this direction. This "Fast Casual" part of the fast food market is growing at about 8 percent a year, while the traditional quick service market is only growing at 2 percent to 3 percent a year.

Along with Nitro Brew Coffee and Dream Donuts the company is experimenting with a new look. The hockey tradition is still evident with a lucky loonie embedded in the floor. There are stools instead of chairs and booths alongside tables. There is a counter that displays a variety of new Dream Donuts—which rotates every few weeks—and

Courtesy of Tim Hortons

freshly made sandwiches. While guests can still enjoy their traditional double double, they can also customize their own coffee, order Nitro Brewed beverages, espressos and lattes, specialty teas and more. The employees are sporting a new look as well, with grey and black replacing Tim Hortons traditional brown and beige uniforms.

The company is using the new store to get instant feedback on the changes.

Sources: Alicja Siekierska, "Nitro Cold Brew, Anyone? Inside Tim Hortons' New Innovation Café in Downtown Toronto, "Yahoo Finance website, July 25, 2019, https://ca.finance.yahoo.com/news/fancy-doughnuts-and-nitro-cold brews-inside-tim-hortons; Cassandra Szklarski; "Tim Hortons Tries Luring Millennials With Nitro Coffee, Upscale Doughnuts," July 28, 2019, Global News, https://globalnews.ca/news/5294682/tim-hortons-millennial-customers-rebrand/; Justin Dallaire, "A Look at Tim Hortons' Yearlong Turnaround," Strategy, July 16, 2019, https://strategyonline.ca/2019/07/16/breaking-down-tim-hortons-yearlong-turnaround/.

franchising. Examples are legal, medical, accounting, and personal-care services. Most of the major airlines are now using online services to sell tickets directly to consumers, which results in lower distribution costs for the airline companies. Other companies with standardized service packages have developed indirect channels that place the service in more convenient locations for their customers. Bank ATMs located in gas stations and hotel lobbies are a good example of standardizing a service and intensifying distribution by relying on indirect channels.

The *location* of a service most clearly reveals the relationship between its target market strategy and its distribution strategy. For time-dependent service providers, such as airlines, physicians, and dentists, *scheduling* is often a more important factor.

11-3e | Physical Evidence Strategy

Closely associated with managing place strategies to maintain service quality is managing the physical evidence surrounding the service delivery. Physical evidence provides cues to the level of service quality the customer can expect. All four categories of service processes can benefit from attention paid to both the physical environment in which the service is being offered and the quality of the equipment used to deliver the service. For example, when you arrive at your dental appointment, old equipment may lead you to question the ability of the dentist to provide the best oral care with the least amount of pain.

11-3f | Promotion Strategy

Consumers and business users have more trouble evaluating services than goods because services are less tangible. In turn, marketers have more trouble promoting intangible services than tangible goods. Here are four promotion strategies for services:

- *Stressing tangible cues:* A tangible cue is a concrete symbol of the service offering. To make their services more tangible, hotels will turn down beds in the evening and leave a mint on the pillow, ensure concierge staff are attentive, and offer free newspapers outside the room door each morning.

- *Using personal information sources:* A personal information source is someone consumers are familiar with (such as a celebrity) or someone they know or can relate to personally. Service companies can set up blogs and stimulate customer interaction on the blogs to generate positive word of mouth. Facebook, Twitter, LinkedIn, and other social media sites are used by service companies in their promotion strategy to capitalize on the potential for consumer discussion around their service

Celebrity is a powerful promotional tool for services and non-profits alike.

offerings. Of course, there is always the possibility of negative word of mouth, which requires a comprehensive and often swift crisis communication plan.

- *Creating a strong organizational image:* One way to create an image is to manage the evidence, including the physical environment of the service facility, the appearance of the service employees, and the tangible items associated with a service, such as the company's website, stationery, and brochures. Canadian Tire employees all wear red uniforms, and the red logo and the colour red predominates in all communications.

- *Engaging in postpurchase communication:* Postpurchase communication refers to the follow-up activities that a service company might engage in after a customer transaction. Emails, letters, and other types of follow-up are excellent ways to demonstrate to the customer that their feedback matters.

11-3g | Price Strategy

Considerations in pricing a service are similar to the pricing considerations to be discussed in Chapter 12. However, the unique characteristics of services present special pricing challenges.

First, to price a service, it is important to define the unit of service consumption. For example, should pricing be based on the specific task (such as washing the car) or should it be time based (such as the amount of time it takes to wash the car)? Some services include the consumption of goods. Restaurants charge for the food and drink consumed, not for the table and chairs that have been used.

Second, for services that comprise multiple elements, the issue is whether pricing should be based on a bundle of elements or whether each element should be priced separately. Often a bundle price is used because consumers don't want to pay "extra" for every element in the service, and it is administratively easier for the service company. Alternatively, customers may not want to pay for service elements they do not use.

Marketers should set performance objectives when pricing each service. Three categories of pricing objectives have been suggested[12]:

- *Revenue-oriented pricing* focuses on maximizing the surplus of income over costs. This is the same approach that many manufacturing companies use. A limitation of this approach is that determining costs can be difficult for many services.

- *Operations-oriented pricing* seeks to match supply and demand by varying prices. For example, matching hotel demand to the number of available rooms can be achieved by raising prices at peak times and decreasing them during slow times.

- *Patronage-oriented pricing* tries to maximize the number of customers using the service. Thus prices vary with different market segments' ability to pay, and methods of payment (such as credit) are offered to increase the likelihood of a purchase. Senior citizen and student discounts at movie theatres and restaurants are examples of patronage-oriented pricing.[13]

A company may need to use more than one type of pricing objective. In fact, all three objectives may need to be included to some degree in a pricing strategy, although the importance of each type may vary depending on the type of service provided, the prices that competitors are charging, the differing ability of various customer segments to pay, or the opportunity to negotiate price. For customized services (such as construction services), customers may also have the ability to negotiate a price.

11-3h | Productivity Strategy

Because services are often tied to a service provider and because the delivery of a service cannot be inventoried if supply exceeds demand, it is critical that the service company work to manage the supply or the availability of the service without affecting service quality. Such a strategy is often referred to as capacity management. A trip to Florida during your February break is likely much more expensive than the same trip in September. Student demand for holidays to Florida is high in February, and hotels and airlines try to capitalize on the demand. In September, on the other hand, school has just started, and students and families are thus otherwise engaged, so hotels and airlines offer lower prices to stimulate demand. After all, the plane still has to fly despite empty seats, and the hotels are still open despite empty rooms. This method of capacity management is called *off-peak pricing*.

11-4 | RELATIONSHIP MARKETING IN SERVICES

Many services involve ongoing interaction between the service organization and the customer. Thus these services can benefit from relationship marketing, the strategy described in Chapter 1, as a means of attracting, developing, and retaining customer relationships. The idea is to develop strong loyalty by creating satisfied customers who will buy additional services from the company and are unlikely to switch to a competitor. Satisfied customers are also likely to engage in positive word-of-mouth communication, thereby helping to bring in new customers.

Many businesses find it more cost-effective to hang on to the customers they have than to focus only on attracting new customers. It has been estimated that companies can spend almost five times to market to a new customer than an existing one.[14]

Services that purchasers receive on a continuing basis (e.g., smartphones services, banking, and insur-

ance) can be considered membership services. This type of service naturally lends itself to relationship marketing. When services involve discrete transactions (e.g., a movie screening, a restaurant meal, or public transportation), it may be more difficult to build membership-type relationships with customers. Nevertheless, services involving discrete transactions may be transformed into membership relationships by using marketing tools. For example, the service could be sold in bulk (e.g., a subscription to a theatre season or a commuter pass on public transportation). Or a service company could offer special benefits to customers who choose to register with the company (e.g., loyalty programs for hotels and airlines). While the registration process and subsequent use of the loyalty card at every purchase is designed to reward the consumer for repeat buying, the data gathered by the company based on each purchase allows for targeted communication with the customer, which serves to further enhance the service–customer relationship.[15]

Relationship marketing can be practised at four levels:

- *Level 1: Financial.* Pricing incentives are used to encourage customers to continue doing business with a company. Frequent flyer programs are an example of level 1 relationship marketing. This level of relationship marketing is the least effective in the long term because its price-based advantage is easily imitated by other companies.

- *Level 2: Social.* This level of relationship marketing also uses pricing incentives but seeks to build social bonds with customers. The company stays in touch with its customers, learns about their needs, and designs services to meet those needs. Level 2 relationship marketing is often more effective than level 1 relationship marketing.

- *Level 3: Customization.* A customized approach encourages customer loyalty through intimate knowledge of individual customers (often referred to as customer intimacy) and the development of one-to-one solutions to fit customer needs.

- *Level 4: Structural.* At this level, the company again uses financial and social bonds but adds

internal marketing
treating employees as customers and developing systems and benefits that satisfy their needs

structural bonds to the formula. Structural bonds are developed by offering value-added services that are not readily available from other companies. Many high-end hotels leave treats in repeat guests' hotel rooms when they celebrate special events, such as a bottle of wine for a couple celebrating an anniversary. Marketing programs like this one have the strongest potential for sustaining long-term relationships with customers.[16]

11-5 | INTERNAL MARKETING IN SERVICE COMPANIES

Services are performances, so the quality of a company's employees is an important part of building long-term relationships with customers. Employees who like their jobs and are satisfied with the company they work for are more likely to deliver superior service to customers. Their superior service, in turn, increases the likelihood of retaining customers. Thus it is critical that service companies practise **internal marketing**, which means treating employees as customers and developing systems and benefits that satisfy their needs. While this strategy may also apply to goods manufacturers, it is even more critical in service companies. This is because in service industries, employees deliver the brand promise— their performance as a brand representative—directly to consumers. To satisfy employees, companies have designed and instituted a wide variety of programs, such as flextime, onsite daycare, investments in wellness, and compassionate-care top-up payments.

Companies like Google have designed and instituted a wide variety of programs such as flextime, on-site daycare, and concierge service for their employees.

HABITAT FOR HUMANITY

Habitat for Humanity is a non-profit organization that started in the United States in the early 1970s. The Canadian organization began in 1985. The aim of the organization is to "bring communities together to help families build strength, stability, and independence through affordable housing."

The organization achieves this goal by building single-family homes and multi-unit developments as well as rehabilitating existing structures. The organization does not give the homes away. The prospective home-owner must meet certain criteria such as being able to make affordable mortgage payments, be in need of better housing, and be able to contribute at least 500 volunteer hours to the projects. Once accepted for home ownership, the future homeowner will help build their home and take classes in personal finance and home maintenance. At the end of the project the home is purchased with no down payment at a fair market value price and a mortgage. The mortgage is arranged with no interest, and payments are geared to the family's income.

The future homeowner is not the only person or group helping to build these homes. Volunteers in each building project community also help out. The volunteers could be helping to build the homes or preparing food for those building. Companies like Home Depot and Whirlpool also help out. These companies and many others like them either donate money or products needed to build the homes. The Government of Canada also helps with the projects by donating funds.

Habitat for Humanity Canada also has retail outlets called ReStore. These outlets sell items donated by local businesses or individuals. The items include surplus building materials from local building projects or furniture in good repair that families no longer require.

Habitat for Humanity Canada is an example of a non-profit organization that pulls communities together to provide low-income families with affordable homes. In 2019, the organization built over 250 homes across the country.

Jonny White/Alamy Stock Photo

Sources: Habitat for Humanity Canada website, https://habitat.ca, accessed August 21, 2019; Habitat for Humanity International website, https://habitat.org, accessed August 21, 2019; Trina Berlo, Habitat for Humanity Builds Two New Homes in Stayner, Creemore Echo, February 16, 2018, http://creemore.com/habitat-for-humanity-builds-two-homes-stayner/.

11-6 | NON-PROFIT ORGANIZATION MARKETING

A **non-profit organization**, also referred to as **not-for-profit,** is an organization that exists to achieve some goal other than the usual business goals of profit, market share, and return on investment. Both non-profit organizations and private-sector service companies market intangible products, and both often require the customer to be present during the production process. Both for-profit and non-profit services vary greatly from producer to producer and from day to day, even from the same producer. An example of a non-profit organization that has more than service is Habitat for Humanity described in the box.

Canada's non-profit and voluntary sector includes over 170 000 organizations from small local charities to large organizations such as hospitals. In Canada, more than two million people are employed in the non-profit sector, generating 8.1 percent of the nation's gross domestic product, more than is generated from retail.[17]

The non-profit sector includes many organizations that support those who are disadvantaged, as well as hospitals, colleges, and universities. If hospitals, colleges, and universities are removed from the picture, the remaining organizations are what Statistics Canada calls the core non-profit sector,

> **non-profit organization (not-for-profit)**
> an organization that exists to achieve a goal other than the usual business goals of profit, market share, or return on investment

which accounts for about 2.4 percent of GDP, more than three times that of the motor vehicle industry. It is often assumed that the government funds charities and non-profits, but that is not the case; in fact, sale of goods and services account for more than 45 percent of the total income of the core non-profit sector.[18]

11-6a | What Is Non-profit Organization Marketing?

Non-profit organization marketing is the effort by non-profit organizations to bring about mutually satisfying exchanges with target markets. Although these organizations vary substantially in size and purpose and operate in different environments, most perform the following marketing activities:

- Identifying the customers they want to serve or attract (although they usually use another term, such as *clients, patients, members,* or *donors*);

- Explicitly or implicitly specifying objectives;

- Developing, managing, and maintaining programs and services;

- Deciding on prices to charge (although they may use other terms, such as *fees, donations, tuition, fares, fines,* or *rates*);

- Scheduling events or programs, and determining where they will be held or where services will be offered; and

- Communicating their availability through both online and offline media vehicles. Non-profit marketing companies must engage in marketing communication, and it needs to be recognized and valued as a means to build awareness of the non-profit's mission. As in for-profit marketing, marketing communications in the non-profit sector can help to develop a better understanding of the target consumer, thereby ensuring communication strategies that differentiate the non-profit in the highly competitive market. Many non-profits are involved in policy change, and marketing communications can play a large role in building awareness and understanding of the issues. For many non-profits, fundraising is a key activity to support the ability to deliver their programs and services. Building awareness of the non-profit's mission helps to build donor engagement for funding opportunities.

non-profit organization marketing
the effort by non-profit organizations to bring about mutually satisfying exchanges with target markets

11-6b | Unique Aspects of Non-profit Organization Marketing Strategies

Like their counterparts in for-profit business organizations, non-profit managers develop marketing strategies to bring about mutually satisfying exchanges with their target markets. However, marketing in non-profit organizations is unique in many ways—including the setting of marketing objectives, the selection of target markets, and the development of appropriate marketing mixes.

OBJECTIVES In the private sector, the profit motive is both an objective for guiding decisions and a criterion for evaluating results. Non-profit organizations do not seek to make a profit for redistribution to owners or shareholders. Rather, their focus is often on generating enough funds to deliver the service while covering expenses.

Most non-profit organizations are expected to provide equitable, effective, and efficient services that respond to the wants and preferences of their multiple constituencies, which may include users, donors, politicians, appointed officials, the media, and the general public. Non-profit organizations place great emphasis on building and maintaining relationships with a variety of constituent groups. Non-profit organizations cannot measure their success or failure in strictly financial terms.

Managers in the non-profit sector are challenged to demonstrate achievement of multiple, diverse, and often intangible objectives, which can make prioritizing objectives, making decisions, and performance evaluation difficult.

TARGET MARKETS Two issues relating to target markets are unique to non-profit organizations:

- *Apathetic or strongly opposed targets:* Private-sector organizations usually give priority to developing those market segments that are most likely to respond to particular offerings. In contrast, some non-profit organizations must, by nature of their service, target those who are apathetic about or strongly opposed to receiving their services, such as vaccinations or psychological counselling.

- *Pressure to adopt undifferentiated segmentation strategies:* Non-profit organizations are sometimes forced to adopt undifferentiated strategies (see Chapter 7). Today however, as non-profits become more sophisticated in their data management, they are recognizing the value of data mining to find like prospects to target with differentiated strategies. Sometimes they fail to recognize the advantages of targeting, or an undifferentiated approach may appear to offer economies of scale and low per-capita costs. In other instances, non-profit organizations are pressured or required to serve the maximum number of people targeting the average user.

POSITIONING DECISIONS Many non-profit organizations use a complementary positioning strategy. The main role of many non-profit organizations is to provide services, with available resources, to those who are not adequately served by private-sector organizations. As a result, the non-profit organization must often complement, rather than compete with, the efforts of others. The positioning task is to identify underserved market segments and to develop marketing programs that match their needs rather than target the niches that are most profitable. For example, a university library may see itself as complementing the services of the public library rather than as competing with it.

PRODUCT DECISIONS Three product-related characteristics distinguish business organizations from non-profit organizations:

- *Benefit complexity:* Non-profit organizations often market complex and emotional behaviours or ideas. Examples are the need to exercise or eat properly and the need to quit smoking. The benefits that a person receives are complex, long term, and intangible, and therefore are more difficult to communicate to consumers.

- *Benefit strength:* The benefit strength of many non-profit offerings is not immediate or is indirect. What are the direct, personal benefits to you of driving within the required speed limit or volunteering at your local hospice or putting out only one bag of garbage per week? In contrast, most private-sector service organizations can offer customers immediate and direct personal benefits.

- *Involvement:* Many non-profit organizations market products that elicit very low involvement ("Prevent forest fires) or very high involvement ("Stop smoking"). The typical range for private-sector goods is much narrower. Traditional promotional tools may be inadequate to motivate adoption of either low- or high-involvement products; take, for example, the pink ribbon pins that we all have come to associate with breast cancer.

In pursuit of new and sustainable funding and of ways and means to support their clients, some non-profits have launched social enterprises. A social enterprise is a cause-driven business whose primary reason for being is to improve social objectives and serve the common good.[19] As an example, YWCA Hamilton runs a catering/wholesale/café initiative called At the Table. Revenue generated from At the Table sales is reinvested into the organization to support the many programs and services offered by YWCA Hamilton in support of women, girls, and their families. One of the programs offered is the Transitional Housing and Shelter program, where women are provided housing and support as they seek to turn their lives around from a past challenged by mental illness, addictions, violence, homelessness, food insecurity, and precarious employment. A key component of the At the Table social enterprise is offering the women in the program the opportunity to work in the At the Table kitchen, gaining employable skills in the food service sector.[20]

Courtesy of YWCA Hamilton

PLACE (DISTRIBUTION) DECISIONS A non-profit organization's capacity for distributing its service offerings to potential customer groups when and where they want them is typically a key variable in determining the success of those service offerings. For example, many universities

JHVEPhoto/Shutterstock.com

Canadian Blood Services has placed a heavy emphasis on mobile donor sites that set up at the donor's place of business, in essence intensifying distribution.

and colleges have one or more satellite campus locations and offer online courses to provide easier access for students in other areas.

The extent to which a service depends on fixed facilities has important implications for distribution decisions. Services such as those offered by a community food bank are limited by the space the food bank has to store the food.

PROMOTION DECISIONS Many non-profit organizations are explicitly or implicitly prohibited from advertising, thus limiting their promotion options. Other non-profit organizations simply do not have the resources to retain advertising agencies, promotion consultants, or marketing staff. However, non-profit organizations have a few special promotion resources to call on:

- *Professional volunteers:* Non-profit organizations often seek out marketing, sales, and advertising professionals to help them develop and implement promotion strategies. In some instances, an advertising agency donates its services in exchange for potential long-term benefits. Donated services create goodwill, personal contacts, and general awareness of the donor's organization, reputation, and competency.

- *Sales promotion activities:* Sales promotion activities that make use of existing services or other resources are increasingly being used to draw attention to the offerings of non-profit organizations. Sometimes non-profit charities even team up with other companies for promotional activities. Special events are a great way to reach many targets while partnering with both for-profit and non-profit companies. A perfect example is the Running Room, which offers non-profits the opportunity to associate with its sponsored runs. Runners can choose to run and raise money for the charity when registering for the run.

- *Public relations:* Public relations is a valuable tool for non-profits. But organizations must ensure that their message is compelling and meaningful. One form of public relations used often by non-profits is public service advertising. A **public service advertisement (PSA)** is an announcement that promotes a program of a non-profit organization or of a federal, provincial or territorial, or local government. Unlike a commercial advertiser, the sponsor of the PSA does not pay for the time or space. Instead, these are donated by the medium as a public service. PSAs are used, for example, to help educate students about the dangers of misusing and abusing prescription drugs, as well as where to seek treatment for substance abuse problems.

- *Social media:* Non-profits generally want to promote a message so that people will come together bound by a common goal. Social media can amplify the message by its ability to connect groups of people. Social media allow non-profits to share their message to build community and to create action. Non-profits are embracing podcasting, blogging, and social networking because, for very little money, they allow non-profits to build relationships and engage with their stakeholders. As more and more social media tools are created to make the use of various social media sites easier and increasingly more measureable, non-profits' ability to maximize the potential of social media for engagement and relationship building will continue.

PRICING DECISIONS Five key characteristics distinguish the pricing decisions of non-profit organizations from those of the profit sector:

- *Pricing objectives:* The main pricing objective in the profit sector is revenue or, more specifically, profit maximization, sales maximization, or target return on sales or investment. Many non-profit organizations must also be concerned about revenue. Often, however, non-profit organizations seek to either partially or fully defray costs rather than achieve a profit for distribution to stockholders. Non-profit organizations also seek to redistribute income through the delivery of their service. Moreover, they strive to allocate resources fairly among individuals or households or across geographic or political boundaries.

- *Nonfinancial prices:* In many non-profit situations, consumers are not charged a monetary price but instead must absorb nonmonetary costs. Nonmonetary costs include time and maybe even embarrassment, depending on the service being provided.

- *Indirect payment:* Indirect payment through taxes is common to marketers of free services, such as libraries, fire protection, and police protection. Indirect payment is not a common practice in the profit sector.

- *Separation between payers and users:* By design, the services of many charitable organizations are provided to those who are relatively poor and are largely paid for by those who are better off financially. Although examples of separation between payers and users can be found in the profit sector (such as insurance claims), the practice is much less prevalent.

- *Below-cost pricing:* An example of below-cost pricing is university tuition. Virtually all private and public colleges and universities price their services below their full costs.

public service advertisement (PSA)
an announcement that promotes a program of a non-profit organization or of a federal, provincial or territorial, or local government

AWAKE CHOCOLATE
CONTINUING CASE

Essential Service of Caffeine

Given that Awake Chocolate is a for-profit maker of a consumer packaged good—and not a service—finding a fitting topic for this chapter seemed to be a stretch. Then the world changed in early 2020, and would never be the same again. One of the positive outcomes of the COVID-19 pandemic was the way for-profit businesses came to the aid of non-profit organizations. A delicate proposition to be sure, seeing as most small businesses during that time were hanging by a thread.

For Awake Chocolate, the first public announcement of how it would help came, like all of the brand's marketing communications, through the "voice" of Nevil, the beloved owl, brand mascot. This had long been Awake's *inbound* marketing strategy—to communicate through Nevil, something discussed in later chapters.

Appropriately breaking away from the normally cheeky writing style, Nevil posted a message on Instagram on March 26 (see Figure 1).

This set into motion a flurry of social media posts, first by Awake to communicate its offering, then hundreds of healthcare workers responding with pictures of themselves, enjoying, and according to some post captions, "living" off Awake Chocolate.

For-profit, service-based companies have their own unique challenges, described in this chapter, including the "4 I's" of services (intangibility, inseparability, inconsistency, and inventory). But non-profit organizations are usually serviced based, and have one additional, and significant hindrance—money. As in very little of it.

So when the COVID-19 pandemic struck, it not only decimated businesses large and small—see WestJet's hard decision to wipe out the jobs of half of its employees—but also made non-profits that much more vulnerable. Many companies felt a genuine compulsion to lend a hand in any way possible. For Awake, the match between the over-tired, double-shifted frontline medical workers provided an appropriate giveback for the brand.

"Thousands of healthcare workers will get to try our chocolate at a time when they could surely use the extra energy," explained Deremo. "And it's uplifting to

Figure 1

know that we're supporting them during what is a really stressful time. I have a feeling that many of the recipients will become future customers, but even if they don't, it's still a good outcome for us." At the time of writing, the duration of the pandemic was unknown, but Deremo insisted that Awake would be involved in a significant way for as long as it continued. "We also plan to continue healthcare support for as long as this lasts. Our plan going forward is to donate 10 percent of online sales back to the healthcare community in the form of free chocolate."

The feedback from the community suggests that Awake's gesture was received gratefully.

Wrote one medical student on Instagram in response to the Awake giveaway, "These are lifesavers. I literally recommend them to any busy soul. There's one in my purse or white coat at all times. It's caffeinated chocolate that you can use as a substitute for grabbing a coffee, for an afternoon pick me up on those long days."[1]

As discussed in subsequent chapters, Awake had already figured out how to leverage the words of its fans during business as usual. During the COVID-19 pandemic, however, the endearing words from essential service workers spoke even more loudly.

QUESTIONS

1. Go back into Awake's social media posts in 2020 and pull out a post made by the company as to what it was doing as a community service during the COVID-19 crisis. View the comments made by healthcare workers, or any essential service workers, who received Awake's product. Comment on how you think Awake was perceived in its role at this time.

2. Non-profit organizations and service-based businesses face different challenges than those who make consumer or B2B goods. And yet all companies have some element of service to them. Identify and describe the service aspect demonstrated by Awake during the crisis.

3. CEO Adam Deremo called Awake's donation of free product to essential service providers something that he and his team felt obligated to do. How would you evaluate the level at which Awake's gesture was perceived in terms of altruism?

NOTE

1. https://www.instagram.com/awakechocolate (accessed April 6, 2020).

Product Decisions, Part 3 Case

Hershey's Focus on Innovation

When you are the Senior Director of Marketing for the Canadian arm of a 125-year-old American company, what do you do to become the number one confectionary brand in the country? For the Hersey chocolate company, you introduce new products and new packages and change your strategies to target Gen Z and millennial snackers.

The Hershey company was started by Milton S. Hershey in 1894, and the company's corporate head office has the unique address of 19 East Chocolate Avenue, Hershey PA, United States. The company also has offices throughout the world including Brazil, Canada, India, Korea, and Mexico, among others.

When the Canadian marketing team wanted to develop a new chocolate bar, they chose a different way of going through the development process. Working with the crowdsourcing platform Crowdiate, the team provided a brief to a global group of creative people who were asked to provide ideas for a new product, the form the product should take, a new product concept template, and a list of ingredients. The result was 115 new product ideas from 18 different countries. The ideas were refined until the final concept—The Ice Cream Shoppe—concept remained. The Crowdiate approach was successful because it provided a collaborative approach to idea generation that was disciplined and provided feedback quickly.

The result of the Ice Cream Shoppe concept was three new candy bars: Cookies 'N' Mint, Birthday Cake, and Strawberries 'N' Crème. The candy bars are aimed at millennial parents and include an ingredient that causes a freezing sensation when the consumer bites into them. The promotional activities to support the launch included eye-catching packaging, television, online videos, and social media.

While the Canadian arm of the company was developing new candy bars, the corporate marketing team was working on developing new packaging for the entire brand (150 products). The new packaging had to look good on store shelves, and on consumers' mobile devices for online shoppers. Two additional criteria for the new packaging were that it had to work in the customer's kitchen and be easy to open. The result of the design process was to move to a bag that could stand up on its own. The current packaging was a bag that sat flat on the store shelf, which was convenient for shipping and stacking on shelves, but did not permit the product inside to be seen. To go along with the new stand-up package there would be a new branding design that included bright colours to attract the attention of consumers.

The team developing new packaging included not only people from the marketing department but also manufacturing and digital commerce. Changing the packaging on 150 items was no small task for manufacturing. This group had to figure out how to change the equipment that bagged the candy, and how the new packaging would fit into cartons for shipping.

The digital commerce representative on the team viewed the new packaging as part of a bigger project to improve the company's digital presence on all products. The chief digital commerce officer said, "If you don't

Julie Pratt

Julie Pratt

merchandise the digital shelf correctly, people may choose not to shop with you in the digital or the physical store."

The last part of the new packaging design process was to get the retailer to display the products in a favourable way on store shelves. To accomplish this, the company redesigned its Global Customer Insights Centre (GCIC) in Hershey, which hosts retailers to demonstrate how to set up their store display. The centre caters displays to each retailer; some displays are candy aisles, some are self-checkout displays, and others are point-of-purchase displays. Hershey also shared its research with the retailers. For example, data analytic research showed that customers often purchased Kit Kat bars with their morning coffee, so Hershey showed retailers how to display Kit Kat bars with coffee.

The Hershey chocolate company may have been in business for 125 years but it is moving rapidly into the age of digital marketing.

SOURCES

Hershey Company website, www.thehersheycompany.com/en_us/home.html, accessed May 17, 2020; Christopher Lombardo, "Hershey Crowd-Sourced Ideas For New Ice Cream Bars," Strategy Online, https://strategyonline.ca/2020/05/13/hershey-crowd-sourced-ideas-for-new-ice-cream-bars/, May 13, 2020; Catherine Phillips, "2019 MOY: Jackson Hitchon Sweetens Hershey," Strategy Online, https://strategyonline.ca/2019/11/12/2019-moy-jackson-hitchon-sweetens-hershey/, November 12, 2019; Crystal Lindell, "How the 125-Year-Old Hershey Company Continues to Innovate," Candy Industry website, www.candyindustry.com/articles/88674-how-the-125-year-old-hershey-company-continues-to-innovate, May 14, 2019.

QUESTIONS

1. Go to the Hershey website, review its product line, and comment on the product mix, product lines and product line depth.

2. Pick five different products that the Hershey company makes. What stage of the product life cycle are these products in? What marketing strategies would you make given the life cycle stage these products are in?

3. What type of branding strategy does the Hershey company use for its products? Do you think it is effective? Why or why not?

4. Discuss how effective the new product development process is by using a crowdsourcing platform like Crowdiate. Are there ways to make the process more effective?

12 | Setting the Right Price

"Price is what you pay, value is what you get."

—Warren Buffett[1]

12-1 | THE IMPORTANCE OF PRICE AND THE PRICING PROCESS

Price means one thing to the consumer and something else to the seller. To the consumer, price is the cost of something. To the seller, price is revenue, the primary source of profits. In the broadest sense, price allocates resources in a free-market economy.

Marketing managers are frequently challenged by the task of price setting, but they know that meeting the challenge of setting the right price can have a significant impact on the company's bottom line. Organizations that successfully manage prices do so by creating a pricing infrastructure within the company. This means defining pricing goals, searching for ways to create customer value, assigning authority and responsibility for pricing decisions, and creating tools and systems to continually improve pricing decisions. The importance of creating the right pricing strategy cannot be overstated. But there are two aspects of pricing that must be considered: the internal pricing (determined by financial and accounting formulas) and the external pricing determinants (determined by an understanding of marketing, demand, and the external environment). Keeping both in mind will help ensure that companies establish a price that satisfies not only the bottom line but also the customer.

12-1a | What Is Price?

Price is that which is given up in an exchange to acquire a good or service. It is typically the money exchanged for the good or service, but it may also include the time lost while waiting to acquire the good or service.

Consumers are interested in obtaining a reasonable price, which refers to the perceived value at the time of the transaction. The price paid is based on the satisfaction consumers *expect* to receive from a product and not necessarily the satisfaction they *actually* receive. Price can relate to anything with perceived value, not just money. When goods and services are exchanged, the trade is called *barter*.

price
that which is given up in an exchange to acquire a good or service

12-1b | The Importance of Price to Marketing Managers

Prices are the key to revenues, which in turn are the key to profits for an organization. **Revenue** is the price per unit charged to customers multiplied by the number of units sold. Revenue is what pays for every activity—for all the **costs** the company incurs for production, finance, sales, distribution, overhead, and so on. Costs are the combined financial value of all inputs that go into the production of a company's products, both directly and indirectly. What's left over (if anything) or the revenue minus expenses is **profit**. Managers usually strive to charge a price that will earn a fair profit.

Revenue = Price per unit × Units sold

Profit = Revenue − Costs (fixed + variable)

Moreover, price invariably creates a perception of quality to customers. While customers are more savvy than ever, they still usually associate a high price with high quality and vice versa—especially when comparing similar products. This puts the onus on the company to ensure that the price befits the value.

To earn a profit, managers must choose a price that is neither too high nor too low, a price that equals the perceived value to target consumers. If, in consumers' minds, a price is set too high, the perceived value will be less than the cost, and sale opportunities will be lost. Conversely, if a price is too low, the consumer may perceive it as a great value, but the company loses revenue it could have earned by charging a higher, but acceptable, price.

Trying to set the right price is one of the most stressful and pressure-filled tasks of the marketing manager, as attested to by the following trends in the consumer market:

- Potential buyers carefully evaluate the price of each product against the value of existing products.

revenue
the price per unit charged to customers multiplied by the number of units sold

costs
the combined financial value of all inputs that go into the production of a company's products, both directly and indirectly

profit
revenue minus expenses

- Increased availability of bargain-priced private and generic brands puts downward pressure on overall prices.

- Companies try to maintain or regain their market share by cutting prices.

- Internet and mobile access makes comparison shopping seamless and in many cases results in downward pressure on price.

In the business market, buyers are also becoming more price sensitive and better informed. Marketing information systems enable organizational buyers to compare price and performance with great ease and accuracy. Improved communication and the increased use of direct marketing and computer-aided selling have also opened up many markets to new competitors. Finally, competition in general is increasing, so some installations, accessories, and component parts are being marketed as indistinguishable commodities.

12-2 | THE PRICING PROCESS

Now that we know what pricing is and why it is important, we need to look at the process of setting the right price. There is no easy formula here; while there are numbers, there are also considerations that go into setting a price that go beyond numbers.

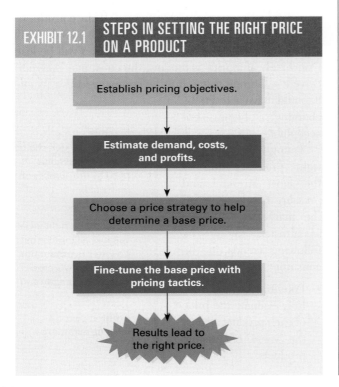

EXHIBIT 12.1 STEPS IN SETTING THE RIGHT PRICE ON A PRODUCT

Establish pricing objectives.

↓

Estimate demand, costs, and profits.

↓

Choose a price strategy to help determine a base price.

↓

Fine-tune the base price with pricing tactics.

↓

Results lead to the right price.

Setting the right price on a product is a four-step process (see Exhibit 12.1).

12-2a | Step 1—Establishing Pricing Objectives

The first step in setting the right price is to establish pricing objectives derived from the company's overall objectives. Those objectives fall into three categories: profit oriented, sales oriented, and status quo. With a good understanding of the marketplace and of the consumer, a manager can sometimes tell very quickly whether an objective is realistic.

All pricing objectives have trade-offs that managers must weigh. A profit-maximization objective may require a bigger initial investment than the company can commit or wants to commit. A sales-oriented objective, such as reaching the desired market share, often means sacrificing short-term profit, because without careful management, long-term profit objectives may not be met. Meeting the competition, a status quo objective, is the easiest pricing objective to implement, but it can also be short-sighted and costly.

In all situations, when managers set about establishing pricing objectives, they must consider the product's demand, costs, profits, and so forth, as it progresses through its life cycle. This process usually means trade-offs occur in meeting the target customer's needs, being competitive, having considerations for changing economic conditions, and meeting the company's corporate objectives. What follows is an explanation of the three main pricing objectives and their potential impact on overall corporate objectives.

PROFIT-ORIENTED PRICING OBJECTIVES
Profit-oriented objectives are profit maximization, satisfactory profits, and target return on investment.

- **Profit maximization:** Profit maximization means setting prices so that total revenue is as large as possible relative to total costs. Profit maximization does not always signify unreasonably high prices, however. Both price and profits depend on the type of competitive environment a company faces, such as whether it is in a monopoly position (i.e., the company is the only seller) or in a much more competitive situation. Although this goal may sound impressive to the company's owners, it is not good enough for planning.

When attempting to maximize profits, managers can try to expand revenue by increasing customer satisfaction, or they can attempt to reduce costs by operating more efficiently. A third possibility is to attempt to do both. Some companies may focus too much on cost reduction at the expense of the customer. When companies rely too heavily on customer service, however, costs tend to rise to unacceptable levels. A company can maintain or slightly cut costs while increasing customer loyalty through customer service initiatives, loyalty programs, customer relationship management programs, and allocating resources to programs that are designed to improve efficiency and reduce costs.

- **Satisfactory profits:** Satisfactory profits are a reasonable level of profits. Rather than maximizing profits, many organizations strive for profits that are satisfactory to the shareholders and management—in other words, a level of profits consistent with the level of risk an organization faces. In a risky industry, a satisfactory profit may be 35 percent. In a low-risk industry, it might be 7 percent. Satisfactory profits are often connected to corporate social responsibility (CSR), where companies may forgo a blind pursuit of profits to focus on the environment, a safe work environment, and other CSR initiatives. Tentree is a Canadian apparel brand named for its value proposition—to plant 10 trees for each item sold. This is a profit-eating proposition to begin with, and further eroding the bottom line is Tentree's pledge to operate its manufacturing in a transparent and responsible manner.[2]

- **Target return on investment:** The most common profit objective is a target **return on investment (ROI)**, sometimes called the company's return on total assets. ROI is determined by dividing net profits after tax by total assets. ROI measures management's overall effectiveness in generating profits with the company's available assets. The higher the company's ROI, the better off the company is. Many companies use a target ROI as their main pricing goal. ROI is a percentage that puts a company's profits into perspective by showing profits relative to investment.

iStock.com/South_agency

ROI is calculated as follows:

$$\text{Return on investment} = \frac{\text{Net profits after tax}}{\text{Total assets}}$$

Generally, companies seek ROIs in the 10 to 30 percent range. In some industries, such as the grocery industry, however, a return of less than 5 percent is common and acceptable. A company with a target ROI can predetermine its desired level of profitability. The marketing manager can use the standard, such as 10 percent ROI, to determine whether a particular price and marketing mix are feasible. In addition, however, the manager must weigh the risk of a given strategy even if the return is in the acceptable range.

SALES-ORIENTED PRICING OBJECTIVES

Sales-oriented pricing objectives are often based on market share or total sales maximization.

- **Market share:** Market share is a company's product sales as a percentage of total sales for that industry. Sales can be reported in dollars or in units of product. However, market share is usually expressed in terms of revenue and not units.

  Many companies believe that maintaining or increasing market share is an indicator of the effectiveness of their marketing mix. Larger market shares have indeed often meant higher profits, thanks to greater economies of scale, market power, and the ability to recruit and compensate top-quality management. Conventional wisdom also says that market share and ROI are strongly related. For the most part they are; however, many companies with low market share survive and even prosper. To succeed with a low market share, companies need to compete in industries with slow growth and few product changes. Ferrari, the Italian sports car manufacturer, is one example of such a company. Otherwise, companies must compete in an industry that makes frequently purchased items, such as consumer convenience goods.

  The conventional wisdom regarding market share and profitability isn't always reliable, however. Because of extreme competition in some industries, many market share leaders either do not reach their target ROI or

> **return on investment (ROI)**
> net profits after tax divided by total assets
>
> **market share**
> a company's product sales as a percentage of total sales for that industry

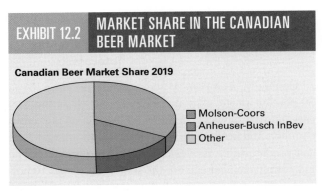

EXHIBIT 12.2 **MARKET SHARE IN THE CANADIAN BEER MARKET**

Canadian Beer Market Share 2019

- Molson-Coors
- Anheuser-Busch InBev
- Other

Source: Adapted from Statista, "Market share of companies within the Canadian brewing industry as of June 2017" https://www.statista.com/statistics/339828/market-share-of-the-canadian-brewing-industry/.

actually lose money. Procter & Gamble switched from market share to ROI objectives after realizing that profits don't automatically follow as a result of a large market share. Still, for some companies, the struggle for market share can be all-consuming.

Exhibit 12.2 shows the market share of sales in the Canadian beer industry in 2019. Note the dominance of global conglomerates Anheuser-Busch InBev (owners of Budweiser, Labatt, and others) and Molson-Coors Brewing Company, together owning just under 50 percent of all beer sales in Canada. The market share of the larger companies in the beer industry in Canada has been under pressure in resent years. This pressure can be attributed to a number of factors such as changing consumer tastes, an industry in the mature stage of the life cycle, and the proliferation of new entrants into the craft beer market in Canada. Changing consumer tastes are the result of the older baby boomers and the younger millennials drinking less beer and moving to higher-priced craft beers. The growth in craft beer sales in Canada provides would-be start-ups with a built-in excuse for profit-based pricing. Craft beer consumers expect a different kind of beer, produced from higher-quality ingredients, and therefore expect a higher price; they see value in the product more than the price. The challenge for craft brewers is finding that balance where perceived benefit is not outweighed by price. An industry in the mature stage results in mergers and acquisitions as a way to maintain or increase market share.[3]

Research organizations, such as Nielsen and Information Resources Inc., provide excellent market share reports for many different industries. These reports enable companies to track their performance in various product categories over time.[4]

- *Sales maximization:* Rather than strive for market share, companies sometimes try to maximize sales. A company with the objective of maximizing sales will ignore profits, competition, and the marketing environment as long as sales are rising.

If a company is strapped for funds or faces an uncertain future, it may try to generate a maximum amount of cash in the short run. Management's task when using this objective is to calculate which price–quantity relationship generates the greatest cash revenue. Sales maximization can also be effectively used on a temporary basis to sell off excess inventory. It is not uncommon to find Christmas cards, ornaments, and other seasonal items discounted at 50 to 70 percent off retail prices after the holiday has ended.

Maximization of cash should never be a long-run objective because cash maximization may mean little or no profitability.

STATUS QUO PRICING OBJECTIVES Status quo pricing seeks to maintain existing prices or to meet the competition's prices. This third category of pricing objectives has the major advantage of requiring little planning, but it is essentially a passive policy.

Often, companies competing in an industry with an established price leader simply meet the competition's prices. These industries typically have fewer price wars than those with direct price competition. In other cases, managers regularly shop competitors' stores to ensure that their prices are comparable.

Status quo pricing often leads to suboptimal pricing. This occurs because the strategy ignores customers' perceived value of both the company's goods and services and those offered by its competitors. Status quo pricing also ignores demand and costs. Although the policy is simple to implement, it can lead to a pricing disaster.

12-2b | Step 2—Estimating Demand, Costs, and Profits

After establishing pricing objectives, managers must estimate demand, costs, and profit. (A more detailed discussion of how to calculate demand, costs, and profits can be found in the online appendix—Marketing Math—but for now we examine these concepts at a high level.) Estimating costs is relatively simple as it consists of adding up the separate costs of each input that goes into a finished product. These are called *variable costs* as they will vary based upon the number of

status quo pricing
a pricing objective that maintains existing prices or meets the competition's prices

DEMAND THROUGH THE PRODUCT LIFE CYCLE

As a product moves through its life cycle, the demand for the product and the competitive conditions tend to change:

- *Introductory stage:* Management usually sets prices high during the introductory stage of a product. One reason is that the company hopes to recover its development costs quickly. In addition, demand originates in the core of the market (the customers whose needs ideally match the product's attributes) and thus is relatively inelastic. On the other hand, if the target market is highly price sensitive, management often finds it better to price the product at or below the market level.

- *Growth stage:* As the product enters the growth stage, prices generally begin to stabilize for several reasons. First, competitors have entered the market, increasing the available supply. Second, the product has begun to appeal to a broader market, often lower-income groups. Finally, economies of scale are lowering costs, and the savings can be passed on to the consumer in the form of lower prices.

- *Maturity stage:* Maturity usually brings further price decreases as competition increases and inefficient, high-cost companies are eliminated. Distribution channels become a significant cost factor, however, because of the need to offer wide product lines for highly segmented markets, extensive service requirements, and the sheer number of dealers necessary to absorb high-volume production. The manufacturers that remain in the market toward the end of the maturity stage typically offer similar prices. At this stage, price increases are usually cost initiated, not demand initiated. Nor do price reductions in the late phase of maturity stimulate much demand. Because demand is limited and producers have similar cost structures, the remaining competitors will probably match price reductions.

- *Decline stage:* The final stage of the life cycle may see further price decreases as the few remaining competitors try to salvage the last vestiges of demand. When only one company is left in the market, prices begin to stabilize. In fact, prices may eventually rise dramatically if the product survives and moves into the specialty goods category, as have horse-drawn carriages and vinyl records.

products produced. However, there are other costs of running a business that the price of each product must also help to cover. These *fixed costs* stay the same over time, regardless of production. The craft breweries that we discussed earlier would count what they spend on water, hops, barley, bottles, labelling, and packaging as variable costs; property tax on their brewery and payroll of administrative staff would be examples of fixed costs.

DEMAND **Demand** is the quantity of a product that will be sold in the market at various prices for a specified period. The quantity of a product that people will buy depends on its price. Estimating demand can be tricky, especially for a new product that hasn't yet been tested in the market. There are methods of getting some general idea of demand, such as researching historical sales data on similar products. Companies can use that information as a basis of estimating demand through the product's life cycle, which asserts that demand will change as a product goes through four distinct phases. (This concept is discussed more deeply in Chapter 10.) However, estimating demand requires a little more of a scientific approach in order to get closer to the truth.

ELASTICITY OF DEMAND The estimation of demand must begin with some broad assumptions associated with the fundamentals of economics—namely, **price sensitivity** and **price elasticity of demand**. Price sensitivity refers to consumers' varying levels of desire to buy a

demand
the quantity of a product that will be sold in the market at various prices for a specified period

price sensitivity
consumers' varying levels of desire to buy a given product at different price levels

price elasticity of demand
a measurement of change in consumer demand for a product relative to the changes in its price

given product at different price levels. Price elasticity of demand measures the change of consumer demand for a product relative to the changes in its price.

There are mathematical calculations used to find precise answers to the questions posed by the concepts of sensitivity and elasticity (see the online appendix), by using one proven economic tool to demonstrate price sensitivity and a set of categories to help us understand elasticity.

Price sensitivity is commonly demonstrated using the demand curve, which shows the often-inverted relationship between demand and price. That is, it demonstrates a common behavioural truth in the market that you, as a consumer, have exhibited since you first started making purchase decisions: You are generally more willing to buy a product as its price lowers. Marketers, of course, realize this common truth as well, but plotting it on a graph demonstrates it with greater accuracy. Suppose, for instance, a craft brewer is grappling over the average price for a pint of its beer at the brewery's onsite pub. The company has done enough research to see that other pubs are selling pints of beer for anywhere between $5 and $10. Curious as to how price increases of $1 might affect demand, they conduct an experiment that shows the following:

Price	Units Sold
$10	10
$9	12
$8	14
$7	16
$6	18
$5	20

The table is reasonably self-explanatory, but when applied to a line graph (see Exhibit 12.3), the story becomes clearer, showing the relationship between price and demand. All things being equal, the lower the price, the greater the demand. Conversely, the higher the price, the lower the demand. This rule of thumb, like most things in life, has its exceptions, but those are better explained in the context of economics and behavioural science.

The demand curve is helpful, but really only in showing us what we already know. Price changes will invariably result in changes of quantity demanded. But even this general assertion will depend on the type of product and the prevailing market environment. And this is where the concept of price elasticity of demand comes in handy.

As discussed, price elasticity of demand refers to the degree of change in demand relative to changes in price. Mathematical calculations can be used to demonstrate this concept with great precision, but for the purposes of this discussion, we can divide price elasticity of demand into two categories: elastic demand and inelastic demand. *Elastic demand* occurs when changes in price greatly change levels of demand, whereas *inelastic demand* exists when changes in price have little or no impact on demand. Therefore, we can classify different types of products as either elastic or inelastic (see Exhibit 12.4).

BREAK-EVEN ANALYSIS As stated above, the demand curve and elasticity serve to tell us only what we already know. Alone, they don't really help marketers decide exactly where to set the price. One more essential tool is needed here to help bring together the concepts of demand, costs, and profit. That tool is break-even analysis.

As discussed, the two biggest questions marketers must answer when pricing their product are these:

1. How much does it cost to bring the product to market?

2. How much is the market willing to pay for the product?

As all for-profit companies go into business to generate a profit, the desirable goal is to have a number for

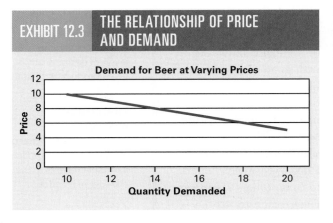

EXHIBIT 12.3	THE RELATIONSHIP OF PRICE AND DEMAND

Demand for Beer at Varying Prices

EXHIBIT 12.4	ELASTICITY OF DEMAND	
	Characteristics	**Product Examples**
Elastic	• Nonessential • Many alternatives • Maslow's Social, Esteem Needs	• Smartphones • Fashion • Automobiles
Inelastic	• Essential • Few alternatives • Maslow's Physiological Needs	• Home heating and electricity • Basic food staples • Winter boots

question 2 that is greater than the number for question 1. Break-even analysis helps us get partway there.

Break-even analysis calculates the threshold of either units sold or total revenue required that a company must meet to cover its costs. Moreover, it demonstrates that beyond this threshold profit will occur.

Like the demand curve, break-even analysis is based on a foundation of mathematics and represented with a line graph. Here is the formula for calculating the break-even point (BEP):

BEP = Fixed costs/(Variable price per unit − Variable cost per unit)

The denominator in this equation represents the margin or profit earned on each sale of each product. In other words, using our craft brewery example, it accounts for the variable costs of producing each pint of beer (beer ingredients, beer-making labour, etc.). However, as discussed previously, the goal of the price is not only to cover these variable costs but also to cover fixed costs, which is why we place those in the numerator of the formula. Using our craft brewery's pub operation, let's demonstrate this concept. Suppose the owners have used their demand curve and decided that they want to sell each pint of beer for $8. Suppose further that they have calculated the variable costs of each pint to be $2. Referring to their monthly budget, they have determined that the fixed costs of running their brewery pub each month are $6000. Using our formula above, the owners of the brew pub would calculate their break-even point (BEP) as follows:

BEP = $6000/($8 − $2)

BEP = $6000/$6

BEP = 1000

The BEP in this example is 1000, meaning that the brew pub must sell 1000 pints to cover the costs of making and serving the beer, as well as contribute to the monthly costs of running the pub. However, two caveats need to be mentioned here. First, the pub is naturally going to be selling other products besides pints of beer, such as other beverages and food menu items. Second, the 1000 units sold represents the BEP only, meaning that is the number of units sold required to cover costs. Every pint sold beyond 1000 represents profit, which is the ultimate goal of the brewery and all other for-profit businesses. The online appendix for this chapter goes into more detail on the theory and mathematics involved in break-even analysis, including examples of both break-even volume (as demonstrated above) and break-even price.

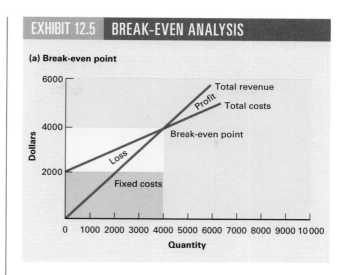

EXHIBIT 12.5   BREAK-EVEN ANALYSIS

(a) Break-even point

Exhibit 12.5 illustrates the concept of break-even analysis. Note that fixed costs remain the same regardless of units sold, and total costs increase with each unit produced. The total revenue line in turn begins at zero, but as it grows it eventually catches up to the total costs. The point at which it does so is the exact BEP. Everything beyond this point is profit.

Despite the rigour of demand curve and break-even calculations, the marketer is still left with a fundamental question when it comes to setting the actual price: What will the market bear? Let's look at one of our key challenges of price setting—estimating demand. In practice, the marketer will not know for sure until the product is offered for sale at a given price and the market responds accordingly. If the company has a hard time keeping the product in stock, there's a good chance that the price is too low. Conversely, if the product isn't moving at all, a likely cause is that the market is reacting to a price it feels is too high for the value offered.

Now that this section has brought us closer to setting that optimal price, let's proceed to choosing a price strategy.

12-2c | Step 3—Choosing a Price Strategy

The basic, long-term pricing framework for a good or service should be a logical extension of the pricing goals, while working within estimates of costs and demand. The marketing manager's

break-even analysis the calculation of number of units sold, or total revenue required, that a company must meet to cover its costs, beyond which profit occurs

EXHIBIT 12.6 PRODUCT-CYCLE PRICING STRATEGIES

	Introduction	Growth	Maturity	Decline
High	Penetration	Penetration	Status quo (lead down)	
Medium	Status quo	Status quo (lead down)	Status quo (maintain)	
Low	Skimming	Skimming	Skimming	Status quo (maintain)

chosen **price strategy** defines the initial price for a product and the intended direction for price movements over the product life cycle (see Exhibit 12.6).

The price strategy sets a competitive price in a specific market segment that is based on a well-defined positioning strategy (see Chapter 7). Changing a price level from medium to high may require a change in the product itself, the target customers served, the promotional strategy, or the distribution channels.

A company's freedom in pricing a new product and devising a price strategy depends on the market conditions and the other elements of the marketing mix. If a company launches a new item resembling several others already on the market, its pricing freedom will be restricted. To succeed, the company will probably need to charge a price close to the average market price of similar competitors' products. In contrast, a company that introduces a totally new product with no close substitutes will have considerable pricing freedom.

Strategic pricing decisions tend to be made without an understanding of the likely response from either buyers or the competition. Managers often make tactical pricing decisions without reviewing how they may fit into the company's overall pricing or marketing strategy. Many companies make pricing decisions and changes without an existing process for managing the pricing activity. As a result, many of them do not have a serious pricing strategy and do not conduct pricing research to develop their strategy.[5]

On the other hand, those companies that conduct both research and serious planning for creating a pricing strategy are endeavouring to understand the environment that their product has entered or is currently in. These companies first consider their current product positioning, the product's demand and costs, the company's long-term goals, and the product life-cycle stage, and then select from three basic approaches: price skimming, penetration pricing, and status quo pricing.

PRICE SKIMMING Price skimming is sometimes called a *market-plus approach to pricing* because it denotes a high price relative to the prices of competing products. The term **price skimming**, referring to a high introductory price, often coupled with heavy promotion, is derived from the phrase "skimming the cream off the top." Companies often use this strategy for new products when the product is perceived by the target market as having unique customer benefits. Often, companies will use skimming and then lower prices over time, known as *sliding down the demand curve*. We saw this happening with products such as flat-screen televisions and hybrid cars. Other manufacturers maintain skimming prices throughout a product's life cycle.

Price skimming works best when the market is willing to buy the product even though it carries an above-average price. Companies can also effectively use price skimming when a product is well protected legally, when

price strategy
a basic, long-term pricing framework that defines the initial price for a product and the intended direction for price movements over the product life cycle

price skimming
a high introductory price, often coupled with heavy promotion

Hybrid cars were introduced at a high price and promoted heavily.

DOLLARAMA—THE GREAT CANADIAN SUCCESS STORY

What started in 1910 as the S. Rossy Inc. store on Craig Street in Montreal has morphed into the Dollarama success story with more than 1200 stores across the country. The original stores were based on the general merchandise format common at the time. A major growth spurt started in 1973 when Larry Rossy, grandson of the original owner, took over the company after the death of his father. In 1992, with 44 locations in Quebec, the concept of the stores changed. The company converted one of its stores to a pricing strategy where everything in the store was $1.00 or less. From the beginning this new pricing strategy was a huge success, and the company changed all its stores to this pricing format. Building on the success of the original stores, the company started a major expansion program opening stores across Canada. In 2009, the company changed its pricing platform slightly to include prices up to $2.00. Today the company has moved the highest price point to $4.00 and has expanded store locations to include Latin America.

Sources: Pat McKeough, "Earnings up 6% for Dollarama Despite Increased Competition," TSI Network website, www.tsinetwork.ca/daily-advice/growth-stocks/earnings-up-6-for-dollarama-despite-increased-competition/, May 24, 2019; Dollarama website, www.dollarama.com, accessed February 20, 2020; Tara Deschamps, "Dollarama Shifts Strategy to Least Expensive Products to Maintain Growth," The Record website, www.therecord.com/news-story/9070980-dollarama-shifts-strategy-to-least-expensive-products-to-maintain-growth, December 6, 2018.

it represents a technological breakthrough, or when it has in some other way blocked the entry of competitors. Managers may follow a skimming strategy when production cannot be expanded rapidly because of technological difficulties, shortages, or constraints imposed by the skill and time required to produce a product. As long as demand is greater than supply, skimming is an attainable strategy.

A successful skimming strategy enables management to recover its product development costs quickly. Even if the market perceives an introductory price as being too high, managers can lower the price. Companies often feel it is better to test the market at a high price and then lower the price if sales are too slow. Successful skimming strategies are not limited to products. Well-known athletes, lawyers, and hairstylists are experts at price skimming. Naturally, a skimming strategy will encourage competitors to enter the market.

PENETRATION PRICING Penetration pricing is at the opposite end of the spectrum from skimming. **Penetration pricing** means charging a relatively low price for a product initially as a way to reach the mass market. The low price is designed to capture a large share of a substantial market, resulting in lower production costs. If a marketing manager has decided that the company's pricing object is to obtain a large market share, then penetration pricing is a logical choice.

Penetration pricing does mean lower profit per unit. Therefore, to reach the BEP, the company requires a higher volume of sales than needed under a skimming policy. The recovery of product development costs may be slow. As you might expect, penetration pricing tends to discourage competition.

A penetration strategy tends to be effective in a price-sensitive market. As discussed previously, price should decline more rapidly when demand is elastic (i.e., demand for a product is price sensitive) because the market can be increased in response to a lower price. Also, price sensitivity and greater competitive pressure should lead either to a stable low price or to a lower initial price and then a later, relatively slow decline in the price.

Although Walmart is typically associated with penetration pricing, other chains have also done an excellent job of following this strategy.

penetration pricing
a relatively low price for a product initially as a way to reach the mass market

Dollarama stores, those bare-bones, strip-mall chains that sell staples at cut-rate prices, are now one of the fastest-growing retailers in Canada. Dollarama stores are located in both small towns and large metropolitan areas with small stores in inner-city neighbourhoods or suburbs. Parking is readily available, and shoppers can be in and out in less time than it takes to hike across a jumbo Walmart parking lot.[6]

If a company has a low fixed-cost structure and each sale provides a large contribution to those fixed costs, penetration pricing can boost sales and provide large increases in profits—but only if the market size grows or if competitors choose not to respond. Low prices can attract additional buyers to the market. The increased sales can justify production expansion or the adoption of new technologies, both of which can reduce costs. And, if companies have excess capacity, even low-priced business can provide incremental dollars toward fixed costs.

Penetration pricing can also be effective if an experience curve will cause costs per unit to drop significantly. The experience curve proposes that per-unit costs will decrease as a company's production experience increases. Manufacturers that fail to take advantage of these effects will find themselves at a competitive cost disadvantage relative to others that are further along the curve.

One of the advantages of penetration pricing is that it can make it difficult for the competition to compete. However, penetration pricing also means gearing up to sell a large volume at a low price. If the volume or demand fails to materialize, the company will face losses. Penetration pricing can also prove disastrous for a prestige brand that adopts the strategy in an effort to gain market share and fails.

STATUS QUO PRICING The third basic price strategy a company can choose is status quo pricing, also called *meeting the competition* or *going-rate pricing*. It means charging a price identical to or very close to the competition's price.

Although status quo pricing has the advantage of simplicity, its disadvantage is that the strategy may ignore demand or cost, or both. If the company is comparatively small, however, meeting the competition may be the safest route to long-term survival.

base price
the general price level at which the company expects to sell the good or service

quantity discount
a unit price reduction offered to buyers buying either in multiple units or at more than a specified dollar amount

After managers have set pricing goals; estimated demand, costs, and profits; and chosen a pricing strategy, they should set a base price. A **base price** is the general price level at which the company expects to sell the good or service. The general price level is correlated with the actions taken in the first three steps of the price-setting process.

12-2d | Step 4—Using a Price Tactic

Once a base price has been determined, a series of price tactics are offered to help fine-tune the base price to make sure it satisfies the company and customer.

Fine-tuning techniques are short-run approaches that do not change the general price level. They do, however, result in changes *within* a general price level. These pricing tactics allow the company to adjust for competition in certain markets, meet ever-changing government regulations, take advantage of unique demand situations, and meet promotional and positioning goals. Fine-tuning pricing tactics include various sorts of discounts, geographic pricing, and other pricing tactics.

MARKUP Before proceeding with a long, and still nonexhaustive list of pricing tactics, it is important to point out that all for-profit companies enter into a business endeavour with the intention of earning a profit. Thus no matter what tactic or fine-tuning approach a business takes in setting its price, it must first attend to profit, which results from some form of markup. Markup, in fact, pervades all three pricing strategies discussed in the previous section as well. Markup is the profit-producing device of price and thus must be a component of each pricing tactic. Because there are several different markup methods, ranging from the nonmathematical to the mathematical, you are encouraged to review the Markup Pricing section in the online appendix for this chapter.

DISCOUNTS AND ALLOWANCES A base price can be lowered through discounts and allowances. Managers use the various forms of discounts to encourage customers to do what they would not ordinarily do, such as paying cash rather than using credit, taking delivery out of season, or performing certain functions within a distribution channel.[7] The following are the most common tactics:

- *Quantity discounts:* When buyers are charged a lower unit price when buying either in multiple units or at more than a specified dollar amount, they are receiving a **quantity discount**. For example, if a customer purchases a single product, they will pay $2.00 but if the customer purchases 10 they will pay $1.90 per product. A **cumulative quantity discount** is a deduction from list price that applies to the buyer's total purchases made during a specific period; it is intended to encourage customer loyalty. For example, if the customer purchases the 10 products over a year, they will pay $1.90 per item even if these products are purchased one at a time. In contrast, a **noncumulative quantity discount** is a deduction from list price that applies to a single order rather than to the total volume of orders placed during a certain period. It is intended to encourage orders in large quantities.

- *Cash discounts:* A **cash discount** is a price reduction offered to a consumer, an industrial user, or a marketing intermediary in return for prompt payment of a bill. For example, if an invoice says 2/10, net 30, the purchaser will receive a 2 percent discount if the account is paid within 10 days. The customer will have to pay the full amount within 30 days if the discount is not taken advantage of. Prompt payment saves the seller carrying charges and billing expenses and allows the seller to avoid bad debt.

- *Functional discounts:* When distribution channel intermediaries, such as wholesalers or retailers, perform a service or function for the manufacturer (for example, setting up retail displays or extending credit), they must be compensated. This compensation, typically a percentage discount from the base price, is called a **functional discount** (or **trade discount**). Functional discounts vary greatly from channel to channel, depending on the tasks performed by the intermediary.

- *Seasonal discounts:* A **seasonal discount** is a price reduction for buying merchandise out of season (for example, buying new ski equipment in March and accepting delivery in July). It shifts the storage function to the purchaser. Seasonal discounts also enable manufacturers to maintain a steady production schedule year-round.

VALUE-BASED PRICING Value-based pricing, also called *value pricing*, is a pricing tactic that has grown out of the quality movement. Instead of determining prices on the basis of costs or competitors' prices, value-based pricing starts with the customer, considers the competition, and then determines the appropriate price. The basic assumption is that the company is customer driven, seeking to understand the attributes customers want in the goods and services they buy and the value of that bundle of attributes to customers. Because very few companies operate in a pure monopoly, however, a marketer using value-based pricing must also determine the value of competitive offerings to customers. Customers determine the value of a product (not just its price) relative to the value of alternatives. In value-based pricing, therefore, the price of the product is set at a level that seems to the customer to be a good price compared with the prices of other options.

Because companies like Walmart, Costco, and Dollarama have had a strong impact on the grocery industry in Canada, rival supermarkets are adopting value-based pricing as a defensive move. Shoppers in competitive markets are seeing prices fall or at least remain constant as general merchants such as Walmart push rivals to match its value prices. Numerous regional grocery chains have switched to value pricing. In the past, they offered weekly specials to attract shoppers and then made up the lost profit by keeping nonsale prices substantially higher. Now, Costco, Walmart, and Dollarama have conditioned consumers to expect inexpensive goods every day.[8]

DYNAMIC PRICING
When competitive pressures are high, a company must know when it should raise or lower prices to maximize its revenue. More and more companies are tuning to **dynamic pricing** to help adjust prices; it is the

cumulative quantity discount
a deduction from list price that applies to the buyer's total purchases made during a specific period

noncumulative quantity discount
a deduction from list price that applies to a single order rather than to the total volume of orders placed during a certain period

cash discount
a price reduction offered to a consumer, an industrial user, or a marketing intermediary in return for prompt payment of a bill

functional discount (trade discount)
a discount to distribution channel intermediaries such as wholesalers and retailers for performing channel functions

seasonal discount
a price reduction for buying merchandise out of season

value-based pricing
a pricing tactic that sets the price at a level that seems to the customer to be good value compared with the prices of other options

dynamic pricing
the ability to change prices very quickly, often in real time

ability to change prices very quickly, often in real time. Dynamic pricing originated with the airlines, which are limited by fixed capacity; however, the new thinking is that dynamic pricing can be used in any industry where demand or supply fluctuates. Uber, for example, uses dynamic pricing by raising fares when more people need rides and vice versa. Dynamic pricing relies on technology in order to monitor supply and demand, adjust prices, and inform potential customers of the current prices. Customers can then decide whether to make a purchase or wait for a price change. In order to make sure they are getting the best prices, many consumers keep Amazon and other e-commerce sites open on their smartphones while shopping in-store. Rather than sticking with set prices that give them the profit margins they want, physical retailers increasingly have to tweak their pricing in real time to match, or at least approach, those of their rivals.

GEOGRAPHIC PRICING Because many sellers ship their wares to a nationwide or even a worldwide market, the cost of freight can greatly affect the total cost of a product. Sellers may use several different geographic pricing tactics to moderate the impact of freight costs on distant customers.

In some cases, the company adds the cost of shipping to the price. This price tactic requires the buyer to absorb the freight costs from the shipping point. The farther buyers are from sellers, the more they pay, because transportation costs generally increase with the distance merchandise is shipped. This pricing tactic means that customers living in the Far North pay considerably more than those living in southern Canada. If the marketing manager wants total costs, including freight, to be equal for all purchasers of identical products, the company will adopt uniform delivered pricing. In this case, the seller pays the actual freight charges and bills every purchaser an identical, flat freight charge.

Sometimes a marketing manager wants to equalize total costs among buyers within large geographic areas—but not necessarily in all of the seller's market area. The marketing manager may modify the base price with a zone-pricing tactic. Rather than using a uniform freight rate for its total market, the company divides it into segments or zones and charges a flat freight rate to all customers in a given zone. Honda, for example, has standardized freight charges on its vehicles, which are based on costs from the point of origin to a specific region.

In other cases, the seller pays all or part of the actual freight charges and does not pass them on to the buyer.

JETS DONUT
Official Donut of the Winnipeg Jets
$1.19
plus tax

The manager may use this tactic in intensely competitive areas or as a way to break into new market areas.

OTHER PRICING TACTICS Unlike geographic pricing, other pricing tactics are unique and defy neat categorization. Managers use these tactics for various reasons; for example, to stimulate demand for specific products, to increase store patronage, and to offer a wider variety of merchandise at a specific price point. Other pricing tactics include a single-price tactic, flexible pricing, professional services pricing, price lining, loss-leader pricing, odd–even pricing, price bundling, two-part pricing, and pay-what-you want pricing.

- *Single-price tactic:* A merchant using a single-price tactic offers all goods and services at the same price (or perhaps two or three prices). Netflix is an example of a single-price tactic where for a nominal amount per month, members can watch unlimited movies and TV episodes on their TVs and computers. Dollarama stores are another example of retailers using the single-price tactic.

- *Flexible pricing:* **Flexible pricing** (or **variable pricing**) means that different customers pay different prices for essentially the same merchandise bought in equal quantities. This tactic is often found in the sale of shopping goods, specialty merchandise, and most industrial goods except supply items. Car dealers and many appliance retailers commonly follow the practice. It allows the seller to adjust for competition by meeting another seller's price. Thus a marketing manager with a status quo pricing objective might readily adopt the tactic. Flexible pricing also enables the seller to close a sale with price-conscious consumers.

- *Professional services pricing:* **Professional services pricing** is used by people with experience, training, and often certification by a licensing board—for example, lawyers, dentists, and family counsellors. Professionals typically charge customers at an hourly rate, but sometimes fees are based on the solution of a problem or performance of an act (such as an eye examination) rather than on the actual time involved.

- *Price lining:* When a seller establishes a series of prices for a type of merchandise, it creates a price line. **Price lining** is the practice of offering a product line with several items at specific price points. Price lining is often used for electronics where there is a top of the line, a mid-range price point and a bargain model. Price lining reduces confusion for both the salesperson and the consumer.

- *Loss-leader pricing:* **Loss-leader pricing** is selling a product near or even below cost in the hope that shoppers will buy other items once they are in the store. This type of pricing appears weekly in the advertising of supermarkets. Loss-leader pricing is normally used on well-known items that consumers can easily recognize as bargains. The goal is not necessarily to sell large quantities of loss-leader items but to try to appeal to customers who might shop elsewhere.[9]

  Loss-leader pricing is not limited to products. Health and fitness clubs often offer a one-month free trial as a loss leader.

- *Odd–even pricing:* **Odd–even pricing** (or **psychological pricing**) means using odd-numbered prices to connote a bargain and even-numbered prices to imply quality. For years, many retailers have priced their products in odd numbers—for example, $99.95—to make consumers feel they are paying a lower price for the product.

- *Price bundling:* **Price bundling** is marketing two or more products in a single package for a special price. For example, Microsoft offers suites of software that bundle spreadsheets, word processing, graphics, electronic mail, Internet access, and groupware for networks of microcomputers. Price bundling can stimulate demand for the bundled items if the target market perceives the price as a good value.

  Bundling has also been used in the telecommunications industry. Companies offer local service, long-distance service, Internet service, wireless, and even cable TV in various menus of bundling. Telecom companies use bundling as a way to protect their market share and fight off competition by locking customers into a group of services. For consumers, comparison shopping may be difficult since they may not be able to determine how much they are really paying for each component of the bundle. A related price tactic is **unbundling**, or reducing the bundle of services that comes with the basic product.

  The purchase of season's tickets to a concert series, sporting event, or other activity is another example of price bundling. When you visit a fast

Slavoljub Pantelic/Shutterstock.com

single-price tactic
offering all goods and services at the same price (or perhaps two or three prices)

flexible pricing (variable pricing)
different customers pay different prices for essentially the same merchandise bought in equal quantities

professional services pricing
used by people with experience, training, and often certification by a licensing board; fees are typically charged at an hourly rate but may be based on the solution of a problem or performance of an act

price lining
offering a product line with several items at specific price points

loss-leader pricing
a product is sold near or even below cost in the hope that shoppers will buy other items once they are in the store

odd–even pricing (psychological pricing)
odd-numbered prices connote bargains, and even-numbered prices imply quality

price bundling
marketing two or more products in a single package for a special price

unbundling
reducing the bundle of services that comes with the basic product

COULD THE NICKEL BE NEXT?

While it is a very common pricing tactic, odd–even pricing might be running into a problem—the death of the penny. In early 2013, the Royal Canadian Mint officially stopped producing the Canadian one-cent coin. This means that retailers have had to make changes to their prices, at a cost of more than $100 000 for some large organizations (that's a lot of pennies!). Rounding has also become an issue, as prices that were using odd pricing of 99 cents may be rounded up if customers are not paying with credit, debit, or cheque. Just as consumers have become accustomed to a world without the penny, there is talk of eliminating the nickel. Desjardins, Canada's leading financial cooperative based in Quebec, thinks that the nickel should also be eliminated. The organization is advocating for only three coins under a dollar—10-cent, 20-cent, and 50-cent coins. The odd-even pricing tactic may become even odder in the future.

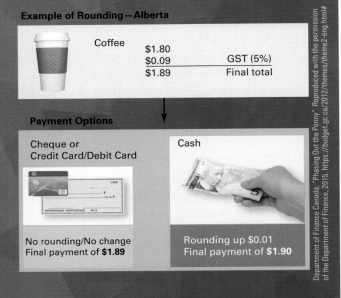

Example of Rounding—Alberta

Coffee	$1.80	
	$0.09	GST (5%)
	$1.89	Final total

Payment Options

Cheque or Credit Card/Debit Card

No rounding/No change
Final payment of **$1.89**

Cash

Rounding up $0.01
Final payment of **$1.90**

Department of Finance Canada, "Phasing Out the Penny". Reproduced with the permission of the Department of Finance, 2015. https://budget.gc.ca/2012/themes/theme2-eng.html#

Sources: John Rieti, "5 Odd Questions about the Death of the Penny," CBC News, February 1, 2013, www.cbc.ca/news/canada/5-odd-questions-about-the-death-of-the-penny-1.1353684 (accessed August 11, 2014); and Royal Canadian Mint, "Phasing Out the Penny," www.mint.ca/store/mint/learn/phasing-out-the-penny-6900002#. UtQ7oRZ23ww (accessed August 11, 2014); Pete Evans, "Canada Will Scrap the Nickel Within 5 Years, Desjardins Predicts," CBC News, https://www.cbc.ca/news/business/desjardins-nickel-cash-1.3563961, May 3, 2016; Mario Canseco, "Canadians Happy Without Penny, Not Ready to Abandon Nickel," Research Co., https://researchco.ca/2019/12/06/canada-penny-nickel/, December 6, 2019.

food restaurant you often encounter price bundling. McDonald's Happy Meals and Value Meals are bundles, and customers can trade up these bundles by super sizing them. Super sizing provides a greater value to the customer and creates more profits for the fast food chain.

- *Two-part pricing:* **Two-part pricing** means charging two separate amounts to consume a single good or service. Health and fitness clubs charge a membership fee and then a flat fee each time a person uses certain equipment or facilities.

Consumers sometimes prefer two-part pricing because they are uncertain about the number and the types of activities they might use, such as at an amusement park. Two-part pricing can increase a seller's revenue by attracting consumers who would not pay a high fee even for unlimited use.

- *Pay what you want:* **Pay-what-you-want pricing** allows the customer to chose the amount they want to pay for a good or service. To many people, paying what you want or what you think something is worth is a very risky tactic. Obviously, it would not work for expensive durables like cars. Imagine someone paying $1 for a new BMW! Yet this model has worked in varying degrees in digital media marketplaces, restaurants, and other service businesses. Social

Professional services pricing

ALPA PROD/Shutterstock.com

two-part pricing
charging two separate amounts to consume a single good or service

pay-what-you-want pricing
allows the customer to choose the amount they want to pay for a good or service

The Hudson Bay Company was investigated by the Competition Bureau for advertising mattress sleep sets as clearance items when in fact the products they were selling were being ordered directly from the factory.

pressures can come into play in a "pay-what-you-want" environment because an individual does not want to appear poor or cheap to their peers.

12-3 | THE LEGALITY AND ETHICS OF SETTING A PRICE

Some pricing decisions are subject to government regulation. Companies and marketers need to be aware of the laws within the Competition Act before establishing any pricing strategy. The act covers legal and ethical issues relating to deceptive pricing, price fixing, predatory pricing, resale price maintenance, and price discrimination.

Both alleged and proven unethical pricing practices can have serious consequences for the companies and the marketing managers involved.

12-3a | Bait Pricing

In contrast to loss leader pricing, which is a genuine attempt to give the consumer a reduced price, bait pricing is deceptive. **Bait pricing** is a price tactic that tries to get the consumer into a store through false or misleading price advertising and then uses high-pressure selling to persuade the consumer to buy more expensive merchandise instead.

The Hudson Bay Company (HBC) was investigated by the Competition Bureau for advertising mattress sleep sets as clearance items when in fact the products being sold were being ordered directly from the factory. Another problem was that the "regular price" advertised was so inflated that the company was unlikely to sell any at that price. A large difference between the advertised regular price and sale price is one of the triggers for the Competition Bureau to investigate the situation. Under the Competition Act the fine for a first-time offender can be as high as $10 million. The Hudson Bay Company agreed to pay a $4.5 million fine and an additional $500 000 toward legal and investigative costs in order to settle the charge.[10]

> **bait pricing**
> a price tactic that tries to get consumers into a store through false or misleading price advertising and then uses high-pressure selling to persuade consumers to buy more expensive merchandise instead

12-3b | Deceptive Pricing

Deceptive pricing refers to promoting a price or price saving that is not actually available. It occurs when the seller leads the purchaser to believe that they can receive or are receiving the good or service at the promoted or reduced price. Sellers who use deceptive pricing typically promote a low price on a product for which they have very little stock, or no stock at all, with the intent of selling the customer another, higher-priced product as a substitute. This tactic is also called a *bait and switch*. To avoid the perception of using this tactic, marketers must ensure that they have adequate stock on hand or that they clearly indicate the limited quantities available at the reduced price; if the stock quickly sells out; they should offer rain cheques.

A second form of deceptive pricing occurs when a seller promotes a discount from a regular price that, in fact, has not been the regular price for a significant time.

Other deceptive pricing practices include selling a product at a price above the advertised price (a civil court issue) and double ticketing, in which a product is sold for more than the lowest of two or more prices tagged on it (a criminal offence).

12-3c | Price Fixing

Price fixing occurs when two or more companies conspire to set the prices they will charge for their products or services. It can be done by establishing a floor, or lowest price, in a bidding situation or by simply setting the market price that the consumer will pay. Proving an allegation of price fixing is often a very difficult and lengthy process.

One recent case involved the price of bread. Canada Bread and Weston Bakeries, the country's two largest producers of bread, buns, bagels, and naan, devised a scheme known as 7/10. The bakeries would increase the wholesale price of bread by seven cents and then convince retailers to increase the price to the customer by 10 cents. The practice continued for 16 years and involved the bread-producing companies

deceptive pricing
promoting a price or price saving that is not actually available

price fixing
an agreement between two or more companies to set the price they will charge for a product or service

predatory pricing
the practice of charging a very low price for a product with the intent of driving competitors out of the market or the business

In Canada, the price fixing of bread went on for 16 years before the scheme came to light.

and several grocery store chains including Loblaw Companies Ltd., Walmart Canada Corp., Sobeys Inc., Metro Inc., and Giant Tiger Stores. The scheme came to light only when a representative from Loblaws informed the Competition Bureau of the practice; the company received immunity from charges. The fines for price fixing in Canada can be substantial—up to $25 million and imprisonment for up to 14 years or both. Loblaws did not get off completely because the company offered $25 gift cards to customers as a way of refunding the money that customers overpaid for bread over the years.[11]

12-3d | Predatory Pricing

Although a normal business strategy might be to set prices low to lure business away from the competition and gain market share, such action must be done within reason. **Predatory pricing** occurs when a company sets its prices very low with the intention of driving its competition out of either the market or the business. To do this, the company lowers its price below its average variable cost for an extended time—more time than is typical of any short-term loss leader that might be used to attract business or move excess inventory. Once the very low price has eliminated any competitor that cannot afford to operate at that price, the company will raise its prices. Predatory pricing situations are difficult to prove as evidence must show a willful intent to destroy the competition.

The airline industry has been the target of predatory pricing investigations. The Canadian airline industry has only two main companies, making predatory pricing easier for the large carriers. WestJet's discount arm, Swoop, has been investigated for its low prices on some Canadian routes, particularly the Edmonton to Hamilton route. The price charged by Swoop for this route was $69 including airport fees and taxes. Flair Airlines, a discount carrier based in British Columbia, has accused Swoop of undercutting fares to limit the competition in this market, as Flair discontinued flying the Edmonton to Hamilton route. This type of compliant will be heard by the Competition Tribunal, which will ultimately decide if this is an example of predatory pricing or fair competition.[12]

12-3e | Resale Price Maintenance

Producers usually take the time to research where they want their products to be positioned with regard to price and quality, and in relation to their competitors, so that they achieve their desired profit goals. They cannot, however, dictate the retailer's selling price or determine a floor price. Producers may give their channel members a manufacturer's suggested retail price (MSRP) and even indicate the MSRP by way of a label on the product, but they cannot discriminate against any retailers that do not follow their recommendations. In Canada, **resale price maintenance**, producers' attempts to control the price of their products in retail stores, is illegal. However, companies operating both in Canada and in the United States will find that resale price maintenance is legal south of the border, and, thus, such companies may need two separate pricing policies.

12-3f | Price Discrimination

Price discrimination is the practice of charging different prices to different buyers for goods of like grade and quality within relatively the same period to substantially reduce the competition. This type of price discrimination does not apply to services, end-users, or consumers; thus movie theatres and dry cleaners, for example, can charge different prices for students and seniors or charge different prices on various days of the week.

Producers can legally offer promotional (push) incentives to channel members, but they must do so on a proportional basis; that is, sale prices and any savings can be in relation to and proportional to transactional or logistical costs. Sellers may also lower their prices to buyers in their efforts to meet competitive challenges. Note that the Competition Act also makes it illegal for buyers to use their influence of purchasing power to force discriminatory prices or services.

Six elements are necessary for price discrimination to occur:

1. Two or three instances of discrimination must have occurred over time.

2. The sales in question must have occurred within a relatively short time.

3. The products sold must be commodities or tangible goods.

4. The seller must charge different prices to two or more buyers for the same product.

5. The products sold must be of the same quality and grade.

6. The buyers of the goods must be competitors.

resale price maintenance
attempts by a producer to control the price of their products in retail stores

AWAKE CHOCOLATE
CONTINUING CASE

Sell Value over Price

Price serves many different purposes for an organization, not the least of which is getting paid. In fact, of the 4 P's it is the only one that actually stands as a cash in-flow, as making products, getting them to market, and finally promoting them usually represent costs. Price has to cover those costs of each unit sold, and that is the first consideration a company makes when establishing its price: how much did it cost to produce the product? A close second consideration would come from asking how much the customer is willing to pay.

In his role as chief financial officer, Dan Tzotzis, was of course deeply involved in setting the price for Awake chocolates, but he knew decision went beyond costs and demand. "Everything begins and ends with the consumer, and so we tried to adopt what their lens would be on the value proposition," he recalled. "When trying to devise a price for both Canada and the US, we had to consider what price would they be willing to pay." Just as covering costs represents the very lowest price a company could charge for a product, the price customers are willing to pay—an indicator of demand—represents the highest price point assignable to a product.

But estimating what the market will bear is much more difficult than calculating costs. Fortunately for Awake, a contextual pricing reference had been set. "There was a precedent set in the market by energy drinks: to charge twice the price for half the can size. Because consumers were willing to pay a premium for functional products." With a clear nod to the trailblazing price brashness of Red Bull, Tzotsis and his team performed some supplementary market research to gain confidence that they too could charge a premium for their product.

Predicting how much a customer group is willing to pay for a product, however, regardless of the premium, is difficult, especially for a new product. As this chapter makes clear, one of the only immutable laws in marketing is that, in most cases, quantity demanded decreases as price increases. This economic theory of the demand curve is fairly reliable—but not all the time.

"We thought very carefully about what we could set as our price, and what we ultimately landed on was suggested retail prices of $1.99 for our bars and $0.79 for our bites. So our regular-sized bars were priced the same as what traditional confectionary companies were charging for their 'king' bars. Consumers were then familiar with these price points. Their familiarity with energy drinks, and their premium price, at least gave us a precedent that consumers would also be familiar with a premium price attached to a regular-sized bar."

The actual price that a product would have on a store shelf was out of Awake's hands. But, as Tzotzis argued, at that price, everyone would be happy with their margins and customers would be satisfied that the steeper price was worth it due to the premium nature of the product.

In the consumer packaged goods industry, the average profit margin for companies runs anywhere between 45 and 55 percent (author interview with Dan Tzotzis, January 26, 2020), but at the time of the launch of Awake's first products, the company would have been content with a margin of 35 percent. "But if we weren't able to create perceived value at any price with our customers, then margin is a moot point. It is that they understand and appreciate the value Awake chocolate offers, at our premium pricing, that has allowed us to thrive. If they did not see that value, we'd be dead in the water."

QUESTIONS

1. Using the theory from this chapter, identify the pricing objective, pricing strategy, and any pricing tactics you believe are a part of Awake's approach to pricing.

2. Have a look at comparable products, either in your campus's store or online. Create a table to show the different price points between Awake and its competitors. Why do you think there are any differences?

3. When Dan speaks about "perceived value," what is he describing: the price, the functional benefit of the product, or both? Explain.

AWAKE Chocolate

Pricing Decisions, Part 4 Case

Pricing Tactics at Costco

What started in San Diego, California, in 1976 has grown to over 750 outlets globally and introduced consumers to a new concept in shopping. Sol Price, the founder, had a vision to change the way people shopped. The first stores were called The Price Club and were open only for business customers. Businesses could purchase a membership that would allow them to take advantage of lower prices on business supplies and other wholesale items. Instrumental in developing the Price Club concept was Executive Vice President Jim Sinegal, who left the company in 1983 to open the first Costco, with partner Jeff Brotman. Costco followed the same membership format but allowed businesses and consumers to shop in its warehouse-style stores. The two companies operated independently until 1993 when they merged.

Today Costco Wholesale is incredibly successful. The company has had an annual sales growth rate of over 6 percent for the last five years as compared to Walmart, which has seen annual sales grow at just over 1.5 percent for the same period. The company owes its success to several factors including sticking to its original principles, efficient operations, and value pricing.

The company's principles include a commitment to quality, an entrepreneurial spirit, and a focus on its employees. Costco carries fewer products than a traditional store; it chooses products based on quality, price, and features to provide customers with a good variety of quality products at a good price. As part of the strategy, Costco has developed their branded products under the Kirkland label; every Kirkland product has been created specifically for the company, hand selected, and tested in order to provide customers with a quality product at a good price. The entrepreneurial spirit is part of the corporate culture at Costco and ensures that everyone within the organization

works to exceed member expectations. Employees are paid fair salaries and benefits to attract and keep a workforce of positive thinking, high-energy employees, another way of keeping costs down because it eliminates the costs of always training new employees.

Costco has also designed its operations to ensure the lowest possible costs. Stores are in low-rent areas that are accessible to large urban populations but where costs to build large warehouse-style stores are lower. This also allows the stores to have large parking areas. One recently opened store in Alberta is 149 000 square feet with parking for more than 775 cars and 800 shopping carts.

The warehouse-style stores allow products that are sold in larger quantities to be displayed on pallets or open shelving units. This allows for lower setup costs and fewer employees needed to restock shelves. The store merchandise fits into four categories: food and sundries, fresh food, soft lines (clothing), and hard lines (appliances and electronics). Many stores also carry ancillary services including gas bars, pharmacies, food courts, hearing aid centres, and optical centres.

A major factor in the consideration of pricing for Costco is revenue the company receives from memberships (more

Pictures_n_Photos/Shutterstock.com

than 12 million members in Canada). There are membership programs for consumers and another for businesses. Consumer memberships are at two levels: the basic membership costs $60 a year and the higher level—called the executive level—costs an additional $60 a year. Members at the higher level of membership account for just under 40 percent of Costco customers but account for more than 60 percent of sales. Research also shows that organizations that use the membership format enjoy higher levels of trust with their members.

Another pricing tactic that Costco uses effectively is loss-leader products, including its rotisserie chickens and hot dogs. In one year, the company sold more than 130 million hot dog and soda combinations at $1.50 from its in-store food counters. Costco owns and operates a factory in California that produces more than 250 million hot dogs a year, allowing the company keep the price low.

Keeping operating costs down and using pricing tactics has been a successful combination for Costco. Sales at Costco have been growing each year and the company is making money in a low-margin business. It has been estimated that the company has an average profit margin of over 10 percent on merchandise but the profit margin on the Kirkland-branded products is higher.

SOURCES

Costco website, www.costco.ca/about-us.html, accessed April 7, 2020; Justin Dallaire, "Membership Organizations Enjoy High Levels Of Trust," Strategy Online, "Costco Opens it 100th Warehouse in Canada," Canadian Grocer website, www.canadiangrocer.com/top-stories /headlines/costco-opens-its-100th-warehouse-in -canada-82529, August 23, 2018; Chris Powell, "Costco Canada Has No Plans to Eliminate Polish Hot Dog," Canadian Grocer website, www.canadiangrocer.com /top-stories/headlines/costco-canada-has-no-plans -to-eliminate-polish-hot-dog-81870, July 12, 2018; Amit Singh, "How Costco Manages It Inventory and Supply Chain," marketrealist.com/2019/12/analyzing-costcos- inventory-supply-chain-management-strategies/, December 31, 2019.

QUESTIONS

1. Go to the Costco.ca website. Review the membership options and the features of each. Discuss whether the memberships are value for money from the customer point of view. Discuss the advantages of the membership from the company point of view.

2. Go to the Costco.ca website. Review some of the larger products available such as appliances. Visit the websites of other companies that also sell the same products. Compare the prices. Are Costco prices significantly lower?

3. Costco claims to use value-based pricing. Explain what value-based pricing is. Discuss whether Costco uses value-based pricing effectively.

4. Costco uses loss-leader pricing for rotisserie chickens and for the hot dog and soft drink combo at its food counter. Explain what loss-leader pricing is and discuss the effectiveness of this pricing tactic.

13 | Marketing Channels and Supply Chain Management

LEARNING OUTCOMES

13-1 Explain the nature of marketing channels

13-2 Identify different channel intermediaries and their functions

13-3 Describe the types of marketing channels

13-4 Summarize how to make channel strategy decisions

13-5 Recognize how to handle channel relationships

13-6 Learn about supply chain management

13-7 List channel and distribution challenges in global markets

"Content is king, but distribution is queen. And she wears the pants."

—Jonathan Perelman, Buzzfeed[1]

13-1 | THE NATURE OF MARKETING CHANNELS

13-1a | Change the Channel

The concept of a channel often makes one think of other meanings than the one meant in this chapter: a type of media (i.e., television channels), a form of passage (e.g., the English Channel), or a method of communication (e.g., diplomatic channel). All describe a passage of something from one place to another. Marketing channels describe the journey taken by marketing offerings from those who produce them to those who consume them. As you take this journey, you will become increasingly aware of how complicated and important the marketing channels process has become.

Aside from transportation truck with a large company logo driving by, or a retail employee stocking a shelf, consumers don't often consider the advantages of marketing channels (or channels of distribution). And what place can provide is significant—a source of competitive advantage that is unrivalled by any of the other three Ps of the marketing mix. It is becoming increasingly difficult to gain a competitive advantage based on product, price, or promotion. Because of constant innovation and technology transfer, products have a hard time standing apart and have become commoditized, meaning there is little to differentiate between different offerings within a product category. Thanks to globalization, companies can find cheap means of production for their product, thus keeping prices within a competitive range. Oversaturation of the marketplace with constant communication with and promotion to customers has left many customers seeking a way to distance themselves from the promotional noise.

But as pointed out by Jonathan Perelman at the beginning of this chapter, distribution channels have earned their place in the marketing discussion.

Channels of distribution can achieve competitive advantage through a thoughtful strategy that takes advantage of several trends:

- Continual push for growth in most companies
- Increased vertical integration in channels
- Greater role of information technology

Ultimately, the main reason a well-operated channel of distribution provides such a fundamental competitive advantage that it is very difficult and expensive to emulate.

While it is easy to point toward companies that are huge in size and success, it is helpful to look at much smaller companies to discover how advantageous marketing channels can be. For every Amazon that blows away the competition thanks to its large size and buying power, there exist numerous successes that are smaller in size but can have a great impact on a marketing channel.

For example, one such "small" success is Eight Ounce Coffee from Calgary, Alberta. The success of Eight Ounce has not gone unnoticed; the company ranked in the top five of Canada's Fastest-Growing Wholesale and Distribution Companies in both 2019 and 2018, according to *Canadian Business Magazine*.[2]

Among the numbers that stand out for Eight Ounce is its incredible revenue growth—an increase of 1354 percent[3] from 2013 to 2018. But the truly astonishing numbers are the number of products (hundreds) and brands (over 60) that Eight Ounce offers directly to baristas and coffee shops across Canada. Eight Ounce provides a wide array of offerings—from Japanese heat-resistant glassware to a case of 12 oat milk—and does so in a very personal way.

The Eight Ounce wholesale website is easy to use and nothing like many business-to-business sites, which are often bland and impersonal. The site has a look and feel like another huge player in the distribution market: Amazon.

Eight Ounce uses its website to go beyond its role as a wholesaler, by offering end consumers the chance to

Courtesy of Eight Ounce Coffee

purchase many of the company's products. This type of vertical integration spurs Eight Ounce Coffee's growth, and provides a great example of how marketing intermediaries do not have to be nameless and faceless corporate structures in order to be successful.

13-1b | The Marketing Channel and Intermediaries Defined

A **marketing channel** (also called a **channel of distribution** or *distribution channel*) is a business structure of interdependent organizations that ease the transfer of ownership as products move from producer to business user or consumer. Marketing channels represent the *place* or *distribution* function in the marketing mix (product, price, promotion, and place). The marketing channel is all about getting the right product to the right place at the right time.

Many different types of organizations participate in marketing channels. **Channel members** (also called *intermediaries*) comprise all parties in the marketing channel that negotiate with one another, buy and sell products, and facilitate the change of ownership between buyer and seller as they move products from the manufacturer into the hands of the final consumer. An important aspect of marketing channels is the joint effort of all channel members to create a continuous and seamless supply chain. The **supply chain** is the connected chain of all the business entities, both internal and external to the company, that perform or support the marketing channel functions.

marketing channel (channel of distribution)
a set of interdependent organizations that handle products and often transfer ownership of products as they move from producer to business user or consumer

channel members
all parties in the marketing channel that negotiate with one another, buy and sell products, and facilitate the change of ownership between buyer and seller as they move the product from the manufacturer into the hands of the end customer

supply chain
the connected chain of all the business entities, both internal and external to the company, that produce the product and perform or support the marketing channel functions

discrepancy of quantity
the difference between the amount of product produced and the amount an end-user wants to buy

13-1c | How Intermediaries Help the Supply Chain

As products move through the supply chain, channel members facilitate the distribution process through three key actions: providing specialization and division of labour, overcoming discrepancies, and providing contact efficiency.

PROVIDING SPECIALIZATION AND DIVISION OF LABOUR According to the concept of specialization and division of labour, breaking down a complex task into smaller, simpler tasks and then allocating them to specialists will both create greater efficiency and lower average production costs. Manufacturers achieve economies of scale through producing large quantities of a single product.

Marketing channels can also attain economies of scale through specialization and division of labour by aiding producers who lack the financing or expertise to market directly to end-users or consumers. In some cases, as with most consumer convenience goods, such as soft drinks, the cost of marketing directly to millions of consumers—taking and shipping individual orders—makes no sense.

For this reason, producers hire channel members, such as wholesalers and retailers, to do what the producers are not equipped to do or what channel members are better prepared to do. Channel members can do some things more efficiently than producers because they have built good relationships with their customers. Therefore, their specialized expertise enhances the overall performance of the channel.

OVERCOMING DISCREPANCIES Marketing channels also aid in overcoming discrepancies of quantity, assortment, time, and space created by economies of scale in production. For example, let's say that Maple Leaf Foods produces 2000 units of Natural Bacon in one day. No one consumer is likely to buy that amount at once. Maple Leaf would seek to distribute those units throughout its vast array of retailers in order for the product not to spoil and to meet the needs of consumers across Canada. The quantity produced to achieve low unit costs has created a **discrepancy of quantity**, which is the difference between the amount of product produced and the amount an end-user wants to buy. However, by storing the product and distributing it in the appropriate amounts, marketing channels overcome quantity discrepancies by making products available in the quantities that consumers desire.

SUPPLY CHAIN IN CANADA LOSES THE "MANAGEMENT"

In September 2019, the Supply Chain Management Association announced that it had changed its name to Supply Chain Canada. This simplification of name was meant to describe a much deeper and involved representation of the field of supply chain management. The association of supply chain providers has been around for more than 100 years, but the change in name was done to help broker the group's entrance into the new economic realities. President and CEO of Supply Chain Canada Christian Buhagiar stated: "The new name and look are part of a transformation that we have undertaken as the association enters its second century."[4] The field of supply chain management is seen by students as not as "professional" as other fields, with images of forklifts and shipping containers coming to mind before strategic operational decision making. With its new name, Supply Chain Canada is hoping to shift industry's perceptions to a field that uses the newest technologies, from AI to Blockchain, to help provide a sustainable competitive advantage for companies that can look beyond product offerings, price decisions, and promotional campaigns.[5]

Mass production creates discrepancies of not only quantity but also assortment. A **discrepancy of assortment** occurs when a consumer does not have all the items needed to receive full satisfaction from a product. For pancakes to provide maximum satisfaction, several other products are required to complete the assortment. At the very least, most people want a knife, a fork, a plate, butter, and syrup. Even though Quaker is a large consumer-products company, it does not come close to providing the optimal assortment to go with its Aunt Jemima pancakes. To overcome discrepancies of assortment, marketing channels assemble in one place many of the products necessary to complete a consumer's needed assortment.

A **temporal discrepancy** is created when a product is produced but a consumer is not ready to buy it. Marketing channels overcome temporal discrepancies by maintaining inventories in anticipation of demand. For example, manufacturers of sunscreen offer their product at retailers year-round, despite consumer demand being concentrated only during the summer months. Channel intermediaries will make the product available whenever it is needed, even taking into consideration the extra hours needed to produce for a special order or unique circumstances.

Furthermore, because mass production requires many potential buyers, markets are usually scattered over large geographic regions, creating a **spatial discrepancy**. Often global, or at least nationwide, markets are needed to absorb the outputs of mass producers. Marketing channels overcome spatial discrepancies by making products available in locations convenient to consumers. For example, if all the Aunt Jemima pancake mix is produced in Peterborough, Ontario, then the Quaker Oats Company must use an intermediary to distribute the product to other regions of Canada.

PROVIDING CONTACT EFFICIENCY The third need fulfilled by marketing channels is the contact efficiency provided by reducing the number of stores customers must shop in to complete their purchases.

discrepancy of assortment
the lack of all the items a customer needs to receive full satisfaction from a product or products

temporal discrepancy
a product is produced but a customer is not ready to buy it

spatial discrepancy
the difference between the location of a producer and the location of widely scattered markets

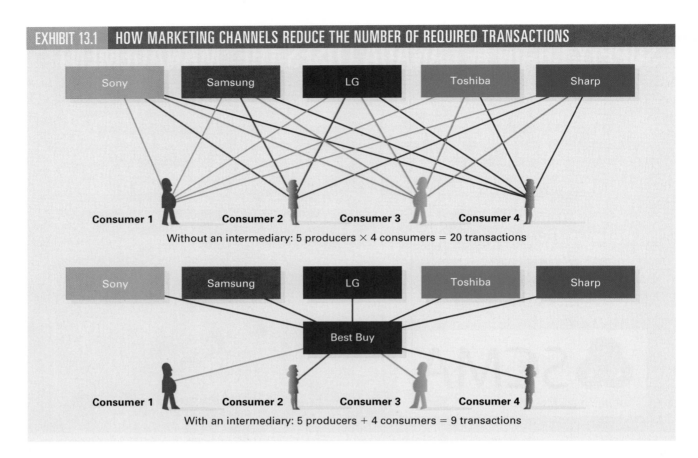

Without an intermediary: 5 producers × 4 consumers = 20 transactions

With an intermediary: 5 producers + 4 consumers = 9 transactions

Suppose you had to buy your milk at a dairy and your meat at a stockyard. You would spend a great deal of time, money, and energy shopping for just a few groceries. Supply chains simplify distribution by reducing the number of transactions required to move products from manufacturers to consumers and by making an assortment of goods available in one location.

Consider the example illustrated in Exhibit 13.1. Four consumers each want to buy a new LED television. Without a retail intermediary, such as Best Buy, television manufacturers Sony, Samsung, LG, Toshiba, and Sharp would each have to make four contacts to reach the four buyers who are in the target market, for a total of 20 transactions. However, when Best Buy acts as

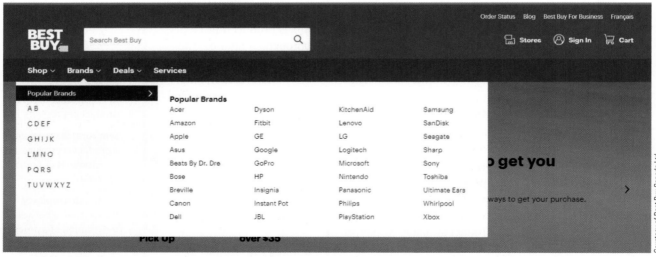

an intermediary between the producer and customers, each producer makes only one contact, reducing the number of transactions to nine. Each producer sells to one retailer rather than to four customers. In turn, customers buy from one retailer instead of from five producers. Information technology has enhanced contact efficiency by making information on products and services easily available online. Shoppers can find the best bargains without physically searching for them and can also search for ratings and feedback on products without having to visit the store.

13-2 | CHANNEL INTERMEDIARIES AND THEIR FUNCTIONS

Channel intermediaries must find a way to work together while simultaneously achieving their business goals and objectives. Intermediaries in a channel will have to negotiate with one another, decide on terms of ownership transfer between buyers and sellers, and coordinate the physical movement of finished products from the manufacturer to the final consumer.

What separates intermediaries is the fundamental idea of ownership or title. *Taking title* means that an intermediary made the decision to own the merchandise and control the terms of the sale—for example, price and delivery date. Retailers and merchant wholesalers are examples of intermediaries that take title to products in the marketing channel and resell them. **Retailers** are companies that sell mainly to consumers and business customers. Retailers will be discussed in more detail in Chapter 14.

The main characteristics that determine what type of intermediary should be used by a manufacturer (producer) are as follows:

- Product characteristics, which may require a certain type of wholesaling intermediary, include whether the product is standardized or customized, the complexity of the product, and the gross margin of the product. For example, a customized product, such as insurance, is sold through an insurance agent or broker that may represent one or multiple companies. In contrast, a standardized product, such as a chocolate bar, is sold through a merchant wholesaler that takes possession of the product and reships it to the appropriate retailers.

- Buyer considerations that affect the wholesaler choice include how often the product is purchased and how long the buyer is willing to wait to receive the product. For example, at the beginning of the

school term, a student may be willing to wait a few days for a textbook if it means paying a lower price by ordering through an online portal like Amazon or directly from the publisher's website. Thus, this type of product can be distributed directly. But if the student waits to buy the book until right before an exam and needs the book immediately, the student will need to purchase it for full price at the school bookstore or pay even more by adding on high shipping charges to have it delivered quickly from an online site.

- Market characteristics that determine the wholesaler type include the number of buyers in the market and whether they are concentrated in a general location or are widely dispersed. Chocolate bars and textbooks, for example, are produced in one location and consumed in many other locations. Therefore, a merchant wholesaler is needed to distribute the products. In contrast, in a home sale, the buyer and seller are localized in one area, which facilitates the use of an agent or a broker relationship.

13-2a | Channel Functions Performed by Intermediaries

Retailing and wholesaling intermediaries in marketing channels perform several essential functions that enable the flow of goods between producer and buyer. The three basic functions that intermediaries perform are summarized in Exhibit 13.2.

Although individual members can be added to or deleted from a channel, someone must still perform these essential functions. They can be performed by producers, end-users or consumers, channel intermediaries such as wholesalers and retailers, and sometimes by nonmember channel participants. For example, if a manufacturer decides to eliminate its private fleet of trucks, it must still move the goods to the wholesaler. This task may be accomplished by the wholesaler, which may have its own fleet of trucks, or by a nonmember channel participant, such as an independent trucking company. Nonmembers also provide many other essential functions that may at one time have been provided by a channel member. For example, research companies may perform the research function; advertising agencies may provide the promotion function; transportation and storage companies, the physical distribution function; and banks, the financing function.

retailer
a channel intermediary that sells mainly to consumers and business customers

EXHIBIT 13.2 MARKETING CHANNEL FUNCTIONS PERFORMED BY INTERMEDIARIES

Type of Function	Description
Transactional functions	*Contacting and promoting:* Contacting potential customers, promoting products, and soliciting orders
	Negotiating: Determining how many goods or services to buy and sell, type of transportation to use, when to deliver, and method and timing of payment
	Risk taking: Assuming the risk of owning inventory
Logistical functions	*Physically distributing:* Transporting and sorting goods to overcome temporal and spatial discrepancies
	Storing: Maintaining inventories and protecting goods
	Sorting: Overcoming discrepancies of quantity and assortment
	Sorting out: Breaking down a heterogeneous supply into separate homogeneous stocks
	Accumulating: Combining similar stocks into a larger homogeneous supply
	Allocating: Breaking a homogeneous supply into smaller and smaller lots ("breaking bulk")
	Assorting: Combining products into collections or assortments that buyers want available at one place
Facilitating functions	*Researching:* Gathering information about other channel members and customers
	Financing: Extending credit and other financial services to facilitate the flow of goods through the channel to the final consumer

13-3 | TYPES OF MARKETING CHANNELS

A product can take many routes to reach its final customer. Marketers search for the most efficient channel from the many alternatives available. Marketing a consumer convenience good, such as gum or candy, differs from marketing a specialty good, such as a Coach handbag. The next sections discuss the structures of typical and alternative marketing channels for consumer and business-to-business products.

13-3a | Channels for Consumer Products

Exhibit 13.3 illustrates the four ways manufacturers can route products to consumers. Producers use the **direct channel** to sell directly to customers. Direct-marketing activities—including telemarketing, mail-order and catalogue shopping, and online shopping—are a good example of this type of channel structure. Direct channels have no intermediaries. Producer-owned stores and factory outlet stores—such as clothing companies Stanfield's and Le Château—are examples of direct channels. Direct marketing and factory outlets are discussed in more detail in Chapter 14.

By contrast, an *agent/ broker channel* is fairly complicated and is typically used in markets characterized by many small manufacturers and many retailers that lack the resources to find each other. Agents or brokers bring manufacturers and wholesalers together for negotiations, but they do not take title to merchandise. Ownership passes directly to one or more wholesalers and then to retailers. Finally, retailers sell to the ultimate consumer of the product. For example, a food broker represents buyers and sellers of grocery products. Canadian-based Westrow Food Group positions itself as "Your Turnkey Solution to the Canadian Market." Its focus is on what it calls the "perimeter fresh aisles" in grocery stores: seafood, deli, bakery, and produce. Unlike some food brokers in Canada, Westrow attempts to cover the entire Canadian market by offering services relating to setting up key accounts, retail and merchandise reporting, and other administrative tasks. The company's focus is to take on tasks that are often challenging for companies seeking to enter the geographically vast Canadian retail market.[6]

Most consumer products are sold through distribution channels similar to the other two alternatives: the retailer channel and the wholesaler channel. A *retailer channel* is most common when the retailer is large and can buy in large quantities directly from the manufacturer. Chapters Indigo is an example of a retailer that often bypasses a wholesaler. Online entities such as Shopify offer entrepreneurs and small businesses the opportunity sell wholesale to other businesses while simultaneously selling to consumers. A *wholesaler channel* is commonly used for low-cost and low-involvement items that are frequently purchased, such as candy, gum, and magazines.

direct channel
a distribution channel in which producers sell directly to customers

EXHIBIT 13.3 | MARKETING CHANNELS FOR CONSUMER PRODUCTS

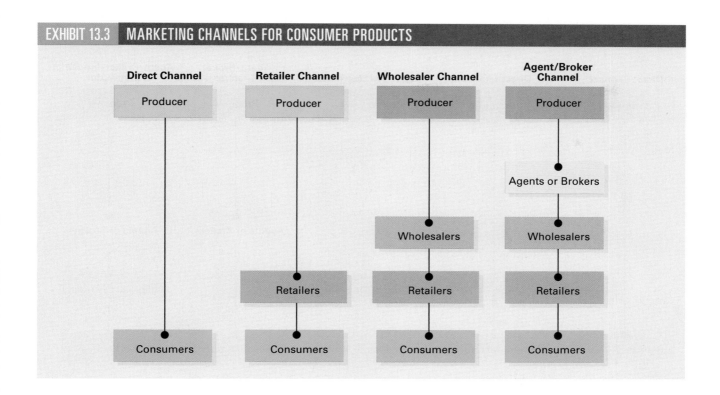

What's in a Name? Direct Channels vs. Direct Marketing

Marketing has a number of terms that are similar and, unfortunately, used interchangeably. Marketing strategies devised by companies and online bloggers are often disguised as marketing tactics (see Chapter 3). Direct channels are often confused with direct marketing. However, *direct channels*, as you have already read, have to do with companies providing a direct line to the end customers without intermediaries. On the other hand, *direct marketing* is a promotional effort to promote directly to consumers using different media, both traditional (e.g., mail) and digital (e.g., email). As your understanding of marketing grows, it is important to keep terms such as these distinct.

13-3b | Channels for Business and Industrial Products

As Exhibit 13.4 illustrates, five channel structures are common in business and industrial markets. First, direct channels are typical in business and industrial markets.

For example, manufacturers buy large quantities of raw materials, major equipment, processed materials, and supplies directly from other manufacturers. Manufacturers that require suppliers to meet detailed technical specifications often prefer direct channels. The direct communication required between Chrysler Canada and

EXHIBIT 13.4 CHANNELS FOR BUSINESS AND INDUSTRIAL PRODUCTS

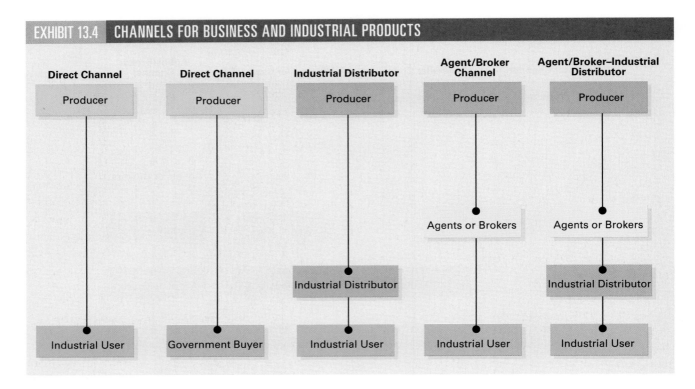

its suppliers, for example, along with the tremendous size of the orders, makes anything but a direct channel impractical. The channel from producer to government buyers is also a direct channel. Since much government buying is done through bidding, a direct channel is attractive.

Companies selling standardized items of moderate or low value often rely on *industrial distributors*. In many ways, an industrial distributor is like a supermarket for organizations. Industrial distributors are wholesalers and channel members that buy and take title to products. Moreover, they usually keep inventories of their products and sell and service them. Often, small manufacturers cannot afford to employ their own sales force. Instead, they rely on manufacturers' representatives or selling agents to sell to either industrial distributors or users, such as Sysco.

Many manufacturers and customers are bypassing distributors and going direct, often online. Companies looking to take on more intermediary duties from the supply chain have created online exchanges. For example, retailers that use the Worldwide Retail Exchange to make purchases (which in the past would have required telephone or face-to-face sales calls) save approximately 15 percent on their purchasing costs.

dual distribution (multiple distribution)
the use of two or more channels to distribute the same product to target markets

Finally, a different type of online marketplace emerging more frequently is a private exchange. Private exchanges allow companies to automate their supply chains while sharing information only with select suppliers. Dell, IBM, and Hewlett-Packard, for example, use private exchanges to manage their inventory supplies and reduce distribution and freight costs.[7]

13-3c | Alternative Channel Arrangements

Producer rarely use just one type of channel to move product; they usually employ several different or alternative channels, which include multiple channels, nontraditional channels, and strategic channel alliances.

MULTIPLE CHANNELS When a producer selects two or more channels to distribute the same product to target markets, this arrangement is called **dual distribution** (or **multiple distribution**). As more people have access to the Internet and embrace online shopping, an increasing number of retailers are choosing to use multiple distribution channels. For example, Starbucks sells its products not only in its retail locations but also on grocery store shelves. Nestlé paid more than $7 billion in 2018 for the worldwide rights to sell Starbucks coffee in grocery stores.[8] Not only will Nestlé have control over Starbucks products like ground coffee and coffee pods, but also it will be able to sell other Starbucks-owned brands like Seattle's Best Coffee and Teavana. The Starbucks

Sheila Fitzgerald/Shutterstock.com

deal for Nestlé netted the company more than $250 million in 2019 alone.[9]

NONTRADITIONAL CHANNELS Often nontraditional channel arrangements help differentiate a company's product from the competition. Nontraditional channels include the Internet, mail-order channels, and infomercials. Although nontraditional channels may limit a brand's coverage, for a producer serving a niche market, they provide a way to gain market access and customer attention without having to establish channel intermediaries.

Nontraditional channels can also provide another avenue of sales for larger companies. For example, vending machines, which are often associated with dispensing pop, snacks, or cash, are taking on new roles. Sometimes you can find non-food products in vending machines, such as the short-lived experiment of Redbox movie rentals in Canada from 2012 to 2015. There are also surgical mask vending machines in Japan, pet food for stray animals in vending machines in Turkey, and vending machines stocked with cars in China.[10]

STRATEGIC CHANNEL ALLIANCES Companies often form **strategic channel alliances**, which are cooperative agreements between business companies to use one of the manufacturer's already established channels. Alliances are used most often when the creation of marketing channel relationships may be too expensive and time-consuming. The Nestlé–Starbucks partnership has allowed Starbucks to gain a foothold in the grocery market, and Nestlé has not had to give up control of its higher-end Nespresso line of products to the grocery store aisles since it can focus on delivering Starbucks products as higher-end options for grocery store consumers. The success in alliances is especially true in global markets where cultural differences, distance, and other barriers can prove challenging. This is particularly true for Nestlé as it has been able to leverage its alliance with Starbucks to access more than 50 international markets.

13-4 | MAKING CHANNEL STRATEGY DECISIONS

Devising a marketing channel strategy requires several critical decisions. Supply chain managers must decide what role distribution will play in the overall marketing strategy. In addition, they must be sure that the channel strategy chosen is consistent with product, promotion, and pricing strategies. In making these decisions, marketing managers must determine which factors will influence the choice of channel and the appropriate level of distribution intensity.

13-4a | Factors Affecting Channel Choice

The selection of marketing channel depends on the supply chain manager's desired distribution channel objectives with regard to coverage, costs, and control of the products. First, the supply chain manager analyzes several factors that often interact. These factors can be grouped as market factors, product factors, and producer factors.

MARKET FACTORS Among the most important market factors affecting the choice of distribution channel are target customer considerations. Specifically, supply chain managers should answer the following questions: Who are the potential customers? What do they buy? Where do they buy? When do they buy? How do they buy? Additionally, the choice of channel depends on whether the producer is selling to consumers or to industrial customers. Industrial customers tend to buy in larger quantities and often require more customer service than consumers. In contrast, consumers usually buy in very small quantities and sometimes do not mind if they receive little or no service, such as when shopping in discount stores like Walmart.

The geographic location and the size of the market are also important in channel selection. As a rule, if the target market is concentrated in one or more specific areas, then direct selling through a sales force is appropriate. When markets are more widely dispersed,

strategic channel alliances
cooperative agreements between business companies to use one of the manufacturer's already established distribution channels

Perishable products spoil if they don't reach customers in time, so they tend to benefit from shorter, more direct marketing channels.

Arina P Habich/Shutterstock.com

intermediaries are less expensive. The size of the market also influences channel choice. Generally, larger markets require more intermediaries. For instance, Procter & Gamble has to reach millions of consumers with its many brands of household goods. As a result, it needs many intermediaries, including wholesalers and retailers.

PRODUCT FACTORS Products that are more complex, customized, and expensive tend to benefit from shorter and more direct marketing channels. These types of products sell better through a direct sales force. Examples are pharmaceuticals, scientific instruments, and aerospace. On the other hand, the more standardized a product is, the longer its distribution channel can be and the greater the number of intermediaries that can be involved. For example, with the exception of flavour and shape, the formula for chewing gum is about the same from producer to producer. Chewing gum is also very inexpensive, so the distribution channel for gum tends to involve many wholesalers and retailers.

The product's life cycle is also an important factor in choosing a marketing channel. In fact, the choice of channel may change over the life of the product. As products become more common and less intimidating to potential users, producers tend to look for alternative channels. Brokerhouse Distributors, a leading wholesale supplier in Canada, started out selling vending machines, but now offers customers an array of products. Instead of just selling machines that dispense chocolate bars or cans of soft drinks, Brokerhouse provides the hospitality industry in Canada with everything from professional milk frothers to water coolers.[11]

Another factor is the delicacy of the product. Perishable products, such as vegetables and milk, have a relatively short lifespan. Therefore, they require fairly short marketing channels. Today, consumers' desire for fresh and organic produce has led to a renewed growth across Canada in farmers' markets and in businesses delivering these products from the farm directly to consumers' homes. In the last Canadian census, close to 25 000 Canadian farms reported selling agriculture products directly to consumers.[12]

PRODUCER FACTORS In general, producers with large financial, managerial, and marketing resources are better able to use more direct channels. These producers have the ability to hire and train their own sales force, warehouse their own goods, and extend credit to their customers. Smaller or weaker companies, on the other hand, must rely on intermediaries to provide these services. Compared with producers that have only one or two product lines, producers that sell several products in a related area are able to choose channels that are more direct, so their sales expenses can be spread over more products.

A producer's desire to control pricing, positioning, brand image, and customer support also tends to influence channel selection. For instance, companies that sell products with exclusive brand images, such as designer perfumes and clothing, usually avoid channels in which discount retailers are present, preferring instead to sell their wares only in expensive stores to maintain an image of exclusivity. Many producers have opted to risk their image, however, and test sales in discount channels. Some well-recognized brands will work directly with discount retailers like Dollarama to get overstock and

McCain Foods channels are varied across Canada, depending on the nature of the product it sells— from French fries for consumers to appetizers for restaurants.

The Canadian Press/Lethbridge Herald-David Rossiter

discontinued items on to a Dollarama shelf and for Dollarama, getting these "rejects" can be profitable business.[13]

13-4b | Levels of Distribution Intensity

Organizations have three options for intensity of distribution: intensive distribution, selective distribution, or exclusive distribution.

INTENSIVE DISTRIBUTION

Intensive distribution is a form of distribution aimed at maximum market coverage. **Coverage** refers to ensuring product availability in every outlet where potential customers might want to buy it. If buyers are unwilling to search for a product (as is true of convenience goods and operating supplies), then the product must be very accessible to buyers.

Most manufacturers pursuing an intensive distribution strategy sell to a large percentage of the wholesalers willing to stock their products. Retailers' willingness (or unwillingness) to handle items tends to control the manufacturer's ability to achieve intensive distribution. For products like soft drinks it is important that manufacturers get the product out to as many different retailers as possible. Whether it is at a five-star restaurant or a vending machine at a postsecondary institution, soft drink providers try to be in as many places as consumers would expect them to be when looking for a soft drink.

SELECTIVE DISTRIBUTION

Selective distribution is achieved by screening dealers and retailers to eliminate all but a few in any single area. Because only a few are chosen, the consumer must seek out the product. Canada Goose, the famous and successful Canadian outfitter, initially sold its product almost exclusively to scientists and actors working in extreme winter conditions. Eventually the company offered its products in select stores in Europe, and in 2016 began opening up its own branded stores. While you still cannot buy Canada Goose products everywhere, more retailers (like Sporting Life) are carrying the expensive yet popular Canadian apparel company's products.[14]

Rich Fury/Getty Images

Selective distribution strategies often hinge on a manufacturer's desire to maintain a superior product image so as to be able to charge a premium price.

EXCLUSIVE DISTRIBUTION

The most restrictive form of market coverage is **exclusive distribution**, which is a form of distribution that involves only one or a few dealers within a given area. Because buyers may have to search or travel extensively to buy the product, exclusive distribution is usually confined to consumer specialty goods, a few shopping goods, and major industrial equipment. Sometimes, exclusive territories are granted by new companies (such as franchisers) to obtain market coverage in a particular area. Limited distribution may also serve to project an exclusive image for the product. With increased confidence placed in buying online by consumers, more companies can afford to create an exclusive distribution setup, simply by creating an online portal through their website to exclusively sell their products.

Retailers and wholesalers may be unwilling to commit the time and money necessary to promote and service a product unless the manufacturer guarantees them an exclusive territory. This arrangement shields the dealer from direct competition and enables it to be the main beneficiary of the manufacturer's promotion efforts in that geographic area. In an exclusive distribution, channels of communication are usually well established because the manufacturer works with a limited number of dealers rather than many accounts.

Exclusive distribution also takes place within a retailer's store rather than a geographic area—for example, when a retailer

intensive distribution
a form of distribution aimed at having a product available in every outlet where target customers might want to buy it

coverage
ensuring product availability in every outlet where potential customers might want to buy it

selective distribution
a form of distribution achieved by screening dealers to eliminate all but a few in any single area

exclusive distribution
form of distribution that involves only one or a few dealers within a given area

does not sell many other competing brands. Companies like Loblaw are increasingly turning to their own product lines in order to meet the needs of consumers. The Canadian food retail giant has three well-known private label brands: No Name, President's Choice, and Life Brand.[15]

13-5 | HANDLING CHANNEL RELATIONSHIPS

A marketing channel is more than a set of institutions linked by economic ties. Social relationships play an important role in building unity among channel members. A critical aspect of supply chain management, therefore, is managing the social relationships among channel members to achieve synergy. The basic social dimensions of channels are power, control, leadership, conflict, and partnering.

13-5a | Channel Power, Control, and Leadership

Channel power is a channel member's capacity to control or influence the behaviour of other channel members. **Channel control** occurs when one channel member intentionally affects another member's behaviour. To achieve control, a channel member assumes channel leadership and exercises authority and power. This member is termed the **channel leader**, or **channel captain**. In one marketing channel, a manufacturer may be the leader because it controls new-product designs and product availability. In another marketing channel, a retailer may be the channel leader because it wields power and control over the retail price, inventory levels, and post-sale service.

The exercise of channel power is a routine element of many business activities in which the outcome is often greater control over a company's brands. Indigo is considered to be a channel captain in the world of Canadian book publishing. When Chapters and Indigo merged in 2001, the newly combined entity was forced to sell 23 stores to adhere to federal competition laws.[16] Indigo has strict rules for book distributors—if you don't have physical distribution capabilities (i.e., a physical warehouse) you will not be working with the company.[17] The book retailer provides unparalleled distribution of books across Canada, and if you are an aspiring author, publisher, or distributor, you probably want to build a strong relationship with Indigo.

13-5b | Channel Conflict

Inequitable channel relationships often lead to **channel conflict**, which is a clash of goals and methods among distribution channel members. In a broad context, conflict may not be bad. Often it arises because staid, traditional channel members refuse to keep pace with the times. Removing an outdated intermediary may result in reduced costs for the entire supply chain. The Internet has forced many intermediaries to offer online services, such as merchandise tracking and inventory availability.

Conflicts among channel members can be due to many different situations and factors. Often, conflict arises because channel members have conflicting goals, as was the case with Apple and its distributors. Conflict can also arise when channel members fail to fulfill expectations of other channel members—for example, when a franchisee does not follow the rules set down by the franchiser or when communications channels break down between channel members. Further, ideological differences and different perceptions of reality can also cause conflict among channel members. For instance, some retailers, believing the customer is always right, may offer a very forgiving return policy. Conversely, some wholesalers and manufacturers may feel that people often try to get something for nothing or don't follow product instructions carefully. These differing views of allowable returns will undoubtedly conflict with those of retailers.

Conflict within a channel can be either horizontal or vertical. **Horizontal conflict** is a channel conflict that occurs among channel members on the same level, such as two or more different wholesalers or two or more

---

channel power
a marketing channel member's capacity to control or influence the behaviour of other channel members

channel control
one marketing channel member intentionally affects another member's behaviour

channel leader (channel captain)
a member of a marketing channel who exercises authority and power over the activities of other channel members

channel conflict
a clash of goals and methods among distribution channel members

horizontal conflict
a channel conflict that occurs among channel members on the same level

different retailers that handle the same manufacturer's brands. This type of channel conflict is found most often when manufacturers practise dual or multiple distributions. Horizontal conflict can also occur when channel members feel that other members on the same level are being treated differently by the manufacturer, such as only some channel members receiving substantial discounts. An example of a horizontal conflict is a turf war, where a manufacturer does not clearly stipulate the geographical ranges and restrictions for its distributors. This leads to conflict between the two distributors, which are both at the same level in the distribution channel system.

Many regard horizontal conflict as healthy competition. Much more serious is **vertical conflict**, which occurs between different levels in a marketing channel, most typically between the manufacturer and wholesaler or the manufacturer and retailer. Producer-versus-wholesaler conflict occurs when the producer chooses to bypass the wholesaler and deal directly with the consumer or retailer.

Dual distribution strategies can also cause vertical conflict in the channel, such as when high-end fashion designers sell their goods through their own boutiques and luxury department stores. Similarly, manufacturers experimenting with selling to customers directly over the Internet create conflict with their traditional retailing intermediaries. Producers and retailers may also disagree over the terms of the sale or other aspects of the business relationship. Some manufacturers use a pricing tactic called resale price maintenance, where a supplier may try to prevent a reseller from selling its products at a low price. The tactics used can involve agreements or even threats. This is considered illegal by Canada's Competition Bureau.[18]

13-5c | Channel Partnering

Regardless of the locus of power, channel members rely heavily on one another. Even the most powerful manufacturers depend on retailers to sell their products; and even the most powerful retailers require the products provided by suppliers. In sharp contrast to the adversarial relationships of the past between buyers and sellers, contemporary management emphasizes the development of close working partnerships among channel members. **Channel partnering**, or **channel cooperation**, is the joint effort of all channel members to create a supply chain that serves customers and creates a competitive advantage. Channel partnering is vital if each member is to gain something from other members. By cooperating,

The key to the success of Ionity is the collaboration and cooperation of businesses and governments across Europe.

retailers, wholesalers, manufacturers, and suppliers can speed up inventory replenishment, improve customer service, and reduce the total costs of the marketing channel.

Channel alliances and partnerships help supply chain managers create the parallel flow of materials and information required to leverage the supply chain's intellectual, material, and marketing resources. The rapid growth in channel partnering is due to new technology and the need to lower costs. Collaborating channel partners meet the needs of customers more effectively, thus boosting sales and profits. Forced to become more efficient, many companies are turning formerly adversarial relationships into partnerships.

An example of a successful channel alliance is seen in the creation of Ionity, a charging station for electric vehicles. Car companies that normally compete for customer business—Ford, Mercedes, BMW, and Volkswagen—worked together in 2017 to create a standard high-power voltage station for their electric vehicles in the European market. Ionity is one network for multiple car companies' products, and was created to provide a consistent experience for

vertical conflict
a channel conflict that occurs between different levels in a marketing channel, most typically between the manufacturer and wholesaler or between the manufacturer and retailer

channel partnering (channel cooperation)
the joint effort of all channel members to create a supply chain that serves customers and creates a competitive advantage

electric vehicle drivers, no matter what logo is on their steering wheel. As of late 2019, Ionity had over 150 charging stations across Europe, with the goal of reaching 400 by the end of 2020.[19]

13-6 | MANAGING THE SUPPLY CHAIN

A supply chain consists of a group of companies working together to produce, handle, and distribute products to an end customer. Many modern companies are turning to **supply chain management** to coordinate and integrate all the activities performed by supply chain members into a seamless process, from the source to the point of consumption, ultimately giving supply chain managers total visualization of the supply chain, both inside and outside the company, and gaining a competitive advantage.

Supply chain management is mostly customer driven. In the mass-production era, manufacturers produced standardized products that were pushed down through the supply channel to the consumer. In today's marketplace, however, products are being driven by customers, who expect to receive product configurations and services matched to their unique needs. The focus is on pulling products into the marketplace and partnering with members of the supply chain to enhance customer value. Customizing an automobile is now possible because of new supply chain relationships between the automobile manufacturers and the after-market auto-parts industry.[20]

This reversal of the flow of demand from a push to a pull has resulted in a radical reformulation of market expectations and traditional marketing, production, and distribution functions. Integrated channel partnerships allow companies to respond with the unique product configuration and mix of services demanded by the customer. Today, supply chain management is both a *communicator* of customer demand that extends from the point of sale all the way back to the supplier, and a *physical flow* process that engineers the timely and cost-effective movement of goods through the entire supply pipeline.

supply chain management
a management system that coordinates and integrates all the activities performed by supply chain members into a seamless process, from the source to the point of consumption, resulting in enhanced customer and economic value

13-6a | Benefits of Supply Chain Management

Supply chain management is both a key means of differentiation for a company and a critical component in marketing and corporate strategy. Companies that focus on supply chain management commonly report lower costs of inventory, transportation, warehousing, and packaging; greater supply chain flexibility; improved customer service; and higher revenues. Research has shown a clear relationship between supply chain performance and profitability.

A company that has benefited greatly from the use of supply chain is the fashion retailer Zara. In order to stay ahead in the fashion game, Zara has turned the world of supply chain upside down. Instead of starting with fashions and designs that are then put through the supply chain, Zara scans the external environment for the trends that are most likely to be sought after in the global fashion industry. These trends are analyzed and sent to Zara designers who create products that are reflective of the fashion trends. The key for Zara is in the plural "designers"; as most competitors, such as H&M, have a head designer, which limits the ability to be truly innovative and "fashion forward."

Zara's agile supply chain is executed due to multiple manufacturing, distribution, and retail centres around the world. Local partners are used to provide raw materials, and state-of-the-art software is applied to all levels of its supply chain. Zara averages about 10 to 15 days to bring a new item from concept to the shop floor. Competitors like UK-based retailer Asos take from four to six weeks.[21]

This flexibility in and control of a supply chain has translated into business success for Zara. It achieved sales of over CDN$38 billion in 2018 to 2019, with more than 2000 stores worldwide, and 300 new stores in 2018 to 2019 alone.[22]

Xurxo Lobato/Cover/Getty Images

Zara's nimble supply chain allows the company to bring new trends to market in a fraction of the time of other fashion retailers.

13-6b | Managing Logistics in the Supply Chain

Critical to any supply chain is orchestrating the physical means through which products move through it. **Logistics** is the process of strategically managing the efficient flow and storage of raw materials, in-process inventory, and finished goods from point of origin to point of consumption. As mentioned earlier, supply chain management coordinates and integrates all the activities performed by supply chain members into a seamless process. The supply chain consists of several interrelated and integrated logistical components: (1) sourcing and procurement of raw materials and supplies, (2) production scheduling, (3) order processing, and (4) inventory control.

The **logistics information system** is the link connecting all the logistics components of the supply chain. The components of the system include, for example, software for materials acquisition and handling, warehouse management and enterprise-wide solutions, data storage and integration in data warehouses, mobile communications, electronic data interchange, radio-frequency identification (RFID) chips, and the Internet. Working together, the components of the logistics information system are the fundamental enablers of successful supply chain management.

The **supply chain team**, in concert with the logistics information system, orchestrates the movement of goods, services, and information from the source to the consumer. Supply chain teams typically cut across organizational boundaries, embracing all parties that participate in moving the product to market. The best supply chain teams also move beyond the organization to include the external participants in the chain, such as suppliers, transportation carriers, and third-party logistics suppliers. Members of the supply chain communicate, coordinate, and cooperate extensively.

13-6c | Sourcing and Procurement

One of the most important links in the supply chain occurs between the manufacturer and the supplier. Purchasing professionals are on the front lines of supply chain management. Purchasing departments plan purchasing strategies, develop specifications, select suppliers, and negotiate price and service levels.

The goal of most sourcing and **procurement** activities is to reduce the costs of raw materials and supplies. Purchasing professionals have traditionally relied on tough negotiations to get the lowest price possible from suppliers of raw materials, supplies, and components.

Perhaps the biggest contribution purchasing can make to supply chain management, however, is in the area of vendor relations. Companies can use the purchasing function to strategically manage suppliers to reduce the total cost of materials and services: through enhanced vendor relations, both buyers and sellers can develop cooperative relationships that reduce costs and improve efficiency with the aim of lowering prices and enhancing profits.

13-6d | Production Scheduling

In traditional mass-market manufacturing, production begins when forecasts call for additional products to be made or when inventory control systems signal low inventory levels. The company then makes a product and transports the finished goods to its own warehouses or those of intermediaries, where the goods wait to be ordered by retailers or customers. For example, many types of convenience goods, such as toothpaste, deodorant, and detergent, are manufactured on the basis of past sales and demand and then sent to retailers to resell. Production scheduling that is based on pushing a product down to the consumer obviously has its disadvantages, the most notable being that companies risk making products that may become obsolete or that consumers don't want in the first place.

In a customer "pull" manufacturing environment, which is growing in popularity, production of goods or services is not scheduled until an order is placed by the customer specifying the desired configuration. This process, known as **mass customization**, or **build-to-order**,

logistics
the process of strategically managing the efficient flow and storage of raw materials, in-process inventory, and finished goods from point of origin to point of consumption

logistics information system
the link that connects all the logistics functions of the supply chain

supply chain team
a group of individuals who orchestrate the movement of goods, services, and information from the source to the consumer

procurement
the process of buying goods and services for use in the operations of an organization

mass customization (build-to-order)
a production method whereby products are not made until an order is placed by the customer; products are made according to customer specifications

Harvey's creates a "just-in-time" experience for its customers when the company offers a variety of options and alternatives that are fresh and in front of their customers.

Courtesy of Harvey's Canada

uniquely tailors mass-market goods and services to the needs of the individuals who buy them. Companies as diverse as BMW, Dell, Levi Strauss, Mattel, and a host of online businesses are adopting mass customization to maintain or obtain a competitive edge.

As more companies move toward mass customization —and away from mass marketing—of goods, the need to stay on top of consumer demand is forcing manufacturers to make their supply chains more flexible. Flexibility is critical to a manufacturer's success when responding to dramatic swings in demand. To meet consumers' demand for customized products, companies must adapt their manufacturing approach or even create a completely new process. An excellent example of mass customization matched with new technology is Invisalign. Customers visit a dentist or doctor to inquire about cosmetic dentistry as an option to improve the alignment of their smile. A digital scan is performed without the invasiveness of other dental techniques like braces or dentures. Information from the scan is then sent to a facility in Mexico where an individualized scan is developed among thousands of other for smiles worldwide. Doctors in over 100 countries have used the Invisalign system for their patients, from children through adults. The Invisalign system provides customization for each individual

just-in-time production (JIT)
a process that redefines and simplifies manufacturing by reducing inventory levels and delivering raw materials just when they are needed on the production line

order processing system
a system whereby orders are entered into the supply chain and filled

mouth, but does so on a massive scale—more than 7.5 million people have used the Invisalign system.[23]

JUST-IN-TIME MANUFACTURING An important manufacturing process common today among manufacturers is just-in-time manufacturing. Borrowed from the Japanese, **just-in-time production (JIT)**, sometimes called *lean production,* requires manufacturers to work closely with suppliers and transportation providers to get necessary items to the assembly line or factory floor at the precise time they are needed for production. For the manufacturer, JIT means that raw materials arrive at the assembly line in guaranteed working order "just in time" to be installed, and finished products are generally shipped to the customer immediately after completion. For the supplier, JIT means supplying customers with products in just a few days, or even a few hours, rather than weeks. For the ultimate end-user, JIT means lower costs, shorter lead times, and products that more closely meet the consumer's needs. Companies that have taken the leap to JIT have found substantial impacts on their business operations. Fast food companies like Harvey's have everything on hand for customers, but will not make the final product until the customer arrives, pays for their order, and makes their specific request.

13-6e | Order Processing

The order is often the catalyst that sets the supply chain in motion, especially in build-to-order environments. The **order processing system** processes the requirements of the customer and sends the information into the supply chain via the logistics information system. The order goes to the manufacturer's warehouse. If the

Today's companies rely on sophisticated software to help them control inventories.

product is in stock, the order is filled and arrangements are made to ship it. If the product is not in stock, it triggers a replenishment request that finds its way to the factory floor.

Proper order processing is critical to good service. As an order enters the system, management must monitor two flows: the flow of goods and the flow of information. Good communication among sales representatives, office personnel, and warehouse and shipping personnel is essential to accurate order processing. Shipping incorrect merchandise or partially filled orders can create just as much dissatisfaction as stockouts or slow deliveries. The flow of goods and information must be continually monitored so that mistakes can be corrected before an invoice is prepared and the merchandise shipped.

Order processing is becoming more automated through the use of computer technology known as **electronic data interchange (EDI)**. EDI replaces the paper documents that usually accompany business transactions, such as purchase orders and invoices, with electronic transmission of the needed information. A typical EDI message includes all the information that would traditionally be included on a paper invoice, such as product code, quantity, and transportation details. The information is usually sent via private networks, which are more secure and reliable than the networks used for standard email messages. Most importantly, the information can be read and processed by computers, significantly reducing costs and increasing efficiency. Companies that use EDI can reduce inventory levels, improve cash flow, streamline operations, and increase the speed and accuracy of information transmission. EDI also creates a closer relationship between buyers and sellers.

EDI works hand in hand with retailers' *efficient consumer response* programs to ensure the right products are on the shelf, in the right styles and colours, at the right time, through improved techniques for tracking inventory, ordering, and distribution. Canadian Pacific Railway, one of Canada's oldest companies, uses EDI for its interactions with suppliers and other partners. CP is one of the few companies to provide information about EDI on its About page. There, CP lists the rules for EDI, detailing transaction types and available software.

13-6f | Inventory Control

The **inventory control system** develops and maintains an adequate assortment of materials or products to meet a manufacturer's or a customer's demands. Inventory decisions, for both raw materials and finished goods, have a significant impact on supply chain costs and the level of service provided. If too many products are kept in inventory, costs increase—as do risks of obsolescence, theft, and damage shrinkage. If too few products are kept on hand, then the company risks product shortages, angry customers, and ultimately lost sales. The goal of inventory management, therefore, is to keep inventory levels as low as possible while maintaining an adequate supply of goods to meet customer demand.

As you would expect, JIT has a significant impact on reducing inventory levels. Because supplies are delivered exactly when they are needed on the factory floor, little inventory of any kind is needed, and companies can order materials in smaller quantities. Those lower inventory levels can give companies a competitive edge through the flexibility to halt production of existing products in favour of those gaining popularity with consumers. Savings also come from having less capital tied up in inventory and from the reduced need for storage facilities. At the retail level, the reduced need for storage

electronic data interchange (EDI)
information technology that replaces the paper documents that usually accompany business transactions, such as purchase orders and invoices, with electronic transmission of the needed information to reduce inventory levels, improve cash flow, streamline operations, and increase the speed and accuracy of information transmission

inventory control system
a method of developing and maintaining an adequate assortment of materials or products to meet a manufacturer's or a customer's demand

Using 3DP technology, objects are built to precise specifications using raw materials at or near the location where they will be consumed.

space allows for more extensive use of the retail store's area (its real estate space) for the display of more products to its customers.

13-7 | DISTRIBUTION CHALLENGES IN WORLD MARKETS

With the spread of free-trade agreements and treaties, global marketing channels and management of the supply chain have become increasingly important to corporations that export their products or manufacture abroad.

13-7a | Developing Global Marketing Channels

electronic distribution
a distribution technique that includes any kind of product or service that can be distributed electronically, whether over traditional forms such as fibre-optic cable or through satellite transmission of electronic signals

Manufacturers introducing products in global markets must decide which type of channel structure to use. Using company salespeople generally provides more control and is less risky than using foreign intermediaries. However, setting up a sales force in a foreign country also involves a greater commitment, both financially and organizationally.

Channel structures and types abroad may differ from those in North America. For instance, the more highly developed a nation is economically, the more specialized its channel types. Therefore, a marketer wanting to sell in Germany or Japan will have several channel types to choose from. Conversely, developing countries, such as India, Ethiopia, and Venezuela, have limited channel types available: typically, these countries have few mail-order channels, vending machines, or specialized retailers and wholesalers.

13-7b | Electronic Distribution

Electronic distribution is the most recent development in the logistics arena. Broadly defined, **electronic distribution** includes any kind of product or service that can be distributed electronically, whether over traditional forms such as fibre-optic cable or through satellite transmission of electronic signals. Companies like E*TRADE, Apple (iTunes), and Movies.com have built their business models around electronic distribution.

In the near future, however, electronic distribution will not be limited only to products and services that are mostly composed of information that can therefore be easily digitized. For example, experiments with **three-dimensional printing (3DP)** have been successful in industries such as auto parts, biomedical, and even fast food. Using 3DP technology, objects are built to precise specifications using raw materials at or near the location where they will be consumed. Lowe's Home Improvement Stores hopes to alleviate the need to carry vast quantities of rarely purchased inventory by installing kiosks where customers can design and print their own doorknobs, lamps, and replacement parts.[24] Shipping raw materials such as powdered brass or ceramic composite is cheaper than shipping finished products because these materials can be packaged in perfectly cubic containers, making transportation much more efficient and cost effective. Raw materials are used only when they are needed, so virtually no waste is produced during printing. The potential uses for 3DP are virtually endless. Of recent note, 3D printer manufacturer ByFlow has partnered with FoodInk and 3DSamba to open FoodRush, the first pop-up restaurant where "prepared" meals can be 3D printed for immediate consumption. Ingredients for dishes such as salads, fish and chips, and even steak are turned into a pulp and are combined together to make creations that are printed and eaten on the spot![25]

Many industry experts project that 3DP (also referred to as *additive manufacturing*) will radically transform the ways global supply chains work by changing the basic platforms of business. With 3DP, smaller, localized supply chains will become the norm, and small manufacturers will produce many more custom products than ever before over very short lead times. Research shows that additive manufacturing has the potential to lower the energy needed to produce goods by as much as 5 percent and lower carbon emissions as well.[26] Furthermore, because such platforms will remove much of the need for transportation of finished goods to distribution centres and retailers, 3DP is expected to have a very positive impact on businesses' carbon footprints and the environment. At the same time, these platforms should make it possible to deliver unique goods more quickly, creating perceptions of better service.

three-dimensional printing (3DP)
the creation of three-dimensional objects via an additive manufacturing (printing) technology that layers raw material into desired shapes

AWAKE CHOCOLATE
CONTINUING CASE

A Taste for Channel Success

It's rare for a food product to trace its success back to when it was able to mask the flavour of its most important ingredient. But that is the case for Awake Chocolate. And solving this huge challenge started in a very unconventional place.

February 12, 2011: Dan Tzotzis' kitchen. This is when and where the first prototype of an Awake bar was created. The three founders of Awake, whom you now should know, plus a friend, put together ingredients to create a chocolate bar infused with caffeine. But the biggest challenge was dealing with that key ingredient. The amount of caffeine that Awake wanted to put into its bars, Dan noted, "would completely ruin the taste of chocolate. Caffeine (in a more pure form) is a bitter and heinous ingredient." The aftertaste lasts 90 minutes.

"We found a way that we mask the taste of caffeine, coating the caffeine in a food-based ingredient (soybean oil), [and] rendering the caffeine tasteless," said Dan. They secured the "masked caffeine" from a supplier in the United States and realized they had a viable proposition—all thanks a supplier that to this day remains part of Awake's marketing channel.

As Dan said: "Had we not discovered this supplier, we would not have been able to proceed." Awake has continued to be thankful for its marketing channel members. From the start, it relied on a chocolate manufacturer to navigate the tricky world of food ingredients. Dan remembered: "We worked with our current manufacturing facility and told them what kind of taste profile we were looking for in a chocolate bar. … and they … brought our vision to life."

Dan was effusive in his praise: "We had a lot of help from our current manufacturing facility. When you're trying to commercialize this on a grander scale, we needed the help of experts. We knew what we knew [and used] the experts of those in the field to bring it to life for us."

And this has become the formula for success for Awake Chocolate. From Dan's Kitchen to today, the company is always seeking out assistance from its supply chain and marketing channel in order to achieve its overarching vision. With a singular focus on quality in its channel network, Awake has been able to achieve great levels of success. As Adam stated, "The first, second, and third priorities when we started was taste." And when a singular focus drives either side of your supply chain and marketing channels, the result can be very satisfying—without the bitter aftertaste.

QUESTIONS

1. Create an infographic using a free online software program. On the infographic, draw out the channel system that Awake Chocolate uses. Be sure to include important characteristics for success from the textbook and your course notes.

2. Using information from previous chapters, provide some specific reasons that Awake Chocolate has been so successful with using nontraditional channels.

3. Describe the factors of a strong supply chain that Awake Chocolate will have to adhere to if it wants to continue to create new product innovations in the future.

Radu Bercan/Shutterstock.com

AWAKE
CAFFEINATED CHOCOLATE™

14 | Retailing

LEARNING OUTCOMES

14-1 Discuss the importance of retailing in the Canadian economy

14-2 Explain the ways in which retailers can be classified and the major types of retail operations

14-3 Discuss nonstore retailing techniques and franchising

14-4 Define franchising and describe its two basic forms

14-5 List the major tasks involved in developing a retail marketing strategy

14-6 Discuss retail product and service failures and means to improve

14-7 Discuss retailer and retail consumer trends that will affect retailing in the future

"You can't get away with retail being just a transactional space anymore. Customers want an experience. Retailers need to make their experience memorable—even before it starts and after it ends."

—Anne Forkutza, Creative Strategist, iQmetrix[1]

14-1 | THE ROLE OF RETAILING

Retailing—all the activities directly related to the sale of goods and services to the ultimate consumer for personal, nonbusiness use—has enhanced the quality of our daily lives. When we shop, whether online or in store, for a variety of products and services, we are involved in retailing.

Retailing affects all of us directly or indirectly. The retailing industry is one of the largest employers in Canada and is an industry being pushed to innovate. A retailer is a market intermediary that sells goods and services to the final consumer. Retailers ring up over $600 billion in sales annually, contributing over $100 billion to Canada's GDP.[2] The retail sector is the largest industry in Canada, employing over 2 million people.[3] Global retailers are successfully entering the Canadian market and challenging domestic retailers. Canadian consumers are changing quickly and expect retailers to anticipate their changing needs and offer personalized shopping experiences. Consumers continue to shop online from every device and invest a significant amount of their time in social media. Technology also been changing the retail experience for consumers with smart shopping carts and apps that allow you order before you even enter the store. Shopping is becoming more of a social experience with more and more retailers adding additional features like restaurants in their stores. The Canadian economy is heavily dependent on retailing, and although many of the jobs are casual and young workers dominate the industry, it serves as a key driver to our economy.[4]

retailing
all the activities directly related to the sale of goods and services to the ultimate consumer for personal, non-business use

The retailing landscape in Canada is dotted with small independents surrounded by large chains. Successful retailers are those that have built trusted relationships with their shoppers. The market research company BrandSpark International conducted a study of more than 5000 Canadians to identify their most trusted retailers and found that the most trusted retailers across Canada included Ikea and Home Depot. The most trusted in the auto parts and accessories category is the iconic Canadian retailer Canadian Tire, and the most trusted in the discount store category was Dollarama.[5]

14-2 | CLASSIFICATION AND TYPES OF RETAIL OPERATIONS

A retail establishment can be classified according to its ownership, level of service, product assortment, and price. Traditionally, retailers fall into several types of stores based on their classification, such as a department store or supermarket, but recently retailers have started to combine these formats.

14-2a | Classification of Retail Operations

Classification of retailers by ownership is straightforward and simple; however, retailers use the classification variables of level of service, product assortment, and price to position themselves in the competitive marketplace. Positioning is the strategy used to influence how consumers perceive a product or company in relation to all competing products or companies. These four variables can be combined in several ways to create distinctly different retail operations.

OWNERSHIP Retailers can be broadly classified by form of ownership: independent, part of a chain, or a franchise outlet. Retailers owned by a single person or partnership and not operated as part of a larger retail institution are **independent retailers**. Around the world, most retailers are independent, operating one or a few stores in their community.

independent retailers retailers owned by a single person or partnership and not operated as part of a larger retail institution

In many communities there is a resurgence of local independent retail, particularly in specialty gift shops.

Chain stores are owned and operated as a group by a single organization. Under this form of ownership, the head office for the entire chain handles many administrative tasks. The head office also buys most of the merchandise sold in the stores. Gap and Starbucks are examples of chains.

Franchises, such as Subway and Tim Hortons, are owned and operated by individuals but are licensed by a larger supporting organization. The franchising approach combines the advantages of independent ownership with those of the chain store organization. Franchises are discussed in more detail later in the chapter.

LEVEL OF SERVICE The level of service that retailers provide can be classified along a continuum, from full service to self-service. Some retailers, such as exclusive clothing stores, offer high levels of service. They provide alterations, credit, delivery, consulting, liberal return policies, layaway, gift wrapping, and personal shopping. By contrast, retailers such as factory outlets and warehouse clubs offer virtually no services. After stock is set out for sale, the customer is responsible for any information gathering, acquisition, handling, use, and product assembly. At the extreme low end of the service continuum, a retailer may take the form of a product kiosk or vending machine.

PRODUCT ASSORTMENT The third basis for positioning or classifying stores is by the breadth and depth of their product line. Specialty stores—for example, Maison Birks—have the most concentrated product assortments, usually carrying single or narrow product lines but in considerable depth. On the other end of the spectrum, full-line discounters typically carry broad assortments of merchandise with limited depth. For example, Costco carries automotive supplies, household cleaning products, furniture, and appliances. Typically, though, it carries a very limited

selection of appliances. In contrast, a specialty appliance store such as Goemans Appliances, a family-owned and -operated retailer with eight locations in southwestern Ontario, carries a seemingly endless number of makes and models of every appliance imaginable.

Other retailers, such as factory outlet stores, may carry only part of a single line. Nike stores sell only certain items of its own brand. Discount specialty stores, such as Best Buy and Toys "R" Us, carry a broad assortment in concentrated product lines, such as electronics and toys.

PRICE Price is a fourth way to classify and position retail stores. Traditional department stores and specialty stores typically charge the full suggested retail price. In contrast, discounters, factory outlets, and off-price retailers use low prices as a major lure for shoppers.

The price level of a retailer generally matches the **gross margin** percentage. For example, a traditional jewellery store (specialty store) has high prices and high gross margins of approximately 50 percent. Gross margins can decline as a result of markdowns on merchandise during sale periods and price wars among competitors, when stores lower their prices on certain items in an effort to win customers.

14-2b | Major Types of Retail Operations

Recently, retailers have been experimenting with alternative formats that make it difficult to categorize them by the traditional classifications. For instance, supermarkets are expanding their nonfood items and services. Loblaw Companies Limited has been highly successful with the launch of the Joe Fresh brand. Discounters like Walmart have added groceries; drugstores like Shoppers Drug Mart, which is now owned by Loblaws Companies Inc., are becoming more like convenience stores; and department stores, and even some discounters, are experimenting with smaller stores. Nevertheless, many stores still fall into one of the basic types. (See Exhibit 14.1.)

DEPARTMENT STORES **Department stores** such as the Hudson's Bay Company house several departments

chain stores
stores owned and operated as a group by a single organization

franchise
retailers that are owned and operated by individuals but are licensed by a larger supporting organization

gross margin
the amount of money the retailer makes as a percentage of sales after the cost of goods sold is subtracted

department store
a retail store that has several departments under one roof, carrying a wide variety of shopping and specialty goods

under one roof, carrying a wide variety of shopping and specialty goods, including apparel, cosmetics, housewares, electronics, and sometimes furniture. Purchases are generally made within each department rather than at one central checkout area. Each department is treated as a separate buying centre, but central management sets broad policies about the types of merchandise carried and price ranges. Central management is also responsible for the overall advertising program, credit policies, store expansion, customer service, and so on. While large independent department stores are not as common as in the past, there appears to be a renaissance. Simons, the Quebec-based, family-run department store is expanding across Canada with stores in Edmonton, Vancouver, and Toronto.[6] The Bay, which operates Hudson's Bay department stores across Canada, also operates Saks Fifth Avenue and Lord & Taylor in the United States.[7]

SPECIALTY STORES Specialty stores allow retailers to refine their segmentation strategies and tailor their merchandise to specific target markets. A typical specialty store carries a deeper but narrower assortment of merchandise within a single category of interest. The specialized knowledge of its salespeople allows for more attentive customer service. The Children's Place and Running Room are well-known specialty retailers.

Courtesy of Running Room Canada Inc.

SUPERMARKETS Supermarkets are large, departmentalized, self-service retailers that specialize in food and some nonfood items. Some conventional supermarkets are being replaced by much larger *superstores*. Superstores meet the needs of today's customers for convenience, variety, and service by offering one-stop shopping for many food and nonfood needs, as well as services such as pharmacists, florists, on-site prepared meals for takeaway, sit-down restaurants, photo processing kiosks, and banking centres. Some even offer optical shops, and many now have gas stations. This tendency to offer a wide variety of nontraditional goods and services under one roof is called **scrambled merchandising**.

To stand out in an increasingly competitive marketplace, supermarkets are tailoring their marketing strategies to appeal to specific consumer segments and individual consumers by utilizing the data captured through their *loyalty marketing programs*.

DRUGSTORES Drugstores stock pharmacy-related products and services as their main draw, but they also carry an extensive selection of over-the-counter (OTC) medications, cosmetics, health and beauty aids, seasonal merchandise, specialty items such as greeting cards and a limited selection of toys, and even refrigerated convenience foods. As competition has increased from mass merchandisers and supermarkets that have their own pharmacies, drugstores have added services such as 24-hour drive-through pharmacies and low-cost health clinics staffed by nurse practitioners. Drugstores are also selling more food products, including perishables.

CONVENIENCE STORES Convenience stores can be defined as miniature supermarkets, carrying a limited line of high-turnover convenience goods. There are over 12000 convenience stores in Canada, generating over $350 million in revenue.[8] These self-service stores, such as Quickie Convenience, and Alimentation Couche-Tard, which operates Mac's Convenience and Circle K stores, are typically located near residential areas, and many are open 24 hours, 7 days a week.

DISCOUNT STORES Discount stores compete on the basis of low prices, high turnover, and high volume. Discounters can be classified into following major categories:

- **Full-line discount stores** offer consumers very limited service and carry a much broader assortment of well-known, nationally branded hard goods, including housewares, toys, automotive parts, hardware, sporting goods, and garden

specialty store
a retail store that carries a deeper but narrower assortment of merchandise within a single category of interest

supermarkets
large, departmentalized, self-service retailers that specialize in food and some nonfood items

scrambled merchandising
the tendency to offer a wide variety of nontraditional goods and services under one roof

drugstores
retail stores that stock pharmacy-related products and services as their main draw

convenience store
a miniature supermarket, carrying only a limited line of high-turnover convenience goods

discount store
a retailer that competes on the basis of low prices, high turnover, and high volume

full-line discount stores
retailers that offer consumers very limited service and carry a broad assortment of well-known, nationally branded hard goods

Who Is Shopping Online?

Some retailers offer their product and services only online and others have moved to add an online element to their traditional offering. To develop these retail strategies, companies need to know who is making online purchases and what they are buying.

It turns out that more than 80 percent of Canadians are making purchases online. The highest number of Canadians making online purchases is aged 25 to 34, where 95 percent buy products online. Even those over 65, the smallest group of online shoppers, has more than 60 percent buying products and services online. The number of seniors shopping online increased as they changed their purchase behaviour in response to the COVID-19 virus crisis, but some experts believe that seniors may return to their previous purchasing behaviour when life goes back to normal.

Another study showed that within the 16- to 24-year-old age group there was a difference in online shopping habits between genders. Within

this age group more than 85 percent shopped online. This study showed women shopped online more frequently but men spent more time shopping online. There was also a difference in what men and women were purchasing online. Men were purchasing books and school-related items while women were buying clothes.

Sources: Christopher Lombardo, "Seniors are Embracing Tech and Online Shopping," Online Strategy, https://strategyonline.ca/2020/04/03/seniors-are-embracing-technology-and-online-shopping/, April 3, 2020; "Online Shopping in Canada, 2018," Statistics Canada, www150.statcan.gc.ca/n1/pub/89-28-0001/2018001/article/00016-eng.htm, December 2, 2019; Daniel Calabretta, "How Gen Z is Shopping Online While Staying Home," Strategy Online, https://strategyonline.ca/2020/04/14/how-gen-z-is-shopping-online-while-staying-home/, April 14, 2020.

mass merchandising
a retailing strategy using moderate to low prices on large quantities of merchandise and lower levels of service to stimulate high turnover of products

supercentres
retail stores that combine groceries and general merchandise goods with a wide range of services

specialty discount stores
retail stores that offer a nearly complete selection of single category merchandise and use self-service, discount prices, high volume, and high turnover

items, in addition to clothing, bedding, and linens. Full-line discounters use the retailing strategy of **mass merchandising**: the use of moderate to low prices on large quantities of merchandise and lower levels of service to stimulate high turnover of products. Dollarama is an example of a full-line discount store.

- **Supercentres** extend the full-line concept to include groceries and general merchandise with a wide range of services, such as pharmacy, dry cleaning, portrait studios, hair salons, optical shops, and restaurants—all in one location. Walmart stores have evolved to supercentres where customers are drawn in by groceries, but end up purchasing other items from the full-line discount inventory.

- Single-line **specialty discount stores** offer a nearly complete selection of merchandise within a single category and use self-service, discount prices, high volume, and high turnover to their advantage. A **category killer** such as Best Buy is a specialty discount store that heavily dominates its narrow merchandise segment.

- **Warehouse membership clubs** are limited-service merchant wholesalers that sell a limited selection of brand-name appliances, household items, and groceries to members, small businesses, and groups. The product mix is generally quite wide and the items are often sold in bulk at discounted prices in exchange for a membership fee. Merchandise is displayed without any frills and inventory turns over quickly. Currently,

EXHIBIT 14.1 | TYPES OF STORES AND THEIR CHARACTERISTICS

Type of Retailer	Level of Service	Product Assortment	Price	Gross Margin
Department store	Moderately high to high	Broad	Moderate to high	Moderately high
Specialty store	High	Narrow	Moderate to high	High
Supermarket	Low	Broad	Moderate	Low
Drugstore	Low to moderate	Medium	Moderate	Low
Convenience store	Low	Medium to narrow	Moderately high	Moderately high
Full-line discount store	Moderate to low	Medium to broad	Moderately low	Moderately low
Supercentre	Moderate to low	Broad	Moderate	Moderately low
Specialty Discount Store	Moderate to low	Medium to broad	Moderately low to low	Moderately low
Warehouse Membership Clubs	Low	Broad	Low to very low	Low
Off-Price Retailer	Low	Medium to narrow	Low	Low
Factory Outlet	Low	Narrow	Moderately low	Moderately low
Restaurant	Low to high	Narrow	Low to high	Low to high

the leading store in this category is Costco, with 100 stores across the country.[9]

- An **off-price retailer** such as Winners or Marshall's sells brand-name merchandise at considerable discounts. Off-price retailers often buy the following at below cost: manufacturers' overruns, closeouts on lines, or orders from manufacturers that department stores may have cancelled. Off-price retailers have done very well as their strong value proposition has resonated with the consumer.

- A **factory outlet** is an off-price retailer owned and operated by a single manufacturer; it carries one line of merchandise—its own. By operating factory outlets, manufacturers can regulate where their surplus merchandise is sold and realize higher profit margins than if they disposed of the goods through independent wholesalers and retailers. Often factory outlet stores are grouped together in factory outlet malls.

iStock.com/SeventyFour

RESTAURANTS Restaurants straddle the line between retailing establishments and service establishments. Restaurants do sell tangible products—food and drink—but they also provide a valuable service for consumers in the form of food preparation and food service. Most restaurants could even be defined as specialty retailers, given that most concentrate their menu offerings on a distinctive type of cuisine—for example, Swiss Chalet and Starbucks coffee shops.

14-3 | THE RISE OF NONSTORE RETAILING

The retailing formats discussed so far entail physical stores where merchandise is displayed and to which customers must travel in order to shop. In contrast, **nonstore retailing** provides shopping without visiting a physical location. Nonstore retailing adds a level of convenience for customers who wish to shop from their current locations. Due to broader

category killers
specialty discount stores that heavily dominate their narrow merchandise segment

warehouse membership clubs
limited-service merchant wholesalers that sell a limited selection of brand-name appliances, household items, and groceries to members, small businesses, and groups

off-price retailer
a retailer that sells brand-name merchandise at considerable discounts

factory outlet
an off-price retailer that is owned and operated by a manufacturer

nonstore retailing
provides shopping without visiting a store

changes in culture and society, nonstore retailing is currently growing faster than in-store retailing. The major forms of nonstore retailing are automatic vending, direct retailing, direct marketing (DM), and Internet retailing (or *e-tailing*). In response to the recent successes seen by nonstore retailers, traditional bricks-and-mortar retailers have begun seeking a presence in limited nonstore formats.

14-3a | Automatic Vending

Automatic vending entails the use of machines to offer goods for sale—for example, the vending machines dispensing soft drinks, candy, and snacks typically found in cafeterias and office buildings. Retailers constantly seek new opportunities to sell via vending machines. As a result, modern vending machines today sell merchandise such as toys, sports cards, makeup, office supplies, and even electronics. A key aspect of their continuing success is the proliferation of cashless payment systems in response to consumers' diminishing preference for carrying cash. Modern vending machines are becoming increasingly more interactive with digital screens and video cameras. These "smart" machines can prompt consumers to buy additional products, run advertisements, and track users' purchases to offer frequency discounts.

Vending machines are now equipped to accept mobile payments.

Kyodo News/Getty Images

14-3b | Self-Service Technologies (SST)

Self-service technologies are technological interfaces that allow customers to provide themselves with products or services without the intervention of a service employee. Automatic teller machines, pay-at-the-pump gas stations, and movie ticket kiosks allow customers to make purchases that once required assistance from a company employee. However, as with any sort of self-service technology, self-service technologies come with failure risks due to human or technological error.

Unless customers expect that they can easily recover from such errors, they may end up shopping elsewhere.

14-3c | Direct Retailing

In **direct retailing**, representatives sell products door-to-door, office-to-office, or in at-home sales parties. In Canada alone more than 200 companies use the direct selling model and more than a million direct sales consultants are involved in direct retailing.[10] Companies such as Avon and The Pampered Chef have used this approach for years. Although most direct sellers, like Thirty-one (thirtyonegifts.ca), still encourage the "party" method, the realities of the marketplace have forced them to be more creative in reaching their target customer. Direct sales representatives now hold sales opportunities in offices, parks, libraries, and other common locations. Many direct retailers are also turning to direct mail, the telephone, and social media to reach their target customer.

14-3d | Direct Marketing (DM)

Direct marketing includes techniques used to encourage consumers to make a purchase from their home, office, or other convenient locations. Common techniques are direct mail, catalogues and mail order, and telemarketing. Shoppers using these methods are less bound by traditional shopping situations. Time-strapped consumers and those who live in rural or suburban areas are most likely to be direct-response shoppers because they value the convenience and flexibility provided by DM. DM occurs in several forms:

- **Telemarketing** is the use of communications to sell a product or service and involves both outbound and

automatic vending
the use of machines to offer goods for sale

self-service technologies (SST)
technological interfaces that allow customers to provide themselves with products and/or services without the intervention of a service employee

direct retailing
the selling of products by representatives who work door-to-door, office-to-office, or at in-home parties

direct marketing
techniques used to get consumers to make a purchase from their home, office, or another nonretail setting

telemarketing
the use of telecommunications to sell a product or service; involves both outbound and inbound calls

inbound calls. Outbound sales calls are usually unsolicited, and inbound calls, are usually customer orders made through toll-free 800 numbers or fee-based 900 numbers. Rising postage rates and decreasing long-distance phone rates have made *outbound* telemarketing an attractive DM technique. *Inbound* telemarketing programs are mainly used to take orders, generate leads, and provide customer service. Inbound 800 telemarketing has successfully supplemented direct-response TV, radio, and print advertising for more than 25 years.

- **Direct mail** is a form of direct-response communication delivered directly to consumers' homes. It can be the most efficient or the least efficient retailing method, depending on the quality of the mailing list and the effectiveness of the mailing piece. By using direct mail, marketers can precisely target their customers according to demographics, geography, and even psychographic characteristics. Direct mailers are becoming more sophisticated in targeting the right customers. **Microtargeting** is the use of direct mail techniques that employ highly detailed data analytics in order to isolate potential customers with great precision. Based on census data, lifestyle patterns, past purchase patterns, and credit history, direct marketers can pick out those most likely to buy their products.[11] Micromarketing is also an effective tool for online retailing. Many companies have purchased access to online search engine data, making it easier than ever to pinpoint customer preferences. A customer's online search history enables retailers to match its specific customer wants through targeted digital advertisements.

- **Shop-at-home television networks** such as The Shopping Channel (TSC) produce television shows that display merchandise, with the retail price, to home viewers and use inbound telemarketing to place orders directly using credit cards for payment. This form of retailing has grown significantly in Canada in the recent years, as a variety of innovative and quality products are offered to consumers for viewing and purchase.

14-3e | Online Retailing or E-tailing

Online retailing or **e-tailing** enables a customer to shop over the Internet and have items delivered directly to their door or to a bricks-and-mortar location for pickup. Today global online retailing accounts for more than US$3 trillion in sales and is expected to reach more than US$6.5 trillion by 2023.[12] The top three online sites for Canadian shoppers are amazon.ca, amazon.com, and Costco.ca.[13] Interactive shopping tools and live chats substitute for the in-store interactions with salespeople and product trials that customers traditionally use to make purchase decisions. Shoppers can look at a much wider variety of products online because there are no physical space restrictions. See Exhibit 14.2 for a list of Canada's most trusted e-commerce retailers.

14-3f | Sharing Economy

The **sharing economy** refers to the way connected consumers exchange goods and services with each other through a digital marketplace. This phenomenon has given rise to online exchange communities such as Kijiji or Craiglist, a system of local message boards where users can buy, sell, and trade almost any product or service. Other companies match people looking for specific services, such as ride-sharing services like Uber, vacation rentals such as Airbnb, or grocery shopping and delivery services like Instacart. These companies provide a platform to not only match buyers and sellers but also track ratings and reviews for service providers and clients alike.

In addition to visiting retailer websites for information, consumers are increasingly using social

direct mail
a form of direct-response communication that is delivered directly to consumers' homes

microtargeting
the use of direct marketing techniques that employ highly detailed analytics in order to isolate potential customers with great precision

shop-at-home television network
a specialized form of direct-response marketing whereby television shows display merchandise, with the retail price, to home viewers

online retailing (e-tailing)
a type of shopping available to consumers with access to the Internet

sharing economy
the way connected consumers exchange goods and services with each other through a digital marketplace

EXHIBIT 14.2 | CANADA'S MOST TRUSTED E-COMMERCE RETAILERS

Retail Category	National Most Trusted E-Commerce Retailers
Baby/Children's Clothing	Old Navy, Carter's/OshKosh, The Children's Place (Tie)
Baby Supplies/Gear	Amazon
Beauty & Cosmetics	Sephora
Books	Amazon
Cameras & Photography Supplies	Amazon
Electronics Gaming/Videogames	Amazon
Health & Wellness	Amazon
Home Décor	Amazon/Wayfair (tie)
Home Improvement/Renovation	The Home Depot
Household Cleaning & Laundry Products	Amazon
Housewares/Kitchenware	Amazon
Laptop/Desktop Computers	Best Buy
Major Home Appliances	Amazon
Mattresses	Amazon
Men's Clothing	Amazon
Personal Electronics (Headphones, Bluetooth Speakers, etc.)	Amazon
Pet Food & Supplies	Amazon
Recreation & Outdoor Gear	Amazon
Shoes/Footwear	Amazon
Small Home Appliances	Amazon
Sporting Goods	SportChek
Toys and Games	Amazon
Women's Clothing/Fashion	Amazon/Hudson Bay (tie)

Source: "BrandSpark Canada, 2019 Most Trusted Award Winners – E-Commerce," www.brandspark mosttrusted.com/canada, accessed March 15, 2020.

media applications as both shopping platforms and sources of information. Social networking sites such as Facebook, Instagram, and Twitter enable users to immediately purchase items recommended by their social connections, a phenomenon known as social shopping. Companies are eager to establish direct linkages between social networking platforms and their own websites due to the benefit that a product or service recommended by a friend will receive higher consideration from the potential customer.

franchiser
the originator of a trade name, product, methods of operation, and so on, that grants operating rights to another party to sell its product

franchisee
an individual or a business that pays the franchiser for the right to use its name, product, or business methods

14-4 | FRANCHISING

As mentioned above, a franchise is a continuing relationship in which a franchiser grants to a franchisee the right to operate a business or to sell a product. The **franchiser** originates the trade name, product, methods of operation, and so on. The **franchisee**, in return, pays the franchiser for the right to use its name, product, or business methods. The only country in the world that has more franchises than Canada is the United States. In Canada approximately 1 in 10 working Canadians is directly or indirectly employed in the franchise industry. Over 40 percent of all retail sales in Canada come from franchised companies.[14] There are over 75 000 franchise units in Canada and over 60 percent of these are in the nonfood sectors and industries. A franchise is usually a small company but franchises in Canada generate almost $100 billion in sales annually.[15]

To be granted the rights to a franchise, a franchisee usually pays an initial, one-time franchise fee. The amount of this fee depends solely on the individual franchiser but the average initial franchise fee in Canada is $25 000 and can be considerably higher. This franchise fee covers the costs of training, start-up and ongoing business support, as well as launch fees. In addition to this initial franchise fee, the franchisee is expected to pay royalty fees that are in the range of 0 to 20 percent of gross sales. The franchisee may also be expected to pay advertising fees, which usually cover the cost of promotional materials and, if the franchise organization is large enough, regional or national advertising. There may be other start-up costs such as insurance, furniture, or remodelling of premises. The average total investment needed to start a franchise in Canada is between $150 000 and $200 000.[16]

Two basic forms of franchises are used today: product and trade name franchising and business format franchising. In *product and trade name franchising*, a dealer agrees to sell certain products provided by a manufacturer or a wholesaler. This approach has been used most widely in the auto and truck, soft drink bottling, tire, and gasoline service industries—for example, a local tire retailer may hold a franchise to sell Michelin tires.

Business format franchising is an ongoing business relationship between a franchiser and a franchisee. Typically, a franchiser sells a franchisee the rights to use the franchiser's format or approach to doing business. This form of franchising has rapidly expanded since the 1950s through retailing, restaurant, food-service, hotel and motel, printing, and real estate franchises.

M&M Meat Shops is an example of a Canadian franchise that is currently undergoing a rebranding. They have recently changed their name to M&M Food Market.

Douglas Carr/Alamy Stock Photo

14-5 | RETAIL MARKETING STRATEGY

Retail managers develop marketing strategies based on the goals established by stakeholders and the overall strategic plans developed by company leadership. Strategic retailing goals typically focus on increasing total sales, reducing cost of goods sold, and improving financial ratios such as return on assets or equity. At the store level, more tactical retailing goals include increased store traffic, higher sales of a specific item, developing a more upscale image, and creating heightened public awareness of the retail operation and its products or services. The tactical strategies that retailers use to obtain their goals include having a sale, updating decor, and launching a new advertising campaign. The key strategic tasks that precede these tactical decisions are defining and selecting a target market and developing the retailing mix to successfully meet the needs of the chosen target market.

14-5a | Defining a Target Market

The first task in developing a retail strategy is to define the target market. This process begins with market segmentation, one of the topics of Chapter 7. Successful retailing has always been based on knowing the customer.

Determining a target market is a prerequisite to creating the retailing mix. Target markets in retailing are often defined by demographics, geography, and psychographics. For instance, many retailers are now targeting those between the ages of 25 and 40. Canadian retail companies are finding more success using a different formats than their United States counterparts. In the United States, many retailers have moved to large suburban stores; however, this format is not as successful in Canada because many Canadians in the 25- to 40-year-old age bracket live in urban centres. Canadian retailers are finding that smaller store formats in urban centre are working better. Retailers like Sobey's, with its acquisition of Farm Boy stores, and Ikea are moving to smaller stores in urban centres.[17]

14-5b | Choosing the Retailing Mix

Retailers combine the elements of the retailing mix to come up with a single retailing method to attract the target market. The **retailing mix** consists of six Ps: the four Ps of the marketing mix (product, place, promotion, and price) as well as presentation and personnel (see Exhibit 14.3).

The combination of the six Ps projects a store's (or website's) image, which influences consumers' perceptions. Using these impressions of stores, shoppers position one store against another. A retail marketing manager must ensure that the store's positioning is compatible with the target customers' expectations. As discussed at the beginning of the chapter, retail stores can be positioned on three broad dimensions: service provided by store personnel, product assortment, and price. Management should use everything else—place, presentation, and promotion—to fine-tune the basic positioning of the store.

THE PRODUCT OFFERING The first element in the retailing

> **retailing mix**
> a combination of the six Ps—product, place, promotion, price, presentation, and personnel—used in a single retail method to attract the target market

EXHIBIT 14.3 | THE RETAILING MIX

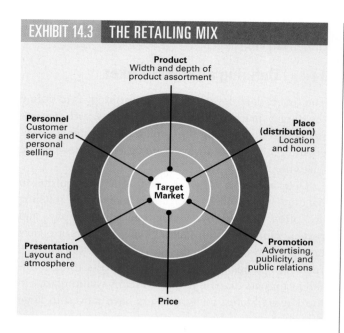

Product
Width and depth of
product assortment

Personnel
Customer
service and
personal
selling

Place
(distribution)
Location
and hours

Target
Market

Presentation
Layout and
atmosphere

Promotion
Advertising,
publicity, and
public relations

Price

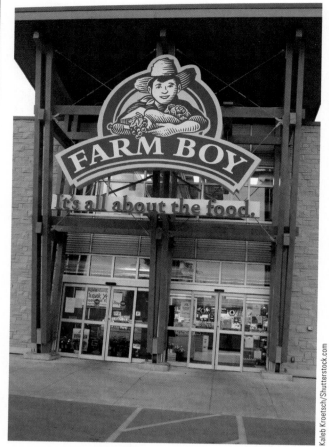

Kaleb Kroetsch/Shutterstock.com

mix is the **product offering**, also called the *product assortment* or *merchandise mix*. Developing a product offering is essentially a question of the width and depth of the product assortment. *Width* refers to the assortment of products offered; *depth* refers to the number of different brands offered within each assortment. Price, store/website design, displays, and service are important to consumers in determining where to shop, but the most critical factor is merchandise selection. This reasoning also holds true for online retailers. Amazon.ca, for instance, offers considerable width in its product assortment with millions of different items, including books, music, toys, videos, tools and hardware, health and beauty aids, electronics, and software. Conversely, online specialty retailers—such as Clearly, which sells optical products—focus on a single category of merchandise, hoping to attract loyal customers with their larger depth of products at lower prices and better customer service. Many online retailers purposely focus on single-product-line niches that could never garner enough foot traffic to support a traditional bricks-and-mortar store.

Retailers decide the product offering on the basis of what their target market wants to buy. Using data mining techniques, retailers analyze past sales, fashion trends, customer requests, competition, and other data sources to determine what the target market most likely will buy. The data they collect in customer relationship management (CRM) databases allows them to gain better insight into who is buying their products and how to build relationships to be rewarded with customer loyalty. Shoppers Drug Mart's successful points program, PC Optimum, is a brilliant tool that collects shopping data. Shoppers Drug Mart is owned by Loblaws and the data mined from the PC Optimum program are used by both organizations to build relationships and improve the consumer's shopping experience. Chapters Indigo's Plum rewards works in the same fashion. The shopping habits of a consumer not only assist the retailer to determine the merchandise selection but also to develop ongoing consumer engagement strategies as past purchase data can be used to build targeted online messaging to the consumer.

PROMOTION Retail promotion strategy includes advertising, public relations and publicity, and sales promotion. The goal is to help position the store or website in consumers' minds. Retailers design intriguing ads, stage special events, engage in social media conversations, and develop specific promotions

product offering
the mix of products offered to the consumer by the retailer; also called the product assortment or merchandise mix

for their target markets. Today's grand openings are a carefully orchestrated blend of advertising, merchandising, goodwill, and glitter. All the elements of an opening—press coverage, social media activity, special events, media advertising, and store displays—are carefully planned. Other promotions that are often used successfully are sales events, coupons, and discounts for certain products or customer groups. Retailers must exercise caution with store promotions that brand cannibalization doesn't occur. **Brand cannibalization** is a situation whereby the promotion intended to draw in new customers simply shifts current customer from buying one brand to another, versus increasing overall sales. In addition, retailers need to be careful to not train customers to buy only when sales are offered.

Retailers' advertising is carried out mostly at the local level. Local advertising by retailers usually provides specific information about their stores, such as location, merchandise, hours, prices, and special sales. In contrast, national retail advertising generally focuses on image. Hudson's Bay Co. emphasizes product mix and pricing in newspaper advertisements, inserts, and flyers on a weekly basis. Advertising campaigns also take advantage of cooperative advertising, another popular retail advertising practice. Traditionally, marketers paid retailers to feature their products in store mailers, or a marketer developed a TV campaign for the product and simply tacked on several retailers' names at the end. Another common form of cooperative advertising involves the promotion of exclusive products. Hudson's Bay Co. teamed up with designer Brian Gluckstein to offer signature products under the Gluckstein label that are sold exclusively at The Bay and thebay.com.[18]

PLACE The retailing axiom "location, location, location" has long emphasized the importance of place to the retail mix. The physical location decision is important first because the retailer is making a large, semipermanent commitment of resources that may reduce its future flexibility. Second, the physical location will affect the store's growth and profitability.

Physical site location begins by choosing a community. Important factors to consider are the area's economic growth potential, the amount of competition, and geography. For instance, Walmart will build in a new community, or an area of a community, that is still under development. Fast-food restaurants tend to place a priority on locations with other fast-food restaurants, because being located in clusters helps to draw customers for each restaurant. Starbucks seeks densely populated urban communities for its stores.

Roman Tiraspolsky/Shutterstock.com

With its own in-store stylists, makeup and perfume retailer Sephora is a popular destination store for shoppers who want to try out a new look.

After settling on a geographic region or community, retailers must choose a specific site. In addition to growth potential, the important factors are neighbourhood socioeconomic characteristics, traffic flows, land costs, zoning regulations, and public transportation. A particular site's visibility, parking, entrance and exit locations, accessibility, and safety and security issues are also considered. Additionally, a retailer should consider how its store would fit into the surrounding environment—for example, the Hudson's Bay Co. would be unlikely to locate one of its new Saks stores next to a Dollarama.

In addition, retailers face the decision as to whether to have a freestanding unit or to become a tenant in a shopping centre or mall.

FREESTANDING STORES An isolated, freestanding location is often used by large retailers of shopping goods such as furniture, cars, or electronics. Ikea tends to utilize a freestanding store location, which likely offers the advantage of low site cost or rent, no nearby competitors, and plenty of parking. On the other hand, it may be difficult to attract customers to a freestanding location, and no neighbouring retailers are around to share costs. To be successful, stores in isolated locations must become destination stores. **Destination stores** are stores consumers seek out and purposely plan to visit.

brand cannibalization the reduction of sales for one brand as the result of the promotion of a current product or brand

destination stores stores that consumers seek out and purposely plan to visit

Websites can also be destinations for shoppers. Well.ca is a destination website for a variety of health, wellness, and baby and beauty products, and trivago.ca is a destination for travellers looking for the best price for a hotel room.

Freestanding units are increasing in popularity as bricks-and-mortar retailers strive to make their stores more convenient to access, more enticing to shop in, and more profitable. Perhaps the greatest reason for developing a freestanding site is greater visibility. Retailers often believe they get lost in huge shopping centres and malls, but freestanding units can help stores develop an identity with shoppers. Also, an aggressive expansion plan may not allow time to wait for the shopping centre to be built. Drugstore chains, such as Shoppers Drug Mart, have been determinedly relocating their existing shopping centre stores to freestanding sites, especially street corner sites for drive-through accessibility.

SHOPPING CENTRES Shopping centres began in the 1950s when Canadians started migrating to the suburbs. The first shopping centres were *strip malls*, typically located along busy streets. They usually included a supermarket, a variety store, and perhaps a few specialty stores. Next, *community shopping centres* emerged, with one or two small department stores, more specialty stores, a couple of restaurants, and several apparel stores. These community shopping centres provided off-street parking and a broader variety of merchandise.

Regional malls offering a much wider variety of merchandise started appearing in the mid-1970s. Regional malls are either entirely enclosed or roofed to allow shopping in any weather. Most are landscaped with trees, fountains, sculptures, and the like to enhance the shopping environment. They have hectares of free parking. The *anchor stores* or *generator stores* (often major department stores) are usually located at opposite ends of the mall to create heavy foot traffic.

According to shopping centre developers, *lifestyle centres* are emerging as the newest generation of shopping centres. Lifestyle centres typically combine outdoor shopping areas that comprise upscale retailers and restaurants, plazas, fountains, and pedestrian streets. The Shops at Don Mills in Toronto is a good example of such a lifestyle mall; it brings together fine restaurants, theatre, and condo living with a park, public spaces, and retail stores. Lifestyle centres appeal to retail developers looking for an alternative to the traditional shopping mall, a concept rapidly losing favour among shoppers.

Many smaller specialty lines are opening shops inside larger stores to expand their retail opportunities without risking investment in a separate store. This strategy reflects a popular trend of **pop-up shops**—tiny, temporary stores that stay in one location for only a short time. Pop-up shops help retailers reach a wide market while avoiding high rent at retail locations. They have become a marketing tool for large retailers who desire to target a new consumer. The Living Vine, a Toronto-based wine importer, used a pop-up store in one of the trendy areas of the city to promote its wines. Customers could sample wines, ask questions of wine experts and order wines by the case. The temporary store was open for only six days. The event was promoted only through social media but it allowed consumers to be exposed to organic and natural wines that normally are available only through special orders.[19]

In addition to the above considerations, retailers must also learn about the legal implications of the arrangement they are entering, whether that be a lease or a purchase contact. Consideration such as leasehold improvements, length of the lease, rent increases, and stipulations regarding subleasing are critical to understand and are likely worth legal advice. The same holds for entering into a purchase contract.

Despite the popularity of shopping malls in the past, they are slowly being replaced with other retail options such as online shopping. In fact, many bricks-and-mortar malls are struggling to survive. Anchor stores such as large department stores have closed many of their locations in recent years due to increased competition from discount stores and speciality retailers.[20]

PRICE Retailing's ultimate goal is to sell products to consumers, and the right price is critical in ensuring sales. Because retail prices are usually based on the cost of the merchandise, an essential part of pricing is efficient and timely buying.

Price is also a key element in a retail store's positioning strategy. Higher prices often indicate a level of quality and help reinforce the prestigious image of retailers, as they do for Harry Rosen and Maison Birks. On the other hand, discounters and off-price retailers, such as TJ Maxx and Winners, offer good value for the money spent.

PRESENTATION The presentation of a retail store helps determine the store's image and positions the retail store in consumers' minds. For instance, a retailer that wants to position itself as an upscale store would use a lavish or sophisticated presentation.

pop-up shops
tiny, temporary stores that stay in one location for only a short time

The atmosphere of MEC helps to position the store.

Henry Birks—part of the Maison Birks chain of stores—uses higher prices to present a prestigious image.

The main element of a store's presentation is its **atmosphere**, the overall impression conveyed by a store's physical layout, decor, and surroundings. The atmosphere might create a relaxed or busy feeling, a sense of luxury or of efficiency, a friendly or cold attitude, a sense of organization or of clutter, or a fun or serious mood. Mountain Equipment Co-op (MEC) uses rustic, unfinished wood to create a casual look to convey an outdoorsy feel.

The layout of retail stores is a key factor in their success. The goal is to use all of the store's space effectively, including aisles, fixtures, merchandise displays, and non-selling areas. In addition to making shopping easy and convenient for the customer, an effective layout has a powerful influence on traffic patterns and purchasing behaviour. IKEA uses a unique circular store layout, which encourages customers to pass all the store's departments to reach the checkout lanes. The shopper thus is exposed to all of IKEA's merchandise assortment.

Layout also includes the placement of products in the store. Many technologically advanced retailers are using a technique called *market-basket analysis* to analyze the huge amounts of data collected through their point-of-purchase scanning equipment. The analysis looks for products that are commonly purchased together to help retailers find ideal locations for each product. Wal-mart uses market-basket analysis to determine where in the store to stock products for customer convenience. Kleenex tissues, for example, are in the paper-goods aisle as well as beside the cold medicines.

The following factors are the most influential in creating a store's atmosphere:

- *Employee type and density:* Employee type refers to an employee's general characteristics—for instance, being neat, friendly, knowledgeable, or service oriented. Density is the number of employees per thousand square feet of selling space. Whereas low employee density creates a do-it-yourself, casual atmosphere, high employee density denotes readiness to serve the customer's every whim.

- *Merchandise type and density:* A prestigious retailer, such as Harry Rosen, carries the best brand names and displays them in a neat, uncluttered arrangement. Discounters and off-price retailers often carry seconds or out-of-season goods crowded into small spaces and hung on long racks by category—tops, pants, skirts, etc.—creating the impression that "We've got so much stuff, we're practically giving it away."

- *Fixture type and density:* Fixtures can be elegant (rich woods), trendy (chrome and smoked glass), or old tables, as in an antiques store. The fixtures should be consistent

atmosphere
the overall impression conveyed by a store's physical layout, decor, and surroundings

with the general atmosphere the store is trying to create.

- *Sound:* Sound can be pleasant or unpleasant for a customer. Music can entice customers to stay in the store longer and buy more or eat quickly and leave a table for others. It can also control the pace of the store traffic, create an image, and attract or direct the shopper's attention. Recent studies show that the type of music played can even influence a customer's choice of product. Ethnic music increases the likelihood of a customer choosing a menu item from the same country, and country western music increases customers' willingness to pay for functional, everyday products.[21]

- *Odours:* Smell can either stimulate or detract from sales. Research suggests that people evaluate merchandise more positively, spend more time shopping, and are generally in a better mood when an agreeable odour is present. Other research shows that certain scents empower consumers and lead to more premium purchases.[22] Retailers use fragrances as an extension of their retail strategy.

- *Visual factors:* Colours can create a mood or focus attention and therefore are an important factor in atmosphere. Red, yellow, and orange are considered warm colours and are used when a feeling of warmth and closeness is desired. Cool colours, such as blue, green, and violet, are used to open up closed-in places and create an air of elegance and cleanliness. Many retailers have found that natural lighting, either from windows or skylights, can lead to increased sales. Outdoor lighting can also affect consumer patronage.

PERSONNEL People are a unique aspect of retailing. Most retail sales involve a customer–salesperson relationship, if only briefly. Sales personnel provide their customers with the amount of service prescribed in the retail strategy of the store.

Retail salespeople serve another important selling function: they persuade shoppers to buy. They must

Pop-Paul-Catalin/Shutterstock.com

therefore be able to persuade customers that what they are selling is what the customer needs. Salespeople are trained in two common selling techniques: trading up and suggestion selling. *Trading up* means persuading customers to buy a higher-priced item than they originally intended to buy. To avoid selling customers something they do not need or want, however, salespeople should take care when practising trading-up techniques. *Suggestion selling*, a common practice among most retailers, seeks to broaden customers' original purchases with related items. For example, if you buy a new printer at Staples, the sales representative will ask whether you want to purchase paper or extra ink cartridges. Suggestion selling and trading up should always help shoppers recognize true needs rather than sell them unwanted merchandise.

Providing great customer service is one of the most challenging elements in the retail mix because customer expectations for service are so varied. What customers expect in a department store is very different from their expectations for a discount store. Customer expectations also change. Ten years ago, shoppers wanted personal one-on-one attention. Today, most customers are happy to help themselves as long as they can easily find what they need.

Customer service is also critical for online retailers. Online shoppers expect a retailer's website to be easy to use, products to be available, and returns to be simple. Online retailers need to design their sites to give their customers the information they need, such as what's new and what's on sale, and consider using suggestive selling.

14-5c | Retailing Decisions for Services

The fastest growing part of our economy is the service sector. Although distribution in the service sector is difficult to visualize, the same skills, techniques, and strategies used to manage inventory can also be used to manage service inventory, such as bank accounts or airline seats. The quality of the planning and execution of distribution can have a major impact on costs and customer satisfaction.

Because service industries are so customer oriented, service quality is a priority. To manage customer relationships, many service providers, such as insurance

Service distribution focuses on four main areas:

- **Minimizing wait times:** Minimizing the amount of time customers wait in line is a key factor in maintaining the quality of service.

- **Managing service capacity:** If service companies don't have the capacity to meet demand, they must either turn away some prospective customers, let service levels slip, or expand capacity.

- **Improving service delivery:** Service companies are now experimenting with different distribution channels for their services. Choosing the right distribution channel can increase the times that services are available or add to customer convenience.

- **Establishing channel-wide network coherence:** Because services are to some degree intangible, service companies also find it necessary to standardize their service quality across different geographic regions to maintain their brand image.

companies, hair salons, and financial services, use technology to schedule appointments, manage accounts, and disburse information.

14-6 | ADDRESSING RETAIL PRODUCT/ SERVICE FAILURES

In spite of retailers' best intentions and efforts to satisfy each and every customer, consumer dissatisfaction can occur. No retailer can be everything to every customer. A product may be located where customers cannot easily find it, an employee may provide mistaken information about a product's features or benefits, a promotional item may be out of stock by the time the customer attempts to purchase, or the item may go on sale shortly after the customer makes the purchase. Customers are generally indifferent to the reasons for retailer errors, and their reactions to mistakes can range widely. In this era of instantaneous and widespread communications via social media, an upset customer can have far-reaching effects.

The best retailers have plans in place not only to recover from inevitable lapses in service but also perhaps to even benefit from them. For these top-performing stores, service recovery is handled proactively as part of an overarching plan to maximize the customer experience. These are some actions that might be taken:

- Notifying customers in advance of stockouts and explaining the reasons certain products are not available;

- Implementing liberal return policies designed to ensure that the customer can bring back any item for any reason (if the product fails to work as planned, or even if the customer simply doesn't like it); and

- Issuing product recalls in conjunction with promotional offers that provide future incentives to repurchase.

In short, the best retailers treat customer disappointments as opportunities to interact with and improve relations with their customers. Evidence indicates that successful handling of such failures can sometimes yield even higher levels of customer loyalty than if the failure had never occurred at all.

14-7 | RETAILER AND RETAIL CONSUMER TRENDS AND ADVANCEMENTS

Though retailing has been around for thousands of years, it continues to change every day. Retailers are constantly innovating, and always looking for new products and services (or ways to offer them) that will attract new customers or inspire current ones to buy in greater quantities or more frequently. Many of the most interesting and effective retail innovations are related to the use of technology and shopping data to help find new and better ways to entice customers into a store or to a website—and then to spend more money once there.

14-7a | Big Data

Retailers decide what to sell on the basis of what their target market wants to buy. Retailers such as Walmart, Loblaws, and Shoppers Drug Mart collect data at the point of sale and throughout the store that provides invaluable customer insights. Through the use of big data analytics, stores like these can determine which products to stock and at what prices, how to manage markdowns, and how to advertise to draw target customers and keep them loyal. Big data analytics will allow for loyalty programs to be improved by personalizing rewards and offers.

Retailers are increasingly using **beacons**—devices that send out connecting signals to customers' smartphones and tablets. These devices recognize when a customer is in or near the store and indicate to an automated system to send the customer a marketing message via email or text. Beacons can also be used by sales associates to offer a discount at the point of sale.

Radio frequency identification (RFID) is not new technology, but its use has increased over the last few years. Traditionally used for inventory management purposes prior to items reaching the sales floor,

Courtney Thorne

retailers have begun using RFID for other purposes. RFID has the potential to make the checkout process easier and faster by allowing customers to scan items before the checkout and automatically process a payment.[23]

14-7b | Shopper Marketing and Analytics

Shopper marketing is an emerging retailing trend that employs market data to best serve customers as they prepare to make a purchase.

Shopper marketing focuses on understanding how a brand's target consumers behave as shoppers in different channels and formats, and then uses this information in business-based strategies and initiatives that are carefully designed to deliver balanced benefits to all stakeholders—brands, channel members, and customers. It may sound simple, but it is anything but. Both manufacturers and retailers now think about consumers specifically while they are in shopping mode. They use **shopper analytics** to dig deeply into customers' shopping attitudes, perceptions, emotions, and behaviours, both online and offline, to learn how their individual shopping experience shapes their behaviour. More and more companies are conducting or participating in big data analytics projects to better understand how shoppers think when they shop at a store or on a website and what factors influence their thinking.

Shopper marketing is becoming increasing popular as a method to improve the shopping experience by aligning brands with retailers' different customer segments. Shopper marketing is also being used to improve supply chain management, allowing the supply chains to react faster to changes. Shopper marketing has increased the need for sophisticated analytics and metrics. As with many modern business efforts, shopper marketing forces managers to coordinate better, measure more, think creatively, and move faster.

14-7c | Future Developments in Retail Management

A retailing trend with great growth potential is the leveraging technology to increase touchpoints with customers and thereby generate greater profitability. As consumers are increasingly willing to use their mobile devices to browse, comparison shop, and pay for their purchases, strategic retailers are rethinking how they appeal to shoppers. One trend is called "showrooming" where customers visit the retail store to examine the product and then make the purchase online. Showrooming and data

beacon
A device that sends out connecting signals to customers' smartphones and tablets

shopper marketing
understanding how one's target consumers behave as shoppers, in different channels and formats, and using this information to develop better retail strategies

shopper analytics
searching for and discovering meaningful patterns in shopper data for the purpose of fine-tuning, developing, or changing market offerings

HBC—THE HUDSON BAY COMPANY

We often look to new innovative young companies to see what to expect in the future for retail but Canada's oldest retail company seems to able to weather most economic storms and keep going. The Hudson Bay Company (HBC) began business on May 2, 1670. Today the company website describes it as "a diversified retailer focused on driving the performance of high-quality stores and their omnichannel platforms and unlocking the value of real estate holdings."[24] The company operates more than 300 stores in Canada and the United States including Hudson's Bay, Saks Fifth Avenue, Saks OFF 5th, and Lord + Taylor. The stores carry products from luxury products to off-price fashion.

Throughout its history the company has not always made successful retail decisions. In the 1970s, the company acquired Zellers and Simpsons, both department stores, and both have since been closed. The company is constantly assessing the different stores it operates. Recent changes include the closure of its Home Outfitter locations, review of its Saks OFF 5th locations, and the sale of its online Gilt operation.

In today's challenging retail environment HBC continues to adapt. The company has recently gone private and is rebranding the remaining retail locations. It even changed its company slogan to "Live a Colourful Life."

Jeff Whyte/Shutterstock.com

Sources: "A Brief History of HBC," HBC website, www.hbcheritage.ca/history/company-stories/a-brief-history-of-hbc, accessed May 5, 2020; Josh Kolm, "HBC to Shutter Home Outfitters," Strategy online, https://strategyonline.ca/2019/02/22/hbc-to-shutter-home-outfitters/, February 22, 2019; Christopher Lombardo, "Hudson's Bay Hopes to Rebound With a Colourful Campaign," Strategy Online, https://strategyonline.ca/2020/03/09/hudsons-bay-hopes-to-rebound-with-a-colourful-campaign/, March 9, 2020.

analysis have led to the development of virtual reality apps that enable the purchaser to view the product where it will be used; for example, clothes on the purchaser or furniture in the room. The increased use of technology has resulted in retailers reducing multiple retail channel systems into a single, unified system for the purpose of creating efficiencies or saving costs—a process called **retail channel omnification**. Efficiencies could come about when retailers reduce the number of outlets, use smaller retail spaces, or hold less inventory.

Not all retailers embrace omnification as the way of the future. Some are using alternative strategies such as click-and-collect or robots. **Click-and-collect** is the practice of buying something online and then travelling to a physical store location to take delivery of the merchandise. Some retailers are using artificial intelligence and robots. Robots are replacing or augmenting retail employees at restaurants, grocery stores, and even airports. The integration of all these new technologies is changing the shopping experience for consumers.

retail channel omnification
the reduction of multiple retail channels systems into a single, unified system for the purpose of creating efficiencies or saving costs.

click-and-collect
the practice of buying something online and then travelling to a physical store location to take delivery of the merchandise

AWAKE CHOCOLATE
CONTINUING CASE

AWAKE Chocolate

Micro Mart, Macro Potential

The days of office workers putting up with stale donuts and marginal coffee could be coming to an end with the introduction of micro marts. Replacing the traditional break room in offices, a micro mart (also referred to as a nano mart) is a like a convenience store that is installed in small spaces to offer some fresh, but mostly prepackaged and prepared food items.

Convenience store industry insiders describe them as such: "Micro marts are found in office buildings, fitness centres, and as small, stand-alone, self-service stores, but they can also be found in the form of small unattended refrigerators at the gas pump that customers can open with an app or credit card to select fresh food products and beverages."[1]

Cofounder Dan Tzotzis recalled how Awake Chocolate came to be part of this new retailing movement: "We stumbled across these micro markets through an engaged operator that brought us in to the 200 that she operated. We saw tremendous success in those micro markets right from the start. So, it led us to explore that market a little bit further."

As they continued to scour postsecondary campuses, Awake began to utilize its relatively small sales force to try and build the company's presence in the micro market world. Dan found the centralized decision making with micro markets a key to building such a strong presence: "Because we had a case study of really strong performance in that segment, we were able to penetrate that market quickly."

Awake cofounder Matt Schnarr described micro marts as "if you could walk into a vending machine." Micro marts are not traditional retail scenarios, and exploit the growth of nontraditional retail channels like vending machines. There is no need for staffing these retail locations, and the reliance on technology and use of security has led to the exponential growth of micro marts.

Being small, micro marts offer many conveniences for customers and businesses. But the lack of size creates challenges for food producers such as Awake. The small Canadian company has made a big imprint in the micro mart world, with a presence in around 15 000 micro markets across the United States, according to Dan Tzotzis.

One of the key reasons for success has to do with having a strong broker, which helps to build relationships with companies that supply micro marts, many of whom had experience with vending machines. As a smaller player, Awake could not rely on gaining shelf space with larger retailers, especially those in Canada charging the slotting fees that can cost hundreds of thousands of dollars in some cases. It had to focus on less traditional retail methods, but ones where consumers were going to be tired—and the workplace certainly fits that bill.

What is also tired is the existing retail industry in Canada. It seems each week there is another retailer operating in Canada about to close up a bricks-and-mortar location and focus on e-commerce, or closing up shop entirely. There had been very little in the way of innovation in retail, until the introduction of the micro mart.

Although there are close to 30 000 micro marts in the United States, according to Tzotzis there are likely no more than 250 in total in Canada. But there are more than 27 000 convenience stores in Canada[2] and thousands more workplaces, so this market is ripe for growth.

QUESTIONS

1. Identify the characteristics of micro marts with respect to the following: level of service (low, moderate, high); product assortment (narrow, medium, broad); price (low, moderate, high) and gross margin (low, moderate, high). Note that variations on these options can be used (e.g., "moderately low").

2. Create a new topic in the online digital resources for this textbook (MindTap) or use your class-specific Learning Management System (LMS) and moderate a discussion around how micro marts are the most important nonstore retailing method in the 21st century.

3. Create a short presentation detailing how Awake Chocolate can create a retail marketing strategy around the micro mart concept.

NOTES

1. Erin Del Conte, "What is a Micro Mart?" CStore Decisions, January 21, 2020. https://cstoredecisions.com/2020/01/21/what-is-a-micro-mart/.

2. James Dunne, "So Long, Soggy Hotdog: The Convenience Store Reinvented," CBC News, July 27, 2019, www.cbc.ca/news/business/convenience-stores-gourmet-foods-1.5226687 (accessed June 24, 2020).

Distribution Decisions, Part 5 Case

Apocalypse ... Soon?

In the last few years, any Canadian walking through their local mall would see an almost inevitable sign: "For Rent."

It is not that Canadian shoppers are unfamiliar with the comings and goings of retailers over the years. Now-forgotten but previously famous Canadian retailers include Woodward's, Zellers, and A&B Sound to name only a few.

There are news items each week describing the next retailer to go under, and the obligatory discussion as to whether this most recent failure is the true indicator for the retail "apocalypse" in Canada.

So what is the easy cause for this most recent round of retail flops? The easy answer is, of course, to blame technology. The omnipresent phone in everyone's pockets can now be used a tiny point-of-sale device, on which consumers can simply scroll, click, purchase, and receive their purchases without leaving their home, car, office, or local dog park.

The number of digital shoppers has increased consistently since 2013; 9 out of 10 Canadian online shoppers own a mobile phone, with 60 percent of them using their phone to make a purchase. Close to 80 percent of Canadian online shoppers state that they bought more in 2018 than they did in 2015.[1]

But it would seem the saturation level for digital ownership, whether phones, laptops, or tablets, will happen in the next few years. At that point there won't be as many newcomers to online shopping; instead companies will be trying to convince Canadians to buy more often.

However, online shopping is not the only reason for bricks-and-mortar retail decline; there has been a shift in retail strategy by most stores. In the 1980s and 1990s, bigger was better, and that included square footage and sheer number of stores. Those decades were dominated by bigger concept stores, like Woodward's, Sears, Zellers, Walmart, and The Bay.

But today, retailers such as the Gap are turning to smaller stores, which results in much better per square foot sales than larger stores.[2]

Some stores are even turning toward using their retail space as a place to fulfill online orders. Specialty clothing and lifestyle retailer Zumiez shut down its warehouse where it filled online orders so that it could shift those duties to its retail stores. The chief executive of Zumiez noted: "Not only does the concept of localized fulfillment mean that we now only have one cost structure to leverage, but we can now get product into customers' hands faster by reducing the order processing time, cutting down the shipping distance to the customer and also offering in-store pickup."[3]

For some retailers, a retail space does not make a lot of sense. Canadian card and stationery retailer Carlton Cards closed all of its retail stores in early 2020. But losing all of that retail space was a relief for the company, especially since it still sells its cards and products in other retail stores like Shoppers Drug Mart.

Bench, another retailer, closed all of its Canadian stores in early 2020.[4] For anyone who had shopped in a Bench store, it might have been a forgettable experience. Parent company Freemark Apparel Brands never seemed to put much effort into making the Bench retail space to be reflective of any sort of brand experience. It made a lot more sense that if the company could not enhance its customers' experiences itself, it should focus on its website and have other intermediaries (e.g., Hudson's Bay) take its products and make a better display and customer experience.

So, clearly just having a retail store is not good enough; aspiring retailers have to work on creating a true customer experience at their stores. Lululemon is a brand that focuses on more than just selling athletic clothes; it offers classes, beverages, and knowledgeable staff to help answer questions.

Apple stores famously have millions of dollars of their products on display, ready for any customer of any age to interact with the technology; the company has spent time and money on creating just the right experience. There are tables available to have repairs completed by the Geniuses who are trained to solve customer problems. Recently, Apple Stores revamped spaces at the back of stores, looking to provide more room for classes and free tutorials.

The kind of success achieved by Apple and Lululemon does point away from an easy and hyperbolic claim of a "retail apocalypse." The 2019 Canadian Shopping Centre Study analyzed the top 30 malls in Canada and showed an increase in productivity per square foot in 21 out of the 30 malls.[5]

But clearly retailers can no longer simply open doors and adorn mannequins in hopes of winning customers away from their phones. There needs to be a product that is pleasing to customers that has attributes and benefits that help to solve a problem that exists in their lives.

And it also helps retailers to see study what is going on around them in the retail environment. Larger malls are becoming destinations for customers to enjoy a wide variety of experiences: movies, food, and entertainment. There are pop-up shops for high-demand retailers, such as Manitobah Mukluks, which may fly in for the holiday season, and then leave the albatross of unwanted space that is likely still being paid for by a previous retailer who was not so in demand.

And even if retailers create an unforgettable physical retail experience, the digital world cannot be ignored. The combination of physical and digital in the omnichannel approach has become a necessity for retailers. The two most recent generations, Y and Z, both crave and demand an experience that can be had in person and on their devices.

This multipronged approach has forced retailers to create better connections, not only in their own digital and physical spaces, but also with intermediaries charged with getting them products for their shelves. Marketing research expert Kruti Desai recently noted, "Next-day delivery is now becoming the norm and it's likely going to keep growing. So, we are seeing how that omnichannel strategy is changing the way retailers are selling their products, storing their products."[6]

The idea that Canadian retail is facing an apocalypse is probably exaggerated. Although there are plenty of trends that are concerning for retailers—everything from international trade wars to anticonsumerism—there exists potential for any retailer willing to look, listen, and learn.

Tada Images/Shutterstock.com

QUESTIONS

1. Create a clear target market for your new retail concept.

2. Discuss how you would create an omnichannel retail strategy for your new store.

3. You hear of a new mattress concept store called Casper. Head to the company's website and look over its offerings. Also have a look for the closest Casper retail location and go visit if possible.

NOTES

1. Melody McKinnon, "2019 Multi-Source Report: What Canadian Online Shoppers Want," Online Business Canada, https://canadiansinternet.com/2019-report-what-canadian-online-shoppers-want (accessed June 24, 2020).

2. Tonya Garcia, "Massive Store Closures Are a Strategy, Not a Sign of a 'Retail Apocalypse,' Experts Say," Market Watch, September 16, 2019, www.marketwatch.com/story/massive-store-closures-are-a-strategy-not-a-sign-of-a-retail-apocalypse-experts-say-2019-09-13 (accessed June 24, 2020).

3. Ibid.

4. Josh Rubin, "Bench Athletic Wear Is Closing All of Its Canadian Stores," *The Toronto Star,* January 23, 2020, www.thestar.com/business/2020/01/23/bench-athletic-wear-is-closing-all-of-its-canadian-stores.html (accessed June 24, 2020).

5. Tonya Garcia, "Massive Store Closures Are a Strategy, Not a Sign of a 'Retail Apocalypse,' Experts Say," Market Watch, September 16, 2019, www.marketwatch.com/story/massive-store-closures-are-a-strategy-not-a-sign-of-a-retail-apocalypse-experts-say-2019-09-13 (accessed June 24, 2020).

6. Mario Toneguzzi, "'Retail Apocalypse' in Canada a Myth: Expert," Retail Insider, June 25, 2019, www.retail-insider.com/retail-insider/2019/6/retail-apocalypse-in-canada-a-myth-expert (accessed June 24, 2020).

15 | Marketing Communications

LEARNING OUTCOMES

15-1 Discuss the role of promotion in the marketing mix

15-2 Apply the communication process to marketing communications

15-3 Outline the goals and tasks of promotion

15-4 Discuss the elements of integrated marketing communications (the promotional mix)

15-5 Discuss promotional goals and the AIDA concept

15-6 Discuss the concept of integrated marketing communications and the factors that affect the promotional mix

"Think like a wise man but communicate in the language of the people."

—W.B. Yeats[1]

15-1 | THE ROLE OF PROMOTION IN THE MARKETING MIX

promotion
communication by marketers that informs, persuades, reminds, and connects potential buyers to a product for the purpose of influencing an opinion or eliciting a response

promotional strategy
a plan for the use of the elements of promotion: advertising, public relations, personal selling, sales promotion, direct-response communication, and social media

The fourth "P" of the marketing mix is, ironically, how most people would define marketing. If this book has taught you nothing else, it should be that marketing is not synonymous with advertising, public relations, selling, social media, and the other concepts discussed in these last few chapters. That said, promotion is as vital to marketing as the principles discussed up to this point. The truth is, no product, no matter how appealing, no matter how competitively priced, and no matter how strategically distributed, can get to its target market without some form of **promotion**—communication that informs, persuades, reminds, and connects potential buyers to a product or service for the purpose of influencing their opinion or eliciting a response.

Promotional strategy is a plan for the optimal use of the elements of promotion (the promotional mix elements): advertising, public relations, sales promotion, personal selling, direct-response communication, and digital marketing. As Exhibit 15.1 shows, the goals of the company's promotional strategy should be in support of overall goals of the firm's marketing mix—product, place (distribution), promotion, and price. Using these overall goals, marketers combine the elements of the promotional strategy (the promotional mix) to form a coordinated and **integrated marketing communications** plan. The promotion plan then

becomes another integral part of the marketing strategy for reaching the target market.

The main function of a marketer's promotional strategy is to convince target customers that the products offered provide a unique benefit to them that is not available with competitors' offerings. Internally, this message reflects a competitive advantage that the business holds over the competition. A competitive advantage, often referred to as its differentiation is the set of unique features of a company and its products that are perceived by the target market as significant and superior to those of the competition. Such features can include high product quality, rapid delivery, low prices, excellent customer service, or any feature not offered by the competition.

In the highly competitive cellphone service market, each Canadian company vies for consumers' business using a variety of differentiation strategies at the product level, and then attempts to convey that message through its promotional content. This is also an integral part of the company's positioning strategy—a key strategic concept, discussed at length in Chapter 7. Effective communications here will suggest unique benefits as well as the company's position, often within a single short tagline or slogan. Of course, everything falls apart if the value proposition falls apart at the product offering level.

Exhibit 15.2 lists the digital service providers

integrated marketing communications
the strategic integration of all promotional mix tactics resulting in a thematically consistent and uniform look and feel regardless of platforms or mediums used

EXHIBIT 15.1 ROLE OF PROMOTION IN THE MARKETING MIX

Overall Marketing Objectives

Marketing Mix
- Product
- Place (distribution)
- Promotion
- Price

Promotional Mix
- Advertising
- Direct marketing
- Public relations
- Sales promotion
- Personal selling
- Digital marketing

Promotion Plan

Target Market

EXHIBIT 15.2 TOP DIGITAL SERVICE PROVIDERS IN CANADA, 2020

Market Position	Company	Brand Position	Subscribers
1	Rogers Communications	Make more possible (Rogers.com)	10.8 Million
2	BCE	The network you choose matters (Bell.ca)	9.6 million
3	Telus Mobility	The future is friendly (Telus.com)	9.2 Million
4	Shaw Communications	Connect to more of what you love (Shaw.ca)	3.2 million
5	Videotron	Helix gets it (referencing Videotron's voice-activated entertainment and management platform)	1.7 million

Source: Floella Church, Most Popular Canadian Telecommunication Companies in 2020 www.ctca.ca/most-popular-canadian-telecomunication-companies/.

dotting the Canadian telecommunications landscape in 2020, along with the claims they were making at the time.

Promotion is a vital component of the marketing mix, informing consumers of a product's benefits and thereby positioning the product in the marketplace.

15-2 | MARKETING COMMUNICATION

Promotional strategy is built upon the foundation of the **communication** process, in which meaning is exchanged through a wide variety of symbols, – most commonly words and images. When a company develops a new product, changes an old one, or simply tries to increase sales or awareness of an existing one, marketers use promotion programs to communicate information necessary to achieve the specific objective. But this is easier said than done. Simple in design and understanding, the communication model is fraught with complexities embedded in the fact that senders and receivers are unique human beings with their own specific way of seeing the world.

Communication can be divided into two major categories: interpersonal communication and mass communication. **Interpersonal communication** is direct, face-to-face communication between two or more people. When communicating face-to-face, each person can see the other's reaction and can respond almost immediately. A salesperson speaking directly with a client is an example of an interpersonal marketing communication.

Mass communication involves communicating a concept or message to large audiences.

communication
the process by which we exchange or share meanings through a common set of symbols

interpersonal communication
direct, face-to-face communication between two or more people

mass communication
the communication of a concept or message to large audiences

Most marketing communication strategies follow this procedure due to the economies of scale present. A single Facebook post or advertisement can reach thousands, whereas face-to-face reaches only those present when the face-to-face communication is exchanged. The downside of mass communication is not only the lack of a personal feeling but also the ability to have a desired effect on the receiver of a message. This effect is decreased when the same message is sent across multiple diverse people. Furthermore, when a company uses mass communication, it does not personally know the people with whom it is trying to communicate, nor is it able to respond immediately to consumers' reactions to its message. Any clutter from competitors' messages or other distractions in the environment can reduce the effectiveness of the mass-communication effort. With so many drawbacks, why keep using mass communication? Simply put, the task is too great to rely on one-by-one acquisition of customers. To account for the shortcomings of mass communication, companies must maintain a consistently appealing and effective interpersonal communications culture. And the face-to-face must be consistent with the messages and positions set forth by the mass strategies. This becomes harder to achieve the larger a company grows, which introduces another paradox. Companies must produce mass media communications to scale their consumer base, but as they do so, they must hire additional personnel to fill HR needs resulting from the growth created by the wider net of communications. The next challenge is to have a growing number of employees, from disparate backgrounds, with untold personality differences and experience levels, *all* communicate in the same way. It can't be done. And it gets even more difficult to manage if companies decide to grow via a franchise model. Now, not only do they have different people responsible for customer interactions, but they have different managers (franchise owners) intent on doing things their way.

Tim Hortons has built an enormous empire in Canada of rabid Tims fans in the multimillions. Each day, Tims

EXHIBIT 15.3 | COMMUNICATION PROCESS

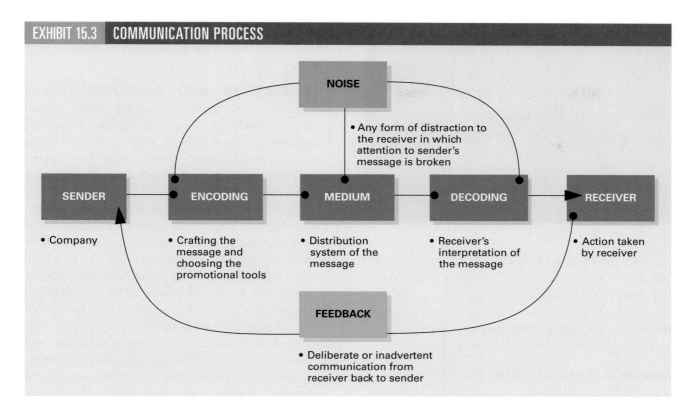

NOISE

• Any form of distraction to the receiver in which attention to sender's message is broken

SENDER — ENCODING — MEDIUM — DECODING — RECEIVER

• Company

• Crafting the message and choosing the promotional tools

• Distribution system of the message

• Receiver's interpretation of the message

• Action taken by receiver

FEEDBACK

• Deliberate or inadvertent communication from receiver back to sender

customers flock to any of the brand's 5000 stores across Canada, having been lured there (in part) by mass communications, such as a "Roll Up the Rim" YouTube commercial. When they arrive at the store, they can be met by a level of interpersonal communications above, below, or exactly within their expectations. All of which is to suggest the importance of excruciating effort put into the encoding portion of the communications process.

15-2a | The Communication Process

Marketers are both senders and receivers of messages. As *senders*, marketers attempt to inform, persuade, remind, and connect with the target market in the hope of achieving a particular course of action. As *receivers*, marketers listen to the target market so they can develop the appropriate messages, adapt existing messages, spot new communication opportunities, and connect with the target audience. In this way, marketing communication is a two-way, rather than one-way, process. The two-way nature of the communication process is shown in Exhibit 15.3.

THE SENDER AND ENCODING The **sender** is the originator of the message in the communication process. In an interpersonal conversation, the sender may be a parent, a friend, or a salesperson. For an advertisement, press release, social media campaign, or a

greeting at a hotel check-in, the sender is the company or organization. Increasingly, hotel chains are buying into everything discussed so far in this chapter. They develop a short punchy tagline, build upon their value proposition to solidify a desired position, then carry that message in all mass and interpersonal communication. Marriott Hotel has gone to great lengths over the last several years to appeal to the business traveller. In 2018 it launched its "Travel Brilliantly" positioning campaign, promising a more seamless, comfortable, and efficient business travel experience. Advertisements, publicity, and loyalty price discount programs all featured the tagline, and then, when travellers arrived at the check-in counter, they were greeted with "How can I help you travel brilliantly?" As mentioned, the mood and attitude to which the message was relayed by one individual in Calgary would have differed from the front desk person in Halifax, but the intent would have been rooted in the same overarching strategy.

Encoding is the conversion of the sender's ideas and thoughts into a

sender
the originator of the message in the communication process

encoding
the conversion of the sender's ideas and thoughts into a message, usually in some combination of words, images, and sound

message, usually in some combination of words, images, and sound. A basic principle of encoding is that what is important is not what the sender says, but rather what the receiver hears. To convey messages that the receiver will hear in the way in which they were intended, marketers use concrete words and visual images.

MESSAGE TRANSMISSION Transmission of a message requires a **channel**—a voice, radio, newspaper, or more than anything else today, some form of social media, as a communication medium. However, mass media aside, theoretically a facial expression or gesture can also serve as a channel. The ubiquity of smartphones in everyone's hands, all containing one or more social media app, makes message transmitting instantaneous.

Reception occurs when the message is detected by the receiver and enters their frame of reference. In a two-way conversation, such as a sales pitch given by a sales representative to a potential client, reception is normally high. In contrast, the desired receivers may or may not detect the message when it is mass communicated because most media are cluttered by **noise**—anything that interferes with, distorts, or slows down the transmission of information. Transmission can also be hindered by situational factors in the physical surroundings, such as light, sound, location, and weather; the presence of other people; or the temporary moods consumers might bring to the situation. While social media has made it easier for senders to get their message out

to target markets, the ease of use is available to everyone and thus a very strategic approach is required to have desired results.

THE RECEIVER AND DECODING Marketers communicate their message through a channel to customers, or **receivers**, who will decode the message. It is important to note that there can be multiple receivers as consumers share their experiences and their recommendations online through social networks and other types of social media, as happened with the campaign used by Billie Eilish to help launch the single "Everything I Wanted." Much as she had done with astonishing success as an independent artist, Eilish took to YouTube to debut the song in late 2019. By then she had been signed to Interscope Records but retained authority to launch new music to her fans in the way they had been accustomed over the years, rather than the age-old record label process of commercial radio exclusives. These online conversations are highly influential and they reach many people quickly and exponentially. Thus, the empowered consumer (receiver) in this new level of engagement is transforming marketing and promotion

channel
a medium of communication—such as a voice, radio, newspaper, or social media—used for transmitting a message

noise
anything that interferes with, distorts, or slows down the transmission of information

receivers
the people who decode a message

as marketers (senders) must constantly try to create, follow, and engage with these conversations. **Decoding** is the interpretation of the language and symbols sent by the source through a channel. Effective communication requires a common understanding or common frame of reference between two communicators. Therefore, marketing managers must ensure a proper match between the message to be conveyed and the target market's attitudes and ideas. The strategy of Interscope Records to allow Billie Eilish to launch a new single her way was a decoding strategy. It required an understanding of the psyche of Eilish's audience (young females) and the astuteness to keep the launch consistent with those that had attracted fans in the first place—the Billie Eilish way.

Even if a message has been received, it will not necessarily be decoded as desired by the sender, because of selective exposure, selective perception, and selective retention. When people receive a message, they tend to manipulate, alter, and modify it to reflect their own biases, needs, knowledge, and culture. Differences in age, social class, education, culture, and ethnicity can lead to messages having little or, worse yet, negative effect. Further, because people don't always listen or read carefully, they can easily misinterpret what is said or written. In fact, researchers have found that consumers misunderstand a large proportion of communications from organizations. The further the reach, the harder it becomes. Global marketers have an even greater challenge as they try to decide if the product's message should be consistent to all geographic segments, or customized. Consistent messaging is more practical, given the impact that the Internet has had on connecting consumers globally, but cultural differences sometimes dictate that location-specific messaging is used, to avoid miscommunication.

FEEDBACK In interpersonal communication, the receiver's response to a message is direct **feedback** to the source. Feedback may be verbal, as in saying, "Yes, I will buy," or nonverbal, as in nodding, smiling, frowning, or gesturing. Feedback can also occur digitally as in the Billie Eilish single release, which generated millions of likes and passionate conversations in both the digital and traditional media landscapes.

Because mass communicators are often cut off from direct feedback, they must rely on market research, social media, or an analysis of viewer responses for indirect feedback. They might use measurements such as click-through rate (CTR) to determine how enticing their messages were in a digital format, even though CTR may reveal nothing more about consumer behaviour.

Indirect feedback like this, however, does provide the analytics necessary to determine if the message is meeting the communication objectives.

The increasing use of online advertising has changed the nature of feedback as it provides for feedback that is interactive, two-way, and often in real time. Marketers can use Web analytics to measure the length of time a consumer stays on a particular page within their website, how often they visit the site, or how many pages they view. These analytics are available instantly, providing the opportunity to make immediate adjustments.

Social media also enables instant feedback by allowing companies to respond immediately to online posts, whether they are on the companies' blogs, hosted on their websites, or social media sites. In traditional communication, a marketer can see the results of consumer behaviour (e.g., a rise or drop in sales) but they must rely on their judgment to explain the behaviour. Today, consumers use social media platforms to comment publicly on marketing efforts. This opens the door for a marketer to engage in a personal, two-way conversation with the consumer. However, because social media conversations occur in real time, and are public, any negative posts or complaints are highly visible. Companies today must therefore allocate devoted social media resources to be not only senders of communications, but also listeners to feedback. Moreover, those resources overseeing the social channels need to be aware of the nuances uniquely inherent to each. For instance, Instagram users tend to respond more favourably to feed posts that possess a certain level of artistic merit. This is exactly how and why the platform was built: "To allow everyone to share beautiful pictures," recalled founder Kevin Systrom on the NPR podcast, "How I Built This" in 2016. Conversely, users of TikTok prefer natural, unrefined, untouched, unfiltered pictures and videos. In that environment, TikTok loyalists will actually become quite vigilant in expressing their disdain for posers on their platform.

Social media has changed the role of the consumer in communications. A consumer who provides a comment on Instagram or YouTube is essentially a sender, meaning the communication model today is much more complicated than in the past. The good news is that these senders can be influencers.

decoding
interpretation of the language and symbols sent by the source through a channel

feedback
the receiver's response to a message

15-3 | THE GOALS OF PROMOTION

People communicate with one another for many reasons. They seek amusement, ask for help, give assistance or instructions, provide information, and express ideas and thoughts. Promotion, on the other hand, seeks to modify behaviour and thoughts in some way. For example, McDonalds, always trying to shift focus away from the fast food stigma, supports a variety of organizations aimed at getting kids active. It also knows a trending social phenomenon when it sees one. After the Toronto Raptors captured their historical NBA Championship in 2019, McDonalds Canada introduced a variety of national promotional tie-ins. By the beginning of the 2019 to 2020 season, McDonalds was not about to release its grip on the Raptors juggernaut, nor the opportunity to continue to reposition itself as a brand celebrating activity. Its "Beyond the Arch" promotion accomplished multiple communication objectives:

1. Associated with the Toronto Raptors by cobranding with the team using licensed trademarks

2. Compelled customers to download and activate the "McD's" app, a requirement to participate in the promotion

3. Drove traffic to McDonalds locations to redeem prizes (the promotion awarded free fries to app users every time the Raptors scored 12 three-pointers in a single game)

Promotion also strives to reinforce existing behaviour—for instance, encouraging consumers to complement their summer barbecues with local craft beers versus a national brand. The source (the seller) hopes to project a favourable image or to motivate a purchase of the company's goods and services.

Promotion can perform one or more of four tasks: *inform* the target audience, *persuade* the target audience, *remind* the target audience, or *connect* the target audience (see Exhibit 15.4). Connecting the target audience is a new task made possible by the increasing acceptance of social media. Often a marketer will try to accomplish two or more of these tasks at the same time.

15-3a | Informing

Informative promotion seeks to convert an existing need into a want or to stimulate interest in a new product. This type of promotion is generally more prevalent during the early stages of the product life cycle. People typically will not buy a product or service or support a non-profit organization until they understand its purpose and its

EXHIBIT 15.4   GOALS OF PROMOTION

Inform

Connect

Persuade

Remind

Note that the goals overlap, as often more than one goal is pursued at any given time.

benefits to them. Complex and technical products, such as automobiles, computers, and investment services often continue to use informative promotion well after the product or service has moved beyond the introductory stage of the product life cycle. This continued promotion is due to the nature of the purchase decision and the risk involved in the purchase. Informative promotion is also important when a new brand is being introduced into an old product class. The new product cannot establish itself against more mature products unless potential buyers are aware of it, value its benefits, and understand its positioning in the marketplace. For example, Tesla, the California-based electric auto company, focuses its messages not only on the gas savings from driving an electric car, but also the higher-order needs Abraham

Maslow defined in his hierarchy, namely social esteem and self-actualization. (Review his important literature in Chapter 5 of this book.)

15-3b | Persuading

Persuasive promotion is designed to stimulate a purchase or an action. Persuasion normally becomes the main promotion goal when the product enters the growth stage of its life cycle. By this time, those in the target market should have general awareness of the product category and some knowledge of how the category can fulfill their wants. Therefore, the company's promotional task switches from informing consumers about the product category to persuading them to buy its brand rather than the competitor's. The promotional message thus emphasizes the product's real and perceived competitive advantages, often appealing to emotional needs, such as love, belonging, self-esteem, and ego satisfaction.

Persuasion can also be an important goal for very competitive, mature product categories, such as many household items and consumer consumables. In a marketplace characterized by many competitors, the promotional message often encourages brand switching and aims to convert some buyers into loyal users. For example, in the case of Proctor and Gamble, the Cincinnati-based consumer packaged goods company with hundreds of different brands under its name (e.g., Tide, Swiffer) goes to great lengths to build and then communicate a culture of social responsibility. It claims this commitment to responsibility and transparency is "what sets us apart." One of the tactical ways it executes on this promise is the implementation of a "Smart Label" initiative, an icon-link in every online product description that takes visitors to a complete breakdown of everything going into a product.

Critics believe that some promotional messages and techniques can be too persuasive, causing consumers to buy products and services they really don't need. However, the counterbalancing argument coming from the capitalistic camp would say communications have no "causal" effect—only intention.

15-3c | Reminding

Reminder promotion is used to keep the product and brand name in the public's mind. This type of promotion prevails during the maturity stage of the life cycle. A reminder promotion assumes that the target market has already been persuaded of the merits of the good or service. Its purpose is simply to trigger a memory. Crest toothpaste and other consumer products often use reminder promotion.

15-3d | Connecting

The increasing acceptance and use of social media are beneficial in helping companies develop relationships with their customers. These relationships, if nurtured properly, can result in increased consumer loyalty, which is highly coveted in the later stages of the product life cycle. Social media allows not only companies to connect with customers, but also customers to connect with each other. The resulting heightened consumer loyalty and connection can create product advocates that promote brands to others through their social networks.

15-4 | THE PROMOTIONAL MIX (AKA INTEGRATED MARKETING COMMUNICATIONS—IMC)

Most promotional strategies use several ingredients—which may include advertising, publicity, sales promotion, personal selling, direct-response communication, and social media—to reach a target market. That combination is called the **promotional mix**. The introduction of digital marketing in the late 1990s brought both the opportunity of leveraging many of these simultaneously but with the challenge of integrating them in a manner that kept the messaging consistent with one to another. Thus, the concept of integrated

promotional mix
the combination of promotional tools—including advertising, publicity, sales promotion, personal selling, direct-response communication, and social media—used to reach the target market and fulfill the organization's overall goals

lev radin/Shutterstock.com

marketing communications (IMC) was born. While the terms *IMC* and *promotional mix* are similar, it is the *integration* term in IMC that modernized the function of promotions from the 2000s forward. It is so widely adopted as a guiding principle of promotions today that the more common term is simply *marketing communications*, or even the compound abbreviation *markcomms*. The proper promotional mix is the one that management believes will meet the needs of the target market and fulfill the organization's overall goals. Data play a very important role in how marketers distribute funding among their promotional mix tactics. The more funds allocated to each promotional tool and the more managerial emphasis placed on each tool, the more important that element is thought to be in the overall mix.

15-4a | Advertising

Almost all companies selling a product or service use advertising, whether in the form of a multimillion-dollar global campaign or a single bus bench in a suburban neighbourhood. **Advertising** is any form of impersonal, one-way mass communication, using time or space owned by an advertising medium company that is paid for by an organization. Traditional media—including out-of-home (OOH), print, radio, and television—were historically the most commonly used mediums to transmit advertisements to consumers. They became popular in this order historically, each outperforming the medium it succeeded. Indeed, advertising revenue essentially funded and built the media industry, and each of these aforementioned media. However, total expenditure on advertising has been tilting more and more to digital options including online banner advertising websites, email, blogs, videos, interactive games, podcasts, flash briefings, and texts. With the increasing fragmentation of traditional media choices and the accelerated use of social media by consumers, marketing budgets are shifting toward buying advertisements on these digital options, including social media. However, as the Internet becomes a more vital component of many companies' promotion

advertising
any form of impersonal, one-way mass communication, using time or space owned by an advertising medium company that is paid for by an organization

public relations
the marketing function that evaluates public attitudes, identifies areas within the organization the public may be interested in, and executes a program of action to earn public understanding and acceptance

and marketing mixes, consumers and lawmakers are increasingly concerned about possible violations of consumers' privacy, forcing social media sites such as Facebook to re-examine their privacy policies.

One of the primary benefits of advertising is its ability to communicate to a large number of people at one time. Cost per contact, therefore, is typically very low. Advertising has the advantage of being able to reach the masses (for instance, through national television networks), but it can also be used to microtarget smaller groups of potential customers by placing ads in special-interest sections of local newspapers, or, more currently, an ad on a platform like LinkedIn that will reach only certain people with specific words in their job description. Although the cost per contact in advertising is very low, the total cost to advertise is typically very high because frequency is required. This is an advertising concept which accurately asserts that ads must be seen or heard multiple times in order for desired impact to have a chance. Therefore, it's not enough to buy one television ad in the evening news. Advertisers must buy multiple occasions, which drives up the total ad-buy price. Chapter 16 examines advertising in greater detail.

15-4b | Public Relations (PR) and Publicity

Organizations that are concerned with how they are perceived by their target markets often spend large sums to build a positive public image. PR, and one of its inherent tactics, publicity, is a mass communication tool that is not paid for in terms of space but can be used to earn public understanding and acceptance. Publicity is as much a *result* of public relations as it is a *tactic* of **public relations**. That is, it can be planned or unplanned in earning media coverage. For example, when Apple stages its lavish new product announcements every September, this is a planned event intended to generate publicity (and it does so very well). It is therefore a planned PR tactic. However, when a celebrity is seen wearing the latest Apple Watch, that generates unplanned publicity. Public relations, as a whole, is a communications tool that evaluates public attitudes, identifies areas within the organization the public may be interested in, and executes a program of action. Publicity attempts to use media to help an organization communicate with its customers, suppliers, shareholders, government officials, employees, and the community in which it operates. Marketers use publicity not only to maintain a positive image but also to educate the public about the company's goals and objectives, introduce new products, reinforce a product's positioning, achieve a competitive advantage, and help support the sales effort. It must be stated, however, that publicity has an equal and opposing negative force in which media reports about a company's shortcomings. In the worst case, such as Volkswagen's cover-up of its emissions reporting process, the publicity can result in costly fines, stock price decreases, and a drop in trust.

Heinz capitalized on some great publicity with a short-lived but long-in-the-making advertising campaign for Heinz ketchup. During an episode in Season six of the series *Mad Men,* Don Draper, the creative director with the fictional advertising agency Stirling, Cooper, Draper, Pryce, pitched an unconventional ad campaign entitled "Pass the Heinz." The campaign featured mouth-watering images of food that were missing a key ingredient—ketchup. In the episode, Heinz executives turned down the campaign, stating, "I want to see the bottle. I want to see the product." Today Heinz executives think Don Draper was completely correct on positioning, and so, with the direction of their current advertising agency David, they recreated the three ads exactly as presented in Season six. The campaign ran in the *New York Post* and *Variety* and on outdoor billboards in New York City in early spring 2017. The back story to this campaign was so interesting and unique that it was talked about in the media, creating significant publicity for Heinz and generating greater awareness than that which would have been achieved with the campaign's limited media buy.[2]

As demonstrated by Heinz, a public relations program can generate favourable **publicity**—public information about a company, a product, a service, or an issue appearing in the mass media as a news item. Social media sites such as Twitter can provide large amounts of publicity quickly. Organizations generally do not pay for the publicity and are not identified as the source of the information, but they can benefit from it.

Although organizations do not directly pay for publicity, it should not be viewed as "free." Preparing news releases, staging special events, and persuading media personnel to broadcast or print publicity messages costs money. Public relations and publicity are examined further in Chapter 16.

15-4c | Sales Promotion

Sales promotion consists of all marketing activities that stimulate consumer purchases in the near term. Sales promotion is generally a short-run tool used to stimulate immediate increases in demand. Sales promotion can be aimed at end consumers, business-to-business customers, or a company's employees. Sales promotions include price discounts, free samples, contests and sweepstakes, premiums, trade shows, and coupons. Increasingly, companies such as Groupon and WagJag have combined social networks and sales promotion. All social mediums have become sales promotions platforms for companies as well. Furthermore, in the spirit of IMC, organizations will often spread the same message across multiple platforms as well as traditional media as both an ad-buy and sales promotion.

Marketers often use sales promotion to improve the effectiveness of other ingredients in the promotional mix, especially advertising and personal selling. Adding value to the brand is the main intent of sales promotion, which makes it a particularly valuable activity for promoting new brands or brands in highly competitive marketplaces. Research shows that sales promotion complements advertising by yielding faster short-term sales responses. In many instances, more money is spent on sales promotion than on advertising. Sales promotion is discussed in more detail in Chapter 17.

15-4d | Personal Selling

Personal selling is a purchase situation involving a personal, paid-for communication between two people in an attempt to influence each other. Here, both the buyer and the seller have specific objectives they want to accomplish. The buyer may need to minimize cost or ensure a quality product, whereas the salesperson may need to maximize revenue and profits, which in turn, result in some form of personal financial compensation.

A traditional method of personal selling is a planned presentation to one or more prospective buyers for the purpose of making a sale. Whether the personal selling takes place face to face or over the phone, it attempts to persuade the buyer to accept a point of view. This traditional view of personal selling has been stigmatized to create the perception that the objectives of the salesperson come at the expense of the buyer, creating a win–lose situation.

Today, personal selling is characterized by the relationship that develops between a salesperson and a buyer. Initially, this concept was more typical

publicity
a public relations tactic that, when used proactively, is intended to generate media coverage (earned media) about an organization or person

sales promotion
all marketing activities that stimulate consumer purchases in the near term

personal selling
a purchase situation involving a personal, paid-for communication between two people in an attempt to influence each other

in business-to-business selling situations, involving the sale of products such as heavy machinery and computer systems, which tend to take a long time to close and often result in modifications to the product to meet the unique needs of the buyer. More recently, both business-to-business and business-to-consumer selling have tended to focus on building long-term relationships rather than on making a one-time sale.

Relationship selling emphasizes a win–win outcome and the accomplishment of mutual objectives that benefit both buyer and salesperson in the long term. Rather than focusing on a quick sale, relationship selling attempts to create a long-term, committed relationship that is based on trust, increased customer loyalty, and a continuation of the relationship between the salesperson and the customer. Personal selling, like other promotional mix elements, is increasingly dependent on the Internet. Most companies use their websites to attract potential buyers seeking information on products and services and to drive customers to their physical locations, where personal selling can close the sale. Personal selling is discussed further in Chapter 17.

15-4e | Direct-Response Communication

Direct-response communication, often referred to as *direct marketing*, is the communication of a message directly from an organization and directly to an intended individual target audience. The objective is to generate profitable business results through targeted communications to a specific audience. Direct-response communication uses a combination of relevant messaging and offers that can be tracked, measured, analyzed, stored, and leveraged to drive future marketing initiatives.

Direct-response communication has grown in importance in IMC programs for many reasons, but two factors have played key roles: (1) the results of the communication program can be measured and, hence, immediately altered (if necessary) to improve performance; and (2) the use of the Internet as a communication tool provides one-to-one communication to the intended target, which is the foundation of direct-marketing communication.

Direct-marketing communication uses a variety of media to deliver the personalized message, including television and radio, referred to as *direct-response broadcast*; newspaper and magazines, referred to as *direct-response print*; the telephone, referred to as *telemarketing*; the Internet, both email and websites; and postal mail, referred to as *direct mail*. The most common form of direct-response communication is direct mail.

Direct-response communication can be highly successful because the consumer often finds the targeted communication to be more appealing as it is more personal. Direct marketing is designed to meet consumers' unique needs. Potential buyers can learn about the product and make a purchase at the same time. Direct response is discussed further in Chapter 16.

15-4f | Online Marketing, Content Marketing, and Social Media

Online marketing is communication delivered through the Internet and/or mobile devices. The rapid growth of consumers' use of the Internet and its pervasive impact on consumers' daily lives have led to new communication opportunities for marketers. The Internet creates real-time, two-way communication with consumers. This allows the marketer to alter the message to better suit the consumer. Not only can consumers immediately respond to the marketer's message with further inquiries or even a purchase, but also, as a result of email and social media, they can also share it instantly with their friends and family. The penetration of Internet usage has also created the opportunity for marketers to become publishers of content that is easily accessible to consumers through marketers' email marketing, search engine optimization, paid search, and display advertising strategies that pull the consumer to the company's website or social media channels, to engage them with the content and thus the brand. Content created by marketers adds value to a brand and can help to reinforce a brand's positioning in the marketplace relative to competition.

In 2019, during the seemingly endless self-created destruction of high-profile men's reputations, Gillette strategically chose to pivot away from its decades-old tagline, "The Best a Man Can Get," over to "The Best Men Can Be." The subtle change of a passive verb was the big idea at the centre of a traditional and digital media blitz. YouTube alone received over 30 million views, many of which were negative about how the brand was portraying men (Youtube.com/Gillette). However, a different customer base, including women, was born out of the goodwill generated by the message, which could not have been completed without social media.

direct-response communication
communication of a message directly from a marketing company and directly to an intended individual target audience

online marketing
two-way communication of a message delivered through the Internet to the consumer

#thebestmencanbe

Finally, as the second decade of the 2000s came to a close, **influencer marketing** was quickly becoming an important tactic within the digital strategy. Customers were beginning to put more stock into personal endorsements from influencers than corporate messages. These influencers were not the celebrities who had been a staple in the ad-world for decades; they were everyday people hawking everything from protein bars to legal advice. What made them influential was not only the reach they had attained within the various platforms but also the specific type of customer they were reaching. Organizations knew that these influencers had developed strong reputations with their audiences, and that this value was worth compensating influencers, either in kind or in cash, for endorsing a brand.

Social media are promotion tools used to facilitate conversations and other interactions among people. Consumers can hold intimate conversations with companies that can be shared through "likes" on Facebook and Instagram and retweets on Twitter. In the same way, social media allow consumers to speak to one another—often in a public forum, such as Facebook, providing instantaneous and wide-reaching word of mouth. **Social media** include blogs; microblogs, like Twitter; video platforms, such as YouTube and TikTok; podcasts; and social networks, such as Instagram, Facebook, Pinterest, and LinkedIn. The consumer who uses social media is in control of the message, the medium, and the response. This increased consumer empowerment can be frightening for companies, but they have come to see that when used properly, social media has value. Indeed, social media has become a "layer" in promotional strategies. Social media is ubiquitous. Social media has created a completely new way for marketers to manage their image, connect with consumers, and generate interest in and desire for their products. If the marketer can listen and learn, they can engage more successfully. Marketers are using social media as an integral aspect of their campaigns and as a way to extend the benefits of traditional media. Social media is discussed in more detail in Chapter 18.

15-4g | The Communication Process and the Promotional Mix

The elements of the promotional mix differ in their ability to affect the target audience. Exhibit 15.5 outlines differences among the promotional mix elements with respect to mode of communication, marketer's control over the communication process, amount and speed of feedback, direction of message, marketer's control over the message, identification of the sender, speed in reaching large audiences, and message flexibility.

From Exhibit 15.5, you can see that most elements of the promotional mix are indirect and impersonal when used to communicate with a target market, providing only one direction of message flow. For example, advertising, public relations, and sales promotion are generally impersonal, one-way means of mass communication controlled by the marketer. Because these elements of the promotional mix provide no opportunity for direct feedback, altering the promotional message and adapting to changing consumer preferences, individual differences, and personal goals is difficult to do quickly.

Personal selling, on the other hand, is personal, two-way communication offering the opportunity to adjust the message as required. Personal selling, however, is very slow in dispersing the marketer's message to large audiences. Direct-response communication is meant to be targeted, two-way communication but the extent of the personalization is dependent on the medium used to reach the intended target.

The Internet has changed the landscape tremendously. Both the marketer and the consumer, with the consumer often in control, are now sharing the communication space. Consumers can pass judgment on a brand or the brand's message in a public forum, through online posts (whether they're asked to do so or not), and they can alter the communication message immediately or create their own. This is referred to as **consumer-generated content**.

Astute marketers, recognizing that consumers trust each other more than they trust brands, have created campaigns that encourage the consumer to create consumer-generated content. Many new products have been successfully launched, and established products have continued to remain relevant, on the basis of consumer-generated

influencer marketing leveraging the influential power of individuals, as thought leaders, to gain trust of a target market

social media collection of online communication tools that facilitate conversations online; when used by marketers, social media tools encourage consumer empowerment

consumer-generated content any form of publicly available online content created by consumers; also referred to as user-generated content

EXHIBIT 15.5

CHARACTERISTICS OF THE ELEMENTS IN THE PROMOTIONAL MIX (INCLUDING DIRECT-RESPONSE COMMUNICATION)

	Advertising	Public Relations	Sales Promotion	Personal Selling	Direct-Response Communication	Social Media Online Marketing, Content Marketing
Mode of Communication	Indirect and impersonal	Usually indirect and impersonal	Usually indirect and impersonal	Direct and face-to-face	Direct but often impersonal	Indirect but instant
Marketer's Control over the Situation	Low	Moderate to low	Moderate to low	High	Some, depending on medium used	Some, depending on medium used
Amount of Feedback	Little	Little	Little to moderate	Much	High	High
Speed of Feedback	Delayed	Delayed	Varies	Immediate	Varies	Immediate
Direction of Message	Flow one-way	One-way	Mostly one-way	Two-way	Mostly two-way	Two-way/multiple ways
Marketer's Control over Message Content	Yes	No	Yes	Yes	Some	Varies
Identification of Sender	Yes	No	Yes	Yes	Yes	Yes
Speed in Reaching Large Audience	Fast	Usually fast	Fast	Slow	Slow	Fast
Message Flexibility	Same message to all audiences	Usually no direct control over message audiences	Same message to varied target	Tailored to prospective buyer	Tailored to prospective target	Tailored to prospective target—the most targeted

content. WestJet is so consumer-content driven that it built a series of ads in 2019 around third-party travel review hub, "TripAdvisor" and specifically how, by way of passenger reviews, it had named WestJet Canada's best airline three years in a row. This didn't merely associate WestJet's accomplishment to some nebulous industry ranking system no one had heard of; rather, it leveraged the power of a universal opinion hub as a form of source credibility to make the accomplishment relatable.

As a result of the impact of social media, as well as the proliferation of new platforms, tools, and ideas, promotional tactics can also be categorized according to media types—paid, earned, or owned (see Exhibit 15.6). **Paid media** are based on the traditional advertising model, where a brand pays for media space. Traditionally, paid media included television, magazine, outdoor, radio, or newspaper advertising. Now, increasingly, paid media come in the form of display advertising on websites or pay-per-click advertising on search engines, such as Google. Paid media are quite important, especially as they migrate to the Web. **Earned media** are based on the traditional publicity model. The idea is to get people talking about the brand—whether through media coverage (as in traditional public relations) or through word of mouth (through sharing on social media sites). Search engine optimization (SEO), where companies embed key words into content to increase their positioning on search results, can also be considered earned media. **Owned media** are those where brands become publishers of their own content to maximize

paid media
a category of promotional tactic based on the traditional advertising model whereby a brand pays for advertising space

earned media
a category of promotional tactic based on a public relations model that gets customers talking about products or services

owned media
a category of promotional tactic based on brands becoming publishers of their own content to maximize the brands' value to consumers

Markus Mainka/Shutterstock.com

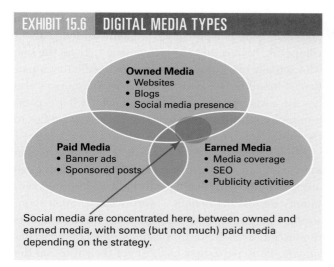

EXHIBIT 15.6   DIGITAL MEDIA TYPES

Owned Media
- Websites
- Blogs
- Social media presence

Paid Media
- Banner ads
- Sponsored posts

Earned Media
- Media coverage
- SEO
- Publicity activities

Social media are concentrated here, between owned and earned media, with some (but not much) paid media depending on the strategy.

Source: Adapted from Dave Fleet, "Why Paying Bloggers for Posts Changes the Game," DaveFleet.com, December 12, 2010, http://davefleet.com/2010/12/bloggers-money=posts-game (accessed May 17, 2017).

brand value to the customer. Owned media are often referred to as **branded content or inbound content**. Owned media include a company's own website and its official presence on Facebook, Twitter, YouTube channels, blogs, and other platforms. These media are controlled by the brand but continually keep the consumer in mind. This type of media can be highly engaging by encouraging consumer conversation and can be very cost-effective if consumer engagement leads to online sharing.

15-5 | PROMOTIONAL GOALS AND THE AIDA CONCEPT

The ultimate goal of any promotion is to have someone buy a good or service or, in the case of non-profit organizations, to take some action (such as donate online). A classic model for achieving promotional goals is called the **AIDA concept**.[3] The acronym stands for *attention, interest, desire*, and *action*—the stages of consumer involvement with a promotional message.

This model proposes that consumers respond to marketing messages in a cognitive (thinking), affective (feeling), and conative (doing) sequence. First, a promotion manager may focus on attracting a consumer's *attention* by training a salesperson to use a friendly greeting and approach, by using music that is relevant to the target, or by using bold headlines, movement, bright colours, and other similar creative devices in an advertisement. Next, a good sales presentation, demonstration, or advertisement creates *interest* in the product and then,

by illustrating how the product's features will satisfy the consumer's needs, arouses desire. Finally, a special offer or a strong closing sales pitch may be used to obtain purchase action.

The AIDA concept assumes that promotion propels consumers along the following four steps in the purchase-decision process:

1. *Attention:* The advertiser must first gain the attention of the target market. A business cannot sell its product if the market does not know that the good or service exists. In an attempt to regain relevance at a time when it was squeezed out of the denim category it had created, Levi's tried reaching out to a younger demographic with an investment in building its brand. In 2011, Levi's brought in Proctor and Gamble executive Charles Burgh, who concurred: "[Levi's] hadn't been investing in building the brand, we hadn't been investing in innovation, we were really disconnected with the consumer, our advertising was not working."[4] Burgh and his team moved quickly. By 2016 they had acquired the naming rights to the brand new football stadium in the company's hometown of San Francisco, and a new tagline, "Live in Levi's." They also invested heavily in research and development to compete with the "athleisure wear" segment. The Superbowl, held in Levi's Stadium in 2016, signalled to the world that the brand was back.

2. *Interest:* Simple awareness of a brand seldom leads to a sale. The next step is to create interest in the product. In the case of Levi's, its purchase of the Eureka Innovation Lab pushed forward new industry standards including a four-way stretch fabric and a marketing team devoted exclusively to the women's division of the company.

3. *Desire:* Levi's newfound focus on women in the late teens–20, which resulted in the creation of the "wedgie" jean, helped increase women's sales almost 30 percent from 2018 to 2019.[5] The hiring of an AI officer in 2019 also signalled to the world that Levi's would not be content to fade into

branded (or inbound) content
creation of engaging bespoke content as a way to promote a particular brand that attracts and builds relationships with consumers

AIDA concept
a model that outlines the process for achieving promotional goals in terms of stages of consumer involvement with the message; the acronym stands for *attention, interest, desire*, and *action*

the background anymore. All of this led Levi's, a 165-year-old company to its initial public offering in March 2019.[6]

4. *Action:* One of the remaining challenges Levi's had by 2019 was that a large percentage of women were wearing yoga pants or sweatpants instead of jeans. Certainly the aforementioned four-way stretch fabric had helped, but women still needed to see someone else, preferably famous, wearing and looking great in Levi's. Enter Beyoncé and her appearance in 2019 at Coachella where she was rocking Levi's cut-offs. Needless to say, consumer action soon followed.[7]

Most buyers involved in high-involvement purchase situations pass through the four stages of the AIDA model on their way to making a purchase, but a repeat purchase or a low-risk purchase may not require the consumer to pass through all four stages. The promoter's task is to first determine where on the purchase ladder most of the target consumers are located and to then design a promotion plan to meet their needs. The AIDA concept does not explain how all promotions influence purchase decisions. The model suggests that promotional effectiveness can be measured by consumers progressing from one stage to the next. However, despite the commonly accepted AIDA model, there is some debate around the order of the stages and whether consumers go through all steps. A purchase can occur without interest or desire, such as when a low-involvement product is bought on impulse. Regardless of the order of the stages or consumers' progression through these stages, the AIDA concept helps marketers by suggesting which promotional strategy will be most effective.[8]

If taken too literally, the AIDA model has its limitations. "Action" as the end goal suggests a purchase (or a donation, in the case of a charity). However, a single purchase or donation is not the end goal. Marketers are concerned about loyalty—continual purchase behaviour. Hence, marketers develop IMC programs that turn the action into loyalty. A brand-loyal consumer can become a brand advocate.

15-5a | AIDA and the Promotional Mix

Exhibit 15.7 depicts the relationship between the promotional mix and the AIDA model. It shows that, although advertising does have an impact in the later stages, it is most useful in gaining attention for goods or services. In contrast, personal selling reaches fewer people at first. Salespeople are more effective at creating customer interest for merchandise or a service and

at creating desire. For example, advertising may help a potential computer purchaser to gain knowledge about competing brands, but the salesperson may be the one who actually encourages the buyer to decide that a particular brand is the best choice. The salesperson also has the advantage of having the product, such as a computer, physically there to demonstrate its capabilities to the buyer.

Public relations' greatest impact is gaining attention for a company, good, or service. Many companies can attract attention and build goodwill by sponsoring community events that benefit a worthy cause. Such sponsorships project a positive image of the business and its products into the minds of consumers and potential consumers. Book publishers push to get their titles on the bestseller lists of major publications such as *The Globe and Mail,* to be included in the yearly CBC Canada Reads series, and to get their authors included in literary events throughout the country.

Sales promotion's greatest strength is in creating strong desire and purchase intent. Frequent-buyer sales promotion programs, popular among retailers, allow consumers to accumulate points or dollars that can later be redeemed for goods. Frequent-buyer programs tend to increase purchase intent and loyalty and encourage repeat purchases.

Social media are a strong way to gain attention and interest in a brand, particularly if content goes viral. It can then reach a massive audience. Social media are also effective at engaging with customers and enabling companies to maintain interest in a brand if properly managed.

EXHIBIT 15.7	THE PROMOTIONAL MIX AND THE AIDA MODEL			
	Attention	**Interest**	**Desire**	**Action**
Advertising	●	●	◐	○
Public Relations	●	●	●	○
Sales Promotion	◐	◐	●	◐
Personal Selling	◐	●	●	●
Direct Marketing	◐	●	●	●
Social Media	◐	●	●	●

● Very effective   ◐ Somewhat effective   ○ Not effective

15-6 | INTEGRATED MARKETING COMMUNICATIONS AND THE PROMOTIONAL MIX

As discussed at the beginning of this chapter, ideally, marketing communications from each promotional mix element (advertising, public relations, sales promotion, personal selling, direct-response communication, and social media) should be integrated—that is, the message reaching the consumer should be the same regardless of whether it is from an advertisement, a salesperson in the field, a magazine article, a Facebook page, or a coupon in a newspaper insert.

Consumers do not think in terms of the six elements of promotion. Instead, everything is an "ad." The only people who recognize the distinctions among these communications elements are the marketers themselves. So, unfortunately, when planning promotional messages, some marketers treat each of the promotion elements separately, failing to integrate the communications efforts from one element to the next.

To prevent this disjointed communication, companies today have adopted the concept of IMC. IMC is the careful coordination of all promotional messages—traditional advertising, public relations, sales promotion, personal selling, direct-response communication, and social media—for a product or service to ensure the consistency of messages at every contact point where a company meets the consumer. Following the concept of IMC, marketing managers carefully work out the roles that various promotional mix tools will play in the communications strategy. The timing of promotional activities is coordinated, and the results of each campaign are carefully monitored to improve future use of the promotional mix tools.

The IMC concept continues to grow in popularity for several reasons. First, the proliferation of thousands of media choices and the continued use of social media by all age groups has made communication a more complicated task. Instead of promoting a product through only mass-media options, such as television and magazines, promotional messages today can appear in a variety of sources.

Further, the mass market is highly fragmented. The traditional broad market groups that marketers promoted to in years past have been replaced by selectively segmented markets requiring niche marketing strategies that rely on well-integrated communication campaigns. Finally, marketers have slashed their advertising spending in favour of promotional techniques that generate immediate sales responses, those that are more easily measured, and those that offer heightened consumer engagement. Online advertising has thus earned a bigger share of the budget because of its measurability, the immediacy of feedback, and its success at engaging the individual consumer. The interest in IMC is largely a reaction to the scrutiny that marketing communications has come under and, particularly, to suggestions that uncoordinated promotional activity leads to a strategy that is wasteful and inefficient.

15-6a | Factors Affecting the Promotional Mix

Promotional mixes vary a great deal from one product and one industry to the next. Normally, advertising and personal selling are used to promote goods and services supported and supplemented by sales promotion. Public

A FINE BALANCE

Tea is the second-most-consumed beverage next to water, and consumption is growing. Tea drinkers have on average 11 types of tea in their cupboard.[9] Tetley is the leading tea brand in the category in Canada, but as Canadians increase their consumption of tea, competition within the category has intensified, providing consumers much in the way of variety. Such a competitive landscape requires innovation to stay relevant to the consumer. Tetley's latest launch is a line of "Super Teas" fortified with everything from echinacea and zinc to vitamin B. To reinforce the new positioning, Tetley created the "notyouraveragecupoftea" IMC campaign, which included a television/YouTube ad featuring the juxtaposition of tea in the lives of athletes, firefighters, motorcyclists, and performing artists—all singing, in deliberately offbeat rhythms, "I'm the Little Teacup." The fully integrated campaign was designed to drive awareness of the Super Teas, as well as the idea that the tea drinker no longer fit the age-old stereotype.[10]

relations helps to develop a positive image for the organization and the product line. Social media have been used more for consumer goods, but business-to-business marketers are increasingly using them as well. A business may choose not to use all six promotional elements in its promotional mix, or it may choose to use them only in varying degrees. The particular promotional mix chosen by a business for a product or service depends on several factors: the nature of the product, the stage in the product life cycle, target market characteristics, the type of buying decision, funds available for promotion, and whether a push or a pull strategy will be used.

NATURE OF THE PRODUCT Characteristics of the product itself can influence the promotional mix. For instance, a product can be classified as either a business product or a consumer product (refer to Chapters 9 and 10). As business products are often custom-tailored to the buyer's exact specifications, they are typically not well suited to mass promotion. Therefore, producers of most business goods, such as computer systems or industrial machinery, rely more heavily on personal selling than on advertising. However, advertising can still serve a purpose in promoting business goods as a strategic campaign in a trade publication can help locate potential customers for the sales force.

In contrast, because consumer products generally are not custom made, they do not require the selling

iStock.com/miodrag ignjatovic

Producers of consumer goods typically use a pull strategy to bring customers to a traditional or virtual storefront.

efforts of a company representative to tailor them to the user's needs. Thus consumer goods are promoted mainly through advertising or social media to create brand familiarity. Sales promotion, the brand name, and the product's packaging are about twice as important for consumer goods as for business products.

The costs and risks associated with a product also influence the promotional mix. As a general rule, when the costs or risks of buying and using a product increase, persuasive personal selling becomes more important. The more expensive the item is, whether it be a consumer or business good, the more important it is that a salesperson be available to assure buyers that they are spending their money wisely and not taking an undue financial risk. Social risk is also an issue. When a consumer is purchasing specialty products such as jewellery or clothing, a salesperson can be useful to guide the decision.

STAGE IN THE PRODUCT LIFE CYCLE The product's stage in its life cycle is a factor in designing a promotional mix (see Exhibit 15.8). During the *introduction stage,* the basic goal of promotion is to inform the target audience that the product is available. Initially, the emphasis is on the general product class—for example, electric cars. This emphasis gradually changes to gaining attention for a particular brand, such as the Nissan Leaf or the Tesla. Typically, both extensive advertising and public relations inform the target audience of the product class or brand and heighten awareness levels. Companies use owned media here to manage the message and to provide consumers with the information they seek to become knowledgeable about the product class and the brand. Sales promotion encourages early trial of the product, and personal selling gets retailers to carry the product.

EXHIBIT 15.8 **FACTORS AFFECTING THE PROMOTIONAL MIX**

- Nature of the Product
- Stage in the PLC
- Push or Pull Strategy
- Promotional Mix
- Target Market Factors
- Promotional Funds Available
- Type of Buying Decision

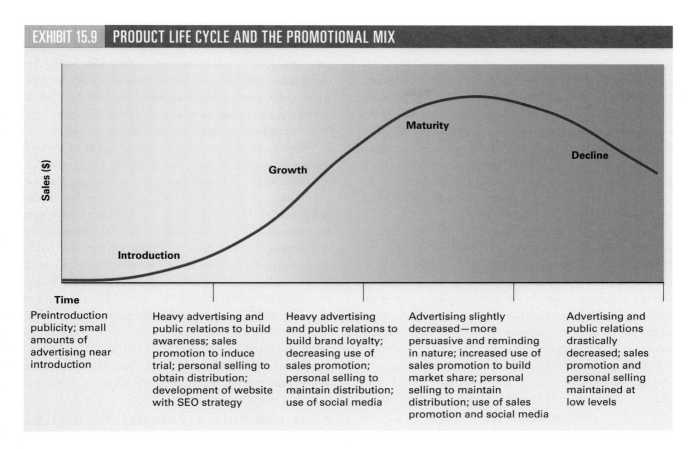

EXHIBIT 15.9 PRODUCT LIFE CYCLE AND THE PROMOTIONAL MIX

| Preintroduction publicity; small amounts of advertising near introduction | Heavy advertising and public relations to build awareness; sales promotion to induce trial; personal selling to obtain distribution; development of website with SEO strategy | Heavy advertising and public relations to build brand loyalty; decreasing use of sales promotion; personal selling to maintain distribution; use of social media | Advertising slightly decreased—more persuasive and reminding in nature; increased use of sales promotion to build market share; personal selling to maintain distribution; use of sales promotion and social media | Advertising and public relations drastically decreased; sales promotion and personal selling maintained at low levels |

When the product reaches the *growth stage* of the life cycle, the promotion blend may shift. Often a change is necessary because different types of potential buyers are targeted. Although advertising and public relations continue to be major elements of the promotional mix, sales promotion can be reduced because consumers need fewer incentives to purchase. The promotional strategy is to emphasize the product's differential advantage over the competition. Persuasive promotion is used to build and maintain brand loyalty during the growth stage. Social media can be quite effective here as they can be used to heighten consumer engagement, create online conversations about the brand, and establish peer-to-peer advice, resulting in brand preference. By this stage, personal selling has usually succeeded in achieving adequate distribution for the product.

As the product reaches the *maturity stage* of its life cycle, competition becomes fiercer and thus persuasive; reminder advertising is more strongly emphasized. Sales promotion comes back into focus as product sellers try to increase their market share. Social media, in particular the innovative use of social media, such as the encouragement of consumer-generated content, can keep the brand top of mind with consumers.

All promotion, especially advertising, is reduced as the product enters the *decline stage*. Nevertheless,

personal selling and sales promotion efforts may be maintained, particularly at the retail level.

TARGET MARKET CHARACTERISTICS A target market that is characterized by widely scattered potential customers, highly informed buyers, and brand-loyal repeat purchasers generally requires a promotional mix with more advertising, social media, and sales promotion, and less personal selling. Sometimes, however, personal selling is required even when buyers are well informed and geographically dispersed. Although industrial installations may be sold to well-educated people with extensive work experience, salespeople must be present to explain the product and work out the details of the purchase agreement.

Businesses often sell goods and services in markets where potential customers are difficult to locate. Social media and direct-response print advertising can be used to find these customers. The consumer is invited to call for more information, mail in a reply card for a detailed brochure, or visit a website to receive more information.

TYPE OF BUYING DECISION The promotional mix also depends on the type of buying. For routine consumer decisions, such as buying toothpaste, the most effective promotion calls attention to the brand or reminds the consumer about the brand and its distinguishing characteristics. Advertising, social media, and sales promotion are the most productive promotion tools to use for routine decisions.

If the decision is neither routine nor complex, advertising, social media, in particular branded content, and public relations help establish awareness for the good or service. Take, for example, the purchase of hiking shoes. Although the consumer may have never bought hiking shoes before, their need for a pair has heightened their awareness of options. An advertisement, an Instagram post by an outdoor lifestyle influencer, or a review on a website will help to establish the brand preference in the purchase decision.

In contrast, consumers who make complex buying decisions are more extensively involved. They rely on large amounts of information to help them reach a purchase decision. Personal selling is effective in helping these consumers decide. For example, consumers thinking about buying a car often depend on a salesperson to provide the information they need to reach a decision. Again, social media are playing an important role here as purchasers seek advice from peers to acquire the information they need to make the right brand decision. Print advertising may also be used for high-involvement purchase decisions because it can often provide a large amount of information to the consumer.

AVAILABLE FUNDS Money, or the lack of it, may easily be the most important factor in determining the promotional mix. A small, undercapitalized manufacturer may rely heavily on social media for a good online SEO strategy that places the company's website in the top few

results as well as publicity to create demand. If the situation warrants a sales force, a financially strained company may turn to manufacturers' agents, who work on a commission basis with no advances or expense accounts. Even well-capitalized organizations may not be able to afford the advertising rates of highly rated television programs or printed publications with strong circulation.

When funds are available to permit a mix of promotional elements, a business will generally try to optimize its return on promotion dollars while minimizing the *cost per contact,* or the cost of reaching one member of the target market. In general, the cost per contact is very high for personal selling, public relations, and sales promotions, such as samplings and demonstrations. On the other hand, given the number of people national advertising and social media reach, they have very low cost per contact. Usually, a trade-off is made among the funds available, the number of people in the target market, the quality of communication needed, and the relative costs of the promotional elements. There are plenty of low-cost options available to companies without a huge budget. Many of these include online strategies and public relations efforts, in which the company relies on free publicity.

PUSH AND PULL STRATEGIES The last factor that affects the promotional mix is whether a push or a pull promotional strategy will be used. Manufacturers may use aggressive personal selling and trade advertising to convince a wholesaler or a retailer to carry and sell their merchandise. This approach is known as a **push strategy** (see Exhibit 15.10). The wholesaler, in

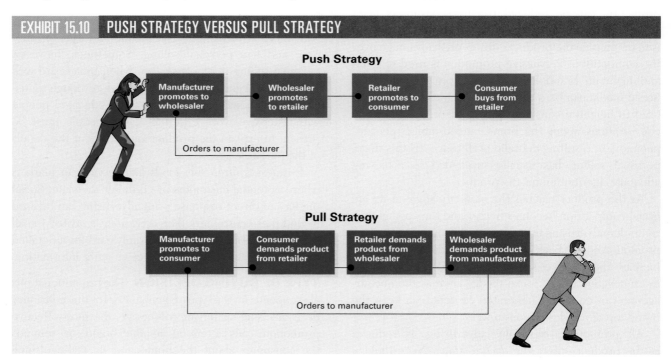

EXHIBIT 15.10 PUSH STRATEGY VERSUS PULL STRATEGY

Push Strategy

Manufacturer promotes to wholesaler → Wholesaler promotes to retailer → Retailer promotes to consumer → Consumer buys from retailer

Orders to manufacturer

Pull Strategy

Manufacturer promotes to consumer → Consumer demands product from retailer → Retailer demands product from wholesaler → Wholesaler demands product from manufacturer

Orders to manufacturer

turn, must often push the merchandise forward by persuading the retailer to handle the goods. The retailer then uses advertising, displays, and other forms of promotion to convince the consumer to buy the pushed products. This concept also applies to services.

At the other extreme is a **pull strategy**, which stimulates consumer demand to obtain product distribution. Rather than trying to sell to the wholesaler, the manufacturer using a pull strategy focuses its promotional efforts on end consumers or opinion leaders. Social media and content or branded marketing are the most recent (and best) example of a pull strategy. The idea is that social media content does not interrupt a consumer's experience with media (like a television commercial interrupts the viewing of a show). Instead the content invites customers to experience it on social media or a website. This encourages more engaged behaviour between consumers and a brand, thereby heightening brand knowledge and encouraging a desire to seek out the brand to purchase. Heavy sampling, introductory consumer advertising, cents-off campaigns, and couponing are also all part of a pull strategy.

Rarely does a company use a pull or a push strategy exclusively. Instead, the mix will usually emphasize one of these strategies. For example, pharmaceutical companies generally use a push strategy, through personal selling and trade advertising, to promote their drugs and therapies to physicians. Sales presentations and advertisements in medical journals give physicians the detailed information they need to prescribe medication to their patients. Most pharmaceutical companies supplement their push promotional strategy with a pull strategy targeted directly to potential patients through advertisements in consumer magazines and on television.

push strategy
a marketing strategy that uses aggressive personal selling and trade advertising to convince a wholesaler or a retailer to carry and sell particular merchandise

pull strategy
a marketing strategy that stimulates consumer demand to obtain product distribution

AWAKE CHOCOLATE
CONTINUING CASE

Nevil, the Communicator

For many people, even today, the reference to "the owl" on the packaging is more of a memory jogger of Awake bars than the Awake name itself. Nevil, as he was officially dubbed at his conception in 2012, was immediately adopted by the founders of Awake for the many things he and his nocturnal likeness stood for.

"It started in a really pragmatic way. We found an experienced brand design agency to work with us as a partner. And we laid out for them three or four ideas of how we wanted people to feel about our brand," explained CEO Adam Deremo. "And they took those ideas and created a whole bunch of different visual representations of what the brand could look like. And when we looked at all of these concepts, all three of us immediately looked at Nevil and said, 'Yep, that's our brand.'"

The importance of this branding element cannot be understated from a marketing communications standpoint. Companies of all stripes, in all industries, often struggle with brandmarks, pictorials, and abstracts in trying to create a fitting association between a name and a symbol. And even then, they often find what they've created is difficult to represent across the marketing functions of packaging, and integrated marketing communications. For Awake, Nevil checked off all the boxes.

Speaking of the caricature, Deremo comments, "It looks hand-drawn, which distinguishes us in confectionary. The fact that it's an owl is a cue to nocturnal activity, which makes sense for a caffeine brand. And the fact that he became our mascot gave us licence to do all of our brand communications from the viewpoint of Nevil."

Integrated marketing communications, the topic of this chapter, is both an academic concept and an actual business directive as to how companies should handle marketing communications in the 2020s. IMC suggests that all messaging be similar in intangible categories such as attitude and tone, as well as in tangible things like colours, fonts, and taglines. Having Nevil's presence and voice across all communications tools discussed in the last four chapters instantly gave Awake Chocolate a perceived sense of coordination in its messaging.

But even with that utility built into its communications, Deremo, who, as CEO is, for all intents and purposes, also the CMO (Chief Marketing Officer), claimed that the company can still do better at tightening up their communications, making them even more consistent and coordinated—the ultimate goal of the integrated marketing communications concept. "One of the important things we did early on was develop a brand style guide, so that anyone who was ever going to be involved with marketing communications would be walked through the style guide. It's kind of like our north star of our communications." You can imagine the challenges of having multiple content creators, senior and junior, newly hired and established, all having to somehow create the exact same voice for Nevil.

Typically associated with brand development, the style guide is also as much about integrated communications because it sets a standard for consistency as well as addresses the topics to cover and the tone to use when covering them. As mentioned in the Awake case in Chapter 11, during the COVID-19 crisis, as the voice of the brand, Nevil was forced to embody a persona more of compassion and caring than levity and lightness.

Chapters 16 to 18 of this book focus on the various subcomponents of integrated marketing communications. As you proceed through the remaining chapter cases, you will see how Nevil is the common thread connecting the subcomponents. As such, Nevil is more than just a branding element; he is the chief storyteller for Awake Chocolate.

QUESTIONS

1. **Jump on to Awake's social media channels and select one or two posts from two or more different platforms (e.g., Instagram and Twitter). Comment on the style and tone of the posts. Note whether you believe the language, tone and attitude of Nevil are consistent across the platforms and posts.**

2. **Continue y audit of Awake's marketing communications by visiting the company's corporate website at www.awakechocolate.com. Review, compare, and comment on the consistency with which the web content matches the social media content.**

3. **Using either your campus store, or a social media photograph, take a look at the point-of-purchase displays (POP) used by Awake. These are the cardboard display boxes manufactured by the company to be used by retailers. Again, compare and comment on the consistency with which the POP matches the different communications channels discussed in the previous questions.**

AWAKE Chocolate

16 | Advertising, Public Relations, and Direct Response

LEARNING OUTCOMES

16-1 Define advertising and understand the effect of advertising

16-2 Identify the major types of advertising

16-3 Discuss the creative decisions in developing an advertising campaign

16-4 Describe media evaluation and selection techniques and how media are purchased

16-5 Discuss the role of public relations in the promotional mix

16-6 Discuss the role of direct-response communication in the promotional mix

"Advertising is based on one thing: happiness."

—Don Draper, *Mad Men*

16-1 | WHAT IS ADVERTISING?

In Chapter 1, we learned that marketing is about understanding the needs of the customer. It helps to shape a business's products and services, based on an understanding of what the customer is looking for. We learned that marketing is about engaging in a *conversation* with that customer and guiding the delivery of what is required to satisfy those needs. *Advertising can help to start the conversation.*

In Chapter 15, we defined *advertising* as any form of impersonal, one-way mass communication, using time or space owned by an advertising medium company that is paid for by an organization. Despite many predictions of its demise, advertising not only continues to be a popular form of promotion but also the amount spent on it continues to grow year over year.[1] Indeed, while digital marketing may have disrupted traditional forms of media, it has single-handedly breathed new life into advertising, with some estimates

of worldwide digital ad-spend to double between 2018 and 2023.[2]

Of course, there are a number of other advertising media or media types that marketers can use to help start the conversation, but there is no doubt that almost any organization's media spend *must* allocate dollars to digital. This holds true in Canada where over 50 percent of advertising budgets are spent on digital.[3] Of the traditional media types; print, out-of-home, and broadcast, television places second in spending, but it is rapidly becoming a distant second.

This is not to say that companies are not producing video forms of advertising. On the contrary, they're producing more of it, but they're buying time and space primarily on Google (YouTube) and Facebook (Instagram), rather than network television. In fact, the only existing opportunities for advertisers to gain the attention of their customers, using television as a medium, are during live sports or awards shows. And even that is hit and miss, as so many consumers now skip through or over ads.

16-1a | Advertising and Market Share

According to Interbrand, an international agency, the top two companies by brand valuation were Apple at $234 billion and Google at $168 billion in its 2019 study.[4] Apple, of course, derives most of its revenue from the sale of consumer electronics such as computers, tablets, and phones, whereas Google's main revenue stream is from advertising; a significant portion of that would come from Apple, trying to ensure it remains at the top of any Google search. In fact, Apple is analogous to most companies that can afford advertising today—buying space and time from other companies in order to maintain brand awareness, and market share.

The challenge for marketers has always been to determine the most appropriate advertising budget. For decades, companies could draw reasonable correlations between sales and advertising expenditure over time, and then use a **percentage of sales** approach to decide on their advertising budget. A company might spend, for instance, $50 000 on advertising and achieve gross annual sales of $500 000 thus concluding that a future sales projection would require a 10 percent of sales spend on advertising. But in the end, this was still just a guess, potentially attaching too much, or too little, influence on sales to advertising.

However, the analytics available with digital advertising today, such as **click-through rate (CTR)** and **pay per click (PPC)** allow advertisers infinitely more data on the effectiveness of their ads. CTR is a ratio of clicks on an ad by viewers to the number of viewers to whom the ad was exposed. Thus, if a company's ad on Facebook is exposed to 100 000 people, and 2300 click through it, then a CTR of 2.3 percent has been achieved, which, incidentally, is a reasonably impressive measurement. PPC, on the other hand is a payment system hedging in favour of the advertiser, whereby the media owner (say Facebook) gets paid only when a user clicks on an ad.

percentage of sales
a method of determining an advertising budget in which a percentage of forecast sales is calculated as the amount to spend on advertising

click-through rate (CTR)
the ratio of clicks on an ad by viewers to the number of viewers to whom the ad was exposed

pay per click (PPC)
a digital advertising payment method in which the advertiser pays the media company, through which the ad is placed, each time a user clicks on a digital ad placed within the media company's space

SUPPORTING A CLIMATE STRIKE

Swedish student activist Greta Thunberg became a household name in 2019, first publicly shaming world leaders at the United Nations Climate Change Summit, then being named person of the year for *Time Magazine*. That autumn, Thunberg's voice, and that of thousands of others, helped organize Climate Strike marches at dozens of locations globally. Sensing the obligation to stand united with strikers, companies like Patagonia, Ben & Jerry's, and Lush cosmetics used a variety of communications tools, including advertising to show their support. But these were not gestures of customer nor corporate pressure; they came from brands self-aware enough to know that they had a definitive role to play in giving a voice to the problem.

Swedish teenager Greta Thunberg further ignited climate change activism among citizens and brands.

16-1b | The Effects of Advertising on Consumers

Advertising affects consumers' daily lives, informing them about products and services and influencing their attitudes, beliefs, and ultimately purchases. Advertising affects the TV programs people watch, the content of the newspapers they read, the politicians they elect, the medicines they take, and the toys their children play with. Recently, due to the surge of our attention on digital, and subsequent use of digital advertising platforms, it is safe to say that we, the consumer, now affect advertising in ways never before felt by advertisers. As opined in his book, *Marketing Rebellion* (2019), Mark Schaefer notes that companies have had to live with the reality that they no longer control the message, and thus have to acknowledge that customers, consumers, shoppers, and buyers are driving the conversation as much as the advertisers themselves. Consequently, the balance of power has shifted to a point now where we see consumers and advertisers having influence on one another.

Though advertising cannot change consumers' deeply rooted values and attitudes, it may succeed in transforming a person's negative attitude toward a product into a positive one. For instance, serious or dramatic advertisements are more effective at changing consumers' negative attitudes. Humorous ads have been found to increase the viewer's involvement in the ad, thereby increasing the impact of the advertisement's message.[5] Advertising also reinforces positive attitudes toward brands. When consumers have a neutral or favourable frame of reference for a product or brand, advertising often positively influences them. When consumers are already highly loyal to a brand, they may buy more of it when advertising and promotion for that brand increase.[6]

Advertising can also affect the way consumers rank a brand's attributes. In past years, car ads emphasized brand attributes such as speed and fuel efficiency. Today, car manufacturers have added safety, technology, customization, and environmental considerations to the list.

16-2 | MAJOR TYPES OF ADVERTISING

The company's promotional objectives determine the type of advertising it uses. If the goal of the promotion plan is to improve the image of the company or the industry, **institutional advertising** may be used. In contrast, if the advertiser wants to enhance the sales of a

institutional advertising
a form of advertising designed to enhance a company's image rather than promote a particular product

specific good or service, **product advertising**, which promotes the benefits of a specific good or service, is used.

16-2a | Institutional Advertising

Historically, advertising in Canada has been product oriented. Today, many companies market multiple products and need a different type of advertising. Institutional advertising, or corporate advertising, promotes the corporation as a whole and is designed to establish, change, or maintain the corporation's identity. It usually does not ask the audience to do anything but maintain a favourable attitude toward the advertiser and its goods and services. Ideally, this favourable attitude will transfer to the products being marketed by the company, thereby creating a competitive advantage over other companies.

In 2019, 11 years removed from its listeriosis scandal in which 22 people died, Maple Leaf foods was in proactive rather than reactive mode. That is, the company had long since exhausted its crisis communications with regards to the incident (which incidentally became a case study in the proper way to handle a corporate crisis). Maple Leaf's "Let's Be Honest" ad campaign demonstrated how it was now aggressively in the process of positioning itself not only as a leader in food safety but also in corporate transparency. Using humour, rationality, and emotional strategic appeals, the campaign featured a collage of young children caught lying to their parents. The sequences, submitted by parents as part of a Maple Leaf contest, were edited together into a series of ads, all of which ended in a close-up of the Maple Leaf "Natural Selections" line of packaged lunch meats and the list of ingredients. The voiceover then proudly states, "Parents don't always get a straight answer, but when it comes to ingredients, we put the ingredients right on the package." The campaign further entrenched Maple Leaf's pursuit of trust.

Advocacy advertising is a form of institutional advertising in which an organization expresses its views on a particular issue or cause. Companies have increased their investment in advocacy advertising, as the benefits of publicly supporting social issues and causes that their target consumer is committed to has proven valuable.

16-2b | Product Advertising

Unlike institutional advertising, product advertising promotes the benefits of a specific good or service. The product's stage in its life cycle often determines whether

Unbox 5 FREE meals with our Boxing Week deal! 🥡 😋 Try Goodfood today for farm-fresh ingredients and delicious recipes.

MAKEGOODFOOD.CA
5 FREE MEALS in your 1st box
Canada's #1 Online Grocery Service

Courtesy of Goodfood

Preparing for Boxing Day 2019, Canadian-based meal-in-a-box, do-it-yourself company Good Food took out a series of digital ads across various platforms, including Facebook, not only incentivizing customers to take advantage of their "freemium," but also to start repositioning themselves as a "grocery service."

the product advertising used is pioneering advertising, competitive advertising, or comparative advertising.

PIONEERING ADVERTISING Pioneering **advertising** is intended to stimulate primary demand for a new product or product category. Heavily used during the introductory stage of the product life cycle, pioneering advertising offers consumers in-depth information about the benefits of the product class. Pioneering advertising also seeks to create interest. Pharmaceutical companies often use pioneering advertising.

product advertising
a form of advertising that promotes the benefits of a specific good or service

advocacy advertising
a form of advertising in which an organization expresses its views on a particular issue or cause

pioneering advertising
a form of advertising designed to stimulate primary demand for a new product or product category

COMPETITIVE ADVERTISING Companies use competitive or brand advertising when a product enters the growth phase of the product life cycle and other companies begin to enter the marketplace. Instead of building demand for the product category, the goal of **competitive advertising** is to influence demand for a specific brand. During this phase, promotion often becomes less informative and, instead, appeals more to emotions. Advertisements may begin to stress subtle differences between brands, with heavy emphasis on building recall of a brand name and creating a favourable attitude toward the brand. Automobile advertising has long used very competitive messages, drawing distinctions on the basis of factors such as quality, performance, and image.

COMPARATIVE ADVERTISING Comparative advertising directly or indirectly compares two or more competing brands on one or more specific attributes. Some advertisers even use comparative advertising against their own brands. Products experiencing sluggish growth or those entering the marketplace against strong competitors are more likely to employ comparative claims in their advertising.

Before the 1970s, comparative advertising was allowed only if the competing brand was veiled and unidentified. In 1971, the Federal Trade Commission (FTC) in the United States fostered the growth of comparative advertising, claiming it provided consumers with useful information. In Canada, advertisers should err on the side of caution when using comparative advertising. There are a number of key restrictions including creating a false impression (ensuring what is being said is true and the visuals do not distort the message), ensuring the advertisement is not misleading, and ensuring all that is said in the ad is accurate. Should a named competitor feel that the ad is misrepresenting its product, claims can be made to an appropriate regulatory body, as well as with the Advertising Standards Council.[7]

competitive advertising
a form of advertising designed to influence demand for a specific brand

advertising campaign
a series of related advertisements focusing on a common theme, slogan, and set of advertising appeals

advertising objective
a specific communication task that a campaign should accomplish for a specified target audience during a specified period

advertising appeal
a strategy used by the advertiser to engage the attention of a viewer, reader, listener, and/or potential customer

16-3 | CREATIVE DECISIONS IN ADVERTISING

Advertising strategies are typically organized around an advertising campaign. An **advertising campaign** is a series of related advertisements focusing on a common theme, known in advertising circles as "the big idea." It is the embodiment of imagery, creative copy (words), audio, and a slogan, all revolving around set of advertising appeals. It is a specific advertising effort for a particular product that extends for a defined period of time.

Before any creative work can begin on an advertising campaign, it is important to determine what goals or objectives the advertising should achieve. An **advertising objective** is the specific communication task that a campaign should accomplish for a specified target audience during a specified period. The objectives of a specific advertising campaign often depend on the overall corporate objectives, the product being advertised, and, according to research, where the consumer is with respect to product adoption. The consumer's position in the AIDA process (see Chapter 15) helps to determine whether the advertising objective is to create awareness, arouse interest, stimulate desire, or create a purchase.

The DAGMAR approach (Defining Advertising Goals for Measured Advertising Results) establishes a protocol for writing advertising objectives. According to this method, all advertising objectives should precisely define the target audience, the desired percentage change in a specified measure of effectiveness, and the time frame during which that change is to occur.

Once the advertising objectives are defined, creative work can begin on the advertising campaign. Specifically, creative decisions include identifying product benefits, developing and evaluating advertising appeals, executing the message, and evaluating the effectiveness of the campaign.

16-3a | Identifying Product Benefits

A well-known rule of thumb in the advertising industry is "Sell the sizzle, not the steak." In other words, the advertising goal is to sell the benefits of the product, not its attributes. Customers do not buy attributes; they buy benefits. An attribute is simply a feature of the product, such as quality of the clothing in the case of Lululemon apparel. The benefit is how the consumer will feel when wearing the clothing. In Lululemon bottoms, tops, hoodies, and other pieces, the customer feels aligned with values of fitness, health, community, and fashion.

Marketing research and intuition are usually used to unearth the perceived benefits of a product and to rank consumers' preferences for these benefits.

EXHIBIT 16.1 COMMON ADVERTISING APPEALS

Rational	Informs consumers whether the product will save them money, make them money, or otherwise enhance their lives	Walmart: Save money, live better
Emotional/ Sentimental	Appeals to consumers in a way that pulls at their heartstrings and engages them in a way that makes them feel myriad emotions	Dove Real Beauty
Fear	Makes consumers feel as though they will be at worst, in danger, and at least missing out (FOMO) by not buying a product or participating in the message being promoted	Michelin: Because so much is riding on your tires
Negative	Rallies consumers to a brand by bringing them against a negative force. Typically there is an institutional element to these appeals.	Always: Like a Girl
Humour	Uses anything from mild amusement to outright slapstick to get people to remember a message because it made them laugh	M&M Chocolate Bar: Eat You Alive
Sex	Entices consumers toward a product through physical attraction. This appeal has evolved from sexist ads of the 1950s to 1980s to an appeal that uses physical attractiveness in less overt ways. Often advertisers will use this appeal in combination with humour in order to divert or even contradict the sexual approach	Old Spice: I Am a Man
Influencer	Uses experts, celebrities, or other forms of thought leader to influence consumers through the idea that "expert is always right"	Turkish Airlines: 5 Senses with Dr Oz

16-3b | Developing and Evaluating Advertising Appeals

An **advertising appeal** identifies a reason for a person to buy a product. Developing advertising appeals, a challenging task, is generally the responsibility of the creative people in the advertising agency. Advertising appeals typically play off consumers' emotions or address consumers' needs or wants.

Advertising campaigns can leverage one or more advertising appeals. Often the appeals are quite general, thereby allowing the company to develop a number of subthemes or mini-campaigns using both advertising and sales promotion. Several possible advertising appeals are listed in Exhibit 16.1.

Choosing the most appropriate appeal normally requires market research. Criteria for evaluation include desirability, exclusiveness, and believability. Desirability is usually achieved only after the ad successfully attracts the *attention* of the target market, before generating *interest* by the customer in the product, and then becoming *desirable* to the target market. This represents the first three components of the AIDA process:

1. Attention: Customer is drawn to the ad

2. Interest: Customer becomes interested in the subject of the ad

3. Desire: Customer feels a need that can be solved by the subject in the ad

4. Action: Customer decides to adopt the idea (buy the product) being advertised

The ad must also appear to be exclusive or unique; consumers must be able to distinguish the advertiser's message from competitors' messages. Most important,

Bloomberg/Getty Images

the appeal should be believable. An appeal that makes extravagant claims not only wastes promotional dollars but also creates ill will toward the advertiser.

The way in which the benefit is presented, within the advertising appeal selected for the campaign, becomes what advertisers call its **unique selling proposition (USP)**. The USP often becomes all or part of the campaign's slogan. The Maple Leaf Natural Selections campaign, discussed earlier in this chapter, was based not on what was in the packaged meats produced by the company, but the trust parents should have that Maple Leaf will tell the truth about what's in the package. The big idea was that anybody can stuff meat into a plastic sack—only Maple Leaf can be trusted to tell you what's in it. The company transformed the crisis it had experienced almost a decade earlier into a reason it can be trusted today. If anyone knows food safety, it's Maple Leaf Foods.

unique selling proposition (USP)

a desirable, exclusive, and believable advertising appeal selected as the theme for a campaign

16-3c | Executing the Message

Message execution is the way an advertisement presents its information. Again, the AIDA plan (see Chapter 15) is a good blueprint for executing an advertising message. Any ad should immediately draw the attention of the reader, viewer, or listener. The advertiser must then use the message to hold interest, create desire for the good or service, and ultimately motivate a purchase.

The style in which the message is executed is one of the most creative elements of an advertisement. Exhibit 16.2 lists examples of executional styles used by advertisers. Executional styles often dictate what type of media is used to convey the message. Scientific executional styles lend themselves well to print advertising, where more information can be conveyed. Testimonials by athletes are one of the more popular executional styles.

"Slice of Life" is one of the more common means of executing a message as it demonstrates the product being used in an everyday situation, usually by normal people doing normal things. Procter & Gamble has built an empire using this style, showing myriad household products being used at home.

Sometimes a company will modify its executional styles to make its advertising more relevant or to make it stand out among competitive advertisements. A&W advertisements that include the A&W "guy" have evolved over the past few years from a pure humour appeal, to include a good deal of rationality, to even emotional as we remember A&W as the quick-service restaurant that cares about quality meals without treating animals inhumanely. In the fall of 2019, A&W launched a "change is good" IMC campaign, inviting customers to share their feelings on A&W's moves toward greater sustainability in its operations. The now ubiquitous A&W guy is shown responding to people who have posted, by video-calling them and discussing their positive feelings toward the brand.

16-3d | Postcampaign Evaluation

Evaluating an advertising campaign can be a demanding task. How can one be sure that the change in product awareness, sales, or market share is solely the result of the advertising campaign? Many advertising campaigns are designed to create an image. But how does one measure whether the intended image has been created? So many variables shape whether a product or service has achieved its objectives that determining the true impact of the advertising campaign is often impossible. Nonetheless, marketers spend considerable time studying advertising effectiveness and its probable impact on sales, market share, or awareness.

EXHIBIT 16.2	TEN COMMON EXECUTIONAL STYLES FOR ADVERTISING
Slice of Life	Depicts people in settings where the product would normally be used. For example, young couple receiving financial advice from an agent at Scotia Bank in the "Richer than you think" campaign.
Lifestyle	Shows how well the product will fit in or enhance the consumer's lifestyle. For example, P&G's Swiffer being used to quickly pick up dust and pet fur in a busy home.
Spokesperson/Testimonial	Can feature a celebrity, a company official, or a typical consumer making a testimonial or endorsing a product. For example, Galen Weston appears in television ads with regular consumers, promoting the launch of the new PC Plus program.
Fantasy	Creates a fantasy for the viewer built around use of the product. For example, Subaru showing a driver and family effortlessly speeding around tight corners in a snowstorm.
Humorous	Advertisers often use humour in their ads to break through the clutter and be memorable. For example, Amazon Alexa installed in unexpected items.
Real/Animated Product Symbols	Creates a character that represents the product in advertisements. For example, Telus animals have become product symbols.
Mood or Image	Builds a mood or an image around the product, such as peace, love, or beauty. For example, J'adore by Dior perfume ads present the iconic fragrance as the ultimate expression of femininity, luxury, and sexuality through the use of beautiful actresses and images.
Demonstration	Shows consumers the expected benefit. Many consumer products use this technique. For example, Tide laundry detergent is famous for demonstrating how its product will clean clothes whiter and brighter.
Musical	Conveys the message of the advertisement through song. Example: The 1971 classic from Coca-Cola, "I'd Like to Teach the World to Sing."
Scientific	Uses research or scientific evidence to depict a brand's superiority over competitors. Example: Aleve pain relief stating its longer lasting pain relief effects than competitor Tylenol

Testing ad effectiveness can be done either before or after the campaign. Before a campaign is released, marketing managers use pretests to determine the best advertising appeal, layout, and media vehicle. After advertisers implement a campaign, they use several monitoring techniques to determine whether the campaign has met its original goals. Even if a campaign has been highly successful, advertisers still typically do a postcampaign analysis to identify how the campaign might have been more efficient and which factors contributed to its success.

Automated media buying, or **programmatic buying**, improves the effectiveness of media buying by providing more efficient and effective buying, thereby creating real-time evaluation. Programmatic buying is the automated buying and selling of online advertising, using platform-driven data. It therefore schedules ads for clients based upon platform-specific user data. At the moment, programmatic buying accounts for a large component of digital media buying. However, technology advances are making the practice possible for traditional media

as well. While programmatic buying doesn't assess the impact of the creative on the achievement of objectives, it does allow for instantaneous media placement evaluation and subsequent media placement alterations to improve achievement of objectives.[8] It is anticipated that in the not-too-distant future we will see more brands experimenting with programmatic buying, thereby creating individualized messages and media selection.

16-4 | MEDIA DECISIONS IN ADVERTISING

A major decision for advertisers is the choice of **medium**—the channel used to convey a message to a target market. **Media planning**, therefore, is the series of decisions advertisers make regarding the selection and use of media to allow the marketer to optimally and cost-effectively communicate the message to the target audience. Specifically, advertisers must determine which types of media will best communicate the benefits of their product or service

programmatic buying
using an automated system to make media buying decisions in real time

medium
the channel used to convey a message to a target market

media planning
the series of decisions advertisers make regarding the selection and use of media, allowing the marketer to optimally and cost-effectively communicate the message to the target audience

A&W Food Services of Canada Inc.

EXHIBIT 16.3   ADVERTISING SPENDING IN CANADA BY MEDIUM

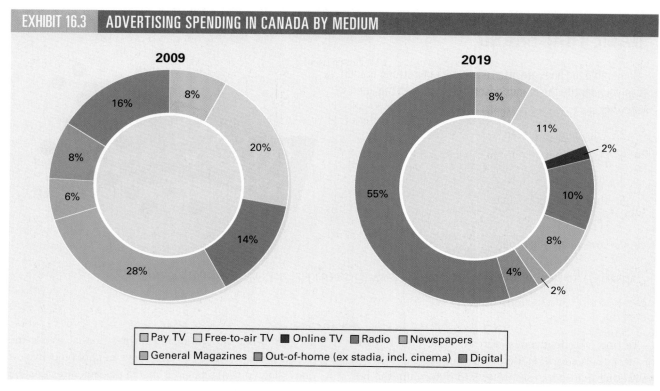

Source: Adapted from: https://www.statista.com/statistics/237295/advertising-spending-in-canada-by-media/.

to the target audience and when and for how long the advertisement will run.

Media selection is affected by the target market and the promotional objectives, as well as by the advertising appeal and execution decisions. Both creative and media decisions are made at the same time. Creative work cannot be completed without knowing which medium will be used to convey the message to the target market. In many cases, the advertising objectives dictate the medium and the creative approach to be used. For example, if the objective is to demonstrate how fast a product operates, the best medium to show this action is likely a video shown on television, in theatres, on social media, or all of these.

In 2019, Canadian advertising expenditures totalled over $15 billion, which represented the fifth consecutive year of overall growth in the industry.[9] (See Exhibit 16.3.) Traditional media—television, radio, print, and out-of-home accounted for roughly one-third of the spend—while digital occupied the majority. Canadian advertising expenditures are expected to continue a slow growth in the coming years with digital spending increasing, and traditional advertising decreasing. Most of the growth in digital spending, beyond display advertising on social media platforms, will be fuelled by advertising on mobile devices such as smartphones and tablets.[10] Mobile's share

of total digital ad spending is close to 50 percent, and the share of digital spending accounted for by mobile will continue to grow.[11]

16-4a | Media Types

Advertising media are channels that advertisers use in mass communication. The traditional advertising media of newspapers, magazines, radio, television, out-of-home media, and direct response are being challenged by digital media. Digital media are evolving to meet new consumer trends and to respond to the proliferation of data made possible by technology. Exhibit 16.4 summarizes the advantages and disadvantages of traditional versus digital channels.

NEWSPAPERS The advantages of newspaper advertising include geographic selectivity, flexibility, and timeliness. Newspaper readers are highly engaged, as professional journalists, editorialists, and opinion leaders create content. Because copywriters can usually prepare newspaper ads quickly and at a reasonable cost, local merchants can reach their target market almost daily. Because newspapers are generally a mass-market medium, they may not be the best vehicle for marketers trying to reach a very narrow market; however, newspapers have innovated by creating special sections that

Medium	Advantages	Disadvantages
Newspapers	Geographic selectivity and flexibility; short-term advertiser commitments; news value and immediacy; year-round readership; high individual market coverage; co-op and local tie-in availability; short lead time; highly credible	Little demographic selectivity; limited colour capabilities; low pass-along rate; may be expensive
Magazines	Good reproduction, especially for colour; demographic selectivity; regional selectivity; target market selectivity; relatively long advertising life; high pass-along rate	Long-term advertiser commitments; slow audience buildup; limited demonstration capabilities; lack of urgency; long lead time
Radio	Selectivity and audience segmentation; low cost; immediacy of message; can be scheduled on short notice; relatively no seasonal change in audience; highly portable; short-term advertiser commitments; entertainment carryover	No visual treatment; short advertising life of message; high frequency required to generate comprehension and retention; distractions from background sound; commercial clutter
Television	Ability to reach a wide, diverse audience; low cost per thousand (CPM); creative opportunities for demonstration; immediacy of messages; entertainment carryover; demographic selectivity with cable specialty stations; emotional medium	Short life of message; some consumer skepticism about claims; high campaign cost; little demographic selectivity with network stations; long-term advertiser commitments; long lead times required for production; commercial clutter
Out-of-Home Media	Repetition; moderate cost; flexibility; geographic selectivity; high creativity	Short message; lack of demographic selectivity; high "noise" level distracting audience
Digital and Mobile	Fastest-growing medium; ability to reach a narrow target audience; relatively short lead time required for creating Web-based advertising; moderate cost; ability to engage consumers as video content grows	Ad exposure relies on "click-through" from banner ads; measurement for social media needs much improvement; 80% of adults access the Internet; not all consumers use social media

target specific market segments. However, newspaper advertising also encounters many distractions from competing ads and news stories. In response to consumer demand for real-time information, newspapers' content is now distributed to smartphones, tablets, and desktop computers with more than 25 percent of Canadians reading news across all four channels. Newspapers have embraced social media, with writers establishing their own Twitter accounts and Facebook pages that readers can follow to get up-to-the-minute news. Newspaper advertising spending is expected to experience more erosion as readership in the traditional format continues to decline.[12]

The main sources of newspaper ad revenue are local retailers, classified ads, and cooperative advertising. In **cooperative advertising**, the manufacturer and the retailer split the costs of advertising the manufacturer's brand. Cooperative advertising encourages retailers to devote more effort to the manufacturer's lines, such as a Sport Chek ad promoting a sale on Nike running shoes.

MAGAZINES One of the main advantages of magazine advertising is its target market selectivity. Magazines are published for virtually every market segment, offering meaningful target market engagement. Consumers who choose to read magazines spend considerable time doing so. Readers have high acceptance of the advertisements they see in a magazine, and readers are often driven to websites to seek additional information. Nevertheless, the magazine industry in Canada is

© Pixellover RM 4/Alamy

experiencing considerable challenges as readers migrate away from printed publications to online reading. In fact, Rogers Media has revamped its magazine content strategy to reduce emphasis on print publications and increase investment in digital content. As an example, it ceased print publication of *Flare*, *MoneySense*, and *Canadian Business* to provide only digital versions of their content and through apps.[13]

RADIO As an advertising medium, radio offers selectivity and audience segmentation, low unit and production costs, timeliness, and geographic flexibility. Local advertisers are the most frequent users of radio

cooperative advertising
an arrangement in which the manufacturer and the retailer split the costs of advertising the manufacturer's brand

advertising. Like newspapers, radio lends itself well to cooperative advertising.

The ability to target specific audience segments based upon their listening preferences in music, talk, sports, and so on, is a major selling point for radio stations. Radio listeners tend to listen habitually and at predictable times. However, radio is losing ground with millennials as they shift their audio listening to other options such as Sirius-XM, Spotify, Google Play, or podcasts. Radio is responding by offering online streaming and mobile apps such as iHeartRadio.

Radio is still a highly effective medium for retailers, automobile dealers, and impulse products. Radio often enhances a media plan that combines other media because of the ability to inexpensively increase reach and frequency, particularly among commuters.

TELEVISION Television broadcasters are made up of national, regional, and specialty and digital networks, independent stations, and pay-television services. As a result, the television audience has become highly fragmented, which makes targeting segments easier, but with lower reach in terms of total audiences. Television still delivers wide and diverse audiences, but the golden age of television, where half of the country would be glued to the same show, at the same time are over.

In today's digital world and with Canadians' high consumption of online video, some are questioning the role of television. Yet Canadians continue to spend more time with television than any other medium. Canadians still prefer watching television on their larger television screens rather than their computer screens because the former offers the best overall sound and visual experience, making it a highly engaging and influential medium. While Canadians' online video consumption is high relative to other countries, live traditional television viewing still continues to be the norm.

Canadians often multitask while watching television. They are just as likely to be on their mobile device, laptop, or tablet while the television is on. Given this viewing behaviour, television advertisers are using the television commercial to drive the viewer to a website for further brand engagement.

PVRs—personal video recorders—are found in over half of all Canadian homes but their penetration has slowed as Canadians engage in

cord cutting
discontinuing or never committing to a TV cable or satellite provider

infomercial
a 30-minute or longer advertisement that looks more like a TV talk show than a sales pitch

alternative ways to access video, such as streaming and video on demand (VOD). For cable companies a real threat is "**cord cutting**"—discontinuing or never committing to a TV cable or satellite provider. In response to this trend, and the wave of penetration by Netflix and other streaming platforms, Canada's major cable providers offer their own VOD platforms including both paid and free content. Disney Plus, the much-anticipated Disney entrant into this space in late 2019, was as much an industry indicator as any other competitive move. Disney execs called it "the future of the company" prelaunch, and immediate response from the market proved encouraging, with over 10 million sign-ups the first day.[14]

Of course, the value to viewers of streaming services, beyond the variety and on-demand flexibility, is that there are no advertisements. Advertisers are faced again with the need to explore new strategies for gaining consumer attention in the face of a new threat.

Advertising time on television can be very expensive, especially for network and popular cable channels. Specials events and first-run prime-time shows for top-ranked TV programs command the highest rates for a typical 30-second spot. **Infomercials** continue to be a successful television format as they are relatively inexpensive to produce and air. Advertisers use infomercials when the information to be presented to the consumer is relatively complicated.

OUT-OF-HOME MEDIA Outdoor, or out-of-home, advertising is a flexible, low-cost medium that may take a variety of forms. Examples are billboards, skywriting, giant inflatables, transit shelters, street columns, interior and exterior bus and subway signs, signs in sports arenas and airports, and ads painted on cars, trucks, water towers, manhole covers, and even people. Out-of-home is showing modest growth in advertising spending, as marketers incorporate a digital element in the campaign whether through the use of technology innovations or integrated campaigns that include a digital component. For example, transit shelters offer interactivity, entire bus shelters can be interactive 3D advertisements, and entire buses or train interiors or exteriors can be covered with ads. Another recent technology innovation is the use of beacons, which are small devices that enable content-related interactions with someone near the out-of-home property. As an example, a beacon-enabled billboard can send a notification to a mobile device of a person standing in the area of the beacon. The billboard may be advertising a new yogurt, and the notification to the person's mobile device could be for a discount on the yogurt at a store in the vicinity.[15]

CASHMERE LENDS A HAND

Cashmere bathroom tissue knows that public bathrooms are too quiet, and for many people, a "shy bladder" creates an uncomfortable problem. Bathroom tissue is largely bought on price with little brand loyalty. In an effort to drive consumer decision making past price, Cashmere created a cheeky campaign using out-of-home advertising. The company inserted a device in 400 washroom stalls that, when activated, streams classical music. The stall user can control the volume, ensuring that a person's "shy bladder syndrome" is effectively managed.

TOO SHY TO GO?

Live stream our playlist to cover the sound of your stream at
NowStreaming.ca

Cashmere
BATHROOM TISSUE

Courtesy of Kruger Products L.P., makers of Cashmere Bathroom Tissue

Another type of out-of-home media is place-based media, which communicates to consumers where they live, work, and play. Their content is created to be personalized and relevant. A variety of place-based media allows marketers to reach the right consumer at the right place at the right time, such as washroom ads in bars, restaurants, schools, and fitness facilities. The Cashmere bathroom tissue ad (see box) is an example of place-based out-of-home advertising, and when you consider that approximately 70 percent of all brand decisions are made at the point of purchase, place-based media can be critical to include in the media mix.

Outdoor advertising offers tremendous geographic selectivity, making it ideal for promoting both products and local businesses. One of the main advantages of outdoor media over other media is its very high exposure frequency and very low clutter from competing ads. Outdoor advertising can also be customized to local marketing needs, which is why local businesses are often the leading outdoor advertisers in any given region.

THE INTERNET Internet advertising revenue continues to grow, with **mobile advertising** fuelling this growth. The trend in our reliance on mobile devices for everything from entertainment to education has created a domino effect where website owners have created more user-friendly mobile versions of their sites, thereby attracting eyeballs, which in turn creates advertising revenue.

As previously stated, Canadians are highly engaged online, spending more hours online than anyone else in the world. Online activity is still most often undertaken via a desktop computer, but increasingly (particularly among the 18-to-34-year-old group) a mobile device is used. In 2018, there were more than 25 million smartphones in use in Canada, with the number expected to reach 30 million by 2023.[17]

Mobile phones are intensely personal devices, accompanying the owners at all times. Social media is the number one reason Canadians are online, with almost 60 percent of us engaged with one or more platforms followed closely by mobile messaging at 57 percent.[18] Canadians are more likely to access social media sites on their smartphones than their desktop and are more likely to spend more time on social media sites when they visit them via their smartphones. However, in a report issued by digital media analytics firm NapoleanCat usage by Canadians of both Facebook and Instagram were in decline year over year from 2018 to 2019, but still incredibly popular.[19]

As consumers use the Internet more and more, marketers are increasingly investing in digital campaigns that include search engine marketing, display advertising (banner ads), social media advertising (such as Facebook ads), email marketing, and mobile marketing.

Including advertising messages in Web-based, mobile, console, or hand-held video games to advertise or promote a product, service, or idea, referred to as **advergaming**, is still popular. Some games

mobile advertising
advertising that displays text, images, and animated ads via mobile phones or other mobile devices that are data-enabled

advergaming
placing advertising messages in Web-based or video games to advertise or promote a product, a service, an organization, or an issue

amount to virtual commercials; others encourage players to buy in-game items and power-ups to advance; and still others allow advertisers to sponsor games or buy ad space for product placements. Many of these are social games played on Facebook or mobile networks, where players can interact with each other. **Social gaming** sites, which allow for social interaction between players, are also popular locations for digital ads, particularly campaigns targeting a younger population.

16-4b | Media Selection Considerations

An important element in any advertising campaign is the **media mix**, the combination of media to be used. Media mix decisions are typically based on several factors: cost per contact, reach, frequency, target market considerations, flexibility of the medium, noise level, and the lifespan of the medium.

Cost per thousand (CPM) is the cost of reaching 1000 people. This is a measure of efficiency for dollars spent on advertising. The lower the number, the more efficient the ad spend. Superbowl advertising is often ridiculed for its exorbitant price of advertising (over $5 million in 2020); however, the total number of people viewing the televised event made the CPM relatively low.

Cost per contact is the cost of reaching one member of the target market. It is a more specific variation on the cost per thousand (CPM) metric discussed previously. Naturally, as the size of the audience increases, so does the total cost. Like CPM, cost per contact enables an advertiser to compare media vehicles, such as television versus radio, magazine versus newspaper, or one website versus another. The advertiser might then pick the vehicle with the lowest cost per contact to maximize advertising punch for the money spent.

Cost per click (CPC), like click-through rate (CTR) discussed earlier, is a means of measuring effectiveness of digital advertising. However, unlike CTR, which shows a percentage of how many times an ad is clicked versus merely seen, CPC reveals how much it costs to have a viewer actually do the clicking. Although there are several variations, this option enables the marketer to pay only for "engaged" consumers—those who clicked on an ad.

Reach is the number of different target consumers who are exposed to a message at least once during a specific period, usually four weeks. Media plans for product introductions and attempts at increasing brand awareness usually emphasize reach. For example, an advertiser might try to reach 70 percent of the target audience during the first three months of the campaign. Reach is related to a medium's ratings, generally referred to in the industry as *gross ratings points,* or GRP. A television program with a higher GRP means that more people are tuning in to the show and the reach is higher. Accordingly, as GRP increases for a particular medium, so does cost per contact.

Because the typical ad is short-lived and because often only a small portion of an ad may be perceived at one time, advertisers repeat their ads so that consumers will remember the message. **Frequency** is the number of times an individual is exposed to a message during a specific period. Advertisers use average frequency to measure the intensity of a specific medium's coverage. For example, Red Bull GmbH, the Austrian company selling the energy drink Red Bull, might want an average exposure frequency of five for its Red Bull television ads to ensure the Red Bull company slogan, "Red Bull gives you wings," is well entrenched in the target consumers' minds. In other words, Red Bull wants each television viewer to see the ad an average of five times.

Media selection is also a matter of matching the advertising medium with the product's target market. If marketers are trying to reach teenage females, they might select advertising on the retailer Sephora's website. A medium's ability to reach a precisely defined market is its **audience selectivity**. Some media vehicles, such as general newspapers and network television, appeal to a wide cross-section of the population. Others—such as *Zoomer, Runners World,* HGTV, and Christian radio stations—appeal to very specific groups.

The *flexibility* of a medium can be extremely important to an advertiser. For example, because of layouts and design, the lead time for magazine advertising is

social gaming
playing an online game that allows for social interaction between players on a social media platform

media mix
the combination of media to be used for a promotional campaign

cost per contact
the cost of reaching one member of the target market

cost per click
the cost associated with a consumer clicking on a display or banner ad

reach
the number of target consumers exposed to a commercial at least once during a specific period, usually four weeks

frequency
the number of times an individual is exposed to a given message during a specific period

audience selectivity
the ability of an advertising medium to reach a precisely defined market

Michael D. Brown/Shutterstock.com

Courtesy of Molson Coors Canada

This Molson commercial sings the praises of multiculturalism. With the climate created by the US immigration and refugee ban announced by President Donald Trump in early 2017, this advertisement, which was originally created and aired before Canada Day 2016, resurfaced on social media. In less than a week, the ad received more than 10 million views. And it all happened without Molson or its advertising agency doing anything, but rather by consumers using it to speak to the political climate of the time.[20]

considerably longer than for other media types and so is less flexible. By contrast, radio and Internet advertising provide maximum flexibility. If necessary, an advertiser can change a radio ad on the day it is to air.

Noise level is the level of distraction of the target audience in a medium. Noise can be created by competing ads, as when a street is lined with billboards or when a television program is cluttered with ads from competing sponsors. Whereas newspapers and magazines have a high noise level, direct mail is a private medium with a low noise level. Typically, no other advertising media or news stories compete for direct-mail readers' attention at the same time.

Media have either a short or a long *lifespan,* which means that messages can either quickly fade or persist as tangible copy to be carefully studied. A radio commercial may last less than a minute, but advertisers can overcome this short lifespan by repeating radio ads often. In contrast, a magazine has a relatively long lifespan, which is further increased by a high pass-along rate.

Media planners have traditionally relied on the factors we've just discussed for selecting an effective media mix, with reach, frequency, and cost often being the overriding criteria. Well-established brands with familiar messages probably need fewer exposures to be effective, whereas newer or unfamiliar brands likely need more

exposures to become familiar. In addition, today's media planners have more media options than ever before.

The proliferation of media channels is causing *media fragmentation* and forcing media planners to pay as much attention to where they place their advertising as to how often the advertisement is repeated. Therefore, marketers should evaluate reach *and* frequency when assessing the effectiveness of advertising. In certain situations, it may be important to reach potential consumers through as many media vehicles as possible. When this approach is considered, however, the budget must be large enough to achieve sufficient levels of frequency to have an impact. In evaluating reach versus frequency, the media planner ultimately must select an approach that is most likely to result in the ad being understood and remembered when a purchase decision is being made.

Advertisers also evaluate the qualitative factors involved in media selection, including, in the television medium, for instance, attention paid to the commercial and the program, involvement, program liking, lack of distractions, and other audience behaviours that affect the likelihood that a commercial message is being seen and, ideally, absorbed. While advertisers can advertise their product in as many media as possible and repeat the ad as many times as they like, the ad still may not be effective if the audience is not paying attention. Research on audience attentiveness for television, for example, shows that the longer viewers stay tuned to a particular program, the more memorable they find the commercials.

16-4c | Media Scheduling

After choosing the media for the advertising campaign, advertisers must schedule the ads. A **media schedule** designates the media to be used (such as magazines, television, or radio), the specific vehicles (such as Home Depot website, the TV show *The Blacklist* or *Kim's Convenience*, or the Saturday edition of *The Globe and Mail*), and the insertion dates of the advertising.

Media schedules are divided into four basic types (see Exhibit 16.4):

media schedule
designation of the media, the specific publications or programs, and the insertion dates of advertising

continuous media schedule
a media scheduling strategy in which advertising is run steadily throughout the advertising period; used for products in the later stages of the product life cycle

flighted media schedule
a media scheduling strategy in which ads are run heavily every other month or every two weeks, to achieve a greater impact with an increased frequency and reach at those times

pulsing media schedule
a media scheduling strategy that uses continuous scheduling throughout the year coupled with a flighted schedule during the best sales periods

seasonal media schedule
a media scheduling strategy that runs advertising only during times of the year when the product is most likely to be purchased

- Products in the later stages of the product life cycle, which are advertised on a reminder basis, use a **continuous media schedule**. A continuous schedule allows the advertising to run steadily throughout the advertising period. Examples are Boston Pizza, which may have a television commercial on Global every Wednesday at 7:30 and billboards in 14 major cities across Canada over a 12-week period.

- With a **flighted media schedule**, the advertiser may schedule the ads heavily every other month or every two weeks to achieve a greater impact with an increased frequency and reach at those times. Movie studios might schedule television advertising on Wednesday and Thursday nights, when moviegoers are deciding which films to see that weekend.

Courtesy of Modo Yoga

- A **pulsing media schedule** combines continuous scheduling with a flighted media schedule. Continuous advertising is simply heavier during the best sale periods. A retail department store may advertise year-round but place more advertising during certain sale periods, such as Thanksgiving, Christmas, and back-to-school.

- Certain times of the year call for a **seasonal media schedule**. Modo Yoga and other fitness facilities tend to follow a seasonal strategy, placing greater emphasis on January as New Year's resolutions are being made.

Research comparing continuous media schedules versus flighted ones found that continuous schedules for television advertisements are more effective in driving sales than flighted schedules. The research suggests that it may be more important to get exposure as close as possible to the time when a consumer makes a purchase. Therefore, the advertiser should maintain a continuous schedule over as long a period as possible. Often called *recency planning*, this theory of scheduling is now commonly used for scheduling television advertising for frequently purchased products, such as Coca-Cola or Tide detergent. Recency planning's main premise is that advertising works by influencing the brand choice of people who are ready to buy. Mobile advertising is one of the more promising tactics for contacting consumers when they are thinking about a specific product, as demonstrated throughout the chapter.

16-4d | Media Buying

Media buyers in advertising agencies purchase media. Media are bought through a negotiation process, although flat rates do exist for most media companies. Advertising agencies are compensated on a percentage basis, usually between 12 and 15 percent, for the media they buy. The All media to be purchased is negotiable, despite published rate cards, and media rates really are a result of supply and demand. TV rates for a highly rated program that everyone wants to buy airtime on, the Super Bowl, for example, will be higher than the rates for another program that has much lower reach. However, with the proliferation of media choices today, advertisers, no matter the size of the budget, should be able to create impactful media buys. Media buyers need to be challenged to build media plans that achieve the clients' objectives at the lowest possible cost, but when agency compensation for media is commission based, this can be a challenge.

16-5 | PUBLIC RELATIONS

The first part of this chapter has been devoted to advertising, also known as "paid media." The greatest strength of advertising is that once it's paid for, it has guaranteed exposure. Conversely, the biggest weakness with advertising is overexposure and the fatigue the public has with advertising in general. This is where "earned media" becomes a desirable counterpunch for companies attempting to gain attention to their target markets. Earned media, also referred to (somewhat oxymoronically) as "free advertising" occurs through any number of deliberate tactics by a company to create newsworthy content, which justifies media coverage. This process is rooted in the IMC tool known as public relations.

Public relations is the element in the promotional mix that evaluates public attitudes, identifies issues that may elicit public concern, and executes programs to gain public understanding and acceptance. Public relations is a vital link in a progressive company's marketing communication mix. Marketing managers plan public relations campaigns that fit into overall marketing plans and focus on targeted audiences. These campaigns strive to maintain a positive image of the corporation in the eyes of the public. As such, they should capitalize on the factors that enhance the company's image and minimize the factors that could generate a negative image. In Canada, public relations practitioners can become members of the Canadian Public Relations Society (CPRS, www.cprs.ca/aboutus), which oversees the practice of public relations for the benefit and protection of public interest.

Publicity is the effort to capture media attention—for example, through articles or editorials in publications or through human-interest stories on radio or television programs. Corporations usually initiate publicity by issuing a media release that furthers their public relations plans. A company that is about to introduce a new product or open a new store may send out media releases in the hope that the story will be published or broadcast. Savvy publicity can often create overnight sensations or build up a reserve of goodwill with consumers. Corporate donations and sponsorships can also create favourable publicity.

Public relations departments may perform any or all of the following functions:

- *Media relations:* placing positive, newsworthy information in the news media to attract attention to a product, a service, or a person associated with the company or institution

- *Product publicity:* publicizing specific products or services

- *Corporate communication:* creating internal and external messages to promote a positive image of the company or institution

- *Public affairs:* building and maintaining national or local community relations

- *Lobbying:* influencing legislators and government officials to promote or defeat legislation and regulation

- *Employee and investor relations:* maintaining positive relationships with employees, shareholders, and others in the financial community

- *Crisis management:* responding to unfavourable publicity or a negative event

16-5a | Major Public Relations Tools

Public relations professionals commonly use several tools, many of which require an active role on the part of the public relations professional, such as writing media releases and engaging in proactive media relations. Sometimes, however, these techniques create their own publicity.

PRODUCT PUBLICITY Publicity is instrumental in introducing new products and services. Publicity can help advertisers explain the special features of their new product by prompting free news stories or positive word of mouth. During the introductory period, an especially innovative new product often needs more exposure than conventional paid advertising affords. Public relations professionals write media releases, develop videos, and post messages and

A Cause Worth Tweeting About

Since September 2010, Bell Canada has been dedicated to removing the stigma associated with mental health through a number of initiatives, the most noteworthy being the Bell Let's Talk Day, held in January each year. Olympian Clara Hughes is the spokesperson for this multiactivity cause campaign. Since the campaign's inception, $80 million has been invested in mental health initiatives within Canadian communities, on the strength of Canadians participating in Let's Talk Days. In January 2019, over 145 million long-distance and mobile calls, texts, tweets, and Facebook shares contributed to the growing fund of over $100 million raised since the program began. Perhaps Bell's greatest accomplishment with the initiative is that 86 percent of Canadians say they are more aware of mental health issues since the Let's Talk campaign began.[21]

Ryan Reynolds
@VancityReynolds

That which shall be named! Talk about it. Dance about it. Cry about it. But don't keep quiet about it.
#MaximumEffort
#BellLetsTalk twitter.com/bell_letstalk/...

---

videos on social media sites in an effort to generate news about their new product. They also jockey for exposure of their product or service at major events, on popular television and news shows, or in the hands of influential people. The concept of "influencer" has taken on a life of its own with the digital revolution of corporate communications. Once solely the domain of A-list actors and athletes, influencers today can work on behalf of a company targeting only a small market niche. The massive reach of social platforms, particularly Instagram, allow companies to redirect advertising budgets toward influencer marketing, simply by finding how popular individuals are within the company's target market (measured by followers), then compensating said influencer for mentions or placements within their posts.

However, the practice of paying influencers to promote a company's product, while often effective, places it somewhere between advertising and public relations as a promotional tool. Remember advertising is all about "paid space," while PR is about gaining exposure on the merit of newsworthiness. Influencer marketing somehow finds its way as a new category of the communications mix alongside these two standards.

PRODUCT PLACEMENT Marketers are increasingly using product placement to reinforce brand awareness and create favourable attitudes. **Product placement** is a strategy that involves getting a product, service, or company name to appear in a movie, television show, radio program, magazine, newspaper, video game, video or audio clip, book, or commercial for another product; on the Internet; or at special events. Good product placement—that is, product placement that reinforces brand personality and positioning—is placement whereby the brand is used in an appropriate context and by those that represent the brand's target group. Good product placement can also add a sense of realism to a movie, television show, video game book, or similar vehicle. More than two-thirds of all product placements are in movies and television shows, but placements in alternative media are growing, particularly on the Internet and in video games. Digital technology now enables companies to "virtually" place their products in any audio or video production. Virtual placement not only reduces the cost of product placement for new productions but also enables companies to place their products in previously produced programs such as reruns of television shows. Overall, companies obtain valuable product exposure, brand reinforcement, and increased sales through product placement. *The Amazing Race Canada* is a prime example of a television program full of product placement—air carriers, credit card companies, automobiles and retailers, entertainment venues, and gas stations.

product placement
a public relations strategy that involves getting a product, service, or company name to appear in a movie, television show, radio program, magazine, newspaper, video game, video or audio clip, book, or commercial for another product; on the Internet; or at special events

SPONSORSHIP Sponsorships are a public relations strategy that provide a way for companies to get in front of audiences who would otherwise ignore, dismiss, or fail to even notice advertising.

With **sponsorship**, a company spends money to support an issue, a cause, or an event that is consistent with corporate objectives, such as improving brand awareness or enhancing corporate image. Most commonly, companies sponsor events, such as festivals and fairs, conventions, expositions, sporting events, arts and entertainment spectaculars, and charity benefits. Sports and entertainment sponsorship are the top two areas where dollars are being spent, followed by causes. Like each of Canada's other three banks (RBC, Scotiabank, and TD-CanadaTrust) CIBC has a significant stake in the way it is perceived amongst Canadians. Following each quarterly report, media is quick to release details of how much richer these four companies become, often resulting in negative perceptions. Therefore, the bank aims to show itself as a strong corporate citizen. CIBC's sponsorship of "Run for the Cure" began in 1997, five years after the run itself had begun. It was a formal partnership between the financial institution and the Canadian Cancer Society aimed to raise funds for breast cancer research. The October event is now as much a part of the Canadian calendar as Thanksgiving, with over 80 000 participants and $16 million in annual funds raised.[22]

A special type of sponsorship, **cause-related marketing**, involves the association of a for-profit company with a non-profit organization. Through the sponsorship, the company's product or service is promoted, and money is raised for the non-profit. In a common type of cause-related sponsorship, a company agrees to donate a percentage of the purchase price for a particular item to a charity, but some arrangements are more complex. Both CIBC's Run for the Cure and Bell Canada Let's Talk campaign are examples of sponsorship activities, but are also cause marketing, whereby the

investment of funds by a for-profit company is to increase awareness of a social cause.

More and more companies are employing similar strategies either for social or environmental causes. However, as such strategies become more common, the cynicism of the public becomes equally heightened. It is therefore important to attend to details of managing the way such programs are executed; to ensure significant financial contribution is made by the company, and that funds raised are demonstrably channelled to targeted causes, in order to avoid public backlash. That said, a strategically planned and well-executed ongoing cause-marketing program will engage both consumers and employees, giving an organization a competitive advantage.

When an advertiser attempts to position itself with an event but has not been sanctioned as an official sponsor, the advertiser is participating in **ambush marketing**. There are plenty of examples of ambush marketing surrounding the Olympics because of the strong reach of the Olympic Games coverage, yet the high cost of being an official Olympic sponsor.

EXPERIENTIAL People are an effective form of media and can deliver key messages about a brand to the consumer in a personal way. When trained people (ambassadors) communicate with consumers in a natural setting, they can offer deeper brand engagement. **Experiential marketing** is a form of marketing that helps the consumer experience the brand. When combined with brand ambassadors, the resulting experience can create a more memorable and emotional connection between the consumer and the brand. Adidas Sporting Goods hired an agency to train a

sponsorship
a public relations strategy in which a company spends money to support an issue, a cause, or an event that is consistent with corporate objectives, such as improving brand awareness or enhancing corporate image

cause-related marketing
a type of sponsorship involving the association of a for-profit company with a non-profit organization; through the sponsorship, the company's product or service is promoted, and money is raised for the non-profit

ambush marketing
when an advertiser attempts to position itself with an event but is not sanctioned as an official sponsor

experiential marketing
a form of advertising that focuses on helping consumers experience a brand such that a memorable and emotional connection is formed between the consumer and the brand

Jonny White/Alamy Stock Photo

Nike has historically capitalized on the Olympic Games by creatively associating itself with the games without paying the significant sponsorship dollars.

team of ambassadors that engaged with running groups at a variety of retail partners across Canada. The purpose was to undertake wear-testing and receive feedback of Adidas running apparel.

16-5b | Managing Unfavourable Publicity

Although marketers try to avoid unpleasant situations, crises do happen. In our free-press environment, with extremely social media–savvy consumers, publicity is not easily controlled, especially in a crisis. **Crisis management** is the coordinated effort to handle the effects of unfavourable publicity or an unexpected unfavourable event, ensuring fast and accurate communication in times of emergency.

An example from late 2019 that ties together elements from advertising, social media, public relations, publicity and crisis management is Peloton, the stationary bike brand that soared to prominence in the category. The company produced a television/digital ad titled, "The Gift that Gives Back" just in time for the Christmas shopping season. The ad depicts a woman receiving a Peloton for Christmas one year earlier from her husband, then chronicling her life in a series of selfie videos for the entire year. Created to appear as a series of amateur selfies ultimately suggesting how the bike transformed the woman's life, the ad was the subject of swift and vengeful scorn. The backlash came from an overwhelming sentiment that the ad objectified women. Social media channels lit up with disdain and PR critics lambasted the com-

crisis management
a coordinated effort to handle all the effects of either unfavourable publicity or an unexpected unfavourable event

pany, which remained silent for days in the aftermath—one of the first no-no's in crisis management. After what was considered a disingenuous apology from the CEO days after the crisis, prompted by what many saw as a response to stem the tide of stock value decline, Peloton somehow benefited from the incident with an overall increase in sales.

16-6 | DIRECT-RESPONSE COMMUNICATION

Direct-response communication is often referred to as *direct marketing*. It involves generating profitable business results through targeted communications to a specific audience. Direct-response communication uses a combination of relevant messaging and offers that can be tracked, measured, analyzed, stored, and leveraged to drive future marketing initiatives.

Direct-response communication provides the opportunity for one-to-one communication resulting in more targeted messaging and relationship building. Not-for-profits, whose objective is to raise awareness and generate donations, rely heavily on this form of communication because it can be tailored, its effectiveness is measurable, and it builds relationships that are key to effective stewardship.

Direct-response communication can be successful because the targeted communication is often more appealing to the consumer than mass-market communication. It is designed to meet consumers' unique needs, and they can learn about the product and make a purchase all at one time.

When creating a direct-response marketing campaign, keep in mind the following six key elements:

- *The offer:* The offer is the catalyst that stimulates the consumer to respond to the sales proposition in the message. The more time-sensitive the offer, the more immediate the need for a response.

- *The creative:* Special considerations are needed when developing a direct-response campaign; industry experts exist to assist marketers in this task.

- *The media:* To deliver a personalized message, direct-response communication can use television, radio, newspapers, magazines, telephone, the Internet, mail, or any combination of these media.

- *Response and tracking mechanism:* The strength of direct-response communication is the ability to track results and report progress relative to the communication objective.

- *Customer call service:* Because direct response is built around an immediate consumer response, a call centre should exist to handle the calls.

- *Protection of privacy legislation*: By definition, direct marketing requires organizations to communicate directly with members of their target market using personal information (emails, addresses, phone numbers, etc.). Such privileged information must be handled with extreme care.

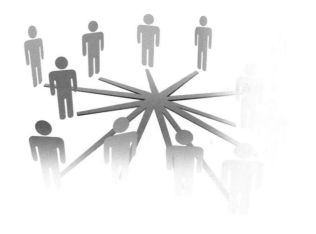

Michael D Brown/Shutterstock.com

16-6a | The Tools of Direct-Response Communication

TELEMARKETING Telemarketing refers to outbound (a company calling the customer) and inbound (a customer calling the company) sales calls to secure an order. Inbound telemarketing is what we do each time we call a number to place an order. Outbound telemarketing is what we often are annoyed by. In Canada consumers can voluntarily register on a **Do Not Call List (DNCL)**. Companies that use telemarketing must update their database every 30 days to ensure that those registered on the DCNL are not contacted. Companies will be fined if they are found in violation of the DNCL.

DIRECT MAIL Direct mail refers to printed communications distributed to the consumer via Canada Post or independent contractors. The key is that the material is delivered directly to the consumer. Direct mail has two forms—addressed and unaddressed—and addressed direct mail generally receives higher response rates. A successful campaign must obviously reach the right person, be read by that person, and be persuasive enough to lead to a response. A critical element in a direct-mail campaign is the mailing list. Mailing lists can be internal (such as a company-created database) or can be rented or purchased from companies that specialize in lists. Another critical element is the creative—the envelope must be interesting and intriguing enough to be opened, and the enclosed letter must be persuasive enough to prompt a response. The dramatic rise in postage rates puts the success of direct mail as a communications tool in question.

DIGITAL DIRECT MARKETING

COMPANY WEBSITES Company websites are wonderful public relations and direct marketing tools as they are used to introduce new products; promote existing products; provide information to the media, including through social media news releases; obtain consumer feedback; communicate legislative and regulatory information; showcase upcoming events; provide links to related sites (including corporate and noncorporate blogs, Facebook, Twitter, LinkedIn, and Instagram); release financial information; interact with customers and potential customers; and perform many more marketing activities. Social media are playing a larger role in how companies interact with customers online. Indeed, online reviews (good and bad) from opinion leaders and other consumers help marketers sway purchasing decisions in their favour.

The reason corporate websites are considered a direct marketing tool is because of the use of cookies. These small files exchanged between web servers and visitors to websites are what make it possible for you to be directly targeted by a digital ad or other call to action after having visited the website of the company now reaching you directly.

Canada's Anti-Spam Legislation, established in 2014, went into full force in 2017. In it, the use of cookies was permitted, without gaining permission from the user. However, by late 2019, more and more companies were publishing a disclaimer, also known as "cookie consent" on their landing page, essentially warning visitors that they can and will be tracked by cookies, and information discovered about them will very likely be used to target them with ads.

The Internet, and specifically social media, has breathed new life into direct-response marketing as a promotional tool. By definition, any digital marketing is also direct marketing, as one of the most important things it does is gather information about potential customers. Visits to a corporate website, as discussed previously, will use cookies to track the visitor. If the visitor interacts within the site, by providing any personal

Do Not Call List (DNCL) a free service whereby Canadians register their telephone number to reduce or eliminate phone calls from telemarketers

information, for instance, it is assumed that consent has been given.

The same can be said for social media. By interacting with an organization's Facebook, YouTube, Instagram, or LinkedIn page in any fashion, users are setting themselves up to be targeted. If you follow a company you will most certainly receive targeted and personal messages from the company. Email is another, albeit older and most obvious, direct marketing tool. Once an email address is obtained by a company, whether by its website or social media, the email is used to acquire new customers or convince customers to purchase something immediately. Email communication can be a cost-effective direct-response tool; it provides the recipient with the opportunity to seek additional information or to place an order with the click of a mouse.

direct-response broadcast
advertising that uses television or radio and includes a direct call to action asking the consumer to respond immediately

direct-response television (DRTV)
advertising that appears on television and encourages viewers to respond immediately

direct-response print
advertising in a print medium that includes a direct call to action

DIRECT-RESPONSE BROADCAST Direct-response broadcast uses television and radio. **Direct-response television (DRTV)** refers to television commercials that end with a call to action. DRTV can vary in length: short-form DRTVs can be 15, 30, 60, 90, or 120 seconds. Long-form DRTVs typically run for 30 to 60 minutes and are often referred to as *infomercials*. Because the return on investment with direct response is measured and is a critical key success factor, marketers don't want to pay regular rates for the spots. Stations offer discounts on inventory not sold, which explains why much DRTV is seen at odd hours in the day. Direct-response radio isn't as widely used as direct-response television because of the nature of radio as a medium (portable and no visuals), but some advertisers will create messaging around the call-to-action tool (the phone number) to enhance the success of radio as a direct-response medium.

DIRECT-RESPONSE PRINT Direct-response print includes newspapers, magazines, and inserts. Often marketers will want to capitalize on the subscriber base of the magazine or newspaper to reach a certain demographic or psychographic. However, the decline in subscribers to these types of publications is affecting this tool. An ad is a direct-response print ad if it includes a direct call to action.

AWAKE CHOCOLATE
CONTINUING CASE

Terms of Engagement

Over the years, Awake has leveraged customer feedback through direct-response marketing, to not only tell its story but also make product decisions.

For reasons discussed in the next chapter, Awake's primary communications vehicle is sampling—a form of sales promotion. CEO Adam Deremo admitted sampling is more effective for his company than advertising, because Awake simply could not compete with major confectionary companies in advertising expenditures. However, there are other tools in the marketer's tool kit with which to tell the brand's story. Historically, those other options are public relations, direct response, and personal selling. While this book devotes an entire chapter to digital/social media, it is widely considered to be simply the modern form of direct-response marketing. In the old days, this meant "junk mail," physical items that would show up, usually uninvited, in our mailboxes, delivered by Canada Post. These days, digital junk mail has another name: spam. But is by no means the only way to use this important tool. Digital marketing includes a pantheon of new ways for businesses to engage directly with their customers.

"Social media is a really great listening vehicle for our brand," opined Deremo. "We launched with only a solid milk chocolate product. But when we were thinking of expanding into new flavours, we ran polls on Facebook. We listened to what our consumers said. We literally turned that choice over to our followership." Moreover, rather than simply humouring its followers, Awake made a significant, perhaps risky, business decision by going with the majority vote. "They voted for caramel, and that was the flavour that we launched."

In this way, Awake turned social media channels into a highly effective public relations tool, as well as one for research and development. "If you're willing to read through comments people leave on social media, you'll find valuable information. We, in fact use consumer comments a lot to show our retail buyers what consumers are saying about our product. In that sense our consumer comments become an important part of our sales process to our customers. In some cases, those comments have been quite persuasive."

A random scroll through Awake's facebook page bears out the argument made by Deremo:

Nevil: Friday is here friends. May your weekend be caffeinated and excellent!

Follower 1: Why are your products so hard to find!!! How about selling them at Stater Bros or Walgreens!!

Follower 2: Or Sam's Club!!

This sort of unsolicited feedback, begging for Awake Chocolate in some of America's largest grocery retailers, speaks to the power of the brand and the value of direct-response marketing as well as both a PR and personal selling tool.

QUESTIONS

1. At the time of this writing, Adam Deremo and his team had used SEO advertising (search engine optimization) only, as opposed to the many forms of media display advertising discussed in this chapter. However, as the brand has grown, the thought of mainstream advertising, or display advertising, was becoming more feasible. Do some research to determine if you can find any evidence of Awake advertising in this form, and comment as to its effectiveness in your opinion.

2. This chapter covers the concept of public relations, but the term comes up only in passing in this case. Using theoretical concepts in the chapter, explain how Awake uses its direct-response marketing also as a public relations tactic.

3. Scroll through Awake's Facebook feed and find an example, not covered in this case, that demonstrates its use of this platform as a market research tool. Explain your findings using direct quotes and dates from the page.

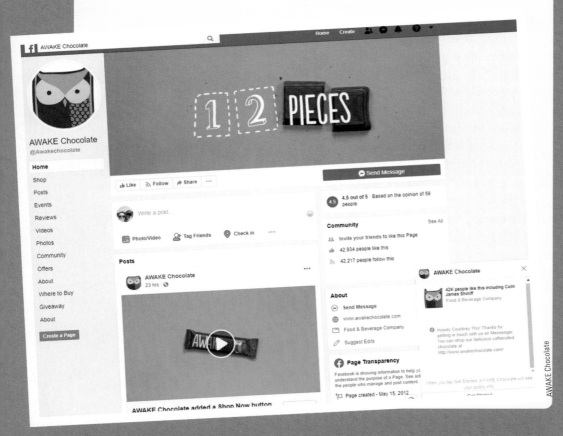

AWAKE Chocolate

17 | Sales Promotion and Personal Selling

LEARNING OUTCOMES

17-1 Define and state the objectives of sales promotion

17-2 Discuss the most common forms of consumer sales promotion

17-3 Discuss the most common forms of trade sales promotion

17-4 Describe personal selling

17-5 Discuss the key differences between relationship selling and traditional selling

17-6 List the steps in the selling process and discuss key issues

"Make a customer, not a sale."

—Katherine Barchetti[1]

17-1 | WHAT IS SALES PROMOTION?

Advertising, publicity, and direct response, as we learned in Chapter 16, can help create and maintain knowledge of a brand's positioning, improving the likelihood that the consumer will choose that brand over others. But with today's plethora of goods and services, how can marketers increase the likelihood that the consumer will continue to see their brand as number one and buy it repeatedly? Equally important, how can they increase the likelihood that the consumer will buy the brand for the first time? Marketing managers use the tools discussed in Chapter 16 as well as sales promotion and personal selling tactics discussed in this chapter.

Sales promotion is a communications tool that provides a short-term incentive to the consumer, or members of the distribution channel, as a motivation to try or purchase a good or service immediately. Sales promotions are used in these cases because they can have more effect on behaviour than they do on attitudes.

For over 30 years, Tim Horton's "Roll Up the Rim" sweepstakes served as the poster child of the way sales promotions should work. The fun of playing along with the contest matched with the anticipation of possibly winning a prize routinely drove up coffee sales during its winter run. Eventually becoming as ubiquitous as the brand itself, and its brand nomenclature—"double double"—"Roll Up the Rim" was a hit, until it collided with the tidal wave of concern over the excessive corporate waste it created. At the conclusion of the 2019 campaign, the executive team had had enough, and vowed to change the contest in 2020 to have a reduced environmental impact.

The reworked model of "Roll Up the Rim" wasn't announced until March 2020, roughly one month after the usual time the contest commenced in previous years. The plan was to halve the event's length and to supplement in-store participation through virtual participation via the Tim's app.[2] However, at the last minute, the company was compelled to go all digital, due to health concerns over the COVID-19 virus that gripped the world in 2020. In a public statement, Tim Hortons stated that it is not "the right time for team members in our restaurants to collect rolled-up tabs that have been

in people's mouths during the current public health environment."[3]

And so, with uncharacteristic subtlety, and a cascade of both controllable and uncontrollable forces, "Roll Up the Rim" was downsized forever. There was some speculation that growing discontent with the waste created by "Roll Up the Rim" alone would have eventually caused the pivot, but the slow demise of this once-textbook example of a sales promotion may have been supplanted by another Tim Horton's sales promotion—a loyalty program. It too, however, underwent significant changes in early 2020 due to what Restaurant Brands International Inc. CEO Jose Cil described as attracting "far more guests to our loyalty program far more quickly than we had planned."[4] This ballooning effect of expanding membership resulted in millions of dollars in loyalty-based drinks and donuts gifted to customers in 2019, and was partially to blame for Tim's overall sagging financial performance that year.

When the program was tweaked in 2020, two things were clear. First there was going to be more reliance upon the loyalty-based program than ever, as it transitioned over to a fully digital experience (no more use of Tims cards). Second, as CTV News reported, while more intensity would drive the loyalty strategy, reward redemption was going to rely on increased purchases.[5]

But while both "Roll up the Rim" and "Tims Rewards" were showing some signs of fatigue or financial liability, there was no sign, nor would there ever be, that Tim Hortons would begin moving away from sales promotion as a marketing communications tool.

Sales promotion is a key element in an integrated marketing communications (IMC) program because, as with the Tim Horton's example, it stimulates sales, albeit the goal is to have sales exceed the costs of the giveaways that drew attention in the first place. In contrast to traditional advertising media, sales promotion is relatively easy to measure. Marketers know the precise number of samples handed out, the number of clicks through to a website, or the number of contest entries received. The Internet is providing even greater opportunities as Instagram, YouTube, and other social media sites are being used to deliver sales promotion offers, providing instant two-way communication.

Sales promotion strategies are playing a greater role in communication plans as a result of increased competition and the increasing use of online marketing tools and social media.

17-1a | The Sales Promotion Target

Sales promotion is usually targeted toward either of two distinctly different markets. Sales promotion targeted to the final consumer is referred to as **consumer sales promotion**. **Trade sales promotion** is directed to members of the marketing channel, such as wholesalers and retailers.

consumer sales promotion
activities, such as price discounts, to incentivize consumer purchases

trade sales promotion
activities, such as price discounts, to incentivize current or prospective clientele to make purchases

17-1b | The Objectives of Sales Promotion

The purpose of sales promotion is to effect behaviour in a short time. Immediate purchase is, in fact, its main goal. The objectives of a promotion depend on the general behaviour of target consumers (see Exhibit 17.1) and the stage in the product life cycle. In the introductory stage of the product life cycle, sales promotion techniques are used to gain channel member support, as the company works to build distribution and to achieve trial by the final consumer. As the product moves through the product life cycle, the company's objectives change, as does the behaviour of the target consumer. For example, marketers who are targeting loyal users of their product in the late growth and maturity stages of the product life cycle need to reinforce existing behaviour or increase product usage. In this situation, loyalty programs work well. With over 70 percent of purchase decisions made in-store, and with the increasing use of digital technologies by the shopper (more often than not the female head of household), loyalty programs that are accessed by mobile devices are increasing in effectiveness.

Canadian Tire replaced its paper money concept in 2018 with a purely online loyalty program before creating the Triangle Rewards loyalty program. This new program allowed customers to earn points not only at Canadian Tire stores and gas bars, but also at sister retail brands SportChek, Marks, PartSource, and Atmosphere. This program also drove traffic to Canadian Tire's digital store where special, "online only" deals could be purchased. In addition, the Canadian Tire Triangle Mastercard issues Canadian Tire Money as a percentage of purchases not only at Canadian Tire stores and the other aforementioned brands, but also at all other stores where Mastercard is accepted.[6]

Canadian Tire, Tim Hortons, and, in fact, any company now doing sales promotions online are practising direct response marketing as well, since online engagement by definition, is predicated on two-way communication between seller and buyer. In both cases, also, particularly the topsy-turvy evolution of Roll Up the Rim, a third marketing communications strategy was employed. Public relations was required to communicate the first reworking of the contest, and then again mere weeks later, to explain the abolishment of cups altogether. All of which points toward the notion of IMC, to which these last few chapters are dedicated.

Once marketers understand the dynamics occurring within their product category and have determined the particular consumers and consumer behaviours they want to influence, they can then select the appropriate promotional tools to achieve these goals.

EXHIBIT 17.1	TYPES OF CONSUMERS AND SALES PROMOTION GOALS	
Type of Buyer	**Desired Results**	**Sales Promotion Examples**
Loyal customers People who buy a particular brand most of the time or all of the time	Reinforce behaviour, increase consumption, change purchase timing	• Loyalty marketing programs, such as frequent-buyer cards or frequent-shopper clubs • Bonus packs that give loyal consumers an incentive to stock up or offer premiums in return for proof of purchase
Competitor's customers People who buy a competitor's product most of the time or all of the time	Break loyalty, persuade to switch to another brand	• Sampling to introduce another brand's superior qualities compared with competing brands • Sweepstakes, contests, or premiums that create interest in the product
Brand switchers People who buy a variety of products in the category	Persuade to buy one brand more often	• Any promotion that lowers the price of the product, such as coupons, price-off packages, and bonus packs. A promotion that adds value to a product such as a contest. • Trade deals that help make the product more readily available than competing products
Price buyers People who consistently buy the least expensive brand	Appeal with low prices or supply added value that makes price less important	• Coupons, price-off packages, refunds, or trade deals that reduce the price of the brand to match or undercut the price of the brand that would have otherwise been purchased

Source: Adapted from *Sales Promotion Essentials*, 3rd ed., by Don E. Schulz, William A. Robinson, and Lisa A. Petrison. © McGraw-Hill Education.

17-2 | TOOLS FOR CONSUMER SALES PROMOTION

Marketing managers must decide which consumer sales promotion devices to use in a specific campaign. The methods chosen must suit the objectives to ensure success of the overall promotion plan.

17-2a | Discounts and Coupons

As consumers, we are hardwired to sniff out deals in our purchasing. As discussed in Chapter 1, price is one half of the value equation. The lower the price, the more we usually value in the offering. Thus, when a seller lowers the price of a product, it tends to have a gravitational pull to our attention—particularly if it is a product that we are interested in purchasing.

Price discounts come in myriad formats. The most obvious is a percentage price discount. This is simply reducing an original, or regular, price by a set percentage such as 10 percent, 20 percent, or 50 percent. Discounting can also just be in the form of a dollar amount, which is really just another way of representing percentage, but sometime it has more pull. Car dealerships like to visibly show the Manufacturers Suggested Retail Price (MSRP) on the window sticker of a new car in the show room, then use erasable white paint to write the "reduced price" (e.g., from $49 900 to $44 900), or perhaps even more effective, bold incentivising language like "slashed by $5000!")

In lower price consumer categories, price discounts can be applied to the purchase of more than one item. Claire's and Justice, tween girls fashion and accessory retailers offer almost everything at a discount, when compared to the "original price," that is readily and visibly displayed. These stores also take advantage of the fact that all of their items are value priced, and "feel" (at least to a tween girl and her parent) that buying 3 T-shirts for $36 is infinitely better than buying one for $18 … even though said parent and daughter intended to leave the store with only one T-shirt.

Price discounting can be interpreted and even scrutinized by consumerists as being somewhat manipulative, so users of this tactic must ensure that they are familiar with, and obeying, retail regulations.

A **coupon** is a certificate that entitles consumers to an immediate price reduction when they buy the product. Coupons are a particularly good way to encourage product trial and repurchase. They are also likely to increase the amount of a product bought. Coupons can be distributed in a variety of ways, such as

JHVEPhoto/Shutterstock.com

directly on the package, on the shelf in store, at the cash register, on a coupon wall as you enter the store, in weekly flyers, in a free-standing insert (FSI), and through various digital delivery methods, such as daily deal sites, like Groupon, that can be accessed via a computer or the consumer's tablet or smartphone. Both consumer goods producers and retailers can also issue coupons through their own websites or social media channels. In-store coupons are still popular because they directly influence customers' buying decisions. Instant coupons on product packages and electronic coupons issued at the counter now achieve much higher redemption rates because consumers are making more in-store purchase decisions.

Canadians continue to use their mobile devices to research and shop, creating yet another coupon distribution method for companies. A variety of cellphone mobile apps exist for coupons, saving the consumer from clipping coupons and remembering to redeem them at the checkout. Canadians, particularly those aged 18 to 34, are interested in receiving coupons on their mobile devices, either via email or text message, which they then conveniently use at a point of purchase for savings.[7] As the use of smartphones as mobile wallets grows, so will the use of mobile couponing. Digital coupons can have up to 10 times higher redemption than paper coupons, so they do work.[8] Social media are also increasingly being used as a couponing distribution method. Facebook introduced Offers a few years ago, which allows businesses to post an offer such as a coupon on their Facebook page. Consumers can click on the Offer and have it sent to their email address for redemption at point of purchase. Over 53 percent of Canadians "like"

coupon
a certificate that entitles consumers to an immediate price reduction when they buy the product

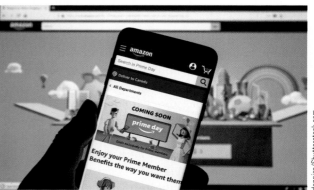

purchaser must usually mail in a rebate form and some proof of purchase, the reward is not immediate. Manufacturers prefer rebates for several reasons. Rebates allow manufacturers to offer price cuts to consumers directly. Manufacturers have more control over rebate promotions because they can be rolled out and stopped quickly. Further, because buyers must fill out forms with their names, addresses, and other data, manufacturers use rebate programs to build customer databases. Perhaps the best reason of all to offer rebates is that although rebates are particularly good at enticing a purchase, most consumers never bother to redeem them.

17-2c | Premiums

A **premium** is an extra item offered to the consumer, usually in exchange for some proof that the promoted product has been purchased. Premiums reinforce the consumer's purchase decision, increase consumption, and persuade nonusers to switch brands. Premiums that are developed as collectibles can encourage brand loyalty. A classic example of a longstanding premium program is the McDonald's Happy Meal, where a small toy is included with the meal, usually a "bite-sized" version of a popular kids movie character. Movie theatres got into the act as well, including the small toy to go along with the kids' snack pack of popcorn, drink, and candy. But premiums aren't limited to small inexpensive trinkets designed to trigger adult purchase decisions based upon their children's demands. The word free crosses all demographics, instilling an urgency to "buy now" in otherwise intelligent adults. Canada's big telecom providers, Rogers, Telus, and Bell, have been doing this for years, offering endless high-end premiums,

Amazon's basic interface serves as a freemium for the company, to which many users willingly upgrade to reap the perceived benefits of Amazon Prime, the premium model.

pages on Facebook to receive deals or coupons, and over 40 percent follow brands or retailers on Twitter to receive immediate information on deals and coupons.

17-2b | Rebates

Rebates are cash refunds given for the purchase of a product during a specific period. They are similar to coupons in that they offer the purchaser a price reduction; however, because the

rebates
cash refunds given for the purchase of a product during a specific period

premium
an extra item offered to the consumer, usually in exchange for some proof of purchase of the promoted product

like smartphones, tablets, and televisions, in exchange for our signature on a usage contract.

A close cousin to premium is the "**freemium**," popularized by consumer tech companies ranging from music streaming service Spotify to the professional networking site, LinkedIn. Setting up an account on these and other services is free, and comes with varying degrees of functionality. Sooner or later, however, as the user experience expands, so too does the cost of participating in the enhanced experience.

Premiums can also include more product for the regular price, such as two-for-the-price-of-one bonus packs or packages that include more of the product. Another possibility is to attach a premium to the product's package.

17-2d | Loyalty Marketing Programs

Loyalty marketing programs and **frequent-buyer programs** reward loyal consumers for making multiple purchases. Loyalty marketing programs are designed to build long-term, mutually beneficial relationships between a company and its key customers.

A recent study by consulting firm Bain & Company reported that increasing consumer retention by 5 percent could boost a company's profits by 25 to 95 percent![9] In highly competitive marketplaces, loyalty programs can enhance profitability by discouraging brand switching. A recent study conducted of North American consumers found that on a per-person basis, members were actively engaged in only about 7 of the 13.4 loyalty programs that they belonged to. Not being able to participate in the program on their mobile device and dissatisfaction with the loyalty program website are two key reasons that members do not engage with programs they have signed on to. A good loyalty program should support the brand promise, be personalized to the member, encourage redemption through an easy-to-navigate website and be accessed on a smartphone. If loyalty programs can improve personalization, satisfaction levels increase significantly. Members who redeem their points for relevant rewards (personalization) and instantly in-store are far more likely to be satisfied with the loyalty program. The more satisfied members are with the loyalty program experience, the more likely they are to become a brand ambassador and for the program to meet the promotion objectives.[10]

Well-established loyalty programs can provide marketers with data on consumer purchases, including what they buy, when they buy, and even sometimes why they buy. Such data can be used to create more personalized and sophisticated marketing programs. In the 1990s,

The Canadian Press/Fernando Morales/The Globe and Mail

Loblaws started the consumer loyalty program PC Points, which has evolved to the current PC Optimum program. This loyalty program uses points as currency for purchases made in store. The program is personalized, so with each scan of the loyalty card, consumer purchase data are recorded and weekly customized "offers" are provided to the member via their mobile device or online. The customized offers are based on purchase history and often encourage consumers to buy more products by offering bonus points on items. By simply scanning the loyalty card at the checkout, the member can redeem accumulated points for free groceries. As a product enhancement, the loyalty program is linked to PC Financial Cards and Shoppers Drug Mart. If the consumer uses a PC credit or debit card for purchases, additional points are collected.[11] With Canadians exhibiting limited loyalty to grocery retailers, Loblaws hopes this program will keep them coming back.

Cobranded credit cards are an increasingly popular loyalty marketing tool. Royal Bank, Scotiabank, Canadian Tire, Costco, Holt Renfrew, and Aeroplan are only a few of the companies sponsoring cobranded Visa, MasterCard, or American Express cards.

17-2e | Contests and Sweepstakes

Contests and sweepstakes are generally designed to create interest in a good or service and, thereby,

freemium
an initially "free" offering, to use a service with limited functionality, which serves as an enticement to pay a "premium" to receive an enhanced experience

loyalty marketing program
a promotional program designed to build long-term, mutually beneficial relationships between a company and its key customers

frequent-buyer program
a loyalty program in which loyal consumers are rewarded for making multiple purchases of a particular good or service

to encourage brand switching. *Contests* are promotions in which participants use some skill or ability to compete for prizes. A consumer contest usually requires entrants to submit a proof of purchase and answer questions, complete sentences, or write a paragraph about the product. Winning a *sweepstakes*, on the other hand, depends on chance, and participation is free. Sweepstakes usually draw about ten times as many entries as contests do.

While contests and sweepstakes may draw considerable interest and publicity, they are generally not effective tools for generating long-term sales. To increase their effectiveness, sales promotion managers must make certain the award will appeal to the target market. Offering several smaller prizes to many winners instead of one huge prize to just one person can often increase the effectiveness of the promotion, but there's no denying the attractiveness of a jackpot-type prize. Tim Hortons' classic Roll Up the Rim to Win is an example of a sweepstakes that combines both large and small prizes to ensure many winners, although its reign may be in jeopardy due to declining interest, environmental backlash, and the COVID-19 outbreak.

17-2f | Sampling

Sampling allows the customer to try a product or service for free. Sampling has been proven to increase sales, so it's no surprise that new consumer products often rely on sampling to build the business.

Samples can be mailed directly to the customer, delivered door to door, packaged with another product, or demonstrated and distributed at a retail store or service outlet. Sampling at special events is a popular, effective, and high-profile distribution method that permits marketers to piggyback onto fun-based consumer activities—including sporting events, college and university fests, fairs and festivals, beach events, and even chili cook-offs.

With the growth of social media, online sampling has become popular. Branded products run contests through social media sites, connect with fans, show commercials, and offer samples of new products in exchange for "liking" the brand. Recognizing the role of influencers in purchase decisions, marketers engage with bloggers as a way to create widespread influence. Bloggers are offered products to try, and good blogs will differentiate between products that have been offered by companies and products that they have purchased themselves. Such a level of transparency increases trust and the value of the reviews to the reader of the blog. Minute Rice launched an influencer marketing campaign, #WeekdayWin. A number of food bloggers who were parents were engaged to share recipes that could be made in 15 minutes and addressed the daily challenges young families face in feeding children: picky eaters and a lack of time. The goal was to create conversations about dinnertime challenges and position Minute Rice as the easy, affordable, and healthy third ingredient in a balanced meal accompanied by a protein and vegetable.[12]

17-2g | Shopper Marketing

Shopper marketing used to be referred to as point-of-purchase (POP) promotion. As part of an IMC program, shopper marketing focuses on the consumer from the point at which the need is stimulated through to selection and purchase of the item. Shopper marketing strategy leverages that knowledge to create effective point-of-purchase opportunities in the store to engage and influence the shopper. It includes promotions such as *shelf talkers* (signs attached to store shelves), shelf extenders (attachments that extend shelves so products stand out), ads on grocery carts and bags, end-of-aisle and floor-stand displays, television monitors at supermarket checkout counters, in-store audio messages, and audiovisual displays. One big advantage of shopper marketing is that it offers manufacturers a captive audience in retail stores. With the majority of brand decisions made in-store, point of purchase is a critical tool in the promotion mix.

17-3 | TOOLS FOR TRADE SALES PROMOTION

Whereas consumer promotions *pull* a product through the channel by creating demand, trade promotions *push* a product through the distribution channel. When selling to members of the distribution channel, manufacturers use many of the same sales promotion tools used in consumer promotions such as sales contests, premiums, and point-of-purchase displays. Several tools, however, are unique to manufacturers and intermediaries.

- *Trade allowances:* A **trade allowance** is a price reduction offered by manufacturers to intermediaries, such as wholesalers and retailers. The price

sampling
a promotional program that allows the consumer the opportunity to try a product or service for free

trade allowance
a price reduction offered by manufacturers to intermediaries, such as wholesalers and retailers

reduction or rebate is given in exchange for a specific activity, such as allocating space for a new product or buying a product during a promotional period. For example, a local Best Buy could receive a special discount for running its own promotion on a Bose Bluetooth speaker.

- *Push money:* Intermediaries receive **push money** as a bonus for pushing the manufacturer's brand through the distribution channel. Often the push money is directed toward a retailer's salespeople.

- *Training:* Sometimes a manufacturer will train an intermediary's personnel if the product is rather complex—as frequently occurs in the computer and telecommunications industries. Running shoe retail salespeople in specialty running retailers are trained by manufacturers to ensure they can sell the right shoe for the right runner.

- *Free merchandise:* Often a manufacturer offers retailers free merchandise in lieu of quantity discounts— "Buy 10 cases and get 11." Occasionally, free merchandise is used as payment for trade allowances normally provided through other sales promotions.

- *Store demonstrations:* Manufacturers can also arrange with retailers to perform an in-store demonstration. In the wine industry, the sommelier is often invited to a restaurant for an evening to demonstrate the winery's wines and provide suggestions to guests of the restaurant that evening.

- *Co-op advertising:* Co-op advertising is a partnership between channel members with the intent of sharing in the cost of advertising directed at the final consumer to improve sales. More often than not, the partnership is between the manufacturer (who is named in the advertisement) and the retailer. The manufacturer repays the retailer for all or some of the cost of the advertisement.

- *Business meetings, conventions, and trade shows:* Trade association meetings, conferences, and conventions are important aspects of sales promotion and a growing, multibillion-dollar market. At these shows, manufacturers, distributors, and other vendors can display their goods and describe their services to customers and potential customers. Trade shows have been uniquely effective in introducing new products; they can establish products in the marketplace more quickly than advertising, direct marketing, or sales calls. Companies participate in trade shows to attract and identify new prospects, serve current customers, introduce new products, increase corporate image,

At trade shows, vendors can display current and new products, and share their current service offerings to existing and new customers.

test the market response to new products, enhance corporate morale, and gather competitive product information.

Trade promotions are popular among manufacturers for many reasons. Trade sales promotion tools help manufacturers gain new distributors for their products, obtain wholesaler and retailer support for consumer sales promotions, build or reduce dealer inventories, and improve trade relations. Car manufacturers annually sponsor dozens of auto shows for consumers. The shows attract millions of consumers, providing dealers with both increased store traffic and good leads.

17-4 | PERSONAL SELLING

Personal selling is direct communication between a sales representative and one or more prospective buyers in an attempt to influence each other in a purchase situation. In a sense, all businesspeople are salespeople. An individual may be a plant manager, a chemist, an engineer, or a member of any profession and yet still have to sell. During a job search, applicants must sell themselves to prospective employers in the interview.

Personal selling offers several advantages over other forms of promotion. Personal selling may also work better than other forms of promotion given certain customer and product characteristics. Generally speaking, personal selling becomes more important

push money
money offered to channel intermediaries to encourage them to push products—that is, to encourage other members of the channel to sell the products

ADVANTAGES OF PERSONAL SELLING

- Personal selling provides a detailed explanation or demonstration of the product. This capability is needed especially for goods and services that are complex or new.

- The sales message can be varied according to the motivations and interests of each prospective customer. Moreover, when the prospect has questions or raises objections, the salesperson is there to provide explanations. In contrast, advertising and sales promotion can respond only to the objections the copywriter thinks are important to customers.

- Personal selling can be directed to only qualified prospects. Other forms of promotion include some unavoidable waste because many people in the audience are not prospective customers.

- Personal selling costs can be controlled by adjusting the size of the sales force (and resulting expenses) in one-person increments. On the other hand, advertising and sales promotion must often be purchased in fairly large amounts.

- Personal selling is considerably more effective than other forms of promotion in obtaining a sale and gaining a satisfied customer.

- Personal selling is capable of forming relationships in a more meaningful way between seller and buyer. Relationship building, in fact, is at the core of personal selling.

EXHIBIT 17.2	COMPARISON OF PERSONAL SELLING AND SALES PROMOTION
Conditions Where Personal Selling Makes Sense	**Conditions Where Sales Promotion Makes Sense**
High-involvement purchase decisions	Low-involvement purchase decisions
New and unknown products in the introductory stage of the product life cycle	Established products, in the growth or mature stages of the product life cycle
High-priced products	Low-priced products
Products that require demonstration or learning	Products that are widely adopted and understood
Products that are customizable	Products that are uniform
Specialty and unsought products	Convenience and shopping products
Services	Goods
Business to business	Business to consumer
Examples: car, home, tattoo artist B2B purchases such as property, plant, or equipment	**Examples:** groceries, underwear, fast food, gardening equipment

17-5 | RELATIONSHIP SELLING

Until recently, marketing theory and practice concerning personal selling focused almost entirely on a planned presentation to prospective customers for the sole purpose of making the sale. Today, personal selling emphasizes the relationship that develops between a salesperson and a buyer; or, in the case of B2B, a sales team and a buying team. The traditional sales process emphasized persuasion; today, the sales process is a multistage process that involves building, maintaining, and enhancing interactions with customers to develop long-term satisfaction through mutually beneficial partnerships. The sales process today is often referred to as **relationship selling** or **business development**. With relationship selling, the objective is to build long-term relationships with consumers and buyers. The focus is on building mutual trust between the buyer and seller through the delivery of anticipated, long-term, value-added benefits to the buyer.

Business development reps (BDR), therefore, need to become consultants, partners, and problem solvers for their customers. They strive to build long-term relationships with key accounts by developing trust over time. The emphasis shifts from a one-time sale to a long-term relationship in which the salesperson works with the customer to develop solutions to enhance the customer's bottom line. Research has shown that positive

as the number of potential customers decreases, as the complexity of the product increases, and as the value of the product grows (see Exhibit 17.2). For highly complex goods, such as business jets or private communication systems, a salesperson is needed to determine the prospective customer's needs, explain the product's basic advantages, propose the exact features and accessories that will meet the client's needs, and establish a support plan for installation or use.

relationship selling (business development)
a multistage sales process that involves building, maintaining, and enhancing interactions with customers for the purpose of developing long-term satisfaction through mutually beneficial business partnerships

EXHIBIT 17.3	KEY DIFFERENCES BETWEEN TRADITIONAL SELLING AND BUSINESS DEVELOPMENT	
Selling	**Business Development**	
Creates revenue by closing deals with customers	Identifies customers for whom the company can provide a solution, and follows with a gradual relationship-building process	
Relies on business development to identify and seed relationships	Relies on sales to cement financial commitments from customers	
Involves sales reps	Involves business development reps (BDR)	
Comprises mostly establishing trust and maintaining relationship	Comprises mostly research, analysis, and customer relationship management	

Source: Leslie Ye, "Sales vs. Business Development: Differences, Similarities, & Job Titles to Hire For," Hubspot, June 4, 2019.

customer–salesperson relationships contribute to trust, increased customer loyalty, and the intent to continue the relationship with the salesperson.[13] Thus relationship selling promotes a win–win situation for buyer and seller. The immediacy of communication provided by email and mobile messaging allows the relationship between buyer and seller to develop more quickly and strengthen sooner.

The result of business development, or relationship selling, tends to be loyal customers who purchase from the company time after time. A relationship-selling strategy focused on retaining customers costs a company less than constantly prospecting and selling to new customers.

Relationship selling provides many advantages over traditional selling in the consumer goods market. Still, relationship selling is more often used in selling situations for installation goods, such as heavy machinery or computer systems, and services, such as airlines and insurance, than for consumer goods. Exhibit 17.3 lists the key differences between traditional personal selling and relationship or business development. As you can see, while they are different roles, they are complementary, if not interdependent, on one another.

17-6 | THE SELLING PROCESS

Completing a sale requires several steps. The **sales process**, or **sales cycle**, is simply the set of steps a salesperson goes through to sell a particular product or service. The sales process or cycle can be unique for each product or service, depending on the features of the product or service, the characteristics of customer segments, and the internal processes in place within the company, such as how leads are gathered.

Some sales take only a few minutes, but others may take much longer to complete. Sales of technical products, such as a Bombardier rail vehicle, and customized goods and services typically take many months, perhaps even years, to complete. On the other end of the spectrum, sales of less technical products, such as office supplies, are generally more routine and may take only a few days. Whether a salesperson spends a few minutes or a few years on a sale, seven basic steps make up the personal selling process:

1. Generating leads
2. Qualifying leads
3. Approaching the customer and probing needs
4. Developing and proposing solutions
5. Handling objections
6. Closing the sale
7. Following up

Like other forms of promotion, these steps of selling follow the AIDA (attention, interest, desire, action) concept discussed in Chapter 15. Once a salesperson has located a prospect with the authority to buy, the salesperson tries to get the prospect's attention. The salesperson can generate interest through an effective sales proposal and presentation that have been developed after a thorough needs assessment. After developing the customer's initial desire (preferably during the presentation of the sales proposal), the salesperson closes by trying to get an agreement to buy. Follow-up after the sale, the final step in the selling process, not only lowers cognitive dissonance but also may open up opportunities to discuss future sales. Effective follow-up can also lead to repeat business in which the process may start all over again at the needs assessment step.

Exhibit 17.4 outlines the objectives of each step in the selling process and some key activities that occur at each step.

Traditional selling and relationship selling follow the same basic steps; however, they differ in the relative importance placed on key steps in the process. Traditional selling efforts are transaction oriented, focusing on generating as many leads as possible, making as many presentations as possible, and closing as many sales as possible. In contrast, the salesperson practising relationship selling emphasizes an upfront investment in the

sales process (sales cycle)
the set of steps a salesperson goes through to sell a particular product or service

EXHIBIT 17.4 | STEPS IN THE SELLING PROCESS

Step	Objective	Comments
1. Generating leads	Identification of those companies and people most likely to buy	Leads can be generated through advertising, websites, trade shows, direct mail, and telemarketing. Networking is a great tool for generating leads. Referrals from current clients are strong leads.
2. Qualifying leads	To determine if the lead has a recognized need, the buying power, and the receptivity and accessibility to meet and discuss the potential deal	It can be more cost effective to use a sales support person or a prequalification system to complete the qualification process. Company websites are useful here.
3. Approaching the customer and probing needs	To gather information and decide how best to approach the prospect	Information sources include websites, directories, colleagues who may know the prospect, and current company salespeople. The ultimate goal is to conduct a *needs assessment* of the prospect to build a client profile.
4. Developing and proposing solutions	To create the solution and prepare the presentation that will effectively deliver the solution	To present successfully, the salesperson must be well prepared. Engaging the customer in the presentation is critical, and the presentation should be explicitly tied to the prospect's expressed interest.
5. Handling objections	To be prepared to engage in *negotiation*-type discussions with the customer	The ability to handle objections must be rehearsed so that they are handled flawlessly in the presentation. If the salesperson is not confident in handling an objection, it is best to be honest, acknowledge the objection, and communicate that an answer will be forthcoming.
6. Closing the sale	To obtain a commitment	The most difficult part of the presentation is often the close. A good salesperson will know, as the presentation evolves, how to close by observing signals provided by the client. This point in the selling process involves negotiation to ensure all parties' needs are met.
7. Following up	To ensure that the customer is satisfied	The salesperson must ensure that the promises made during the presentation are all met. To ensure repeat sales, the customer must not feel abandoned.

lead generation (prospecting)
identification of those companies and people most likely to buy the seller's offerings

cold calling
a form of lead generation in which the salesperson approaches potential buyers without any prior knowledge of the prospects' needs or financial status

referrals
recommendations to a salesperson from a customer or business associate

networking
the use of friends, business contacts, co-workers, acquaintances, and fellow members in professional and civic organizations to identify potential clients

time and effort needed to uncover each customer's specific needs and wants and meet them with the product or service offering. By doing the homework upfront, the salesperson creates the conditions necessary for a relatively straight-forward close. Then a salesperson with strong relationship selling skills will follow up regularly to build and maintain a long-term relationship, as it is far more expensive to gain a new customer than it is to retain a current one. Relationship-selling theorists suggest that in addition to knowing the client well, salespeople should develop mutual trust with their prospect at the outset. Salespeople must sell themselves before they can sell the product. The goal from the outset is to ensure that the customer trusts that the salesperson is committed to continually meeting their needs in the most efficient and effective way possible.

17-6a | Some Key Issues in Each Step of the Selling Process

Lead generation or **prospecting** is the lifeblood of an effective sales team as it ensures new customers are constantly being sought. Before the advent of more sophisticated methods of lead generation, most prospecting was done through **cold calling**—a form of lead generation in which the salesperson approaches potential buyers without any prior knowledge of the prospects' needs or financial status. Although this method is still used, many sales managers have realized the inefficiencies of having their top salespeople use their valuable selling time cold calling, and today this form of prospecting is often left to an internal sales support person.

A highly effective tool for gaining new clients or **referrals** is **networking**. Networking is using friends, business contacts, coworkers, acquaintances, and fellow members in professional and civic organizations to identify potential clients. Indeed, some national networking clubs have been started for the sole purpose of generating leads and providing valuable business advice.

Social media are also providing an opportunity for networking. LinkedIn is one such example. LinkedIn, a member-based social media tool with demonstrated effectiveness for creating connections and online networking, offers Sales Navigator, an online tool that helps sales professionals easily find and engage with the right prospects through social selling.

Social selling is about leveraging your social network to find the right prospects, build trusted relationships, and through such activities achieve sales targets. Social selling techniques can lead to better leads, enhancing the sales prospecting process and eliminating the need for cold calling. With social selling and tools such as LinkedIn's Sales Navigator, the salesperson can build and maintain relationships within a much larger network far more efficiently. To enhance the success of social selling, salespeople should ensure that they have created a professional brand for themselves. With the breadth of contacts that can be acquired through social selling, buyers can be selective, choosing only to work with salespeople whom they trust. A salesperson who demonstrates knowledge of the industry and is an active participant in the industry through a LinkedIn profile and other social media is more likely to be trusted.

A close cousin to social selling is the **Trojan Horse method**. Here, explains Steven Woessner in his book *Profitable Podcasting*, the trick is to simply get a prospective customer's attention long enough to demonstrate your value as a solution provider. In Woessner's case, he recruits guests for his podcast, for whom he feels his consulting would be valuable. After having the prospect participate in an interview in during Steven is able to showcase his knowledge of marketing and business, often the prospect asks him what it would cost to leverage his expertise.[14]

The Trojan Horse method can be scaled through all social media channels, but especially through LinkedIn, where the userbase is predominantly employed, or employable adults in search of information, networking, and interacting with like minds. Simply writing a weekly blogpost on Linkedin will also help bolster the profile of an entrepreneur as a thought leader.

Leads generated through any method do not necessarily warrant a sales call. **Lead qualification** involves determining the sales prospect's (1) recognized need, (2) buying power, and (3) receptivity and accessibility. Companies must be diligent in ensuring that the lead offers potential. Companies are using social media to drive prospects to their websites and are then using Web analytics to determine potential or to qualify leads. Website analytics offer the opportunity to measure the length of time people stay on a website, what they pay attention to on the website, and how often they return. Companies set up their websites so that visitors are encouraged to register, indicate the products and services they are interested in, and provide information on their time frame and resources. Leads from the website can then be prioritized and transferred to salespeople.

Before the actual sales call, a salesperson needs to conduct as much research as possible on all leads. This process is called the **preapproach** and ensures that the salesperson has enough prospect knowledge to engage them and keep them engaged throughout the actual presentation. A thorough preapproach will ensure a consultative approach to selling. The salesperson's ultimate goal is to conduct a **needs assessment**, a determination of the customer's specific needs and wants and the range of options the customer has for satisfying them. In other words, the salesperson needs to find out as much as possible about the prospect's situation. The salesperson should determine how to maximize the fit between what the company can offer and what the prospective customer wants. As part of the needs assessment, the consultative salesperson must know everything there is to know about the following:

- *The product or service:* The consultative salesperson must be an expert on the product or service, including performance comparisons with the competition, other customers' experiences with the product, and current advertising and promotional campaign messages
- *Customers and their needs:* The salesperson should know more about customers than they know about themselves. The goal of such knowledge is to become a trusted consultant and adviser.

social selling
leveraging social networks to find the right prospects and build trusted relationships to achieve sales goals

Trojan Horse method
demonstrating or displaying a person or company's expertise via social media channels, resulting in recruitment of prospects who are impressed with said expertise and voluntarily come forward with interest in seeking the company's assistance

lead qualification
determination of a sales prospect's (1) recognized need, (2) buying power, and (3) receptivity and accessibility

preapproach
a process that describes the research a salesperson must do before contacting a prospect

needs assessment
a determination of the customer's specific needs and wants and the range of options the customer has for satisfying them

Sales professionals are increasingly using online networking sites, such as LinkedIn, to connect with targeted leads and clients around the world. LinkedIn is a business-oriented social networking site with more than 360 million registered users that allows its members to exchange knowledge, ideas, and opportunities in an online forum, 24 hours a day, 7 days a week.

sales proposal
a formal written document or professional presentation that outlines how the salesperson's product or service will meet or exceed the prospect's needs

sales presentation
a formal meeting in which the salesperson presents a sales proposal to a prospective buyer

negotiation
the process during which both the salesperson and the prospect offer concessions in an attempt to arrive at a sales agreement

follow-up
the final step of the selling process, in which the salesperson ensures that delivery schedules are met, that the goods or services perform as promised, and that the buyer's employees are properly trained to use the products

- *The competition:* The salesperson must know as much about competitor companies and products as about their own company. Competitive intelligence ensures that the salesperson can handle objections well.

- *The industry:* The salesperson must know the impact of economic and financial conditions on the industry, as well as current legislation and regulations.

The result of the research is the creation of a *customer profile* that helps salespeople optimize their time and resources. This profile is then used to develop an intelligent analysis of the prospect's needs in preparation for the development of the presentation.

Once the salesperson has gathered the appropriate information about the client's needs and wants, the next step is to determine whether their company's products or services match the needs of the prospective customer. The salesperson then develops a solution, or possibly several solutions, in which the salesperson's product or service solves the client's problems or meets a specific need.

These solutions are typically presented to the client in the form of a sales proposal presented at a sales presentation. A **sales proposal** is a written document or professional presentation that outlines how the company's product or service will meet or exceed the client's needs. The **sales presentation** is the formal meeting in which the salesperson presents the sales proposal to a prospective buyer. The presentation should be explicitly tied to the prospect's expressed needs and should include the customer in the discussion as much as possible.

Because the salesperson often has only one opportunity to present solutions, the quality of both the sales proposal and presentation can make or break the sale. Salespeople must be able to present the proposal with confidence and professionalism and be prepared to knowledgeably handle any objections.

At the end of the presentation, the salesperson should ask the customer how they would like to proceed. If the customer exhibits signs of being ready to purchase, and all questions have been answered and objections have been met, then the salesperson can try to close the sale. Closing requires courage and skill. If the salesperson has developed a strong relationship with the customer, and the proposal and presentation are well prepared, only minimal efforts are needed to close a sale. However, in all likelihood some negotiation will play a role in closing the sale. **Negotiation** is the process during which both the salesperson and the prospect offer concessions in an attempt to arrive at a sales agreement. Effective negotiators avoid using price as a negotiation tool. Instead, salespeople should emphasize the value to the customer, rendering price a nonissue. Salespeople should also be prepared to ask for trade-offs and should try to avoid giving unilateral concessions.

Once the sale is closed, it is not complete. A basic goal of relationship selling is to motivate customers to come back, again and again, by developing and nurturing long-term relationships. Most businesses depend on repeat sales, and repeat sales depend on thorough and continued **follow-up** by the salesperson. When customers feel abandoned, cognitive dissonance arises, and repeat sales decline. Today, this issue is more pertinent than ever because customers are far less loyal to brands and vendors. Buyers are more inclined to look

THE CANADIAN PROFESSIONAL SALES ASSOCIATION (CPSA)

The Canadian Professional Sales Association (CPSA) is the only organization in Canada to offer the Certified Sales Professional (CSP) designation, which carries with it a recognized standard of excellence. The CSP designation is a sign of a committed, honest, and knowledgeable sales expert with training in the consultative selling method. The CSP designation is well recognized in industry today and validates an individual's sales expertise. Individuals with the CSP designation report that it provides them with a competitive advantage, and 95 percent of them experience an increase in sales after training. The CPSA offers a course called Essential Sales Training with an emphasis on professional selling and selling online. Advanced selling courses are offered, as are programs in sales management. Members who have gone through the training programs find themselves equipped with new ideas and techniques that, combined with their already well-honed tools, ensure continued success.

Source: Learn How Top-Tier Sales Professionals Get Great Results, Canadian Professional Sales Association, 2017, https://www.cpsa.com/learning-development/sales-training (accessed May 2017).

for the best deal, especially in the case of poor after-the-sale follow-up.

17-6b | Personal Selling in a Global Marketplace

More and more Canadian companies are expanding their marketing and selling efforts into global markets. And with Canada's continued low economic growth, companies need to develop business outside Canada. Salespeople selling in foreign markets should tailor their presentation and closing styles to each market. Different personalities and skills will be successful in some countries and absolute failures in others. For instance, if a salesperson is an excellent closer and always focuses on the next sale, doing business in Latin America might be difficult because Latin Americans typically want to take a long time building a personal relationship with their suppliers.

While there has been a focus on the countries of Brazil, Russia, India, and China (BRIC) of late, companies also need to recognize the opportunities in Middle Eastern countries. The cultural, language, and religious differences in doing business in different countries can be learned and hence should not be a barrier to effective business development. Recognizing the importance of doing business abroad, a growing number of business schools are working to expose graduates to these markets and the cultural nuances that will increase the success of business relationships.[15]

17-6c | The Impact of Technology on Personal Selling

E-commerce, or buying, selling, marketing, collaborating with partners, and servicing customers electronically using the Internet, has had a significant impact on personal selling. Virtually all companies are involved in e-commerce and consider it to be necessary to compete in today's marketplace. For customers, the Web has become a powerful tool, providing accurate and up-to-date information on products, pricing, and order status. The Internet also cost-effectively processes orders and services requests. Although on the surface the Internet might look like a threat to the job security of salespeople, it actually releases sales reps from tedious administrative tasks, resulting in more time to focus on the needs of their clients.

Experts agree that a relationship between the salesperson and customer will always be necessary. When used appropriately, technology can improve the effectiveness and efficiency of the salesperson and can and does improve customer relationships. Information readily available to salespeople through Internet research helps the salesperson to work from a strong knowledge base when meeting customers for the first time. Smartphones, iPads, laptops, and email ensure that customers and salespeople can be connected all day, every day. This 24/7 connectedness can result in customer needs being handled in a timely and efficient manner, reinforcing the customer–salesperson relationship. As mentioned earlier, trust is a key component of the relationship, and technology can help to build and maintain that trust.

AWAKE CHOCOLATE
CONTINUING CASE

AWAKE Chocolate

Strategic Sampling

In the previous chapter, we talked about how Awake Chocolate uses direct response marketing, via social media engagement, rather than spending a lot on advertising. In this chapter, we talk about how the same brand goes all in on sampling, a form of sales promotion, as a means of incentivizing consumer and B2B sales.

Promotional strategies, like any of the other 4 Ps is first customer-centric, but then product-centric. The way in which a company tells its story—the epitome of promotions—will vary depending upon who its market is, and what problem they are solving, as well as and the form, function, and life-cycle stage of the product. In the case of Awake Chocolate, the only logical way to spread the word early was through product sampling.

"We've always been of the belief," confirmed CEO Adam Deremo, "that the most persuasive marketing tool we have is putting a sample into someone's hands." Simple enough, one could argue: just slap a giant decal on a vehicle, and hit the road for some good old-fashioned guerrilla marketing. However, again, with the customer in mind, as well as the product, Awake has been strategic in selecting the right sampling conditions. "We're very opportunistic in sponsoring [and sampling in] events where we think potential consumers are going to be found. So we do lots of campus philanthropy events, campus club events, and office sampling." It is also common for Awake's retail partners to use the same tactic in their stores, giving out samples as a means of instigating purchase.

Being opportunistic is a key advantage in promotions, especially when coupled with agility. A company's ability to respond quickly to events can be the difference between elevating brand awareness significantly; falling behind competitors; or worse, being perceived as irrelevant or invisible. As mentioned in Chapter 11, Awake's ability to service frontline health workers during the 2020 COVID-19 pandemic not only positioned it as a brand that cared but also showcased the utility the product provided—helping essential service workers stay alert in order to help the flood of patients during that time. "We gave away one thousand boxes of our chocolate—the equivalent of 25 000 cups of coffee—through that support program. We then committed 10 percent of online sales to the effort. The need was so great that we had more requests than we could fulfill during the first phase of the program."

As mentioned, promotional strategy should be predicated on the needs of the consumer and the type of product. As Deremo pointed out, it was difficult, especially at the beginning, to explain the benefit of his product in any way other than taste. "It's really hard to articulate in words the feeling of invigoration you get when you eat something that's got 50 mg of caffeine in it. If you just think about the copy-writing challenge of explaining that in a short, catchy sentence, it's really hard. And we've worked with some very talented creatives who have not been able to crack the code on that."

In addition to being a practical way of communicating the value of Awake Chocolate, it turns out sampling is also more efficient for smaller brands. Deremo continues, "As a resource-constrained brand, we will never be able to outspend Hershey or Mars (on advertising), but we may be able to out-sample them in certain markets."

The main goal of sales promotions, which distinguishes it as a promotional tactic over other members of the IMC mix, is to move product now. Whereas advertising is often about building brand awareness and planting a seed in a consumer's mind to be rolled out for a future purchase, sales promotion is all about getting people to buy, almost on the spot. Thus, you can appreciate why Awake takes advantage of the same psychological strategy in handing out its bars and bites.

QUESTIONS

1. In this case, Awake CEO Adam Deremo asserted that it is difficult to describe in words the sensation and flavour of Awake chocolate. For the purposes of argument, try the following experiment. Find something at your campus store (or a food item in your backpack for that matter), and write how it "feels" to eat it, as if explaining it to someone who has not tried it before.

2. Recall a recent occasion where you were offered a free sample of a product in a retail location or event. Try to reflect honestly as to what, if any, impact that sample might have had on a future purchase of the product sampled.

3. Awake's first products hit store shelves in 2013. Now, several years later, the company continues to use sampling as its major promotional strategy, even in places where the brand value is well known. What purpose does sampling serve under these circumstances?

AWAKE Chocolate

18 | Social Media and Digital Strategies

LEARNING OUTCOMES

18-1 Describe social media's role in an integrated marketing communication plan

18-2 Describe the social media tools in a marketer's toolbox, and explain how they are useful

18-3 Understand the mobile infrastructure supporting social and digital marketing

18-4 Explain the role of search, and distinguish between SEO and SEM

18-5 Describe general guidelines involved in a social media campaign

"Our head of social media is the customer."

—Unknown spokesperson, McDonald's[1]

18-1 | WHAT IS SOCIAL MEDIA'S ROLE IN INTEGRATED MARKETING COMMUNICATIONS?

While the Worldwide Web quickly made Internet use pervasive in the late 1990s, social media made the Web use ubiquitous 10 years later. Now in the 2020s, it is unfathomable to imagine a time without social media. But commercializing that attention took longer than expected, and even now stakeholders of social media are constantly striving to gain maximum efficiency from its overall reach and its complex roster of different players. Indeed, as a tool within the marketer's promotional toolkit, or integrated marketing communications (IMC), it has been a boon perhaps not seen since television reached its diffusion state in the 1950s and 1960s. The eyeballs have just moved from one large screen to multiple smaller ones.

Social media has not only revolutionized where we pay attention, but also is where we receive our news, as well as where we discuss the news. When a helicopter carrying Kobe Bryant, his daughter, and seven other people, crashed into a foggy hillside outside Los Angeles, most people found out about it via their preferred social medium. It wasn't on the front page of a newspaper—or even a newspaper's website. Although many would have rushed to websites of *The National Post* or *New York Times* or CBC to confirm the tragedy had occurred, they would have heard it first through social media.

The impetus was then upon thought leaders, influencers, and related brands to not only become involved in the dialogue, but also to do so in a manner that came across as sincere and not self-serving. Nike, one of the brands most closely associated with Kobe Bryant, chose to respect the families of all involved by waiting a day before posting a photo of Kobe with the company's deepest sympathies on January 27, 2020.[2] The post appeared consistently across all of Nike's social media channels.

Nike had signed a $40 million endorsement deal with Kobe Bryant in 2004, which spawned a best-selling

basketball shoe line, estimated to have been worn by up to 25 percent of NBA players.[3] After Kobe's death, Nike promptly sold out of Kobe gear online and proceeds of those sales went to the Kobe and Vanessa Bryant Family Foundation.[4]

The potential for a PR crisis was not lost on Nike. The suddenness of the event, coupled with Bryant's high stature, put enormous pressure on Nike's communications team to churn out consistent messages across multiple channels, and respond not only to the rabid NBA/Kobe fanbase, but also to journalists who would be weighing in on Nike's response to the loss of one of its star spokespeople. Knowing that most people received news of the tragedy first through social media, Nike was able to not only control its side of the story, but also use direct messaging based upon the narrative created by Kobe fans and Nike fans alike. This would not have been possible when crisis communication came in the form of press conferences and live radio announcements.

And thus continues the love–hate relationship marketers have always had with the very mediums used to amplify their story. Nevertheless, the pluses significantly outweigh the negatives. To borrow concepts from previous chapters: reach would appear to be unlimited as the world goes mobile, with computers in our pockets everywhere we go, and target messaging has a precision that would make surgeons envious. These

A day following the tragic helicopter accident that resulted in the death of Kobe Bryant, his daughter Gianna, and seven others, Nike took to social media platforms to share its profound sadness and extend deepest sympathies, noting that Kobe was a beloved member of the Nike family.

communications economies of scale are yet another compelling reason to have a digital communications strategy in place within a company's overarching IMC strategy. Ignore it at your peril.

Social media as communication tools provide marketers with the opportunity not only to respond immediately but also to listen. Marketers who listen can tap into comarketing—capitalizing on consumer input to create message content. Comarketing relies on a continual dialogue with the consumer, who is empowered to vocalize likes and dislikes. Astute marketers use this information for continual improvement, as a source for message content, and to get ideas for mass-market campaigns.[5]

Social media offer more sophisticated methods of measuring the impact and effectiveness of the conversations, which is critical for the creation of new and innovative marketing communication campaigns. Likes, follows, subscriptions, shares, tweets, retweets, and so on, are all common metrics now across social media platforms. Instagram, its parent company Facebook, Twitter, LinkedIn, YouTube, Pinterest, and TikTok all realize that their success rests on two things: the narcissistic behaviour of humans and that that behaviour attracts attention unlike anything the world has ever seen—thus creating unheard-of reach for brands that wish to jump into the deep end. But the single biggest difference between these media and traditional media, is the content producers.

Traditional media was once the exclusive domain of people with some sort of formal training or experience in performing or journalism; however, on social media anyone and everyone can produce content. And those who produce the content that attracts the most attention are sought by brands in the same way advertisers used to flock to the most popular TV sitcoms and dramas. These new media stars are appropriately called "**influencers**," due to the sway they hold over the thousands or millions who follow their every move on social media. Brands compensate influencers to mention, promote, or sometimes just provide a product placement within their social media posts. Determining who these influencers are is much easier than it was in the past to quantify the popularity of TV entertainers. Important metrics like views, likes, and follows are readily available in each of the platforms.

Given the tremendous reach and impact of influencers, representation of influencers has begun;

influencer
a person who has accumulated a sufficient following on one or more social media platforms to be considered to have an influence on consumer behaviour

Exhibit 18.1 — Social Media's Most Powerful Influencers

Influencer/ Nationality	Followers in Millions (Sum of YouTube, Instagram, Facebook, Twitter followers)	Claim to Fame
Felix Kjellberg/Sweden	119	"PewDiePie" produces largely inappropriate adult oriented content
Whindersson Nunes/Brazil	77.2	Standup comic and funny photos
Logan Paul/USA	56	Humour and surprise
El Rubius/Spain	61.7	Memes, games, personal blog
Dude Perfect/USA	66	5 former basketball players doing tricks with balls and bottles
Cameron Dallas/USA	46.6	Actor/Model
Zoe Sugg/UK	37.4	Fashion/beauty blogger
Lele Pons/ USA-Venezuela	51.2	Comedy
Liza Koshy	39.6	Actor/comedy
Huda Kattan	41.2	"Huda Beauty"/fashion and makeup

Source: https://mediakix.com/blog/top-influencers-social-media-instagram-youtube/.

influencer agencies perform the same tasks as actor or athlete agents. They line up work, negotiate the highest possible compensation, and take a commission. The size of these payouts can be huge, and so even a small percentage can be lucrative for an agent. Exhibit 18.1 highlights social media's most powerful influencers as of late 2019, collected by MediaKix, a leading social media influencer agency.

Canadians are online addicts, ranking first in time spent online at 36.3 hours per month—one full hour longer than our American counterparts, who place second.[7]

18-1a | How Canadians Use Social Media

If Canadians are online addicts, with 46 percent of us admitting to using our phones while using the washroom, social media are our drugs of choice.[8] According to Insights West, a Vancouver-based technology tracking and market research firm, 82 percent of Canadians are on Facebook; 63 percent on YouTube; 39 percent on Instagram; and 29 percent on Twitter.[9] These measurements are skewed somewhat by demographics, and sometimes surprisingly so. For instance, most of Instagram's loyalty comes from 18- to 45-year-olds, Facebook from those

Content Is King

Ali Salman, noted online marketing strategist and head of Rapid Boost Marketing, asserts that both Gen X and Gen Y rely on social media to stay connected with one another and with the world in general. Furthermore, he continues, these cohorts possess the greatest purchasing power, so being where their eyeballs are is critical. Beyond this, however, Salman notes the importance of not only being online, but also engaging in "social proof," which earns trust and positions companies as authorities within industries. Forty-seven percent of Canadian business owners recognize the importance of social media, he adds, but only half of that number are engaging with their customers there on a daily basis. A social media plan is so crucial, Salman insists, that companies must either allocate their own resources to manage it, or contract it out to an agency.[6]

over 45, and YouTube's from mostly from those over 55.[10] Smartphone penetration in Canada is close to 75 percent, and it is clearly the most popular way to access social media sites. Smartphones have become an indispensable part of day-to-day living; many people will not leave home without them and use them throughout the day for many activities beyond phone conversation, thus transforming behaviour. While viewing traditional media, many consumers are doing other things, such as watching a Twitter feed on their smartphones.

Importantly for marketers, 70 percent of Canadians follow at least one brand or company on social media, and 24 percent actually interact with those brands.[11] But not all interactions are positive. Many users take to social media to vent their frustrations about the brands or companies they follow. Fifty percent of Canadians used Facebook to complain about a company, while 23 percent did the same via Twitter.[12] Addressing these complaints in the threads created by users is one of the most important reasons to have full-time resources in place for social media management.

The unprecedented penetration of smartphones and the continual advances in digital devices and social media tools have resulted in consumers who are willing to use a variety of media platforms. Today's consumer may have started watching a program on TV, continued watching it on a smartphone on the way home from school, and finished watching it in bed on a tablet. Therefore, marketers must create campaigns that deliver content on many platforms. For example, Netflix leverages some of that very content to populate its many social media platforms. It then actively participates in the conversations it starts. In January 2020, Netflix posted a clip from its show, "Sex Education" in which poet Erin May Kelly recites one of her poems as the scene plays out on a bus bound for school. Kelly was discovered via social media by Netflix producers, who decided to insert her into the script. The excerpt was posted January 28, and one day later had received over 1.2 million views and over 1000 comments.[13]

With online spending by marketers outpacing TV spending in 2020.[14] One can see that marketers today are embracing online and social media alongside traditional media. The resulting shift from one-to-many communication to many-to-many communication provides tremendous opportunity as well as tremendous risk. Social media transfer control to the audience, so the audience can be in control of the message, the medium, or the response—or all three. This distribution of control is difficult for some companies to adjust to, but influencer and consumer engagement can be significantly more successful.

Embracing this redistribution of control and using consumers to develop and market products is called crowdsourcing. **Crowdsourcing** describes how the input of many people can be leveraged to make decisions that used to be based on the input of only a few people. 15 Asking consumers to provide feedback on marketing campaigns and products and responding to the feedback increases the chances of success and also creates brand advocates.

SOCIAL COMMERCE

Social commerce is a subset of e-commerce that involves the interaction and user contribution aspects of social media to assist in the online buying and selling of products and services.[16] Social commerce relies on user-generated content on websites to help consumers with purchases. This stems

crowdsourcing
the use of consumers to develop and market products

social commerce
a subset of e-commerce that involves the interaction and user contribution aspects of social media to assist in the online buying and selling of products and services

from the human behaviour relying upon social proof to make decisions, as asserted by Dr. Robert Chialdini in his book *Influence: The Psychology of Persuasion*. In it, Chialdini listed six principles of influence, including social proof—our rationalization of decisions based on the common behaviour of others.[17]

Pinterest quickly grabbed the position of market leader in the social commerce space as it basically defined the category of social commerce. Users collect ideas and products from all over the Web and pin favourite items to individually curated pinboards. Other users browse boards by theme, keyword, or product; click on what they like; and are then either taken to the original site or are able to re-pin the item on their own pinboard. Another social commerce site gaining in popularity is Etsy, a marketplace where people around the world connect to buy and sell unique goods. Etsy gives users the opportunity to share on Facebook, Twitter, and Pinterest boards. Social commerce sites often include ratings and recommendations (like Amazon.ca) and social shopping tools like those provided by Pinterest. In general, social commerce sites are designed to help consumers make more informed decisions on purchases.

18-2 | THE TOOLS OF SOCIAL ENGAGEMENT

It is important for marketers to engage with customers on social media for all of the reasons listed above, and a number of tools and platforms can be employed as part of an organization's social media strategy. Social networks, media creation and sharing sites, social news sites, blogs, microblogs location-based

social networking sites
websites that allow individuals to connect—or network—with friends, peers, business associates, and brands

social networking sites, review sites, audio, and virtual worlds and online gaming all have their place in a company's social marketing plan. These are all tools in a marketing manager's toolbox, available when applicable to the marketing plan but not necessarily to be used all at once. Because of the breakneck pace at which technology changes, this list of resources will surely look markedly different five years from now; more tools emerge every day and branding strategies must keep up. For now, the resources highlighted in this section remain a marketer's strongest set of platforms for conversing and strengthening relationships with customers.

18-2a | Social Networks

As discussed, **social networking sites** allow individuals to connect—or network—with friends, peers, business associates and their favourite brands. Connections may be made on the basis of shared interests, shared environments, or personal relationships. Depending on the site, connected individuals may be able to send each other messages, track each other's activity, see each other's personal information, share multimedia, or comment on each other's blog and microblog posts. Depending on its goals, a marketing team might engage several social networks as part of its social media strategy. At the same time, companies need to look at the landscape of social media, and be proactive to change in users and user habits within these platforms.

For instance, Facebook is the largest social network in sheer volume of accounts, but Instagram (which Facebook acquired in 2012) is rapidly catching up. LinkedIn was, and still is, primarily a professional social network; however, the nature of content on LinkedIn has begun overlapping with Facebook, with more personal anecdotal information being published. Meanwhile, Google-owned YouTube is growing in popularity with baby boomers—presumably due to its endless and instant supply of "how-to-do-or-fix-anything" videos. Twitter, Pinterest, and Snapchat each have their place in the palette of colours making up the social media spectrum. And then there's TikTok. At the time of this writing, the quirky, yet phenomenally growing "tween network" had amassed over half a billion followers and was the most downloaded iPhone app in Canada in 2019.[18] What to make of this growth, and the Gen Z audience driving it, is still a head-scratcher for marketers. Formerly named Musical.ly, the lip-syncing app was purchased by Chinese company ByteDance in 2017,

EXHIBIT 18.2 SOCIAL MEDIA CHANNELS, REGISTERED USERS

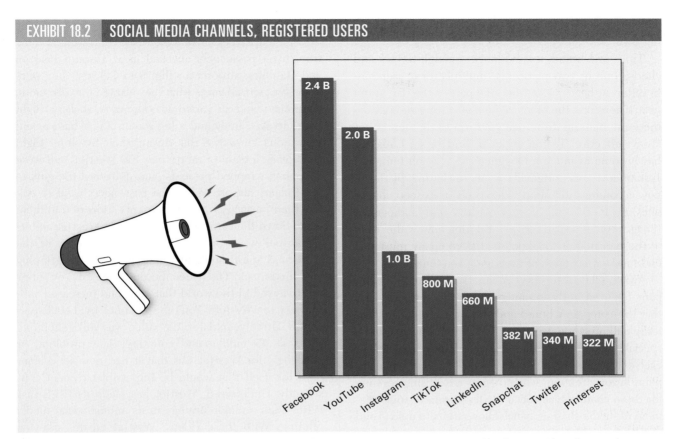

- 2.4 B — Facebook
- 2.0 B — YouTube
- 1.0 B — Instagram
- 800 M — TikTok
- 660 M — LinkedIn
- 382 M — Snapchat
- 340 M — Twitter
- 322 M — Pinterest

Sources: Adapted from https://thenextweb.com/podium/2020/01/30/digital-trends-2020-every-single-stat-you-need-to-know-about-the-internet/; https://www.omnicoreagency.com/linkedin-statistics/.

then with 100 million users, and rebranded as TikTok.[19] But to assume that the hundreds of millions of users to download and use the app since then are all of the same demographic would be a mistake.[20] Gary Vaynerchuk, as rabid and prolific a social media user if there ever was one, says,

> Everybody has an excuse for why TikTok is not right for them. Either it's too young, too small, only for certain people … they forget that it's just a means for communication and you can put anything you want into the pipelines. People are too quick to say "no" to things they haven't even tried when, in reality, it could be the thing that gets you to where you want to be.[21]

It's estimated that 4.5 billion people use the Internet and most of them, 3.8 billion, are also on at least one social media channel.[22] Globally, over six hours per day is spent online per person, and Facebook has over 2.4 billion users, making it the most popular social networking site (see Exhibit 18.2).[23]

Canada-based social media management company Hootsuite released a report in January 2020 that ranked the social media channels by global reach based upon registered users.

At one time, companies would choose social media channels based solely upon which one(s) best connected with their customers. What many have learned the hard way is that the overlap between these channels is beginning to have more to do with daily routine than standard demographics such as gender and age. For instance, a 34-year-old female office manager might get up in the morning and view her Instagram feed due to its image-oriented, bite-sized consumption. Seeing something of newsworthiness, she might then jump on to her Twitter feed to see how the people she's following might be reacting to news. Once at work, she might then in turn, open up her LinkedIn account, and perhaps share thoughts on posts made by others—or post something of her own. Lunchtime might be spent on Pinterest, viewing anything from clothes to carpets from brands she loves. Some humorous videos on YouTube might get her through the 3:00 stagnation period, and by home time and dinner, in a more relaxed state, she might take in and react to Facebook posts. She will likely want to spend some time viewing what her son or daughter are putting on TikTok, either through their account or her own.

Thus, as a brand, it is no longer enough to pick and choose one or two platforms; multiplatform users are in different headspaces from one part of the day to the next. Therefore, the practical idea of cutting and pasting the same message from one platform to the next is not always effective. Twitter exists in short verse; LinkedIn has become as much a blogging site as a job hub; and Instagram, while originally a photo-sharing platform, now accommodates short video posts in its feed, longer ones in IGTV, and live broadcasts and audiograms (images containing voiceover). Yet somehow, within each of these customer touchpoints, the company must stay on brand with consistent messaging and tone.

Awake Chocolate CEO Adam Duremo of the company featured in the running case in this textbook, says that the company's brand and standards guideline, typically outlining how logos can and cannot be used, has a special section that provides examples of how to write for each of the different platforms.[24] Due to the intense competition for attention, which begets advertising revenue for these channels, all social media sites have some element of media-sharing, which allows users to upload and distribute multimedia content, such as videos, photos, or audio. Today, organizations can tell compelling brand stories through videos, photos, and audio.

Photo-sharing sites allow users to archive and share photos. Linkedin, Twitter, Instagram—and its parent Facebook—all offer free photo hosting services that can be used by individuals and businesses alike.

Video creation and distribution have also gained popularity among marketers because of video's rich ability to tell stories. YouTube dominates business video sharing, with over 90 percent of marketers who share videos saying they do so through YouTube. Creative marketers wanting to increase consumer engagement develop campaigns that encourage consumers to create product usage videos. Such user-generated content, if used strategically, can be a powerful tool for brands.

In one of the great social media campaigns in Canadian business history, if social media metrics are any indication, WestJet emotionally engaged viewers during Christmas 2013 with a holiday YouTube video showing WestJet employees making the wishes of travellers come true. After passengers checked in at Toronto Pearson and Hamilton airports for flights to Calgary, they were asked by a virtual Santa what they wanted for Christmas. Responses were as varied as computers, socks, a flight home to see family and a big-screen TV. What passengers didn't know was that during their five-hour flight to Calgary, a team of more than 150 WestJet staff went shopping, wrapped presents, and delivered the gifts to the Calgary airport. When the passengers went to collect their baggage, wrapped presents addressed to them came down the carousel. The action by WestJet and its employees was wonderful, in the truest sense of the Christmas spirit, and the resulting video was gripping and emotional. The video became one of YouTube's most viewed in the world that year, and increased subscribers to WestJet's YouTube channel by 11 000 percent.[25] Three years later, the video was still generating views at 45 million and counting. The problem, or challenge, for WestJet was that it had now set a standard for itself that would be impossible to meet consistently. Undeterred, WestJet has made its Christmas Wish video a major strategy in its annual social media offering. With these videos, WestJet creates growing brand engagement that would have been hard to achieve with a traditional television ad—and it would have been unaffordable.[26]

Not coincidentally, given its brand heritage, WestJet also pencils in a social media campaign every April 1, as part of an April Fool's tradition that dates back to a time before social media or Internet, when, in their cheeky way, the company would issue far-fetched stories as news releases to traditional media, many of whom went along with the gag.

18-2b | Social News Sites

Social news sites allow users to post news stories and multimedia on a platform, such as Reddit or Digg, for readers to then vote on. The more interest from readers, the more votes the post gets, and thus the higher it is ranked. Marketers have found that these sites are great for promoting campaigns. If marketing content posted to a social news site is voted up, discussed, and shared enough to be listed among the most popular topics of the day, it can go viral. Social bookmarking sites, such as StumbleUpon and Reddit, are similar to social news sites but the objective of their users is to collect, save, and share interesting and valuable links. The result is peer networks that are linked by a common interest.

media-sharing sites
websites that allow users to upload and distribute multimedia content such as videos and photos

social news sites
websites that allow users to decide which content is promoted on a given website by voting that content up or down

18-2c | Blogs

Blogs have become staples in many social media strategies and are often a brand's social media centrepiece. Blogs allow marketers to create content in the form of posts, which ideally build trust, thought leadership, and a sense of authenticity in customers. Once posts are made, audience members can provide feedback through comments. Because the comments section of a blog post opens a dialogue and gives customers a voice, it is one of the most important avenues of conversation between brands and consumers.

Blogs can be divided into two broad categories: **corporate or professional blogs** and **noncorporate blogs**, such as personal blogs. Corporate blogs are sponsored by a company and have become a critical element in reinforcing corporate image, for communicating with customers, and for adding value. Whole Foods Market Inc. has a blog that does all of that. It features recipes, product information, how-to articles, and much more. The blog features a number of different writers, as well as the CEO. The blog allows the company to communicate Whole Foods Market Inc.'s image. In contrast, noncorporate blogs are independent and not associated with the marketing efforts of any particular company or brand. Because these blogs contain information not controlled by marketers, they are perceived to be more authentic than corporate blogs. Noncorporate blogs are really the birthplace of blogging—a space where anybody can be an expert on anything. The credibility of the noncorporate blogger is in the hands of the online community. People may follow, congregate, and accumulate around the blogger due to the blogger's expertise and/or unique blog product, or they will reject or ignore the blogger due to the lack of an interesting or credible offering. Whether blogs are about beer, fashion, or funerals, the ones that generate the widest reach are the ones that marketers should pay attention to and communicate with—as they would with traditional media channels. This is part of media relations in the era of social media. Whether bloggers are reviewing a product they have sourced themselves or are sampling a product, the review can be a critical influencer to purchase for those reading the blog.

A case can also be made for posting blogs on existing social media platforms, as opposed to burying them somewhere in a corporate website, never to be seen. LinkedIn, the professionals' social media hub, has become the perfect setting for such communication. With a built-in audience of corporate leaders, networkers, thinkers, and job seekers, LinkedIn's platform encourages individual account holders and employees of companies to post blogs of any size. They can be microblogs, along the same lines as Twitter, or they can be much longer—a deep dive into an issue or event relevant to the company or its industry.

Recently, users of Instagram and Facebook have found a middle ground between the microblogging of Twitter and long form on LinkedIn. Cirque de Soleil trapeze artists Enya White and Shelli Epstein chronicled their ups and downs with lengthy posts during their entire 2019 to 2020 world tour of "Lucia." These checked several boxes: provided Cirque unpaid media exposure, provided the artists with content with which to engage their fans, and provided fans with ways to communicate with the artists.

18-2d | Microblogs

Microblogs are blogs with strict limits on the length of posts. Twitter, the most popular microblogging platform, requires that posts be no more than 280 characters. Other microblogging platforms are Tumblr, Google Buzz, and Qaiku.

Twitter is effective for disseminating breaking news, promoting longer blog posts and campaigns, sharing links, keeping in touch, announcing events, and promoting sales. When a company follows, retweets, responds to potential and current customers' tweets, and tweets content that inspires customers to engage with the brand or the company, Twitter users quickly establish a foundation for how the narrative of any trending story will evolve. Research has found that when operated correctly, corporate Twitter accounts are well respected and well received. Twitter can be used to build communities; aid in customer service; gain prospects; increase awareness; and, in the case of non-profits, raise funds.

More than anything else, Twitter demonstrates relevance, whether as a person or a brand. If you're not involved in conversations the world, or at least your customers, are having, then you are conspicuous by your absence.

blogs
publicly accessible Web pages that function as interactive journals, whereby readers can post comments on the authors' entries

corporate or professional blogs
blogs that are sponsored by a company or one of its brands and maintained by one or more of the company's employees

noncorporate blogs
independent blogs that are not associated with the marketing efforts of any particular company or brand

microblogs
blogs with strict post-length limits

Social media managers must have their hands on the pulse of all conversations taking place on Twitter and become involved in those conversations in order to maintain relevance.

Twitter recorded more engagements regarding Kobe Bryant's death in a 24-hour period than it did regarding President Trump's impeachment hearing for the entire week.[27] Eerily, in the hours after his death, fans, journalists, and companies alike descended upon Bryant's Twitter feed, focusing on his final tweet, in which he celebrated LeBron James surpassing him for third place in the NBA's all-time scoring list. If there was ever a tweet that "blew up" as the hyperbole goes, this was it. Two million likes and over half million retweets, and hundreds of millions of engaged comments resulted before the end of the day following Bryant's death.[28]

Kobe Bryant
@kobebryant

Continuing to move the game forward @KingJames. Much respect my brother #33644

---

location-based social networking sites
websites that combine the fun of social networking with the utility of location-based GPS technology

review sites
websites that allow consumers to post, read, rate, and comment on opinions regarding all kinds of products and services

18-2e | Location-Based Social Networking Sites

Location-based social networking sites combine the fun of social networking with the utility of location-based GPS technology. Foursquare, one of the most popular location sites, treats location-based micronetworking as a

game: users earn badges and special statuses that are based on the number of visits they make to particular locations. Users can write and read short reviews and tips about businesses, organize meet-ups, and see which Foursquare-using friends are nearby. Foursquare updates can also be posted to linked Twitter and Facebook accounts for followers and friends to see. In a recent survey, only 13 percent of people claimed to use the location-based social platforms, while almost all of them use other social channels like Facebook.[29] Unfortunately, the added value offered by location-based sites like Foursquare just isn't perceived. Facebook provides the ability to share your location with your network, and Facebook, Twitter, Instagram, Pinterest, and other more robust sites provide all that Foursquare offers and more.

18-2f | Review Sites

Individuals tend to trust other people's opinions when it comes to purchasing. According to Nielsen Media Research, more than 80 percent of consumers said that they trusted online consumer opinions as much as they do their own friends.[30] This percentage is much higher than that of consumers who trust traditional advertising. Based on the early work of Amazon and eBay to integrate user opinions into product and seller pages, countless websites have sprung up that allow users to voice their opinions across every segment of the Internet market. Some of the more popular general business review sites are Google My Business, Yelp, Foursquare, Facebook, Amazon, and Tripadvisor. However, the proliferation of review sites dives deeply and endlessly into specific industries and social issues. **Review sites** allow consumers to post, read, rate, and comment on opinions regarding all kinds of products and services. Review sites can enhance consumer engagement opportunities for those marketers who follow and respond to consumer posts about their products or services.

iStock.com/Prostock-Studio

18-2g | Audio: Podcasts and Beyond

A podcast, another type of user-generated media, is a digital audio or video file that is distributed serially for other people to listen to or watch. **Podcasts** can be streamed online, played on a computer, uploaded to a portable media player (like an iPod), or downloaded onto a smartphone. Podcasts are like radio shows that are distributed through various means and not linked to a scheduled time slot.

In 2019, a significant year of growth for podcast consumption and production, 24 percent of Canadian adults indicated they had listened to a podcast in the last month, having their choice of over 700 000 podcasts available through multiple players, but mostly Apple iTunes and Spotify.[31]

The combination of rising popularity in podcasts, and the rapidly growing smart speaker space is also giving rise to a new audio format dominated by Amazon and Google. Despite Apple pioneering the category with its voice-assistant, Siri, Amazon's Alexa and Google's assistant have quickly taken the number one and two positions with regards to units sold. Both provide opportunities for members of the public to create voiced content, called "Flash Briefings" (Amazon) and "Actions" (Google). The format, launched in the mid-2010s, has taken some time to generate widespread use, but many experts predict that once we realize the practicality of using our voice more often than our hands, the "voice-first" space will accelerate quickly.

18-2h | Virtual Worlds and Online Gaming

Virtual worlds and online gaming present additional opportunities for marketers to engage with consumers. These include massive multiplayer online games (MMOGs), such as World of Warcraft and The Sims Online, as well as online communities. Growth is expected to continue in this area as consumer devices,

such as virtual reality headsets, start to become more mainstream. Statista predicts the VR hardware space to double by 2022, topping over \$16B.[32] While unfamiliar to and even intimidating for many traditional marketers, the field of virtual worlds is an important, viable, and growing consideration for social media marketing.

One area of growth is social gaming. An increasing number of people are playing games within social networking sites like Facebook or on their mobile devices by downloading game apps. Some of the more popular games available for download on smartphones include Candy Crush, Minecraft, and Roblox. Such games are attractive because they can be played in just five minutes, perhaps while commuting home from school or work. A growing trend among mobile games is to use mobile ads to generate revenue for the game-makers. But the biggest splash in this space during the mid-2010s was Pokémon GO, a free, location-based reality game in which Pokémon characters are made to appear on players' phones (using their GPS systems) as if they were standing (or crouching) right around the corner, behind a tree, or on the other side of a house. The object is to capture and/or battle the Pokémon. Even as of early 2020, Pokémon players could still be seen clustering around suburban locales, playing along with the game.

18-2i | Evaluation and Measurement of Social Media

Social media are revolutionizing the way organizations communicate with stakeholders. Given the relative ease and efficiency with which organizations can use social media, a positive return on investment (ROI) is likely, but as for anything else, the greater a company's investment in time, money, and human resources, the greater return it can expect. Hootsuite, the global leader in social media management software, provides a relatively simple equation for calculating social media ROI:

ROI = (Profit/Social media investment) × 100

Put simply, if you can attribute \$1000 in sales directly to a social campaign that costs \$500 (salaries, search engine optimization, etc.), you could easily calculate the profit as \$500 (\$1000 – \$500). Entering these into the equation above, you would arrive at an ROI of 100 percent.

ROI = (\$500/\$500) × 100

But as Hootsuite blogger Sarah Dawley points out, the equation has its limits because, like

podcasts
digital audio or video file that is distributed serially for other people to listen to or watch

any other tool within the IMC portfolio, not all revenue can be attributed to the message. In the same way, not all "return" should be measured by sheer revenue—but it's a start.[33]

Some marketers accept that this unknown variable and focus on social media are less about ROI than about deepening relationships with customers; others work tirelessly to better understand the measurement of social media's effectiveness. While literally hundreds of metrics have been developed to measure social media's value, these metrics are meaningless unless they are tied to key performance indicators.[34] For example, a local coffee shop manager may measure the success of her social media presence by her accumulated number of friends on Facebook and followers on Twitter. But these numbers depend entirely on context. The rate of accumulation, investment per fan and follower, and comparison to similarly sized coffee shops are all important variables to consider. Without context, measurements are meaningless.

Some social media metrics to consider are the following:

1. *Buzz:* Volume of consumer-related buzz for a brand based on posts and impression, by social channel, by stage in the purchase channel, by season, and by time of day

2. *Interest:* Number of likes, fans, followers, and friends; growth rates; rate of going viral or pass-along; and change in pass-along over time

3. *Participation:* Number of comments, ratings, social bookmarks, subscriptions, page views, uploads, downloads, embeds, retweets, Facebook posts, pins, and time spent with social media platforms

4. *Search engine ranks and results:* Increases and decreases on searches and changes in key words

5. *Influence:* Media mentions, influences of bloggers reached, influences of customers reached, and second-degree reach based on social graphs

6. *Sentiment analysis:* Positive, neutral, and negative sentiment; trends of sentiment; and volume of sentiment

7. *Website metrics:* Clicks, click-through rates, and percentage of traffic. The main issue is to start with good measurable objectives, determine what needs to be measured, and figure it out.

Even with this list, marketers and budget decision makers are still left with a raft of uncertainty. Only items 4 and 7 produce legitimate measurable data, from which some degree of change (positive or negative) can be

linked to investment in social media tactics. Like advertising or any other component of the IMC tool kit, except personal selling and sales promotions, it is impossible to quantify with certainty the financial ROI associated with social media.

18-2j | The Changing World of Social Media

As you read through the chapter, some of the trends that are noted may already seem ancient to you. There will also be other trends and platforms that were not here when this book was written in late 2019 and early 2020.

18-3 | MOBILE'S ROLE IN DIGITAL MARKETING

While much of the excitement in digital marketing has been based on websites and new technology uses, much of the growth lies in new platforms. These platforms have grown beyond smartphones and tablets and into wearable technology, such as the Apple Watch, Samsung Watch, Google-owned Fitbit, and Samsung Gear VR. The major implication of this development is that consumers are gaining multiple ways to access the Internet and thus companies and their products. The wearable trend will continue, and at times falter (see Google Glass and Snapchat's Spectacles) but until technology finds a way to untether us from our phones, those computers in our pockets will continue to be our life support for communication, information, and entertainment.

18-3a | Mobile and Smartphone Technology

By 2020, for the first time, more Internet traffic was via smartphones than computers. There are over 27 million smartphone users in Canada, and the usage figures suggest that they have become a necessary tool for everyday living.[35] Sixty-six percent of Canadians access the Internet every day from their smartphone, and very few smartphone users ever leave their home without them.[36] Canadians use their smartphones to search for information, to watch videos, for social networking, and for traditional communication. Canadians download and use apps on their smartphones for a multitude of reasons, and they often multimedia-task; almost 50 percent of Canadians claim to use their phone while doing other things, such as watching television.[37]

In 2012, mobile advertising revenue in Canada was $160 million, representing a 1.3 percent share of reported media, and in 2013 it more than doubled to $290 million; by 2020, it had risen to over $8 billion.[38]

Rawpixel.com/Shutterstock.com

Tablet penetration was spurred in 2015 by the launch of "phablets"—portable enough to be a phone but large enough to be a tablet. Apple's iPhone 6+ ushered in this trend in full, although some of its competitors had been manufacturing larger mobile phones for some time. The most likely type of advertising winner as a result of tablet/phablet penetration was video, and Canadians lead the way in online video viewership growth, offering marketers a highly engaging communication opportunity.

The low barriers to entry that have been created by the standardization of mobile platforms, the seemingly reduced concerns (especially among the younger population, who are the largest mobile users) over the once-worrisome privacy issues, and the portability of the smartphones are all reasons for the popularity and growth of mobile marketing. In addition, mobile marketing is measurable; metrics and usage statistics make it an effective tool for gaining insight into consumer behaviour, and mobile marketing's response rate is higher than that of traditional media types, further fuelling its popularity and growth.

One use for bar-code scanning apps is the reading and processing of Quick Response (QR) codes. When scanned by a smartphone's QR reader app, a QR code takes the user to a specific site with content about or a discount for products or services.

The smartphone trend called near *field communication* (NFC) uses small chips hidden in or behind products that, when touched by compatible devices, will transfer the information on the chip to the device. In Canada, NFC offers the opportunity for mobile payments via your smartphone.

18-3b | The Second Coming of Text

One more thing our phones provide for us is instant messaging. While this was one of the first utilities of the smart phone in 2010, it has not become obsolete but is on the rise. In its 2019 report, SMA explains that a staggering 95 percent of text messages are opened and

COMMON MOBILE MARKETING TOOLS

- **SMS (Short Message Service):** 160-character text messages sent to and from smartphones. SMS is typically integrated with other tools.

- **MMS (Multimedia Messaging Service):** Similar to SMS but allows for the attachment of images, video, ringtones, and other multimedia to text messages.

- **Mobile Websites (MOBI and WAP Websites):** Websites designed specifically for viewing and navigation on mobile devices.

- **Mobile Ads:** Visual advertisements integrated into text messages, applications, and mobile websites. Mobile ads are often sold on a cost-per-click basis.

- **Bluetooth Marketing:** A signal is sent to Bluetooth-enabled devices that allows marketers to send targeted messages to users based on their geographic locations.

- **Smartphone Applications (Apps):** Software designed specifically for mobile and tablet devices. These apps include software to turn phones into scanners for various types of bar codes.

responded to within 3 minutes, and 64 percent of those who receive text messages perceive them in a more positive light than, say, posts on social media.[39] Thus, despite the lack of vibrant imagery, emotional or humorous video, or contemplative blogs.

18-3c | Apps and Widgets

Millions of applications or **apps** have been developed for the mobile market. These apps allow you to listen to music, track your calorie intake, play games, book a hotel, practise yoga, or find your way home. LeBron James was the first A-list athlete/celebrity to became a spokesperson for an app, the mindfulness and meditative app, Calm. But the developers and founders of the app, launched in 2012, had done their homework long before signing LeBron. By 2019, and prior to the announced partnership, Calm had been riding the growing trend in matters of mental health and had built a company with a valuation of $1 billion.[41]

apps
short for *applications*; free or purchased software programs that are downloaded to run on smartphones, tablet computers, and other mobile devices

How long will it be before even an app so reliant upon a nondistracted experience with its users, will give into the temptation of ad revenue?

While some marketers focus their apps on connectivity, Nike created Nike+ to provide both utility and connectivity. Using an iPhone's GPS capabilities, users can track their running and cycling routes and examine mapping and details of their pace and calories burned. Information on treadmill runs and other exercise details can be entered manually as well, so as a training tool this app can provide powerful information to the user. In addition, activities can be shared online with other runners and athletes.

Web widgets, also known as gadgets and badges, are software applications that run entirely within existing online platforms. Essentially, a Web widget allows a developer to embed a simple application, such as a weather forecast, horoscope, or stock market ticker, into

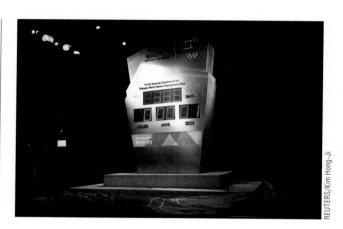

REUTERS/Kim Hong-Ji

a website, even if the developer did not write (or does not understand) the application's source code. From a marketing perspective, widgets allow customers to display company information (such as current promotions, coupons, news, or countdown clocks) on their own websites.

18-4 | SEARCH: SEO AND SEM

In the time it takes you to read this sentence, well over 100 000 Web searches will have been performed on Google. For proof, pause here and visit www.internet livestats.com/one-second/#google-band. There, a real-time count is generated for each Google search. Anywhere. At the time of this writing, the count was at 82 000 per second.[42] Why is this important? Because online search is a fully engrained human behaviour, and marketers must understand how it works. Before getting into how to use search, it is important to break it down into its various fundamental terms.

Search engine optimization (SEO) is a process that marketers take to optimize the chance of search engines,

Cyberstock/Alamy Stock Photo

Calm, a meditation and mindfulness app, was moderately popular. Then, LeBron James got involved and changed its trajectory entirely.

THE DIGITAL MARKETING INSTITUTE INDICATES THREE KEY AREAS ON WHICH MARKETERS SHOULD FOCUS THEIR SEO STRATEGY:

- *Quality content:* Having great quality content sends a message to search engines that your website and business is delivering a legitimate good or service. Part of the way they assess you is via link building and keywords.

- *User experience:* Is your website designed for users to have a frictionless experience? Is it fast and easy to navigate? Can users meet their end goals (e.g.: making a purchase) with ease?

- *Link patterns:* Are you backlinking to authority sites? Where are your inbound links coming from?

Source: SDigital Marketing Institute, "SEO vs SEM: How Do They Work Together," https://digitalmarketinginstitute.com/en-ca/blog/how-do-seo-and-sem-work-together-in-2018.

"driven" by persons looking for information online, to produce their company's website, name, products or all three, when people perform those online searches. Search engines, primarily Google, respond to searches by people by scouring the web in nanoseconds looking to match the user's search request with optimal results for *that* user. How effectively a company shows up in that complex algorithm can and should be controlled as much as possible by the company's marketing department, thus, optimizing the company's chance for success. It is ironic that even super-human efforts in this regard do not guarantee anything. But with no SEO strategy, chance of success is zero.

Therefore, the question is, "how do we optimize our searchability?" This is usually meant within the context of "**organic traffic**"—that is, search results based solely on SEO tactics, and not paid tactics. These will be covered next in the section of **search engine marketing (SEM)**. For now, we will look at areas that marketers can control to optimize their searchability.

The above steps should be seen as a very high-level guideline as to minimum requirements to set up an SEO strategy. Unless marketing managers are SEO experts, this is one of those newer areas of digital marketing for which a very specific and specialized skillset is required. With that expertise obtained, a deep dive would be recommended into each of the steps.

If SEO maximizes a company's chance to be ranked high in one of those 100 000 searches per second based only on no-cost tactics such as keywords, tagging, website design, and so on, SEM is generally explained as the "paid search" partner in manipulating search. Given the millions, and growing, number of websites vying for attention in searches, there is little chance for a small or new company to get a toe-hold without paying for it. This is analogous to trying to achieve press coverage through a PR campaign, but never receiving it due to the lack of newsworthiness to your story; at some point an ad-spend becomes necessary. SEM is the paid component of search whereby paid advertisements appear as top results on search engines.

Keyword is a very important concept for both SEO and SEM. Think about your savviness as a digital searcher of information. For example, you know that if you're hoping to adopt a dog from a local animal shelter, you probably wouldn't use the words *dog, rescue, adopt,* or *shelter* by themselves. Using them together would make your search more effective, but would still return results of no relevance. Your search strategy must start by thinking like your customers. Knowing today's slang, jargon, street language, as well as predictable standard verbiage is vital to maximizing your SEO and SEM. However, with SEM, you are paying to have your company's website show up, when words are used by online searchers. So when there's potential profit in the game, keyword knowledge becomes even more important; as a result, many cottage industries, and companies within them, such as Wordstream, have arisen in the wake of SEM.

search engine optimization (SEO)
a process that marketers take to optimize the chance of search engines, "driven" by people looking for information online, to produce their company's website, name, products or all three

organic traffic
online search results based upon unpaid (SEO) tactics

search engine marketing (SEM)
the practice of using paid advertisements that appear on the results page of a search engine to market a business

18-5 | DESIGNING A DIGITAL MARKETING STRATEGY

To effectively use the tools in the social media, mobile, and search toolbox, marketers need a clearly outlined digital marketing plan. This is linked to the marketing plan, and should fit appropriately into the objectives and steps in those plans. It is important to continue to research throughout the development of the digital marketing plan to keep abreast of the rapidly changing digital world. A detailed digital marketing plan is outside the scope of this chapter and book, but in order to give you a reasonable overview, we'll refer to a guideline provided by HubSpot, a leading global digital marketing service, founded in Boston in 2004.[43]

18-5a | The Listening System

Successful preparation and execution of a digital strategy rests on an obvious but often overlooked assumption—that companies have systems in place to track their customers in the digital space. Listening to customers and industry trends and continually revising the digital marketing plan to meet the needs of the changing global and localized uses of digital are keys to successful digital marketing strategies. Numerous industry leaders are sharing some of their best practices. For example, HubSpot practises what it preaches—namely the benefits of building valuable content online and then using social media to pull customers to its website. Social engine profiles have increased HubSpot's website traffic, which has made its lead-generation program much more effective.

DIGITAL MARKETING PLAN AT A GLANCE

1. *Build your customer personas:* This detailed exercise forces you to understand your target market in the ways explained in previous chapters. It is vital when attempting to communicate with them that you not only know ages, genders, and values, but also behaviours with regard to social media channel preferences, mobile use, and keyword use.

2. *Develop goals:* Make these SMART, ensuring that specific, measurable, attainable, relevant, and time-bound statements are used to describe the 5 Ws. "Increase followers" is a goal but not a SMART goal. "Increase Instagram followers from 5000 to 10 000 by July 2022" is more specific, measurable, and time bound. If it is also attainable and relevant (does your target market use Instagram?), then it is a much more useful goal.

3. *Evaluate and identify the tools to be used:* This chapter has covered the big three digital tool categories: social, mobile, and search. Within each is a pantheon of options, which a properly prepared digital campaign must be surgical in preparing and executing. A "peanut butter" strategy of spreading a marketing message everywhere is *not* strategic. Select the tools appropriate for the audience and the goals. HubSpot efficiently categorizes your tools another way:

   – *Owned:* your website: social media profiles, blogs, podcasts, etc.

   – *Earned:* word-of-mouth

   – *Paid:* SEM or other forms of digital exposure in which a "toll" is paid to the messaging pipeline (Google, Facebook, influencers)

4. *Audit and plan the owned media component:* The audit part of this is often overlooked but worth mentioning. Making sure that website, social media profiles, blogs, podcasts, etc., all have a consistent look and feel, and language is vital. The planning part, again, is beyond what can be covered in this book, but this would include the actual content creation.

5. *Audit and plan the earned media component:* As above with owned media, it is important to ensure your network is informed, as members therein should be prepared to spread the word-of-mouth that a digital strategy requires.

6. *Audit and plan the paid media component:* Once again, an audit (and review) of any previous paid campaigns is in order to determine effectiveness.

7. *Bring it all together:* While this is a rather obvious, and at the same time, nebulous step, it is included to ensure that the aforementioned parts do not spin off into an orbit of their own. Bringing it all together is, therefore, not only a final step of preparation, but it applies also to implementation. For this, a project management mindset (or a planning tool) is recommended.

Source: Adapted from Hudson, Elissa, *Digital Strategy Guide*, HubSpot, January 2020.

EXHIBIT 18.3   EIGHT STAGES OF EFFECTIVE LISTENING

Stage	Description	Resources Required	Purpose
Stage 1: Being without an objective	The organization has established a listening system but has no goals.	Social media notification tools (Google Alerts)	To keep up with brand and competitor information
Stage 2: Tracking brand mentions	The organization tracks mentions in social space but has no guidance on next steps.	A listening platform with key word report capabilities (Radian6)	To track discussions, understand sentiment, and identify influencers to improve overall marketing strategy
Stage 3: Identifying market risks and opportunities	The organization seeks discussions online that may result in identification of problems and opportunities.	A listening platform with a large staff dedicated to the client (Converseon)	To seek out discussions and report to other teams, such as product development and sales; these teams then engage the customers directly or conduct further research
Stage 4: Improving campaign efficiency	The organization uses tools to acquire real-time data on marketing efficiency.	Web analytics software (Google Analytics)	To gather a wealth of information about consumers' behaviour on their websites (and social media)
Stage 5: Measuring customer satisfaction	The organization collects information about satisfaction, including measures of sentiment.	Insight platforms that offer online focus group solutions	To measure the impact of satisfaction or frustration during interaction
Stage 6: Responding to customer inquiry	The organization identifies customers where they are (e.g., Twitter).	A customer service team is allowed to make real-time responses	To generate a high sense of satisfaction for customers
Stage 7: Understanding customers better	The organization adds social information to demographics and psychographics to gain better consumer profiles.	Social customer relationship management (CRM) systems to sync data	To create a powerful analytical tool by marrying the organization's database and social media
Stage 8: Being proactive and anticipating customer demands	The organization examines previous patterns of data and social behaviour to anticipate needs.	Advanced customer database with predictive application (yet to be created)	To modify the social media strategy to pre-empt consumer behaviour modifications on the basis of trends

Sources: Jeremiah Owyang, "Web Strategy Matrix: The Eight Stages of Listening," *Web Strategy*, November 10, 2009; and Jim Sterne, *Social Media Metrics* (Hoboken, NJ: John Wiley & Sons, 2010).

After determining how to integrate the social strategy into the greater IMC strategy, the next action a marketing team should take when initiating a social media campaign is simple—it should just listen. Developing an effective listening system is necessary to both understanding and engaging an online audience. Marketers must not only hear what is being said about the brand, the industry, the competition, and the customer but also pay attention to who is saying what. The specific ways that customers and noncustomers rate, rank, critique, praise, deride, recommend, snub, and generally discuss brands are all important. Negative comments and complaints are of particular importance, both because they can illuminate unknown brand flaws and because they are the comments that tend to go viral. Thus, social media have created a new method of market research: customers telling marketers what they want and need (and don't want and need). Online tools, such as Google Alerts, Google Blog Search, Twitter Search, and others, are helpful in the development of efficient, effective listening. But there are probably none more trusted, more established, nor more ubiquitous in the space than Canadian-based Hootsuite. Created by Vernon, BC–born Ryan Holmes in 2008, Hootsuite has over 15 million users in 175 countries.[44] Its multiple uses and customizable interface help users deploy messages across all social channels efficiently, and it also tracks mentions, user habits, and patterns to assist companies in the daunting task of nonstop surveillance. In Exhibit 18.3, social media strategist Jeremiah Owyang outlines eight stages of effective listening. Listening to customers communicate about one's own brand can be very revealing, but using social media is also a great way to monitor competitors' online presences, fans, and followers. Paying attention to the ways that competing brands attract and engage with their customers can be particularly enlightening for both small businesses and global brands.

AWAKE CHOCOLATE
CONTINUING CASE

Influencers at the Ready

Influencer marketing is to small brands, like Awake, and even those much smaller, their answer to celebrity endorsements. Ever since marketing communications have existed, mega-brands fawned over mega-stars in the hopes, usually justified, that that brand association would translate into sales and market share. It continues to be a tried-and-true strategy, which we witness routinely in television advertising, particularly when Super Bowl rolls around, and the beer and auto giants trot out their highly paid celebs.

But companies like Awake cannot use multimillion dollar endorsement deals, nor, at this point would they even wish to. However, they can, and do, use social media influencers, defined in this chapter as "a person who has accumulated a sufficient following on one or more social media platforms, to be considered to have an influence on consumer behaviour."

In CEO Adam Deremo's opinion, the role of a social media influencer goes beyond this. "I think influencers have supplanted public relations. So instead of going to a PR agency, it somehow makes sense to go directly to an influencer who has their own followership. And there are market places online where you can search for just the kind of influencer you desire, using some pretty sophisticated targeting tools." Awake has always leveraged the strengths of its biggest fans as brand ambassadors and influencers. It then showcases them across its social media channels, of course while they are enjoying Awake Chocolate products.

Needless to say, mascot Nevil comes back into play here by utilizing the massive reach of one of Awake's influencers, lifestyle blogger Sarah Nicole Landry on Instagram on February 1, 2020.

At the time of this writing, Nicole had well over a million followers on Instagram, making her bona-fide "Instagram famous." And her reach certainly boded well for Awake's reach. "She hit our radar because she is from southern Ontario, so highly locally relevant," recalled Deremo. Her celebrated blog site, featuring real, raw, and often emotional social commentary from a woman's perspective, was in alignment with Awake's brand. "We reached out to propose a collaboration, and she was receptive because she felt our products were a good fit for her lifestyle."

But not all of Awake's influencers are that prolific, and in fact Deremo insisted, "A lot of the influencers we've partnered with would be considered 'micro' influencers, with followerships ranging from 2000 to 10 000."

In terms of compensation, Deremo dispels another myth. "Our experience is that you can still find really good influencers who are willing to do it just for the opportunity to get some of your product. Which I think is a fair trade." Having said this, he foresees a time, sooner or later, when the product for service payment method will be replaced by a purely monetary exchange. "You can tell, even over the last two or three years, that space is getting monetized more and more each day."

That day may already be here. According to Influencer Marketing Hub, Influencer marketing has continued to grow over the past few years, from a $1.7 billion industry in 2016 and expected to reach $6.5 billion in 2019.[1]

What makes it a hot commodity is the personal level of engagement that it can create. Unlike celebrities who never establish a relationship with a fan in supporting the product they have been asked to support, social media influencers have, in many cases, developed a first-name basis with many of their followers. Thus, when they support a brand like Awake, they cannot only draw new attention to a company but also solidify opinions already held. This increasing influence of influencers, and the increasing compensation they command, is not lost on Deremo. "The biggest challenge we've had with the in-kind model is that it doesn't scale all that well. It's definitely easier to move the social needle when you're executing a paid model with the help of an agency."

As always, communications decisions ultimately come down to asking, "Who is it we are trying to reach?" For Deremo, that audience has become fairly clear. "Our primary shopper is a millennial woman, most often between 25 and 34," asserts Deremo. "So, we try to partner with influencers who would have currency with that cohort." But here's where behavioural segmentation intersects with demographics. "The brand connection has to be authentic," he concedes. "They truly have to like the brand in order to be motivated to post about it."

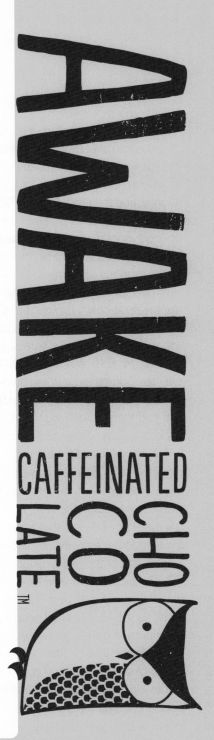

QUESTIONS

1. **Visit Awake's Instagram page. Identify an influencer, who just entered the feed over the last few months, and discuss why that person might have been recruited by Awake.**

2. **With the market value of influencer marketing likely over $7 billion by the time you read this, is it still right for Awake to still be paying in chocolate rather than money?**

3. **Is Sarah Nicole (AKA @thebirdspapaya) still acting as an influencer for Awake? Scroll through Instagram posts to find out. Identify any other influencers Awake has recruited in the meantime, and discuss, based on what you now know about Awake, whether you find this influencer to be a good fit for the brand.**

NOTE

1. "The State of Influencer Marketing," Influencer Marketing Hub, https://influencer marketinghub.com/influencer-marketing-2019-benchmark-report (accessed June 25, 2020).

Promotion Decisions, Part 6 Case

Connection in a Contagion

For all of the contempt, much of it justified, placed upon digital communications from its humble beginnings in the late 1990s, even its most fervent critics were relieved to have access from March 11, 2020, onward. While some might argue the exact date the COVID-19 pandemic went from someone else's problem to everyone's problem, for the next months sometimes it seemed that the only thing holding the world's inhabitants together was the Internet and the various social media channels coursing through it.

While sports network camera crews caught some of the breaking chaos live prior to the NBA game between the Oklahoma Thunder and the Utah Jazz, it was through social media that news spread quickly that night. Very quickly. At 8:10 pm ET, ESPN reporter Royce Young tweeted: Something is going on here. Thunder head medical staffer Donnie Strack just grabbed the three officials and told them something. All players were just told to go back to their bench. We're seconds from tipoff.[1]

He was describing what might be considered the tipping point of COVID-19's arrival in North America. It was an otherwise routine mid-season game, between two of the smallest markets in the NBA, in a region where news can still travel slowly—but that tweet set in motion a flurry of social media activity. What made it newsworthy was that a Utah Jazz player, Rudy Gobert, had tested positive for COVID-19 earlier in the week. At 8:14 pm, Young tweeted that the game had been called. Before the end of the night, the NBA season had been suspended. By the end of the month, the entire planet was in lockdown.

Publications like *Forbes* took the position that social media created as much of a pandemic as the virus itself; *Forbes* cited the distortions, half-truths, memes, and outright lies pulsing through Twitter, Facebook, and Instagram in those panic-driven first few weeks.[2] However, there is little doubt that the world needed to sort through the news via online communication during that surreal time in 2020.

These were already platforms that much of the world's population had chosen to use as its primary source of information, news, entertainment, and personal interaction. It was inevitable that the dark side of social media would emerge during the pandemic. However, the same social media would become a lifeline not only individuals connecting with loved ones but also small businesses trying to generate any revenue.

As *Time* magazine's Alejandro De La Garza commented March 16, 2020, "Social media is both offering a window into our collective response to the coronavirus outbreak, as well as shaping our reaction in the first place—for good and for ill."[3] By the end of March, even the most passive users of social media had glommed on to one channel or another for any number of reasons—to be informed, to be entertained, or to be connected—during a period where isolation wasn't merely a voluntary social condition; it was the law.

The flood of attention on social media channels provided a significant opportunity, as well as a perilous trap, for companies desperately trying to remain solvent while appearing both compassionate, empathetic, and relevant. Opportunity because so many eyes were on the platforms, seeking to be informed and connected. Perilous because no crisis is an appropriate time to be seen as taking advantage. And of course, no crisis goes on very long before being contaminated by profiteers looking to benefit from the anxiety of a vulnerable population. But while the social media companies were doing their best to mitigate misinformation and panic-purchase tactics, such as the illicit advertising and selling of protective masks and toilet paper, stomping everything out became increasingly difficult as the crisis unfolded.

Nevertheless, by the end of March, there was a sense that social media was actually serving as a predominantly valid place to engage, connect, and become informed. *New York Times* writer Kevin Rose opined on March 17, "Already, social media seems to have improved, with more reliable information than might have been expected from a global pandemic. And while the ways we're substituting for in-person interaction aren't perfect, we are seeing an explosion of creativity as people try to use technology as a bridge across physical distances."[4]

For their part, companies were driven to digital communications, including social media, to keep a lifeline with current and prospective customers. Rumble Boxing Studio, in Calgary, for instance, began offering free "Rumble Boxer Body" workouts over IGTV, (Instagram Television) on March 27, 2020. Rumble "tribe" members who wanted more could subscribe to receive paid online workouts on for $19.99 per month (www.rumbleboxing.com). Like so many businesses, Rumble could not afford to shut down indefinitely. In fact, it had been mere days away from opening up its first location in Vancouver's high-end Yaletown district. While critics might have scoffed at the "freemium" tactic of generating sales, the gym made good on its promise to connect with its community for free, while providing an opt-in value to those willing to pay for additional connections.

Unfortunately, a startling number of companies continued to advertise across social media platforms without changing the content of their ads to acknowledge that they were even aware of the pandemic.

For its part, WestJet, Canada's second largest airline, took to multiple channels, including YouTube and LinkedIn, March 24 with a video message from CEO Ed Sims. In it, he described the devastating economic impact the pandemic had brought to his industry and his company. He transparently announced, with raw emotion, how 6900 employees had lost their jobs on that day. In the same message, he made a promise to personally recommend any of them for employment elsewhere. As of March 27, the LinkedIn post had received almost 20 000 views, 400 likes, and over 50 comments—the vast majority positive.[5] For this company that had scrappily clawed its way from obscurity in the mid 1990s to being an international carrier, with plans for further expansion in the early 2020s, coronavirus had eviscerated its trajectory inside a single month. But, true to its brand, the airline was quick to get ahead of negative press by controlling the narrative of the story, using social media.

At the time of this writing, experts couldn't agree as to how long the virus would continue to be active,

Girts Ragelis/Shutterstock.com

especially with no vaccine expected until late 2021. What was clear, however, was that for the duration of the pandemic, and for months afterward, a "social recession," would linger. Coined by *Vox* magazine's Ezra Klein, the term referred to lingering loneliness brought about by self-isolation.[6] As a result, reliance on social media by the billions of global users already plugged in, and newly recruited users, was bound to accelerate, providing prudent and empathetic companies an opportunity to comfort, engage, and stand by their customers at a safe social distance.

QUESTIONS

1. At the time you are reading this case, the world will be much different than the time when it was written. Perform a quick social media audit of a company of your choice. Go back to its posts within the month of March 2020. Make a list of posts the company made as it was responding to the COVID-19 pandemic, and analyze how, in your opinion, it reacted to news of the spread of the pandemic.

2. Using your institution's resources, research case studies about businesses that survived or perished due to the COVID-19 pandemic in 2020. Cite specific ways those companies used social media to maintain connections with their stakeholders, including employees, customers, investors, and news media.

3. Is there any lingering impact today with regards to a "social recession" as referenced in this case? What company(ies) have done an admirable job in empathizing and engaging with that segment of their audience? Explain.

4. As you read this case, the memories of COVID-19 in 2020 may be still fresh in your mind, or perhaps somewhat faded. You will also have some context as to what role social media played as a connector between companies and customers. Based upon this context, comment on how and/or if the general use of digital communications has changed significantly since the outbreak.

NOTES

1. Ed Savitz, "Listening to Social Media Cues Doesn't Mean Ceding Control," Forbes, https://www.forbes.com/sites /ciocentral/2012/08/04/listening-to-social-media-cues -doesnt-mean-ceding-control/#53552b27cd52.

2. Aaron Rose, "The Night the NBA Stopped" *Sports Illustrated*, March 18, 2020, www.si.com/nba/raptors/news/the-night -the-nba-stopped-PcAVNs39HUO9kjLIPgXfcw (accessed June 24, 2020).

3. Billy Bambrough, "Coronavirus COVID-19 Will Go Down in History as the Social Media and Bitcoin Pandemic" *Forbes*, March 23, 2020, www.forbes.com/sites /billybambrough/2020/03/23/coronavirus-covid -19-will-go-down-in-history-as-the-social-media-and -bitcoin-pandemic/#220da0113c10 (accessed June 24, 2020).

4. Alejandro De La Garza, "How Social Media Is Shaping Our Fears of—and Response to—the Coronavirus," March 16, 2020, https://time.com/5802802/social-media-coronavirus (accessed June 24, 2020).

5. Kevin Roose, "The Coronavirus Crisis Is Showing Us How to Live Online," *The New York Times*, March 17, 2020, www .nytimes.com/2020/03/17/technology/coronavirus-how -to-live-online.html (accessed June 24, 2020).

6. LinkedIn, Westjet, www.linkedin.com/company/westjet (accessed June 24, 2020).

7. Kevin Roose, "The Coronavirus Crisis Is Showing Us How to Live Online."

adopter a consumer who was satisfied enough with their trial experience with a product to use it again. p. 186

advergaming placing advertising messages in Web-based or video games to advertise or promote a product, a service, an organization, or an issue. p. 317

advertising any form of impersonal, one-way mass communication, using time or space owned by an advertising medium company that is paid for by an organization. p. 292

advertising appeal a strategy used by the advertiser to engage the attention of a viewer, reader, listener, and/or potential customer. p. 310

advertising campaign a series of related advertisements focusing on a common theme, slogan, and set of advertising appeals. p. 310

advertising objective a specific communication task that a campaign should accomplish for a specified target audience during a specified period. p. 310

advocacy advertising a form of advertising in which an organization expresses its views on a particular issue or cause. p. 309

AIDA concept a model that outlines the process for achieving promotional goals in terms of stages of consumer involvement with the message; the acronym stands for *attention, interest, desire,* and *action.* p. 297

ambush marketing when an advertiser attempts to position itself with an event but is not sanctioned as an official sponsor. p. 323

anonymized data data from which personally identifiable information has been removed. p. 71

applied research an attempt by marketers to use research to develop new or improved products. p. 28

apps short for *applications*; free or purchased software programs that are downloaded to run on smartphones, tablet computers, and other mobile devices. p. 357

aspirational reference groups groups that an individual would like to join. p. 85

assurance the knowledge and courtesy of employees and their ability to convey trust. p. 199

atmosphere the overall impression conveyed by a store's physical layout, decor, and surroundings. p. 275

attitude a learned tendency to respond consistently toward a given object. p. 93

audience selectivity the ability of an advertising medium to reach a precisely defined market. p. 318

automatic vending the use of machines to offer goods for sale.

baby boomers people born between 1947 and 1965. pp. 26, 268

bait pricing a price tactic that tries to get consumers into a store through false or misleading price advertising and then uses high-pressure selling to persuade consumers to buy more expensive merchandise instead. p. 233

base price the general price level at which the company expects to sell the good or service. p. 228

basic research pure research that aims to confirm an existing theory or to learn more about a concept or phenomenon. p. 28

beacon a device that sends out connecting signals to customers' smartphones and tablets. p. 277

belief an organized pattern of knowledge that an individual holds as true about their world. p. 93

benefit segmentation the process of grouping customers into market segments according to the benefits they seek from the product. p. 121

big data the exponential growth in the volume, variety, and velocity of information and the development of complex new tools to analyze and create meaning from such data. p. 65

blogs publicly accessible Web pages that function as interactive journals, whereby readers can post comments on the authors' entries. p. 353

brainstorming the process of getting a group to think of unlimited ways to vary a product or solve a problem. p. 181

brand a name, term, symbol, design, or combination thereof that identifies a seller's products and differentiates them from competitors' products. p. 163

brand cannibalization the reduction of sales for one brand as the result of the promotion of a current product or brand. p. 273

brand equity the value of company and brand names. p. 164

brand loyalty a consistent preference for one brand over all others. p. 164

brand mark the elements of a brand that cannot be spoken. p. 164

brand name that part of a brand that can be spoken, including letters, words, and numbers. p. 164

branded (or inbound) content creation of engaging bespoke content as a way to promote a particular brand that attracts and builds relationships with consumers. p. 297

break-even analysis the calculation of number of units sold, or total revenue required, that a company must meet to cover its costs, beyond which profit occurs. p. 225

business analysis the second stage of the screening process, where preliminary figures for demand, cost, sales, and profitability are calculated. p. 181

business product a product used to manufacture other goods or services, to facilitate an organization's operations, or to resell to other customers. p. 157

business services complementary and ancillary actions that companies undertake to meet business customers' needs. p. 104

business-to-business (B2B) marketing the process of matching capabilities between two nonconsumer entities to create value for both organizations and the "customer's customer"; also referred to as *business marketing*. p. 96

buyer for export an intermediary in the global market that assumes all ownership risks and sells internationally for its own account.

buying centre all those people in an organization who become involved in the purchase decision. p. 107

campaign management developing product or service offerings customized for the appropriate customer segment and then pricing and communicating these offerings to enhance customer relationships. p. 146

cannibalization a situation that occurs when sales of a new product cut into sales of a company's existing products. p. 126

cash discount a price reduction offered to a consumer, an industrial user, or a marketing intermediary in return for prompt payment of a bill. p. 229

category killers specialty discount stores that heavily dominate their narrow merchandise segment. p. 267

causal research a type of conclusive research that focuses on the cause and effect of two variables and attempts to find some relationship between them. p. 54

cause-related marketing a type of sponsorship involving the association of a for-profit company with a non-profit organization; through the sponsorship, the company's product or service is promoted, and money is raised for the non-profit. p. 323

chain stores stores owned and operated as a group by a single organization. p. 264

channel a medium of communication—such as a voice, radio, newspaper, or social media—used for transmitting a message. p. 288

channel conflict a clash of goals and methods among distribution channel members. p. 252

channel control one marketing channel member intentionally affects another member's behaviour. p. 252

channel leader (channel captain) a member of a marketing channel who exercises authority and power over the activities of other channel members. p. 252

channel members all parties in the marketing channel that negotiate with one another, buy and sell products, and facilitate the change of ownership between buyer and seller as they move the product from the manufacturer into the hands of the end consumer. p. 242

channel partnering (channel cooperation) the joint effort of all channel members to create a supply chain that serves customers and creates a competitive advantage. p. 253

channel power a marketing channel member's capacity to control or influence the behaviour of other channel members. p. 252

click through rate (CTR) the ratio of clicks on an ad by viewers to the number of viewers to whom the ad was exposed. p. 307

click-and-collect the practice of buying something online and then travelling to a physical store location to take delivery of the merchandise. p. 279

closed-ended question an interview question that asks the respondent to make a selection from a limited list of responses.

cobranding placing two or more brand names on a product or its package. p. 167

code of ethics a guideline to help marketing managers and other employees make better decisions. p. 32

cognitive dissonance the inner tension that a consumer experiences after recognizing an inconsistency between behaviour and values or opinions. p. 78

cold calling a form of lead generation in which the salesperson approaches potential buyers without any prior knowledge of the prospects' needs or financial status. p. 340

commercialization the decision to market a product. p. 184

communication the process by which we exchange or share meanings through a common set of symbols. p. 286

Competition Bureau the federal department charged with administering most marketplace laws. p. 17

competitive advantage the set of unique features of a company and its products that are perceived by the target market as significant and superior to the competition. p. 41

competitive advertising a form of advertising designed to influence demand for a specific brand. p. 310

competitive intelligence (CI) an intelligence system that helps managers assess their competition and vendors in order to become more efficient and effective competitors. p. 71

compiled lists customer lists that are developed by gathering names and addresses gleaned from telephone directories and membership rosters, sometimes enhanced with information from public records, such as census data, auto registrations, birth announcements, business start-ups, or bankruptcies. p. 142

component lifestyles mode of living that involves choosing goods and services that meet one's diverse needs and interests rather than conforming to a single, traditional lifestyle. p. 22

concentrated targeting strategy a strategy used to select one segment of a market to target marketing efforts. p. 125

concept test evaluation of a new-product idea, usually before any prototype has been created. p. 181

conclusive research a more specific type of research that attempts to provide clarity to a decision maker by identifying specific courses of action. p. 54

consumer behaviour how consumers make purchase decisions and how they use and dispose of purchased goods or services; also includes the factors that influence purchase decisions and product use. p. 74

consumer decision-making process a five-step process used by consumers when buying goods or services. p. 75

consumer product a product bought to satisfy an individual's personal wants. p. 157

consumer sales promotion activities, such as price discounts, to incentivize consumer purchases. p. 331

consumer-generated content any form of publicly available online content created by consumers; also referred to as user-generated content. p. 295

continuous media schedule a media scheduling strategy in which advertising is run steadily throughout the advertising period; used for products in the later stages of the product life cycle. p. 320

control provides the mechanisms both for evaluating marketing results in light of the plan's objectives and for correcting actions that do not help the organization reach those objectives within budget guidelines. p. 47

convenience product a relatively inexpensive item that merits little shopping effort. p. 158

convenience store a miniature supermarket, carrying only a limited line of high-turnover convenience goods. p. 265

cooperative advertising an arrangement in which the manufacturer and the retailer split the costs of advertising the manufacturer's brand. p. 315

cord cutting discontinuing or never committing to a TV cable or satellite provider. p. 316

core competencies key unique strengths that are hard to imitate and underlie the functioning of an organization. p. 41

core service the most basic benefit the consumer is buying. p. 203

corporate or professional blogs blogs that are sponsored by a company or one of its brands and maintained by one or more of the company's employees. p. 353

corporate social responsibility a business's concern for society's welfare. p. 29

cost competitive advantage being the low-cost competitor in an industry while maintaining satisfactory profit margins. p. 42

cost per click the cost associated with a consumer clicking on a display or banner ad. p. 318

cost per contact the cost of reaching one member of the target market. p. 318

costs the combined financial value of all inputs that go into the production of a company's products, both directly and indirectly. p. 219

coupon a certificate that entitles consumers to an immediate price reduction when they buy the product. p. 331

coverage ensuring product availability in every outlet where potential customers might want to buy it. p. 251

credence quality a characteristic that consumers may have difficulty assessing even after purchase because they do not have the necessary knowledge or experience. p. 197

crisis management a coordinated effort to handle all the effects of either unfavourable publicity or an unexpected unfavourable event. p. 324

crowdsourcing the use of consumers to develop and market products. p. 349

culture the set of values, norms, attitudes, and other meaningful symbols that shape human behaviour and the artifacts, or products, of that behaviour as they are transmitted from one generation to the next. p. 83

cumulative quantity discount a deduction from list price that applies to the buyer's total purchases made during a specific period. p. 229

customer relationship management (CRM) a system that gathers information about customers that can help to build customer loyalty and retain those loyal customers. p. 132

customer satisfaction customers' evaluation of a good or service in terms of whether it has met their needs and expectations. p .7

customer value the relationship between benefits and the sacrifice necessary to obtain those benefits. p. 8

customer-centric a philosophy under which the company customizes its product and service offerings based on data generated through interactions between the customer and the company. p. 138

data mining an analytical process that compiles actionable data on the purchase habits of a company's current and potential customers; the process of sorting through large sets of data to find patterns and relationships. pp. 67, 137

data visualization presenting data in a pictorial or graphical format. p. 67

data warehouse a type of database specifically designed to collect and organize large sets of data used for analytics. p. 67

database where electronic data is collected, organized, and stored for easy retrieval. p. 63

deceptive pricing promoting a price or price saving that is not actually available. p. 233

decision confirmation the reaffirmation of the wisdom of the decision a consumer has made. p. 78

decline stage a long-run drop in sales. p. 191

decoding interpretation of the language and symbols sent by the source through a channel. p. 289

demand the quantity of a product that will be sold in the market at various prices for a specified period. p. 223

demographic segmentation segmenting markets by age, gender, income, ethnic background, occupation, and family life cycle. p. 117

demography the study of people's vital statistics, such as their age, race and ethnicity, and location. p. 23

department store a retail store that has several departments under one roof, carrying a wide variety of shopping and specialty goods. p. 264

depth interview an interview that involves a discussion between a well-trained researcher and a respondent who is asked about attitudes and perspectives on a topic. p. 57

derived demand demand in the business market that comes from demand in the consumer market. p. 102

descriptive research a type of conclusive research that attempts to describe marketing phenomena and characteristics. p. 54

destination stores stores that consumers seek out and purposely plan to visit. p. 273

development the stage in the product development process in which a prototype is developed and a marketing strategy is outlined. p. 182

diffusion the process by which the adoption of an innovation spreads. p. 186

direct channel a distribution channel in which producers sell directly to customers. p. 246

direct-response broadcast advertising that uses television or radio and includes a direct call to action asking the consumer to respond immediately. p. 326

direct-response television (DRTV) advertising that appears on television and encourages viewers to respond immediately. p. 326

direct-response print advertising in a print medium that includes a direct call to action. p. 326

direct mail a form of direct-response communication that is delivered directly to consumers' homes. p. 269

direct marketing techniques used to get consumers to make a purchase from their home, office, or another non-retail setting. p. 268

direct retailing the selling of products by representatives who work door-to-door, office-to-office, or at in-home parties. p. 268

direct-response communication communication of a message directly from a marketing company and directly to an intended individual target audience. p. 294

discount store a retailer that competes on the basis of low prices, high turnover, and high volume. p. 265

discrepancy of assortment the lack of all the items a customer needs to receive full satisfaction from a product or products. p. 243

discrepancy of quantity the difference between the amount of product produced and the amount an end-user wants to buy. p. 242

discretionary income the amount of money people have to spend on nonessential items. p. 19

disposable income the amount of money people have to spend after taxes. p.19

diversification a strategy of increasing sales by introducing new products into new markets. p. 41

Do Not Call List (DNCL) a free service whereby Canadians register their telephone number to reduce or eliminate phone calls from telemarketers. p. 325

drugstores retail stores that stock pharmacy-related products and services as their main draw. p. 265

dual distribution (multiple distribution) the use of two or more channels to distribute the same product to target markets. p. 248

dumping the sale of an exported product at a price lower than that charged for the same or a like product in the home market of the exporter. p. 248

dynamic pricing is the ability to change prices very quickly, often in real time. p. 229

earned media a category of promotional tactic based on a public relations model that gets customers talking about products or services. p. 296

electronic data interchange (EDI) information technology that replaces the paper documents that usually accompany business transactions, such as purchase orders and invoices, with electronic transmission of the needed information to reduce inventory levels, improve cash flow, streamline operations, and increase the speed and accuracy of information transmission. p. 257

electronic distribution a distribution technique that includes any kind of product or service that can be distributed electronically, whether over traditional forms such as fibre-optic cable or through satellite transmission of electronic signals. p. 258

empathy caring, individualized attention paid to customers. p. 199

empowerment delegation of authority to solve customers' problems quickly—usually by the first person who learns of the customer's problem. p. 138

encoding the conversion of the sender's ideas and thoughts into a message, usually in some combination of words, images, and sound. p. 286

environmental factors noncontrollable factors caused by natural disasters, which negatively or positively affect organizations. p. 21

environmental scanning the collection and interpretation of information about forces, events, and relationships in the external environment that may affect the future of the organization or the implementation of the marketing plan. p. 39

ethics the moral principles or values that generally govern the conduct of an individual or a group. p. 31

ethnographic research the study of human behaviour in its natural context; involves observation of behaviour and physical setting. p. 61

evaluation gauging the extent to which the marketing objectives have been achieved during the specified period. p. 46

evoked set (consideration set) a group of the most preferred alternatives resulting from an information search, which a buyer can further evaluate to make a final choice. p. 77

exchange people giving up one thing to receive another thing they would rather have. p. 8

exclusive distribution a form of distribution that involves only one or a few dealers within a given area. p. 251

experience curves curves that show costs declining at a predictable rate as experience with a product increases. p. 42

experience quality a characteristic that can be assessed only after use. p. 197

experiential marketing a form of advertising that focuses on helping consumers experience a brand such that a memorable and emotional connection is formed between the consumer and the brand. p. 323

experiment a method a researcher uses to gather primary data to determine cause and effect. p. 61

exploratory research an informal discovery process that attempts to gain insights and a better understanding of the management and research problems. p. 54

express warranty a written guarantee. p. 172

extensive decision making the most complex type of consumer decision making, used when considering the purchase of an unfamiliar, expensive product or an infrequently purchased item; requires the use of several criteria for evaluating options and more time for seeking information. p. 80

external information search the process of seeking information in the outside environment. p. 76

factory outlet an off-price retailer that is owned and operated by a manufacturer. p. 267

family brand the marketing of several different products under the same brand name. p. 166

family life cycle (FLC) a series of stages determined by a combination of age, marital status, and the presence or absence of children. p. 119

feedback the receiver's response to a message. p. 289

flexible pricing (variable pricing) different customers pay different prices for essentially the same merchandise bought in equal quantities. p. 231

flighted media schedule a media scheduling strategy in which ads are run heavily every other month or every two weeks, to achieve a greater impact with an increased frequency and reach at those times. p. 320

focus group a small group of recruited participants engaged in a non-structured discussion in a casual environment. p. 58

follow-up the final step of the selling process, in which the salesperson ensures that delivery schedules are met, that the goods or services perform as promised, and that the buyer's employees are properly trained to use the products. p. 342

four Ps product, price, place, and promotion, which together make up the marketing mix. p. 45

franchise retailers that are owned and operated by individuals but are licensed by a larger supporting organization. p. 264

franchisee an individual or a business that pays the franchiser for the right to use its name, product, or business methods. p. 270

franchiser the originator of a trade name, product, methods of operation, and so on, that grants operating rights to another party to sell its product. p. 270

freemium an initially "free" offering to use a service with limited functionality, which serves as an enticement to pay a "premium" to receive an enhanced experience. p. 335

frequency the number of times an individual is exposed to a given message during a specific period. p. 318

frequent-buyer program a loyalty program in which loyal consumers are rewarded for making multiple purchases of a particular good or service. p. 335

full-line discount stores retailers that offer consumers very limited service and carry a broad assortment of well-known, nationally branded hard goods. p. 265

functional discount (trade discount) a discount to distribution channel intermediaries such as wholesalers and retailers for performing channel functions. p. 229

gap model a model identifying five gaps that can cause problems in service delivery and influence customer evaluations of service quality. p. 199

Generation X people born between 1966 and 1978. p. 25

Generation Y people born between 1979 and 2000. p. 24

Generation Z people born between 1995 and 2009. p. 23

generic product a no-frills, no-brand-name, low-cost product that is simply identified by its product category. p. 165

generic product name a term that identifies a product by class or type and cannot be trademarked. p. 167

geodemographic segmentation clusters potential customers into neighbourhood lifestyle categories. pp. 117, 121

geographic segmentation segmenting markets by region of a country or the world, market size, market density, or climate. p. 116

global brand a brand with at least 20 percent of the product sold outside its home country or region. p. 164

green marketing the development and marketing of products designed to minimize negative effects on the physical environment. p. 31

gross domestic product (GDP) the total market value of all goods and services produced in a country for a given period.

gross income the amount of money people earn before taxes and expenses. p. 19

gross margin the amount of money the retailer makes as a percentage of sales after the cost of goods sold is subtracted. p. 264

growth stage the second stage of the product life cycle when sales typically grow at an increasing rate, many competitors enter the market, large companies may start to acquire small pioneering companies, and profits are healthy. p. 191

heterogeneity the variability of the inputs and outputs of services, which causes services to tend to be less standardized and uniform than goods. p. 198

horizontal conflict a channel conflict that occurs among channel members on the same level. p. 252

ideal self-image the way an individual would like to be. p. 89

implementation the process that turns a marketing plan into action assignments and ensures that these assignments are executed in a way that accomplishes the plan's objectives. p. 46

implied warranty an unwritten guarantee that the good or service is fit for the purpose for which it was sold. p. 172

independent retailers retailers owned by a single person or partnership and not operated as part of a larger retail institution. p. 263

individual branding the use of different brand names for different products. p. 166

inflation a measure of the decrease in the value of money, expressed as the percentage reduction in value since the previous year. p. 19

influencer a person who has accumulated a sufficient following on one or more social media platforms to be considered to have an influence on consumer behaviour influencer marketing. p. 348

influencer marketing leveraging the influential power of individuals, as thought leaders, to gain trust of a target market. p. 295

infomercial a 30-minute or longer advertisement that looks more like a TV talk show than a sales pitch. p. 316

informational labelling package labelling designed to help consumers make proper product selections and to lower their cognitive dissonance after the purchase. p. 169

innovation a product perceived as new by a potential adopter. p. 186

inseparability the inability of the production and consumption of a service to be separated; consumers must be present during the production. p. 198

institutional advertising a form of advertising designed to enhance a company's image rather than promote a particular product. p. 308

intangibility the inability of services to be touched, seen, tasted, heard, or felt in the same manner that goods can be sensed. p. 196

integrated marketing communications the strategic integration of all promotional mix tactics resulting in a thematically consistent and uniform look and feel regardless of platforms or mediums used. p. 284

intensive distribution a form of distribution aimed at having a product available in every outlet where target customers might want to buy it. p. 251

interaction the point at which a customer and a company representative exchange information and develop learning relationships. p. 138

internal information search the process of recalling information stored in one's memory. p. 76

internal marketing treating employees as customers and developing systems and benefits that satisfy their needs. p. 208

interpersonal communication direct, fact-to-face communication between two or more people. p. 286

introductory stage the full-scale launch of a new product into the marketplace. p. 189

inventory control system a method of developing and maintaining an adequate assortment of materials or products to meet a manufacturer's or a customer's demand. p. 257

involvement the amount of time and effort a buyer invests in the search, evaluation, and decision processes of consumer behaviour. p. 79

joint demand the demand for two or more items used together in a final product. p. 102

just-in-time production (JIT) a process that redefines and simplifies manufacturing by reducing inventory levels and delivering raw materials just when they are needed on the production line. p. 256

knowledge management the process by which learned information from customers is centralized and shared for the purpose of enhancing the relationship between customers and the organization. p. 138

lead generation (prospecting) identification of those companies and people most likely to buy the seller's offerings. p. 340

lead qualification determination of a sales prospect's (1) recognized need, (2) buying power, and (3) receptivity and accessibility. p. 341

learning (CRM) in a CRM environment, the informal process of collecting customer data through customer comments and feedback on product or service performance. p. 138

learning a process that creates changes in behaviour, immediate or expected, through experience and practice leveraging the influential power of individuals, as thought leaders, to gain trust of a target market. p. 92

lifestyle a mode of living as identified by a person's activities, interests, and opinions. p. 89

lifetime value (LTV) analysis a data manipulation technique that projects the future value of the customer over a period of years by using the assumption that marketing to repeat customers is more profitable than marketing to first-time buyers. p. 144

limited decision making the type of decision making that requires a moderate amount of time for gathering information and deliberating about an unfamiliar brand in a familiar product category. p. 79

location-based social networking sites websites that combine the fun of social networking with the utility of location-based GPS technology. p. 354

logistics information system the link that connects all the logistics functions of the supply chain. p. 255

logistics the process of strategically managing the efficient flow and storage of raw materials, in-process inventory, and finished goods from point of origin to point of consumption. p. 255

loss-leader pricing a product is sold near or even below cost in the hope that shoppers will buy other items once they are in the store. p. 231

loyalty marketing program a promotional program designed to build long-term, mutually beneficial relationships between a company and its key customers. p. 335

manufacturer's brand the brand name of a manufacturer. p. 165

market people or organizations with needs or wants and the ability and willingness to buy. p. 114

market development a marketing strategy that involves attracting new customers to existing products. p. 40

market opportunity analysis (MOA) the description and estimation of the size and sales potential of market segments that are of interest to the business and the assessment of key competitors in these market segments. p. 44

market penetration a marketing strategy that tries to increase market share among existing customers by using existing products. p. 39

market segment a subgroup of people or organizations sharing one or more characteristics that cause them to have similar product needs. p. 114

market segmentation the process of dividing a market into meaningful, relatively similar, and identifiable segments or groups. p. 114

market share a company's product sales as a percentage of total sales for that industry. p. 221

marketing the activities that develop an offering in order to satisfy a customer need. p. 3

marketing analytics the use of data to optimize marketing decisions. p. 52

marketing audit a thorough, systematic, periodic evaluation of the objectives, strategies, structure, and performance of the marketing organization. p. 47

marketing channel (channel of distribution) a set of interdependent organizations that handle products and often transfer ownership of products as they move from producer to business user or consumer. p. 242

marketing company era a strong emphasis on the marketing concept and development of a more comprehensive approach to understanding the customer. p. 5

marketing dashboard marketing metrics and insights from marketing analytics are compiled in one place. p. 68

marketing environment the entire set of situational conditions, both internal (strengths and weaknesses) and external (opportunities and threats), within which a business operates. p. 37

marketing information systems (MIS) help companies collect, analyze, and communicate information throughout the organization. p. 67

marketing mix a unique blend of product, price, place, and promotion, strategies designed to produce mutually satisfying exchanges with a target market. p. 45

marketing objective a statement of what is to be accomplished through marketing activities. p. 44

marketing research the process of planning, collecting, and analyzing data relevant to a marketing decision. p. 52

marketing strategy the activities of selecting and describing one or more target markets and developing and maintaining a marketing mix that will produce mutually satisfying exchanges with target markets. p. 44

marketing-controlled information source a product information source that originates with marketers promoting the product. p. 77

Maslow's hierarchy of needs a method of classifying human needs into five categories in ascending order of importance: physiological, safety, social, esteem, and self-actualization. p. 91

mass communication the communication of a concept or message to large audiences. p. 286

mass customization (build-to-order) a strategy that uses technology to deliver a strategy that uses technology to deliver customized services on a mass basis; a production method whereby products are not made until an order is placed by the customer; products are made according to customer specifications. pp. 204, 255

mass merchandising a retailing strategy using moderate to low prices on large quantities of merchandise and lower levels of service to stimulate high turnover of products. p. 266

maturity stage a period during which sales increase at a decreasing rate. p. 191

measurement error an error that occurs when the information desired by the researcher differs from the information provided by the measurement process. p. 56

media mix the combination of media to be used for a promotional campaign. p. 318

media planning the series of decisions advertisers make regarding the selection and use of media, allowing the marketer to optimally and cost-effectively communicate the message to the target audience. p. 313

media schedule designation of the media, the specific publications or programs, and the insertion dates of advertising. p. 320

media-sharing sites websites that allow users to upload and distribute multimedia content such as videos and photos. p. 352

medium the channel used to convey a message to a target market. p. 313

Mercosur the largest Latin American trade agreement.

microblogs blogs with strict post-length limits. p. 353

microtargeting the use of direct marketing techniques that employ highly detailed analytics in order to isolate potential customers with great precision. p. 269

mission statement a statement of the business's value based on a careful analysis of benefits sought by present and potential customers and an analysis of existing and anticipated environmental conditions. p. 38

mobile advertising advertising that displays text, images, and animated ads via mobile phones or other mobile devices that are data-enabled. p. 317

modified rebuy a situation where the purchaser wants some change in the original good or service. p. 108

morals the rules people develop as a result of cultural values and norms. p. 31

motives driving forces that cause a person to take action to satisfy specific needs. p. 91

multiculturalism the peaceful and equitable coexistence of different cultures, rather than one national culture, in a country. p. 26

multiplier effect (accelerator principle) the phenomenon in which a small increase or decrease in consumer demand can produce a much larger change in demand for the facilities and equipment needed to make the consumer product. p. 102

multisegment targeting strategy a strategy that chooses two or more well-defined market segments and develops a distinct marketing mix for each. p. 125

mystery shoppers researchers posing as customers who gather observational data about a store and collect data about customer–employee interactions. p. 60

need a state of being where we desire something that we do not possess but yearn to acquire. pp. 3, 76

need recognition the result of an imbalance between actual and desired states. p. 76

needs assessment a determination of the customer's specific needs and wants and the range of options the customer has for satisfying them. p. 341

negotiation the process during which both the salesperson and the prospect offer concessions in an attempt to arrive at a sales agreement. p. 342

networking the use of friends, business contacts, co-workers, acquaintances, and fellow members in professional and civic organizations to identify potential clients. p. 340

new product a product new to the world, new to the market, new to the producer or seller, or new to some combination of these. p. 177

new task buy a situation requiring the purchase of a product for the first time. p. 108

new-product strategy a plan that links the new-product development process with the objectives of the marketing department, the business unit, and the corporation. p. 178

niche competitive advantage the advantage achieved when a company seeks to target and effectively serve a single segment of the market. p. 43

niche one segment of a market. p. 125

noise anything that interferes with, distorts, or slows down the transmission of information. p. 288

nonaspirational reference groups (dissociative groups) groups that influence our behaviour because we try to maintain distance from them. p. 86

noncorporate blogs independent blogs that are not associated with the marketing efforts of any particular company or brand. p. 353

noncumulative quantity discount a deduction from list price that applies to a single order rather than to the total volume of orders placed during a certain period. p. 229

nonmarketing-controlled information source a product information source that doesn't originate from the company(ies) making the product. p. 77

nonprobability sample any sample in which little or no attempt is made to have a representative cross-section of the population. p. 55

non-profit organization an organization that exists to achieve a goal other than the usual business goals of profit, market share, or return on investment. p. 210

non-profit organization marketing the effort by non-profit organizations to bring about mutually satisfying exchanges with target markets. p. 209

nonstore retailing provides shopping without visiting a store.

norms the values and attitudes deemed acceptable by a group. pp. 85, 267

North American Industry Classification System (NAICS) an industry classification system developed by the United States, Canada, and Mexico to classify North American

business establishments by their main production processes. p. 106

observation research a systematic process of recording the behavioural patterns of people, objects, and occurrences with or without questioning them. p. 60

odd-even pricing (psychological pricing) odd-numbered prices connote bargains, and even-numbered prices imply quality. p. 231

off-price retailer a retailer that sells brand-name merchandise at considerable discounts. p. 267

on-demand marketing: delivering relevant experiences, integrated across both physical and virtual environments, throughout the consumer's decision and buying process. p. 150

one-to-one marketing an individualized marketing method that uses data generated through interactions between carefully defined groups of customers and the company to build long-term, personalized, and profitable relationships with each customer. p. 126

online marketing two-way communication of a message delivered through the Internet to the consumer. p. 294

online research panel is a sample of persons who have agreed to complete surveys via the Internet. p. 63

online retailing (e-tailing) a type of shopping available to consumers with access to the Internet. p. 269

open-ended question an interview question that encourages an answer phrased in the respondent's own words. p. 60

opinion leader an individual who influences the opinions of others. p. 86

optimizers business customers who consider numerous suppliers, both familiar and unfamiliar, solicit bids, and study all proposals carefully before selecting one. p. 122

order processing system a system whereby orders are entered into the supply chain and filled. p. 256

organic traffic online search results based upon unpaid (SEO) tactics. p. 359

original equipment manufacturers (OEMs) individuals and organizations that buy business goods and incorporate them into the products that they produce for eventual sale to other producers or to consumers. p. 105

owned media a category of promotional tactic based on brands becoming publishers of their own content to maximize the brands' value to consumers. p. 296

paid media a category of promotional tactic based on the traditional advertising model whereby a brand pays for advertising space. p. 296

Pareto Principle (80/20 rule) a principle holding that approximately 20 percent of all customers generate around 80 percent of the demand. p. 122

pay per click (PPC) a digital advertising payment method in which the advertiser pays the media company, through which the ad is placed, each time a user clicks on a digital ad placed within the media company's space. p. 307

pay-what-you-want pricing allows the customer to choose the amount they want to pay for a good or service. p. 232

penetration pricing a relatively low price for a product initially as a way to reach the mass market. p. 226

percentage of sales a method of determining an advertising budget in which a percentage of forecast sales is calculated as the amount to spend on advertising. p. 307

perception the process by which people select, organize, and interpret stimuli into a meaningful and coherent picture. p. 90

perceptual mapping a means of displaying or graphing, in two or more dimensions, the location of products, brands, or groups of products in customers' minds. p. 128

perishability the inability of services to be stored, ware-housed, or inventoried. p. 198

personal selling a purchase situation involving a personal, paid-for communication between two people in an attempt to influence each other. p. 293

personality a way of organizing and grouping the consistency of an individual's reactions to situations. p. 89

personally identifiable information data that can be used to identify a particular person. p. 71

persuasive labelling package labelling that focuses on a pro-motional theme or logo; consumer information is secondary. p. 169

pioneering advertising a form of advertising designed to stimulate primary demand for a new product or product cat-egory. p. 309

planned obsolescence the practice of modifying products so those that have already been sold become obsolete before they actually need replacement. p. 162

planning the process of anticipating future events and deter-mining strategies to achieve organizational objectives in the future. p. 36

podcasts digital audio or video file that is distributed serially for other people to listen to or watch. p. 355

point-of-sale interactions communications between cus-tomers and organizations that occur at the point of sale, usually in a store. p. 139

pop-up shops tiny, temporary stores that stay in one location for only a short time. p. 274

position the place a product, brand, or group of products occupies in consumers' minds relative to competing offerings. p. 127

positioning a process that influences potential customers' overall perception of a brand, a product line, or an organiza-tion in general. p. 127

preapproach a process that describes the research a sales-person must do before contacting a prospect. p. 341

predatory pricing the practice of charging a very low price for a product with the intent of driving competitors out of the market or the business. p. 233

predictive modelling a data manipulation technique in which marketers try to determine, based on some past set of

occurrences, the odds that some other occurrence, such as an inquiry or a purchase, will take place in the future. p. 144

premium an extra item offered to the consumer, usually in exchange for some proof of purchase of the promoted product. p. 334

price bundling marketing two or more products in a single package for a special price. p. 231

price elasticity of demand a measurement of change in con-sumer demand for a product relative to the changes in its price. p. 223

price fixing an agreement between two or more companies to set the price they will charge for a product or service. p. 233

price lining offering a product line with several items at specific price points. p. 231

price sensitivity consumers' varying levels of desire to buy a given product at different price levels. p. 223

price skimming a high introductory price, often coupled with heavy promotion. p. 226

price strategy a basic, long-term pricing framework that defines the initial price for a product and the intended direc-tion for price movements over the product life cycle. p. 226

price that which is given up in an exchange to acquire a good or service. p. 218

primary data information that is collected for the first time and is used for solving the particular problem under investi-gation. p. 56

primary membership groups groups with which individuals interact regularly in an informal, face-to-face manner. p. 85

private brand a brand name owned by a wholesaler or a retailer. p. 165

probability sample a sample in which every element in the population has a known statistical likelihood of being selected. p. 55

procurement the process of buying goods and services for use in the operations of an organization. p. 255

product advertising a form of advertising that promotes the benefits of a specific good or service. p. 309

product anything, both favourable and unfavourable, received by a person in an exchange for possession, consumption, atten-tion, or short-term use. p. 156

product category all brands that satisfy a particular type of need. p. 189

product development a marketing strategy that entails the creation of new products for current customers. p. 40

product differentiation a positioning strategy that some companies use to distinguish their products from those of com-petitors. p. 127

product item a specific version of a product that can be desig-nated as a distinct offering among an organization's products. p. 160

product life cycle (PLC) a concept that traces the stages of a product's acceptance, from its introduction (birth) to its decline (death). p. 188

product line a group of closely related product items.

product line depth the different versions of a product item in a product line. p. 160

product line extension adding products to an existing product line to offer more options to consumers. p. 162

product line length the number of product items in a product line. p. 160

product mix all products that an organization sells. p. 160

product mix width the number of product lines an organization offers. p. 160

product modification changing one or more of a product's characteristics. p. 161

product offering the mix of products offered to the consumer by the retailer; also called the product assortment or merchandise mix. p. 272

product placement a public relations strategy that involves getting a product, service, or company name to appear in a movie, television show, radio program, magazine, newspaper, video game, video or audio clip, book, or commercial for another product; on the Internet; or at special events. p. 322

product/service differentiation competitive advantage the provision of a unique benefit that is valuable to buyers beyond simply offering a low price. p. 43

production era a focus on manufacturing and production quantity in which customers are meant to choose based on what is most abundantly available. p. 4

professional services pricing used by people with experience, training, and often certification by a licensing board, fees are typically charged at an hourly rate, but may be based on the solution of a problem or performance of an act. p. 231

profit revenue minus expenses. p. 219

programmatic buying using an automated system to make media buying decisions in real time. p. 310

promotion communication by marketers that informs, persuades, reminds, and connects potential buyers to a product for the purpose of influencing an opinion or eliciting a response. p. 284

promotional mix the combination of promotional tools—including advertising, publicity, sales promotion, personal selling, direct-response communication, and social media—used to reach the target market and fulfill the organization's overall goals. p. 291

promotional strategy a plan for the use of the elements of promotion: advertising, public relations, personal selling, sales promotion, direct-response communication, and social media. p. 284

psychographic segmentation market segmentation on the basis of personality, motives, lifestyles, and geodemographic categories. p. 119

psychological factors tools that consumers use to interact with their world, recognize their feelings, gather and analyze information, formulate thoughts and opinions, and take action. p. 90

public relations the marketing function that evaluates public attitudes, identifies areas within the organization the public may be interested in, and executes a program of action to earn public understanding and acceptance. p. 292

public service advertisement (PSA) an announcement that promotes a program of a non-profit organization or of a federal, provincial or territorial, or local government. p. 212

publicity a public relations tactic that, when used proactively, is intended to generate media coverage (earned media) about an organization or person. p. 293

pull strategy a marketing strategy that stimulates consumer demand to obtain product distribution. p. 303

pulsing media schedule a media scheduling strategy that uses continuous scheduling throughout the year coupled with a flighted schedule during the best sales periods. p. 320

purchasing power a comparison of income versus the relative cost of a set standard of goods and services in different geographic areas. p. 19

push money money offered to channel intermediaries to encourage them to push products—that is, to encourage other members of the channel to sell the products. p. 336

push strategy a marketing strategy that uses aggressive personal selling and trade advertising to convince a wholesaler or a retailer to carry and sell particular merchandise. p. 303

pyramid of corporate social responsibility a model that suggests corporate social responsibility is composed of economic, legal, ethical, and philanthropic responsibilities and that the company's economic performance supports the entire structure. p. 30

quantity discount a unit price reduction offered to buyers buying either in multiple units or at more than a specified dollar amount. p. 228

reach the number of target consumers exposed to a commercial at least once during a specific period, usually four weeks. p. 318

real self-image the way an individual actually perceives themself to be. p. 89

rebates cash refunds given for the purchase of a product during a specific period. p. 334

receivers the people who decode a message. p. 288

recency-frequency-monetary (RFM) analysis the analysis of customer activity by recency, frequency, and monetary value. p. 144

recession a period of economic activity characterized by negative growth, which reduces demand for goods and services. p. 20

reciprocity a practice where business purchasers choose to buy from their own customers. p. 103

reference group a group in society that influences an individual's purchasing behaviour. p. 85

referrals recommendations to a salesperson from a customer or business associate. p. 340

relationship commitment a business's belief that an ongoing relationship with another company is so important that the relationship warrants maximum efforts at maintaining it indefinitely. p. 98

relationship marketing a strategy that focuses on keeping and improving relationships with current customers. p. 7

relationship selling (business development) a multistage sales process that involves building, maintaining, and enhancing interactions with customers for the purpose of developing long-term satisfaction through mutually beneficial business partnerships. p. 336

reliability the ability to perform a service dependably, accurately, and consistently. p. 199

repositioning changing consumers' perceptions of a brand in relation to competing brands. p. 129

resale price maintenance attempts by a producer to control the price of their products in retail stores. p. 235

research design specifies which research questions must be answered, how and when data will be gathered, and how the data will be analyzed. p. 54

response list a customer list that includes the names and addresses of individuals who have responded to an offer of some kind, such as by mail, telephone, direct-response television, product rebates, contests or sweepstakes, or billing inserts. p. 142

responsiveness the ability to provide prompt service. p. 199

retail channel omnification the reduction of multiple retail channels systems into a single, unified system for the purpose of creating efficiencies or saving costs. p. 278

retailer a channel intermediary that sells mainly to consumers and business customers. p. 245

retailing all the activities directly related to the sale of goods and services to the ultimate consumer for personal, nonbusiness use. p. 262

retailing mix a combination of the six Ps—product, place, promotion, price, presentation, and personnel— used in a single retail method to attract the target market. p. 271

return on investment (ROI) net profits after tax divided by total assets. p. 221

revenue the price per unit charged to customers multiplied by the number of units sold. p. 219

review sites websites that allow consumers to post, read, rate, and comment on opinions regarding all kinds of products and services. p. 354

routine response behaviour the type of decision making exhibited by consumers buying frequently purchased, low-cost goods and services; requires little search and decision time. p. 79

sales era hard selling to the customer, who has greater choice thanks to more competition in the marketplace. p. 4

sales presentation a formal meeting in which the salesperson presents a sales proposal to a prospective buyer. p. 342

sales process (sales cycle) the set of steps a salesperson goes through to sell a particular product or service. p. 339

sales promotion all marketing activities that stimulate consumer purchases in the near term. p. 293

sales proposal a formal written document or professional presentation that outlines how the salesperson's product or service will meet or exceed the prospect's needs. p. 342

sample a subset from a larger population. p. 55

sampling a promotional program that allows the consumer the opportunity to try a product or service for free. p. 336

sampling error an error that occurs when a sample does not represent the target population. p. 56

satisficers business customers who place their order with the first familiar supplier to satisfy their product and delivery requirements. p. 122

scaled-response question a closed-ended question designed to measure the intensity of a respondent's answer. p. 60

scrambled merchandising the tendency to offer a wide variety of nontraditional goods and services under one roof. p. 265

screening the first filter in the product development process, which eliminates ideas that are inconsistent with the organization's new-product strategy or are obviously inappropriate for some other reason. p. 181

search engine marketing (SEM) the practice of using paid advertisements that appear on the results page of a search engine to market a business. p. 359

search engine optimization (SEO) a process that marketers take to optimize the chance of search engines, "driven" by people looking for information online, to produce their company's website, name, products or all three. p. 359

search quality a characteristic that can be easily assessed before purchase. p. 197

seasonal discount a price reduction for buying merchandise out of season. p. 229

seasonal media schedule a media scheduling strategy that runs advertising only during times of the year when the product is most likely to be purchased. p. 320

secondary data data previously collected for any purpose other than the one at hand. p. 54

secondary membership groups groups with which individuals interact less consistently and more formally than with primary membership groups. p. 85

segmentation bases (variables) characteristics of individuals, groups, or organizations. p. 115

selective distortion a process whereby consumers change or distort information that conflicts with their feelings or beliefs. p. 90

selective distribution a form of distribution achieved by screening dealers to eliminate all but a few in any single area. p. 251

selective exposure the process whereby a consumer decides which stimuli to notice and which to ignore. p. 90

selective retention a process whereby consumers remember only information that supports their personal feelings or beliefs. p. 90

self-concept how consumers perceive themselves in terms of attitudes, perceptions, beliefs, and self-evaluations. p. 89

self-regulation programs voluntarily adopted by business groups to regulate the activities of their members. p. 18

self-service technologies (SST) technological interfaces that allow customers to provide themselves with products and/or services without the intervention of a service employee. p. 268

sender the originator of the message in the communication process. p. 286

sentiment analysis the use of text analysis to mine and categorize unstructured data from social media posts. p. 69

service mark a trademark for a service. p. 167

service the result of applying human or mechanical efforts to people or objects. p. 196

sharing economy the way connected consumers exchange goods and service with each other through a digital marketplace. p. 269

shop-at-home television network a specialized form of direct-response marketing whereby television shows display merchandise, with the retail price, to home viewers. p. 269

shopper analytics searching for and discovering meaningful patterns in shopper data for the purpose of fine-tuning, developing, or changing market offerings. p. 278

shopper marketing promotion set up at the retailer's location to build traffic, advertise the product, or induce impulse buying. p. 278

shopping product a product that requires comparison shopping because it is usually more expensive than a convenience product and is found in fewer stores. p. 158

simulated (laboratory) market testing the presentation of advertising and other promotion materials for several products, including the test product, to members of the product's target market. p. 184

single-price tactic offering all goods and services at the same price (or perhaps two or three prices). p. 231

social acceleration the concept of exponentially rapid growth starting with human desire for improved products, spurring competitive pursuit of market share, driving innovation and technology, and resulting in a higher standard of living, but with new socio-environmental problems. p. 29

social class a group of people who are considered nearly equal in status or community esteem, who regularly socialize among themselves both formally and informally, and who share behavioural norms. p. 84

social commerce a subset of e-commerce that involves the interaction and user contribution aspects of social media to assist in the online buying and selling of products and services. p. 349

social gaming playing an online game that allows for social interaction between players on a social media platform. p. 318

social media collection of online communication tools that facilitate conversations online; when used by marketers, social media tools encourage consumer empowerment. p. 295

social networking sites websites that allow individuals to connect—or network—with friends, peers, business associates, and brands. p. 350

social news sites websites that allow users to decide which content is promoted on a given website by voting that content up or down. p. 352

social selling leveraging social networks to find the right prospects and build trusted relationships to achieve sales goals. p. 341

socialization process the passing down of cultural values and norms to children. p. 87

societal marketing era looking not only at the customer but expanding marketing efforts to include aspects from the external environment that go beyond a company's customers, suppliers, and competitors. p. 6

spatial discrepancy the difference between the location of a producer and the location of widely scattered markets. p. 243

specialty discount stores retail stores that offer a nearly complete selection of single category merchandise and use self-service, discount prices, high volume, and high turnover. p. 265

specialty product a particular item with unique characteristics for which consumers search extensively and for which they are very reluctant to accept substitutes. p. 159

specialty store a retail store that carries a deeper but narrower assortment of merchandise within a single category of interest. p. 265

sponsorship a public relations strategy in which a company spends money to support an issue, a cause, or an event that is consistent with corporate objectives, such as improving brand awareness or enhancing corporate image. p. 323

status quo pricing a pricing objective that maintains existing prices or meets the competition's prices. p. 222

stimulus any unit of input affecting one or more of the five senses: sight, smell, taste, touch, hearing. p. 76

straight rebuy a situation in which the purchaser reorders the same goods or services without looking for new information or new suppliers. p. 109

strategic business unit (SBU) a subgroup of a single business or a collection of related businesses within the larger organization. p. 37

strategic channel alliances cooperative agreements between business companies to use one of the manufacturer's already established distribution channels. p. 249

strategic planning the leadership and managerial process of establishing the organization's objectives and then determining how to achieve them given internal resources and the evolving marketing environment. p. 36

structured data data that is easily defined and organized. p. 68

subculture a homogeneous group of people who share elements of the overall culture and also have their own unique cultural elements. p. 84

supercentres retail stores that combine groceries and general merchandise goods with a wide range of services. p. 266

supermarkets large, departmentalized, self-service retailers that specialize in food and some nonfood items. p. 265

supplementary services a group of services that support or enhance the core service. p. 203

supply chain management a management system that coordinates and integrates all the activities performed by supply chain members into a seamless process, from the source to the point of consumption, resulting in enhanced customer and economic value. p. 254

supply chain team an entire group of individuals who orchestrate the movement of goods, services, and information from the source to the consumer. p. 255

supply chain the connected chain of all the business entities, both internal and external to the company, that produce the product and perform or support the marketing channel functions. p. 242

survey research the most popular method for gathering primary data, in which a researcher interacts with people to obtain facts, opinions, and attitudes. p. 58

sustainable competitive advantage an advantage that cannot be copied by the competition. p. 43

SWOT analysis identifying internal environment of strengths (S) and weaknesses (W) as well as external opportunities (O) and threats (T). p. 39

tangibles the physical evidence of a service, including the physical facilities, tools, and equipment used to provide the service. p. 199

target market a group of people or organizations for which an organization designs, implements, and maintains a marketing mix intended to meet the needs of that group. p. 14

telemarketing the use of telecommunications to sell a product or service; involves both outbound and inbound calls. p. 268

temporal discrepancy a product is produced but a customer is not ready to buy it. p. 243

test marketing the limited introduction of a product and a marketing program to determine the reactions of potential customers in a market situation. p. 182

three-dimensional printing (3DP) the creation of three-dimensional objects via an additive manufacturing (printing) technology that layers raw material into desired shapes. p. 259

touch points all possible areas of a business where customers have contact with that business. p. 139

trade allowance a price reduction offered by manufacturers to intermediaries, such as wholesalers and retailers. p. 336

trade sales promotion activities, such as price discounts, to incentivize current or prospective clientele to make purchases. p. 331

trademark the exclusive right to use a brand or part of a brand. p. 167

triple bottom line a business philosophy seen as the pursuit of profit while also benefiting society and the environment. p. 29

Trojan Horse method demonstrating or displaying a person or company's expertise via social media channels, resulting in recruitment of prospects who are impressed with said expertise, and voluntarily come forward with interest in seeking the company's assistance. p. 341

trust confidence in an exchange partner's reliability and integrity. p. 98

two-part pricing charging two separate amounts to consume a single good or service. p. 232

unbundling reducing the bundle of services that comes with the basic product. p. 231

undifferentiated targeting strategy a marketing approach that views the market as one big market with no individual segments and thus uses a single marketing mix. p. 124

unique selling proposition (USP) a desirable, exclusive, and believable advertising appeal selected as the theme for a campaign. p. 310

universal product codes (UPCs) a series of thick and thin vertical lines (bar codes), readable by computerized optical scanners that match the codes to brand names, package sizes, and prices. p. 170

unsought product a product unknown to the potential buyer or a known product that the buyer does not actively seek. p. 159

unstructured data data that is not easily defined and organized. p. 69

Uruguay Round an agreement created by the World Trade Organization to dramatically lower trade barriers worldwide.

usage-rate segmentation dividing a market by the amount of product bought or consumed. p. 122

value the enduring belief shared by a society that a specific mode of conduct is personally or socially preferable to another mode of conduct. p. 83

value-based pricing a pricing tactic that sets the price at a level that seems to the customer to be a good value compared with the prices of other options. p. 229

vertical conflict a channel conflict that occurs between different levels in a marketing channel, most typically between the manufacturer and wholesaler or between the manufacturer and retailer. p. 253

want a particular product or service that will satisfy a need. p. 76

warehouse membership clubs limited-service merchant wholesalers that sell a limited selection of brand-name appliances, household items, and groceries to members, small businesses, and groups. p. 267

warranty a confirmation of the quality or performance of a good or service. p. 172

web survey and design systems software systems specifically designed for web questionnaire construction and delivery. p. 63

ENDNOTES

Chapter 1

1. Dan Shewan, "23 Brilliant Marketing Quotes You'll Wish You'd Said," WordStream, December 19, 2017, www.wordstream.com/blog/ws/2015/12/09/marketing-quotes (accessed June 10, 2020).

2. Robert J. Keith, "The Marketing Revolution," SAGE Journals, January 1, 1960, journals.sagepub.com/doi/abs/10.1177/002224296002400306?journalCode=jmxa (accessed June 10, 2020).

3. Peter F. Drucker, *Management: Tasks, Responsibilities, Practices*, New York: Harper and Row, 1973.

4. "Enrich Not Exploit Sustainability Report 2016," The Body Shop, 2016, www.thebodyshop.com/about-us/our-commitment/enrich-not-exploit-sustainability-report-2016 (accessed June 10, 2020).

5. Imogen Watson, "Body Shop Outlines Plans to Improve 'Slow' Progress on Green Goals," May 14, 2019, www.thedrum.com/news/2019/05/14/body-shop-outlines-plans-improve-slow-progress-green-goals (accessed June 10, 2020).

6. "The End of Interruption—Why Interruption Is An Outdated Marketing Strategy," July 5, 2018, www.ie.edu/exponential-learning/news-events/news/end-interruption-interruption-outdated-marketing-strategy (accessed June 10, 2020).

7. Valarie A. Zeithaml, Mary Jo Bitner, and Dwayne D. Gremler, *Services Marketing*, 4th ed. (New York: McGraw-Hill Irwin, 2006), 110.

8. Diane Kaemingk, "Reducing Customer Churn for Banks and Financial Institutions," August 29, 2018, www.qualtrics.com/blog/customer-churn-banking (accessed June 10, 2020).

9. Vadim Kotelnikov, "Customer Retention: Driving Profits Through Giving Customers Lots of Reasons to Stay," e-COACH, www.1000ventures.com/business_guide/crosscuttings/customer_retention.html (accessed June 10, 2020).

10. Christine Moorman, "Why Apple Is a Great Marketer," *Forbes*, October 7, 2012, www.forbes.com/sites/christinemoorman/2012/07/10/why-apple-is-a-great-marketer (accessed June 10, 2020).

11. Vanessa Mitchell, "Report: Marketing Skills Gap Just Getting Bigger," January 17, 2019, www.cmo.com.au/article/656333/report-marketing-skills-gap-just-getting-bigger/ (accessed June 10, 2020).

12. Joe Andrulis, "The Marketing Department Has a Marketing Problem," August 22, 2016, www.campaignlive.com/article/marketing-department-marketing-problem/1406321 (accessed June 10, 2020).

Chapter 2

1. Quote Addicts, https://www.linkedin.com/pulse/thought-provoking-quotes-from-simon-sinek-slava-khabovets-mba (accessed June 10, 2020).

2. Michael E. Porter, "How Competitive Forces Shape Strategy," *Harvard Business Review,* March 1979 (accessed May 30, 2017).

3. Competition Bureau, www.competitionbureau.gc.ca (accessed September 15, 2014).

4. "The Canadian Code of Advertising Standards," Advertising Standards Canada, www.adstandards.com/en/Standards/canCodeOfAdStandards.aspx (accessed December 3, 2016).

5. Jason Vermes, "'It Basically Means Nothing': Why Some Economists Are Skeptical of the Term Middle Class," August 2019.

6. "Special Reports—What Difference Does Learning Make to Financial Security?," Employment and Social Development Canada, January 2008, www4.hrsdc.gc.ca/.3ndic.1t.4r@-eng.jsp?iid=54 (accessed August 28, 2011).

7. Chris Fournier, Erik Hertzberg, and Natalie Wong, "Canadians Are Feeling the Debt Burn," Bloomberg Businessweek, March 26, 2019, www.bloomberg.com/news/articles/2019-03-26/canadians-are-feeling-the-debt-burn (accessed June 10, 2020).

8. Doug Murray, "Where Do Canadians Spend the Most Money Each Year?" Slice, June 25, 2019, https://www.slice.ca/money/photos/where-canadians-spend-most-money/ (accessed June 10, 2020).

9. Ibid.

10. Mark Abadi and Katie Warren, The 10 Most Liveable Cities in the World, September 4, 2019, *Business Insider.*

11. Reinhard Ellwanger, Benjamin Sawatzky, and Konrad Zmitrowicz, "Factors Behind the 2014 Oil Price Decline," Bank of Canada, Autumn 2017, https://www.bankofcanada.ca/wp-content/uploads/2017/11/boc-review-autumn2017-ellwanger.pdf (accessed June 10, 2020).

12. John Gibson, "Alberta Recession, One of the Most Severe Ever, TD Report Finds," CBC News, July 18, 2016, www.cbc.ca/news/canada/calgary/td-economics-report-alberta-recession-gdp-forecast-1.3684056 (accessed June 10, 2020).

13. "Nearly $1 Billion of Oils Sands Activity Lost Due to Fort McMurray Fires So Far, Report Estimates," *Financial Post*, May 17, 2016, http://business.financialpost.com/news/energy/nearly-1-billion-of-oilsands-production-lost-due-to-fort-mcmurray-fires-so-far-report-estimates?__lsa=af8a-8573 (accessed December 3, 2016).

14. "Is Generation Z Glued to Technology? 'It's Not an Addiction; It's an Extension of Themselves,'" Global News, June 19, 2018, https://globalnews.ca/news/4253835/generation-z-technology-addiction (accessed June 10, 2020).

15. "Exploring Canadian Values," Nanos Research, October 2016, https://www.nanos.co/wp-content/uploads/2017/07/2016-918-values-populated-report-w-tabs-r.pdf (accessed April 2020).

16. "Definition of Family," The Vanier Institute of the Family, www.vanierinstitute.ca/definition_of_family#.Umhz7Pkqhng (accessed October 22, 2013).

17. "Thinking about Families: An Interview with Katherine Scott, Director of Programs, Vanier Institute of the Family," *Transition Magazine,* Winter 2010, 5–7, http://vanierinstitute.ca/include/get.php?nodeid=220 (accessed October 21, 2013).

18. Ibid.

19. Aaron Saltzman, "Smartphones and Children: Unstoppable Trend Leaves Parents with Questions and Fears," CBC News, November 17, 2015, www.cbc.ca/news/business/children-smartphones-1.3321564 (accessed June 10, 2020).

20. Karen Mazurkewich, "Tweens & Technology," *National Post*, August 10, 2010, www.mhoneill.com/106B/articles/tween%20power.pdf (accessed August 29, 2011).

21. John Herrman, "How TikTok Is Rewriting the World," March 10, 2019, *The New York Times,* https://www.nytimes.com/2019/03/10/style/what-is-tik-tok.html (accessed July 13, 2020).

22. Alex Hern, "TikTok Video Sharing App Fined for Collection of Children's Data," February 28, 2019, https://www.theguardian.com/technology/2019/feb/28/tiktok-video-sharing-app-fined-for-collection-of-childrens-data (accessed July 13, 2020).

23. Is Generation Z Glued to Technology? It's Not an Addiction: It's an Extension of Themselves, Global News, 2018.

24. Doug Norris, PhD, "Millennials: The Generation DuJour," Environics Analytics, January 22, 2016, www.environicsanalytics.ca/blog-details/ea-blog/2016/01/22/millennials-the-generation-du-jour (accessed December 4, 2016).

25. Karen Kroll, "Yes, Millennials and Boomers Can Work Together," *Forbes*, www.forbes.com/sites/zurich/2015/07/31/yes-millennials-and-boomers-can-work-together-heres-how-to-help/#6df9b98d7d36 (accessed June 10, 2020).

26. "Myths, Exaggerations, and Uncomfortable Truths: The Real Story behind Millennials in the Workplace," IBM Institute for Business Value, February 19, 2015, https://www-935.ibm.com/services/us/gbs/thoughtleadership/millennialworkplace (accessed June 10, 2020).

27. Karen Akers, "Generation Y: Marketing to the Young and the Restless," *Successful Promotions*, January/February 2005, 33–38.

28. Sarah Boesveld, "Gen Y and Millennial Moms Having More Kids and Abandoning Helicopter Parenting," *National Post*, April 24, 2014, http://news.nationalpost.com/news/gen-y-and-millennial-moms-having-more-kids-and-abandoning-helicopter-parenting (accessed December 5, 2016).

29. Layton Han, "Gen X: The New Luxury Buyers and How to Reach Them," MediaPost, May 30, 2012, www.mediapost.com/publications/article/175754/gen-x-the-new-luxury-buyers-and-how-to-reach-them.html (accessed February 18, 2014).

30. Timothy Dewhirst, "Who Is Generation X? If Only Marketers Knew," *Globe and Mail*, January 25, 2016, www.theglobeandmail.com/report-on-business/rob-commentary/who-is-generation-x-if-only-marketers-knew/article28365604 (accessed June 10, 2020).

31. "More Canadians Are 65 and over Than under Age 15, Statscan Says," CBC News, September 29, 2015, www.cbc.ca/news/business/statistics-canada-seniors-1.3248295 (accessed June 10, 2020).

32. Don Pittis, "How to Prepare the Economy for the Baby Boom Bust: Don Pittis," CBC News, April 15, 2019, www.cbc.ca/news/business/boomers-bust-1.5088836 (accessed June 10, 2020).

33. Ibid.

34. "Census Metropolitan Area and Census Agglomeration Definitions," Statistics Canada, September 17, 2010, www.statcan.gc.ca/pub /93-600-x/2010000/definitions-eng.htm (accessed October 23, 2013).

35. "Canada's Population Tops 36 Million for First Time," CBC News, March 16, 2016, www.cbc.ca /news/canada/stats-can-36-million-canada -population-1.3494677 (accessed December 5, 2016).

36. Martin Turcotte and Mireille Vézina, "Migration from Central to Surrounding Municipalities in Toronto, Montréal and Vancouver," *Canadian Social Trends*, Statistics Canada catalogue no. 11-008-X, 90, Winter 2010, www.statcan.gc .ca/pub/11-008-x/2010002/article/11159-eng.pdf (accessed October 23, 2013).

37. "Canada's Population Tops 36 Million, as Immigrants, Refugees Swell Numbers," CBC News, September 29, 2016, www.cbc.ca/news /business/canada-population-2016-1.3783959 (accessed December 5, 2016).

38. "Young, Suburban and Mostly Asian: Canada's Immigrant Population Surges," *National Post*, May 8, 2013, http://news.nationalpostcom/2013/05/08 /young-suburban-and-mostly-asian-canadas -immigrant-population-surges (accessed October 25, 2013).

39. "2018 Annual Report to Parliament on Immigration," Government of Canada, www.canada.ca /en/immigration-refugees-citizenship/corporate /publications-manuals/annual-report-parliament -immigration-2018/report.html (accessed June 10, 2020).

40. Ibid.

41. Ibid.

42. merriam-webster.com.

43. Adapted from Alison DeNisco Rayome, "5 tech trends your business can't afford to ignore," TechRepublic, May 21, 2019, https://www.techre public.com/article/5-tech-trends-your-business -cant-afford-to-ignore/ (accessed April 2020). Used with permission of TechRepublic.com Copyright© 2020. All rights reserved.

44. This section is adapted from Archie B. Carroll, "The Pyramid of Corporate Social Responsibility: Toward the Moral Management of Organizational Stakeholders," *Business Horizons*, July–August 1991, 39–48; see also Kirk Davidson, "Marketers Must Accept Greater Responsibilities," *Marketing News*, February 2, 1998, 6.

45. Kasturi Rangan, Lisa Chase, and Sohel Karim, "The Truth About CSR," *Harvard Business Review*, January–February 2015, https://hbr.org/2015/01 /the-truth-about-csr (accessed December 7, 2016).

46. Julia Howell, "The Bottom Line of Corporate Community Giving," Imagine Canada, October 22, 2012, https://www935.ibm.com/services/us/gbs /thoughtleadership/millennialworkplace (accessed June 10, 2020).

47. "Clorox's Canada Office Leads the Way in Sustainability," Strategy Online, http://strategyonline .ca/2018/10/30/cloroxs-canada-office-leads-the-way -in-sustainability (accessed June 10, 2020).

48. "Greenlist™," S. C. Johnson, www.scjohnson. ca/en/scj_greenlist.aspx (accessed October 25, 2013).

49. Based on Edward Stevens, *Business Ethics* (New York: Paulist Press, 1979). Used with permission of Paulist Press.

50. Anusorn Singhapakdi, Scott J. Vitell, and Kenneth L. Kraft, "Moral Intensity and Ethical Decision-Making of Marketing Professionals," *Journal of Business Research*, 36, 3, 1996, 245–255; and

Ishmael P. Akaah and Edward A. Riordan, "Judgments of Marketing Professionals about Ethical Issues in Marketing Research: A Replication and Extension," *Journal of Marketing Research*, XXVI, 1989, 112–120.

Chapter 3

1. Emily Steel, "Google's Rivals Unite on Ads," *The Wall Street Journal*, September 15, 2011.

2. Justin Dallaire, "View from the C-Suite: Bon-Look Finesses Its Retail Strategy," Strategy, http://strategyonline.ca/2019/09/17/view -from-the -c-suite-bonlook-finesses-its-retail-strategy (accessed June 15, 2020).

3. Emily Jackson, "Tim Hortons Launches All-Day Breakfast Across Canada," *Financial Post*, July 23, 2018, https://business.financialpost.com/news/retail -marketing/tim-hortons-all-day-breakfast-canada (accessed June 15, 2020).

4. "Tim Hortons Opens First Location in China," CBC News, February 26, 2019, www.cbc.ca/news /business/tim-hortons-china-1.5033616 (accessed June 15, 2020).

5. "A Double Double™ You Can Eat! Introducing the New Tim Hortons Double Double™ Coffee Bar" Tim Hortons website, January 30, 2019. www.timhortons.com/ca/en/corporate/news-release .php?id=11399 (accessed June 15, 2020).

6. Melissa Dunne, "Retail as a Community Hub," Strategy Online, May 8, 2019, http://strategyonline. ca/2019/05/08/retail-as-a-community-hub (accessed June 15, 2020).

7. Adamkasi, "Competitive Advantage of WestJet," November 18, 2018, www.competitiveadvantag eanalysis.com/competitive-advantage-of-westjet (accessed June 15, 2020).

8. Lydia Couture, Aaron Sydor, Jianmin Tang, "Industry Productivity in the Manufacturing Sector: The Role of Offshoring: Statistics Canada, Publication 11F0027M, no. 98, June 2015.

9. Jetlines website, www.jetlines.com/en (accessed June 15, 2020).

10. Government of Canada website, https:// innovation.ised-ised.canada.ca/s/list-liste?language =en&token=a0B0b00000GBoqEAH (accessed September 28, 2019).

11. Jason McBride, "How to Build a Driverless Car," *Toronto Life*, May 13, 2019 (accessed June 15, 2020).

12. Tangerine website, www.tangerine.ca/en/ways -to-bank (accessed June 15, 2020).

13. Lance Anderson, "Loblaws to Begin Carrying Nicecream from Chimp Treats Peterborough Company's Frozen Fruit Dessert to Start Appearing on Shelves on Wednesday," *The Peterborough Examiner*, September 4, 2018, www.thepeterbor oughexaminer.com/news-story/8879712-loblaws -to-begin-carrying.

14. The Greenhouse juice company website, https://greenhousejuice.com (accessed September 29, 2019).

Chapter 4

1. Tamer El Araby, "Market Research in the Digital World," July 7, 2015, Nielsen Insights, www.nielsen .com/eg/en/insights/news/2015/market-research-in -the-digital-age.html.

2. "Center-Stores Doing Just Fine, Thank You," *Quirk's Marketing Research Review*, January 2016, 14-16

3. "Canadian Internet Use Survey," Statistics Canada, October 29, 2019, www150.statcan.gc.ca /n1/daily-quotidien/191029/dq191029a-eng.htm (accessed June 15, 2020).

4. Tony L. Whitehead, "Basic Classical Ethnographic Research Methods," *Cultural Ecology of Health and Change*, July 17, 2005, www.scribd.com /document/164547014/Classical-Ethno-Methods (accessed June 15, 2020).

5. Jo Bowman, "The Rise of People-Watching Research Carried out by Brands," Raconteur, September 1, 2016, www.raconteur.net /business /the-rise-of-people-watching-research-carried-out -by-brands (accessed February 2017).

6. "Understanding Online Research Panels," dataSpring website, June 2019, www.d8aspring .com/understanding-online-research-panels (accessed June 15, 2020).

7. "Number of Smartphone Users in Canada from 2013 to 2023," statista website, February 27, 2020, www.statista.com/statistics/467190/forecast-of-smart phone-users-in-canada (accessed June 15, 2020).

8. "Facebook by the Numbers: Stats, Demographics & Fun Facts," Omni Core website, www .omnicoreagency.com/facebook-statistics (accessed June 15, 2020).

9. Hootsuite website, https://hootsuite.com (accessed June 15, 2020).

10. "Data Visualization: What It Is and Why It Matters," *What It Is and Why Matters | SAS*, www .sas.com/en_us/insights/big-data/data-visualization .html (accessed June 15, 2020).

11. Janko Roettgers, "Google Will Keep Reading Your Emails, Just Not for Ads," *Variety*, June 23, 2017, www.variety.com/2017/digital/news/google-gmail-ads -emails-1202477321 (accessed June 15, 2020).

12. DJ Pangburn, "How-And Why-Apple, Google, and Facebook Follow You Around in Real Life." *Fast Company*, December 22, 2017, www.fastcompany .com/40477441/facebook-google-apple-know-where -you-are (accessed June 15, 2020).

13. Jason Murdock, " Facebook Is Tracking You Even If You Don't Have an Account." *Newsweek*, April 17, 2018, www.newsweek.com /facebook-tracking-you-even-if-you-dont-have -account-888699 (accessed June 15, 2020).

14. Tim Moynihan, "Alexa and Google Home Record What You Say. But What Happens to That Data?" *Wired*, June 3, 2017, www.wired .com/2016/12/alexa-and-google-record-your-voice (accessed June 15, 2020).

15. Katie Lobosco, "Talking Barbie Is Too Creepy for Some Parents." *CNNMoney*, Cable News Network, March 12, 2015, money.cnn.com /2015/03/11/news/companies/creepy-hello-barbie /index.html (accessed June 15, 2020).

16. David Baser, "Hard Questions: What Data Does Facebook Collect When I'm Not Using Facebook, and Why?" *Facebook Newsroom*, April 16, 2018, newsroom.fb.com/news/2018/04 /data-off-facebook (accessed June 15, 2020).

17. Steven Musil, "Facebook Acknowledges It Shared User Data with Dozens of Companies." *CNET*, CNET, July 1, 2018, www.cnet.com/news /facebook-acknowledges-it-shared-user-data-with -dozens-of-companies (accessed June 15, 2020).

18. Mark Bergen and Jennifer Surane, "Google and Mastercard Cut a Secret Ad Deal to Track Retail Sales." *Bloomberg.com*, August 30, 2018, www.bloomberg.com/news/articles/2018-08-30 /google-and-mastercard-cut-a-secret-ad-deal-to -track-retail-sales (accessed June 15, 2020).

19. Scott Berinato, "There's No Such Thing as Anonymous Data." *Harvard Business Review*, July 24, 2015, hbr.org/2015/02/theres-no-such-thing-as -anonymous-data (accessed June 15, 2020).

Chapter 5

1. John Dudovskiy, "Telsa Segmentation, Targeting and Positioning: Overview," Research Methodology website, October 13, 2018, https://research -methodology.net/telsa-segmentation-targeting-and -positioning-overview.

2. Fitbit website, www.fitbit.com/en-ca/shop /versa?color=petal (accessed June 16, 2020).

3. J. Clement, "Social Networking in Canada— Statistics & Facts," Statista website, September 18, 2019, www.statista.com/topics/2729/social -networking-in-canada (accessed June 16, 2020).

4. Ronald Alsop, "The Best Corporate Reputations in America: Johnson & Johnson (Think Babies!) Turns Up Tops," *Wall Street Journal*, September 23, 1999, B1; and Alsop, "Survey Rates Companies' Reputations, and Many Are Found Wanting," *Wall Street Journal*, February 7, 2001, B1.

5. Josh Kolm, "BC Dairy Taps Influencers for Multicultural Campaign," Strategy Online, August 1, 2019, http://strategyonline.ca/2019/08/01/bc -dairy-taps-influencers-for-multicultural-campaign (accessed June 16, 2020).

6. "Klout Alternatives," Finance online website, https://alternatives.financesonline.com/p/klout (accessed July 3, 2020).

7. Josh Kolm, "What Influences Canadian Fashion Shoppers?," *Strategy*, http://strategy online.ca/2019/10/16/what-influences-canadian -shoppers.

8. "Men vs. Women: The Gender Divide of Car Buying," cjponyparts website, www.cjponyparts. com/resources/men-vs-women-car-buying, April 13, 2020 (accessed July 3, 2020).

9. "Gender Marketing: Definition and Implementation," ionos website, www.ionos.ca/digitalguide /online-marketing/online-sales/gender-marketing -definition-and-implementation, September 14, 2017.

10. Marion Chan, "Look Who's Buying Groceries Now," *Canadian Grocer*, July 8, 2015, www .canadiangrocer.com/blog/look-who%E2%80%99s -buying-groceries-now-55466 (accessed June 16, 2020).

11. Josh Kolm, "Holiday Spending Expected to Rise Slightly," Strategy online, October 17, 2019, http://strategyonline.ca/2019/10/17/holiday -spending-expected-to-rise-slightly (accessed June 16, 2020).

12. Nora J. Rifon and Molly Catherine Ziske, "Using Weight Loss Products: The Roles of Involvement, Self-Efficacy and Body Image," in *1995 AMA Educators' Proceedings*, ed. Barbara B. Stern and George M. Zinkhan (Chicago: American Marketing Association, 1995), 90–98.

13. Melissa Dunne, "Home Hardware Paints with AR," Strategy Online, August 1, 2019 https:// strategyonline.ca/2019/08/01/home-hardware -paints-with-ar (accessed July 3, 2020).

14. "Segmentation," Environics Analytics, www .environicsanalytics.com/en-ca/data/segmentation (accessed June 16, 2020).

15. Sarah Hall, "What Color Is Your Cart?" *Self*, September 1999, www.godiva.com (accessed January 2006).

16. Joshua Rosenbaum, "Guitar Maker Looks for a New Key," *Wall Street Journal*, February 11, 1998, B1, B5.

17. Elizabeth J. Wilson, "Using the Dollarmetric Scale to Establish the Just Meaningful Difference in Price," in *1987 AMA Educators' Proceedings*, ed. Susan Douglas et al. (Chicago: American Marketing Association, 1987), 107.

18. Sunil Gupta and Lee G. Cooper, "The Discounting of Discounts and Promotion Thresholds," *Journal of Consumer Research*, December 1992, 401–411.

19. Mark Stiving and Russell S. Winer, "An Empirical Analysis of Price Endings with Scanner Data," *Journal of Consumer Research*, June 1997, 57–67; and Robert M. Schindler and Patrick N. Kirby, "Patterns of Rightmost Digits Used in Advertised Prices: Implications for Nine-Ending Effects," *Journal of Consumer Research*, September 1997, 192–201.

20. Harley Davidson website, www.harley -davidson.com (accessed June 16, 2020).

Chapter 6

1. Alan Collins, "About This Site, My Background & My Confessions About HR," *Success in HR*, https://successinhr.com/about (accessed June 16, 2020).

2. Industry Canada, "Consumer Trends: Chapter 2 —Consumers and Changing Retail Markets," July 27, 2012, www.ic.gc.ca/eic/site/oca-bc.nsf/eng /ca02096.html (accessed February 2017).

3. Kanetix Ltd., "Ready to Plug-In for Lower Insurance Premiums?", January 5, 2018, www .kanetix.ca/resources/ready-to-plug-in-for-lower -insurance-premiums (accessed June 16, 2020).

4. "Shaping the Future of Marketing: B2B," Canadian Marketing Association, www.the-cma .org /disciplines/b2b (accessed February 2017).

5. Robert M. Morgan and Shelby D. Hunt, "The Commitment-Trust Theory of Relationship Marketing," *Journal of Marketing*, 58, 3, 1994, 23.

6. Ibid.

7. Javier Marcos Cuevas, Saara Julkunen, and Mika Gabrielsson, "Power Symmetry and the Development of Trust in Interdependent Relationships: The Mediating Role of Goal Congruence," *Industrial Marketing Management*, 48, July 2015, 149–159, http://dx.doi.org/10.1016/j.indmarman .2015.03.015.

8. IE Executive Education, "The End of Interruption—Why Interruption Is an Outdated Marketing Strategy," July 5, 2018, www.ie.edu /exponential-learning/news-events/news/end -interruption-interruption-outdated-marketing -strategy (accessed June 16, 2020).

9. "About the IMP Group," Industrial Marketing and Purchasing Group, www.impgroup.org/about .php (accessed February 2017).

10. Hans Greimel, "Toyota Leans on Denso in Keiretsu Comeback," *Automotive News*, www.autonews.com/article/20180910/OEM 10/180919956/toyota-leans-on-denso-in-keiretsu -comeback (accessed June 16, 2020).

11. Scott C. Hammond and Lowell M. Glenn, "The Ancient Practice of Chinese Social Networking: Guanxi and Social Network Theory," June 30, 2004, https://journal.emergentpublications.com/article /the-ancient-practice-of-chinese-social-networking -guanxi-and-social-network-theory (accessed July 3, 2020).

12. Ben Foldy, "As GM Strike Stretches On, Supply Chain Starts to Suffer," *The Wall Street Journal*, September 19, 2019, www.wsj.com/articles /as-gm-strike-stretches-on-supply-chain-starts-to -suffer-11568931201 (accessed June 16, 2020).

13. Lin Ai and Michael Burt, "Walking the Silk Road: Understanding Canada's Changing Trade Patterns," The Conference Board of Canada, December 2012, www.conferenceboard.ca/e -library/abstract.aspx?did=5266 (accessed February 2017).

14. Industry Canada, "Summary—Canadian Industry Statistics," March 11, 2020, www.ic.gc.ca /app/scr/app/cis/summary-sommaire/41(accessed January 2020).

15. Buy and Sell, "Goods and Services," February 4, 2020, https://buyandsell.gc.ca/goods-and-services (accessed June 16, 2020).

16. Statistics Canada, "Table 2—Employment by Class of Worker and Industry, Seasonally Adjusted," www150.statcan.gc.ca/n1/daily-quotidien/191206 /t002a-eng.htm (accessed June 16, 2020).

17. Matevž Rašković and Barbara Mörec, "Determinants of Supplier-Buyer Relationship Competitiveness in Transnational Companies," *Economic and Business Review*, 15 (1), 2013, 5–31, www.ebrjournal.net/ojs/index.php/ebr/article /download/211/pdf (accessed February 2017).

18. Canadian Internet Registration Authority, "2019—Canada's Internet Factbook," https://cira .ca/resources/corporate/factbook/canadas-internet -factbook-2019 (accessed June 16, 2020).

19. Ibid.

20. Business Development Bank of Canada, "Strong Online Presence Drives Growth: BDC Study," July 9, 2019, www.bdc.ca/en/about/mediaroom/news _releases/pages/strong-online-presence-drives -growth.aspx (accessed June 16, 2020).

21. Isabelle Kirkwood, "Report: Cybersecurity Is the Achilles' Heel of Canadian Tech Businesses,"*Betakit Incorporated*, February 6, 2019, https://betakit.com/report-cybersecurity -is-the-achilles-heel-of-canadian-tech-businesses/ (accessed June 16, 2020).

22. Canadian Radio-television and Telecommunications Commission, "Communications Monitoring Report 2019," https://crtc.gc.ca/pubs/cmr2019-en .pdf (accessed June 16, 2020).

23. Content Marketing Institute, "B2B Content Marketing 2020," https://contentmarketinginstitute .com/wp-content/uploads/2019/10/2020_B2B _Research_Final.pdf (accessed June 16, 2020).

24. Doug Camplejohn, "The Best Ways to Use Social Media to Expand Your Network," *Harvard Business Review*, March 7, 2019, https://hbr.org /2019/03/the-best-ways-to-use-social-media-to -expand-your-network (accessed June 16, 2020).

25. IronPaper, "How Effective Is Linkedin for B2B Marketing? These 20 Stats Say it All," March 13, 2018, www.ironpaper.com/webintel/articles/how -effective-is-linkedin-for-b2b-marketing-these -20-stats-say-it-all (accessed June 16, 2020).

Chapter 7

1. Brainy Quotes, "Warren Buffett Quotes," www.brainyquote.com/quotes/warren_buffett _385064 (accessed July 6, 2020).

2. The Coca-Cola Company, Coca-Cola, www.coca -cola.ca/homepage (accessed June 22, 2020).

3. Canada Goose Inc., https://canadagoose.com (accessed June 22, 2020).

4. "Case Studies: Manufacturing Case Study: Arc'teryx," Environics Analytics, www.environicsan alytics.ca/arc'teryx (accessed January 14, 2017).

5. Josh Kolm, "Walmart Opens New Urban Supercentre Concept," *Strategy Online*, May 30, 2019, http://strategyonline.ca/2019/05/30/walmart -opens-new-urban-supercentre-concept (accessed June 22, 2020).

6. CrossFit, Inc., "Crossfit Kids Certificate Course," www.crossfit.com/certificate=course/kids (accessed June 22, 2020).

7. Statistics Canada, "Census Profile, 2016 Census," August 9, 2019, www12.statcan.gc.ca

/census-recensement/2016/dp-pd/prof/details/page.cfm?Lang=E&Geo1=PR&Code1=01&Geo2=&Code2=&SearchText=Canada&SearchType=Begins&SearchPR=01&B1=All&TABID=1&type=0 (accessed June 22, 2020).

8. MarketResearch.com, "Generation Z as Future Customers, Forecast to 2027," June 22, 2020, www.marketresearch.com/Frost-Sullivan-v383/Generation-Future-Customers-Forecast-12220876 (accessed January 17, 2020).

9. The Nielsen Company, "Millennials on Millennials: Why We Matter," May 14, 2018, www.nielsen.com/ca/en/insights/report/2018/millennials-on-millennials (accessed June 22, 2020).

10. David Parkinson, Janet McFarland, and Barrie McKenna, "Boom, Bust and Economic Headaches," *The Globe and Mail*, January 5, 2017, www.theglobeandmail.com/globe-investor/retirement/the-boomer-shift-how-canadas-economy-is-headed-for-majorchange/article27159892 (accessed June 22, 2020).

11. Statistics Canada, "Seniors Online," Catalog No. 978-0-660-30335-2, April 15, 2019, www150.statcan.gc.ca/n1/en/pub/11-627-m/11-627-m2019024-eng.pdf?st=_ss9BnCN (accessed June 22, 2020).

12. Kristyn Anthony, "Are Brands Ready for a Gender-Fluid Future?," *Strategy Online*, January 7, 2020, http://strategyonline.ca/2020/01/07/are-brands-ready-for-a-gender-fluid-future (accessed June 22, 2020).

13. Stephanie Hirschmiller, "Why Millennial Men Don't Shop Like Previous Generations," *Footwear News*, July 5, 2019, https://footwearnews.com/2019/business/features/men-shopping-behavior-internet-sustainability-1202786224 (accessed February 2020).

14. Statistics Canada, "Estimates of the Number of Census Families as of July 1st," April 30, 2020, https://www150.statcan.gc.ca/t1/tbl1/en/tv.action?pid=1710006101 (accessed June 22, 2020).

15. PepsiCo, Inc., Aquafina, www.aquafina.com/en-us/our-products.html#flavor-splash (accessed June 22, 2020).

16. "The Evolving Canadian Population," Environics Analytics, July 7, 2016, www.environicsanalytics.ca/footer/news/2016/07/07/the-evolving-canadian-population (accessed January 17, 2017).

17. PRIZM5: Marketer's Handbook, Environics Analytics, www.environicsanalytics.ca/prizm5 (accessed January 24, 2020).

18. Product2Market, "Benefit Segmentation Examples," https://product2market.walkme.com/benefit-segmentation-examples (accessed June 22, 2020).

19. Gene Marks, "What's the Rush? A Grocery Chain Starts a Check-out Line for People Who Want to Take It Slow," *Washington Post*, February 23, 2017, www.washingtonpost.com/news/on-small-business/wp/2017/02/23/whats-the-rush-a-grocery-chain-starts-a-check-out-line-for-people-who-want-to-take-it-slow (accessed June 22, 2020).

20. Christopher Lombardo, "Sobeys Rolls Out Sensory-Friendly Shopping Nationally," *Strategy Online*, December 4, 2019, http://strategyonline.ca/2019/12/04/sobeys-rolls-out-sensory-friendly-shopping-nationally (accessed June 22, 2020).

21. Justin Dallaire, "What's Behinds Gap's Woes?," *Strategy Online*, January 21, 2020, http://strategyonline.ca/2020/01/21/whats-behind-gaps-woes (accessed June 22, 2020).

22. Infinit Nutrition, "My Custom Fuel Blend," www.infinitnutrition.us/create-a-formula (accessed June 22, 2020).

23. Justin Dallaire, "BMW Dresses Up Luxury Real Estate," Strategy Online, August 2, 2019, http://strategyonline.ca/2019/08/02/bmw-dresses-up-luxury-real-estate (accessed June 22, 2020).

24. The Clorox Company, Green Works, https://greenworkscleaners.com (accessed June 22, 2020).

25. Hudson's Bay Company, www3.hbc.com (accessed June 22, 2020).

26. HelloFresh, www.hellofresh.ca (accessed June 22, 2020).

27. Brunico Communications Ltd., "Snap it With Pepsi," Shopper Innovation + Activation Award website, https://shopperinnovationawards.strategyonline.ca/winners/winner/2018/?e=56320&w=Snap+it+with+Pepsi (accessed June 22, 2020).

28. Justin Dallaire, "Check It Out: Nike's Church of Basketball," *Strategy Online*, August 23, 2018, http://strategyonline.ca/2018/08/23/check-it-out-nikes-church-of-basketball (accessed June 22, 2020).

29. Daniel Calabretta, "McDonald's Restarts Debate About the Big Mac Bacon," Strategy Online, January 21, 2020, http://strategyonline.ca/2020/01/21/mcdonalds-restarts-the-debate-about-the-big-mac-bacon (accessed June 22, 2020).

30. Susan Gunelius, "Kia Rolls out Brand Repositioning Ad Campaign," Corporate Eye, January 9, 2015, www.corporate-eye.com/main/kia-rolls-out-brand-repositioning-ad-campaign (accessed June 22, 2020).

31. Alice Tybout and Brian Sternthal, "Brand Positioning," in *Kellogg on Branding: The Marketing Faculty of the Kellogg School of Management*, ed. Tim Calkins et al. (Hoboken, NJ: John Wiley & Sons, Inc., 2005).

32. Ibid.

Chapter 8

1. Statalytics, "Amazon & Customer Experience: 13 Quotes from Jeff Bezos," November 6, 2016, https://www.satalytics.com/jeff-bezos (accessed June 16, 2020).

2. Darrell K. Rigby and Dianne Ledingham, "CRM Done Right," *Harvard Business Review*, November 2004, 2, https://hbr.org/2004/11/crm-done-right (accessed July 3, 2020).

3. Adrian Payne and Pennie Frow, "A Strategic Framework for Customer Relationship Management," *Journal of Marketing*, 69, 2005, 167–176, http://ns2.academicroom.com/sites/default/files/article/118/files_articles_Strategic%20Framework%20for%20Customer%20Relationship%20Management.pdf (accessed December 2019).

4. OnDemand5.com, www.ondemand5.com (accessed December 2019).

5. Gabriel Swain, "14 Mind-Blowing Statistics That Prove the Need for a CRM," *Agile CRM*, February 28, 2019, www.agilecrm.com/blog/statistics-that-prove-the-need-for-a-crm (accessed December 2019)

6. Jeff Sweat, "Keep 'Em Happy," *Internet Week.com*, January 28, 2002.

7. Sony PlayStation, www.playstation.com/en-ca, and "SAP Customer Success Story: Playstation.com Chooses mySAP CRM," http://h71028.www7.hp.com/enterprise/downloads/playstation.pdf (accessed August 3, 2011).

8. Tom Drake, "What Every Student Needs to Know About the SPC Card," *Drake Money Inc.*, July 4, 2019, https://maplemoney.com/spc-card (accessed June 16, 2020).

9. SPC, "Get the Card," www.spccard.ca/about.aspx (accessed August 31, 2011).

10. CBC/Radio Canada, "Potential Scope of Desjardins Data Breach Widens to Include Another 2 Million Credit Card Holders," December 10, 2019, www.cbc.ca/news/canada/montreal/potential-scope-of-desjardins-data-breach-widens-to-include-another-2-million-credit-card-holders-1.5391021 (accessed June 16, 2020).

11. Random House, *Random House Webster's Unabridged Dictionary*, 2nd ed. (New York: Random House Reference, 2005).

12. "Database Software Markets: Worldwide Overview & Outlook, 2015–2030; Major Players Are Oracle, Microsoft, IBM, SAP & Amazon," November 12, 2019, https://newsfilter.io/articles/database-software-markets-worldwide-overview--outlook-2015-2030---major-players-are-oracle-microsoft-ibm-sap--amazon-3144c97eb6b73164db2e0d93e4972725 (accessed June 16, 2020).

13. Susan Fournier and Jill Avery, "Putting the 'Relationship' Back into CRM," *MIT Sloan Management Review*, March 23, 2011, http://sloanreview.mit.edu/article/putting-the-relationship-back-into-CRM (accessed August 5, 2014).

14. Bond Brand Loyalty, "Redux: The New Story of Loyalty," *The Loyalty Report*, 2019, https://cdn2.hubspot.net/hubfs/352767/TLR%202019/Bond_CAN_TLR19_Exec%20Summary_Launch%20Edition.pdf (accessed June 16, 2020).

15. Ibid.

16. Ibid.

17. "Ingersoll-Rand Company Limited Maximizes Customer Focus with Expanded CRM Capabilities," Oracle, June 2006, www.ediguys.net/pages/SCIS/ingersoll-rand-siebel-casestudy.pdf (accessed August 5, 2014); and Darrell K. Rigby and Dianne Ledingham, "CRM Done Right," *Harvard Business Review*, November 2004, 2, https://hbr.org/2004/11/CRM-done-right (accessed August 5, 2014).

18. Mario Toneguzzi, "Indigenous Footwear Brand 'Manitobah Mukluks' Launches Aggressive Canadian Retail Store Strategy," *Retail Insider*, October 24, 2019, www.retail-insider.com/retail-insider/2019/10/manitobah-mukluks-canada-retail-expansion (accessed June 16, 2020).

19. Clara Shih, "Customer Relationship Automation Is the New CRM," *Harvard Business Review*, October 28, 2016, https://hbr.org/2016/10/customer-relationship-automation-is-the-new-CRM (accessed November 23, 2016).

20. Geoff Williams, "On-Demand Services That Can Make Your Life Easier," *U.S. News and World Report*, June 26, 2015, http://money.usnews.com/money/personal-finance/articles/2015/06/26/5-on-demand-services-that-can-make-your-life-easier (accessed February 9, 2017).

Chapter 9

1. Gerald C. Lubenow, "Job Talks about His Rise and Fall," *Newsweek*, September 29, 1985, www.newsweek.com/jobs-talks-about-his-rise-and-fall-207016 (accessed June 16, 2020).

2. "Life on the Digital Edge," Accenture, 2014, www.accenture.com/t20150523T040714__w__/us-en/_acnmedia/Accenture/Conversion-Assets/Microsites/Documents14/Accenture-Augmented-Reality-Customer-Experience-Drive-Growth.pdf, 6.

3. Todd Wasserman, "P&G Tries to Absorb More Low-End Sales," *BrandWeek*, September 26, 2005, 4.

4. Todd Wasserman, "P&G Seeks Right Ingredient to Wash Out Laundry Woes," *BrandWeek*, August 8, 2005, 5.

5. Amelia Tait, "How Aggressively Cute Toys for Adults Became a $686 Million Business,"

Voxmedia, August 13, 2019, www.vox.com/the -goods/2019/8/13/20798910/funko-pop-vinyl -figurines-collectibles (accessed June 16, 2020).

6. Janet Adamy, "Heinz Sets Overhaul Plans in Motion," *Wall Street Journal*, September 20, 2005, A4.

7. "Dictionary," American Marketing Association, www.marketingpower.com/_layouts/dictionary .aspx?dLetter=B (accessed March 2017).

8. Brad VanAuken, "What Is a Global Brand?" *Branding Strategy Insider*, February 19, 2010, www.brandingstrategyinsider.com/2010/02/what-is -a-global-brand.html#.WMLSGhgZNok (accessed March 2017).

9. "Nielsen: Store Brand Consumers Evolving in Canada," www.pgstorebrands.com/top -story -nielsen__store_brand_consumers _evolving_in _canada-7010.html (accessed March 2017).

10. Rebecca Harris, "The Rising Power of Private Label," *Canadian Grocer*, July 11, 2018, www .canadiangrocer.com/worth-reading/the-rising -power-of-private-label-81826 (accessed June 16, 2020).

11. Claus Enevoldsen, "Marketing Case Study: How Airbnb and Flipboard Teamed Up to Introduce Experiences," *Flipboard*, March 30, 2017, https://about .flipboard.com/business/marketing-case_study-airbnb -and-flipboard (accessed June 16, 2020).

12. Omar El Akkad, "Canadian Court Clears Way to Trademark Sounds," *Globe and Mail*, March 28, 2012, www.theglobeandmail.com/globe-investor /canadian-court-clears-way-to-trademark-sounds /article4096387 (accessed March 2017).

13. Lauren Feiner, "Amazon Is Tackling Its Counterfeit Problem by Letting Brands Delete Knockoffs Themselves," *CNBC*, February 28, 2019, www.cnbc.com/2019/02/28/amazon-announces -project-zero-to-reduce-counterfeit-products.html (accessed June 16, 2020).

14. Deborah Ball, "The Perils of Packaging: Nestlé Aims for Easier Openings," *Wall Street Journal*, November 17, 2005, B1.

15. Ilario Grasso Macola, "Hellmann's Canada Commits to Using 100% Recyclable Packaging," *Packaging Gateway*, February 5, 2020, www .packaging-gateway.com/news/hellmanns-canada -commits-to-using-100-recyclable-packaging/ (accessed June 16, 2020).

16. Shane Fowler, "'Shameful': Cannabis Customers Floored by the Amount of Plastic Packing on Their Pot," *CBC/Radio-Canada*, October 22, 2018, www.cbc.ca/news/canada/new-brunswick /cannabis-packaging-excess-1.4870682 (accessed June 16, 2020).

17. Peter J. Schmitt, "Future Cannabis Industry Leaders Will Focus on Sustainability and Social Impact," *GreenEntrepreneur*, February 5, 2020, www.greenentrepreneur.com/article/345097 (accessed June 16, 2020).

18. Government of Canada, Competition Bureau, "Guide to the *Consumer Packaging and Labelling* Act," www.competitionbureau.gc.ca/eic/site/cb-bc .nsf/eng/01248.html.

19. The Canadian Press, "Kraft Heinz Acknowledges 'Mayochup' Can Have Very Different Meaning," *Global News*, May 19, 2019, https://globalnews.ca/news/5294292/mayochup -cree-translation (accessed June 16, 2020).

Chapter 10

1. "36_James Dyson," *Fast Company*, September 24, 2003, www.fastcompany.com/3019288/36james -dyson (accessed June 16, 2020).

2. Josh Kolm, "What Are Canadians' Favourite New Products?," *Strategy*, February 6, 2019, https://strategyonline.ca/2019/02/06/what-are -canadians-favourite-new-products (accessed June 16, 2020).

3. "Every 2 Minutes, a New Product Is Launched to the U.S. Marketplace; Here Are the Products That Broke Through the Noise and Redefined Innovation in 2019," *The Nielsen Company*, December 3, 2019, www.nielsen.com/us/en /press-releases/2019/every-2-minutes-a-new -product-is-launched-to-the-u-s-marketplace -here-are-the-products-that-broke-through-the -noise-and-redefined-innovation-in-2019 (accessed June 16, 2020).

4. "The Most Innovative Companies 2019," *Boston Consulting Group*, March 21, 2019, www.bcg.com /en-us/publications/collections/most-innovative -companies-2019-artificial-intelligence-platforms -ecosystems.aspx (accessed June 16, 2020).

5. "The World's Most Innovative Companies," *Forbes Media*, www.forbes.com/innovative -companies/list/#tab:rank (accessed June 16, 2020).

6. Tracey Lindeman, "16 Amazing Things Invented by Canadians," CBC, www.cbc.ca/television/16 -amazing-things-invented-by-canadians-1.4195223 (accessed July 8, 2020).

7. Justin Dallaire, "Tim Hortons Expands Retail Product Lineup," *Strategy*, February 6, 2019, https://strategyonline.ca/2019/02/06/tim-hortons -expands-retail-product-lineup (accessed June 16, 2020).

8. "The 2019 Best New Product Awards," *Canadian Living*, www.canadianliving.com/life-and -relationships/community-and-current-events /feature/the-2019-best-new-product-awards (accessed June 16, 2020).

9. "SYLVANIA Natural Series with TruWave Technology to Deliver Best Alternative to Natural Light," *The Associated Press*, February 10, 2020, https://apnews.com/Business%20Wire/cf96d84fe3ff 4750a2e10a146ca23b88 (accessed June 16, 2020).

10. Video Doorbell webpage, *Ring*, https://shop .ring.com/collections/doorbell-cameras?medium =tsa&gclid=CjwKCAiAvonyBRB7EiwAadauqa ZTNCI2NnAKSTspgBGagZEh5kAP49gTV9 MnPxMY5So_qAqJvnUfmhoCF8MQAvD_Bw E&gclsrc=aw.ds&?cb= (accessed June 16, 2020).

11. Darrell Etherington, "Apple's New Product Strategy," Crunch Network, May 30, 2013, https:// techcrunch.com/2013/05/30/apples-new-product -strategy (accessed June 16, 2020).

12. Kris Carlon, "LG's New Product Strategy: Unnecessary or Inevitable?," *Android Authority*, March 1, 2018, www.androidauthority.com /lg-product-strategy-842091 (accessed June 16, 2020).

13. Gary Fraser and Bryan Mattimor, "Slow Down, Speed Up New Product Growth," *Brandweek*, January 11, 2005, 18.

14. Dennis Beers, "Dewalt and Its Customer-Driven Innovation," Consumer Value Creation, March 4, 2017, https://consumervaluecreation .com/2017/03/04/dewalt-and-its-customer-driven -innovation (accessed June 16, 2020).

15. Alden Wicker, "Fashion Brands Turn to Hackathons to Crack Sustainability Strategies," *Vogue Business*, February 11, 2020, www.voguebusiness .com/technology/fashion-brands-turn-to-hackathons -to-crack-sustainability-strategies-lvmh-moncler -kering-prada-group (accessed June 16, 2020).

16. Sellers, "P&G: Teaching an Old Dog New Tricks," 174.

17. Chris Penttila, "Keeping It Fresh," *Entrepreneur*, April 2005, 88.

18. Trade Commissioner Service, "Canada's Innovation Strengths and Priorities," November 21, 2019, www.tradecommissioner.gc.ca/innovators -innovateurs/strategies.aspx?lang=eng (accessed June 16, 2020).

19. Ibid.

20. Shara Tibken, "Apple Invests $250 Million in Corning for Future iphone Glass Research," *CNET*, September 17, 2019, www.cnet.com/news/apple -invests-250-million-in-corning-for-future-iphone -glass-research (accessed June 16, 2020).

21. Patrick Lucas Austin, "The Real Reason Google Is Buying Fitbit," *TIME*, November 4, 2019, https://time.com/5717726/google-fitbit (accessed June 16, 2020).

22. Scott Mautz, "3 Actions That Tip the Scales and Move You From Failure to Success," *Inc.*, January 1, 2020, www.inc.com/scott-mautz/3-actions-that -tip-scales-move-you-from-failure-to-success.html (accessed June 16, 2020).

23. SPharm Canada, "The Drug Review and Approval Process in Canada," https://spharm-inc .com/the-drug-review-and-approval-process-in -canada-an-eguide (accessed June 16, 2020).

24. Stacey Nguyen, "The 7 Best Crowdfunding Sites of 2020," *The Balance Small Business*, November 20, 2019, www.thebalancesmb.com/best-crowdfunding -sites-4580494 (accessed June 16, 2020).

25. Lasse Skovgaard Jense and Ali Gürcan Özkil, "Identifying Challenges in Crowdfunded Product Development: A Review of Kickstarter Projects," *Design Science*, Cambridge University Press, 2018, www.cambridge.org/core/services/aop -cambridge-core/content/view/F2659234936 B8349EAF5AFCFBA2199E8/S2053470118 000148a.pdf/identifying_challenges_in_crowd funded_product_development_a_review_of _kickstarter_projects.pdf (accessed June 16, 2020).

26. McDonald's Corporation Newsroom, "McDonald's Tests New Plant-Based Burger in Canada," September 26, 2019, https://news .mcdonalds.com/news-releases/news-release -details/mcdonalds-tests-new-plant-based-burger -canada-plt (accessed June 16, 2020).

27. Barrett J. Brunsman, "P&G to Test Market Refillable Skin Care Packaging to Cut Plastic Waste," *Cincinnati Business Courier*, June 5, 2019, www.bizjournals.com/cincinnati/news/2019/06/05/ p-g-to-test-market-refillable-skin-care-packaging .html (accessed June 16, 2020).

28. Hannah Fleishman, "13 Businesses with Brilliant Global Marketing Strategies," *Hubspot*, January 22, 2019, https://blog.hubspot.com /marketing/global-marketing-and-international -business (accessed June 16, 2020).

29. Amanda Bourlier, "Getting to Know the Early Adopters," *Canadian Grocer*, January 11, 2019, www.canadiangrocer.com/top-stories/getting-to -know-the-early-adopters-84969 (accessed June 16, 2020).

30. Kevin J. Clancy and Peter C. Krieg, "Product Life Cycle: A Dangerous Idea," *Brandweek*, March 1, 2004, 26.

31. James Daly, "Restart, Redo, Recharge," *Business 2.0*, May 1, 2001, 11.

Chapter 11

1. BrainyQuote, "Steve Jobs Quotes," www. brainyquote.com/quotes/steve_jobs_737723 (accessed July 6, 2020).

2. Statistics Canada, "Employment by Industry, Monthly, Unadjusted for Seasonality," www150. statcan.gc.ca/t1/tbl1/en/tv.action?pid=1410020101 (accessed June 19, 2020).

3. Statistics Canada, Gross Domestic Product (GDP) at Basic Prices, by Industry, Monthly (×1,000,000) www150.statcan.gc.ca/t1/tbl1/en /tv.action?pid=3610043401 (accessed June 19, 2020).

4. Dinah Eng, "Building Great Service at the Four Seasons," Research Gate, April 1, 2016, www .researchgate.net/publications/301583992_Building _Great_Service_at_the_Four-Seasons (accessed April 28, 2017); Micah Solomon, "Four Seasons' Customer Service: Consulting the Systems Behind the Click of a Hotel Door," Forbes, www.forbes .com/sites/micahsolomon/213/11/17/secret _shopping_four_seasons (accessed August 5, 2019).

5. Saje company website, www.saje.ca (accessed August 5, 2019).

6. Valarie Zeithaml, Mary Jo Bitner, and Dwayne D. Gremler, Services Marketing: Integrating Customer Focus across the Firm, 4th edition (New York; McGraw-Hill, 2006).

7. S. Lock, "Online Travel Market—Statistics & Facts," Statista.com, https:/www.statista.com /topics/2074/online-travel-market (accessed July 3, 2018).

8. Dwayne Gremler, Mary Jo Bitner, and Valarie Zeithaml, Services Marketing (New York; McGraw Hill, 2012).

9. Zeithalm, Bitner, and Gremler. Services Marketing: Integrating Customer Focus Across the Firm.

10. Much of the material in this section is based on Christopher H. Lovelock and Jochen Wirtz, Services Marketing, 5th edition (Upper Saddle River NJ: Prentice Hall, 2004).

11. "Top Six Ways to Customize Your Favourite Starbucks Drink," Starbucks, https://stories .starbucks.ca/en/stories/2019/top-six-ways-to -customize-your-favourite-starbucks-drink (accessed June 19, 2020).

12. Lovelock and Wirtz, Services Marketing.

13. Jochen Wirtz and Christopher H. Lovelock, Services Marketing: People, Technology and Strategy, 8th Edition (Upper Saddle River, NJ: Prentice Hall, 2016).

14. Iris Kuo, "How to Keep Them Coming Back," Inc., April 2016, 80–81.

15. Ibid.

16. Much of the material in this section is based on Dwayne Gremler, Mary Jo Bitner, and Valarie Zeithamel, Services Marketing (New York: McGraw Hill), 2012.

17. "Sector Impact," Imagine Canada, http ://sectorsource.ca/research-and-impact/sector -impact (accessed June 19, 2020).

18. Ibid.

19. Amyann Cadwell, "What Is a Social Enterprise? Simple Definition and Three Examples," The Good Trade, www.thegoodtrade.com/features/what-is-a -social-enterprise (accessed June 19, 2020).

20. At the Table website, www.atthetablecatering. com/about (accessed June 19, 2020).

Chapter 12

1. Warren Buffett, Letter to Berkshire Hathaway Shareholders, February 27, 2009, www.berkshire hathaway.com/letters/2008ltr.pdf (accessed August 14, 2017).

2. Tentree website, www.tentree.ca (accessed June 17, 2020).

3. Justin Dallaire, "How Beverage Alcohol Brands Can Tap Millennial Sobriety," strategy online, November 5, 2019, strategyonline.ca/2019/11/05 /how-beverage-alcohol-brands-can-tap-millennial -sobriety (accessed June 17, 2020); Lucie Couillard, "Breweries in Canada," IBISWorld Industry Report 31212CA, October 2019www.ibisworld.ca/reports /reportdownload.aspx?cid=124&rtid=101 (accessed June 17, 2020).

4. Nielsen website, www.nielsen.com/ca/en (accessed June 17, 2020); Information Resources Inc. website, www.iriworldwide.com/en-CA (accessed June 17, 2020).

5. Thomas T. Nagle and George Cressman, "Don't Just Set Prices, Manage Them," Marketing Management, November/December 2002, 29–33; Jay Klompmaker, William H. Rogers, and Anthony Nygren, "Value, Not Volume," Marketing Management, June 2003, 45–48; and Alison Wellner, "Boost Your Bottom Line by Taking the Guesswork Out of Pricing," Inc., June 2005, 72–82.

6. Dollarama website, www.dollarama.com (accessed June 17, 2020); "Out-Discounting the Discounter," BusinessWeek, May 9, 2004, 78–79; an interesting article on shoppers who use penetration pricing to their advantage is Edward J. Fox and Stephen J. Hoch, "Cherry-Picking," Journal of Marketing, 69, 1, 2005, 46–62.

7. Bruce Alford and Abhijit Biswas, "The Effects of Discount Level, Price Consciousness, and Sale Proneness on Consumers' Price Perception and Behavioral Intention," Journal of Business Research, September 2002, 775–783. See also V. Kumar, Vibhas Madan, and Srini Srinivasan, "Price Discounts or Coupon Promotions: Does It Matter?," Journal of Business Research, September 2004, 933–941.

8. Hollie Shaw, "Why Walmart and Costco Keep Stealing Market Share from Canada's Grocery Giants," Financial Post, May 7, 2018, business .financialpost.com/news/retail-marketing/why -walmart-and-costco-keep-stealing-market-share -from-domestic-giants-loblaw-metro-and-sobeys (accessed June 17, 2020).

9. David Bell, Ganesh Iyer, and V. Padmanabhar, "Price Competition under Stockpiling and Flexible Consumption," Journal of Marketing Research, 49, 2002, 292–303.

10. "Hudson's Bay Co to Pay $4.5 Million to Close Deceptive Pricing Probe: Competition Bureau," May 8, 2019, Financial Post, business.financialpost. com/news/retail-marketing/hbc-to-pay-4-5m-to -close-deceptive-pricing-probe-competition-bureau (accessed June 17, 2020); Danial Hnatchuk, "The Competition Bureau Applies Strict Standards to Retail Price Claims in Canada," smartbigger website, March 13, 2017, www.smartbiggar.ca /insights/publication/the-competition-bureau -applies-strict-standards-to-retail-price-claims -in-canada (accessed June 17, 2020).

11. "Price Fixing," Government of Canada website, February 22, 2018, www.smartbiggar.ca/insights /publication/the-competition-bureau-applies-strict -standards-to-retail-price-claims-in-canada (accessed June 17, 2020); Aleksandra Sagan, "Bakers, Grocers Involved in 16-year Price-Fixing Conspiracy: Competition Bureau," CTV News website, January 31, 2018, www.ctvnews.ca /canada/bakers-grocers-involved-in-16-year-price -fixing-conspiracy-competition-bureau-1.3783528 (accessed June 17, 2020); James Brander, "Is Price Fixing a Major Problem in Canada?" Maclean's, January 2, 2018, www.macleans.ca/opinion/is-price -fixing-a-major-problem-in-canada (accessed June 17, 2020).

12. Eric Atkins, "Rival Accuses WestJet Discount Airline Swoop of Predatory Pricing with $1 Fares," The Globe and Mail, January 23, 2020, www.theglobeandmail.com/business/article-flair -airlines-accuses-westjet-discount-airline-swoop -of-predatory; "Why Predatory Pricing in Canada's Airline Industry Must Stop," Red Deer Advocate, February 15, 2019, www.reddeeradvocate.com /opinion/why-predatory-pricing-in-canadas-airline -industry-must-stop (accessed June 17, 2020).

Chapter 13

1. AdExchanger, "Content Is King, Distribution Is Queen and She Wears the Pants," November 12, 2013, www.adexchanger.com/data-driven-thinking /content-is-king-distribution-is-queen-and-she -wears-the-pants (accessed June 19, 2020).

2. "Meet Canada's Fastest-Growing Wholesale & Distribution Companies: 2019 Growth 500," Canadian Business, September 12, 2019, www .canadianbusiness.com/lists-and-rankings/growth -500/2019-wholesale-distribution-fastest-growing -companies (accessed June 19, 2020).

3. Ibid.

4. "Supply Chain Management Association becomes Supply Chain Canada," Canadian Manufacturing, September 13, 2019, www .canadianmanufacturing.com/supply-chain/supply -chain-management-association-becomes-supply -chain-canada-238741 (accessed June 19, 2020).

5. Ibid.

6. Westrow Food Group website. https://www .westrow.com/ (accessed December 2019)

7. Nicole Harris, "'Private Exchanges' May Allow B-to-B Commerce to Thrive after All," Wall Street Journal, March 16, 2001, B1; Michael Totty, "The Next Phase," Wall Street Journal, May 21, 2001, R8.

8. The Associated Press, "Nestle Takes Over Sales of Starbucks in Grocery Aisles," CTV News, May 7, 2018, www.ctvnews.ca/business/nestle -takes-over-sales-of-starbucks-in-grocery -aisles-1.3918038 (accessed June 19, 2020).

9. Corinne Gretler, "Nestle Sees $250 Million Boost for Starbucks Products," Bloomberg, November 19, 2019, www.bloomberg.com/news /articles/2019-11-19/nestle-sees-250-million-sales -boost-for-starbucks-products (accessed June 19, 2020).

10. "The Wackiest Vending Machines in the World," CBC/Radio-Canada, January 24, 2019, www.cbc.ca/radio/undertheinfluence/the-wackiest -vending-machines-in-the-world-1.4990661 (accessed June 19, 2020).

11. "About Brokerhouse," Brokerhouse Distributors Inc., www.brokerhousedist.com/About.aspx (accessed February 2017).

12. Statistics Canada, "Farms Reporting Selling Agricultural Products Directly to Consumers in the Year Prior to the Census," May 1, 2020, www150 .statcan.gc.ca/t1/tbl1/en/tv.action?pid=3210044701 (accessed June 19, 2020).

13. Peter J. Thompson, "Dollarama Beats Expectations with 5.3% Rise in Sales," Financial Post, https://business.financialpost.com/news/retail -marketing/canadas-dollarama-beats-quarterly -same-store-sales-estimates (accessed June 19, 2020).

14. Canada Goose Inc., "Our History," www. canadagoose.com/ca/en/our-history.html (accessed June 19, 2020).

15. Loblaw Companies Limited, "About Us," www .loblaw.ca/en/about-us.html (accessed June 19, 2020).

16. Marina Strauss and Jacquie McNish, "Chapters, Indigo agree to Put 23 Stores on Block," The Globe and Mail, April 11, 2018, www.theglobeand-mail.com/report-on-business/chapters-indigo-agree-to-put-23-stores-on-block/article1179369 (accessed June 19, 2020).

17. Indigo, "FAQ for Book Publishers," www
.chapters.indigo.ca/en-ca/book-publishers-faq
(accessed June 19, 2020).

18. Competition Bureau Canada, "Price
Maintenance," February 22, 2018, www
.competitionbureau.gc.ca/eic/site/cb-bc.nsf
/eng/h_03210.html (accessed June 19, 2020).

19. Nora Manthey, "EU: Ionity Now Runs Over
150 High Power Charging Sites," Electrive.com,
October 13, 2019, www.electrive.com/2019/10/13
/eu-ionity-now-runs-over-150-high-power-charging
-sites (accessed June 19, 2020).

20. Jonathan Welsh, "Auto Makers Now 'Slam'
Cars Right in the Factory," *Wall Street Journal*,
October 30, 2001, B1.

21. Kati Chitrakorn, "Mango Is Building a Faster
Fashion Brand," *Vogue Business*, December 4,
2019, www.voguebusiness.com/consumers/spanish
-label-mango-approach-to-fast-fashion (accessed
June 19, 2020).

22. Maryam Cockar, "Zara Owner Posts Higher
Annual Revenue and Profits," *Independent*,
March, 13, 2019, www.independent.ie/world-news
/zara-owner-posts-higher-annual-revenue-and
-profits-37908654.html (accessed June 19, 2020).

23. Align Technology, Inc., "The Company Behind
the Smile," www.aligntech.com/about (accessed
June 19, 2020).

24. Barbara Thau, "Make It Yourself; Lowe's Tests
Profit Potential of 3D Printed, Personalized Products," *Forbes*, September 8, 2016.

25. Guy Routledge, "3D Printing Food for an
Entire Restaurant Menu," The Food Rush, April
27, 2016, www.thefoodrush.com/blog/3d-printing
-food-for-an-entire-restaurant-menu (accessed
March 14, 2017); "Home," 3DLT, www.3dlt.com
(accessed March 2015).

26. Hans-Georg Kaltenbrunner, "How 3D Printing
Is Set to Shake Up Manufacturing Supply Chains,"
Guardian, November 25, 2014; M. Gebler, et al.,
"A Global Sustainability Perspective on 3D Printing
Technologies," ScienceDirect, www.sciencedirect
.com/science/article/pii/S0301421514004868
(accessed June 19, 2020).

Chapter 14

1. "Disruption in Retail: From Product to Pixels,"
Deloitte and the Retail Council of Canada, www
.retailcouncil.org/sites/default/files/documents
/Deloitte-RCC-2015-BC-Retail-Study.pdf (accessed
February 5, 2017).

2. Emma Bedford, "Sales of Retail Trade in Canada
from 2012 to 2019 (in billions Canadian dollars),"
Statista, www.statista.com/statistics/431661/sales
-of-retail-trade-in-canada (accessed June 19, 2020);
Erin Duffin, "Gross Domestic Product (GDP) of
Canada in January 2020 by Industry," Statista,
www.statista.com/statistics/594293/gross-domestic
-product-of-canada-by-industry-monthly (accessed
June 19, 2020).

3. Emma Bedford, "Number of Employees of
the Retail Trade Industry in Canada from 2008
to 2019 (in millions)," Statista, www.statista.com
/statistics/454100/number-of-employees-of-the-retail
-trade-industry-canada (accessed June 19, 2020).

4. Alexandra Mae Jones, "Things Will Never be the
Same Again: What Will the Retail Landscape Look
Like in 2020?" CTV News, www.ctvnews.ca/lifestyle
/things-will-never-be-the-same-again-what-will-the
-retail-landscape-look-like-in-2020-1.4744311
(accessed June 19, 2020).

5. "Study Ranks Canada's Most Trusted Retailers,
and One Dominates," Retailer Insider, www
.retail-insider.com/retail-insider/2018/7/canada
-most-trusted-retailers-brandspark (accessed June
19, 2020).

6. Simons, www.simons.ca/en/simons/our-history
--a22865 (accessed June 19, 2020).

7. The Hudson Bay Company, www3.hbc.com/hbc
/about-us (accessed June 19, 2020).

8. "Summary—Canadian Industry Statistics," Statistics Canada, www.ic.gc.ca/app/scr/app/cis/summary
-sommaire/44512 (accessed June 19, 2020).

9. "Costco Opens Largest Warehouse in Canada,"
Canadian Grocer, www.canadiangrocer.com/top
-stories/headlines/costco-opens-largest-warehouse
-in-canada-88064 (accessed July 8, 2020).

10. "Industry Statistics and Research," Direct
Sellers Associations, www.dsa.ca/industry-statistics
-and-research (accessed June 19, 2020).

11. Tianyi Jiang and Alexander Tuzhilin, "Dynamic
Microtargeting: Fitness-based Approach to Pre-
dicting Individual Preferences," *Knowledge and
Information Systems*, 19, no. 3 (2009): 337–360.

12. J. Clement, "Global Retail E-Commerce
Sales 2014–2023," Statista, www.statista.com
/statistics/379046/worldwide-retail-e-commerce
-sales (accessed June 19, 2020).

13. Gerard Montasell, "Most Popular Online
Stores in Canada in 2018, by E-commerce Net Sales
(in million U.S. Dollars)," Statista, www.statista
.com/statistics/871090/canada-top-online-stores
-canada-ecommercedb (accessed June 19, 2020).

14. "Canadian Franchise Statistics," www.franchise
101.net/canadian-franchise-statistics (accessed June
19, 2020).

15. "CFA 2018 Accomplishments Report,"
Canadian Franchise Association, www.cfa.ca
/our-services/education-information/research
/CFAAccomplishments Report_2018.pdf (accessed
June 19, 2020).

16. "Canadian Franchise Statistics," www.franchise
101.net/canadian-franchise-statistics (accessed June
19, 2020).

17. DeAnn Campbell, "How Canadian Retailers
Can Flex to Reach Gen Z and Beyond,"
Retailer Insider, www.retail-insider.com/retail
-insider/2020/2/how-canadian-retailers-can-flex-to
-reach-gen-z-and-beyond (accessed June 19, 2020).

18. Hudson Bay, www.thebay.com/c/home
/glucksteinhome (accessed June 19, 2020).

19. Christopher Lombardo, "Not a Wine Shop
Pop-Up Uncorks in Toronto," Strategy Online,
https://strategyonline.ca/2019/10/30/not-a-wine
-shop-pop-up-wine-shop-uncorks-in-toronto
(accessed June 19, 2020).

20. Aleksandra Sagan, "Online Shopping Not
the Only Factor Behind Canada's Dying Malls,"
Toronto Star, March 11, 2018 www.thestar.com
/business/2018/03/11/online-shopping-not-the-only
-factor-behind-canadas-dying-malls.html (accessed
June 19, 2020); Daniel Calabretta, "Shopping
Visits Predicted to Hold Steady in Months
Ahead," Strategy Online, https://strategyonline
.ca/2020/03/16/canadian-store-visits-predicted-to
-hold-steady-in-coming-months (accessed June 19,
2020).

21. A. C. North, L. P. Sheridan, and C. S. Areni,
"Music Congruity Effects on Product Memory,
Perception, and Choice," *Journal of Retailing*, 92,
no. 1 (2015): 82–95.

22. A. V. Madzharov, L. G. Block, and M. Morrin,
"The Cool Scent of Power: Effects of Ambient
Scent on Consumer Preferences and Choice
Behavior," *Journal of Marketing*, 79, no. 1 (2015):
83–96.

23. Matthew Stern, "Walmart's Checkout Pilot
Puts Shoppers in the Fast Lane," Retail Wire,
https://retailwire.com/discussion/walmarts
-checkout-pilot-puts-shoppers-in-the-fast
-lane (accessed June 19, 2020).

24. "Appraisals of Hudson's Bay Company's
Real Estate Portfolio Available at HBC.com,"
BusinessWire, November 9, 2019, www
.businesswire.com/news/home/20191119005567
/en/Appraisals-Hudson%E2%80%99s-Bay
-Company%E2%80%99s-Real-Estate-Portfolio
(accessed June 19, 2020).

Chapter 15

1. "Quotes," www.quotes.net/quote/6791 (accessed
June 16, 2020).

2. Tim Nudd, "60 Years Late, Heinz Approves
Don Draper's 'Pass the Heinz' Ads and Is Actually Running Them," *Adweek*, March 13, 2017,
www.adweek.com/creativity/50-years-later-heinz
-approves-don-drapers-pass-the-heinz-ads-and-is
-actually-running-them (accessed June 16, 2020).

3. The AIDA concept is based on the classic
research of E. K. Strong, Jr., as theorized in *The
Psychology of Selling and Advertising* (New York:
McGraw-Hill Book Co., 1925); and "Theories of
Selling," *Journal of Applied Psychology*, 9, 1, 75–86.

4. Sapna Maheshwari, "Levi's, Whose Jeans Are
a Rugged Symbol of Americana, Prepares to Go
Public," *New York Times*, March 18, 2019, www
.nytimes.com/2019/03/18/business/levis-jeans-ipo
.html (accessed October 2019).

5. Ibid.

6. Ibid.

7. Ibid.

8. Daniel J. Howard and Thomas E. Barry, "A
Review and Critique of the Hierarchy of Effects in
Advertising," *International Journal of Advertising*,
9, 2, 1990, 121–135.

9. Tea and Herbal Association of Canada, www
.tea.ca/wp-content/uploads/2016/08/2015-Tea-Fact
-Sheet.pdf (accessed June 16, 2020).

10. Tetley, "Not Your Average Cup of Tea," www
.tetley.ca/en/our-range/super-teas (accessed June
16, 2020).

Chapter 16

1. Lucas Shaw, "TV Industry Sees Sharp Drop in
Advertising in 2019," 2019, https://www.bloomberg
.com/news/articles/2019-12-09/tv-industry-suffers
-steepest-drop-in-ad-sales-since-recession.

2. Internet Advertising Spending Worldwide
from 2007 to 2020, by Format, Statista website,
www.statista.com/statistics/276671/global-internet
-advertising-expenditure-by-type (accessed June
19, 2020).

3. Lucas Shaw, "TV Industry."

4. "Iconic Moves—Transforming Customer Expectations," Interbrand Best Global Brands 2019,
www.interbrand.com/wp-content/uploads/2019/10
/Interbrand_Best_Global_Brands_2019.pdf
(accessed April 2020).

5. "Does Humor Make Ads More Effective?,"
Knowledge Point, www.millwardbrown.com
/Libraries/MB_Knowledge_Points_Downloads
/MillwardBrown_KnowledgePoint_HumorIn
Advertising.sflb.ashx (accessed September 18, 2014).

6. Tom Duncan, *Integrated Marketing Communications* (Burr Ridge, IL: McGraw-Hill, 2002), 257.

7. Sharon Groom and Brett Stewart, "Comparative
Advertising—The Basics," Canadian Marketing
Association, www.the-cma.org/disciplines
/advertising/archive/comparative-advertising
(accessed April 29, 2017).

8. Russell O'Sullivan, "What Is Programmatic Marketing, Buying and Advertising?," *State of Digital*, October 26, 2015, www.stateofdigital .com/what-is -programmatic-marketing-buying-and-advertising (accessed May 8, 2017).

9. "Media Spending in Canada from 2007 to 2019, by medium," Statista, December 2018, www .statista.com/statistics/237295/advertising-spending -in-canada-by-media/ (accessed June 19, 2020).

10. Rody, Bree, "Growth in Canadian Ad Spend to Slow across Most Media: Study," Media in Canada, April 13, 2017.

11. "Mobile Captures Nearly Half of Canada's Digital Ad Spend," *eMarketer*, March 16, 2016, www.emarketer.com/Article/Mobile-Captures -Nearly-Half-of-Canadas-Digital-Ad-Spend /1013706 (accessed June 19, 2020).

12. Chris Powell, "Newspaper Advertising Outpaces Time Spent Reading Them," Marketing, September 7, 2016, http://marketingmag.ca/media /newspaper -advertising-outpaces-time-spent -reading-them-182551 (accessed June 19, 2020).

13. "Industry Profiles: Magazine Publishing— Interim Update," Ontario Media Development Corporation, November 2016, www.omdc.on.ca /collaboration/research_and_industry_information /industry_profiles/Magazine_Industry_Profile.htm (accessed May 1, 2017).

14. J. Solsman, "Disney Plus Is Here; Netflix is Watching," CNET, November 12, 2019.

15. Kristine Lyrette, "Media Channels: Out of Home," *Media Digest*, 2017, p. 144.

16. P. Briggs, Canada Digital Ad Spending 2019, Emarketer, 2019. Toronto.

17. "Number of Smartphone Users in Canada from 2018 to 2020 (in millions)" Statista website, April 2020, www.statista.com/statistics/467190/forecast -of-smartphone-users-in-canada (accessed June 19, 2020).

18. "Which kind of smartphone apps do you use regularly?" Statista website, June 2019, www.statista.com/forecasts/998495/smartphone -app-usage-by-type-in-canada (accessed June 19, 2020).

19. Jan Pokrop, "Instagram & Facebook User Statistic in Canada" NapoleonCat website, July 2019, https://napoleoncat.com/blog/instagram -user-demographics-in-canada-march-2017 (accessed June 19, 2020).

20. Susan Krashinsky Robertson, "Molson Canadian Ad Gets Second Life in Light of Trump Immigration Ban," *The Globe and Mail*, February 8, 2017, www.theglobeandmail.com/report-on -business/industry-news/marketing/molson-canadian -ad-gets-second-life-in-light-of-trump-immigration -ban/article33957985 (accessed June 19, 2020).

21. Dr. Ryan Todd, "A Decade Later, Bell Let's Talk Has Exposed the Mental Health-Care System," *Winnipeg Sun*, January 27, 2020, https://winnipegsun.com/opinion/columnists/a -decade-later-bell-lets-talk-has-exposed-the-mental -health-care-system (accessed June 19, 2020).

22. Christopher Lombardo, "CIBC Run for the Cure keeps its 'promise'," Strategy Online, September 11, 2019, https://strategyonline.ca /2019/09/11/cibc-run-for-the-cure-keeps-its -promise (accessed June 19, 2020).

Chapter 17

1. Ekaterina Walter, "40 Eye-Opening Customer Service Quotes," Forbes, March 4, 2014, www .forbes.com/sites/ekaterinawalter/2014/03/04/40-eye -opening-customer-service-quotes/#59bf399e6b7b (accessed July 14, 2020).

2. Rebecca Gao, "The New Roll Up the Rim, Explained," *Chatelaine*, March 8, 2020, www .chatelaine.com/food/roll-up-the-rim-tim-hortons -2020-faq (accessed June 24, 2020).

3. "Tim Hortons Announces Changes to Roll Up the Rim to Win in Light of Current Public Health Environment," Cision, March 7, 2020, https://www.newswire.ca/news-releases /tim-hortons-r-announces-changes-to-roll-up-the -rim-to-win-r-in-light-of-current-public-health -environment-831161016.html (accessed June 24, 2020).

4. Brooklyn Neustaeter and Jeremiah Rodriguez, "This Is How Tim Hortons Is Revamping Its Rewards Program, and What It Means to You," CTV News, February 11, 2020, https://www .ctvnews.ca/canada/this-is-how-tim-hortons-is -revamping-its-rewards-program-and-what-it -means-to-you-1.4806723 (accessed June 24, 2020).

5. Ibid.

6. Keph Senett, "Canadian Tire Credit Cards: We Break Down the Triangle Rewards Program and Triangle Mastercards," *Moneysense*, January 24, 2020, https://www.moneysense.ca/spend/credit -cards/canadian-tire-mastercard-credit-card-and -rewards-breakdown (accessed June 24, 2020).

7. www.ipsos-na.com/news-polls/pressrelease .aspx?id=7071 (accessed April 16, 2017).

8. Josh Kolm, "Burning Questions: Seeking the Best in Digital Coupons," Strategy, April 13, 2017, http://strategyonline.ca/2017/04/13/burning -questions-seeking-the-best-in-digital-coupons (accessed June 24, 2020).

9. Kelvin Claveria, "13 Customer Loyalty Stats, Including the Ineffectiveness of Loyalty Programs," Vision Critical, November 22, 2016, www.vision critical.com/customer-loyalty-stats (accessed June 24, 2020).

10. The 2016 Bond Loyalty Report, Brand Loyalty and Visa, http://info.bondbrandloyalty .com/hubfs/Resources/2016_Bond_Loyalty _Report_Executive_Summary_US_Launch _Edition .pdf?t=1492093294940 (accessed April 16, 2017).

11. Clay Pearn, "Loyalty Case Study: Loblaws' PC Plus," Smile.io, February 28, 2017, www.sweet toothrewards.com/blog/loyalty-case-study-loblaws -pc-plus (accessed June 24, 2020).

12. Josh Kolm, "Minute Rice Targets Time-Strapped Moms," Strategy, February 6, 2017, http://strategyonline.ca/2017/02/06/minute-rice -targets-time-strapped-moms (accessed June 24, 2020).

13. Ahsan Azim, "The Effect of Salesperson Trust, Preferential Treatment & Commitment on Customer's Loyalty" March 2013, http:// irmbrjournal.com/papers/1367572812.pdf.

14. S. Woessner, "Profitable Podcasting," Gildan Media, 2017.

15. Denise Deveau, "Cultural Barriers, Perceptions Keeping Canadians from Exploring Hot Global Markets," *Financial Post*, October 28, 2013, http://business.financialpost.com/2013/10/28 /cultural-barriers-perceptions-keeping-canadians -from-exploring-hot-global-markets (accessed June 24, 2020).

Chapter 18

1. Patrick Sayler, "Listening to Social Media Cues Doesn't Mean Ceding Control" Forbes, August 4, 2012, www.forbes.com/sites/ciocentral/2012/08/04 /listening-to-social-media-cues-doesnt-mean -ceding-control/#14b60097cd52 (accessed June 24, 2020).

2. www.linkedin.com/company/nike/ (accessed June 24, 2020).

3. Voytko, Lisette, "Nike Says It Sold Out of Kobe Bryant Products Instead of Pulling Them from Stores," January 28, 2020, *Forbes*, www.forbes .com/sites/lisettevoytko/2020/01/28/nike-and-some -resellers-reportedly-suspend-kobe-bryant-merch -sales-to-limit-profiteering/#4a752e9677e2 (accessed June 24, 2020).

4. Ibid.

5. Megan Haynes, "Trending in 2014," Strategy, December 12, 2013, http://strategyonline.ca /2013/12/12/trending-in-2014 (accessed June 24, 2020).

6. "Internet Use in Canada," CIRA Internet Factbook 2016, Canadian Internet Registration Authority, https://cira.ca/factbook/domain -industry-data-and-canadian-Internet-trends /internet-use-canada (accessed June 24, 2020).

7. "2017: Canadians Love Social Media, But Canadian Businesses Hate to Embrace It!" Rapid Boost Marketing, November 20, 2016, http ://rapidboostmarketing.com/canadians-love -social-media-but-canadian-businesses-hate-to -embrace-it (accessed June 24, 2020).

8. "2019 Canada's Internet Factbook," 2019, Cira, https://cira.ca/resources/corporate/factbook /canadas-internet-factbook-2019 (accessed June 24, 2020).

9. "Consumer Usage of Media Social Media Platforms Continues to Grow, Despite Privacy Concerns Around Targeted Advertising and News Feeds," June 26, 2019, Insights West, https://insightswest.com/news/2019-canadian -social-media-insights-report (accessed June 24, 2020).

10. www.insightswest.com/wp-content/uploads /2019/06/Rep_IW_CDNSocialMediaInsights _June2019.pdf.

11. "Consumer Usage of Media Social Media Platforms Continues to Grow, Despite Privacy Concerns Around Targeted Advertising and News Feeds."

12. Ibid.

13. www.instagram.com/netflix (accessed June 24, 2020).

14. Paul Briggs, "Canada Digital Ad Spending 2019." March 28, 2019, eMarketer, www.emarketer .com/content/canada-digital-ad-spending-2019 (accessed June 24, 2020).

15. Jeff Howe, Crowdsourcing: Why the Power of the Crowd Is Driving the Future of Business (New York, NY: Three Rivers Press, 2009), 32.

16. "The 2010 Canada Digital Year in Review," comScore, March 8, 2011, www.comscore.com /Insights/Presentations-and-Whitepapers /2011/2010-Canada-Digital-Year-in-Review (accessed June 24, 2020).

17. Robert Chialdini, *Influence: The Psychology of Persuasion*, Harper Collins, 2007.

18. Usman Qureshi, "Whatsapp Tops the List of World's Most Downloaded Apps in Q1 2019," April 2019, iPhone Canada, www.iphoneincanada .ca/news/whatsapp-worlds-most-downloaded-app (accessed June 24, 2020).

19. Dami Lee, "The Popular Musical.ly App Has Been Rebranded as TikTok," August 2, 2018, The Verge, www.theverge.com/2018/8/2/17644260 /musically-rebrand-tiktok-bytedance-douyin (accessed June 24, 2020).

20. Simon Kemp, "Digital Trends 2020: Every Single Stat You Need to Know About the Internet," Podium, https://thenextweb.com /podium/2020/01/30/digital-trends-2020-every

-single-stat-you-need-to-know-about-the-internet (accessed June 24, 2020).

21. www.youtube.com/watch?v=Qn3vJU4dWec.

22. Simon Kemp, "Digital Trends 2020: Every Single Stat You Need to Know About the Internet."

23. Ibid.

24. Adam Duremo, Personal interview, January 2020.

25. https://shortyawards.com/6th/westjet-christmas-miracle-real-time-giving.

26. "WestJet Airlines Ltd. Performs Christmas Marketing Miracle with Viral Video," *Financial Post*, December 11, 2013, http://business.financialpost.com/2013/12/11/westjet-airlines-ltd-performs-christmas-marketing-miracle-with-viral-video (accessed January 2014).

27. Michael Nuñez, "Kobe Bryant's Death Prompts More Facebook, Twitter Discussion Than Trump's Impeachment," January 28, 2020, *Forbes*, www.forbes.com/sites/mnunez/2020/01/28/kobe-bryants-death-prompts-more-facebook-twitter-discussion-than-trumps-impeachment/#7ddb05c33a4b (accessed June 24, 2020).

28. Ibid.

29. Denis Metev, "41+ Must Know Foursquare Statistics in 2020," Review 42, September 5, 2019, https://review42.com/foursquare-statistics (accessed June 24, 2020).

30. Craig Bloem, "84 Percent of People Trust Online Reviews As Much as Friends. Here's How to Manage What They See." Inc., www.inc.com/craig-bloem/84-percent-of-people-trust-online-reviews-as-much-.html (accessed June 24, 2020).

31. "Share of Adults Who Listened to a Podcast on the Last Month in Canada from Fall 2010 to Spring 2019," September 2019, Statista, www.statista.com/statistics/788900/canadian-adults-frequency-listening-podcasts (accessed June 24, 2020).

32. "Virtual Reality (VR) Statistics and Facts," Statista, www.statista.com/topics/2532/virtual-reality-vr (accessed June 24, 2020).

33. Sarah Dawley, "A Comprehensive Guide to Social Media ROI" (blog), Hootsuite, May 16, 2017, https://blog.hootsuite.com/measure-social-media-roi-business (accessed June 24, 2020).

34. David Berkowitz, "100 Ways to Measure Social Media," Marketers Studio, November 17, 2009, www.marketersstudio.com/2009/11/100-ways-to-measure-social-media-.html (accessed January 2014).

35. "Number of Smartphone Users in Canada from 2018 to 2024 (in millions)," February 2019, Statista, www.statista.com/statistics/467190/forecast-of-smartphone-users-in-canada/ (accessed June 24, 2020).

36. Ibid.

37. "Our Mobile Planet: Canada—Understanding the Mobile Consumer," Google, May 2013, http://services.google.com/fh/files/misc/omp-2013-ca-en.pdf (accessed January 2014).

38. Paul Briggs, "Canada Digital Ad Spending 2019," March 28, 2019, eMarketer, www.emarketer.com/content/canada-digital-ad-spending-2019 (accessed June 24, 2020).

39. Justin Grossbard, "The Growth of Text Messaging for Businesses in 2020," March 23, 2020, SMS Comparison, www.smscomparison.com/mass-text-messaging/2019-growth/ (accessed June 24, 2020).

40. Portia Crowe, "Snap Is Going Public at a $24 Billion Valuation," March 1, 2017, Business Insider, www.businessinsider.com/snapchat-ipo-price-2017-3 (accessed June 24, 2020).

41. Simon Ogus, "Lebron James Partners with Unicorn App Calm That Focuses on Your Mental Fitness," December 25, 2019, *Forbes*, www.forbes.com/sites/simonogus/2019/12/25/lebron-james-partners-with-unicorn-app-calm-that-focuses-on-your-mental-fitness/#31891ece37d3 (accessed June 24, 2020).

42. www.internetlivestats.com, 2020.

43. "Helping Millions Grow Better," HubSpot, www.hubspot.com/our-story?_ga=2.189432427.1181076698.1580428290-800241294.1580428290 (accessed June 24, 2020).

44. "Hootsuite," Wikipedia, https://en.wikipedia.org/wiki/Hootsuite (accessed March 28, 2017).

Chapter 19

1. "Trade Set to Plunge as COVID-19 Pandemic Upends Global Economy," World Trade Organization, April 8, 2020, www.wto.org/english/news_e/pres20_e/pr855_e.htm (accessed June 24, 2020).

2. Nick Cunningham, "Oil Tanks on Fears of Global Economic Crisis," Oilprice.com, February 24, 2020, https://oilprice.com/Energy/Oil-Prices/Oil-Tanks-On-Fears-Of-Global-Economic-Crisis.html (accessed June 24, 2020).

3. Foxy Originals, https://foxyoriginals.com/pages/designer-profile (accessed June 24, 2020).

4. McCain company, www.mccain.com/information-centre/media-assets (accessed June 24, 2020).

5. Joe Castaldo, "What Really Went Wrong with Target Canada," *Marketing*, January 22, 2016, www.marketingmag.ca/brands/what-really-went-wrong-with-target-canada-166300 (accessed June 24, 2020).

6. "Canada's Top 10 Imports," World's Top Exports, www.worldstopexports.com/canadas-top-10-imports (accessed February 1, 2020).

7. "Exports of Goods and Services (% of GDP)," World Bank, https://data.worldbank.org/indicator/NE.EXP.GNFS.ZS?locations=CA (accessed June 24, 2020).; "Imports of Goods and Services (% of GDP)," World Bank, https://data.worldbank.org/indicator/NE.IMP.GNFS.ZS (accessed June 24, 2020).

8. "OEC—Canada (CAN) Exports, Imports, and Trade Partners," OEC, https://oec.world/en/profile/country/can (accessed June 24, 2020).

9. "Trade and Small and Medium-sized Enterprises," Government of Canada website, www.international.gc.ca/trade-commerce/sme-pme/sme-roles-pme.aspx?lang=eng (accessed June 24, 2020).

10. Pierre Cleroux, "Canada: A Powerful Brand," Business Development Bank of Canada, www.bdc.ca/en/about/sme_research/pages/canada_powerful_brand.aspx (accessed June 24, 2020).

11. "Quality in What We Make," Roots, www.roots.com/on/demandware.static/-/Sites-Roots-Corporate-Library/default/dw8c340791/content/ABOUT_ROOTS_MASTER/quality.htm (accessed June 24, 2020).

12. Claire Manuel, "Coca-Cola's 5by20 Recipe to Empower 5 Million Women by 2020," Ethical Corp, June 20, 2018, www.ethicalcorp.com/coca-colas-5by20-recipe-empower-5-million-women-2020 (accessed June 24, 2020); "5by20," Coca Cola website, www.coca-colacompany.com/shared-future/women-empowerment (accessed July 6, 2020).

13. Lucia Peters, "13 International McDonald's Items That Will Give You Major Fast Food FOMO," Bustle, May 21, 2019, www.bustle.com/p/13-international-mcdonalds-items-that-will-give-you-major-fast-food-fomo-16991111 (accessed June 24, 2020).

14. "IKEA in China: Big Furniture Retail Adapts to the Chinese Market," Daxue Consulting, January 22, 2020, https://daxueconsulting.com/ikea-in-china (accessed June 24, 2020).

15. "Mistakes in Advertising," LEO Network, www.learnenglish.de/mistakes/HorrorMistakes.html (accessed September 15, 2014).

16. "GNI per capita, Atlas Method (Current US$)," The World Bank, https://data.worldbank.org/indicator/NY.GNP.PCAP.CD (accessed July 6, 2020).

17. Ibid.

18. Maureen O'Hare, "World's Most Expensive Cities to Live In," CNN, March 18, 2020, www.cnn.com/travel/article/worlds-most-expensive-cities-2020/index.html (accessed June 24, 2020).

19. Amrita Banta, "Chinese and Indian Consumers Both Love Luxury, But Their Preferences Differ Widely," Luxury Society, May 13, 2019, www.luxurysociety.com/en/articles/2019/05/chinese-and-indian-consumers-love-luxury-their-preferences-differ-widely (accessed June 24, 2020).

20. Ibid.

21. Ethan Lou, "What a Trade War With China Would Do to Canada," *Maclean's*, June 28, 2019, www.macleans.ca/news/canada/what-a-trade-war-with-china-would-do-to-canada (accessed June 24, 2020).

22. "Doing Business, 2020," World Bank Group, https://openknowledge.worldbank.org/bitstream/handle/10986/32436/9781464814402.pdf.

23. Kaveh Waddell, "Why Google Quit China—and Why It's Heading Back," *The Atlantic*, January 19, 2016, www.theatlantic.com/technology/archive/2016/01/why-google-quit-china-and-why-its-heading-back/424482 (accessed June 24, 2020).

24. Andy Blatchford, "Russian Sanctions Starting to Bite into Canadian Export Outlook," CBC News, January 2, 2015, www.cbc.ca/news/business/russian-sanctions-starting-to-bite-into-canadian-export-outlook-1.2888500 (accessed June 24, 2020).

25. Mercosur, www.mercosur.int/en/about-mercosur/mercosur-countries (accessed June 24, 2020).

26. "Mercosur Trade Bloc—Benefits for Canada," Government of Canada, www.international.gc.ca/trade-commerce/trade-agreements-accords-commerciaux/agr-acc/mercosur/benefits-avantages.aspx?lang=eng (accessed June 24, 2020).

27. World Trade Organization, www.wto.org/english/thewto_e/whatis_e/wto_dg_stat_e.htm (accessed June 24, 2020).

28. "North American Free Trade Agreement (NAFTA)— Resources," Government of Canada, www.international.gc.ca/trade-commerce/consultations/nafta-alena/toolkit-outils.aspx?lang=eng (accessed June 24, 2020).

29. "A New Canada-United States-Mexico Agreement," Government of Canada, www.international.gc.ca/trade-commerce/trade-agreements-accords-commerciaux/agr-acc/cusma-aceum/index.aspx?lang=eng (accessed July 7, 2020).

30. "Trade and Investment Agreements," Government of Canada, www.international.gc.ca/trade-commerce/trade-agreements-accords-commerciaux/agr-acc/index.aspx?lang=eng (accessed June 24, 2020).

31. "Agreement Overview," Government of Canada, www.international.gc.ca/trade-commerce/trade-agreements-accords-commerciaux/agr-acc/ceta-aecg/overview-apercu.aspx?lang=eng (accessed June 24, 2020).

32. "Brexit: All You Need to Know About the UK Leaving the EU," BBC, February 17, 2020,

www.bbc.com/news/uk-politics-32810887 (accessed June 24, 2020).

33. "Canada's Participation at the 2019 G20 Summit," Government of Canada, www.international.gc.ca/gac-amc/campaign-campagne/g20/index.aspx?lang=eng (accessed June 24, 2020).

34. Dylan Matthews, "Are 26 Billionaires Worth More Than Half the Planet? The Debate, Explained," Vox, January 22, 2019, www.vox.com/future-perfect/2019/1/22/18192774/oxfam-inequality-report-2019-davos-wealth (accessed June 24, 2020).

35. Lan Ha,"Four Key Groups of Urban Consumers to Watch," Euromonitor, April 3, 2019, https://blog.euromonitor.com/four-key-groups-of-urban-consumers-to-watch (accessed June 24, 2020).

36. Emma Bedford, "Value of Icewine Exported From Canada in 2018, By Country of Destination," Statista, August 29, 2019, www.statista.com/statistics/556172/ice-wine-export-value-canada-destination (accessed June 24, 2020).

37. Rylan Higgins, "Transparency Is Really About Consumer Guilt, and Company Image, and Shareholder Peace of Mind," CBC, May 8, 2017, www.cbc.ca/news/opinion/transparency-garment-industry-1.4096227 (accessed June 24, 2020).

38. "Skechers Launches Joint Venture in South Korea," Business Wire, November 10, 2016, www.businesswire.com/news/home/20161110005045/en/SKECHERS-Launches-Joint-Venture-South-Korea (accessed June 24, 2020).

39. "How Procter & Gamble Is Conquering Emerging Markets," The Motley Fool, October 27, 2013, www.fool.com/investing/general/2013/10/27/how-procter-gamble-is-conquering-emerging-markets.aspx (accessed June 24, 2020).

40. "What Is Selling Where? Pringles Chips," Wall Street Journal, April 24, 2013, D3.

41. Eva Dou and Jenny W. Hsu, "How Convenient: In Taiwan the 24/7 Store Does It All," Wall Street Journal, May 16, 2014, www.wsj.com/articles/SB10001424052702304518704579520371243903680 (accessed June 24, 2020).

42. Michael Zakkour, "Why Starbucks Succeeded in China: A Lesson for All Retailers," Forbes, August 24, 2017, www.forbes.com/sites/michaelzakkour/2017/08/24/why-starbucks-succeeded-in-china-a-lesson-for-all-retailers/#434f357d7923 (accessed June 24, 2020).

43. "Global Scale Meets Local Color," Marketing News, October 2016, 25, 27.

44. "Amazon Invades India," Fortune, January 1, 2016, 63–71.

45. Ibid.

46. Ibid.

47. "Countertrade," http://allaboutcountertrade.blogspot.ca (accessed November 20, 2016).

INDEX

Entries for key terms are highlighted in **bold**.

A

Accelerator principle, 102
Accessory equipment, 104, 158
Addressed direct mail, 325
Adidas, 323–324
Adopter, 185–187, 192
Adopter categories, 185–187, 192
Advantages and disadvantages of primary data, 56
Advergaming, 317
Advertising, 292
Advertising, major types of comparative advertising, 310
institutional advertising, 308–309
Advertising, public relaions, and direct response, 303
advertising and market share, 307
advertising defined, 306
creative decisions in advertising, 310–313
direct -response communication, 324–326
effects of advertising on consumers, 308
major types of asvertising, 308–310
media decisions in advertising, 313–320
public relations, 320–324
Advertising appeal, 310–311, 313–314
Advertising campaign, 183, 201, 271, 273, 293, 310–312, 318, 320
Advertising media, 306, 314–315, 319–320, 331
Advertising objective, 310, 314
Advertising Standards Canada (ASC), 18
Advocacy advertising, 309
Aeroplan, 335
Age, 87–88
Age segmentation, 117–118
AggregateIO, 143
AIDA concept, 297–298
Air Canada, 101, 148
Air Miles, 147
Airbnb., 5, 77, 167, 269
Airlines, low-cost, 42, 234
Aldo, 138
Alimentation Couche-Tard, 265
Alphabet, 181
Alternative channel arrangements
multiple channels, 248–249
nontraditional channels, 249
Amazing Race Canada, 322
Amazon, 28–29, 67, 70, 77, 153–154, 166–168, 198, 270, 312, 334, 350, 354
Ambush marketing, 323
Anchor stores, 274
Anheuser-Busch InBev, 222
Anonymized, 71
Ansoff's strategic opportunity matrix, 39–40
Anti-Spam Legislation, 18, 325
Apple, 10, 27–29, 33, 70, 91, 102, 128, 156, 162, 166–167, 176, 179–180, 182, 191, 252, 258, 283, 292, 307, 355–357
Apple Watch, 182, 292, 356

Applied research, 28, 179–180
Apps, 356–357
Artificial intelligence (AI), 28
ASC (Advertising Standards Canada), 18
Aspirational reference groups, 85, 92
Assurance, 199
At the Table, 211
Athleta, 125
Atmosphere, 272, 275–276
Attitude, 93
Audience selectivity, 318
Audit, marketing, 47
Augmented reality, 157, 185, 190
Australia, 170
Automatic vending, 268
Automobile advertising, 310
Avon products, 268
Awake Chocolate
customer feedback, 327–328
customer relationship management in, 151–152
customer response during COVID-19, 213–215
flavour masking, 260–261
idea behind, 12–13
influencer marketing, 362–363
integrated marketing communications in, 304–305
marketing research, 72–73
marketing strategy, 48–49
in micro markets, 280–281
new product development, 193–194
operational objective, 34–35
packaging, 173–174
pricing strategy, 236–237
promotional strategy, 344–345
target market, 130–131
taste and consumer decision process, 94–95
Axe deodorant, 158, 170

B

B2B (business-to-business) marketing, 96 *See also* Business marketing
B2B Content Marketing Benchmarks Report, 110–111
Baby boomers, 23–26, 89, 117–118, 221–222, 349–350
Bacon, 125, 129, 161, 242
Badges, 354, 358
Bait and switch, 234
Bait pricing, 233
Banana Republic, 125
Bar code, 170, 357
Barchetti, Katherine, 330
Bar-code scanning apps, 357
Base price, 220, 228–230
Bases for segmenting consumer markets, 115–116, 148–149
benefit segmentation, 121
criteria for successful segmentation, 123
demographic segmentation, 116–123

psychographic segmentation, 119–121
usage-rate segmentation, 122
Bases for segmenting consumer markets
demographic segmentation, 116–119
geographic segmentation, 116
Basic research, 28, 180
Beacon, 277
Beacon-enabled billboard, 316
Beacons, 277–278, 316
Beer industry, 222
Belief, 12, 22, 83–84, 93, 98, 120, 151, 308, 344
Beliefs and attitudes, 93
Bell Canada, 147, 323
Let's Talk campaign, 322–323
Bell Helicopter, 107
Below-cost pricing, 212
Benefit segmentation, 121
Benefits of online research communities, 64
BEP (break-even point), 225
Best Buy, 244, 263, 266, 270, 337
Bezos, Jeff, 132
Big data, 16, 62, 65–67, 70, 150, 277–278
Big data analytics, 278
Big Mac, 129, 198
Bilingual labelling, 171
Bill 101 (Quebec), 17
Billboard advertising, 293, 316, 319
Black & Decker, 129, 159
BlackBerry, 10, 166
Blockbuster, 191
Bloggers, 247, 297, 336, 353, 356
Blogs, 353
Bluetooth marketing, 357
BMO, 33, 166
BMW, 127, 148, 232, 253, 256
Body image, 89
Body Shop, 6
Bond Brand Loyalty report, 146
Book publishers, 298
Booz Allen Hamilton, 178, 180
Bose speakers, 337
Boston Consulting Group, 176
Bounty Basic, 161
Brainstorming, 58, 181
Brand, 163
Brand cannibalization, 273
Brand equity, 164, 167
Brand image, 93
Brand loyalty, 123, 146, 148, 161, 164, 199, 301, 317, 334
Brand mark, 164
Brand name, 164
Branded (or inbound) content, 297
Branded content, 297, 302
Branding
benefits of, 164
branding strategies, 164–167
Branding and packaging, global issues, 170–172
Break-even analysis, 224–225
Break-even point (BEP), 225
Brexit, 143
BRIC countries, 343
Bridgestone Canada, 136–137
Briggs & Stratton, 108
Brokerhouse Distributors, 250
Buffet, Warren, 114

Building relationships, 7–8, 96, 151
Build-to-order, 255–256
Bundling, 230
Burberry knockoffs, 168
Burial plots, 160
Business analysis, 179, 181–182
Business buying behaviour
business marketing online, 110–111
buying centres, 107–108
buying situations, 108–109
evaluation criteria for business buyers, 109
Business customers, 105–107, 122, 238, 245, 293
Business customers, classifying
classification by industry, 106–107
major catagories of customers, 105–106
Business ethics *See* Ethics, 32
Business format franchising, 270
Business marketing
business buying behaviour, 107–109
business vs. consumer marketing, 97–98
classifying business customers, 105–107
defined, 96–97
fundamental aspects of, 102–105
networks and relationship appoach, 98–99
networks in business marketing, 99–101
online, 110–111
Business marketing, fundamental aspects, 90, 147
location of buyers, 103
number of customers, 102–103
types of demand, 102
types of negotiations, 103
use of leasing, 103–104
use of reciprocity, 103
Business marketing online, 110–111
Business mission, 38
Business network, 99–100, 103, 113
Business planning, 41–42
building sustainable competitive advantage, 43–44
competitive advantage, 41
cost competitive advantage, 41–42
niche competitive advantage, 43
product differentiation competitive advantage, 42–43
Business product, 102, 104, 106, 157–158, 246, 300
Business product distributors, 106
Business purching roles, 108
Business services, 104
Business unit level planning, 38
business vs. consumer marketing, 97–98
Business-to-business (B2B) marketing, 96 *See also* Business marketing
Buyer behaviour *See* Consumer decision making
Buyers, 16
location of, 103
Buying, nature of, 107
Buying centre, 107–108, 265
implications of, 107–108
roles in, 107

Buying influence, nature of, 107
Buying processes, 122
Buying situations, 108–109

C

C2C (consumer-to-consumer) marketing See Consumer decision making
C2C (consumer-to-consumer) reviews, 77
CAD/CAM (computer-aided design and computer-aided manufacturing), 42
Calgary Philharmonic Orchestra (CPO), 199
Calm, 358
Camp, Garrett, 50
Campaign management, 146–147
Campbell's Soup, 57, 160–161, 169
lines and product mix, 160–161
Canada Dry Motts, 106
Canadian Anti-Spam Legislation, 18
Canadian Blood Services, 121, 211
Canadian Business, 241, 315
Canadian climate regions, 117
Canadian Code of Advertising Standards, 18
Canadian Food Inspection Agency (CFIA), 170
Canadian Football League (CFL), 203
Canadian Greenhouse Juice Company, 43
Canadian Grocer, 87, 187, 239
Canadian Institute of Marketing, 55
Canadian Intellectual Property Office, 167
Canadian marketers, what's expected of, 33
Canadian Marketing Association (CMA), 18, 33, 98–99
Canadian Professional Sales Association (CPSA), 343
Canadian Public Relations Society (CPRS), 321
Canadian Radio-television and Telecommunications Commission (CRTC), 18
Canadian Tire, 164–165, 206, 263, 332, 335
Candy Crush, 355
Cannibalization, 124, 126
Car ads, 308
Car2Go, 45
Careers in marketing, 10
Carlton Cards, 282
Carter's, 270
Cash discount, 229
Cashmere bathroom tissue, 127, 317
CASL (Canadian Anti-Spam Legislation), 18
Casper, 86
Catalogues and mail-order, 268
Category killers, 267
Causal research, 54
Cause-related marketing, 323
Census, 55, 67, 69, 142, 250, 269
Census metropolitan area (CMAs), 26
Central-location telephone (CLT) facility, 58
Central-location telephone interview, 59
Cents-off deals, 81, 303
Certified purchasing manager (CPM), 107
Certified Sales Professional (CSP) designation, 343
Chain stores, 264
Changes to customer purchasings behviour, 88
Changing consumers' beliefs, 93
Channel, 288
Channel captain, 252

Channel choice, factors affecting
market factors, 249–250
producer factors, 250–251
product factors, 250
Channel conflict, 252–253
Channel control, 252
Channel cooperation, 253
Channel interaction, 140
Channel intermediaries and their functions
channel functions performed by intermediaries, 245–246
marketing channel and intermediaries defined, 242
Channel leader (channel captain), 252
Channel members, 235, 242, 246, 248, 252–253, 260, 278, 337
Channel of distribution, 240–241
See also Marketing channels
Channel partnering (channel cooperation), 253–254
Channel power, 252
Channel relationships, handling
channel conflict, 252–253
channel control, 252
channel leader (channel captain), 252
channel power, 252
channel power, control, and leadership, 252
horizontal conflict, 252–253
vertical conflict, 253–254
Channel strategy decisions, making
factors affecting channel choice, 249–251
levels of distribution intensity, 251–252
Chapters Indigo, 124, 246, 272
Charmin Basic, 161
Chernov, Joe, 2
Chewing gum, 250
Chewy Granola Bars, 183
CI (competitive intelligence), 71, 134, 342
CIBC, 163, 166, 323
Cineplex, 147
Circle K, 265
"Circular economy" movement, 169
Cirque du Soleil, 43, 353
Click-and-collect, 40, 279
Click-through rate (CTR), 307
Climate, 50, 116–117, 164, 170–171, 308, 319
Climate regions, 117
Climate strike, 308
Clorox, 31, 128, 180
Clothing, 19–20, 65, 80, 86–87, 89, 92, 116, 119, 125, 157, 161–162, 189, 238, 246, 250, 266, 270, 282, 300, 310
CLT (central-location telephone) facility, 58
Club Car, 146
Cluster sample, 56
CMA (Canadian Marketing Association), 18, 33, 98–99
CMAs (census metropolitan areas), 26
Coach, 246
Cobranded credit cards, 335
Cobranding, 146, 167, 335
Coca-Cola, 66, 90, 115, 124–125, 127, 142, 167, 170–171, 312, 320
Code of ethics, 18, 32
Cognitive dissonance, 78, 81, 147, 169–170, 339, 342
Cold calling, 340–341
Colour, 109, 188, 279
Commercialization, 134, 179, 184–186
Commitment, 9, 30, 33, 36, 47, 74, 98–99, 138–139, 154, 169, 178,

185, 189–190, 238, 258, 273, 291, 315, 339–340
Communication, 286 See also Marketing communication
Communication gap, 201
Communication process
feedback, 289
message tranmission, 288
receiver and decoding, 288–289
sender and encoding, 287–288
Community shopping centres, 274
Company characteristics, 122
Company websites, 217, 279, 325, 340
Comparative advertising, 309–310
Competition Act, 17, 172, 233, 235
Competition Bureau, 17–18, 31, 233–234, 253
Competitive advantage, 41
building sustainable competitive advantage, 43–44
competitive advantage, 41
cost competitive advantage, 41–42
defined, 41
niche, 43
niche competitive advantage, 43
product differentiation competitve advantage, 42–43
Competitive advantage, importance of strategic planning, 36
Competitive advertising, 309–310, 312
Competitive factors, 16
Competitive intelligence (CI), 71, 134, 342
Competitors, 180
Compiled lists, 142
Complementary branding, 167
Component lifestyles, 22
Component parts and materials, 104, 109
Computer-aided design and computer-aided manufacturing (CAD/CAM), 42
Concentrated targeting, 125
Concentrated targeting strategy, 124–126
Concept test, 181
Conceptual learning, 92
Conclusive research, 54
Conferences and conventions, 337
Consideration set, 77–78
Consolidated Foods Kitchen, 183
Consultants, 180–181
Consultative selling, 343
Consumer behaviour, 74, 79, 83, 86–90, 92–93
elements, 93
understanding, 74–75
Consumer buying decisions, cultural and social factors
culture and values, 83–85
social class, 84
social influences on, 85–87
subculture, 84
Consumer buying decisions, factors influencing, 81–83
Consumer buying decisions, individual
age and family life-cycle stage, 87–88
gender, 87
personality, self-concept, and lifestyle, 89
Consumer buying decisions, psychologica influences
beliefs and attitudes, 93
changing beliefs, 93
consumer behaviour elements, 93
learning, 92
marketing implications of perception, 90–91
motivation, 91–92
perception, 90

Consumer buying decisions, types of, 79–80
consumer involvement, determining factors, 80
cosumer buying decisions, factors influencing, 81–83
involvement, marketing implications, 80–81
Consumer decision making
cultural and social factors, 83–87
importance of understanding consumer behaviour, 74–75
individual influences, 87–89
process, 75–79
psychological influences, 90–93
types of consumer buyer decisions, 79–82
Consumer decision-making process, 75, 78, 81–83
Step 1: need recognition, 75–76
Step 2: information search, 76–78
Step 5: postpurchase behaviour, 78–79
Steps 3 and 4: evaluation of alternatives and purchase, 78
Consumer loyalty, 291, 335
Consumer Packaging and Labelling Act, 17, 170
Consumer privacy, 17–18
Consumer product, 157–158
Consumer products, types
convenience products, 158
shopping products, 158–159
speciality products, 159
Consumer Reports, 76–77
Consumer sales promotion, 331, 333, 337
Consumer-generated content, 295, 301
Consumers' incomes, 18–19
Consumer-to-consumer (C2C) marketing See Consumer decision making
Consumer-to-consumer (C2C) review, 77
Consumer involvement, determining factors, 80
Content marketing, 111, 294, 296
importance of, 111, 294–295
Contests and sweepstakes, 293, 335–336
Continuing case See Awake Chocolate
Continuous media schedule, 320
Contracting product line, 161–162
Control, 47
Convenience products, 158, 191
Convenience sample, 56
Convenience store, 130, 264–265, 267, 280–281
Conventional morality, 32
Cooperative advertising, 273, 315–316, 337
Cooperative branding, 167
Cord cutting, 316
Core and supplementary service products
Core competencies, 38, 41
Core service, 203
Corning, 176
Corporate or professional blogs, 353
Corporate planning, 37–38
Corporate social responsibility (CSR), 29, 220–221
ethical behaviour in business, 31–32
ethical decision making, 32
ethical guidelines, 32–33
green marketing, 31
growth of social responsibilty, 30–31

Corporate social responsibility (CSR) (*continued*)
  introduction, 29–30
  morality and business ethics, 32
  Social responsibility, growth of, 30–31
Corporate-level planning, 38
Cost competitive advantage, 41–42
Cost per click, 317, 358
Cost per contact, 318
Costco, 229, 238–239, 264, 269, 335
Cost-of-living index, 19
Costs, 219
Coupon, 23, 81, 137, 147, 191, 273, 293, 299, 303, 332–334, 358
Coverage, 249, 251
CPM (certified purchasing manager), 107, 315, 318
CPSA (Canadian Professional Sales Association), 343
Craft beer consumers, 222
Cream of Chicken Soup, 160
Creative decisions in advertising
  developing and evaluating
   advertising appeals, 310–311
  executing the message, 312
  identifying product benefits, 310
  postcampaign evaluation, 312–313
Creativity, 47, 123, 166, 181, 185, 315, 365
Creators, 305
Credence quality, 197
CREST model, 15–16, 50
Crest toothpaste, 30, 56, 162, 182
Crisis management, 321, 324
Criteria for successful segmentation, 123
Critics, 63, 291, 324, 364–365
CRM (customer relationship management) See Customer relationship management (CRM)
CRM cycle
  bases for segmenting consumer costs, 148–149
  CRM, future of, 149–150
  leverage customer feedback, 145–148
  Stage 1: (marketing research), 134–136
  Stage 2: (business development), 136–145
  Stage 3 (customer feedback), 145
Cross, 168
CrossFit, 117
Cross-selling, 142, 145–147
Crowdfunding, 183
Crowdsourcing, 216, 349
CSP designation, 343
Culture, 83
Customer data
  capturing, 140
  storing and integrating, 140–141
Customer database, 65–66, 142, 334, 361
Customer feedback, 48, 133–134, 139, 145–146, 186, 327
Customer focus, 10, 64
Customer lifetime value, 143–144
Customer profile, 121, 143, 147, 342
Customer "pull" manufacturing environment, 254–255
Customer purchasing behaviour, changes to, 88
Customer relationship management, 7
Customer relationship management (CRM), 29
  CRM cycle, 134 See also CRM cycle
  defined, 132–133
  the other CRM, 133
Customer relationship marketing, 133–134

Customer satisfaction, 7, 44–45, 140, 144–145, 199–201, 204, 220, 276, 361
Customer segmentation, 143
Customer service, 44, 66–67, 69, 139, 145–149, 163, 201, 220–221, 249, 253–254, 265, 269, 272, 276, 285, 353, 361
Customer value, 7–8, 46, 218, 254
Customer-centric, 137–139, 343–344
  companies, 138
Customers, 179
  identifying the best, 142
Customization/standardization, 204
Cutoffs, 78

D

DAGMAR approach, 310
Data, sharing among apps and program, 70
Data collection concerns
  intrusive methods of data collection, 70
  lack of transparency about data sharing, 70–71
Data collection, intrusive methods of, 70
Data for marketing analytics, categories
  examples of different categories of data, 68–69
Data mining, 7, 67, 137, 142–143, 145, 210, 272
Data sharing, lack of transparency about, 70–71
Data sold to other companies, 70–71
Data used in marketing analytics, 67
Data visualization, 67
Data warehouse, 67, 140, 142–143, 255
Database, 63, 142
Dawley, Sarah, 355
Deceptive pricing, 233–234
Decider, 108
Decision confirmation, 78
Decision maker, 23, 32, 53–54, 62, 67, 71, 87, 107, 111, 115, 356
Decline stage, 189, 223, 301
Decoding, 288–289
Delivery gap, 200, 205
Dell Computer, 248, 256
Demand, 224
  curve, 224–226
  through the product life cycle, 223
Demographic factors
  baby boomers, 26
  ethnic and cultural diversity, 26–27
  Generation X, 25–26
  Generation Y, 24–25
  Generation Z, 23–24
  population shifts, 26
Demographic segmentation, 116–117
Demography, 23–24 See also Generational cohorts
Department store, 168, 253, 263–265, 267, 276, 320
Depth interview, 57
Derived demand, 102–103
Descriptive research, 54, 56–57
Destination stores, 273
Destination website, 274
Development, 183
DeWalt power tools, 129, 179–180
DeWalt's Insights Forum, 180
Dichotomous question, 60
Diet Coke, 127–128, 160

Diffusion, 186–188, 192, 194, 346
  curve, 192
Digg, 352, 354
Digital camera, 192
Digital coupons, 333
digital direct marketing, 325
Digital marketing
  listening system, 360–361
  plan, 360
  strategies, 360
Digital media marketing types, 297
Digital media types, 297
Digital technology See Internet
Direct channel, 246–248, 250
Direct channels vs. direct marketing, 247
Direct competitors, 16, 165
Direct mail, 99, 137, 268–269, 294, 319, 325, 339–340
Direct marketing (DM), 46, 220, 246–247, 250, 268–269, 285, 294, 298, 324–326, 337
  See also Direct-response communication
Direct retailing, 268
Direct-marketing activities, 46, 220, 246–247, 250, 268–269, 285, 294, 298, 324–326
Direct-response broadcast, 326
Direct-response communication
  defined, 324–325
  digital direct marketing, 325–326
  direct mail, 325
  direct-response broadcast, 326
  direct-response print, 326
  direct-response television (DRTV), 326
  telemarketing, 325
  tools of, 325–326
Direct-response print, 294, 301, 326
Direct-response radio, 326
Direct-response television (DRTV), 142, 326
Discontinuous innovations, 178
Discount specialty stores, 264
Discount stores, 19, 249, 263, 265–267, 274
Discrepancy of assortment, 243
Discrepancy of quantity, 242
Discretionary income, 19, 85
Disney See Walt Disney Company
Disney customer magic, 9
Disposable income, 19
Dissociative groups, 86
Distribution challenges in world markets
  developing global marketing channels, 258
  electronic distribution, 258–259
Distribution channel marketing, 145, 148
Distribution channels, 145, 148, 156, 168, 223, 228–229, 240, 242, 246, 248–253, 277, 330, 336–337 See also Marketing channels
Distribution intensity, 249, 252–253
  exclusive distribution, 251–252
  intensive distribution, 251
  levels of, 251–252
  selective distribution, 251
Distributors, 180
Diversification, 41
Do Not Call List (DNCL), 325
Dollarama, 227–230, 250–251, 263, 266, 273
Dom Pérignon, 92
Donating by text, 358
Donna Karan, 168
Double ticketing, 234
Dragon's Den, 12–13

Driverless cars, 42
DRTV (direct-response television), 142, 326
Drucker, Peter, 5
Drugstores, 68, 264–265, 267, 274
Dual distribution, 248, 253
Dual distribution (multiple distribution), 248
Dual distribution strategies, 253
Dun & Bradstreet, 142
Duracell batteries, 167
Dynamic pricing, 229–230
Dyson, James, 176

E

Early adopters, 186–188, 192
Early majority, 186–188, 192
Earned media, 293, 296–297, 321, 360
eBay, 354
E-commerce, 67, 110, 113, 116, 118, 230, 269–270, 281, 343, 349
Economic factors, 8
  consumers' incomes, 18–19
  families today, 22–23
  growth of component lifestyles, 22
  inflation, 19–20
  marketing-oriented values, 22
  purchasing power, 19
  recession, 20–21
  social factors, 21
EDI (electronic data interchange), 257
Education, 6, 18, 20, 84–85, 103, 116, 120, 180, 187, 203, 289, 317
Efficient labour, 42
El Araby, Tamer, 52
Elastic demand, 102, 224
Elasticity of demand, 223–224
Electronic data interchange (EDI), 255, 257
Electronic distribution, 258–259
Email, 326, 333, 339, 343
Empathy, 10, 199, 364–365
Employees, 179
Empowerment, 138–139, 295
Encoding, 287–288
Energy bars, 83
Environics Research Group, 24, 55, 61, 116, 121
Environment, external, 15–16
Environmental factors, 21
Environmental scanning, 15, 39, 71
Errors, types of, 55–56
Esteem needs, 91–92, 224
Estimating costs, 222
Estimating demands, 222–223, 225
E-tailing, 268–269
Ethical behaviour in business See corporate social responility, 31–32
Ethical decision making, 32
Ethical guidelines, 17–18, 32–33
Ethics, 31
Ethnic and cultural diversity, 26–27
Ethnic segmentation, 119
Ethnographic research, 60–61
Etsy, 350
EU (European Union), 149
European Data Protection Directive, 149
European Union (EU), 149
Evaluation, 46–47
  control, 46–47
Evaluators, 108
Evoked set (consideration set), 77–79
Evolution of marketing, 4–7

Exchange
building relationships, 8
conditions of, 8
customer value, 8
market segments, 8
marketing mix, 8
Exclusive distribution, 251
Expectation gap, 201
Expedia, 200
Experience curves, 42, 228
Experience quality, 197
Experiential learning, 92
Experiential marketing, 323
Experiment, 61
Exploratory research, 54, 57, 63
Exporting, 42, 105, 258
Express warranty, 172
Extensive decision making, 80
External environment, 1415
competitive factors, 16
corporate social responility, 29–35
demographic factors, 23–27
economic factors, 18–21
ethical behaviour in business, 29–35
regulatory factors, 16–18
social factors, 21–23
technological factors, 27–29
understanding the, 15–16
External information search, 76–77
External marketing environment, 14–16 *See also* Marketing environment
External marketing research providers, 62

F

Facilitating recycling and reducing environmental damage, 169
Facilitating storage, use, and convenience, 169
Factory outlet, 121, 246, 264, 267
Fairness, 18, 22, 33
Fake brands, 168
Family, 22– 23, 86–88
Family brand, 165–166
Family income, 18
Family life cycle (FLC), 81, 83, 87, 117, 119–120
segmentation, 119
stage, 81, 83, 87, 120
Farm Boy, 271
Fashionistas, 119
Fast-food restaurants, 125, 273
Federal legislation, 17–18
Federal Trade Commission (FTC), 23, 310
FedEx, 167
Feedback, 289
Fidget spinner, 190
Field experiment, 61
Fixed costs, 223, 225, 228
Flare, 315
FLC (family life cycle), 81, 83, 87, 117, 119–120
segmentation, 119
stage, 81, 83, 87, 120
Flexible pricing (variable pricing), 230–231
Flighted media schedule, 320
Flipboard, 167
Fluctuating demand, 102
Focus group, 58
Follow-up, 62, 206, 339, 341–343
Food packaging, 170
Forbes magazine, 176
Forces of competition, 16
Ford, Henry, 4, 7
Ford Motor Company, 4, 253
Forkutza, Anne, 262
Fort McMurray wildfire, 21

Four, The (Galloway), 27
Four additional Ps of marketing of services, 203
Four characteristics of a marketing audit, 47
Four "Is" of service, 213
Four Ps, 39, 45, 97, 132, 134, 136 *See also* Marketing mix
Foursquare, 354
Frame of reference, 129
Franchisee, 252, 270
Franchiser, 251–252, 270
Franchises, 264, 270
Franchising, 206, 264, 270
Free merchandise, 337
Free trade agreements (FTAs), 258
Freemium, 335
Freestanding stores, 273
Frequency, 122–123, 136, 140, 143–144, 255, 268, 292, 315–320
Frequent-buyer program, 298, 332, 335
FTAs (free trade agreements), 258
Full-line discount stores, 365
Functional discount (trade discount), 229
Functional modification, 161
Fundamental aspects of business marketing, 102–105

G

Gadgets, 358
Galaxy series of cellphones, 128
Galloway, Scott, 27
Gap Inc., 125
Gap model, 199–200
Garbage in, garbage out, 53
Garnier Fructis bottles, 167
Gatekeepers, 108
GDP (gross domestic product), 19, 21, 196, 209–210, 262
Gender, 56, 81, 83, 87–88, 116–119, 121, 266, 351, 360
marketing, 87
segmentation, 118
General business review sites, 354
General Electric, 67
General Foods' International Coffees, 183
General Motors, 101, 103, 106
Generation X, 23, 25–26, 117
Generation Y, 23–25, 117 *See also* Millennials
Generation Z, 23–24, 59, 205
Generator stores, 274
Generic product, 164–165, 167–168
Generic product name, 167–168
Generic products versus branded products, 165
Geodemographic segmentation, 121
Geodemographics, 119, 121
Geographic pricing, 228, 230
Geographic segmentation, 116
Gibson Guitar Corporation, 91
Gillette, 178, 185, 293
Gillette Fusion razor, 178
Gillette Mach3 razor, 185
Gilt.com, 279
Glad Press'n Seal, 180
Global brand, 149, 164, 171, 361
Global marketing, 258
Globalization *See* Global marketplace
Globe and Mail, 275, 298, 320, 335
Gluckstein, Brian, 273
Goal congruence, 98
Goemans Appliances, 264
Goodall, Jane, 61
Goodfood, 205, 309
Google, 208
Google Alerts, 361
Google Blog Search, 361

Google Buzz, 353
Google My Business, 354
Google Pixel, 90
Google Play, 316
Gorilla Glass, 180
Government purchases, 106
Government subsidies, 42
Governments, 106
federal, 106
municipal, academic. social, and hospitals (MASH), 106
Green marketing, 31–32
Greenlist process, 31
Gross Domestic Process (GDP), 19, 21, 196, 209–210, 262
Gross income, 19
Gross margin, 245, 264, 267, 281
Gross rating points (GRP), 318
Groupon, 293, 333
Growth stage, 189, 191, 223, 291, 301
GRP (growth rating points), 318
Guanxi, 100, 103

H

H&M, 167, 254
H&R Block, 167
Häagen-Dazs, 186
Habitat for Humanity, 209
Happy Meal, 232, 334
Harley-Davidson, 93
Harry Rosen, 43, 274–275
Harvard Business Review 1979, 16
Harvey's, 256
HBC *See* Hudson's Bay Company (HBC)
Head & Shoulders, 125, 162
Health and fitness clubs, 231–232
Health Canada's Food and Drugs Act & Regulation, 17
Heinz, 162, 170, 293
Hellmans, 169
Hershey's, 216–217
Heterogeneity, 198
Heterogeneous shopping products, 159
Hewlett-Packard, 111, 248
HGTV, 318
High-involvement product purchases, 80, 211, 298, 338
Hilton, 146
Hockey Night in Canada Punjabi, 84
Holmes, Ryan, 361
Holt Renfrew, 335
Home Depot, 209, 263, 270, 320
Home Hardware, 89
Home Outfitters, 279
Homogeneous shopping products, 159
Honda, 119, 230
HootSuite, 64–65, 351, 355, 361
Horizontal conflict, 252–253
Household debt, 19
"How Competitive Forces Shape Strategy" (Porter), 16
Hudson Bay Company (HBC), 147, 233, 264–265, 273, 279, 282
Huggies Pull-Ups, 178
Hughes, Clara, 322
Humanitarian texting, 358
Hyatt Hotels, 203
Hyundai, 129

I

IBM, 24, 107, 111, 144, 248
IBM Institute for Business Value, 24
Idea generation, 179, 216
Idea screening, 179, 181
Ideal self-image, 89, 92
Identify customer relationships, 137–138
iHeartRadio, 316

IKEA, 263, 271, 273, 275
IMC (integrated marketing communications), 291–294
Immigrant languages, 84
IMP Group, 99
Implementation, 30, 36–37, 39, 46–47, 136, 291, 360
Improving customer service, 148
Income segmentation, 118–119
Independent retailers, 263–264
India, 84, 186, 216, 258, 343
Indiegogo, 183
Indigo Books & Music, 41, 124, 153–154, 246, 252
Individual branding, 165–166
Inducing product trial by new customers, 147–148
Industrial distributor, 248
Industrial Marketing and Purchasing Group (IMP Group), 98–99
Industrial Marketing Management magazine, 98
Inelastic demand, 102, 223–224
Infinit Nutrition Canada, 125–126
Inflation, 18–20
Influencer, 348
Influencer marketing, 295
Infomercial, 249, 316, 326
Information processing, 203
Information Resources, Inc., 184, 222
Information search, 75–77, 79
Informational labelling, 169
Informative promotion, 290
Ingredient branding, 167
Initiators, 87, 108
Innovation, 186
Innovators, 5, 186–188, 192
Inseparability, 196, 198, 203, 213
Insights West, 347–348
Institutional advertising, 308–309
Institutions, 106
Insurance, 160
Intangibility, 196, 203, 213
Integrated marketing communications, 285
Integrated marketing communications and promotional mix, 299
available funds, 302
factors affecting the promotional mix, 299–303
nature of product, 300
push and pull strategies, 302–303
stage in product life cycle, 300–301
target market characteristics, 301
type of buying decision, 301–302
Integrated marketing communications (IMC), 291–294
Intel, 166–167
Intensive distribution, 251
Interaction, 138–139
Interaction in business marketing, 99
Interactions of current customer base, understanding, 139
Intermediaries
overcoming discrepancies, 242–245
providing contact efficiency, 243–244
providing specialization and division of labor, 242
Internal information search, 76
Internal marketing, 47, 208
Internal marketing in service companies, 208
International trade *See* Global marketplace
Internet, social media *See* social media
Internet, uses of, 63
mobile marketing research, 64
online focus groups, 63
online research communities, 64

Internet, uses of (*continued*)
    online research panel, 63
    rise of big data, 65
    social media marketing research, 64–65
Internet advertising, 317, 319
Internet of Things (IoT), 28
Interpersonal communication, 286–287, 289
Introductory stage, 189–191, 223, 290, 309, 332, 338
Inventory control system, 255–257
Involvement, 79
Involvement, marketing implications, 80–81
Iögo, 38
iPad, 102, 162, 343
iPhone, 69, 90, 128, 162, 180, 182, 191, 350, 357–358
iPod, 355

J

J.D. Power 2019 Canada retail satisfaction study, 201–202
Jetlines, 42
JIT (just-in-time production), 101, 256–257
Jobs, Steve, 156, 180, 196
Joe Fresh, 264
Joint demand, 101–102
Judgment sample, 55–56
Just-in-time production (JIT), 101, 255–257
Just-noticeable difference, 91

K

Kalanick, Travis, 50
KANETIX.ca, 97–98
Keiretsu, 99–100, 103
KFC, 164, 167
Kickstarter, 183
Knockoffs, 167–168
Knowledge gap, 199, 204
Knowledge management, 138
Kodak, 166
Kruger, 127, 317

L

Lab Telus, 185
Labelling, 17, 131, 156, 169–171, 182, 223
Laboratory testing, 61, 182
Labour costs, 42
Laggards, 187–188, 192
Language, 17, 26–27, 60, 70, 84, 142, 170, 172, 177, 284, 289, 305, 333, 343, 359–360
Laptops, 103, 166, 270, 282, 316, 343
Late majority, 187–188, 192
Lead generation (prospecting), 111, 340, 360
Lead qualification, 341
Learning (CRM), 10–11, 42, 61, 65–67, 72, 81, 90, 92–93, 107, 132, 134, 136, 138, 142, 154, 281, 338
Leasing, 99, 103–104, 274
LeBlanc, Jean-Pierre, 198
LEED-certified appliances, 120
Legislation, federal, 17
Leverage customer feedback, **campaign management**, 146
Levi Strauss, 168, 256
Lexicon Branding, 166
Lexus, 119
LG consumer electronics, 165, 167, 179, 244
Licensing, 117, 231, 264, 290
Lifestyle centres, 274

Lifestyle segmentation, 89, 120–121
Lifestyles, component, 22
Lifetime value (LTV) analysis, 143–144
Limited decision making, 79
LinkedIn, 93, 111, 137, 206, 292, 295, 325–326, 335, 341–342, 348, 350–353, 365–366
Liquor Control Board of Ontario (LCBO), 17
List, response, 142
Listening system, 360–361
Listerine, 162
Lifestyle, 89
Loblaw Companies, 39–40, 43, 112, 165, 234, 252, 264, 272, 277, 335
Location-based social networking sites, 350, 354
Loctite Corporation, 108
Logistics, 8, 235, 246, 254–256, 258
Logistics information system, 255–256
London, Ontario, 184
London Drugs, 143
Lord & Taylor, 265, 279
L'Oréal, 6
Loss leader pricing, 230–231, 233–234, 239
Love, 22, 40, 74, 91, 120, 129–130, 164, 173–174, 213, 286, 291, 312–313, 347, 351, 364
Lower-priced products, 161, 177–178
Lowes, 122
Low-involvement product purchases, 79–81, 246, 298, 338
Loyal customers, 48, 73, 132, 144–146, 272, 332, 339
Loyalty marketing programs, 265, 332, 335
LTV (lifetime value) analysis, 143–144
Lululemon, 85, 128, 163, 282–283, 310

M

Mac's Convenience, 265
Magazine advertising, 77, 102, 315, 318
Mail panel survey, 59
Mail surveys, 59
Mailing list, 269, 325
Maison Birks, 264, 274–275
Major equipment, 104, 158, 182, 247
Mall intercept interview, 58–59
Malley Industries, 105–106
Manufacturer's brand, 165, 253, 315, 337
    versus private brands, 165
Manufacturer's suggested retail price, 235
Maple Leaf Foods, 125, 242, 309, 311
Market, 114
Market density, 116
Market development, 40
Market grouping, 299
Market management approach, 99
Market opportunity analysis (MOA), 44–45
Market penetration, 39–40, 186
Market planning
    marketing mix, 45
    place (distribution) strategies, 46
    pricing strategies, 46
    product strategies, 45–46
    promotion strategies, 46
    setting marketing plan objectives, 44
    target market strategy, 44–45
Market segment, 114
Market segmentation, 114–115
    target markets *See* Target marketing
Market segments, 8

Market share, 221
Marketing
    Awake Chocolate, 12–13
    as career, 10
    defined, 2–4
    evolution of, 4–7
    importance of, 10–13
    marketing, 11
    as part of life, 11
    as skill set, 10–11
    and successful companies, 10
Marketing, external environment
    competitive factors, 16
    regulatory factors, 16–17
    target market, 14–15
    understanding external environment, 15–16
    understanding the, 15–16
Marketing, role of promotion in, 284–286
Marketing analytics, 52
Marketing analytics and strategy, 65–66
    analyzing the data, 67–68
    categories of data for marketing analytics, 68–69
    data used in marketing analytics, 67
    marketing analytics techniques, 69
    organizing the data, 67
Marketing audit, 38, 47
Marketing channel (channel of distribution), 242
Marketing channels and supply chain management, 252–254
    channel intermediaries and their functions, 245–246
    distribution challenges, 258–259
    making channel strategy decisions, 249–252
    managing the supply chain, 254–258
    nature of marketing channels, 240–245
    types of marketing channels, 246–249
Marketing channels, nature of
    changing the channels, 240–242
    channel intermediaries and their functions, 245–246
    how intermediaries help the supply chain, 242–245
    marketing and intermediaries, 242–245
Marketing channels, types of
    alternative channel arrangements, 248–249
    channels for business and industrial products, 247–248
    channels for consumer products, 246–247
Marketing communications
    communication process, 287–289
    goals of promotion, 290–291
    integrated marketing communications and promotional mix, 299–303
    introduction, 287
    promotional goals and AIDA concept, 297–298
    promotional mix (AKA integrated marketing communications—IMC), 291–297
    role of promotion in marketing mix, 284–286
Marketing company era, 5
    customer relationship management, 7
    relationship marketing, 7
Marketing concept, 3, 5–6, 138, 179, 185
Marketing dashboard, 68
Marketing environment, 37
Marketing information systems (MIS), 67

Marketing mix, 45
    place, 8–10
    price, 8
    product, 8
Marketing mixes for services
    people strategy, 205
    physical evidence strategy, 205
    place distribution strategy, 205–206
    price strategy, 206–207
    process strategy, 204–205
    product (service) strategy, 203–204
    productivity strategy, 206
    promotion strategy, 206
Marketing objective, 44, 46–47, 115, 210, 285
Marketing plan, 37–39, 44–47, 69, 189, 321, 350, 360
    elements, 38
    evaluation and control, 46–47
    implementation, 46
Marketing plan objectives, setting, 44
Marketing research, 52
    advantages and disadvantages of primary data, 55
    ethnographic research, 60–61
    experiments, 61
    observation research, 60
    questionnaire design, 59–60
    secondary data, 54–55
    Step 1: identify and formulate the problem, 53–54
    Step 2: plan the research design and gather secondary data, 54–55
    Step 3: specify the sampling procedures, 55–56
    Step 4: collect primary data, 56–61
    Step 5: analyze the data, 61–62
    types of errors, 55–56
Marketing research and analytics, 52–53
    data collection concerns, 70–71
    impact of technology, 62–65
    marketing analytics and strategy, 65–69
    marketing research and analytics, 52–53
    marketing research process, 53–62
    three functional roles of, 53
    when to use, 71
Marketing Research and Intelligence Association (MRIA), 55
Marketing research process, 52–54, 62, 73, 295
    Step 1: Identify and formulate th problem/opportunity, 53–54
    Step 2: plan the research design and gather the secondary data, 54–55
    Step 3: specify the sampling procedures, 55–56
    Step 4: collect primary data, 56–61
    Step 5: analyze the reseach, 61–62
    Step 6: prepare and present the report, 62
    Step 7: provide follow-up, 62
Marketing strategy, 44
Marketing-controlled information source, 77–78
Marketing-level planning, 37–38
Marketing-oriented values, 22
Market-plus approach to pricing, 226
Markup, 228
Marriott, 146, 287–288
Marshall's, 267
MASH (municipal, academic, social and hospitals), 106

Maslow's hierarchy of needs, 91
Mass communication, 286–287, 292, 306, 314
Mass customization (build-to-order), 204, 255–256
Mass marketing, 26, 124, 126–127, 227, 255–256, 299, 314, 324, 348
Mass merchandising, 266
Massive multiplayer online game (MMOG), 355
Mattel, 70, 256
Maturity stage, 189, 191, 223, 291, 300, 332
McCain Foods, 106, 250–251
McDonald's, 91, 129, 147, 168, 183–184, 198, 205, 232, 334, 346
Measurement error, 55–56
MEC *See* Mountain Equipment Co-op (MEC)
Media decisions in advertising, 313–314, 328–330
Internet, 317–318
magazines, 315
managing unfavorable publicity, 324
media buying, 320–321
media scheduling, 320
media selection considerations, 328–330
media types, 314–315
newspapers, 314–315
out-od-home media, 316–317
radio, 315
television, 316
Media fragmentation, 319
Media mix, 317–319
Media planning, 313
Media schedule, 320
Media-sharing sites, 352
Medical and consulting services, 197
Medium, 313
Meeting the competition pricing strategy, 220, 228
Mental stimulus processing, 203
Mercedes-Benz, 92, 120
Merchandise mix, 272
mGive Foundation, 358
MGM, 167
Michelin, 270, 311
Microblogs, 295, 350, 353–354
Microsoft, 28, 166, 176, 231
Microtargeting, 269
Milk, 93, 168, 241, 244, 250
Millennials, 23–25, 87, 93, 117, 128, 130, 205, 216, 222, 316, 363
Minecraft, 355
Minute Rice, 182
Mission statement, 37–39, 44
MMOG (massive multiplayer online game), 355
MMS (multimedia messaging service), 357
MOBI, 357
Mobile, growth of, 111
Mobile advertising, 317, 320, 355–357
Mobile couponing, 333
Mobile marketing research, 64
Mobile marketing tools, 357
Mobile phones, 103, 110–111, 121, 140, 162, 180, 282, 317, 357 *See also* Smartphones
Mobile's role in digital marketing apps and widgets, 357–358
common mobile marketing tools, 357
mobile and smartphone technology, 356–357
search: SEO and SEM, 358–359
second coming of texts, 357
Modified rebuy, 108–109
Modo Yoga Studios, 320
Molson, 319

Molson commercial, 319
Molson-Coors Brewing Company, 222
MoneySense, 315
Morality and business ethics, 32
Morals, 31–32
Most ethical companies, worldwide, 33
Motivation, 81, 83, 88–92, 107, 330, 338
Maslow's hierarchy of needs, 91
Motives, 91–92, 119–120, 210
Motor Vehicle Safety Act, 17
Mountain Equipment Co-op (MEC), 275
MSRP (manufacturer's suggested retail price), 235
Multiculturalism, 26–27, 45, 84, 119, 319
Multinational corporations, 6, 10, 49, 109, 142, 186
Multiple choice question, 60
Multiple distribution, 248, 253
Multiplier effect (accelerator principle), 102
Multisegment targeting strategy, 124–126
Municipal, academic, social and hospitals (MASH), 106
Musk, Elon, 74
Mystery shoppers, 60–61

N

NAFTA (North American Free Trade Agreement), 106
NAICS (North American Industry Classification System), 106
National brand, 21, 165, 290
Natural resources, 20
NCE (Networks of Centres of Excellence), 101
Near field communication (NFC), 357
Need, 2–3, 76
Need recognition, 75–76, 79
Needs assessment, 341
Negative reinforcement, 93
Negotiation, 99, 103, 109, 246, 255, 320, 340, 342
Negotiations, types of, 103
Nestlé, 180, 184, 248–249
Netflix, 28, 66, 69, 77, 124, 187, 191, 230, 316, 349
Network approach, 99–100
Network supplier model, 100
Networking, 99–100, 111, 335, 340–342
Networks, business marketing, 99–101
Networks and relationship approach, business marketing
approach to business marketing, 98–99
interaction in business marketing, 99
relationships in business marketing, 98–101
Networks of Centres of Excellence (NCE), 101
New entrants, 16, 222, 358
New methods of service delivery, 42
New product, 177–178
New product categories, 177
importance of, 177–178
introduction, 176–177
New task buy, 108
Newcomers, 282
New-product development, global issues, 186
New-product development process
business analysis, 181–182
development, 182
idea generation, 179–181
idea screening, 181
strategy, 178–179

test marketing, 182–184
New-product strategy, 178–179, 181
New-producters, spread of
diffusion of innovation, 186–187
marketing implications of the adoption process, 188
product characteristics and rate of adoption, 187–188
Newspaper advertising, 296, 314–315
New-to-the-world products, 178
NFC (near field communications), 357
Niche, 41, 43, 124–125, 191, 211, 249, 272, 299, 322
Niche competitive advantage, 43
Nielsen, 52, 222, 354
Nike, 78, 129, 167, 264, 313, 315, 324, 346–347, 358
Nike+, 358
Nissan, 119, 300
No-frills goods and services, 42
Noise, 35, 240, 287–288, 315, 318–319
Nonaspirational reference groups, 86
Noncorporate blogs, 325, 353
Noncumulative quantity discount, 229
Nonmarketing-controlled information source, 76–77
Nonprobability sample, 55–56
Non-profit organization marketing, 210
defined, 209–210
unique aspects of non-profit organization strategies, 210–212
Non-profit organization (not-for-profit), 209–210
strategies, unique aspects of, 210
Nonstore retailing, 267–270, 281
automatic vending, 268
direct mail, 269
direct marketing (DM), 268
direct retailing, 268
introduction, 267–268
microtargeting, 269
nonstore retailing, rise of, 268
self-service technologies (SST), 268
shop-at-home television networks, 269
telemarketing, 268–269
Norms, 6, 31–32, 83–87, 186–187, 259, 283, 316
North American Free Trade Agreement (NAFTA), 106
North American Industry Classification System (NAICS), 106
NPS (Net Promoter Score), 135

O

Objectives, 210
Observation research, 60
Occupation segmentation, 119
Odd–even pricing (psychological pricing), 231
Odours, 276
OEMs (original equipment manufacturers), 105–106, 178
Off-peak pricing, 206–207
Off-price retailer, 263–264, 266–267, 273–275
Oil, 8, 18, 20–21, 103–105, 260
Olay, 184–185
Old Navy, 125, 270
Omega, 166
Omnichannel retailing, 279, 283
On-demand marketing, 150
OnDemand5, 136–137
One-brand-name strategy, 170
One-to-one marketing, 126–127

One-way mirror marketing, 58
Online activities *See* Internet
Online focus groups, 63, 361
Online marketing, 111, 124, 294, 296, 331, 349
Online networketing sites, 342
Online research panel, 63
Online retailing (e-tailing), 268–269
Online reviews, 325
Online sampling, 336
Online shopping, 59, 138, 246, 248, 266, 274, 282
identities of shoppers, 266
Online surveys, 58–59, 63, 68
Open-ended question, 60, 73
Opinion leader, 86
Optimizers, 122
Optimum, 278
Order processing system, 256
Organic traffic, 359
Original equipment manufacturers (OEMs), 105–106, 178
OshKosh B'gosh, 125, 270
Outbound telemarketing, 269, 325
Outdoor advertising, 317
Out-of-home advertising, 316–317
Outsourcing, 25, 42
Owned media, 296–297, 300, 360
Owyang, Jeremiah, 361

P

P&G *See* Proctor & Gamble (P&G)
Package aesthetics, 171
Packaging, functions, 168–169
Paid media, 296–297, 321
Pampers Kandoo baby wipes, 178
Pareto Principle (80/20 rule), 122, 137
Patronage-oriented pricing, 207
Paul, Logan, 348
Pay per click (PPC), 307
Pay-what-you-want pricing, 232–233
PC Financial Cards, 335
Penetration pricing, 226–228
People processing, 203–204
People-watching-people research, 60
Percentage of sales, 307
Perception, 90
Perceptual mapping, 128
Perel, Johathan, 240
Perishability, 198–199
Perishable products, 250
Personal Information Protection and Electronic Documents Act (PIPEDA), 17–18, 140–142, 149
Personal information source, 206
Personal selling
advantages of, 338
communication advantage, 295
controlling costs of, 337–338
and the internet, 293
push money, 337
relationship selling, 338–339
Personal spending, 20
Personality, 81, 83, 87, 89, 119, 286, 322, 343
Personalization, 69–70, 82, 126, 146–147, 150, 197, 262, 278, 294–295, 317, 324, 335
Personally identifiable information, 71
Persuasive labelling, 169
Persuasive promotion, 156, 291, 301
Petroleum, 122
Phablets, 357
Photo sharing sites, 352
Pinterest, 64, 111, 121, 295, 348, 350–351, 354
Pioneering advertising, 309

PIPEDA (Personal Information Protection and Electronic Documents Act), 17–18, 140–142, 149
Place, 8–10 *See also* Marketing channels
Place (distribution) strategies, 46, 206, 211–212
Planned obsolescence, 162
Planning, 36 *See also* Strategic planning
Planters Creamy peanut butter, 181
Plato, 74
PlayStation, 138
PLC *See* Product life cycle (PLC)
Podcasts, 29, 212, 289, 292, 295, 316, 341, 355, 360
Point of difference, 129
Point-of-sale interactions, 66, 136, 139–140, 282
Pokemon Go, 190, 355
Population shifts, 26
Pop-up shop, 148, 274
Porter, Michael, 16
Porter's five forces of competition, 16
Position, 127
Positioning, 127
    bases, 128–129
    perceptual mapping, 128
    statement, 129
Positive reinforcement, 93, 308
Postconventional morality, 32
Postpurchase behaviour, 75, 78–79
Postpurchase services, 109
Prada, 92, 179
Preapproach, 341
Preconventional morality, 32
Predatory pricing, 233–235
Predictive modelling, 69, 143–145
Premium, 25, 31, 77, 90, 115, 159, 161, 236–237, 251, 276, 293, 332, 334–336
Prepurchase service, 109
President's Choice, 165, 252
Price, 8, 109, 218
Price and the pricing process, importance of, 219–220
    importance of price to marketing managers, 219–220
Price bundling, 230–232
Price discrimination, 233, 235
Price elasticity of demand, 223–224
Price fixing, 233–234
Price lining, 230–231
Price sensitivity, 161, 220, 223–224, 227
Price setting, legality and ethics of
    bait pricing, 233
    deceptive pricing, 234
    predatory pricing, 234–235
    price discrimination, 235
    resale price maintenance, 234–235
Price skimming, 226–227
Price strategy, 206, 220, 225–228
Pricing *See also* Pricing decisions; *also* Pricing process; *also* Pricing strategies
    dynamic pricing, 229–230
    geographic pricing, 230
    other pricing tactics, 230–232
    penetration pricing, 227–228
    price skimming, 226
    status quo pricing, 228
    value-based pricing, 229
Pricing decisions, 212
Pricing objectives, 207, 212, 220–222, 231
Pricing process
    break-even analysis, 224–225
    discounts and allowances, 228–229
    geography pricing, 230

markup, 228
    other pricing tactics, 230–233
    penetration pricing, 227–228
    profit-oriented pricing objectives, 220–221
    sales-oriented pricing objectives, 221–222
    status quo pricing, 228
    status quo pricing objectives, 222
    Step 1: establishing pricing objectives, 220
    Step 2: estimating demand, costs, and profits, 222–225
    Step 3: price strategy, choosing, 225–228
    Step 4: using a pricing tactic, 228
Pricing strategies, 46, 124, 158, 225–228
Primary data, 54, 56–58
    collection, 56–58
Primary membership groups, 85
Primary research, 56–57, 194
Privacy, consumer, 18
Privacy Act, 17–18, 149
Privacy Commissioner, 17–18, 141
Private brand, 165
Private exchange, 248
Private label brand, 165, 252
PRIZM, 89
Probability sample, 55–56
Proctor & Gamble (P&G), 291, 297
Procurement, 22, 255
Producers, 105–106
Product, 8, 156 *See also* Product concepts
Product advertising
    competitive advertising, 309–310
    pioneering advertsing, 309
Product and trade name franchising, 270
Product assortment, 263–264, 267, 271–272, 281
Product category, 68, 78–80, 123, 165, 189, 191, 240, 291, 309–310, 332
Product concepts
    branding, 163–168
    packaging, 168–172
    product items, lines, and mixes, 160–163
    product warranties, 172
    types of consumer products, 157–160
Product decisions, 211
Product design, 42, 74, 126, 191, 252
Product development, 40–41
Product differentiation, 41–43, 127
    competitive advantage, 42–43
Product distribution *See* Marketing channels
Product item, 156, 160–161, 163
    adjustments to product items, lines, and mixes, 161–163
Product life cycle (PLC), 188–189
    decline stage, 191–192
    growth stage, 191
    implications for marketing management, 192
    introductory stage, 189–191
    maturity stage, 191
Product line, 160
Product line contraction, 162–163
Product line depth, 160
Product line extension, 162
Product line length, 160
Product mix, 128, 160–161, 198, 266, 273
Product mix width, 160–161
Product modification, 161–162, 180, 189
Product offering, 14, 16, 45, 72, 124–125, 156, 203, 243, 271–272, 285

Product placement, 318, 322, 348
Product publicity, 321
Product quality, 185
Product strategies, 45–46, 203–204
Product trials, 80, 145, 147, 269, 343
Product-cycle pricing strategies, 226
Production era, 4
Production innovation, 42
Production scheduling, 67, 229, 255
Products, containing and protecting, 169
Products, developing and managing
    global issues in new-product development, 186–188
    new products, importance of, 176–178
    new-product development process, 178–186
    product life cycles, 188–192
Products, promoting, 169
Product/service differentiation competitive advantage, 42–43
Professional services pricing, 230–232
Profit, 219
    maximization, 212, 220
Programmatic buying, 313
Project Zero, 168
Promotion, 284 *See also* Promotional mix
Promotion, goals of
    connecting, 291
    informing, 290–291
    introduction, 290
    persuading, 291
    reminding, 291
Promotion decisions, 212
Promotion strategies, 14, 45–46, 156, 188, 190, 206, 212, 272, 331
Promotional goals
    AIDA and the promotional mix, 298
    AIDA concept, 297–298
Promotional mix, 291–292 *See also* Promotion
    advertising, 292
    communication process, 295
    direct-response communication, 294
    online marketing, content marketing, and social media, 294–295
    personal selling, 293–294
    public relations (PR) and publicity, 292–293
    sales promotion, 293
Promotional strategy, 284–286, 298, 301–303, 345
Prospecting, 339–341
Prototyping, 173, 181–183, 204, 260, 310
Provincial and territorial laws, 17–18
PSA (public service advertisement), 138, 212
Psychographic segmentation, 119–121
Psychographics, 45, 89, 116, 121, 131, 143, 269, 271, 326, 361
Psychological factors, 74–75, 81, 83, 90, 95
Psychological pricing, 231
Public relations, 292
    experiential, 322
    major public relations tools, 321–324
    product publicity, 321–322
Public service advertisement (PSA), 212
Publicity, 293, *See also* Public relations
Pull strategy, 300, 302–303
Pulsing media schedule, 320

Purchaser, 15, 34, 45, 77, 79–81, 87, 103, 107–109, 140, 207, 229–230, 234, 279, 298, 301–302, 334
Purchasing contract, 109
Purchasing power, 18–20, 23–24, 80, 117, 172, 235, 349
Purchasing profiles, 122
Pure research, 28
Push money, 337
Push strategy, 302–303
Pyramid of corporate social responsibility, 30

Q

Qaiku, 353
QR (Quick Response) code, 357
Quaker Oats, 49, 183, 243
Qualitative data collection methods, 57–58
Qualitative research, 56
Quality, 109
Quality modification, 161–162
Quantitative data collection methods, 57–58
Quantitative research, 56–57, 60
Quantity discount, 228–229, 337
Questionnaire design, 59–60, 63
Quick Response (QR) code, 357
Quickie Convenience, 265
Quota, 31, 56
    sample, 56

R

Radio-frequency identification (RFID), 28, 255, 278
Random sample, 56
Rapid Boost Marketing, 348–350
Raw materials, 41, 46, 104, 107–108, 122, 158, 247, 254–259
RBC Royal Bank, 163–164, 166, 323
Reach, 318
"Real heroes" campaign, 118
Real self-image, 89
Reason to believe, 129
Rebates, 142, 334, 337
Receivers, 288
Recency-frequency-monetary (RFM) analysis, 143–144
Recession, 18, 20–21, 25–26, 182, 365
Reciprocity, 99, 103
    use of, 103
Red Bull GmbH, 236, 318
Reddit, 111, 352
Reducing and recycling, 169
Re-engineering, 42
Reference group, 81, 83, 85–86, 92
Referrals, 56, 82, 340
Regulatory factors, 16–17
    federal regulation, 17
    provincal and territorial laws, 17–18
    self-regulation, 18
Reinforcement, 92–93, 147, 322
Reinforcing customer purchase decisions, 147
Relationship building, 134, 145, 148, 152, 212, 324, 338–339
Relationship commitment, 98
Relationship marketing, 6–7, 133–134, 207–208
Relationship marketing era, customer satisfaction, 6–7
Relationship marketing in services, 207–208
Relationship selling (business development), 294, 338–340, 342
Reliability, 43, 51, 62, 98, 120, 198–199
Reminder promotion, 291
Repetition, 92–93, 315

Repositioning, 129, 154, 161–162, 177–178, 290, 309
Resale price maintenance, 233, 235, 253
Research, 28
Research and development (R&D), 45, 101, 179–180, 297, 327
Research design, 54–57, 62
Research design process, 55
Research report, 62
Resellers, 105–106, 122, 165, 253
Response list, 142
Responsiveness, 64, 111, 123, 142, 185, 199, 201
Retail channel omnification, 278
Retail marketing strategy
  choosing the retailing mix, 271–276
  defining a target market, 271
  retailing decisions for services, 276–277
Retail operations, major types of
  category killer, 266
  convenience stores, 265
  department stores, 264–265
  discount stores, 265
  drugstores, 265
  factory outlet, 267
  full-line discount stores, 265
  mass merchandising, 266
  nonstore retailing, 267
  off-price retailer, 267
  online retailing or **e-tailing**, 269
  restaurants, 267
  scrambled merchandising, 265
  sharing economy, 269–270
  specialty discount stores, 266
  specialty stores, 265
  supercentres, 266
  supermarkets, 265
  warehouse membership clubs, 266–267
Retail operations,classification and types of, 264
  level of service, 264
  ownership, 263
  price, 264
  product assortment, 264
Retail product/services failures, addressing, 277
Retail promoton, 272
Retailer, 245
Retailer and retail consumer trends and advantages
  big data, 277–278
  future developments in retail management, 278–279
  shopper analytics and marketing, 278
Retailer channel, 246
Retailer errors, 277
Retailing
  addressing retail product/service failures, 277
  classification and types of retail operations, 263–267
  introduction, 262–263
  retail marketing strategy, 277
  retailer and retail consumer trends and advancements, 277–279
  rise of nonstore retailing, 267–270
  role of retailing, 262–263
Retailing mix, 271–272
Retailing mix, choosing
  freestanding stores, 273–274
  personnel, 276
  place, 273
  presentation, 274–276
  price, 274

product offering, 271–272
  promotion, 272–273
  shopping centres, 274
Retaining loyal customers, 146
Rethinking the consumer decision-making process, 82
Return on investment (ROI), 45, 69–70, 106, 116, 209, 220–222, 326, 355
Revenue, 219
Revenue-oriented pricing, 207
Review sites, 350, 354
Reynolds, Ryan, 322
RFID (radio-frequency identification), 28, 255, 278
RFM (recency-frequency-monetary) analysis, 143–144
Right price, setting
  importance of price and the pricing process, 218–220
  legality and ethics of setting a price, 233–235
  the pricing process, 220–233
Roblox, 355
Robots, 28, 42, 105, 279
Rogers Communications, 77, 163, 286, 334
Rogers Media, 84, 315
ROI (return on investment), 45, 69–70, 106, 116, 209, 220–222, 326, 335
Rolex, 43
Roll Up the Rim, 331
Rolls-Royce, 168
Routine response behaviour, 79
Royal Bank *See* RBC Royal Bank
Royal Canadian Mint, 232
Rubbermaid's Sidekick, 180
Runners World, 318
Running Room, 212, 265
Russia, 343
Ruth's Chris Steak House, 159

S

S. C. Johnson & Son, 31
Safety needs, 91
Saje Natural Wellness, 198
Saks Fifth Avenue, 127, 265, 279
Sales approach, 99, 307
Sales cycle, 339
Sales era, 4–5
Sales maximization, 212, 221–222
Sales orientation, 4, 220–221
Sales presentation, 108, 297, 303, 342
Sales process (sales cycle), 327, 338–339
Sales promotion, 293
  objectives of, 332
  sales promotion target, 331
  tools for consumer sales promotion, 333–336
Sales promotion and personal selling
  personal selling, 337–338
  relationship selling, 338–339
  sales promotion defined, 330–332
  selling process, 329–343
  tools for consumer sales promotion, 333–336
  tools for trade sells promotion, 336–337
Sales proposal, 339, 342
Salesforce, 149
Salesforce Tower, 29
Sales-oriented pricing objectives, 220–221
Salman, Ali, 349
Sample, 55
  types of, 56
Sampling, 54–56, 72, 191, 302–303, 327, 331, 336, 344–345, 353

Sampling error, 56
Samsung, 68–69, 128, 165–166, 191, 244, 356
Samsung Gear VR, 356
Satellite burbs, 121
Satisfactory profits, 42, 220–221
Satisficers, 122
SBU (strategic business unit), 37, 39, 41, 44
Scaled-response question, 60
SCMA (Supply Chain Management Association), 243
Scotiabank, 42, 163, 166, 323, 335
Scrambled merchandising, 265
Screening, 58, 63, 179, 181, 194, 251
Search engine marketing (SEM), 359
Search engine optimization (SEO), 294–296, 301–302, 355, 358–359
Search quality, 197
Sears, 282
Seasonal discount, 229
Seasonal media schedule, 320
Secondary data, 54–57, 116
Secondary data collection, 54–57
Secondary membership groups, 85
Segmentation *See* Market segmentation
Segmentation, criteria for successful, 123
Segmentation bases (variables), 115–116
  descriptors, 123
Segmenting, targeting and positioning
  bases for segmenting consumer markets, 115–123
  criteria for successful segmentation, 123
  market segmentation, 114–115
  positioning, 127–129
  steps in segmenting a market, 123–127
Segmenting a market, steps in, 123–124
Selective distortion, 90
Selective distribution, 251
Selective exposure, 90
Selective retention, 90
Self-actualization, 91–92, 291
Self-administered and one-time mail survey, 59
Self-concept, 81, 83, 86–87, 89
Self-esteem needs, 91–92
Self-image, 89, 92
Self-regulation, 6, 18
  consumer privacy, 18
Self-service technologies (SST), 268
Selling process
  impact of technology, 343
  key issues in each step, 340–343
  personal selling in a glob l market, 343
  steps of, 339–340
Sender, 286–288, 295–296
Sensodyne toothpaste, 45
Sentiment analysis, 69
SEO (search engine optimization), 294–296, 301–302, 355, 358–359
Sephora, 148
Service, 109, 196 *See also* Service organizations
Service delivery, 42, 199–200, 204, 206, 277
Service distribution, 277
Service mark, 167
Service mix, 204
Service organizations, 198, 203–205, 210
Service quality
  evaluating service quality, 199

the gap model of service quality, 199–203
  measuring service quality and customer satisfaction, 201
Services and goods, difference
  heterogeneity, 198
  inseparability, 198
  intangibility, 196–197
  perishability, 198–199
Services and nonprofit organization marketing
  defined, 196
  how services differ from goods, 196–199
  internal marketing in service companies, 208
  marketing mixes for services, 203–207
  non-organization marketing, 209–212
  relationship marketing in services, 207–208
  service quality, 199–203
7-Eleven, 157–158, 162–163, 179–180
Sexier ads, 90
Sharing economy, 269–270
Sharp, 166
Shaw Communications, 286
Shelf extenders, 336
Shop-at-home television network, 269
Shopper analytics, 278
Shopper marketing, 278, 336
Shoppers Drug Mart, 158, 165, 263, 272, 274, 277, 282, 335
Shopping product, 158–159, 191, 338
Showrooming, 279
Simons, 147, 265
Simple random sample, 56
Simulated (laboratory) market testing, 184
Simulated shopping, 61
Sinek, Simon, 14
Single-price tactic, 231
SMART method, 44
SMS (Short Message Service), 357
Snapchat, 111, 128, 157, 350–351
Snowball sample, 56
Social acceleration, 29
Social class, 81, 83–85, 289
Social commerce, 349–350
Social consensus, 32
Social factors, 21, 81, 83, 89
  marketing-oriented values, 22
Social gaming, 318, 355
Social media, 294–295
Social media and digital strategies
  designing a digital marketing strategy, 359–361
  mobile's role in digital marketing, 356–358
  search: SEO and SEM, 358–359
  social media's role in integrated marketing comminications, 346–358
  tools of social engagement, 350–356
Social media growth, 111
Social media marketing research, 64–65
Social media metrics, 352, 356
Social media plan, 349
Social media's role in integrated marketing comminications
  Canadian use of social media, 348–350
  introduction, 346–348
Social needs, 30, 91, 363
Social networking sites, 270, 342, 350–352, 354–355
Social news sites, 350, 352

Social responsibility, growth of, 30–31
Social selling, 341
Social visibility, 80
Socialization process, 87
Societal marketing era, 6
Sonos, 166
Sony, 138, 140, 244
Sourcing and procurement, 255
Spatial discrepancy, 243, 246
Specialty discount stores, 266–267
Specialty product, 158–159, 191, 300
Specialty stores, 264–265, 267, 274
Specialty tea retailers, 206
Spectacles, 356
Sponsorship, 31, 298, 321–322
Sport Chek, 315
Spotify, 316, 335, 355
Sprite, 128, 171
SPSS Predictive Marketing, 144–145
SST (self-service technologies), 268
Standard tissue, 127
Standards gap, 200, 205
Starbucks, 40, 148, 167, 183, 191, 199, 204, 248–249, 264, 267, 273
Starwood Hotels, 146
State of Customer Relationship Management, 134
Statistics Canada, 40, 119
Status quo pricing, 222, 226, 228, 231
Stimulus, 76, 81–82, 90–92, 94, 134, 199, 203
Store brand, 91, 165
Store demonstrations, 337
Store layout, 275
Straight rebuy, 108–109
Strategic alternatives, 39–41
  selecting, 41
Strategic business unit (SBU), 37, 39, 41, 44
Strategic channel alliances, 248–249
Strategic directions
  conducting a SWOT analysis, 39
  linking SWOT to growth strategies, 39–41
  selecting a strategic alternatve, 41
  strategic alternatives—linking SWOT to growth strategies, 39–41
Strategic planning
  business planning for competitive advantage, 41–44
  corporate planning, 38–39
  effective strategic planning, 47
  importance of, 36–39
  market planning, 44–46
  marketing plan, implementation, evaluation, and control, 46–47
  strategic business units, 37–38
  strategic directions, 39–41
Strategic planning, effective, 47–48
Stratified sample, 56
Strip malls, 228, 274
Structured data, 68
Student Advantage, 139
StumbleUpon, 352
Style modification, 161
Subaru, 120, 312, 334
Subculture, 81, 83–84
Substitutes, 16, 33, 159, 185, 187, 190–191, 215, 226, 234, 269
  competitors, 16
Subway, 167, 264
Suggestion selling, 276
Sun Microsystems, 111
Super Bowl commercials, 321, 362
Supercentres, 116, 266–267
Supermarkets, 61, 114, 125, 170, 183, 228, 231, 248, 263–265, 267, 274, 336

Superstores, 265
Supplementary services, 203–204
Suppley chain team, 255
Supplier–buyer relationship, 109
Suppliers, 16
Supplies, 104, 158, 182, 238, 245–246, 251, 255, 257, 264, 270, 339
Supply chain, 242
Supply Chain Canada, 243
Supply chain management, 254
  benefits of, 254
  inventory control system, 257–258
  managing logistics in the supply chain, 254
  order processing, 256–257
  product scheduling, 255–256
  sourcing and procurement, 255
Supply chain team, 255
Survey research, 58–59, 63
Sustainable competitive advantage, 41, 43, 243
Sweepstakes, 142, 293, 330, 332, 335–336
Swiffer, 291
Swiffer Mop, 61
Swiss Chalet, 291, 312
SWOT analysis, 38–39, 41, 49
Systematic sample, 56

T

Tablets, 77, 102, 166, 188, 190–191, 277–278, 282, 307, 314–316, 333, 335, 349, 356–357
Tangerine, 42–43, 166
Tangible cue, 197, 206
Tangibles, 8, 46, 156, 197–199, 202, 205, 234, 266, 303, 318
Target market, 14–15, 44–45, 210
  strategy, 44–45
Target markets, strategies for selecting
  concentrated targeting, 125
  undifferentiated targeting strategy, 124–125
Targeted consumers, 129
Targeted marketing communications, 144–147
TD CanadaTrust, 323
Tea, 115, 167, 205, 299
Teavana, 167, 248
Tech trends, 28–29 *See also* Internet
Technological factors, technology and the future of business, 28–29
Technology, impact research and analytics, uses of the Internet, 63
Technology and the future of business, 28–29
Teenage market, 117
Telecommunications industry, 231
Telecommuting, 28–29
Telemarketing, 246, 268–269, 294, 325, 340
Telephone interviews, 58–59
Television advertising, 320, 362
Telus, 163, 185, 286, 312, 334
Temporal discrepancy, 243
Tentree, 221
Tesla Motors, 8, 74–75, 176, 290, 300
Test marketing, 170, 179, 182–184
  alternatives to, 184
  high cost of, 183
Tetley, 299
Tetley tea, 299–303
Textile Labelling Act, 17
#thebestmencanbe, 295
The Children's Place, 265, 270
The Shops at Don Mills, 274
The Sims Online, 355

Three-dimensional printing (3DP), 258–259
Threshold level of perception, 91
Tide, 81, 166, 291, 312, 320
Tide with Downy, 161
Tim Hortons, 17, 40–41, 84, 163, 178, 184, 205, 264, 286, 330–332, 336
Time savings, 61, 126
TJ Maxx, 274
Toilet paper, 127, 317, 364
Tools for consumer sales promotion
  contests and sweepstakes, 335–336
  discounts and coupons, 333–334
  loyalty marketing programs, 335
  premiums, 334–335
  sampling, 336
  shopper marketing, 336
Tools of social engagement
  audio, 355
  blogs, 353
  evaluation and measurement of social media, 355–356
  microblogs, 353–354
  social media channels, registered users (18.2), 351
  social networks, 350–352
  social news sites, 352
  virtual worlds and online gaming, 355
Toothpaste, 45, 56, 79, 162, 164, 182, 187, 255, 291, 301
Touch points, 139–140, 142, 150
Toyota, 42, 100, 107, 119
Toys "R" Us, 264
Trade agreements, 258
Trade allowance, 336–337
Trade and industry associations, 55
Trade discount, 229
Trade sales promotion, 331, 336–337
  tools for, 336–337
Trade shows, 293, 337, 340
Trademark, 167–168, 243
  violations, 168
Trading up, 276
Transit shelters, 316
Trends in B2B online marketing, 111
Triangle, 332
Trickle-down effect, 101
Tripadvisor, 296, 354
Triple bottom line, 29
Trojan Horse method, 341
Trophy kids, 24
Trudeau, Justin, 22, 25
Trump, Donald, 319, 354
Trust, 98
"Truth About CSR, The," 30
Tumblr, 353
Turf war, 253
TV advertising, 320, 362
Tweens, 23, 117, 333, 350
Twitter search, 361
Two-for-one offers, 81
Two-for-the-price-of-one bonus packs, 335
Two-part pricing, 230, 232
Tybout, Alice M., 129
Types of business products, 104–105
Types of primary data, 57
Types of reference groups, 85

U

Uber, 5, 42, 50–51, 77, 150, 230, 269
UberEats, 50–51
Unbundling, 231
Undifferentiated targeting strategy, 124–127, 210
Unfulfilled needs, 76

Uniform delivered pricing, 230
Unilever, 118, 169–170
Unique selling proposition (USP), 311
Unsought products, 159–160
Unstructured data, 69
Urban core areas, 26
Usage-rate segmentation, 121–122
USP (unique selling proposition), 311

 V

Value, 83
Value pricing, 229, 238
Value propostition, 35, 75, 221, 236, 267, 285, 287
Value-based pricing, 229, 237–238
Vancouver City Savings Credit Union (Vancity), 204
Vanier Institute of the Family, 22
Variable costs, 222–223, 225, 234
Variable pricing, 231
Vending machines, 158, 249, 251, 258, 264, 268, 280
Vendors, 180
Vertical conflict, 253
Virtual pet, 190
Voice search, 29
Volunteers, 209, 212

 W

WagJag, 293
Walmart, 66, 115, 127, 226–228, 233, 237, 248, 263, 265, 272, 274, 276, 281, 310
Walt Disney Company, 7, 9, 316
Want, 76
WAP website, 357
Warehouse membership clubs, 266–267
Warranty, 46, 70, 99, 129, 137, 139, 172
Wearable technology, 356
Web survey and survey design systems, 63
Web widgets, 358
Web-based interactions, 139
Weight Watchers, 167
Whole Foods Market, 353
Wholesaler channel, 246–247
Widgets, 357–358
Wildfires, 21
Windex, 31
Winners, 267
Word-of-mouth communication, 187–188, 200, 360
Worldwide Retail Exchange, 248
Wristbands, 190
Wylie, Chris, 143

 X

Xerox, 166, 168, 182

 Y

Yeats, W. B., 284
Yelp, 354
YouTube, 65, 69, 111, 288–289, 294–295, 297, 299, 306, 326, 331, 348–349, 351–352, 365
Yum! Brands, 164

 Z

Zara, 254
Zone pricing, 230
Zoomer, 318

KEY CONCEPTS

1-1 Define marketing. Marketing is about understanding the needs of the customer. No other aspect of business has this focus. Marketing helps to shape a company's products and services based on an understanding of what the customer is looking for. Marketing is about engaging in a conversation with that customer and guiding the delivery of what is required to satisfy those needs.

1-2 Describe the evolution of marketing. Marketing has been created by an evolution in the use and application of marketing techniques in companies over many decades. The five eras of marketing are the production era, the sales era, the marketing company era, the societal marketing era, and the relationship marketing era. Each one developed a new aspect of what we now know as marketing and contributed to how many view marketing today.

1-3 Define key marketing terms. An understanding of the following terms is fundamental for anyone learning about marketing:

- **Exchange:** people giving up one thing to receive another thing they would rather have

- **Customer value:** the relationship between benefits and the sacrifice necessary to obtain those benefits

- **Market segments:** groups of individuals, families, or companies that are placed together because it is believed that they share similar needs

- **Relationship building:** companies can expand their market share in three ways: attracting new customers, increasing business with existing customers, and retaining current customers

- **The marketing mix:** also known as the four Ps of marketing, these are product, price, place, and promotion. Each of the four Ps must be studied and developed to create a proper strategy to attract a market segment.

KEY TERMS

1-1

marketing the activities that develop an offering in order to satisfy a customer need

need a state of being where we desire something that we do not possess but yearn to acquire

1-2

production era a focus on manufacturing and production quantity in which customers are meant to choose based on what is most abundantly available

sales era hard selling to the customer, who has greater choice thanks to more competition in the marketplace

marketing company era a strong emphasis on the marketing concept and development of a more comprehensive approach to understanding the customer

societal marketing era looking not only at the customer but expanding marketing efforts to include aspects from the external environment that go beyond a company's customers, suppliers, and competitors

customer satisfaction customers' evaluation of a good or service in terms of whether it has met their needs and expectations

relationship marketing a strategy that focuses on keeping and improving relationships with current customers

1-3

exchange people giving up one thing to receive another thing they would rather have

customer value the relationship between benefits and the sacrifice necessary to obtain those benefits

1-4 Explain why marketing matters. Marketing is not just about sales and advertising within a company; it permeates the whole company. There are rewarding careers in marketing, with compensation that is competitive with other fields of business, along with opportunities that go well beyond the cubicle. Successfully understanding marketing means having an ability to analyze and communicate findings, which are important skill sets for anyone who aspires for a career in business. An understanding of marketing allows people to be informed consumers, ones who are not afraid to demand more from the products and services they rely on every day.

KEY CONCEPTS

2-1 Discuss the external environment of marketing, and explain how it affects a company. The external marketing environment consists of competitive, regulatory, economic, social, and technological variables. Marketers cannot control the external environment, but they must understand how it is changing and the effect on the target market. Marketing managers can then create a marketing mix to effectively meet the needs of target customers.

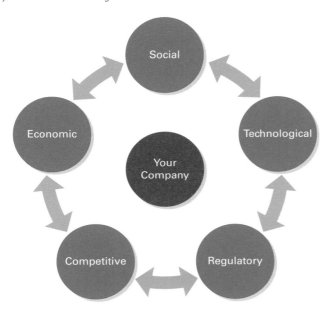

2-2 Describe the competitive factors that affect marketing. Companies face competition from five different areas: direct competitors, who most closely match their value proposition; substitutes, who satisfy similar needs but in different ways; new entrants, who can emerge from nowhere as start-ups challenging for the same market; suppliers, who provide companies with required products but typically charge as much as they can for said products; and buyers, who buy from companies but typically want to pay as little as possible.

2-3 Describe the regulatory factors that affect marketing. All organizations must operate within legal boundaries. In most cases this is in the best interest of all involved; however, marketers must be on top of regulations as they evolve so that they're not blindsided by new laws and regulations that could help (opportunities) or hinder (threats) a business.

2-4 Describe the economic factors that affect marketing. Much like marketers must anticipate external forces of competition and regulations, they must also be the first to see the onset of contractions and expansions in the economy. Signs can be obvious, such as news coverage of changes in economic indicators such as jobs, GDP, and housing. Other times marketers must literally survey their business microscopically, looking for trends in sales. Any combination of shifts in consumer income or recessionary or inflationary trends in the economy will signal to companies that it is time to make adjustments to their strategies.

KEY TERMS

2-1
target market a group of people or organizations for which an organization designs, implements, and maintains a marketing mix intended to meet the needs of that group

2-3
Competition Bureau the federal department charged with administering most marketplace laws

self-regulation programs voluntarily adopted by business groups to regulate the activities of their members

2-4
purchasing power a comparison of income versus the relative cost of a set standard of goods and services in different geographic areas

discretionary income the amount of money people have to spend on nonessential items

disposable income the amount of money people have to spend after taxes

gross income the amount of money people earn before taxes and expenses

inflation a measure of the decrease in the value of money, expressed as the percentage reduction in value since the previous year

recession a period of economic activity characterized by negative growth, which reduces demand for goods and services

environmental factors noncontrollable factors caused by natural disasters, which negatively or positively affect organizations

2-5
component lifestyles mode of living that involves choosing goods and services that meet one's diverse needs and interests rather than conforming to a single, traditional lifestyle

2-6
demography the study of people's vital statistics, such as their age, race and ethnicity, and location

Generation Z people born between 1995 and 2009

Generation Y people born between 1979 and 2000

Generation X people born between 1966 and 1978

baby boomers people born between 1947 and 1965

multiculturalism the peaceful and equitable coexistence of different cultures, rather than one national culture, in a country

CHAPTER REVIEW 2

2-7

basic research pure research that aims to confirm an existing theory or to learn more about a concept or phenomenon

applied research an attempt by marketers to use research to develop new or improved products

2-8

corporate social responsibility a business's concern for society's welfare

triple bottom line a business philosophy seen as the pursuit of profit while also benefiting society and the environment

social acceleration the concept of exponentially rapid growth starting with human desire for improved products, spurring competitive pursuit of market share, driving innovation and technology, and resulting in a higher standard of living, but with new socioenvironmental problems

pyramid of corporate social responsibility a model that suggests corporate social responsibility is composed of economic, legal, ethical, and philanthropic responsibilities and that the company's economic performance supports the entire structure

green marketing the development and marketing of products designed to minimize negative effects on the physical environment

ethics the moral principles or values that generally govern the conduct of an individual or a group

morals the rules people develop as a result of cultural values and norms

code of ethics a guideline to help marketing managers and other employees make better decisions

2-5 Describe the social factors that affect marketing.
Social factors are the most difficult, yet most fascinating of environmental forces to predict. Whether it's behaviour or change in demographics, attitudes, values, or lifestyles, social forces are at the base of just about all other factors. Moreover, they are ultimately at the base of marketing and business as a whole—as marketing, at its simplest level, is the discovery and satisfaction of human needs.

2-6 Explain the importance to marketing managers of current demographic trends.
Today, several basic demographic patterns are influencing marketing mixes. Each generation enters a life stage with its own tastes and biases, and tailoring products to what customers value is key to sales. The cohorts, called Generation Z, Generation Y/ millennials, Generation X, and baby boomers, each have their own needs, values, and consumption patterns. Canada's cultural diversity will increasingly require multicultural marketing.

2-7 Describe the technological factors that affect marketing.
Monitoring new technology is essential to keeping up with competitors in today's marketing environment. Canada excels in basic research and, in recent years, has dramatically improved its track record in applied research. Innovation is increasingly becoming a global process. Without innovation, Canadian companies can't compete in global markets.

2-8 Discuss the role of corporate social responsibility and ethics in business.
Corporate social responsibility (CSR) is a business's concern for social and environmental welfare, often demonstrated by its adherence to the triple bottom line: financial (profit), social (people), and environmental (planet). Business ethics may be viewed as a subset of the values of society as a whole. The ethical conduct of businesspeople is shaped by societal elements, including family, education, religion, and social movements. As members of society, businesspeople are morally obligated to consider the ethical implications of their decisions.

Ethical decision making is approached in three basic ways: (1) the consequences of decisions, (2) rules and laws to guide decision making, and (3) moral development that places individuals or groups in one of three developmental stages: preconventional morality, conventional morality, or postconventional morality.

Many companies develop a code of ethics to help their employees make ethical decisions.

KEY CONCEPTS

3-1 Explain the importance of strategic planning and a business mission statement. Strategic marketing planning is the basis for all marketing strategies and decisions. The marketing plan acts as a guidebook of marketing activities for the marketer. By specifying objectives and defining the actions required to attain them, a marketing plan provides the basis on which actual and expected performance can be compared.

Although there is no set formula, a marketing plan should include elements such as stating the business mission, setting objectives, performing a situation analysis of internal and external environmental forces, selecting target markets, delineating a marketing mix (product, price, place, and promotion) and establishing ways to implement, evaluate, and control the plan.

The mission statement is based on a careful analysis of benefits sought by present and potential customers and an analysis of existing and anticipated environmental conditions. The company's mission statement establishes boundaries for all subsequent decisions, objectives, and strategies. It should focus on the market the organization is attempting to serve rather than on the good or service offered.

3-2 Describe how to conduct business portfolio analysis. In the situation (or SWOT) analysis, the company should identify its internal strengths (S) and weaknesses (W) and also examine external opportunities (O) and threats (T). When examining external opportunities and threats, marketing managers must analyze aspects of the marketing environment in a process called environmental scanning. The six macroenvironmental forces studied most often are social, demographic, economic, technological, political and legal, and competitive.

3-3 Summarize how business planning is used for competitive advantage. A competitive advantage is a set of unique features of a company and its products that are perceived by the target market as significant and superior to those of the competition. Competitive advantages can be divided into three types: cost, product differentiation, and niche strategies. Sources of cost competitive advantages include experience curves, efficient labour, no-frills goods and services, government subsidies, product design, re-engineering, product innovations, and new methods of service delivery. A product/service differentiation competitive advantage exists when a company provides something unique that is valuable to buyers beyond just low price. Niche competitive advantages result from targeting unique segments that have specific needs and wants. The goal of all sources of competitive advantage is to be sustainable.

3-4 Discuss marketing planning, identification of target markets, and elements of the marketing mix.

The target market strategy identifies which market segment or segments to focus on. A market opportunity analysis (MOA) describes and estimates the size and sales potential of market segments that are of interest to the company. In addition, an assessment of key competitors in these market segments is performed. After the market segments are described, one or more may be targeted by the business by (1) appealing to the entire market with one marketing mix, (2) concentrating on one segment, or (3) appealing to multiple market segments by using multiple marketing mixes.

KEY TERMS

3-1

planning the process of anticipating future events and determining strategies to achieve organizational objectives in the future

strategic planning the leadership and managerial process of establishing the organization's objectives and then determining how to achieve them given internal resources and the evolving marketing environment

marketing environment the entire set of situational conditions, both internal (strengths and weaknesses) and external (opportunities and threats), within which a business operates

strategic business unit (SBU) a subgroup of a single business or a collection of related businesses within the larger organization

mission statement a statement of the business's value based on a careful analysis of benefits sought by present and potential customers and an analysis of existing and anticipated environmental conditions

3-2

SWOT analysis identifying internal environment of strengths (S) and weaknesses (W) as well as external opportunities (O) and threats (T)

environmental scanning the collection and interpretation of information about forces, events, and relationships in the external environment that may affect the future of the organization or the implementation of the marketing plan

market penetration a marketing strategy that tries to increase market share among existing customers by using existing products

market development a marketing strategy that involves attracting new customers to existing products

product development a marketing strategy that entails the creation of new products for current customers

diversification a strategy of increasing sales by introducing new products into new markets

core competencies key unique strengths that are hard to imitate and underlie the functioning of an organization

competitive advantage the set of unique features of a company and its products that are perceived by the target market as significant and superior to the competition

cost competitive advantage being the low-cost competitor in an industry while maintaining satisfactory profit margins

experience curves curves that show costs declining at a predictable rate as experience with a product increases

product/service differentiation competitive advantage the provision of a unique benefit that is valuable to buyers beyond simply offering a low price

niche competitive advantage the advantage achieved when a company seeks to target and effectively serve a single segment of the market

sustainable competitive advantage an advantage that cannot be copied by the competition

3-4

marketing strategy the activities of selecting and describing one or more target markets and developing and maintaining a marketing mix that will produce mutually satisfying exchanges with target markets

marketing objective a statement of what is to be accomplished through marketing activities

market opportunity analysis (MOA) the description and estimation of the size and sales potential of market segments that are of interest to the business and the assessment of key competitors in these market segments

marketing mix a unique blend of product, price, place, and promotion, strategies designed to produce mutually satisfying exchanges with a target market

four Ps product, price, place, and promotion, which together make up the marketing mix

3-5

implementation the process that turns a marketing plan into action assignments and ensures that these assignments are executed in a way that accomplishes the plan's objectives

evaluation gauging the extent to which the marketing objectives have been achieved during the specified period

control provides the mechanisms both for evaluating marketing results in light of the plan's objectives and for correcting actions that do not help the organization reach those objectives within budget guidelines

marketing audit a thorough, systematic, periodic evaluation of the objectives, strategies, structure, and performance of the marketing organization

Target Market Options

Entire Market	Multiple Markets	Single Market

The marketing mix (or four Ps) is a blend of product, price, place, and promotion—strategies designed to produce mutually satisfying exchanges with a target market. The starting point of the marketing mix is the product offering. Products can be tangible goods, ideas, or services. Price is what a buyer must give up to obtain a product and is often the easiest to change of the four marketing mix elements. Place (distribution) strategies are concerned with making products available when and where customers want them. Elements of the promotional mix include advertising, direct marketing, public relations, sales promotion, personal selling, and online marketing.

3-5 Explain why implementation, evaluation, and control of the marketing plan are necessary. Before a marketing plan can work, it must be implemented. The plan should also be evaluated to determine whether it has achieved its objectives. Poor implementation can be a major factor in a plan's failure. Control provides the mechanisms for evaluating marketing results in light of the plan's objectives and for correcting actions that do not help the organization reach those objectives within budget guidelines.

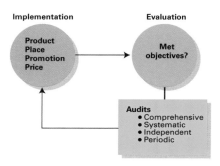

3-6 Identify several techniques that help make strategic planning effective. First, management must realize that strategic planning is an ongoing process and not a once-a-year exercise. Second, good strategic planning involves a high level of creativity. The last requirement is top management's support and cooperation.

KEY CONCEPTS

4-1 Explain marketing research and marketing analytics. Marketing research is about using information-gathering processes to discover the needs of customers and how to better serve those needs. Marketing research is a process, like any other kind of research, and it needs guidelines to follow and direction. Marketing analytics is the use of data to optimize marketing decisions. Marketing research and marketing analytics help decision makers not by solving the problem but by providing information on which decisions can be made. In a company, marketing research can take on any one of three roles: descriptive, diagnostic, and predictive.

4-2 List the steps in the marketing research process. Marketing research is a process of collecting and analyzing data to use in solving specific marketing problems. There are six steps in the process of properly gathering data and creating information used to make marketing decisions. The first step, the most important and strategic decision in the research process, is to identify the problem. The second step is to choose the research design and determine whether to use an exploratory, a descriptive, or a causal approach. The third step is to decide how much secondary and primary data will be collected and then to collect the data. The fourth step is to analyze the data. The fifth step is for researchers to present their report, taking the reams of data and turning them into something actionable for a company's decision makers. The last step is to follow up, and because marketing research is about helping make decisions, it's important that marketing researchers be able to see how their data and information are used in those decisions.

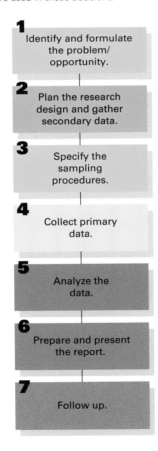

1. Identify and formulate the problem/opportunity.

2. Plan the research design and gather secondary data.

3. Specify the sampling procedures.

4. Collect primary data.

5. Analyze the data.

6. Prepare and present the report.

7. Follow up.

KEY TERMS

4-1

marketing research the process of planning, collecting, and analyzing data relevant to a marketing decision

marketing analytics the use of data to optimize marketing decisions

4-2

research design specifies which research questions must be answered, how and when data will be gathered, and how the data will be analyzed

exploratory research an informal discovery process that attempts to gain insights and a better understanding of the management and research problems

conclusive research a more specific type of research that attempts to provide clarity to a decision maker by identifying specific courses of action

descriptive research a type of conclusive research that attempts to describe marketing phenomena and characteristics

causal research a type of conclusive research that focuses on the cause and effect of two variables and attempts to find some relationship between them

secondary data data previously collected for any purpose other than the one at hand

sample a subset from a larger population

probability sample a sample in which every element in the population has a known statistical likelihood of being selected

nonprobability sample any sample in which little or no attempt is made to have a representative cross-section of the population

measurement error an error that occurs when the information desired by the researcher differs from the information provided by the measurement process

sampling error an error that occurs when a sample does not represent the target population

primary data information that is collected for the first time and is used for solving the particular problem under investigation

depth interview an interview that involves a discussion between a well-trained researcher and a respondent who is asked about attitudes and perspectives on a topic

focus group a small group of recruited participants engaged in a nonstructured discussion in a casual environment

survey research the most popular method for gathering primary data, in which a researcher interacts with people to obtain facts, opinions, and attitudes

open-ended question an interview question that encourages an answer phrased in the respondent's own words

CHAPTER REVIEW 4

closed-ended question an interview question that asks the respondent to make a selection from a limited list of responses

scaled-response question a closed-ended question designed to measure the intensity of a respondent's answer

observation research a systematic process of recording the behavioural patterns of people, objects, and occurrences with or without questioning them

mystery shoppers researchers posing as customers who gather observational data about a store and collect data about customer–employee interactions

ethnographic research the study of human behaviour in its natural context; involves observation of behaviour and physical setting

experiment a method a researcher uses to gather primary data to determine cause and effect

4-3

web survey and design systems software systems specifically designed for web questionnaire construction and delivery

database where electronic data is collected, organized, and stored for easy retrieval

online research panel is a sample of persons who have agreed to complete surveys via the Internet

big data the exponential growth in the volume, variety, and velocity of information and the development of complex new tools to analyze and create meaning from such data

4-4

data warehouse a type of database specifically designed to collect and organize large sets of data used for analytics

marketing information systems (MIS) help companies collect, analyze, and communicate information throughout the organization

data mining the process of sorting through large sets of data to find patterns and relationships

data visualization presenting data in a pictorial or graphical format

marketing dashboard marketing metrics and insights from marketing analytics are compiled in one place

structured data data that is easily defined and organized

unstructured data data that is not easily defined and organized

sentiment analysis the use of text analysis to mine and categorize unstructured data from social media posts

4-5

personally identifiable information data that can be used to identify a particular person

anonymized data data from which personally identifiable information has been removed

4-6

competitive intelligence (CI) an intelligence system that helps managers assess their competition and vendors in order to become more efficient and effective competitors

4-3 Discuss the impact of technology on marketing research and marketing analytics. Technology has an impact on many aspects of our lives, both at home and at work. Online surveys have become a staple of most companies' marketing research efforts because of the ease of implementation. There are also online research panels, online focus groups and online research communities that provide access to respondents with just a click. Mobile technology tools allow people to answer questions on the go, and social networks have created excellent potential pools of respondents. Social media sites such as Facebook or Twitter collect information about the visitors to these sites. Big data may sound intimidating, but technology has allowed companies to mine information about consumers long thought impossible or unreachable.

4-4 Explain how marketing analytics is used to develop a marketing strategy. The goal of marketing analytics is to use data to gain insights and make better decisions. The scope and volume of data available to marketers today allows marketers to use the information gained from marketing analytics to better understand customers, to decide on strategies for products and promotion, as well as to market opportunities. The data collected from various sources is stored in a database, allowing analysts to look for relationships that might not be apparent by any other means. The information from the marketing analytic analysis can be used to make decisions regarding product development and management, promotion, and customer relationships.

4-5 Summarize the concerns related to the collection and use of marketing data. Big data and data analysis have many benefits for the company but there are some downsides from the customers' point of view. The methods of data collection used could be intrusive. Customers are often aware of the uses of the data collected; however, in other situations the data is collected without a clear understanding or consent from the user. The other concern is that companies may share data collected without customers being aware of how and when that data is shared.

4-6 Describe when to conduct marketing research or when to use marketing analytics. When managers have several solutions to a problem, they should not instinctively call for market research or analytics. There are two important considerations before marketing managers decide on market research or analytics. These considerations are the following: will the cost of the research be higher than the additional revenue generated from the results of the research, and can the research be performed in time to make the decision relevant?

KEY CONCEPTS

5-1 **Explain why marketing managers should understand consumer behaviour.** Consumer behaviour describes how consumers make purchase decisions and how they use and dispose of the products they buy. An understanding of consumer behaviour reduces marketing managers' uncertainty when they are defining a target market and designing a marketing mix.

5-2 **Analyze the components of the consumer decision-making process.** The consumer decision-making process begins with need recognition, when stimuli trigger awareness of an unfulfilled want. If additional information is required to make a purchase decision, the consumer may engage in an internal or external information search. The consumer then evaluates the additional information and establishes purchase guideline. Finally, a purchase decision is made.

Consumer postpurchase evaluation is influenced by prepurchase expectations, the prepurchase information search, and the consumer's general level of self-confidence. Cognitive dissonance is the inner tension that a consumer experiences after recognizing a purchased product's disadvantages.

5-3 **Identify the types of consumer buying decisions and discuss the significance of consumer involvement.**

Consumer decision making falls into three broad categories. First, consumers exhibit routine response behaviour for frequently purchased, low-cost items that require very little decision effort; routine response behaviour is typically characterized by brand loyalty. Second, consumers engage in limited decision making for occasional purchases or for unfamiliar brands in familiar product categories. Third, consumers practise extensive decision making when making unfamiliar, expensive, or infrequent purchases. The main factors affecting the level of consumer involvement are previous experience, interest, perceived risk of negative consequences (financial, social, and psychological), situation, and social visibility.

5-4 **Identify and understand the cultural and social factors that affect consumer buying decisions.** Cultural influences on consumer buying decisions include culture and values, subculture, and social class. Culture is the essential character of a society that distinguishes it from other cultural groups. The underlying elements of every culture are the values, language, myths, customs, rituals, laws, and the artifacts, or products, transmitted from one generation to the next. The most defining element of a culture is its values—the enduring beliefs shared by a society that a specific mode of conduct is personally or socially preferable to another mode of conduct. A culture can be divided into subcultures on the basis of demographic characteristics, geographic regions, national and ethnic background, political beliefs, and religious beliefs.

Social factors include external influences such as reference groups, opinion leaders, and family. Consumers seek out others' opinions for guidance on new products, on services and products with image-related attributes, or for those on which attribute information is lacking or uninformative. Consumers may use products or brands to identify with or become a member of a reference group. Opinion leaders are members of reference groups who influence others' purchase decisions. Family members also influence purchase decisions; children tend to shop in patterns similar to those of their parents.

KEY TERMS

5-1
consumer behaviour how consumers make purchase decisions and how they use and dispose of purchased goods or services; also includes the factors that influence purchase decisions and product use

5-2
consumer decision-making process a five-step process used by consumers when buying goods or services

need recognition the result of an imbalance between actual and desired states

stimulus any unit of input affecting one or more of the five senses: sight, smell, taste, touch, hearing

want a particular product or service that will satisfy a need

internal information search the process of recalling information stored in one's memory

external information search the process of seeking information in the outside environment

nonmarketing-controlled information source a product information source that doesn't originate from the company(ies) making the product

marketing-controlled information source a product information source that originates with marketers promoting the product

evoked set (consideration set) a group of the most preferred alternatives resulting from an information search, which a buyer can further evaluate to make a final choice

decision confirmation the reaffirmation of the wisdom of the decision a consumer has made

cognitive dissonance the inner tension that a consumer experiences after recognizing an inconsistency between behaviour and values or opinions

5-3
involvement the amount of time and effort a buyer invests in the search, evaluation, and decision processes of consumer behaviour

routine response behaviour the type of decision making exhibited by consumers buying frequently purchased, low-cost goods and services; requires little search and decision time

limited decision making the type of decision making that requires a moderate amount of time for gathering information and deliberating about an unfamiliar brand in a familiar product category

extensive decision making the most complex type of consumer decision making, used when considering the purchase of an unfamiliar, expensive product or an infrequently purchased item; requires the use of several criteria for evaluating options and more time for seeking information

CHAPTER REVIEW 5

5-4

culture the set of values, norms, attitudes, and other meaningful symbols that shape human behaviour and the artifacts, or products, of that behaviour as they are transmitted from one generation to the next

value the enduring belief shared by a society that a specific mode of conduct is personally or socially preferable to another mode of conduct

subculture a homogeneous group of people who share elements of the overall culture and also have their own unique cultural elements

social class a group of people who are considered nearly equal in status or community esteem, who regularly socialize among themselves both formally and informally, and who share behavioural norms

reference group a group in society that influences an individual's purchasing behaviour

primary membership groups groups with which individuals interact regularly in an informal, face-to-face manner

secondary membership groups groups with which individuals interact less consistently and more formally than with primary membership groups

aspirational reference groups groups that an individual would like to join

norms the values and attitudes deemed acceptable by a group

nonaspirational reference groups (dissociative groups) groups that influence our behaviour because we try to maintain distance from them

opinion leader an individual who influences the opinions of others

socialization process the passing down of cultural values and norms to children

5-5

personality a way of organizing and grouping the consistency of an individual's reactions to situations

self-concept how consumers perceive themselves in terms of attitudes, perceptions, beliefs, and self-evaluations

5-5 Identify and understand the individual factors that affect consumer buying decisions.

Individual factors that affect consumer buying decisions include gender, age, family life-cycle stage, personality, self-concept, and lifestyle. Beyond obvious physiological differences, men and women differ in their social and economic roles, which affect their consumer buying decisions. A consumer's age generally indicates what products they may be interested in purchasing. Marketers often define their target markets by consumers' life-cycle stage, following changes in consumers' attitudes and behavioural tendencies as they mature. Finally, certain products and brands reflect consumers' personality, self-concept, and lifestyle.

5-6 Identify and understand the psychological factors that affect consumer buying decisions.

Psychological factors include perception, motivation, learning, values, beliefs, and attitudes. These factors allow consumers to interact with the world around them, recognize their feelings, gather and analyze information, formulate thoughts and opinions, and take action. Perception allows consumers to recognize their consumption problems. Motivation is what drives consumers to take action to satisfy specific consumption needs. Almost all consumer behaviour results from learning, which is the process that creates changes in behaviour through experience. Consumers with similar beliefs and attitudes tend to react alike to marketing-related inducements.

ideal self-image the way an individual would like to be

real self-image the way an individual actually perceives themself to be

lifestyle a mode of living as identified by a person's activities, interests, and opinions

5-6

psychological factors tools that consumers use to interact with their world, recognize their feelings, gather and analyze information, formulate thoughts and opinions, and take action

perception the process by which people select, organize, and interpret stimuli into a meaningful and coherent picture

selective exposure the process whereby a consumer decides which stimuli to notice and which to ignore

selective distortion a process whereby consumers change or distort information that conflicts with their feelings or beliefs

selective retention a process whereby consumers remember only information that supports their personal feelings or beliefs

motives driving forces that cause a person to take action to satisfy specific needs

Maslow's hierarchy of needs a method of classifying human needs into five categories in ascending order of importance: physiological, safety, social, esteem, and self-actualization

learning a process that creates changes in behaviour, immediate or expected, through experience and practice

belief an organized pattern of knowledge that an individual holds as true about their world

attitude a learned tendency to respond consistently toward a given object

KEY CONCEPTS

6-1 **Describe business marketing.** Business-to-business (B2B) marketing is more than simply using the same aspects of consumer marketing and putting the word *business* in front of the concepts and terms. B2B marketing is about making matches between the capabilities of companies and focusing on active cooperation between parties. This cooperation forms the foundation of how businesses interact as they build value for their organization.

6-2 **Explain the differences between consumer and business marketing.** Business marketing is about an active buyer and active seller. Often consumer marketing focuses on a customer that passively waits for a business to develop an offering based on the 4Ps. The Canadian Marketing Association's definition of business marketing is particularly relevant to our understanding of B2B: "What makes B-to-B different than consumer marketing is the complex nature of *relationships* and *interactions* that form a buying process and customer life cycle that lasts months or years. It involves a network of individuals from buyer, seller, and even third-party partners who have different needs and interests."

6-3 **Summarize the network and relationship approach to business marketing.** Given the importance of relationships and interactions, it is important to stress that trust and commitment form the foundation of solid business-to-business relationships. We talk here about interaction, not transaction. Much of consumer marketing's focus is on getting customers to buy once and hoping they will buy again—a single transaction. With business marketing, the focus shifts to a series of transactions over time that build trust and establish commitment—an interaction. Traditional sales and marketing management approaches rely more on transactions, while a network model looks at interactions. The term *networks* has become a familiar one, given the growth of mobile technologies and social media. The network model in business marketing stresses the interaction among various parties looking for individual gain but not at the expense of the larger network of interconnected companies. Networks have been present in many cultures, including Japan and China, in various forms. What each incarnation of networks shows is the importance of companies working together for mutual gain while ensuring success at the company level.

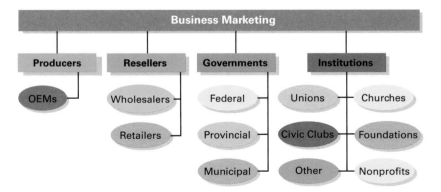

6-4 **State the fundamental aspects of business marketing.** One of the most important and unique aspects of business marketing is how demand is treated, whether derived, inelastic, or joint. Compared with consumer marketing, in business marketing the number of customers is fewer, the location of businesses is strategic, negotiations are important, and understanding reciprocity is essential to learning about business relationships. Business products that are offered as part of a business relationship

KEY TERMS

6-1
business-to-business (B2B) marketing the process of matching capabilities between two nonconsumer entities to create value for both organizations and the "customer's customer"; also referred to as *business marketing*

6-3
relationship commitment a business's belief that an ongoing relationship with another company is so important that the relationship warrants maximum efforts at maintaining it indefinitely

trust confidence in an exchange partner's reliability and integrity

6-4
derived demand demand in the business market that comes from demand in the consumer market

joint demand the demand for two or more items used together in a final product

multiplier effect (accelerator principle) the phenomenon in which a small increase or decrease in consumer demand can produce a much larger change in demand for the facilities and equipment needed to make the consumer product

reciprocity a practice where business purchasers choose to buy from their own customers

business services complementary and ancillary actions that companies undertake to meet business customers' needs

6-5
original equipment manufacturers (OEMs) individuals and organizations that buy business goods and incorporate them into the products that they produce for eventual sale to other producers or to consumers

North American Industry Classification System (NAICS) an industry classification system developed by the United States, Canada, and Mexico to classify North American business establishments by their main production processes

6-6
buying centre all those people in an organization who become involved in the purchase decision

new task buy a situation requiring the purchase of a product for the first time

modified rebuy a situation where the purchaser wants some change in the original good or service

straight rebuy a situation in which the purchaser reorders the same goods or services without looking for new information or new suppliers

are varied, ranging from major equipment purchases to basic supplies. Services to business are unique and more prevalent than in consumer marketing.

6-5 Classify business customers.
To understand the customer landscape in business marketing, it is helpful to categorize business customers into different groups. Most businesses that would be considered major players in business marketing are producers and resellers. However, government; municipal, academic, social, and hospitals (MASH); and non-profits are also important in business marketing. A well-established system to classify companies in North America is the North American Industrial Classification System (NAICS). The NAICS provides a way to identify, analyze, segment, and target business and government markets. Organizations can be identified and compared by using the NAICS numeric codes, which indicate the business sector, subsector, industry group, industry, and country industry. NAICS is a valuable tool for analyzing, segmenting, and targeting business markets.

6-6 Identify aspects of business buying behaviour.
Business buying involves a much larger group of individuals working together to make a decision. While consumers can make decisions on their own or with the aid of the reference group, a business often will have a buying centre from which decisions are made. A buying centre has six types of members: initiator, influencer, gatekeeper, decider, purchaser, and user. Buying also involves understanding the situation in which a company is making a purchase. Companies may be in a new task buy situation: this is the first time they have made this type of purchase. Otherwise, business buyers are in a straight rebuy situation in which they are generally satisfied and buy the same offering again or in a modified rebuy in which some element of the previous offering was unsatisfactory and they are seeking some improvement. Finally, most business purchases are made based on the evaluative criteria of quality, service, and price.

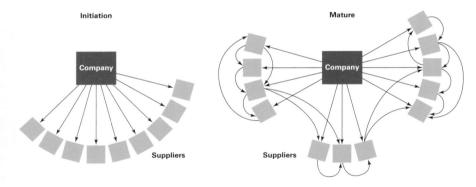

6-7 Describe the ways in which business marketing has gone online.
While much discussion of business marketing is focused on how it differs from consumer marketing, much of what is happening online is similar for both B2B and B2C. Mobile marketing and content marketing are strong trends for business marketers, providing opportunity for both new markets and new relationships but also making it necessary to understand the needs of a more informed marketplace. Social media are another area of growth for business marketing, as seen by the increased use of LinkedIn and other tools.

KEY CONCEPTS

7-1 Describe the characteristics of markets, market segments, and the importance of market segmentation. A market is composed of people or organizations with needs and wants that have both the ability and the willingness to make purchases. A market segment is a subgroup of people or organizations sharing one or more characteristics that cause them to have similar product needs.

Before the 1960s, few businesses targeted specific market segments. Today, segmentation is a crucial marketing strategy for nearly all successful organizations. Market segmentation enables marketers to tailor marketing mixes to meet the needs of particular population segments. Segmentation helps marketers identify consumer needs and preferences, areas of declining demand, and new marketing opportunities.

7-2 Describe the bases commonly used to segment consumer and business markets. Five bases are commonly used for segmenting consumer markets. Geographic segmentation is based on region of a country or the world, market size, market density, or climate. Demographic segmentation is based on age, gender, income, ethnic background, occupation and family life-cycle. Psychographic segmentation is market segmentation based on personality, motives, lifestyles, and geodemographic categories. Benefits sought is a type of segmentation that groups customers according to the benefits they seek in a product. Finally, usage segmentation divides a market by the amount of product purchased or consumed. To enhance the outcome, database-driven analytics are often used.

Business markets can be segmented on two general bases. First, businesses segment markets on the basis of company characteristics, such as customers' geographic location, type of company, company size, and product use. Second, companies may segment customers on the basis of the buying processes those customers use.

7-3 Discuss criteria for successful market segmentation. Successful market segmentation depends on four basic criteria: (1) a market segment must be substantial enough to warrant developing and maintaining a marketing mix; (2) a market segment must be identifiable and measurable; (3) members of a market segment must be accessible to marketing efforts; and (4) a market segment must respond to particular marketing efforts in a way that distinguishes it from other segments.

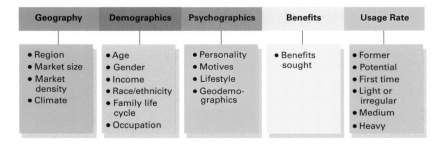

Geography	Demographics	Psychographics	Benefits	Usage Rate
• Region • Market size • Market density • Climate	• Age • Gender • Income • Race/ethnicity • Family life cycle • Occupation	• Personality • Motives • Lifestyle • Geodemo-graphics	• Benefits sought	• Former • Potential • First time • Light or irregular • Medium • Heavy

KEY TERMS

7-1

market people or organizations with needs or wants and the ability and willingness to buy

market segment a subgroup of people or organizations sharing one or more characteristics that cause them to have similar product needs

market segmentation the process of dividing a market into meaningful, relatively similar, and identifiable segments or groups

7-2

segmentation bases (variables) characteristics of individuals, groups, or organizations

geographic segmentation segmenting markets by region of a country or the world, market size, market density, or climate

demographic segmentation segmenting markets by age, gender, income, ethnic background, occupation, and family life cycle

family life cycle (FLC) a series of stages determined by a combination of age, marital status, and the presence or absence of children

psychographic segmentation market segmentation on the basis of personality, motives, lifestyles, and geodemographic categories

geodemographic segmentation clusters potential customers into neighbourhood lifestyle categories

benefit segmentation the process of grouping customers into market segments according to the benefits they seek from the product

usage-rate segmentation dividing a market by the amount of product bought or consumed

Pareto Principle (80/20 rule) a principle holding that approximately 20 percent of all customers generate around 80 percent of the demand

satisficers business customers who place their order with the first familiar supplier to satisfy their product and delivery requirements

optimizers business customers who consider numerous suppliers, both familiar and unfamiliar, solicit bids, and study all proposals carefully before selecting one

7-5

undifferentiated targeting strategy a marketing approach that views the market as one big market with no individual segments and thus uses a single marketing mix

concentrated targeting strategy a strategy used to select one segment of a market to target marketing efforts

niche one segment of a market

CHAPTER REVIEW 7

multisegment targeting strategy a strategy that chooses two or more well-defined market segments and develops a distinct marketing mix for each

cannibalization a situation that occurs when sales of a new product cut into sales of a company's existing products

one-to-one marketing an individualized marketing method that uses data generated through interactions between carefully defined groups of customers and the company to build long-term, personalized, and profitable relationships with each customer

7-6

positioning a process that influences potential customers' overall perception of a brand, a product line, or an organization in general

position the place a product, brand, or group of products occupies in consumers' minds relative to competing offerings

product differentiation a positioning strategy that some companies use to distinguish their products from those of competitors

perceptual mapping a means of displaying or graphing, in two or more dimensions, the location of products, brands, or groups of products in customers' minds

repositioning changing consumers' perceptions of a brand in relation to competing brands

Note that steps 5 and 6 are actually marketing activities that follow market segmentation (steps 1 through 4).

7-4 List the steps involved in segmenting markets. Six steps are involved when segmenting markets: (1) selecting a market or product category for study; (2) choosing a basis or bases for segmenting the market; (3) selecting segmentation descriptors; (4) profiling and analyzing segments; (5) selecting target markets; and (6) designing, implementing, and maintaining appropriate marketing mixes.

7-5 Discuss alternative strategies for selecting target markets. Marketers select target markets by using four different strategies: undifferentiated targeting, concentrated targeting, multisegment targeting, and one-to-one targeting. An undifferentiated targeting strategy assumes that all members of a market have similar needs that can be met by using a single marketing mix. A concentrated targeting strategy focuses all marketing efforts on a single market segment. Multisegment targeting is a strategy that chooses two or more well-defined segments and develops a distinct marketing mixes for each. One-to-one marketing is an individualized marketing method that uses data generated through interaction between carefully defined groups of customers and the company to build long-term, personalized, and profitable relationships with each customer. Successful one-to-one marketing comes from understanding customers and collaborating with them, rather than using them as targets for generic messages. Database technology makes it possible for companies to interact with customers on a personal, one-to-one basis.

7-6 Explain how and why companies implement positioning strategies and how product differentiation plays a role. Positioning is the process that is used to influence potential consumer overall perceptions of a brand, product line, or organization in relation to competitors. The term *position* refers to the place a product, brand, or group of products occupies in consumers' minds relative to competing offerings. To establish a unique position, many companies use product differentiation, emphasizing the real or perceived differences between competing offerings. Products may be differentiated on the basis of attribute, price and quality, use or application, product user, product class, or competitor.

Each car occupies a position in consumers' minds.
Cars can be positioned according to attribute (sporty, conservative, etc.), to price/quality (affordable, classy, etc.), or other bases.
With edgier ads, Cadillac has repositioned itself as a car for younger drivers.

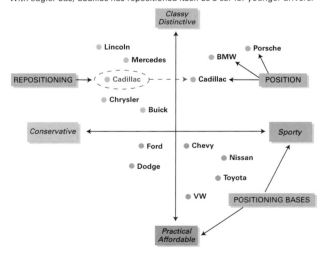

KEY CONCEPTS

8-1 Summarize customer relationship management. In customer relationship management (CRM), a company gathers information about its customers and then uses that information to build loyalty and long-term commitments with those customers. CRM started out as a technology solution for companies looking for data on customers. Much of what was developed was strong from the technology side but did not have the loyalty focus necessary for a true CRM system. CRM must be differentiated from customer relationship marketing, which is more of a customer database than a comprehensive system of tracking and maintaining customer loyalty.

8-2 Explain the CRM cycle. The Government of Canada has taken the lead on customer relationship management by releasing an important report on CRM in Canada. The focus of the report was on developing a process of setting up CRM systems—one that was not too strongly focused on information technology rather than blindly using technology in hopes of creating customer loyalty. What was developed was a three-stage CRM cycle. The first stage of the CRM cycle is focused on using marketing research and general marketing tools to help design and structure a system track customer information. The second stage is called business development, and here the IT tools are used to help track and establish an efficient system of data collection. Finally, the third stage takes action on the data collected and determines what systems of customer retention and loyalty could be established to not only track customers but also begin a two-way interaction that will lead to long-term benefits for both parties.

8-3 Describe the three stages in the CRM cycle: marketing research, business development, and customer feedback. In the first stage of the cycle, there is a renewed focus on marketing as part of CRM. Much of what had been developed for CRM concerned what could be the technology solutions and systems to put in place, rather than spending time on what information and data would be needed to go into these systems. Marketing research techniques, such as competitive intelligence, focus groups, and surveys, are all possible inputs to this first stage of the CRM cycle. As the CRM cycle begins, it becomes clear that CRM is about cross-functional integration of activities in a company that will lead to customer loyalty. The drivers of this process are those with knowledge of marketing strategy.

KEY TERMS

8-1

customer relationship management (CRM) a system that gathers information about customers that can help to build customer loyalty and retain those loyal customers

8-3

data mining an analytical process that compiles actionable data on the purchase habits of a company's current and potential customers

customer-centric a philosophy under which the company customizes its product and service offerings based on data generated through interactions between the customer and the company

learning (CRM) in a CRM environment, the informal process of collecting customer data through customer comments and feedback on product or service performance

knowledge management the process by which learned information from customers is centralized and shared for the purpose of enhancing the relationship between customers and the organization

empowerment delegation of authority to solve customers' problems quickly—usually by the first person who learns of the customer's problem

interaction the point at which a customer and a company representative exchange information and develop learning relationships

touch points all possible areas of a business where customers have contact with that business

point-of-sale interactions communications between customers and organizations that occur at the point of sale, usually in a store

response list a customer list that includes the names and addresses of individuals who have responded to an offer of some kind, such as by mail, telephone, direct-response television, product rebates, contests or sweepstakes, or billing inserts

compiled lists customer lists that are developed by gathering names and addresses gleaned from telephone directories and membership rosters, sometimes enhanced with information from public records, such as census data, auto registrations, birth announcements, business start-ups, or bankruptcies

recency-frequency-monetary (RFM) analysis the analysis of customer activity by recency, frequency, and monetary value

lifetime value (LTV) analysis a data manipulation technique that projects the future value of the customer over a period of years by using the assumption that marketing to repeat customers is more profitable than marketing to first-time buyers

CHAPTER REVIEW 8

predictive modelling a data manipulation technique in which marketers try to determine, based on some past set of occurrences, the odds that some other occurrence, such as an inquiry or a purchase, will take place in the future

campaign management developing product or service offerings customized for the appropriate customer segment and then pricing and communicating these offerings to enhance customer relationships

8-5

on-demand marketing delivering relevant experiences, integrated across both physical and virtual environments, throughout the consumer's decision and buying process

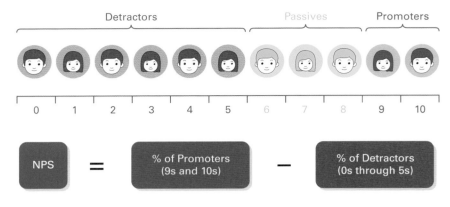

Stage 2 begins with the assumption that the company understands the needs of its customers and have developed an offering that should satisfy them. The first activity in this stage, then, is to identify customer relationships. Using tools such as learning and knowledge management, those relationships are identified, and the nature of the relationships and interactions is used to build a knowledge base. The action then moves to the technology side of CRM by tackling the data needs. Companies need to figure out at this stage how to capture data, store them, and determine which IT tools will best mine them.

Even after the data have been collected and mined, they will get a company only so far in developing effective CRM. At this stage, companies need to look beyond the reams of data and see in there the people and companies that make up their customer base. CRM must be focused on relationship development, not just database development. Companies can use different methods and applications to build customer loyalty. Companies can develop campaigns and loyalty programs, they can try to cross-sell, and they can target their communications. They can look at product trials and distribution channel marketing. All these tools must have one goal: to truly change the way in which customers are managed and build a loyal customer base from a foundation of customer service.

8-4 Identify privacy issues in CRM. The three-stage process of CRM offers numerous options and great potential for data collection, but companies must incorporate strong policies on privacy to protect their customers. Online options are enticing, given the potential access to data, as discussed in Chapter 4 on marketing research, but big data and online options can be a dangerous mix if not managed properly. When developing CRM systems, companies should familiarize themselves with legislation such as the Personal Information Protection and Electronic Documents Act (PIPEDA) and the Privacy Act.

8-5 Determine the future challenges for CRM. The future of CRM is all about looking forward and being proactive. Companies using CRM can no longer rely on CRM to provide historical data and offer suggestions from the past to instruct the future. The future lies in predictive technologies such as those used by Amazon and other online retailers that are able to predict future purchases based on previous interactions with the customer. CRM might become "CRA" with the management of customers turning into the automation of the relationship. This re-think of CRM will take a number of years to be implemented across industries and companies. But as more companies like Amazon and Facebook gain great advantage by predictive and advanced technologies, the future may involve machines being used to help improve the relationship between customer and company.

KEY CONCEPTS

9-1 Define the term *product.* A product is anything, desired or not, that a person or organization receives in an exchange. The basic goal of purchasing decisions is to receive the tangible and intangible benefits associated with a product. Tangible aspects include packaging, style, colour, size, and features. Intangible qualities include service, the retailer's image, the manufacturer's reputation, and the social status associated with a product. An organization's product offering is the crucial element in any marketing mix.

9-2 Classify consumer products. Consumer products are classified into four categories: convenience products, shopping products, specialty products, and unsought products. Convenience products are relatively inexpensive and require limited shopping effort. Shopping products are of two types: homogeneous and heterogeneous. Because of the similarity of homogeneous products, they are differentiated mainly by price and features. In contrast, heterogeneous products appeal to consumers because of their distinct characteristics. Specialty products possess unique benefits that are highly desirable to certain customers. Finally, unsought products are either new products or products that require aggressive selling because they are generally avoided or overlooked by consumers.

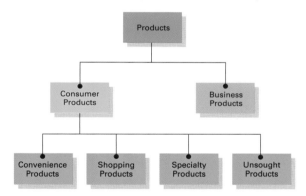

9-3 Define the terms *product item, product line,* and *product mix.* A product item is a specific version of a product that can be designated as a distinct offering among an organization's products. A product line is a group of closely related products offered by an organization. An organization's product mix includes all the products it sells. Product mix width refers to the number of product lines an organization offers. Product line depth is the number of product items in a product line. Companies modify existing products by changing their quality, functional characteristics, or style. Product line extension occurs when a company adds new products to existing product lines.

9-4 Describe marketing uses of branding. A brand is a name, term, or symbol that identifies and differentiates a company's products. Established brands encourage customer loyalty and help new products succeed. Branding strategies require decisions about individual, family, manufacturers, and private brands.

9-5 Describe marketing uses of packaging and labelling. Packaging has four functions: containing and protecting products; promoting products; facilitating product storage, use, and convenience; and facilitating recycling and reducing environmental damage. As a tool for promotion, packaging identifies the brand and its features. It also serves the critical function of differentiating a product from competing products and linking it with related products from the same manufacturer. The label is an integral part of the package and has persuasive and informational functions. In essence, the package is the marketer's last chance to influence buyers before they make a purchase decision.

KEY TERMS

9-1
product anything, both favourable and unfavourable, received by a person in an exchange for possession, consumption, attention, or short-term use

9-2
business product a product used to manufacture other goods or services, to facilitate an organization's operations, or to resell to other customers

consumer product a product bought to satisfy an individual's personal wants

convenience product a relatively inexpensive item that merits little shopping effort

shopping product a product that requires comparison shopping because it is usually more expensive than a convenience product and is found in fewer stores

specialty product a particular item with unique characteristics for which consumers search extensively and for which they are very reluctant to accept substitutes

unsought product a product unknown to the potential buyer or a known product that the buyer does not actively seek

9-3
product item a specific version of a product that can be designated as a distinct offering among an organization's products

product line a group of closely related product items

product mix all products that an organization sells

product mix width the number of product lines an organization offers

product line length the number of product items in a product line

product line depth the different versions of a product item in a product line

product modification changing one or more of a product's characteristics

planned obsolescence the practice of modifying products so those that have already been sold become obsolete before they actually need replacement

product line extension adding products to an existing product line to offer more options to consumers

9-4
brand a name, term, symbol, design, or combination thereof that identifies a seller's products and differentiates them from competitors' products

brand name that part of a brand that can be spoken, including letters, words, and numbers

brand mark the elements of a brand that cannot be spoken

brand equity the value of company and brand names

global brand a brand with at least 20 percent of the product sold outside its home country or region

brand loyalty a consistent preference for one brand over all others

generic product a no-frills, no-brand-name, low-cost product that is simply identified by its product category

manufacturer's brand the brand name of a manufacturer

private brand a brand name owned by a wholesaler or a retailer

individual branding the use of different brand names for different products

family brand the marketing of several different products under the same brand name

cobranding placing two or more brand names on a product or its package

trademark the exclusive right to use a brand or part of a brand

service mark a trademark for a service

generic product name a term that identifies a product by class or type and cannot be trademarked

9-5

persuasive labelling package labelling that focuses on a promotional theme or logo; consumer information is secondary

informational labelling package labelling designed to help consumers make proper product selections and to lower their cognitive dissonance after the purchase

universal product codes (UPCs) a series of thick and thin vertical lines (bar codes), readable by computerized optical scanners that match the codes to brand names, package sizes, and prices

9-7

warranty a confirmation of the quality or performance of a good or service

express warranty a written guarantee

implied warranty an unwritten guarantee that the good or service is fit for the purpose for which it was sold

Courtney Thorne

Nutrition Facts Table
The Nutrition Facts table is a standardized table that lists the nutrient content information of the product, including energy (calories) and 13 core nutrients. This table must be shown on the package in English and in French.

List of Ingredients
The ingredients must be listed in descending order of proportion by weight. This is the weight of each ingredient determined prior to being combined to make the food. This information is required on most prepackaged foods and must be listed in English and in French. It may appear anywhere on the package, except the bottom.

Date Marking
The date marking ("best before") is the predicted amount of time that an unopened food product will retain quality characteristics when stored under the proper conditions. The "best before" date can be listed anywhere on the package, though exceptions exist if it appears on the bottom. It is mandatory that the "best before" date is shown on prepackaged foods if the shelf life is 90 days or less. It is suggested that the best before date is shown on foods if the shelf life longer is than 90 days. The date marking must be shown in English and in French.

Origin Claim
Companies are encouraged to note either Product of Canada or the qualified Made in Canada to help customers quickly and easily identify Canadian made foods. There are specific guidelines about what constitutes a Canadian product.

9-6 Discuss global issues in branding and packaging. In addition to brand piracy, international marketers must address a variety of concerns regarding branding and packaging, including choosing a brand-name policy, translating labels and meeting host-country labelling requirements, making packages aesthetically compatible with host-country cultures, and offering the sizes of packages preferred in host countries.

9-7 Describe how and why product warranties are important marketing tools. Product warranties are important tools because they offer consumers protection and help them gauge product quality.

Express warranty = Written guarantee

Implied warranty = Unwritten guarantee

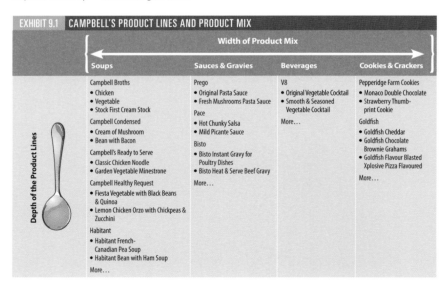

EXHIBIT 9.1	CAMPBELL'S PRODUCT LINES AND PRODUCT MIX			
	Width of Product Mix			
	Soups	**Sauces & Gravies**	**Beverages**	**Cookies & Crackers**
Depth of the Product Lines	Campbell Broths • Chicken • Vegetable • Stock First Cream Stock Campbell Condensed • Cream of Mushroom • Bean with Bacon Campbell's Ready to Serve • Classic Chicken Noodle • Garden Vegetable Minestrone Campbell Healthy Request • Fiesta Vegetable with Black Beans & Quinoa • Lemon Chicken Orzo with Chickpeas & Zucchini Habitant • Habitant French-Canadian Pea Soup • Habitant Bean with Ham Soup More...	Prego • Original Pasta Sauce • Fresh Mushrooms Pasta Sauce Pace • Hot Chunky Salsa • Mild Picante Sauce Bisto • Bisto Instant Gravy for Poultry Dishes • Bisto Heat & Serve Beef Gravy More...	V8 • Original Vegetable Cocktail • Smooth & Seasoned Vegetable Cocktail More...	Pepperidge Farm Cookies • Monaco Double Chocolate • Strawberry Thumbprint Cookie Goldfish • Goldfish Cheddar • Goldfish Chocolate Brownie Grahams • Goldfish Flavour Blasted Xplosive Pizza Flavoured More...

KEY CONCEPTS

10-1 Explain the importance of developing new products and describe the six categories of new products. New products are important to sustain growth and profits and to replace obsolete items. New products can be classified as new-to-the-world products (discontinuous innovations), new product lines, additions to existing product lines, improvements or revisions of existing products, repositioned products, or lower-priced products. To sustain or increase profits, a company must innovate.

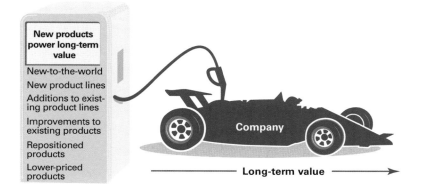

New products power long-term value
- New-to-the-world
- New product lines
- Additions to existing product lines
- Improvements to existing products
- Repositioned products
- Lower-priced products

Company → Long-term value →

10-2 Explain the steps in the new-product development process. First, a company forms a new-product strategy by outlining the characteristics and roles of future products. Then new-product ideas are generated by customers, employees, distributors, competitors, vendors, and internal R&D personnel. Once a product idea has survived initial screening by an appointed screening group, it undergoes business analysis to determine its potential profitability. If a product concept seems viable, it progresses into the development phase, in which the technical and economic feasibility of the manufacturing process is evaluated. The development phase also includes laboratory and use testing of a product for performance and safety. Following initial testing and refinement, most products are introduced in a test market to evaluate consumer response and marketing strategies. Finally, test market successes are propelled into full commercialization. The commercialization process involves starting up production, building inventories, shipping to distributors, training a sales force, announcing the product to the trade, and advertising to consumers.

1. New-product Strategy
2. Idea Generation
3. Idea Screening
4. Business Analysis
5. Development
6. Test Marketing
7. Commercialization

New Product

KEY TERMS

10-1
new product a product new to the world, new to the market, new to the producer or seller, or new to some combination of these

10-2
new-product strategy a plan that links the new-product development process with the objectives of the marketing department, the business unit, and the corporation

brainstorming the process of getting a group to think of unlimited ways to vary a product or solve a problem

screening the first filter in the product development process, which eliminates ideas that are inconsistent with the organization's new-product strategy or are obviously inappropriate for some other reason

concept test evaluation of a new-product idea, usually before any prototype has been created

business analysis the second stage of the screening process, where preliminary figures for demand, cost, sales, and profitability are calculated

development the stage in the product development process in which a prototype is developed and a marketing strategy is outlined

test marketing the limited introduction of a product and a marketing program to determine the reactions of potential customers in a market situation

simulated (laboratory) market testing the presentation of advertising and other promotion materials for several products, including the test product, to members of the product's target market

commercialization the decision to market a product

10-4
adopter a consumer who was satisfied enough with their trial experience with a product to use it again

innovation a product perceived as new by a potential adopter

diffusion the process by which the adoption of an innovation spreads

10-5
product life cycle (PLC) a concept that traces the stages of a product's acceptance, from its introduction (birth) to its decline (death)

product category all brands that satisfy a particular type of need

introductory stage the full-scale launch of a new product into the marketplace

CHAPTER REVIEW 10

growth stage the second stage of the product life cycle when sales typically grow at an increasing rate, many competitors enter the market, large companies may start to acquire small pioneering companies, and profits are healthy

maturity stage a period during which sales increase at a decreasing rate

decline stage a long-run drop in sales

10-3 **Discuss global issues in new-product development.** A marketer with global vision seeks to develop products that can easily be adapted to suit local needs. The goal is not simply to develop a standard product that can be sold worldwide. Smart global marketers also look for good product ideas worldwide.

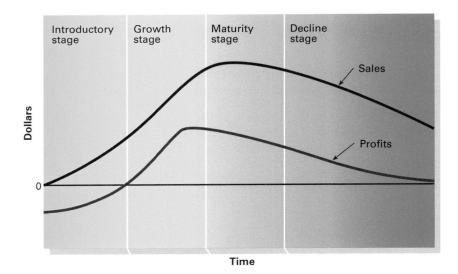

10-4 **Explain the diffusion process through which new products are adopted.** The diffusion process is the spread of a new product from its producer to its ultimate adopters. Adopters in the diffusion process belong to five categories: innovators, early adopters, the early majority, the late majority, and laggards. Product characteristics that affect the rate of adoption include product complexity, compatibility with existing social values, relative advantage over existing substitutes, visibility, and trialability. The diffusion process is facilitated by word-of-mouth communication and communication from marketers to consumers.

Diffusion of Innovations—Adopter Categories

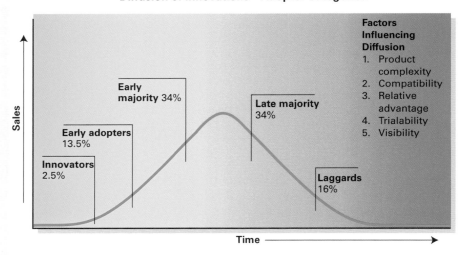

10-5 **Explain the concept of product life cycles.** All brands and product categories have a life cycle with four stages: introduction, growth, maturity, and decline. The rate at which products move through these stages varies dramatically. Marketing managers use the product life-cycle concept as an analytical tool to forecast a product's future and devise effective marketing strategies.

KEY CONCEPTS

11-1 Discuss the differences between services and goods. Services are distinguished by four characteristics. Services are intangible performances because they lack clearly identifiable physical characteristics, making it difficult for marketers to communicate their specific benefits to potential customers. The production and consumption of services occur simultaneously. Services quality is inconsistent because the service depends on elements such as the service provider, individual consumer, location, and so on. Finally, services cannot be inventoried. As a result, synchronizing supply with demand is particularly challenging in the service industry.

Intangible

Inseparable

Perishability

Heterogeneity

11-2 Describe the components of service quality and the gap model of service quality. Service quality has five components: reliability (ability to perform the service dependably, accurately, and consistently), responsiveness (providing prompt service), assurance (knowledge and courtesy of employees and their ability to convey trust), empathy (caring, individualized attention), and tangibles (physical evidence of the service).

The gap model identifies five key discrepancies that can influence customer evaluations of service quality. When the gaps are large, service quality is low. As the gaps shrink, service quality improves. Gap 1, the knowledge gap, is found between customers' expectations and management's perceptions of those expectations. Gap 2, the standard gap, is found between management's perception of what the customer wants and the specifications for service quality. Gap 3, the delivery gap, is found between service quality specifications and delivery of the service. Gap 4, the communications gap, is found between service delivery and what the company promises to the customer through external communication. Gap 5, the perception gap, is found between customers' service expectations and their perceptions of service performance.

11-3 Develop marketing mixes for services. The marketing mix for services adds people, process, productivity, and physical environment to the traditional four Ps of product, price, promotion, and place.

KEY TERMS

11-1

service the result of applying human or mechanical efforts to people or objects

intangibility the inability of services to be touched, seen, tasted, heard, or felt in the same manner that goods can be sensed

search quality a characteristic that can be easily assessed before purchase

experience quality a characteristic that can be assessed only after use

credence quality a characteristic that consumers may have difficulty assessing even after purchase because they do not have the necessary knowledge or experience

inseparability the inability of the production and consumption of a service to be separated; consumers must be present during the production

heterogeneity the variability of the inputs and outputs of services, which causes services to tend to be less standardized and uniform than goods

perishability the inability of services to be stored, warehoused, or inventoried

11-2

reliability the ability to perform a service dependably, accurately, and consistently

responsiveness the ability to provide prompt service

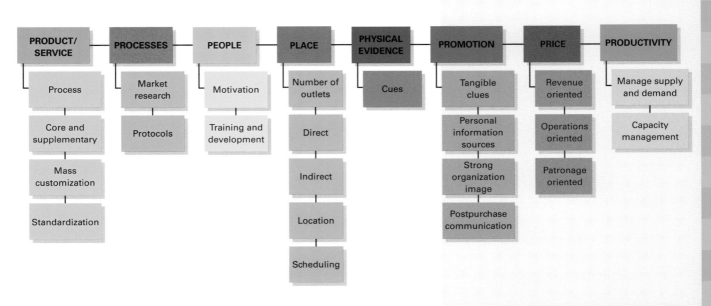

CHAPTER REVIEW 11

assurance the knowledge and courtesy of employees and their ability to convey trust

empathy caring, individualized attention paid to customers

tangibles the physical evidence of a service, including the physical facilities, tools, and equipment used to provide the service

gap model a model identifying five gaps that can cause problems in service delivery and influence customer evaluations of service quality

11-3

core service the most basic benefit the consumer is buying

supplementary services a group of services that support or enhance the core service

mass customization a strategy that uses technology to deliver customized services on a mass basis

11-5

internal marketing treating employees as customers and developing systems and benefits that satisfy their needs

11-6

non-profit organization an organization that exists to achieve a goal other than the usual business goals of profit, market share, or return on investment

non-profit organization marketing the effort by non-profit organizations to bring about mutually satisfying exchanges with target markets

public service advertisement (PSA) an announcement that promotes a program of a non-profit organization or of a federal, provincial or territorial, or local government

11-4 Discuss relationship marketing in services. Relationship marketing in services involves attracting, developing, and retaining customer relationships. Relationship marketing has four levels: level 1 focuses on pricing incentives; level 2 uses pricing incentives and social bonds with customers; level 3 uses intimate knowledge of the customer to create one-to-one solutions; and level 4 uses pricing, social bonds, and structural bonds to build long-term relationships.

11-5 Explain internal marketing in services. Internal marketing means treating employees as customers and developing systems and benefits that satisfy their needs. Employees who like their jobs and are happy with the company they work for are more likely to deliver good service and be brand ambassadors.

11-6 Describe non-profit organization marketing. Non-profit organizations pursue goals other than profit, market share, and return on investment.

Non-profit Organization Marketing

KEY CONCEPTS

12-1 Explain the importance of price and the pricing process. Of the four Ps, price is special. Price is a source of revenue for the company, not a cost centre like many promotional activities. Price involves an understanding of revenues, expenses, and the resulting profit. Many economic factors go into pricing a product or service, but there are also many other factors that are more psychological.

12-2 Describe the four-step pricing process. The four-step pricing process allows for a true understanding of the many factors included in the decisions that must be made in setting a price. The first step is to establish pricing goals. Companies must determine whether they are profit oriented, are focused on meeting a profit objective or a target return, or will look to sales as a way to create their pricing goals. The second step is to estimate demand, costs, and profits. This step is tied in with calculating demand at various price levels, calculating fixed and variable costs, and then determining unit price and quantities required to break even—and to make a profit. There is also a relationship here between the product and, specifically, the product life cycle. The third step is to establish a pricing strategy. Companies can decide to price higher (skimming), lower (penetration), or about the same (status quo) as the competition. Finally, the fourth step is to establish a pricing tactic. Pricing tactics tend to be used once the base price has been established. Tactics include discounts, geographic pricing, flexible pricing, price lining, loss leaders, and odd–even pricing (though this last one might be dying out).

KEY TERMS

12-1
price that which is given up in an exchange to acquire a good or service

revenue the price per unit charged to customers multiplied by the number of units sold

costs the combined financial value of all inputs that go into the production of a company's products, both directly and indirectly

profit revenue minus expenses

12-2
return on investment (ROI) net profits after tax divided by total assets

market share a company's product sales as a percentage of total sales for that industry

status quo pricing a pricing objective that maintains existing prices or meets the competition's prices

demand the quantity of a product that will be sold in the market at various prices for a specified period

price sensitivity consumers' varying levels of desire to buy a given product at different price levels

price elasticity of demand a measurement of change in consumer demand for a product relative to the changes in its price

break-even analysis the calculation of number of units sold, or total revenue required, that a company must meet to cover its costs, beyond which profit occurs

price strategy a basic, long-term pricing framework that defines the initial price for a product and the intended direction for price movements over the product life cycle

price skimming a high introductory price, often coupled with heavy promotion

penetration pricing a relatively low price for a product initially as a way to reach the mass market

base price the general price level at which the company expects to sell the good or service

quantity discount a unit price reduction offered to buyers buying either in multiple units or at more than a specified dollar amount

cumulative quantity discount a deduction from list price that applies to the buyer's total purchases made during a specific period

noncumulative quantity discount a deduction from list price that applies to a single order rather than to the total volume of orders placed during a certain period

CHAPTER REVIEW 12

cash discount a price reduction offered to a consumer, an industrial user, or a marketing intermediary in return for prompt payment of a bill

functional discount (trade discount) a discount to distribution channel intermediaries such as wholesalers and retailers for performing channel functions

seasonal discount a price reduction for buying merchandise out of season

value-based pricing a pricing tactic that sets the price at a level that seems to the customer to be a good value compared with the prices of other options

dynamic pricing is the ability to change prices very quickly, often in real time.

single-price tactic offering all goods and services at the same price (or perhaps two or three prices)

flexible pricing (variable pricing) different customers pay different prices for essentially the same merchandise bought in equal quantities

professional services pricing used by people with experience, training, and often certification by a licensing board, fees are typically charged at an hourly rate, but may be based on the solution of a problem or performance of an act

price lining offering a product line with several items at specific price points

loss-leader pricing a product is sold near or even below cost in the hope that shoppers will buy other items once they are in the store

odd-even pricing (psychological pricing) odd-numbered prices connote bargains, and even-numbered prices imply quality

price bundling marketing two or more products in a single package for a special price

unbundling reducing the bundle of services that comes with the basic product

two-part pricing charging two separate amounts to consume a single good or service

pay what you want pricing allows the customer to choose the amount they want to pay for a good or service

12-3

bait pricing a price tactic that tries to get consumers into a store through false or misleading price advertising and then uses high-pressure selling to persuade consumers to buy more expensive merchandise instead

deceptive pricing promoting a price or price saving that is not actually available

price fixing an agreement between two or more companies to set the price they will charge for a product or service

predatory pricing the practice of charging a very low price for a product with the intent of driving competitors out of the market or the business

resale price maintenance attempts by a producer to control the price of their products in retail stores

12-3 Recognize the legalities and ethics of setting a price. This darker side of pricing introduces us to the concepts of bait pricing, deceptive pricing, price fixing, predatory pricing, resale price maintenance, and price discrimination.

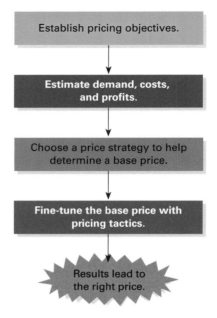

Establish pricing objectives.

Estimate demand, costs, and profits.

Choose a price strategy to help determine a base price.

Fine-tune the base price with pricing tactics.

Results lead to the right price.

KEY CONCEPTS

13-1 Explain the nature of marketing channels. Sometimes referred to as the "forgotten P" of the four Ps, place is an important, albeit overshadowed, element of the marketing mix. The focus of place is on marketing channels (channels of distribution) that guide products from the companies producing them to the consumers or business customers purchasing and using them. The supply chain covers all companies that are responsible for some aspect of developing and distributing a product. Supply chains have intermediaries that end up performing a number of important tasks, including specialization, division of labour, the overcoming of discrepancies, and contact efficiency.

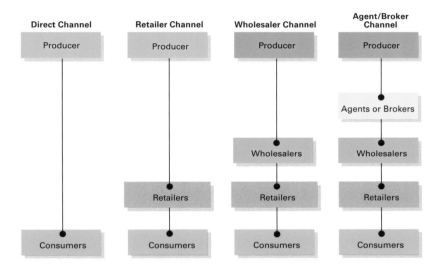

13-2 Identify different channel intermediaries and their functions. The intermediaries in a channel system and supply chain undertake important tasks that are key to a properly functioning distribution system. Intermediaries work with other companies while also ensuring their own companies' success. In determining what type of intermediary to use, a producer should look at a number of factors, including product characteristics, buyer considerations, and market characteristics. Retailers sell mainly to customers. Wholesalers help move goods through the supply chain. Agents and brokers facilitate the exchange of ownership between buyers and sellers.

13-3 Describe the types of marketing channels. Marketing channels are paths to move goods from producer to customer. The most straightforward is called the direct channel: a producer has direct contact with the end customer and does not have to rely on intermediaries. Business channels focus on B2B interactions. In multiple channels, two different types of channels are used to deliver the same product. Nontraditional channels, like vending machines, are intriguing options but with potential risk to the brand and company image. In strategic channel alliances, companies decide to work together to achieve certain supply chain goals.

13-4 Summarize how to make channel strategy decisions. To make the correct decisions when selecting the overall makeup of a channel, companies look at several important factors. The market factors relate to the customer to determine the likely behaviours and patterns that they will display. Product factors deal with the product on offer and, depending on the complexity of the product, will determine how the product

KEY TERMS

13-1

marketing channel (channel of distribution) a set of interdependent organizations that handle products and often transfer ownership of products as they move from producer to business user or consumer

channel members all parties in the marketing channel that negotiate with one another, buy and sell products, and facilitate the change of ownership between buyer and seller as they move the product from the manufacturer into the hands of the end consumer

supply chain the connected chain of all the business entities, both internal and external to the company, that produce the product and perform or support the marketing channel functions

discrepancy of quantity the difference between the amount of product produced and the amount an end-user wants to buy

discrepancy of assortment the lack of all the items a customer needs to receive full satisfaction from a product or products

temporal discrepancy a product is produced but a customer is not ready to buy it

spatial discrepancy the difference between the location of a producer and the location of widely scattered markets

13-2

retailer a channel intermediary that sells mainly to consumers and business customers

13-3

direct channel a distribution channel in which producers sell directly to customers

dual distribution (multiple distribution) the use of two or more channels to distribute the same product to target markets

strategic channel alliances cooperative agreements between business companies to use one of the manufacturer's already established distribution channels

13-4

intensive distribution a form of distribution aimed at having a product available in every outlet where target customers might want to buy it

coverage ensuring product availability in every outlet where potential customers might want to buy it

selective distribution a form of distribution achieved by screening dealers to eliminate all but a few in any single area

exclusive distribution a form of distribution that involves only one or a few dealers within a given area

13-5

channel power a marketing channel member's capacity to control or influence the behaviour of other channel members

channel control one marketing channel member intentionally affects another member's behaviour

channel leader (channel captain) a member of a marketing channel who exercises authority and power over the activities of other channel members

channel conflict a clash of goals and methods among distribution channel members

horizontal conflict a channel conflict that occurs among channel members on the same level

vertical conflict a channel conflict that occurs between different levels in a marketing channel, most typically between the manufacturer and wholesaler or between the manufacturer and retailer

channel partnering (channel cooperation) the joint effort of all channel members to create a supply chain that serves customers and creates a competitive advantage

13-6

supply chain management a management system that coordinates and integrates all the activities performed by supply chain members into a seamless process, from the source to the point of consumption, resulting in enhanced customer and economic value

logistics the process of strategically managing the efficient flow and storage of raw materials, in-process inventory, and finished goods from point of origin to point of consumption

logistics information system the link that connects all the logistics functions of the supply chain

supply chain team an entire group of individuals who orchestrate the movement of goods, services, and information from the source to the consumer

procurement the process of buying goods and services for use in the operations of an organization

mass customization (build-to-order) a production method whereby products are not made until an order is placed by the customer; products are made according to customer specifications

just-in-time production (JIT) a process that redefines and simplifies manufacturing by reducing inventory levels and delivering raw materials just when they are needed on the production line

order processing system a system whereby orders are entered into the supply chain and filled

electronic data interchange (EDI) information technology that replaces the paper documents that usually accompany business transactions, such as purchase orders and invoices, with electronic transmission of the needed information to reduce inventory levels, improve cash flow, streamline operations, and increase the speed and accuracy of information transmission

moves through the channel system. Finally, producer factors connect to the company behind the product and whether it has the necessary size and capabilities to manage a certain type of channel system. Distribution intensity is another important consideration. The three main types of distribution intensity are intensive, selective, and exclusive; each has its own benefits and drawbacks.

13-5 Recognize how to handle channel relationships. The importance of relationships was made evident in Chapter 6 in the discussion of business marketing. With place and distribution, we are once again talking about the need for businesses to work together. However, because business is focused on profit and growth-oriented goals, there is bound to be conflict when companies interact in a marketing channel. Issues of power and control are not surprising in channels, and managing them, along with taking a leadership role, is an important step for any company in a channel. Conflict in a channel can be horizontal, meaning at the same level of intermediary (e.g., distributor versus distributor) between different channels. Conflict can also be vertical within a channel (e.g., distributor versus retailer). But with all of this conflict comes some positive cooperation, and companies work together to make things easier for the entire channel, which also benefits individual companies in the process.

13-6 Learn about supply chain management. Supply chain management strives to coordinate and integrate all the activities involved in getting a product to market. This includes everything from raw materials all the way to the managing of the delivery of the final product to a customer. Logistics is often described as the grease in the wheels of supply chain management, offering the flow and storage necessary for supplies and products to make their way to the necessary points in a channel system. Purchasing and procuring the right items is a vital task in supply chain management.

13-7 List channel and distribution challenges in global markets. Globalization of markets has led to innovations and changes in every market, and channels and distribution are certainly not immune. World markets continue to open up, and with more agreements being ratified by the World Trade Organization, companies now have access to markets and partners that can potentially provide improvements to the existing supply chain.

inventory control system a method of developing and maintaining an adequate assortment of materials or products to meet a manufacturer's or a customer's demand

13-7

electronic distribution a distribution technique that includes any kind of product or service that can be distributed electronically, whether over traditional forms such as fibre-optic cable or through satellite transmission of electronic signals

three-dimensional printing (3DP) the creation of three-dimensional objects via an additive manufacturing (printing) technology that layers raw material into desired shapes

KEY CONCEPTS

14-1 Discuss the importance of retailing in the Canadian economy.
Retailing plays a vital role in the Canadian economy for two main reasons. First, retail businesses contribute to our high standard of living by providing a vast number and diversity of goods and services. Second, retailing employs a large portion of the Canadian working population.

14-2 Explain the ways in which retailers can be classified and the major types of retail operations. Many different kinds of retailers exist. A retail establishment can be classified according to its ownership, level of service, product assortment, and price. On the basis of ownership, retailers can be broadly differentiated as independent retailers, chain stores, or franchise outlets. The level of service retailers provide can be classified along a continuum of full service to self-service. Retailers also classify themselves by the breadth and depth of their product assortments from specialty store to full-line discounter. Last, general price levels also classify a store, from discounters offering low prices to exclusive specialty stores where high prices are the norm.

The major types of retail stores are department stores, specialty retailers, supermarkets, drugstores, convenience stores, discount stores, and restaurants. Department stores carry a wide assortment of shopping and specialty goods, are organized into relatively independent departments, and offset higher prices by emphasizing customer service and decor. Specialty retailers typically carry a narrower but deeper assortment of merchandise, emphasizing distinctive products and a high level of customer service. Supermarkets are large self-service retailers that offer a wide variety of food products and some nonfood items. Drugstores are retail formats that sell mostly prescription and over-the-counter medications, health and beauty aids, cosmetics, and specialty items. Convenience stores carry a limited line of high-turnover convenience goods. Discount stores offer low-priced general merchandise and consist of four types: full-line discounters, specialty discount retailers, warehouse clubs, and off-price retailers. Finally, restaurants straddle the line between the retailing and services industries; although restaurants sell a product, food and drink, to final consumers, they can also be considered service marketers because they provide consumers with the service of preparing food and providing table service.

14-3 Discuss nonstore retailing techniques and franchising.
Nonstore retailing, which provides shopping without visiting a physical location, has four major categories: automatic vending machines, direct retailing, direct marketing, and online or e-tailing. The latest developments in retailing have occurred in the area of online retailing.

14-4 Define franchising and describe its two basic forms. Franchising is a continuing relationship in which a franchiser grants to a franchisee the business rights to operate or to sell a product. Modern franchising takes two basic forms: product or trade-name franchising and business-format franchising.

14-5 List the major tasks involved in developing a retail marketing strategy. Retail management begins with defining the target market, typically on the basis of demographic, geographic, or psychographic characteristics. After determining the target market, retail managers must develop the six variables of the retailing mix: product, promotion, place, price, presentation, and personnel.

KEY TERMS

14-1
retailing all the activities directly related to the sale of goods and services to the ultimate consumer for personal, nonbusiness use

14-2
independent retailers retailers owned by a single person or partnership and not operated as part of a larger retail institution

chain stores stores owned and operated as a group by a single organization

franchise retailers that are owned and operated by individuals but are licensed by a larger supporting organization

gross margin the amount of money the retailer makes as a percentage of sales after the cost of goods sold is subtracted

department store a retail store that has several departments under one roof, carrying a wide variety of shopping and specialty goods

specialty store a retail store that carries a deeper but narrower assortment of merchandise within a single category of interest

supermarkets large, departmentalized, self-service retailers that specialize in food and some nonfood items

scrambled merchandising the tendency to offer a wide variety of nontraditional goods and services under one roof

drugstores retail stores that stock pharmacy-related products and services as their main draw

convenience store a miniature supermarket, carrying only a limited line of high-turnover convenience goods

discount store a retailer that competes on the basis of low prices, high turnover, and high volume

full-line discount stores retailers that offer consumers very limited service and carry a broad assortment of well-known, nationally branded hard goods

mass merchandising a retailing strategy using moderate to low prices on large quantities of merchandise and lower levels of service to stimulate high turnover of products

supercentres retail stores that combine groceries and general merchandise goods with a wide range of services

specialty discount stores retail stores that offer a nearly complete selection of single category merchandise and use self-service, discount prices, high volume, and high turnover

category killers specialty discount stores that heavily dominate their narrow merchandise segment

warehouse membership clubs limited-service merchant wholesalers that sell a limited selection of brand-name appliances, household items, and groceries to members, small businesses, and groups

off-price retailer a retailer that sells brand-name merchandise at considerable discounts

factory outlet an off-price retailer that is owned and operated by a manufacturer

14-3

nonstore retailing provides shopping without visiting a store

automatic vending the use of machines to offer goods for sale

self-service technologies (SST) technological interfaces that allow customers to provide themselves with products and/or services without the intervention of a service employee

direct retailing the selling of products by representatives who work door-to-door, office-to-office, or at in-home parties

direct marketing techniques used to get consumers to make a purchase from their home, office, or another nonretail setting

telemarketing the use of telecommunications to sell a product or service; involves both outbound and inbound calls

direct mail a form of direct-response communication that is delivered directly to consumers' homes

microtargeting the use of direct marketing techniques that employ highly detailed analytics in order to isolate potential customers with great precision

shop-at-home television network a specialized form of direct-response marketing whereby television shows display merchandise, with the retail price, to home viewers

online retailing (e-tailing) a type of shopping available to consumers with access to the Internet

sharing economy the way connected consumers exchange goods and service with each other through a digital marketplace

14-4

franchiser the originator of a trade name, product, methods of operation, and so on, that grants operating rights to another party to sell its product

franchisee an individual or a business that pays the franchiser for the right to use its name, product, or business methods

14-5

retailing mix a combination of the six Ps—product, place, promotion, price, presentation, and personnel—used in a single retail method to attract the target market

product offering the mix of products offered to the consumer by the retailer; also called the product assortment or merchandise mix

brand cannibalization the reduction of sales for one brand as the result of the promotion of a current product or brand

destination stores stores that consumers seek out and purposely plan to visit

14-6 Discuss retail product and service failures and means to improve. In spite of retailers' best intentions and efforts to satisfy each and every customer, consumer dissatisfaction can occur. No retailer can be everything to every customer. The best retailers have plans in place to recover from lapses in service. These plans hinge on honest communication with the customer as often and in as timely a fashion as possible. Good retailers treat customer disappointments as opportunities to improve.

14-7 Discuss retailer and retail consumer trends that will affect retailing in the future. Both small retailers and national chains are using technology to enhance engagement with the consumer and improve their competitiveness. In particular, mobile and social media are the biggest disruptive forces in the industry now.

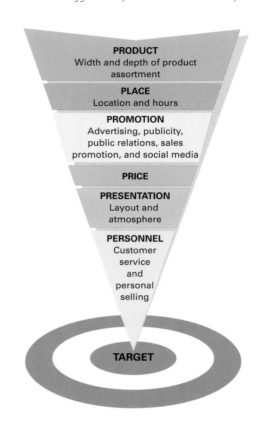

PRODUCT Width and depth of product assortment

PLACE Location and hours

PROMOTION Advertising, publicity, public relations, sales promotion, and social media

PRICE

PRESENTATION Layout and atmosphere

PERSONNEL Customer service and personal selling

TARGET

pop-up shops tiny, temporary stores that stay in one location for only a short time

atmosphere the overall impression conveyed by a store's physical layout, decor, and surroundings

14-7

beacon a device that sends out connecting signals to customers' smartphones and tablets

shopper marketing understanding how one's target consumers behave as shoppers, in different channels and formats, and using this information to develop better retail strategies

shopper analytics searching for and discovering meaningful patterns in shopper data for the purpose of fine-tuning, developing, or changing market offerings

retail channel omnification the reduction of multiple retail channels systems into a single, unified system for the purpose of creating efficiencies or saving costs.

click-and-collect the practice of buying something online and then travelling to a physical store location to take delivery of the merchandise

KEY CONCEPTS

15-1 Discuss the role of promotion in the marketing mix. Promotion is communication by marketers that informs, persuades, reminds, and connects potential buyers of a product to influence their opinion or elicit a response. Promotional strategy is the plan for using the elements of promotion—advertising, public relations, sales promotion, direct response communication, personal selling, and social media—to meet the company's overall objectives and marketing goals. Using these objectives, marketers combine the elements of the promotional strategy to form a coordinated promotion plan. The promotion plan then becomes an integral part of the total marketing strategy for reaching the target market, in addition to product, distribution, and price.

15-2 Apply the communication process to marketing communications. The communication process has several steps. It begins with encoding the message using language and symbols familiar to the receiver. The message is sent through a message channel to the receiver, who decodes the message and provides feedback to the source. Noise in the message channel can distort the message. All of the above applies to any communication involving human beings. When applied to the role of marketing, a company becomes the sender, and customers (or consumers) are the receivers.

15-3 Outline the goals and tasks of promotion. The fundamental goals of promotion are to induce, modify, or reinforce behaviour by informing, persuading, reminding, and connecting. Informative promotion explains a good's or service's purpose and benefits. Promotion that informs the consumer is typically used to increase demand for a general product category or to introduce a new good or service. Persuasive promotion is designed to stimulate a purchase or an action. Promotion that persuades the consumer to buy is essential during the growth stage of the product life cycle, when competition becomes fierce. Reminder promotion is used to keep the product and brand name in the public's mind. Promotions that remind are generally used during the maturity stage of the product life cycle. To create loyal consumers and trade on established consumers, promotion today makes a connection. Social media tools are perfect for creating connection.

15-4 Discuss the elements of integrated marketing communications (the promotional mix). The elements of IMC include advertising, public relations, sales promotion, personal selling, direct-response communication, and social media. Advertising is a form of impersonal, one-way mass communication paid for by the source. Public relations is concerned with a company's public image. Sales promotion is typically used to back up other components of the promotional mix by stimulating immediate demand. Personal selling typically involves direct communication, in person or by telephone. Direct-response communication is targeted communications to a specific audience. Social media are promotional tools that facilitate conversations online and encourage consumer empowerment. Social media include the creation of branded content that builds credibility for a brand and encourages the sharing of messages.

15-5 Discuss promotional goals and the AIDA concept. The AIDA model outlines the four basic stages in the purchase decision-making process, which are initiated and propelled by promotional activities: (1) attention, (2) interest, (3) desire, and (4) action. The components of the promotional mix have varying levels of influence at each stage of the AIDA model.

KEY TERMS

15-1
promotion communication by marketers that informs, persuades, reminds, and connects potential buyers to a product for the purpose of influencing an opinion or eliciting a response

promotional strategy a plan for the use of the elements of promotion: advertising, public relations, personal selling, sales promotion, direct-response communication, and social media

integrated marketing communications the strategic integration of all promotional mix tactics resulting in a thematically consistent and uniform look and feel regardless of platforms or mediums used.

15-2
communication the process by which we exchange or share meanings through a common set of symbols

interpersonal communication direct, fact-to-face communication between two or more people

mass communication the communication of a concept or message to large audiences

sender the originator of the message in the communication process

encoding the conversion of the sender's ideas and thoughts into a message, usually in some combination of words, images, and sound

channel a medium of communication—such as a voice, radio, newspaper, or social media—used for transmitting a message

noise anything that interferes with, distorts, or slows down the transmission of information

receivers the people who decode a message

decoding interpretation of the language and symbols sent by the source through a channel

feedback the receiver's response to a message

15-4
promotional mix the combination of promotional tools—including advertising, publicity, sales promotion, personal selling, direct-response communication, and social media—used to reach the target market and fulfill the organization's overall goals

advertising any form of impersonal, one-way mass communication, using time or space owned by an advertising medium company that is paid for by an organization

public relations the marketing function that evaluates public attitudes, identifies areas within the organization the public may be interested in, and executes a program of action to earn public understanding and acceptance

publicity a public relations tactic that, when used proactively, is intended to generate media coverage (earned media) about an organization or person

sales promotion all marketing activities that stimulate consumer purchases in the near term

personal selling a purchase situation involving a personal, paid-for communication between two people in an attempt to influence each other

direct-response communication communication of a message directly from a marketing company and directly to an intended individual target audience

online marketing two-way communication of a message delivered through the Internet to the consumer

influencer marketing leveraging the influential power of individuals, as thought leaders, to gain trust of a target market

social media collection of online communication tools that facilitate conversations online; when used by marketers, social media tools encourage consumer empowerment

consumer-generated content any form of publicly available online content created by consumers; also referred to as user-generated content

paid media a category of promotional tactic based on the traditional advertising model whereby a brand pays for advertising space

earned media a category of promotional tactic based on a public relations model that gets customers talking about products or services

owned media a category of promotional tactic based on brands becoming publishers of their own content to maximize the brands' value to consumers

branded (or inbound) content creation of engaging bespoke content as a way to promote a particular brand that attracts and builds relationships with consumers

15-5
AIDA concept a model that outlines the process for achieving promotional goals in terms of stages of consumer involvement with the message; the acronym stands for *attention, interest, desire,* and *action*

15-6
push strategy a marketing strategy that uses aggressive personal selling and trade advertising to convince a wholesaler or a retailer to carry and sell particular merchandise

pull strategy a marketing strategy that stimulates consumer demand to obtain product distribution

EXHIBIT 15.7	THE PROMOTIONAL MIX AND THE AIDA MODEL			
	Attention	**Interest**	**Desire**	**Action**
Advertising	●	●	◑	○
Public Relations	●	●	●	○
Sales Promotion	◑	◑	●	◑
Personal Selling	◑	●	●	●
Direct Marketing	◑	●	●	●
Social Media	◑	●	●	●

● Very effective ◑ Somewhat effective ○ Not effective

15-6 Discuss the concept of integrated marketing communications and the factors that affect the promotional mix. Integrated marketing communications is the careful coordination of all promotional messages for a product or service to ensure the consistency of messages at every contact point at which a company meets the consumer—advertising, sales promotion, personal selling, public relations, and social media, as well as direct marketing, packaging, and other forms of communication. Marketing managers carefully coordinate all promotional activities to ensure that consumers see and hear one message. Integrated marketing communications has received more attention in recent years because of the proliferation of media choices, the fragmentation of mass markets into segmented niches, and the decrease in advertising spending in favour of promotional techniques that generate an immediate sales response.

KEY CONCEPTS

16-1 Define advertising and understand the effect of advertising.
Advertising is any form of impersonal, one-way mass communication, using time or space owned by an advertising medium company, that is paid for by an organization. Advertising helps marketers increase or maintain brand awareness and, subsequently, market share.

16-2 Identify the major types of advertising.
The two major types of advertising are institutional advertising and product advertising. The purpose of institutional advertising is to foster a positive company image with all stakeholders. Product advertising is designed mainly to promote goods and services, and it is classified into three main categories: pioneering, competitive, and comparative.

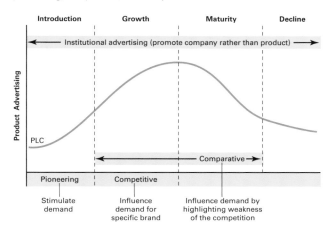

16-3 Discuss the creative decisions in developing an advertising campaign.
Once the goals and objectives of the advertising are defined, creative work can begin. Creative decisions include identifying the product's benefits, developing possible advertising appeals, evaluating and selecting the advertising appeals, executing the advertising message, and evaluating the effectiveness of the campaign.

16-4 Describe media evaluation and selection techniques and how media are purchased.
Media evaluation and selection make up a crucial step in the advertising campaign process. Major types of advertising media include newspapers; magazines; radio; television; outdoor advertising, such as billboards and bus panels; and the Internet. Promotion managers choose the advertising campaign's media mix on the basis of the following variables: cost per contact, reach, frequency, characteristics of the target audience, flexibility of the medium, noise level, and lifespan of the medium. After choosing the media mix, a media schedule designates when the advertisement will appear and the specific vehicles it will appear in. Media are purchased using negotiation and, while rates are published, the cost of various media is based on supply and demand.

16-5 Discuss the role of public relations in the promotional mix.
Public relations is a vital part of a company's promotional mix. Popular public relations tools include new-product publicity, product placement, consumer education, event sponsorship, cause-related marketing, and experiential marketing. An equally important aspect of public relations is managing unfavourable publicity in a way that is least damaging to a company's image.

KEY TERMS

16-1
percentage of sales a method of determining an advertising budget in which a percentage of forecast sales is calculated as the amount to spend on advertising

click-through rate (CTR) the ratio of clicks on an ad by viewers to the number of viewers to whom the ad was exposed

pay per click (PPC) a digital advertising payment method in which the advertiser pays the media company, through which the ad is placed, each time a user clicks on a digital ad placed within the media company's space

16-2
institutional advertising a form of advertising designed to enhance a company's image rather than promote a particular product

product advertising a form of advertising that promotes the benefits of a specific good or service

advocacy advertising a form of advertising in which an organization expresses its views on a particular issue or cause

pioneering advertising a form of advertising designed to stimulate primary demand for a new product or product category

competitive advertising a form of advertising designed to influence demand for a specific brand

16-3
advertising campaign a series of related advertisements focusing on a common theme, slogan, and set of advertising appeals

advertising objective a specific communication task that a campaign should accomplish for a specified target audience during a specified period

advertising appeal a strategy used by the advertiser to engage the attention of a viewer, reader, listener, and/or potential customer

unique selling proposition (USP) a desirable, exclusive, and believable advertising appeal selected as the theme for a campaign

programmatic buying using an automated system to make media buying decisions in real time

16-4
medium the channel used to convey a message to a target market

media planning the series of decisions advertisers make regarding the selection and use of media, allowing the marketer to optimally and cost-effectively communicate the message to the target audience

cooperative advertising an arrangement in which the manufacturer and the retailer split the costs of advertising the manufacturer's brand

cord cutting discontinuing or never committing to a TV cable or satellite provider

infomercial a 30-minute or longer advertisement that looks more like a TV talk show than a sales pitch

mobile advertising advertising that displays text, images, and animated ads via mobile phones or other mobile devices that are data-enabled

advergaming placing advertising messages in Web-based or video games to advertise or promote a product, a service, an organization, or an issue

social gaming playing an online game that allows for social interaction between players on a social media platform

media mix the combination of media to be used for a promotional campaign

cost per contact the cost of reaching one member of the target market

cost per click the cost associated with a consumer clicking on a display or banner ad

reach the number of target consumers exposed to a commercial at least once during a specific period, usually four weeks

frequency the number of times an individual is exposed to a given message during a specific period

audience selectivity the ability of an advertising medium to reach a precisely defined market

media schedule designation of the media, the specific publications or programs, and the insertion dates of advertising

continuous media schedule a media scheduling strategy in which advertising is run steadily throughout the advertising period; used for products in the later stages of the product life cycle

flighted media schedule a media scheduling strategy in which ads are run heavily every other month or every two weeks, to achieve a greater impact with an increased frequency and reach at those times

pulsing media schedule a media scheduling strategy that uses continuous scheduling throughout the year coupled with a flighted schedule during the best sales periods

seasonal media schedule a media scheduling strategy that runs advertising only during times of the year when the product is most likely to be purchased

16-5

product placement a public relations strategy that involves getting a product, service, or company name to appear in a movie, television show, radio program, magazine, newspaper, video game, video or audio clip, book, or commercial for another product; on the Internet; or at special events

sponsorship a public relations strategy in which a company spends money to support an issue, a cause, or an event that is consistent with corporate objectives, such as improving brand awareness or enhancing corporate image

Slice of Life	Depicts people in settings where the product would normally be used. For example, young couple receiving financial advice from an agent at Scotia Bank in the "Richer than you think" campaign.
Lifestyle	Shows how well the product will fit in or enhance the consumer's lifestyle. For example, P&G's Swiffer being used to quickly pick up dust and pet fur in a busy home.
Spokesperson/Testimonial	Can feature a celebrity, a company official, or a typical consumer making a testimonial or endorsing a product. For example, Galen Weston appears in television ads with regular consumers, promoting the launch of the new PC Plus program.
Fantasy	Creates a fantasy for the viewer built around use of the product. For example, Subaru showing a driver and family effortlessly speeding around tight corners in a snowstorm.
Humorous	Advertisers often use humour in their ads to break through the clutter and be memorable. For example, Amazon Alexa installed in unexpected items.
Real/Animated Product Symbols	Creates a character that represents the product in advertisements. For example, Telus animals have become product symbols.
Mood or Image	Builds a mood or an image around the product, such as peace, love, or beauty. For example, J'adore by Dior perfume ads present the iconic fragrance as the ultimate expression of femininity, luxury, and sexuality through the use of beautiful actresses and images.
Demonstration	Shows consumers the expected benefit. Many consumer products use this technique. For example, Tide laundry detergent is famous for demonstrating how its product will clean clothes whiter and brighter.
Musical	Conveys the message of the advertisement through song. Example: The 1971 classic from Coca-Cola. "I'd Like to Teach the World to Sing".
Scientific	Uses research or scientific evidence to depict a brand's superiority over competitors. Example: Aleve pain relief stating its longer lasting pain relief effects than competitor Tylenol

16-6 Discuss the role of direct-response communication in the promotional mix. Direct-response communication is often referred to as direct marketing. It involves the development of relevant messages and offers that can be tracked, measured, analyzed, stored, and leveraged. Popular direct-marketing tools are direct-response broadcast, direct-response print, telemarketing, direct mail, and digital direct marketing. Direct-response communication is designed to generate an immediate response from the consumer through the inclusion of a key element—the offer.

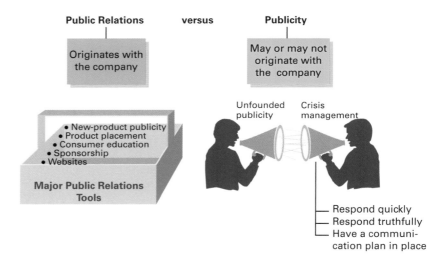

cause-related marketing a type of sponsorship involving the association of a for-profit company with a non-profit organization; through the sponsorship, the company's product or service is promoted, and money is raised for the non-profit

ambush marketing when an advertiser attempts to position itself with an event but is not sanctioned as an official sponsor

experiential marketing a form of advertising that focuses on helping consumers experience a brand

such that a memorable and emotional connection is formed between the consumer and the brand

crisis management a coordinated effort to handle all the effects of either unfavourable publicity or an unexpected unfavourable event

16-6

Do Not Call List (DNCL) a free service whereby Canadians register their telephone number to reduce or eliminate phone calls from telemarketers

KEY CONCEPTS

17-1 Define and state the objectives of sales promotion. Sales promotion consists of those marketing communication activities in which a short-term incentive motivates consumers or members of the distribution channel to purchase a good or service immediately, through either by lowering the price or by adding value. The main objective of sales promotion is to increase trial purchases, consumer inventories, and repeat purchases. Sales promotion is also used to encourage brand switching and to build brand loyalty. Sales promotion supports advertising activities.

17-2 Discuss the most common forms of consumer sales promotion. Consumer forms of sales promotion include coupons and rebates, premiums, loyalty marketing programs, contests and sweepstakes, sampling, and point-of-purchase displays. Coupons are certificates entitling consumers to an immediate price reduction when they purchase a product or service. Coupons are a particularly good way to encourage product trial and brand switching. Similar to coupons, rebates provide purchasers with a price reduction, although it is not immediate. Premiums offer an extra item or incentive to the consumer for buying a product or service. Loyalty programs are extremely effective at building long-term, mutually beneficial relationships between a company and its key customers. Contests and sweepstakes are generally designed to create interest, often to encourage brand switching. Sampling is an effective method of gaining new customers. Finally, point-of-purchase displays set up at the retailer's location build traffic, advertise the product, and induce impulse buying.

17-3 Discuss the most common forms of trade sales promotion. Manufacturers use many of the same sales promotion tools used in consumer promotions, such as sales contests, premiums, and point-of-purchase displays. In addition, manufacturers and channel intermediaries use several unique promotional strategies: trade allowances, push money, training programs, free merchandise, store demonstrations, meetings, conventions, and trade shows.

17-4 Describe personal selling. Personal selling is direct communication between a sales representative and one or more prospective buyers in an attempt to influence each other in a purchase situation. Personal selling offers several advantages over other forms of promotion. Personal selling allows salespeople to thoroughly explain and demonstrate a product. Salespeople have the flexibility to tailor a sales proposal to the needs and preferences of targeted qualified prospects. Personal selling affords greater managerial control over promotion costs and is the most effective method of closing a sale and producing satisfied customers.

17-5 Discuss the key differences between relationship selling and traditional selling. Relationship selling is the practice of building, maintaining, and enhancing interactions with customers to develop long-term satisfaction through mutually

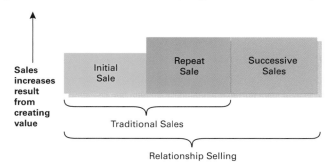

KEY TERMS

17-1

consumer sales promotion activities, such as price discounts, to incentivize consumer purchases

trade sales promotion activities, such as price discounts, to incentivize current or prospective clientele to make purchases

17-2

coupon a certificate that entitles consumers to an immediate price reduction when they buy the product

rebates cash refunds given for the purchase of a product during a specific period

premium an extra item offered to the consumer, usually in exchange for some proof of purchase of the promoted product

freemium an initially "free" offering to use a service with limited functionality, which serves as an enticement to pay a "premium" to receive an enhanced experience

loyalty marketing program a promotional program designed to build long-term, mutually beneficial relationships between a company and its key customers

frequent-buyer program a loyalty program in which loyal consumers are rewarded for making multiple purchases of a particular good or service

sampling a promotional program that allows the consumer the opportunity to try a product or service for free

17-3

trade allowance a price reduction offered by manufacturers to intermediaries, such as wholesalers and retailers

push money money offered to channel intermediaries to encourage them to push products—that is, to encourage other members of the channel to sell the products

17-5

relationship selling (business development) a multistage sales process that involves building, maintaining, and enhancing interactions with customers for the purpose of developing long-term satisfaction through mutually beneficial business partnerships

17-6

sales process (sales cycle) the set of steps a salesperson goes through to sell a particular product or service

lead generation (prospecting) identification of those companies and people most likely to buy the seller's offerings

cold calling a form of lead generation in which the salesperson approaches potential buyers without any prior knowledge of the prospects' needs or financial status

referrals recommendations to a salesperson from a customer or business associate

networking the use of friends, business contacts, coworkers, acquaintances, and fellow members in professional and civic organizations to identify potential clients

social selling leveraging social networks to find the right prospects and build trusted relationships to achieve sales goals

Trojan Horse method demonstrating or displaying a person or company's expertise via social media channels, resulting in recruitment of prospects who are impressed with said expertise, and voluntarily come forward with interest in seeking the company's assistance

lead qualification determination of a sales prospect's (1) recognized need, (2) buying power, and (3) receptivity and accessibility

preapproach a process that describes the research a salesperson must do before contacting a prospect

needs assessment a determination of the customer's specific needs and wants and the range of options the customer has for satisfying them

sales proposal a formal written document or professional presentation that outlines how the salesperson's product or service will meet or exceed the prospect's needs

sales presentation a formal meeting in which the salesperson presents a sales proposal to a prospective buyer

negotiation the process during which both the salesperson and the prospect offer concessions in an attempt to arrive at a sales agreement

follow-up the final step of the selling process, in which the salesperson ensures that delivery schedules are met, that the goods or services perform as promised, and that the buyer's employees are properly trained to use the products

beneficial partnerships. Traditional selling, on the other hand, is transaction focused. That is, the salesperson is most concerned with making one-time sales and moving on to the next prospect. In contrast, salespeople who practise relationship selling typically spend more time understanding a prospect's needs and developing solutions to meet those needs.

KEY DIFFERENCES BETWEEN TRADITIONAL SELLING AND BUSINESS DEVELOPMENT

Selling	Business Development
Create revenue by closing deals with customers	Identify customers for whom the company can provide a solution; followed by a gradual relationship building process
Relies on business development to identify and seed relationships	Relies on sales to cement financial commitments from customers
Involves sales reps	Involves business development reps (BDR)
Comprises mostly establishing trust and maintaining relationship	Comprises mostly research, analysis, customer relationship management

17-6 List the steps in the selling process and discuss key issues.

The selling process is composed of seven basic steps: (1) generating leads, (2) qualifying leads, (3) approaching the customer and probing needs, (4) developing and proposing solutions, (5) handling objections, (6) closing the sale, and (7) following up.

Closing the Sale
Handling Objections
Developing and Proposing Solutions
Approaching Customer
Qualifying Leads
Generating Leads
Follow Up
A Continuing Process

KEY CONCEPTS

18-1 Describe social media's role in an integrated marketing communication plan. Social media include social networks, microblogs, and media-sharing sites, all of which are used by the majority of adults. Smartphones and tablet computers have given consumers greater freedom to access social media on the go, which has increased the use of social media sites. Many advertising budgets are allotting more money to online marketing, including social media, mobile marketing, and search marketing. Social media represent a way for marketers to communicate one-on-one with consumers and to measure the effects of those interactions. Like any other promotional component (e.g., advertising, public relations, sales promotions, and personal selling), it must be integrated into common themes and messages when used together as part of an IMC plan.

18-2 Describe the social media tools in a marketer's toolbox, and explain how they are useful. It is important for marketers to engage with customers on social media for the reasons mentioned throughout this chapter, and a number of tools and platforms can be employed as part of an organization's social media strategy. Social networks, media creation and sharing sites, social news sites, blogs, microblogs location-based social networking sites, review sites, audio, and virtual worlds and online gaming all have their place in a company's social marketing plan. These are all tools in a marketing manager's toolbox, available when applicable to the marketing plan but not necessarily to be used all at once.

Social media tools include:

- Social networks such as Instagram, Facebook, TikTok, LinkedIn, etc.
- Social sharing sites such as YouTube
- Social news sites such as Twitter and Reddit
- Blogs and microblogs, which can be hosted inside a corporate website, or within a social network such as LinkedIn
- Location-based social network sites
- Review sites
- Audio such as podcasts and smart speaker content
- Virtual worlds and gaming

18-3 Understand the mobile infrastructure supporting social and digital marketing. A growing amount of importance in digital marketing lies in new platforms. These platforms have grown beyond smartphones and tablets and into wearable technology, such as the Apple Watch, Samsung Watch, Google-owned Fitbit, and Samsung Gear VR. The major implication of this development is that consumers are gaining multiple ways to access Internet and, thus, companies and their products. The wearable trend will continue, and at times falter (see Google Glass and Snapchat's Spectacles) but until technology finds a way to untether us from our phones, those computers in our pockets will continue to be our life support for communication, information, and entertainment.

18-4 Explain the role of search, and distinguish between SEO and SEM. Search engine optimization (SEO) is a process that marketers use to optimize the chance of search engines producing their company's website, name, products or all three, when people perform online searches. Search engines, primarily Google, respond to searches by scouring the web in nanoseconds to match the user's search request with optimal results for *that* user. How effectively a company shows up in that complex algorithm can,

KEY TERMS

18-1

influencer a person who has accumulated a sufficient following on one or more social media platforms to be considered to have an influence on consumer behaviour

crowdsourcing the use of consumers to develop and market products

social commerce a subset of e-commerce that involves the interaction and user contribution aspects of social media to assist in the online buying and selling of products and services

18-2

social networking sites websites that allow individuals to connect—or network—with friends, peers, business associates, and brands

media-sharing sites websites that allow users to upload and distribute multimedia content such as videos and photos

social news sites websites that allow users to decide which content is promoted on a given website by voting that content up or down

blogs publicly accessible Web pages that function as interactive journals, whereby readers can post comments on the authors' entries

corporate or professional blogs blogs that are sponsored by a company or one of its brands and maintained by one or more of the company's employees

noncorporate blogs independent blogs that are not associated with the marketing efforts of any particular company or brand

microblogs blogs with strict post-length limits

location-based social networking sites websites that combine the fun of social networking with the utility of location-based GPS technology

review sites websites that allow consumers to post, read, rate, and comment on opinions regarding all kinds of products and services

podcasts digital audio or video file that is distributed serially for other people to listen to or watch

18-3

apps short for *applications*; free or purchased software programs that are downloaded to run on smartphones, tablet computers, and other mobile devices

18-4

search engine optimization (SEO) a process that marketers take to optimize the chance of search engines, "driven" by people looking for information online, to produce their company's website, name, products or all three

organic traffic online search results based upon unpaid (SEO) tactics

CHAPTER REVIEW 18

search engine marketing (SEM) the practice of using paid advertisements that appear on the results page of a search engine to market a business

and should, be controlled as much as possible by the company's marketing department, thus, optimizing the company's chance for success. It is ironic that even superhuman efforts in this regard do not guarantee anything, but, with no SEO strategy, chance of success is zero.

SEM (Search Engine Marketing) is generally explained as the "paid search" partner in manipulating search whereby paid advertisements appear as top results on search engines. Given the millions, and growing, number of websites vying for attention in searches, there is little chance for a small or new company to get a toehold without paying for it. This is analogous to trying to achieve press coverage through a PR campaign but never receiving it due to the lack of newsworthiness of your story. At some point an ad spend becomes necessary.

18-5 Describe general guidelines involved in a social media campaign.

To effectively use the tools in the social media, mobile, and search toolbox, marketers need a clearly outlined digital marketing plan. This is linked to the marketing plan and should fit appropriately into the objectives and steps in those plans. It is important to research throughout the development of the digital marketing plan to keep abreast of the rapidly changing digital world. Regardless of how these might change, however, a typical digital marketing strategy would include:

1. Identifying and understanding target customers

2. Developing SMART goals

3. Evaluating and identifying tools to be used

4. Audit and plan the owned media component

5. Audit and plan the earned media component

6. Audit and plan the paid media component

7. Bring it all together

While the above is being executed, a "listening system" should be used to capture feedback coming from those reached, and the company should interact with them accordingly.

NOTES

NOTES

NOTES

NOTES

_____

_____

_____

_____

_____

_____

_____

_____

_____

_____

_____

_____

_____

_____

_____

_____

_____

_____

_____

_____

_____

_____

YOUR FEEDBACK, YOUR BOOK

This resource is built on more than ten years of feedback from students across Canada.

Our research never ends. Continual feedback from you ensures that we keep up with your changing needs.